Red Hat® Linux®
Administrator's
Guide

## Check the Web for Updates

To check for updates or corrections relevant to this book and/or CD-ROM visit our updates page on the Web at **http://www.prima-tech.com/updates**.

## Send Us Your Comments

To comment on this book or any other PRIMA TECH title, visit our reader response page on the Web at **http://www.prima-tech.com/comments**.

## How to Order

For information on quantity discounts, contact the publisher: Prima Publishing, P.O. Box 1260BK, Rocklin, CA 95677-1260; (916) 787-7000. On your letterhead, include information concerning the intended use of the books and the number of books you want to purchase.

# Red Hat® Linux®
## Administrator's
## Guide

*Kerry Cox*

A DIVISION OF PRIMA PUBLISHING

A Division of Prima Publishing

Prima Publishing and colophon are registered trademarks of Prima Communications, Inc. PRIMA TECH is a trademark of Prima Communications, Inc., Roseville, California 95661.

Linux is a registered trademark of Linus Torvalds. The Linux penguin, Tux, is used with permission from Larry Ewing (lewing@isc.tamu.edu). Ewing created this image using The GIMP (www.gimp.org). Modifications to Tux were made by Jim Thompson.

Red Hat, the Red Hat "Shadow Man" logo, RPM, Maximum RPM, the RPM logo, Linux Library, PowerTools, Linux Undercover, Rhmember, Rhmember More, Rough Cuts, Rawhide, and all Red Hat-based trademarks and logos are trademarks or registered trademarks of Red Hat software, Inc. in the United States and other countries.

Microsoft, Windows, Internet Explorer, Notepad, VBScript, ActiveX, and FrontPage are trademarks or registered trademarks of Microsoft Corporation. Netscape is a registered trademark of Netscape Communications Corporation.

*Important:* Prima Publishing cannot provide software support. Please contact the appropriate software manufacturer's technical support line or Web site for assistance.

Prima Publishing and the author have attempted throughout this book to distinguish proprietary trademarks from descriptive terms by following the capitalization style used by the manufacturer.

Information contained in this book has been obtained by Prima Publishing from sources believed to be reliable. However, because of the possibility of human or mechanical error by our sources, Prima Publishing, or others, the Publisher does not guarantee the accuracy, adequacy, or completeness of any information and is not responsible for any errors or omissions or the results obtained from use of such information. Readers should be particularly aware of the fact that the Internet is an ever-changing entity. Some facts may have changed since this book went to press.

ISBN: 0-7615-2157-7
Library of Congress Catalog Card Number: 99-64753
Printed in the United States of America

00 01 02 03 04 HH 10 9 8 7 6 5 4 3 2 1

**Publisher:**
Stacy L. Hiquet

**Marketing Manager:**
Judi Taylor

**Marketing Coordinator:**
Jennifer Breece

**Managing Editor:**
Sandy Doell

**Acquisitions Editor:**
Lynette Quinn

**Senior Editor:**
Kevin Harreld

**Technical Reviewer:**
Charles Coffing

**Copy Editor:**
Andrew Saff

**Interior Layout:**
Marian Hartsough

**Cover Design:**
Prima Design Team

**Indexer:**
Sherry Massey

# Dedication

*I would like to dedicate this book to my dear wife,*
*who provided constant support and encouragement.*
*I never would have completed this book*
*had it not been for her.*

# Acknowledgments

Special thanks go to Laine Berghout for first showing me a Linux machine and demonstrating its potential. Also, I am indebted to Bruno Browning and Read Gilgen for their assistance at the University of Wisconsin-Madison and for providing me with a vocation where I could concentrate not only on my degree but learn Linux. Bruno was extremely patient in my many endless queries. I would like to thank the entire Linux community and the many individuals who patiently answered my postings to newsgroups. They have proven time and again that Open Source software works. I can only hope that my own hand of fellowship has assisted others. Thanks also go out to Brad Parker for his contributions to the wealth of administrative knowledge. Thanks also to John York and Dan Gentry for their feedback on my many user manuals and the reams of instructions that they inherited. Troy Bowman has proven to be a great help providing additional tips and pointers in customizing Linux. I would also like to thank Andrew Bunker for his programming expertise. I never considered myself a programmer, and Andrew has proven that, but nevertheless has been extremely patient and helpful.

I also want to thank the fine people at KSL for their confidence in my abilities and for creating such a great working environment. I am sorely indebted to Owen Smoot, Mark Fenton, Hal Whitlock, and especially Greg James for their help and friendship. Thanks also to Pat Neilson and Kim Hake for their patience with my endless questions and requests.

I would like to thank those at Prima Publishing for their help in getting this book to print. A special thanks goes out to Lynette Quinn for her support and encouragement. Thanks also to my terrific editors who helped me become a better writer than I ever thought I could be. Thank you Kevin Harreld, Charles Coffing, and Andy Saff. I believe it was more than luck on my part that we teamed up and were able to bring this book to print.

# About the Author

**Kerry Cox** is finishing his Ph.D. in German Literature and speaks German, Portuguese, and Russian. He lived two years in Germany, first as an exchange student and later as a fellowship recipient doing fungicidal research at Bayer Industries. He also lived two years in Brazil doing humanitarian service. Kerry has received several awards for his written material in the field of the Humanities and has published both critical literary analyses and short stories. He also developed some of the preliminary work published on the Internet in the field of German Literature. He is co-editor of the Paul Celan Web site and developed the homepage for the International Brecht Society.

Kerry has been working with Linux for almost five years and is currently Systems Administrator for KSL Radio and Television in Salt Lake City, Utah. He manages a large network of Linux and Solaris machines that provide Internet connectivity throughout much of the Western United States. He was previously System Administrator at a large Internet Service Provider, also based in Salt Lake City, and managed the system for another ISP that provided access worldwide via bi-directional satellite transmission.

Some of his other ventures include GNUware.com, a small company providing a compilation of 1,300 Linux programs on one CD. The product is geared for users with low-speed connections who wish to try the vast array of Linux applications.

Kerry now lives in West Jordan, Utah, with his wife and two small boys, ages 5 and 2. With eight networked computers at home, his sons are already becoming familiar with Linux. He is an avid outdoorsman and hikes and fishes in the Uinta Mountains whenever he has a chance.

# Contents at a Glance

# Contents

## PART III   CUSTOMIZING THE SYSTEM . . . . . . . 323

## Chapter 11   Installing Additional Programs . . . . . . . . . 325

# Introduction

The role of a Linux Administrator is not easily defined. You must be a compassionate friend, willing to offer advice, solve problems, and generally give moral support to the more computer-challenged among us. However, you must also be the tyrannical ruler of the network, able to stomp out glitches and fix problems before the users ever realize anything is wrong. If you can balance these two conflicting aspects successfully without becoming schizophrenic, you are well on your way to becoming the perfect administrator.

But, if you are like me, and have discovered that you can't be everything to everyone and you need to simply keep Linux functional for most people, you know that learning all the ins and outs of this brave new operating system can be a challenge—very rewarding at the least—but a challenge nonetheless.

Linux is not very forgiving if you make a mistake. The best way to learn, however, is to make mistakes. But, rather than tinkering with the valuable system that your company bought, learn from other people's mistakes. Don't ruin your day with a fatal mistake typed in late at night. Very few want to share or admit their mistakes, but want only to show their positive achievements. Most Linux books glowingly show the wonderful things Linux can do. This is all very fine, but when bad things start to happen, you need answers fast.

This book attempts to show by example how to fix problems before and after they occur. I attempt to explain in detail what can happen when you don't read the instructions or don't take necessary precautions. Examples are the name of the game. Having learned Linux the hard way (mostly on my own), I have had to make all the fun mistakes.

You are probably one of the many who are either curious about this new operating system and are anxious to try it out on your own machine or who have suddenly found the responsibility for caring and maintaining a Linux system in your workplace, organization, or home. You probably have heard the story of how

Linux came into existence via the efforts of a Finnish graduate student by the name of Linux Torvalds, and how members of the community helped bring it to maturity. Along with that, the term Open Source has probably taken on some meaning, and the whole idea of free software that everyone works on and improves sounds about as utopian as can be. This is what makes Linux so exciting. It is constantly in a state of flux, ever-improving and undergoing renewal by thousands of developers worldwide.

If you are looking at this book now, wondering what it may offer you over the many others currently on the market, let me give you my pitch. I learned Linux the hard way. Back when there were no manuals or books on the market catering to the Linux crowd, I downloaded a copy of Linux from the Red Hat site and began tinkering. I was one of the lucky few successful enough to get a working version on the first try. The rest was painstakingly gained through trial and error.

Today, installing Linux is much easier. Administering, however, can prove to be more challenging. It functions not only as a server but can be a wonderful desktop OS. It operates in much the same way as most systems, only faster, better, and more reliable. There is much more software now on the market and support is becoming easier. As I played with and used Linux, I have taken great pains to document many of the procedures. I still have three large ring binders filled with notes gathered from my journeys through newsgroups, Web sites dedicated to helping other learn Linux, and from my own experiences, both positive and negative, in customizing and administering Linux. This book contains those examples that I have gleaned out of the mire of information over the years.

Because Linux was developed by and for programmers, there is not much in the way of sound documentation. Like increasing layers of strata, the information added to each release of the Linux kernel or Linux programs has covered more and more of the nuances and details that help to fully understand the programs. But, by doing so, they have embedded untold capabilities within each program. They are all flexible and easy to use once you have become familiar with the syntax.

This book is divided up into four major parts, each covering some aspect of Linux administration. Within each section there are several chapters. Each chapter will cover a function of Linux along with examples taken from my own experiences or gathered from others.

# Part I. Getting Started

This section will explain some of the basics concerning installing and configuring a Linux machine. It will take you through the most common hurdles experienced by new and sometimes novice users. It will also look at managing the most basic functions of Linux such as starting up and shutting down the system, moving through the directory structure and understanding shells and file types. This section will also examine the role of root or superuser in basic system administration as well as look at some basic security issues.

# Part II. Administering the System

This section will examine how to add and delete new users to the system. Because Linux allows for true multi-tasking, your Linux machine can support literally hundreds of accounts. Managing all these separate users can be quite a task. This section also looks at the many processes that run simultaneously, each carrying out a specific function. With all this activity, there must be some maintenance and cleaning up done by the system. One chapter will examine just how these tasks can be automated and how, over time, Linux can become a self-maintaining system. However, mistakes do occur and when they happen knowing what to do to fix them is important. This section will also look at performing backups, archiving data, and restoring former data when needed. Linux also allows for logging and checking file systems, not only for errors incurred by programs or processes, but by other individuals. Logging and examining these errors for possible solutions is another important aspect to system administration.

# Part III. Customizing the System

Although a default installation of Linux will meet most user's needs, Linux is also highly configurable and customizable to taste. It will do or perform just about whatever you ask of it. Knowing how to make the proper requests is the key. As the saying goes, "Linux is very friendly; it is just particular about who its friends are." This section helps Linux become your friend. From source code to RPMs, there is always some method of installing new programs. Window Managers or a proper GUI interface to the system have become extremely popular and have made Linux appear as diverse as the many operating systems currently on the market. This section also looks at printing, customizing Linux kernels, and many of the diverse programs now available for Linux. Nearly anything that can be found on proprietary systems can now be found either ported to the Linux platform or an equivalent nearly as good as the closed-source version.

## Part IV. Thinking Outside the Box

Because Linux is a server and is designed to play well with others, understanding how it networks or talks to other computers is crucial to having a well-rounded machine. This section examines how Linux communicates with other Linux machines on a LAN based network or via other transport protocols. It also looks at the protocols involved for networking and how it shares and transmits files. It is designed for both the large business and the home user. Whether it be mounting systems from off a multitude of servers to simply dialing up your ISP, the section offers examples and steps to complete most networking tasks. In addition to transmitting files, this section explores e-mail and security related topics. Configuring your system to prevent most attacks from outside will be needed information to most any administrator.

If you are still reading, then this might be the book for you. I enjoyed writing it and I hope you will enjoy reading it. It was built from notes and records I gathered to help others and hope now to share with a more diverse audience. Don't start at the beginning. Jump right in. I have tried to keep everything compartmentalized so you can both read it through as any text manual, or jump from chapter to chapter, or wade through it from top to bottom. Welcome to the fun and exciting world of Linux, where computing is once again accessible to all. So don't just stand there, buy this book and start having some fun!

# PART I

## Getting Started

# Chapter 1

## Configuring and Installing Red Hat Linux

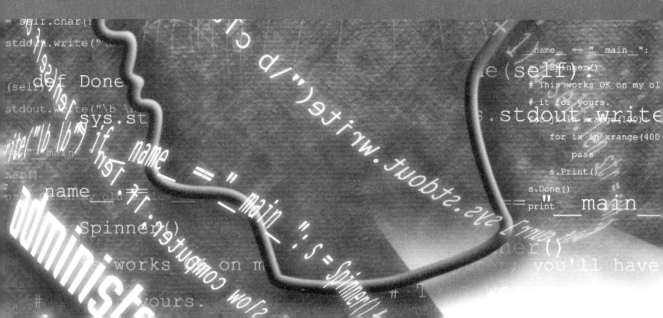

**D**eciding which version or "flavor" of Linux to install is often the most difficult decision that users face when moving to Linux. All distributions of Linux are essentially the same or extremely similar once they are installed. They all use the same Linux *kernel* or core component of the Linux operating system, and though the kernel versions may vary, one release using kernel 2.2.14 while the other uses 2.2.16, their variance is minimal. Each distribution runs nearly the same software. If a desired program does not come pre-installed, chances are it will run on most any distribution with little or no effort, depending upon how recent the release. Many of the programs used under Linux, though designed originally for UNIX, have been ported or implemented for other UNIX-type operating systems, such as AIX, FreeBSD, Solaris, SCO, and other commercial UNIX versions.

Red Hat currently holds a strong position among Linux enthusiasts as the distribution of choice. It was one of the first to employ a simple installation procedure and quickly became one of the most popular releases available. This book will give you a better understanding of how Red Hat functions compared to other distributions. If you are not already using Red Hat Linux, you will soon see why it has quickly come to dominate the American market as the operating system (OS) flavor of choice.

However, it is important to point out that Red Hat Linux is *not* the *only* GNU/Linux. The latter term applies to all flavors of Linux employing the open-source Linux kernel. Red Hat is a specific distribution and should not be confused with the many other distributions currently available. Though it is a popular and easy-to-manage release, it by no means constitutes the one and only version of Linux on the market.

This chapter will look at the following topics:

◆ What other Linux releases are available

◆ How to obtain the Linux OS

◆ What types of hardware are required to install Linux

◆ How to partition the drives

◆ How to install the operating system

# Introducing Red Hat

This book was written for users of Red Hat Linux. Although many books currently on the market detail the vast array of distributions now available, not all users need to know the intricacies of all versions of Linux. Red Hat currently holds dominance as the distribution of choice for many Linux beginners. Focusing on a specific release will assist those just starting out with Linux or those already familiar with it and who are making the change to another "flavor." Many current features associated with Linux were made standard by Red Hat. Those familiar with Red Hat will see similar traits in other distributions.

Because this book incorporates real-life examples of the use of Red Hat Linux, you will be able to follow step-by-step and learn how your own version works. Once you gain confidence in your own abilities with Linux, you can then see how Red Hat relates to other Linux distributions. You will soon see that Red Hat presents a wide variety of choices to all levels of users.

Bear in mind that Linux is a product in development and that some of the more specific examples presented here may appear dated. The developers at Red Hat are striving to improve their product on a daily basis. The material presented in this book, however, should apply to future Red Hat Linux releases for some time to come.

## Contrasting Linux Versions

The only real difference among Linux distributions lies in the installation. This is a secret seldom imparted to the new and uninitiated. Many would have you believe that their version contains features not found elsewhere. Although this may be true to a small degree, all versions still share the core functionality and operability. While some tout easier installation routines, others remain relatively simple. Some utilize a Windows-like graphical user interface (GUI) with splash screens that prompt the user for additional information, while others consider a DOS-like command-line interface the superior method of installation. Most, however, offer the user the choice between the fancier or the simpler method, each of which has its advocates and critics. Many Linux developers believe that flexibility remains key to the further development and acceptance of Linux as a viable alternative operating system—in fact, many consider this flexibility to be one of Linux's strengths over proprietary operating systems.

**NOTE**

Currently, the general trend among distributions appears to be the point-and-click installation method. This is a crucial step for winning over new users to Linux. Many distributions, however, still offer a more robust and flexible command-line interface for novices. Though considered an extremely powerful method of configuring Linux to taste, it remains rather elusive to the novice user, unfamiliar with many of the Linux commands and programs. Red Hat offers both choices. Depending upon the computer's speed and the video card's quality, you can either opt for the GUI installation or the command-line method.

Another difference among the varying Linux flavors is the type of programs that each distribution installs by default or offers to the user during the installation. Generally, only those programs that fall under the *GPL* or *General Public License*, an open-source license that requires all programmers to make any and all changes available to the public, are given as options for the user to install. Commercial software releases, such as BRU2000 (a proprietary backup program), are sometimes bundled with the shrink-wrapped Linux release. Such is the case with Red Hat, which offers commercial programs for testing purposes and then allows you to purchase the full release from the distributor. In cases such as these, source code remains closed or inaccessible for perusal. Only the binary or executable file is installed. These closed-source programs are usually offered on a separate CD, whereas the main Linux CD generally offers programs whose source is accepted as being open to public perusal.

The consensus among Linux enthusiasts, however, is that the source code for all software should be freely and publicly available for consumers to test, modify, and alter. If the program is distributed in binary form—that is, if the source code or text is not available for users to approve or disapprove—that program generally has a more difficult time gaining acceptance among the Linux community. However, once Linux is installed and operational, there are very few, if any, noticeable differences between the different Linux "flavors" or distributions.

## Making the Case for a Free Operating System

As this book was being written, there were over 100 different versions of Linux, each based upon the standard Linux kernel. This number is growing almost on a daily basis, though the trend does appear to be slowing, as several of the smaller releases consolidate. While some of these versions are modifications of existing releases—such as Linux-Mandrake, an offshoot based on the Red Hat release—others are making headway by creating new and innovative methods of installing as well as offering more "bleeding-edge" or untested Beta software. It is also rumored that other software developers will release their own version of Linux, supposedly more compliant with their product. Oracle is one case in point where the operating system will supposedly be designed around the software and not the other way around.

The trend among product developers in the UNIX or Linux field, currently, is to design their software around the operating system. Because many other operating systems developers like to keep their source code away from the public eye—because the code holds the key to their revenue—some proprietary software developers cannot always tailor their code to the OS. This is one of the many complaints currently being voiced against manufacturers such as Microsoft. Without access to the source code of the operating system, many of the programmers work in the dark, hoping that their code will function even after changes are made to the operating system. Measures such as these sometimes result in either the program crashing or the system locking or freezing up.

Many have voiced the same complaint against the Linux kernel and related operating system programs, in that they are changing so quickly developers have a hard time staying current with the latest release. In Linux's favor, though, is that when a program does break, you can trace the source back to the code and offer suggestions or modify the software to run in the event of an outdated library or piece of code.

This is where the claims of Linux enthusiasts are not unfounded. They consistently tout Linux's virtues and report it to be the superior operating system. As a Corel executive stated when announcing plans to port, or develop, the WordPerfect suite for Linux, the operating system is "the ultimate platform for software developers." Many consider Linux to be a robust and extremely dynamic system. Users give testimony of *uptimes* or operating times without a reboot in excess of 100 days when using Linux as a web or print server. Others find it very stable for program development or even for simple desktop applications. Because Linux is still undergoing such active development, many currently consider it not yet ready for enterprise or for mission-critical applications, though several companies are beginning to buck this attitude and are using Linux in increasingly more application servers. The feeling among many is that Linux shows great promise and can presently be used in many instances.

The choice lies with the Linux administrator. In terms of software cost, Linux definitely has the upper hand. But in terms of whether these costs are offset by the need for training or for developing the necessary applications for use on that system, there remains some dispute. With each new and distinct release, there are marked improvements. This book focuses on providing burgeoning Red Hat Linux administrators with real-life examples, clarifying some of the more complicated technical jargon, and conveying difficult concepts or practices to intermediate users.

Though the releases of Linux currently available are diverse, such diversity has its merits. It has resulted in distributions designed exclusively for security issues; others designed as basic minimal installs, several of which can fit on only one floppy disk; and still others designed as the full-blown releases that give the user every bell and whistle imaginable. Many critics of the open-source movement, and even those within the community itself, have voiced the opinion that this fracturing of distributions is similar to what lead several other UNIX versions to fall from grace and out of the mainstream. Though this supposition is still hotly contended, the availability of so many variants does give rise to certain issues. Because so many Linux flavors are available, consumers can choose a distribution for whatever purpose they might need.

This splintering will probably not lead to the downfall of Linux. Rather this gives it an added strength. As long as most programs designed to operate under the Linux cloud can do so under each separate distribution, it can only lead to wider acceptance and development of the OS. However, fragmentation of Linux is a real and potent threat. One way this is being combated is through the process of standardization. Red Hat Linux is hoping to lead the way in standardizing many of the Linux programs by offering a fully customizable release, complete with most every program needed for a regular PC user.

**NOTE**

One Web site dedicated to keeping Linux uniform and preventing further splintering is the Linux Standard Base (http://www.linuxbase.org/). Many of the developers who established this site belong to larger corporations, including Red Hat, which has now accepted the Linux Standard Base as a stock feature of its developmental platform. The core developers responsible for the site also include many Linux developers thoroughly familiar with the Linux kernel and its ongoing evolution.

## Distinguishing the Linux Varieties

The field of Linux distributions is split between commercial releases and lesser-known "hobby" distributions. Most Linux distributions, up until a few years ago, were under development by small groups of Linux enthusiasts. Not much money was available to these developers, so support remained limited. But a few of these distributions became commercial, meaning they gained support by an infra-structure and are being actively developed for the purpose of making money. These comprise many of the well-known distributions that now make up the main body of distributions that retail to Linux users. Red Hat Linux, Caldera OpenLinux, and SuSE Linux are a few of the better-known commercial flavors available. However, plenty other distributions, such as Slackware Linux and Debian GNU/Linux, are noncommercial and fall into the category of "hobby" distributions. These are essentially built and maintained by a few individuals for their own purposes and are distributed without cost or revenue via the Internet. Currently, these distributions make up the bulk of all those available. Though nearly all versions of Linux are available either for download from the Internet or for purchase at a very low cost, there still remains the issue of who is devel-oping the distribution and for what purpose.

Even that is now changing. New releases such as Linux-Mandrake, TurboLinux, and Connectiva Linux, based on other better-known commercial versions, prove that even these newer companies can affect the industry with their own distrib-utions. As the field of Linux continues to mature and to gain popularity, more and more releases should spring into life. This is not to be feared or discouraged but should be viewed as a natural outcome of basing an operating system on open-sourced code. Virtually anyone can splinter off the main body and form his or her own distribution. Though many doubt highly the success rate of the minor releases, several of the larger ones might begin to make a change in the industry.

Many consider Red Hat the de facto standard for beginning Linux users, due to its simple installation routine. Among Linux users, Red Hat is often recom-mended as the choice for novices. That is not to say, however, that it is less suited to the server market, which, according to Red Hat, is its ultimate goal in becom-ing the operating system of choice for home and business use. Because of its fea-tures, the interface is perhaps more arcane than what Windows users have come to expect, but it still offers many more programs available for immediate use than newer Windows NT machines.

> **TIP**
>
> Many sites on the Internet list all the available Linux distributions. Because of the sheer volume of new releases emerging every week, it is not feasible to list all the distributions here. Perusing such sites as the main Linux pages (http://www.linux.org and http://www.linux.com) and the Linux Weekly News page (http://www.lwn.net) should give you a good idea of all the stable and forthcoming releases.

## Considering Pros and Cons

If you have not yet decided on a particular flavor or distribution, take a close look at several of the latest Linux distributions, talk to people who have installed Linux, and find out their impressions. Choose something that will work for you and that will not be too challenging. Above all, talk to those who are familiar with Linux and who have experience, post questions to the newsgroups, read up on the releases via their respective sites, and be willing to look objectively at several different versions before making a final decision.

Each distribution has its good points and bad points. The more well-known commercial distributions are recommended over the lesser-known hobbyist versions. Most distributions, whether commercial or not, have standardized installation routines. They come with a wide assortment of programs and are geared to both desktop and server use. How you decide to utilize Linux depends largely on your own preference or needs. In this book, Red Hat will be the distribution referred to when citing examples or when explaining complicated issues.

> **NOTE**
>
> Red Hat does tend to offer programs that are more cutting-edge and for users more attuned to using the very latest releases. Other distributions, such as Caldera, offer more proven releases of their programs. This is yet another factor that you must take into account when deciding on a Linux distribution. Most versions list the CD contents on their site.

## Taking Initial Steps

Perhaps the most rewarding part of Linux is setting it up for the very first time. Administering the system and running the proper programs requires a lot of time and effort, but I consider installing Red Hat Linux for the first time the most fun part of playing with this unique operating system. For the experience to be a rewarding one, and not a discouraging one for novice users, certain requirements must be met initially. If you follow the steps set forth in this section, your initial encounter with Linux can be a positive one.

## Obtaining the Linux OS

Obtaining the Red Hat Linux software itself is relatively simple. There are a variety of options for getting the latest release. Because the Linux kernel itself is considered open-source, all code must be made available to the consumer. Red Hat offers the latest CD on its own FTP site and on mirrored sites. The contents or the program packages also come in a variety of forms. You can download both the program source or the compiled RPM packages and then install. Red Hat also offers an *ISO image,* or condensed version, of the commercial release, which can then be used to generate an identical copy of the standard distribution CD using nearly any CD writing software.

Here are some options for obtaining a copy of Red Hat Linux:

◆ Go to Red Hat's site and order straight from the manufacturer. If you buy directly, you usually get a shrink-wrapped version along with a 30–90 day customer support option. These releases also come with manuals and various Linux paraphernalia such as bumper stickers or discounts on other Linux merchandise. Costs can range from a low $50 to a high of $150 depending on the support requested or the types of programs that are available for use.

◆ Consult your local computer software distributor. Linux is making strong in-roads to local stores. Copies of Red Hat are available at nearly all major computer superstores and even local computer dealers. This is the fastest way to get your copy. Again, costs can range from $50 to over $150, depending on the type of release.

◆ Purchase a noncommercial version of the CD from one of the many resellers. Cheapbytes (http://www.cheapbytes.com) and Linuxmall (http://www.linuxmall.com) are a few of the most recognized resellers that offer their own version of the major distributions for a low cost. Their prices are much lower, starting at $2 a CD, requiring only an extra $5 or more for shipping and handling. These CDs are exactly the same as the commercial releases, only without the shrink-wrapped packaging or the manuals. However, Red Hat already makes its manuals available on the Internet in hypertext format or on other downloadable CDs. The commercial applications are usually not available on these more economical releases. The Professional release of Red Hat offers several extra CDs that contain commercial software and applications. These resellers offer only the most basic Linux distribution.

◆ Install the operating system directly from your hard drive or via another networked computer. You can do this in a variety of ways. You can either download the code and binary files using an FTP or *File Transfer Protocol* utility from any one of the hundreds of mirror sites throughout the world, do an NFS install from a local networked machine, or load the code directly on your hard drive and then install the OS locally.

◆ Last, if you have a fast Internet connection, you can always download the ISO image of the CD either directly from the main site or from a host of other sites. All that is required is the necessary disk space and bandwidth. Once you have successfully downloaded the ISO image, you can use any sort of CD-burning software to create and distribute your own copy of the CD.

**TIP**

The Metalab site (http://metalab.unc.edu/), located physically in South Carolina, is a good source for procuring either an ISO image of Red Hat Linux or for downloading the software that comes on the CD.

## Evaluating System Requirements

Red Hat Linux demands very little in terms of hardware in order to run. That does not mean that all hardware is fully compatible with Linux, but that you may be able to get Linux up and running on a system that might by today's standards seem obsolete. Because Linux is designed for, and by, its users, it runs on hardware that those users actually use. Some people might see this as limiting, but Red Hat Linux does offer better configuration support than some of its commercial counterparts. Tools such as the Xconfigurator that comes standard with Red Hat Linux allow for faster and easier configuration of the monitor and video cards. Red Hat also provides a high degree of Plug-and-Play (PNP) support for sound and networks cards. Though hardware is normally supported under the kernel and X Server, both of which are present on nearly all Linux distributions, Red Hat has tailored its installation package to accommodate configuration of nearly all hardware types.

One problem with Linux as an open-source model is that some companies do not share the specifications of their hardware with the Linux community. They keep such specifications as proprietary information. Even if they did decide to release the designs for their hardware, those drivers might still fall under the companies' own jurisdiction. Developers of video drivers, for example, would still be dependent upon the manufacturers for code and may be unable to share that code with others depending upon licensing restrictions. Code restrictions violate the very essence of what has contributed to Linux's rise in popularity. The open-source model dictates that the hardware interface must also be available for the public to test and evaluate. Any changes must also remain in the public realm. Efforts have been made to circumvent these limitations, but the progress of developers will remain restricted until manufacturers share more of their proprietary information.

However, in recent months many video-card makers such Matrox and Nvidia have begun sharing their specifications with the Xfree86 community resulting in better performance on the latest Xfree86 4.0 releases. Manufacturers have slowly begun to see the wisdom in sharing code with other developers. This frees up their resources from having to develop for another platform, such as Linux, yet it increases their market share. Normally slow to share their cutting-edge specifications, video-card manufacturers still make designs and chipsets for older models available to the Linux community.

The actual specifications required by Red Hat Linux vary. It is generally accepted that to run the most minimal installation of Linux, an 80386 CPU and 4 megabytes of RAM will suffice. On systems with limited hardware, it is assumed that only the command-line interface will be used. Any sort of installation requiring a GUI will naturally need additional RAM and disk space and a faster processor. Anything surpassing these minimal requirements should function rather well. This includes CPU clones such as those made by AMD and Cyrix. In addition, Linux makes full use of the 32-bit address range of the 386/486 and will utilize all RAM automatically.

When I first started using Linux several years ago, I installed it on an older 486 system with 33 MHz and 8 megabytes of RAM. I had only a 500 megabyte hard drive and a very old 1 megabyte video card. But on my first try, and with modest effort, I succeeded in configuring an older copy of Red Hat 3.0.3 Linux with the 2.0.31 kernel. I even found my older SMC Ethernet card and installed the older Western Digital drivers for it. Once I had AfterStep, a NEXTSTEP look-alike window manager, installed and correctly configured, I obtained a copy of Netscape 3.x from the Internet and had it running. In no time at all I found my older Linux box, made from discarded parts at the University of Wisconsin–Madison, to be quicker and more stable than the Windows 95 machine that I was also utilizing. The Windows machine was a 486 with 66 MHz and had 16 megabytes of RAM, yet I found it to have only half the speed and functionality of my older and, in terms of hardware, slower Linux box.

Stability was also crucial. I was able to keep my Linux box up for over a month whereas my Windows machine required an occasional, sometimes daily, reboot, to clear the memory or to recover from the random crashes. Generally, my first experience with Linux was a very favorable one that set the tone for all my later ventures with Linux.

◆ ◆ ◆

> **TIP**
>
> Naturally, the faster the hardware, the faster Linux will respond. One benefit of Linux is that it utilizes resources much better than its closed-source counterparts, so that on comparable systems, Linux may appear to run even quicker than other operating systems. Get the fastest hardware you can either afford or are willing to use with Linux.

If you are installing additional components such as the X Window interface, 4 to 8 megabytes of RAM is recommended. The interface may be slower, but it will efficiently render images and accommodate more features on a desktop. Generally, the faster the speed and the more RAM, the better. This is true of any operating system, but Linux optimizes faster hardware even better than other operating systems do.

## Configuring Devices

To verify that the components inside the box are actually what they say they are, it is always a good idea to double-check. You can do so either by doing a quick install of Windows on the machine or by moving the parts in question into a Windows machine, and then having Windows confirm their identity. In this respect, Windows does serve a highly useful purpose. Linux is currently developing several different projects to accomplish the same type of hardware verification. By the time that this book is published, there should already be something available for download. KDE already has some preliminary programs that catalog and identify the specifics of most hardware.

If Windows is already installed on the machine and the goal is to migrate to Linux, a quick look through the Device Manager can verify each component's type and make. To locate the Device Manager, click on Start, Settings, Control Panel, System. Click on the second tab, labeled Device Manager. Checking and unchecking each item on the list will give a detailed accounting of the part's manufacturer and model. This feature is especially useful when attempting to identify obscure SCSI and network cards.

Figure 1.1 is a screenshot taken from a sample computer. You can verify the video, network, and sound card without ever having to take the machine apart.

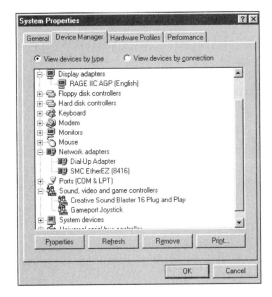

**FIGURE 1.1**

*Windows lists the name, type, and model of each component. Linux is currently developing a similar recognition scheme.*

**TIP**

Linux is not as verbose in its description of hardware components. However, you can still resolve the hardware types under Linux later by consulting the /proc/ directory. Here there are several files that dynamically list CPU information, interrupts, and I/O ports.

Likewise, you can identify some of the more elusive interrupt requests (IRQs) and port settings in the same manner. At the same screen, make sure that the Computer element at the top of the dialog box is highlighted, then click on the Properties button below. The screen shown in Figure 1.2 should appear. Here you can identify the IRQ setting for each card.

However, the newer release of Red Hat Linux already probes many of the ports, video, network, and sound cards. Often, Linux does a better job at identifying all the components than does Windows 95/98 or 2000. If the Linux kernel doesn't automatically recognize a device, several tools exist (such as sndconfig and kudzu), which will accomplish additional probing for devices and let you force IRQ and port settings if you know them. Again, the /proc/ directory lists the different interrupts and ports that Linux uses for each component.

Using the command `cat /proc/interrupts` will show you what interrupts are being used by which devices. The same directory, i.e. /proc/, includes several other dynamic files that will provide information on the CPU, ports, and memory usage.

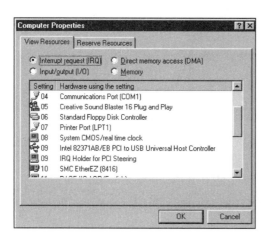

**FIGURE 1.2**

*Become familiar with the various IRQs and port settings required by each component before attempting to make them all talk under Linux.*

While configuring an older machine for one of our employees, I
had partitioned half of a 9 gigabyte SCSI hard drive for Windows
98 while reserving the other half for Linux. The machine had over
196 megabytes of RAM and several peripheral devices, including an
obscure SCSI card. It also had an older network card and an internal tape drive. Windows failed to detect the network card or the
tape drive. It did load a generic driver for the SCSI card so that I
could at least install the operating system. Full configuration of the
machine required several hours of painstaking work. After downloading updated drivers for the network card, I was finally able to
make it function, but I gave up on the tape drive. I was less than
optimistic as I began installing Linux. I had recently purchased a
cheap copy of Red Hat 6.0 and decided to install it on the other 4.5
gigabytes of available hard drive space. Linux detected the network
card without a hitch and then proceeded to inform me that it had
also detected a tape backup device. I had Linux completely installed
and operational in under an hour.

Granted, not all machines are configured or made equally. To quote George
Orwell in *Animal Farm*, ". . . some are more equal than others." Your experience
may not be as positive as mine, but as Linux matures and as manufacturers make
the hardware specifications more accessible, detection of parts and cards will
become even easier.

## Knowing Your Hardware

Before doing any sort of install on your machine, be sure you are familiar with
the computer parts and components. Knowing the history of the hardware also
doesn't hurt. In my case, I knew I had an older SMC network card on my own
computer, but I had to discover on my own that it required the older Western
Digital drivers. Before undertaking any sort of install on Linux, you should be
sure of two things: first, know exactly what cards, chipsets and components make
up your computer, and second, be sure that what you have is compatible with the
Linux release you will be using.

If you have any question as to whether your parts will work with Red Hat, first check the Red Hat site and follow the link to the Hardware Compatibility List. The rule of thumb is that if the part is not listed, it is not supported. You may have to look closely to verify that your parts are or are not listed. (I've had to find out the hard way that many of the older Intel NIC cards that I thought were listed were in fact not supported by even the latest version of Linux. Instead Linux supported the newer cards.) The Hardware Compatibility List is divided into different sections according to type. It is simple to verify that the even the most antiquated sound card is well supported by the latest Red Hat.

It requires only a quick perusal to find several mirrored pages that list the core components currently supported by Linux. The Linux Compatibility HOWTO is probably the most comprehensive. This list goes through all the parts that do and could possibly be integrated into a desktop computer running Linux. The items supported are listed in the following order: motherboards/BIOS, laptops, CPU, memory, video cards, controllers (ranging from hard drives to RAID to SCSI to multiports), network adapters, sound cards, hard drives, tape drives, CD-ROMS, CD writers, removable drives, mice, modems, printers, scanners, and every other possible peripheral imaginable, from joysticks to amateur radios. Because many of the drivers for certain components do overlap, simply knowing what type of chipset your part uses is also quite helpful. This is true in the case of video and Ethernet cards. A particular brand may not be listed by name, but its chip should certainly appear in the list, if supported.

It used to be that only a limited number of parts and accessories worked under Linux, but today nearly any off-the-shelf item will either function under the average Linux install or can be made to function with a bit of effort. If you have components that you are unsure about and the main Red Hat site is unclear as to their compatibility, a quick posting to a newsgroup or consultation with your friendly neighborhood computer guru can quickly dispel any doubts. And if all else fails, there is probably a better or newer part, also likely to be cheaper, available at the nearest computer shop. Also, manufacturers have begun releasing specifications to more and more parts and making more drivers available. Hardware packaging with the term "Works with Linux" has become commonplace. Though you may feel comfortable that your hardware will work, it never hurts to double-check the compatibility lists to verify that your item is listed. If you are still unable to find out, contact the manufacturer. Many companies today make information about their products available on the Internet. Usually a quick visit to their home page will dispel any uncertainty.

> **TIP**
>
> Some of the best places to look for information are on the Linux distributors page and the Linux Documentation Project (LDP) home page. The latter is probably the better choice since it is maintained by an army of volunteers dedicated to publishing information and specifications on all brands of Linux hardware and software and everything else in between. If you can't find an answer there, then someone still needs to write it. The site's current URL is http://www.linuxdoc.org/.
>
> Originally based in North Carolina, the LDP is mirrored on geographically diverse sites and has contributors from all over the globe. The LDP not only provides documentation and helpful HOWTOs, but also hosts a wide array of resources including source code for a vast assemblage of Linux programs and links to resources and guides, documentation, mailing lists, news, and online journals all dedicated to keeping the Linux user up-to-date.

Before taking any steps to install, it helps to write down all the specifications, the card types (including the manufacturer and model number), and any other printed information located on the device. It is far easier to consult your own notes than to attempt to consult the hardware after it is installed and the machine is running. This is especially true for hard drives located in inconvenient places. There have been a couple occasions when I have had to remove a part to verify its product number or chipset.

> **TIP**
>
> You should make a detailed list of every separate component. You can then refer to the list when installing.

# Preparing for the Install

With most Linux distributions and with the newer motherboards, nearly all machines can boot up the Linux installation directly off the CD-ROM. You will first need to consult your motherboard's BIOS to make sure this option is available. Check the option marked "Boot Sequence" or something similar, usually located under the Bios Features Setup, to see whether your machine can initially boot off the CD-ROM. If so, change the configuration to make the CD-ROM the boot drive; then insert the Linux CD and power up the machine. The installation routine should start automatically after verifying the BIOS settings.

On some older machines, only the floppy or hard drive is available for booting the OS. If this is the case, then you must make, borrow, or purchase a boot floppy. Red Hat usually provides a boot floppy with its commercial release along with the CD and manual. However, if one is not available, then you can easily make a boot floppy from software located on the CD. Only two files are needed: rawrite.exe and boot.img. The rawrite (sometimes pronounced *raw write*) file is usually located in a utility directory on the CD. Under the Red Hat release, it is located in a directory called dosutils. The boot.img file is usually found in a directory titled images.

> **CAUTION**
>
> Trying to install one version of a Linux distribution using another version's image will cause problems. Be sure to label the floppy clearly with the correct version. The same is true of mixing bootable images among distributions.

It may be necessary to use additional images located in this same directory, depending upon what type of installation routine you are attempting to use. You can create these images just as readily by using the same process that creates the boot floppy. Other bootable image names are bootnet.img and pcmcia.img. The former is used for booting off a network connection, and the latter is used when installing via a PCMCIA card or a laptop connection. The purpose of each of these files is to create a boot disk.

## Creating a Boot Floppy under Windows

The rawrite.exe file should be copied onto another machine, preferably one that is running either Windows or DOS. It operates by copying the raw image of a file or the information sector by sector onto a floppy disk. The boot.img file is the bootable image of Linux that brings up the CD or installs the drivers for additional installation options such as an NFS or FTP install. The same applies to the other two image files. In addition to providing some programs, this floppy contains a very basic Linux kernel and provides only the necessary drivers to make the CD-ROM functional under Linux so that the rest of the install can proceed normally. The bootnet.img file brings up some basic FTP drivers and allows your machine to recognize either a network or modem connection through which it can then download additional files. The pcmcia.img driver allows for connectivity via the PCMCIA slot on a laptop. When connected to that slot, the pcmcia.img driver recognizes the basic drivers for most Ethernet PCMCIA cards.

You might prefer installing rawrite in the root directory of your Windows machine when creating a boot floppy. The boot.img file goes in the same location. To use rawrite, simply start a DOS window and change into the root directory. Type **rawrite**, and then when prompted type the filename you wish to copy to the floppy. In most cases, you would type **boot.img**. You will need to type the target diskette drive as well. Nearly all Windows machines use a:\ as their primary floppy drive specification. Figure 1.3 shows a sample session.

Once rawrite is done copying the file to the floppy sector by sector, you will get your prompt back. You can now use this floppy on most PCs to boot up the Linux installation program.

## Creating a Boot Floppy Using Linux

The boot image can just as easily be made on a Linux machine. You must have root or superuser permission in order to write to the floppy drive or the /dev/fd0 device. For most users, this is the 1.44 megabyte floppy drive. You may also need to be more specific when listing this device if you have more than one type of floppy drive. A definitive path would be the following: /dev/fd0H1440. This path specifies the initial floppy drive or a:\ drive. If a second floppy drive, or b:\, exists, then the assignment would be /dev/fd1H1440.

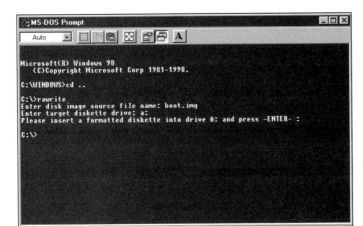

**FIGURE 1.3**

*Use the rawrite.exe program to copy the bootable image to a floppy disk. This disk will no longer be accessible to Windows once it has the image installed.*

> **TIP**
>
> Under UNIX and Linux variants, counting begins with 0. The number 1 is the second number.

To copy over the boot image from the distribution CD, mount the CD itself in Linux and then change to the directory where boot.img is stored. Insert a blank, formatted diskette and type the following:

```
# dd if=boot.img of=/dev/fdH1440 bs=1440k
```

Additional information about the dd command, which copies over files, can be verified by consulting the *man* or manual pages. To refer to the man pages on dd type **man dd** at any command line.

Red Hat has an added feature that makes installing Linux even easier. The Kick-Start method allows a user to set up a specific configuration and then have Linux run the rest of the install process automatically. This is convenient for those users who need to set up multiple Linux machines but who don't have the time to configure each and every option manually.

> **NOTE**
>
> If you know the specific programs you want to install on all machines, you can create a default configuration on the initial machine. You then save this format to a floppy. By simply transferring the same floppy from one computer to the next, you can bypass much of the typing and decision-making.

# Partitioning the Drives

In preparation for any sort of Linux install, you will need to sit down and sketch out some idea of what you want your Linux box to do and where to place each file. Linux is quite versatile in that you can set up separate partitions for different directories. A *partition* is the method by which a single physical disk is divided into multiple logical disks. Each partition is a contiguous section of blocks that is then treated like a separate and distinct physical drive. Although you may have only one drive, you can have several partitions, thus making your computer appear to have several drives. Computers with only a few physical hard drives can have several partitions.

---

### NOTE

Though you may have only one physical hard drive in your machine, if you divide it into four separate partitions, your machine will then treat all four partitions like individual drives, renaming them under Windows as drives C, D, E, and F. Linux will recognize them as devices and will refer to them respectively as /dev/hda1, /dev/hda2, /dev/hda3, and /dev/hda4.

---

Most operating systems allow for this method of sectioning off blocks of information into separate partitions. Some of the basic rules for partitions are:

◆ They cannot overlap.

◆ You cannot mount the same directory on different partitions.

◆ You don't have to partition all the available space on a hard drive. Some space can be left for later to be used with other operating systems or for other partitions.

Once you have decided how you want to set up your system, it is prudent to write down the physical parameters of your configuration. Documenting the setup of your computer cannot be stressed enough. Many people have saved themselves painful hours of stressful reinstallation and retyping by documenting the layout of all the systems. I still have three binders full of notes that I have collected over the years. Though I don't consult them much now, I do occasionally refer to them for specific instructions. Knowing which physical drive holds its respective logical partitions or directories can save you much time and money.

---

### TIP

You can have a partition dedicated entirely to the /home directory or the directory where you keep your own local files. In the case of a reinstall, this allows you to retain all your data while reformatting the other partitions.

---

If you are not used to breaking up directories into different partitions, this can be a bit intimidating, but with a little practice it can prove to be beneficial. Though there may not be much space on some of the older, smaller drives, you can opt to install all your files and directories into one main root or / directory. The root directory is the highest level of all Linux partitions.

## Selecting Mount Points

Red Hat Linux utilizes two different tools for partitioning drives. The one currently touted by Red Hat as being the most dynamic is *Disk Druid*. This tool allows the user to create multiple partitions for each directory. Unlike its predecessor, *fdisk*, Disk Druid is not limited to only four partitions. During the installation phase, you will most likely see Disk Druid as your default partitioning tool. In the latest release of Red Hat, you may opt to use fdisk as well to give the partitions added functionality. Disk Druid can set the partition to only a limited number of partition types.

> **CAUTION**
>
> If you decide to set aside a portion of your Windows partition for Linux, be sure to defragment the drive first so that all files are located in one section of the drive. The remaining space can then be turned over to Linux by using the tools `fips`, included on the CD.

For those unfamiliar with the partitioning schema associated with Linux, Red Hat offers sample mount points for each partition. Rather than attempting to guess at what partition might be needed, Red Hat lists directories—such as /, /boot, /home, /opt, /usr, /usr/local, and /var—as possible mount points for each partition. Though many regard fdisk as the superior tool, Red Hat offers both tools during the install process. To optimize the partitioning schema, you should use a combination of both tools.

There are advantages to command-line tools that allow for the toggling of partition identities such as alternative file system types or formats. The Linux fdisk tool is much more robust than the Microsoft counterpart and can create partitions compliant for a variety of other operating systems, including Windows NT, OS/2, and other operating systems.

> **NOTE**
>
> Using fdisk you can define what type of OS you would like to install on a particular partition. Fdisk allows you to choose between 78 different file formats, anywhere from a Windows 95 file allocation table (FAT) to Novell Netware or even AIX. Fdisk allows you to change a partition's ID to another format by typing **t** at the fdisk command line. You may list all available file types by typing **l** on the same line. Disk Druid presents you initially with only a five or six different file formats.
>
> After installation you can still change the partition format. Type **/sbin/fdisk** and the partition name. A typical command would be **/sbin/fdisk /dev/hda**.

Once you have either set a new partition or changed a partition's ID using fdisk, you will need to write the information to the partition table and then exit. You should use fdisk only during the initial installation or when defining the remaining free space on the drive for another operating system.

As Linux continues to gain importance and notoriety, more and more users are demanding easier- to-use partitioning tools. Red Hat meets many of these demands by further developing Disk Druid and by assisting in setting up separate partitions for both Linux and other operating systems such as Microsoft, DOS, Be, and OS/2. Each can be allotted its own partition. Red Hat also allows you to define which operating system is the default.

## Determining the Function of Your Linux Box

Before partitioning hard drives for use on a Linux machine, you first must answer several questions:

- What is the basic function of this machine?
- What partition will require the most space based on the machine's primary function?
- Will the software need to be reinstalled or upgraded at some later date?
- Will there be a need to expand the existing hardware at some later date?

The first two questions are probably the most important and are linked in purpose. If this Linux box is to function as a web server, it will need more space either on the /home or /usr/local directory. If, however, it is to be a news server and will be hosting thousands of newsgroups, the /var or /usr/local directory will have to be several times larger than the /home directory.

Consider also that files have life expectancies. As mentioned earlier, certain types of files remain on the system for only short durations while other files are permanent once they have been installed. It is useful to keep files with differing turnover rates in alternative partitions. Those files located in /usr/bin and /usr/sbin will probably be around for some time and can be considered stable fixtures in those directories. The space required in these directories probably will not increase significantly over time.

Partition use should be carefully considered in relationship to the file life cycle. Files in directories such as /usr/local and /home have more moderate life expectancies. These can last anywhere from several weeks to months. Thus, their respective partitions can be set somewhat larger. The /var partition and /var/spool rarely keep certain files for more than a week or two and rotate older files out. These two can be set moderately large. There are a couple reasons for setting partitions with dynamic or shorter-life cycles. The space required by your system may change over time and you should allot these partitions room for later growth. Also, empty space helps prevent further fragmentation of files that change over time. These shorter-lived files and their respective directories will not have any bearing on the files in either the /usr or the /home directories and thus will not impact the system's performance.

## Exploring Sample Layouts

Table 1.1 describes a standard partitioning scheme. This example uses a 10 gigabyte hard drive. The system will have no SCSI, just an IDE plugged into the primary master slot on the motherboard. The CD-ROM, meanwhile, is

---

**TIP**

If possible, give yourself enough leeway on all partitions in case an extra partition is needed at some later time. For this reason, you should omit some distinct partitions such as /opt or /usr/local and have their directories reside on either the / or /usr partition. For example, you may want to set aside a /usr partition only if you know you will be adding a larger hard drive later and that the /usr/local directory can then be mounted on this newer drive.

plugged into the secondary slave port. Bear in mind that this example shows just one of many possible methods by which you could split this drive into multiple partitions.

**Table 1.1  A Sample Partitioning Scheme on a Single IDE Drive**

| Partition Name | File System | Size (MB) | Description |
|---|---|---|---|
| / | /dev/hda1 | 500 | Root directory |
| /usr | /dev/hda7 | 2,000 | Binaries and libraries |
| /usr/local | /dev/hda6 | 2,000 | The user's own programs |
| /home | /dev/hda5 | 2,500 | Home directories |
| /var | /dev/hda2 | 500 | Logs and messages |
| /opt | /dev/hda8 | 1,000 | Unique programs |
| /usr/src | /dev/hda3 | 1,000 | Kernel source code |
| swap | /dev/hda4 | 500 | Swap space |

Under Linux, all partitions are treated as devices. Here each partition is configured as a separate device. Linux can handle as many as 16 partitions on one device or physical hard drive. The cryptic label of /dev/hda1 refers to the first partition on device hda, or hard disk drive A. If there are two or more hard drives, then the partitions would be broken up among hdb, hdc, hdd, and so on. Consult Table 1.3 for additional schemes using multiple drives.

The preceding layout is merely a suggested setup for a standard installation. The root directory is kept to a minimum partition size. With earlier Linux distributions, the / or root partition had a limit of 1,024 cylinders or about 540 megabytes.

### NOTE

Red Hat can encounter problems with partitions larger than 8 gigabytes. Another restriction is that the partition containing the Linux kernel has to reside entirely within the first 1024 cylinders of the hard drive. LILO, the program that loads the Linux kernel, has since been fixed to circumvent this limitation. Red Hat 7.0 will be the first version to include the improved LILO.

The /usr directory is allocated more space than other partitions in order to accommodate binary files and the libraries needed by Linux. Red Hat by default places its binary files in /usr/bin. If you plan to use Red Hat Package Managers (RPMs) or binary files, you should keep this partition a generous size.

You should also keep /usr/local relatively spacious since that is where programs compiled by the user are placed. Specifically, the binary files created from compiled source are placed in /usr/local/bin.

The /home directory is kept large for a variety of reasons. It is here that the separate user directories are created. Other important directories are also stored here by default. Under the Red Hat distribution, all HTML and FTP files are stored in /home. If you decide to install the Apache Web server from source rather than using the Red Hat RPM package, the location of your HTML files can change if you go with Apache's default installation. However, you can still specify the default location no matter which method you use.

It is standard practice to use /var to store many of the log and security-related files. These files normally have a shorter life span than other static files, so their turnover rate is relatively high. This means that the /var directory can be kept smaller if you anticipate storing messages for short periods.

The /opt directory has recently become more popular with programs such as Netscape and KDE. This directory is the default location for most of these programs' binary files. It might also be good practice to keep unique directories such as word processor programs in this directory. The /opt directory functions more like a catchall for unique programs and file systems.

The /usr/src directory is unique in that this is where the Linux kernel is stored, configured, and compiled. It is also where Red Hat builds and stores RPMs compiled from source. If you are thinking of doing any developmental work with Red Hat or building RPMs from source, it is prudent to keep this partition separate from the others if you wish to retain the source code for a later reinstall or for organizational or backup purposes.

Swap space is crucial for optimizing speed on your machine. Red Hat protests if you do not dedicate at least a minimal amount of hard drive space as swap space. Older releases of Red Hat would allow you to install without setting aside swap space, but performance would be severely compromised. A good rule of thumb when determining how much disk drive space to be set aside for swap is to partition one and a half to two times your physical RAM.

---

**NOTE**

If you currently have 64 megabytes of RAM on your system, 96 megabytes of swap would be a reasonable amount to devote to swap space. One thing to remember is that swap space and RAM operate together. That means that the 64 megabytes of RAM and the 96 megabytes of swap add up to 160 megabytes of memory. The minimal amount of space that should be set aside for swap space is 16 megabytes. Lastly, under some of the older Red Hat Linux releases, the most space that could be set aside for swap was 128 megabytes of RAM. That limit has since been surpassed in the latest Red Hat releases.

---

Use discretion when setting up the swap space. Don't set so much aside to the detriment of your other partitions. Failure to set up, initialize, or configure swap space correctly can result in poor performance. Red Hat will remind you to set swap space during the installation and will not proceed if you do not set at least a minimum amount of drive space for memory use. Because of how Linux manages its swap space and places working programs on the drive for later reference, there can be too much of a good thing. If swap space is consumed quickly by system programs or doesn't start up correctly, access rates and performance suffer. Swap space greater than three times the size of RAM is probably useless.

The command used to enable swap space is swapon -a. This command is executed from the /etc/rc.d files. As the machine boots up, it reads through the *rc* or *run command* files. These are those files that the operating system reads in order to initialize the system and start various daemons. When the OS finds the swapon command, it activates the swap partitions.

The information about your swap partition is kept in the /etc/fstab file. Here your computer looks for information about the parameters you determined during setup; then, upon bootup, the computer executes these definitions. The swap partitions defined in /etc/fstab have a mount value of none and their type is set to swap. This informs the operating system how to treat each particular partition when the swapon command is issued during the boot up phase or when each partition is mounted.

A similar process is executed when the computer shuts down. As will be mentioned later, powering down a Linux machine is not as simple as turning off the power. If the system is shut down improperly or all power is cut before certain processes can be cleanly halted, file systems and data become corrupted. During the shutdown process, the system executes the swapoff command in order to unmount the swap partitions. If you install Linux properly, you will probably not ever need to use the swapon or swapoff command. You can manually invoke the command, however, when setting aside an additional swap partition or when cleaning up after a system failure. For more information about starting and stopping the computer, see Chapter 2, "Starting Up and Shutting Down."

## Exploring Minimal Layout Schemes

If you are using Linux for more mundane purposes, such as desktop use, or if space is limited, setting up the partitions can be even easier. In such cases, you can place all the directories on one partition. Rather than creating separate partitions, one large standard partition or / is set aside, into which all directories and sub-directories are then placed. Swap will still need its own partition. Table 1.2 shows a sample layout for a single 2.1 gigabyte hard drive.

**Table 1.2  A Sample Layout for a Computer with Limited Hard Drive Space**

| Partition Name | File System | Size (MB) | Description |
| --- | --- | --- | --- |
| / | /dev/hda1 | 2,000 | Root directory |
| swap | /dev/hda7 | 100 | Swap space |

Such a layout is feasible, but not recommended. If one of the directories were to fail or if a reinstall were necessary later, all the files and their contents could become corrupted or would be overwritten. Distributing both system and personal information over several different partitions is a much wiser decision.

## Setting Up Multiple Drives and Partitions

A system with several physical hard drives is even easier to set up. Here it is necessary to place a directory or partition on an actual physical drive. Whether the drives are IDE or SCSI, Linux has the resources to determine the types of drives installed and to assist in their partitioning. Table 1.3 shows a sample configuration for a system similar to that of one of my many machines. I have a 200 MHz Pentium with 64 megabytes of RAM and three actual drives, the first two of which are IDE and the last being SCSI. The table shows how I partitioned the file systems across the three physical drives.

**Table 1.3  A Sample Partitioning Scheme across Three Hard Drives**

| Partition Name | File System | Size (MB) | Description |
| --- | --- | --- | --- |
| / | /dev/hda1 | 400 | Root directory |
| swap | /dev/hda2 | 100 | Swap space |
| /home | /dev/hdb1 | 500 | Home directory |
| /usr | /dev/hdb2 | 500 | Binaries |
| /usr/local | /dev/sda1 | 300 | My own programs |
| /var | /dev/sda2 | 200 | Log messages |

As you can see, the first IDE drive, hda, has only 500 megabytes of space, while the second is about 1,000 megabytes. The third drive, identified by the device label sda (for *SCSI drive*), is also about 500 megabytes.

**CAUTION**

Once you have saved the new partitions and written them to disk, all information formerly found on that drive is lost. Be sure you are absolutely sure that this is what you want before deleting and creating new partitions.

The partitioning format here is much like that of the schemes used earlier in this chapter. You are free to place additional directories in other partitions. However, I have found it useful to keep the partitions to a minimum in case I need to add more drives later. That way a unique directory not allocated to a partition can be dedicated entirely to the new hard drive. This requires adding the new drive device to the /etc/fstab file and then mounting the partition.

The latest Red Hat Linux makes this task simpler with the kudzu utility. Much as Windows can find and determine the type of new hardware placed in the machine, Linux accomplishes the same task and can update the drivers and devices without requiring the installation CD or boot disk. You should run kudzu after installing, replacing, or exchanging hardware. You can usually start kudzu by executing the full command /usr/sbin/kudzu as root or superuser.

## Restoring Lost Partitions

If the unthinkable does happen and the system does crash, making certain partitions unreadable, or if you simply want to reinstall, having taken the time to spread the separate directories across multiple partitions can prove to be advantageous. You will first want to try to access the corrupted file system and correct any errors that might be on the disk. Usually Linux will do this for you with the fsck tool (pronounced by some as *ef es check*). You may need to run fsck manually to clean up the system, in which case knowing the layout of your system will again prove beneficial.

You should reinstall only in worst-case scenarios. However, if you feel that reinstallation is your only option, Red Hat allows you to redefine which partitions to reformat and which to leave alone. For example, during the reinstallation process, you can leave your /home directory's contents untouched while specifying that the /, /usr and /var partitions be reformatted. If you had the foresight to place your personal information in a separate directory such as /home, you will hardly notice that the default binaries are once again in place. If partitions such as /home and /usr/local reside on their own partition, they will remain unaffected.

### NOTE

Many Linux users consider reinstallation to be a carry-over from Windows. Good Linux users usually do not need to reinstall. Usually the corrupted files can be reinstalled without damaging the system further. Consider reinstallation only as a last resort.

In only one instance have I been unable to restore a corrupted file system and needed to reinstall. When I was first learning Linux, a poorly written program blew away much of my root file system and damaged several system files needed to operate Linux. I learned three important lessons that day: first, exercise extreme caution when logged in as root; second, not to implicitly trust just any

Linux software program; third, to spread my directories across separate partitions. Fortunately, I had all my important documents and programs located in both the /home and /usr/local directories, each in their own respective partition. During the reinstall process, I was able to choose those directories that I wanted to reformat and reinstall. For the average user, only the /, /usr, and /var directories need to be reinstalled. The other directories can be left untouched. Linux simply overwrites the chosen partitions and reinstalls the binary files.

Linux takes great pains to make installation and reinstallation as easy as possible. Unlike other proprietary operating systems, Linux allows you to reinstall the complete operating system directly from the CD without compromising existing software. Some believe a good cleanup and periodic reinstall helps to keep disk use down. These activities flush out older links and update the system to the latest compilers and libraries. Careful planning before installing Linux can help circumvent later problems and make the system run more efficiently.

# Installing the Software

You have now familiarized yourself with the hardware and learned what Linux supports. Now, after you have partitioned the drives acceptably, Linux will prompt you to begin the install routine. Red Hat offers you several choices, even before the partitioning process, to choose a Workstation, Server, or Custom option. The first two options are fairly standard, though they can install up to 600 megabytes of programs.

## Defining the Installation Type

The first option, or what is called the Workstation installation, will automatically erase all Linux partitions from the hard drive(s), while the second option, Server, will erase *all* partitions from the computer's hard drive(s). Users should select the third option, Custom, even if they consider themselves Linux neophytes. This option allows for better management and control over the creation of partitions and the selection of programs. There really is no difference between this and the other two alternatives except that with Custom you can choose any and all of the packages that you want.

From here you will be prompted to create partitions and to set the mount points for each. In other words, you need to ensure that each partition has its own distinct directory, as was demonstrated earlier. Red Hat will offer several different choices as to the directories or partitions you can install. The amount of disk space that each partition requires depends upon the computer's function. If you are installing for the first time, you should probably opt for creating only two partitions: root (/) and swap. Once you have decided on the partitions, you can select which partitions to format. If this is a new installation, all partitions should be wiped clean and formatted for the Linux native file system. However, if this is a reinstallation or if you wish to retain the information on existing partitions, then only /, /usr, and /var need to be reformatted. You can choose additional points to format, but this is entirely up to you. Perhaps the best teacher, in this case, is experience. (Besides, I consider installing Linux one of the more enjoyable tasks working with computers.)

## Choosing Your Packages

Once you are ready to install the programs and begin formatting, you will be prompted to choose the packages you want to install. Red Hat is the leader in precompiled source code or binary packages known as *RPMs*. RPM stands for Red Hat Package Manager. The Package Manager portion allows a Linux user to automate the installation of each program fully along with documentation and supporting libraries. The package side of RPMs have doubtlessly made Linux simpler to install and easier to configure. Not only do they make installing programs simpler, but removing or upgrading them is even less a chore. No longer do you have to worry about leftover files or broken links when you remove or upgrade a file. The RPMs take care of all that for you. Again, unlike proprietary software, Red Hat does not require that you step thorough a series of wizards or consult a database to remove a program. A simple one-line command does it all for you. A more complete explanation of RPMs is covered in Chapter 11, "Installing Additional Programs."

Red Hat has carefully divided all the available packages into marked categories or divisions such as Networking, Developmental Programs, and Daemons. This helps you to define the role of your Linux machine (or *Linux box* as many advocates like to term their computers running Linux). Depending on the type of interface that you select when installing Linux, whether it be a full GUI or a more DOS-like install, you may be able to select an entire range of programs rather than having to select each program individually or tediously scroll through a list of options that you may or may not want.

What you choose depends again entirely on the purpose of the machine. If the Linux box is dedicated to functioning as a web server, you can quickly and easily install many of the programs necessary by selecting the appropriate category. By the same token, if you opt for a more complete range of programs, you can easily do so by choosing the requested category either at the outset or after paging through each subtopic.

**TIP**

Be sure to read the description of each package before installing. Many programs might be completely superfluous to your needs and will only take up unnecessary space. Games are one category that can quickly eat up more space than necessary. Calculate available space and the amount consumed by the packages if drive space is at a premium and only a limited install will work. The latest Red Hat will display the amount of drive space needed for all packages before installing.

Choosing what packages to install is not always so intuitive. Red Hat offers explanations of what each program does and where how it functions in terms of category; whether it is a utility, a game, a library, or developmental program. However, as also seen in the *man,* or manual pages, a concise overview of how each program operates and the command-line options, the explanations provided can prove cryptic. For the novice user, this can be rather frustrating. Often, new users opt for a minimal install and then are unable to compile certain programs afterward because the necessary libraries or dependent programs were unavailable. Understanding each program's function is extremely useful.

There are a couple ways new users can familiarize themselves with the available packages. Red Hat allows you the option of highlighting the binary package and then either clicking the Help button or pressing the F1 key to bring up an explanation. The latest GUI install will display the program's function in a caption below the package names and groupings. If you read the caption carefully, it usually will state not only the package's purpose but what other programs may also be dependent and what other packages this binary either supports or complements. When installing, it is always better to err on the side of installing too many programs rather than installing too few, if you have sufficient drive space not only to install the desired programs but also to do work on the machine afterward. You can always uninstall programs later, but it can sometimes prove difficult to determine what programs require installation later.

If disk space is not in short supply, choose a full install. This way you are guaranteed to have all the needed libraries for most any program that you choose to install later. One comforting thought is that even if you choose the most minimal install, Linux will run on the machine. It will boot up, display a prompt, and allow for some very basic functions. If you purchased a release that came with a manual, either on disk or in hard copy format, you should read the distributor's full description as well.

## Exploring the Installation Packages

Table 1.4 shows some of the possible package categories available in the latest Red Hat release along with a brief description of each. The more substantial sections of the install are divided into larger units and then into subcategories.

**Table 1.4 Installation Packages**

| Category | Description |
| --- | --- |
| Applications | These are the main applications that will be needed by Linux. |
| Communications | This section has fax, IRC, and modem programs. |
| Databases | This section includes, postgresql, one of the better open-sourced database programs available. |
| Editors | This section includes various text editors such as emacs, vim, joe, and jed. These are extremely useful for editing text documents on the server itself. |
| Emulators | This section includes dosemu and related programs will allow you to run DOS-based programs under Linux. |
| Engineering | This smaller section deals with scientific applications. |
| Graphics | These programs assist in editing and manipulating images via the command line. |
| Mail | This section features simple mail clients for checking and managing mail from a terminal window. |
| Math | These programs handle mathematics. |
| Networking | This section features tools for managing network resources. |
| News | This section includes various programs for reading and circulating newsfeeds and groups. |

**Table 1.4  Installation Packages** *(continued)*

| Category | Description |
| --- | --- |
| Productivity | This contains, along with other programs, *ical*, a very useful calendaring tool for managing to-do lists and keeping track of your schedule. (I use this every day.) |
| Publishing | This section contains assorted text tools for managing documents and text. |
| Sound | This section features command-line tools for editing or listening to sound files. |
| Base | This section contains the basic files for operating Linux. |
| Kernel | This section contains information on the Linux kernel itself and programs for setting up the file systems and passwords. |
| Daemons | These are programs that run in the background on your system and make your job easier. They are used for logging and sending mail and include other device utilities. |
| Development | This section is of interest to programmers and those who like to see what makes Linux tick or assist in making it work better. |
| Building | These are tools for making your own Linux programs. |
| Debuggers | Includes gdb, perhaps one of the best-known tools for tracking bugs and compilation errors. |
| Languages | This sections contains a wide assortment of computer languages, both textual and graphic. |
| Libraries | Libraries are instructions needed for program development. Linux requires many of these libraries. |
| System | These are system-level developmental tools. |
| Tools | This section contains tools needed by programmers to develop specific packages. |
| Version Control | This section includes rcs and cvs, two very useful utilities for tracking the development of programs and the changes made by programmers. |
| Documentation | This section's usefulness cannot be stressed enough, especially for beginners. Much documentation is already available on the Internet, but local files are also available. This section includes HOWTOs in various languages, manuals, documentation projects, and, most importantly, the man pages. The latest Red Hat release has moved much of the documentation to a separate CD in order to accommodate more programs. |
| Extensions | This section includes several foreign character utilities. |

**Table 1.4 Installation Packages** *(continued)*

| Category | Description |
| --- | --- |
| Games | These are terminal games, some of which are text-based other which have simple graphics. |
| Libraries | These libraries are sometimes needed by additional programs such as games or window managers and not just by the system itself. |
| Networking | Because networking is a growing field, one in which Linux is taking an increasing role, there are several subsections dealing with all aspects of configuring networking under Linux. |
| Admin | These are basic administrative functions, such as FTP, NFS, and caching of DNS. |
| Daemons | These network-related daemons monitor and manage traffic through the system. Here is where caching, DHCP, FTP, newsfeed, sendmail, and web server daemons are located. |
| Development | These utilities are used for DNS or *Domain Name Service* development. |
| News | This section includes newsfeed programs. |
| Utilities | These are additional programs that complement the networking side of Linux. These help to set up and maintain various aspects of both the internal and external network. |
| Shells | These are shells that assist the user in interfacing with the command line under Linux. |
| Utilities | This section features various packages for use under Linux. These utilities include additional functions and features. |
| Archiving | These are programs for backups or compression. |
| Console | These programs manage your video display. |
| File | These programs can help you learn more about the files on your system or manage their use. |
| Printing | These programs assist with sending information to the printer in a recognizable form. |
| System | These programs help configure the system and manage its resources, including information and documentation tools. This section is quite expansive and covers many aspects of Linux use. Be sure to acquaint yourself with what each program does and the basics of its functions. |
| Terminal | These tools help with managing terminals and allowing users to log in. |

**Table 1.4  Installation Packages *(continued)***

| Category | Description |
| --- | --- |
| Text | This section is a crucial part of Linux since so much is still in text format. This section includes tools for checking, comparing, and editing text in files. It also includes various programs such as Perl, sed, and awk that are extremely useful for running checks on larger files or blocks of files. |
| X11 | This section includes the programs and tools needed to set up a graphical working environment. (X11 is a generic name for the GUI.) |
| Amusements | This section offers various graphical diversions. One of the better ones is xearth, which displays a rotating globe on the desktop complete with cities and sunlight. |
| Applications | This section contains several useful graphical programs, including the GIMP, a free image-editing tool similar to Adobe Photoshop. |
| Games | What is any computer without games? Most Linux distributions offer several chess and card games in addition to other unique games found only under Linux. |
| Libraries | This section consists of various X Window or GUI system libraries. |
| Shells | This section includes graphical-oriented shells for accessing command-line interfaces. |
| Utilities | This section includes more graphical programs, including screen savers, image editors, and functional diversions. |
| Window Managers | Here you can choose the type of interface with which you would like to work. The types range from Windows look-alikes to bold new formats. |
| XFree86 | This is a free version of the X-Window system. It is currently under development and provides support to a wide range of video cards. |

The programs that come with a standard Linux release are by no means all the programs available for Linux. They represent merely a selection of programs that, in this case, Red Hat feels are necessary to set up a fully functional Linux box. Linux, unlike most proprietary operating systems, allows you to select from the available programs long after installation; theoretically, the programs remain available indefinitely. That is not the case with other systems, which after installation provide a very minimal selection of tools and programs. In terms of cost,

Linux is by far the better choice. With applications such as Sendmail, Apache, wu-ftpd, and desktop managers and environments such as KDE and GNOME as well as other open-source packages, Linux quickly becomes an economical means of accomplishing much on a limited budget.

> **TIP**
>
> To locate more programs for Linux, you might want refer to the Freshmeat site (http://freshmeat.net/), which keeps a copious database of standard Linux programs along with a detailed description of each. To avoid downloading each separate program, including the larger ones, the GNUware site (http://www.gnuware.com/) offers over 1,000 Linux programs on one CD for a low price. This book provides a complementary copy of the GNUware CDs. They include the source code to over 1,300 free and open-source programs.

In addition to the documentation available while installing, the user's manual—whether it came included in hard copy format, on the CD, or on the distribution's Web site—is always a useful place for information. Again, this documentation will usually list in greater detail facts about each package, its contents, the version, and sometimes even specific details about where the individual programs are placed on the computer during installation. This is especially useful when deciding on how to partition each section and how much space and resources need to be allocated for certain functions.

# Conclusion

The chapters to come will explore more closely many, if not all, of the programs referenced in the preceding segment. Each section will proceed linearly, going from the basic skill sets to the more complex. Each chapter will also be self-contained so that you need not read the book's chapters in sequence to learn specific skills or facts. The next chapter will look at the most basic functions of Linux. These include starting and stopping Linux correctly; optimizing daemons to perform background tasks, and configuring additional settings to improve system performance and security. It will also look more closely at the manner in which Linux boots up, which is extremely useful to understand when debugging problems with the system startup.

# Chapter 2

## Starting Up and
## Shutting Down

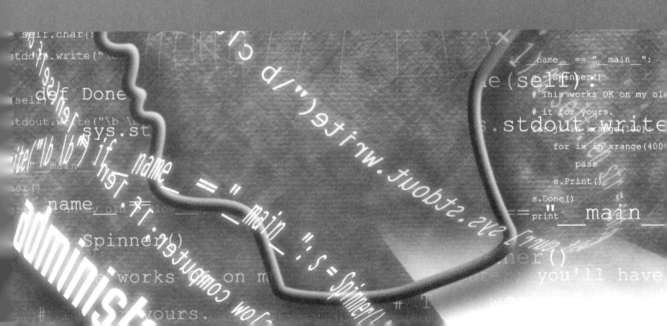

**S**imply turning Linux on and shutting off the power when you are done is not enough to administer a Linux system effectively. Understanding the messages that Linux displays upon bootup is crucial to diagnosing ills and correcting errors. Interpreting these sometimes-cryptic directives will assist you in better managing your Linux system. This chapter will cover the following topics:

- ◆ Understanding how Linux boots up
- ◆ Understanding the Linux system processes
- ◆ Changing run levels under Linux
- ◆ Properly shutting down Linux
- ◆ Troubleshooting boot errors

# Understanding the Linux Bootup Process

Once Linux has been properly installed and appears to be functional, you should familiarize yourself with the manner in which it boots up. Once the BIOS has correctly identified the hardware components, you will be presented with a LILO: prompt. This is where the software takes over from the standard memory tests and BIOS operation. If all has gone well with the installation, as outlined in the previous chapter, Linux should now be ready to start loading and you should be well on your way to running the operating system and related programs.

**NOTE**

This LILO: prompt is an acronym for *Linux loader* and allows the user to enter specific parameters to the bootup or bootstrapping process. Most users need only press the Enter key to start the system. You can also enter other variables if you want Linux to start in single-user mode or if you want to use an alternative *kernel,* or core of the operating system which is responsible for resource allocation, low level hardware interfaces, etc.

To see how to configure alternative kernels and edit the variables associated with LILO:, see Chapter 14, "Building a Custom Kernel."

## Interpreting Console Messages

In general, as Linux begins the bootup sequence, each of the processes as they start up are enabled on the console display and are thus visible to the user. That is, when booting into a regular command-line interface, you will be able to watch as each process starts its initialization sequence. With the latest Red Hat you will see the identification of system hardware and then watch as each daemon or system program either successfully or unsuccessfully starts up. Red Hat will display either a green "OK" next to each process if it starts correctly, or a red "FAILED" if not. Depending upon the speed of the processor, a typical user might be able to see each separate process as the system requires it. Even if the bootup screen displays the processes faster than you may be able to debug or check, you can always check the logs later for any rogue messages if the system sometimes fails to initialize. The bootup process is a critical time for the Linux system since hardware can misfire and customized scripts can prevent other startup sequences.

Some Linux distributions have opted to not display the entire bootup sequence, choosing rather to display a splash screen much like the Microsoft Windows startup does. This is especially true if users have chosen to boot directly into a GUI rather than a command-line interface, where all commands are typed at the command line. Red Hat, however, has opted for a more informative approach. Most users like to see what processes they are running and when they start up. Linux requires some extra care during the startup routine since that can sometimes be the only time that an administrator may see the system boot up for a very long time. Linux enjoys long uptimes, so it is important that you get it right the first time.

---

**NOTE**

Linux is based on the command line. Nearly every feature can be customized, changed, or altered by editing a text file via a console connection or in a terminal window. Though new tools are constantly being developed that allow for point-and-click changes, Linux relies on the simple text editor for most revisions.

---

Understanding how the Linux operating system correctly starts will help in correcting problems with hardware misconfiguration, optimizing the bootup sequence, and changing the daemons or processes that normally run when the operating system is fully functional. A simple change in the kernel or a text error in a startup script can prevent the computer from booting properly and thereby hang the entire process. When this happens, you can properly diagnose of what went wrong by reviewing the messages displayed during the boot process. Linux takes the position that the administrator should be able to see and diagnose any ills with the system. It attempts to be verbose in most situations when either booting up or running separate programs. These variables are taken into account and Linux then provides several approaches to fixing common errors. Linux also provides several different *run levels* or boot levels with varying networking support for each and thus enables you to boot into a safe mode so that you can fix or reinstall corrupted files.

## Reviewing Messages with the dmesg Command

In the Linux bootup process, there are actually two stages. The first is hardware recognition, and the second is the initiation of process daemons or scripts. The first stage is logged by the dmesg command and the second stage is logged to the /var/log/messages file. You can also see the same information that is displayed to the console and logged by dmesg saved here in the messages file. All this information can be reviewed after the machine is running. If there is a problem with the boot sequence, you can probably still reach a command-line prompt and from there examine what errors were generated. This section will cover the first stage of the Linux bootup.

Most Linux users find the bootup sequence extremely informative. With computers using older and slower hardware, you can carefully examine each line and process as it starts and note any inconsistencies. This is useful when building a Linux machine from recycled parts or when piecing together a new box. You can see exactly what hardware is recognized by the operating system and what is not. As CPU speed has increased, Linux now boots up quicker and the entire boot process can become a blur as the messages race by.

Linux provides a simple command to review all the hardware bootup messages after Linux is running. The dmesg command allows the user to see the saved text of the system's bootup process. This information is restricted to only the hardware recognition. This is restricted to the kernel level. Reviewing the dmesg text is a useful tool for identifying hardware issues and checking for needed component support in the default kernel.

Because there is often more text than can fit in a single xterm or console window—it is a good idea to either review the initial text of the message by using the scroll bar or by parsing out the message by using the commands less and more. Either of these two commands allows the user to paginate through the remainder of the message by pressing the space bar or Enter key. Under a console window you can also review previous text within a text editor by selecting the Alt+PageUp and Alt+PageDown keys respectively to review or forward through text. Listing 2.1 is an example of a dmesg request and some sample output.

### Listing 2.1  A Sample dmesg Request on a Vanilla Red Hat 6.2 Install

1. `[root@backup /root]# dmesg | more`

2. `Linux version 2.2.14-5.0 (root@porky.devel.redhat.com) (gcc version egcs-2.91.66 19990314/Linux (egcs-1.1.2 release)) #1 Tue Mar 7 21:07:39 EST 2000`

3. `relocating initrd image:`

4. `    initrd_start:0xc0f96000    initrd_end:0xc0ffff7b`

5. `    mem_start:0xc026c000    mem_end:0xc40ff000`

6. `    initrd_size:0x00069f7b    dest:0xc4095000`

7. `Detected 598860287 Hz processor.`

8. `Console: colour VGA+ 80x25`

9. `Calibrating delay loop... 596.38 BogoMIPS`

10. `Memory: 63616k/66556k available (1060k kernel code, 416k reserved, 976k data, 64k init, 0k bigmem)`

11. `Dentry hash table entries: 262144 (order 9, 2048k)`

12. `Buffer cache hash table entries: 65536 (order 6, 256k)`

13. `Page cache hash table entries: 16384 (order 4, 64k)`

14. `VFS: Diskquotas version dquot_6.4.0 initialized`

15. `L1 I Cache: 64K  L1 D Cache: 64K`

16. `L2 Cache: 512K`

17. `CPU: AMD AMD Athlon(tm) Processor stepping 01`

18. `Enabling extended fast FPU save and restore...done.`

19. `Checking 386/387 coupling... OK, FPU using exception 16 error reporting.`

20. Checking 'hlt' instruction... OK.

21. POSIX conformance testing by UNIFIX

22. mtrr: v1.35a (19990819) Richard Gooch (rgooch@atnf.csiro.au)

23. PCI: PCI BIOS revision 2.10 entry at 0xfdb01

24. PCI: Using configuration type 1

25. PCI: Probing PCI hardware

26. PCI: Enabling I/O for device 00:00

27. Linux NET4.0 for Linux 2.2

28. Based upon Swansea University Computer Society NET3.039

29. NET4: Unix domain sockets 1.0 for Linux NET4.0.

30. NET4: Linux TCP/IP 1.0 for NET4.0

31. IP Protocols: ICMP, UDP, TCP, IGMP

32. TCP: Hash tables configured (ehash 65536 bhash 65536)

33. Initializing RT netlink socket

34. Starting kswapd v 1.5

35. Detected PS/2 Mouse Port.

36. Serial driver version 4.27 with MANY_PORTS MULTIPORT SHARE_IRQ enabled

37. ttyS00 at 0x03f8 (irq = 4) is a 16550A

38. pty: 256 Unix98 ptys configured

39. apm: BIOS version 1.2 Flags 0x03 (Driver version 1.9)

40. Real Time Clock Driver v1.09

41. RAM disk driver initialized:  16 RAM disks of 4096K size

42. VP_IDE: IDE controller on PCI bus 00 dev 39

43. VP_IDE: not 100% native mode: will probe irqs later

44.     ide0: BM-DMA at 0xffa0-0xffa7, BIOS settings: hda:DMA, hdb:pio

45.     ide1: BM-DMA at 0xffa8-0xffaf, BIOS settings: hdc:pio, hdd:pio

46. hda: Maxtor 92041U4, ATA DISK drive

47. hdc: TOSHIBA CD-ROM XM-5302TA, ATAPI CDROM drive

**48.** ide0 at 0x1f0-0x1f7,0x3f6 on irq 14

**49.** ide1 at 0x170-0x177,0x376 on irq 15

**50.** hda: Maxtor 92041U4, 19541MB w/512kB Cache, CHS=2491/255/63

**51.** hdc: ATAPI 4X CD-ROM drive, 128kB Cache

**52.** Uniform CDROM driver Revision: 2.56

**53.** floppy0: no floppy controllers found

**54.** md driver 0.90.0 MAX_MD_DEVS=256, MAX_REAL=12

**55.** raid5: measuring checksumming speed

**56.** raid5: MMX detected, trying high-speed MMX checksum routines

**57.**    pII_mmx   :  1786.128 MB/sec

**58.**    p5_mmx    :  1876.044 MB/sec

**59.**    8regs     :   803.529 MB/sec

**60.**    32regs    :   656.463 MB/sec

**61.** using fastest function: p5_mmx (1876.044 MB/sec)

**62.** scsi : 0 hosts.

**63.** scsi : detected total.

**64.** md.c: sizeof(mdp_super_t) = 4096

**65.** Partition check:

**66.**  hda: hda1 hda2 < hda5 hda6 hda7 hda8 >

**67.** RAMDISK: Compressed image found at block 0

**68.** autodetecting RAID arrays

**69.** autorun ...

**70.** ... autorun DONE.

**71.** VFS: Mounted root (ext2 filesystem).

**72.** (scsi0) <Adaptec AHA-2940A Ultra SCSI host adapter> found at PCI 0/3/0

**73.** (scsi0) Narrow Channel, SCSI ID=0, 3/255 SCBs

**74.** (scsi0) Cables present (Int-50 YES, Ext-50 YES)

**75.** (scsi0) Downloading sequencer code... 423 instructions downloaded

**76.** enable_irq() unbalanced from c481b3c7

**77.** scsi0 : Adaptec AHA274x/284x/294x (EISA/VLB/PCI-Fast SCSI) 5.1.28/3.2.4

**78.**      `<Adaptec AHA-2940A Ultra SCSI host adapter>`

**79.**   `scsi : 1 host.`

**80.**   `(scsi0:0:2:0) Synchronous at 10.0 Mbyte/sec, offset 8.`

**81.**   `Vendor: HP        Model: C1553A        Rev: 9503`

**82.**   `Type:   Sequential-Access        ANSI SCSI revision: 02`

**83.**   `(scsi0:0:4:0) Synchronous at 10.0 Mbyte/sec, offset 8.`

**84.**   `Vendor: HP        Model: C1533A        Rev: 9406`

**85.**   `Type:   Sequential-Access        ANSI SCSI revision: 02`

**86.**   `change_root: old root has d_count=1`

**87.**   `Trying to unmount old root ... okay`

**88.**   `Freeing unused kernel memory: 64k freed`

**89.**   `Adding Swap: 265032k swap-space (priority -1)`

**90.**   `st: bufsize 32768, wrt 30720, max buffers 4, s/g segs 16.`

**91.**   `Detected scsi tape st0 at scsi0, channel 0, id 2, lun 0`

**92.**   `Detected scsi tape st1 at scsi0, channel 0, id 4, lun 0`

**93.**   `eepro100.c:v1.09j-t 9/29/99 Donald Becker`
      `http://cesdis.gsfc.nasa.gov/linux/drivers/eepro100.html`

**94.**   `eepro100.c: $Revision: 1.18 $ 1999/12/29 Modified by Andrey V.`
      `Savochkin <saw@msu.ru>`

**95.**   `eth0: Intel PCI EtherExpress Pro100 at 0xc4860000,`
      `00:A0:C9:6C:2B:6D, IRQ 10.`

**96.**   `Board assembly 678400-001, Physical connectors present: RJ45`

**97.**   `Primary interface chip i82555 PHY #1.`

**98.**   `General self-test: passed.`

**99.**   `Serial sub-system self-test: passed.`

**100.**   `Internal registers self-test: passed.`

**101.**   `ROM checksum self-test: passed (0x49caa8d6).`

**102.**   `Receiver lock-up workaround activated.`

**103.**   `eth1: Intel PCI EtherExpress Pro100 at 0xc4862000,`
      `00:A0:C9:74:C9:FE, IRQ 9.`

**104.**   `Board assembly 678400-001, Physical connectors present: RJ45`

**105.** `Primary interface chip i82555 PHY #1.`

**106.** `General self-test: passed.`

**107.** `Serial sub-system self-test: passed.`

**108.** `Internal registers self-test: passed.`

**109.** `ROM checksum self-test: passed (0x49caa8d6).`

**110.** `Receiver lock-up workaround activated.`

The text that the system produces during the boot process contains much information about the system processes. Your own setup may vary depending upon whether you are using a default Linux install or a customized kernel. The preceding example is taken from a vanilla Red Hat Linux 6.2 install. What appears during the boot process depends on those items or hardware components that are supported in the current working kernel. This stage of the install does not display what daemons or user-defined processes have successfully started but only those items and modules defined in the kernel itself. Linux must first start up the kernel and have it operational before it can initiate any scripts or daemons. Here is the output of dmesg line by line:

◆ Line 1 is the dmesg command used to display the last series of bootup messages. Most users will need to use | `more` to view a paginated display of the entire contents.

◆ Line 2 lists the Linux kernel version currently running on this particular Linux system. Here it is kernel 2.2.14-5.0. The line also displays the GNU C compiler, or gcc, version. The final item denotes the time and date the kernel was last compiled. Here the time and date that the default kernel was compiled was Tuesday, March 7, 2000, at 9:21 p.m. Eastern Standard Time.

---

**NOTE**

For more information about custom kernels and the steps needed to compile and configure your own or an existing kernel, see Chapter 4, "Terminal Shells."

---

◆ Lines 3–6 describe the RAM disk image used by Linux to help in the bootup process. The RAM disk is a clever method used by Linux to get access to other drivers it may need to use hardware vital to booting up (such as SCSI drivers). These messages are simply telling you where in memory the RAM disk resides. The hex numbers are memory locations.

- Line 7 states the processor's speed. The cryptic output translates to a 600 MHz processor.
- Line 8 sets the console display settings at 80 × 25.
- Next, on lines 9–13, Linux completes some system calibrations and then displays the amount of main memory used by the kernel itself. It also displays how much memory is left over for the rest of the system to then utilize.
- Line 14 checks for user-enabled options. Here it initializes disk quotas. This is a useful function if you want to limit the amount of space that each user can have on your system.
- Lines 15 and 16 check the motherboard cache size.
- Line 17 sets the processor type, which in this case is identified as an AMD Athlon processor.
- Lines 18–22 enable additional kernel performance settings.
- Lines 23–26 probe the PCI slots on the motherboard and set up the proper configuration settings.
- Lines 27–33 enable networking protocols such as TCP and IP under the Linux 2.2 kernel. They also set up additional protocols such as ICMP, UDP, and IGMP. Any particular types of socket connections are initialized here as well.
- Line 34 initializes the kernel swap daemon, which then pages out programs and files to swap space.
- Next, lines 35–37 display how the kernel initializes PS/2 and serial ports and assigns them the appropriate IRQs. Next, the kernel sets up the regular tty or serial port and assigns it an IRQ of 4.
- Lines 37–38 assign 256 Unix98 pseudo-terminals or ptys. They are used to produce a terminal for remote login sessions. An example of this is a telnet session via the network to your machine. A login via another machine would spawn a program which then uses any one of the 256 possible /dev/pty terminal sessions.
- Line 39 installs the apm BIOS settings. This will enable the Linux operating system to control the physical hardware. It can then power the computer off when its shutdown sequence is complete. APM is designed primarily for conserving laptop battery power.
- Line 40 installs the Real Time clock driver, which can generate periodic

signals to control timing sensitive applications, and can support alarms. You will have to provide additional settings elsewhere in the software to ensure that the hardware time stays correct.

◆ Line 41 displays the RAM disk drive, which allocates a portion of your physical RAM for saving files and for accessing often used files. This is not always the most effective use of RAM since the Linux buffer cache does the same automatically. Most commonly RAM drives are used during the initial Linux install process.

◆ Next, Linux determines what types of physical hard drives, CD-ROMs, and floppy drives are installed on the computer. This is covered on lines 42–53. There is one Maxtor 20 gigabyte IDE drive, one ATAPI CD-ROM, and no floppy drives.

◆ On lines 54–64, the startup process initializes the RAID code and optimizes the fastest method of computing checksums on the RAID. Locating and mounting RAID devices comes later.

◆ Lines 65–67 list the partition check results. These are the partitions as you set them up during the initial install.

◆ Lines 68–70 show the kernel detecting any additional RAID arrays and beginning the autorun sequence, which attempts to find all drives that belong to each RAID set.

◆ Next, on line 71, the root file system is mounted using the ext2 file format.

◆ Lines 72–79 define the SCSI controller card and verify that certain requirements are met in order for the card to function properly under Linux. The "0:2:0" notation means "channel # : SCSI ID # : LUN".

◆ Once the SCSI card has been properly detected, any peripheral devices are then displayed. The two devices displayed are both SCSI tape backup devices. Linux displays their makeup under lines 80–85. The first has a SCSI ID number of 2 and is an internal HP auto tape loader, while the second is an external single-tape backup device. They are assigned the same driver and identity.

---

**NOTE**

Rather than poring over the dmesg file once the operating system has been loaded, you can reaffirm the identity of your SCSI devices by typing **cat /proc/scsi**. This will display all devices attached to your SCSI card.

- Lines 86 and 87 show how Linux un-mounts the old root boot file and then mounts the root file.
- Line 88 shows how much memory is released by during the startup.
- Line 89 displays the amount of physical swap space mounted for the system's use.
- Line 90 sets the buffer size for the SCSI tape device, or /dev/st.
- Lines 91 and 92 describe the SCSI devices in more detail, now that the kernel is running. Here again you can see the LUN numbers assigned to each respective drive.
- The last series of lines, 93–110, show how Linux begins the networking aspect by detecting the two Ethernet cards. Both are Intel Express 10/100 cards. The first is assigned the designation of eth0, or Ethernet interface 0, and the second eth1. (Remember that Linux begins counting with the number 0 and not the number 1.)

The dmesg command shows only the startup sequence for the hardware and kernel variables. The loading of daemons is yet another aspect to the bootup process and is not handled by the dmesg command. Daemons do not have to be successful in their initialization in order for the machine to start properly or to reach a login prompt. The hardware, however, must boot up properly. Certain daemons might fail to load and will time out. If this occurs, the machine will continue booting but will not load all the daemons. This is true in the case of the sendmail daemon, which hangs if not on a network or if it is unable to determine the machine name. This will not prevent Linux from loading, but will cause a delay in the boot process.

Each system's configuration varies slightly depending upon the distribution, the hardware installed, and the configuration of the kernel. Once all the variables have passed the initial startup sequence, only then will Linux attempt to load any daemons or scripts. This topic will be covered in the next section.

Finally, when all is running the console will display the Red Hat release name and number. This information is based on the text loaded in the /etc/issue file. You can customize this to your own specifications and enter any additional text particular to that machine. Under the release number will be the kernel version and the type of machine on which it is operating. You will then see a login prompt awaiting a username and password.

# Running Daemons in the Background

Linux keeps many processes continuously running. In addition to starting up separate programs when the user calls them, Linux finds it also effective to run *daemons,* or processes that are continuously operational. These can either await requests from the user or that run various operations in the background as determined by system needs. In this manner, background processes can handle programs more quickly and effectively.

A Linux daemon is a *background process*—a process that runs without outputting information to the screen, but which constantly observes and monitors system status and performs tasks automatically. These may or may not be dependent upon the user. You can query a daemon at any time about its status but it will not normally make itself known to the user. Certain daemons are modularized and kept out of the running kernel so that they do not increase the kernel's size and thus slow down Linux's performance. Daemons are started at bootup, right after kernel initializes, and continue to function for as long as the system is running or until the administrator changes their status. This is the second stage of the bootup process and follows the hardware recognition portion. Linux users can start and shut down daemons as different needs arise or when system changes require initialization or updating. However, the entire system manages itself with minimal interaction with users.

Daemons have the responsibility to sort out the incoming stream of data, looking for input that matches the parameters specified by the daemons, and then to determine what priority each command receives. Think of a daemon as a security guard who sits in a back room, watching a vast array of monitors, taking care of specific issues when the need arises. For more information about how processes are managed and prioritized, see Chapter 7, "Identifying Processes."

One function of a daemon is to monitor conditions on the system. One of the most well-known daemons is the *cron* daemon. Short for *chronological,* cron works at particular time intervals to manage automatic processes. It is a text file containing times and specific commands that are initiated by the system at specific intervals. Every few moments it wakes up and checks one of the many *cron files,* or text files containing programs or daemons, to see whether any commands need to be executed. If not, the daemon goes back to sleep, awaiting the next time that it must check for programs. If, upon checking the various files, cron finds a command or text file with a start time that corresponds to the same time on the system clock, the daemon will carry out that command, running until the task is complete.

## Starting Daemons with inetd

As daemons gained popularity among early UNIX, and now Linux, users, they began to slow down system performance since they all started at boot. With so many processes running and vying for memory and CPU usage, serious performance problems developed. BSD created the *inet daemon,* or *inetd,* in response to this issue. This command is a daemon that spawns other daemons as the needs arises. The inetd command became so successful that other versions of UNIX decided to include it as well. Linux is optimized to use inetd for most all its network daemon management. It is this program that sets the standards and limits for many daemon processes. The inetd command is commonly recognized by many today as being the prime daemon and is crucial in maintaining network integrity on Linux systems. Because Linux is most commonly used for Internet-related systems—such as web and FTP servers, telnet, and so on—inetd carries the burden of making sure that these Internet services are configured and started properly. When a request is made to the system for one of these services, it is inetd that spawns the additional Internet daemons as required.

## Understanding System-Specific Daemons

The very first process to start when Linux is powered up is init. It is considered the most important process and as such receives a process ID number, or PID, of 1. PIDs, or process ID numbers, help Linux keep track of each process and also helps the user to make changes or track what the system is doing. Thus init is the first process and spawns many of the later processes. All other processes other than those created by the Linux kernel are descendants of init.

Inetd is the daemon that controls and manages several other daemons, aside from those handled by the kernel or by client processes such as cron, atd, and database daemons. It calls those daemons that are needed by the system to perform various duties. Once they have completed their task, inetd allows them to die gracefully. Like most other daemons, inetd requires root access to run. Since it is what spawns the other daemons, it requires special permissions to perform those tasks that can be done only by or as superuser or root. As such, inetd is extremely powerful and can call certain processes into life and kill them as well.

Inetd, like many daemons and processes, relies upon a configuration file, /etc/inetd.conf, to know exactly what processes can or should not be spawned. The location of this file and many other configuration files is in the /etc directory. However, Linux uses a method of safeguarding many of its more sensitive files, such as inetd.conf, by setting the permissions on the file so that only root can change the file. You can change these permissions on files manually, but should be careful to allow others to change sensitive files such as these.

> **TIP**
>
> Linux often uses configuration files for setting up certain processes. These are easily identifiable by their *.conf* extension.

Other UNIX systems take even more precautions by placing the inetd.conf file one more directory removed from the /etc directory. Solaris, a proprietary UNIX-based system, for example, places the inetd.conf file in an /etc/inet/ directory and creates a symbolic link in /etc to the real file. This does not ensure that no one can inadvertently alter the file but does increase the security. Again, it comes down to the file permissions. Linux protects sensitive files by setting permissions so that only root can make changes. Changing the permissions on this file so that other users besides root can read and write to these files will compromise system security and allow these other users to start their own daemon processes.

## Controlling Access with TCP Wrappers

Another addition to the inetd.conf file that helps Linux maintain control over the ports and to better monitor what services are started is a program called tcp_wrappers. Tcp_wrappers allows better access control and logging of network daemons. Rather than simply starting up the daemons without hesitation, tcp_wrappers employs a system of checks to ensure that those programs are authorized to grant the requested daemon the power to do what it needs to do. The freely available tcp_wrappers program (sometimes referred to as the singular, tcp_wrapper) enhances logging of network functions to the syslog file. Syslog is where Red Hat Linux logs the attempted execution of sensitive programs. This and other logs files are stored in the /var/log directory. See Chapter 19, "Linux Security," for a more comprehensive analysis of system security.

Tcp_wrappers uses the tcpd daemon, which places itself between the inetd daemon and the other sub-daemons. Installing tcp_wrappers involves building the tcpd executable and then configuring the inetd.conf file. Red Hat Linux installs tcp_wrappers by default in the latest release, so no manual tweaking of the files is necessary to gain the best use. Tcpd replaces the standard daemons with its own daemon that functions as a filter on that particular port until the appropriate call is made. tcpd looks at the address from where the request is coming and what it is wanting to use. It then consults the configuration files and decides if the request is allowed.

Tcp_wrappers comes installed by default on nearly all Linux systems. However, if you are using other UNIX-based releases, such as Solaris or AIX, you will need to install tcpd by hand. Red Hat Linux, on the other hand, edits the inetd.conf file by default during the initial installation and can easily be updated using the RPM package. Unless you wish to tighten security further, you probably will not need to edit this configuration file. However, it is important to know what options it controls and how those options affect the system. An explanation of tcp_wrappers is found in Chapter 19.

## Configuring Daemons with the inetd.conf File

Understanding the inetd.conf file can help you comprehend how the system starts up certain functions. Listing 2.2 is an example inetd.conf file taken from a standard Red Hat Linux install. This first example shows how the inetd.conf file looks without tcp_wrappers installed, whereas the second example (Listing 2.3) replaces the configuration with the tcpd program. Those lines with the pound sign preceding them are commented out and their services have been disabled either for security purposes or because they are not needed.

**Listing 2.2  A Section of a Typical inetd.conf File without tcp_wrappers Installed**

```
#
# These are standard services.
#
ftp       stream   tcp   nowait   root   /usr/sbin/ftpd     in.ftpd -1 -a
telnet    stream   tcp   nowait   root   /usr/sbin/telnetd   in.telnetd
```

```
# Shell, login, exec and talk are BSD protocols.
#
shell    stream    tcp    nowait    root    /usr/sbin/rshd    in.rshd
login    stream    tcp    nowait    root    /usr/sbin/rlogind in.rlogind


# Pop and imap mail services et al
#
#pop-2   stream    tcp    nowait    root    /usr/sbin/ipop2d    ipop2d
pop-3    stream    tcp    nowait    root    /usr/sbin/ipop3d    ipop3d
imap     stream    tcp    nowait    root    /usr/sbin/imapd     imapd
```

Listing 2.3 shows the same file with tcp wrappers implemented. Notice how the second-to-last field has been replaced with tcpd or the tcp daemon.

### Listing 2.3  A Default Red Hat Linux inetd.conf File with tcp_wrappers Installed

```
#
# These are standard services.
#
ftp      stream    tcp    nowait    root    /usr/sbin/tcpd    in.ftpd -l -a
telnet   stream    tcp    nowait    root    /usr/sbin/tcpd    in.telnetd


# Shell, login, exec, and talk are BSD protocols.
#
shell    stream    tcp    nowait    root    /usr/sbin/tcpd    in.rshd
login    stream    tcp    nowait    root    /usr/sbin/tcpd    in.rlogind


# Pop and imap mail services et al
#
#pop-2   stream    tcp    nowait    root    /usr/sbin/tcpd    ipop2d
pop-3    stream    tcp    nowait    root    /usr/sbin/tcpd    ipop3d
imap     stream    tcp    nowait    root    /usr/sbin/tcpd    imapd
```

The following is a more detailed explanation of each field in the inetd.conf file:

◆ The first column contains the service name. These service names are linked to specific port numbers whose corresponding service can be found in the /etc/services file for TCP and UDP services.

◆ The second column determines what type of socket will be used for that specific service. There are three different types of sockets: stream, dgram, and raw. Raw sockets are seldom used. Stream sockets, which are commonly used for TCP service, are becoming the most popular. Dgram is implemented in UDP services.

◆ The third column identifies the type of protocol that the daemon will use. The types available are listed in the protocols file, which is located either in the same directory as the services file or in the /etc directory. The protocols are almost always TCP or UDP. Linux, however, remains extremely dynamic and allows for a host of other protocols.

◆ The fourth column is generally set to the variable nowait. This means that the inetd daemon can create new copies of the same daemon. It does not have to wait to respawn itself, but instead can be forked off to generate new versions. If, however, the daemon in question can handle multiple requests this variable should be set to wait so that multiple copies of the same daemon are not forked. Under Red Hat Linux, nowait is an acceptable option.

◆ The fifth column is the name of the user who has permission to run the daemon. This can be set to any user, but generally the service needs to be root in order to bind to ports less than 1024. Therefore, many daemons can only run as root. If, however, a sendmail daemon were running as someone other than root, this variable should be set for that specific user. Another example of this is the fingerd daemon, which is sometimes run as guest, which as its name implies is a user with only limited permissions. It is in this column that the user guest would be specified.

◆ The sixth column lists the arguments to be passed to the daemon executable. In this case, it would either be the daemon itself or the tcpd daemon. tcpd takes as an argument the program to be run should the security check pass.

◆ The last column is the argument used then to spawn the daemon along with any flags or additional options needed to run the process. Notice the in.ftpd daemon command. The command specifies a couple of options to run correctly or to optimize its use.

Tcp_wrappers is available with every Red Hat Linux release. You don't have to install it during installation, though it is recommended to grant the system a higher degree of security. Tcp_wrappers can be installed later. And because it also comes in an RPM format, tcp_wrappers automatically makes the needed changes to the inetd.conf file, so editing the file manually is unnecessary.

# Finding Port Numbers in the /etc/services File

Every service that runs under Linux requires a port number, a specific number to which a client connects to obtain the service. This can be either an external or local service. If the port number of a certain service is not known, you can usually find it in the /etc/services file. This specific file lists all available services such as SMTP, FTP, Telnet, HTTP, and a host of others. Generally, the port numbers for basic Linux services are kept under 1024. These are reserved ports and should only be used for specific services as defined by the Internet Assigned Numbers Authority (IANA). A daemon must be run by root to use these port numbers. For security reasons, it is best to monitor what services are run on ports numbered lower than 1024. Any number higher than 1024 is either open for use or reserved for other network applications.

Listing 2.4 shows a sample excerpt of an /etc/services file. It lists ports 21 through 25 and the services they offer. Generally, all services will be available with any default Red Hat Linux setup. Additional ports such as 110 for the Post Office Protocol (POP) service rarely require tweaking. Editing the /etc/services file does not change the security on your system. The daemon itself must be disabled in either the /etc/inetd.conf file or by editing the startup scripts if you wish to increase the security or usc tcp_wrappers. You may have to add an additional field to the /etc/services if implementing a new service such as Secure Shell (ssh) or when redefining an existing protocol such as POP3 when establishing an additional alias.

Listing 2.4 is a small excerpt from the /etc/services file and shows how each field is configured.

### Listing 2.4  An Excerpt Taken from a Default /etc/services File

```
ftp          21/tcp
fsp          21/udp         fspd
ssh          22/tcp                      # SSH Remote Login Protocol
ssh          22/udp                      # SSH Remote Login Protocol
telnet       23/tcp
# 24 - private
smtp         25/tcp         mail
```

The first column lists the service name as it is mapped to the second column's specific port number and protocol. The next column is a listing of any particular aliases for that same service. For example, *smtp* stands for *Simple Mail Transfer Protocol* and is not a valid request for initiating mail service. A program can query the /etc/services file for the port corresponding to the "smtp" protocol. It then returns port number 25. One can also query the "mail" protocol and also get the port number 25 as a response. You can use either the service name or the alias when referring to a service in /etc/inetd.conf. Another example of an alias (not demonstrated in Listing 2.4) is a whois call that under the alias column could also be a nickname. Querying the whois command will display the port number associated with that particular service. The last column is sometimes a commented-out explanation of what the service does.

## Choosing and Controlling Generic Daemons

Linux allows the administrator to choose what daemons he or she might want to start up automatically. Red Hat has two utilities for determining which services will be made available upon startup. They are, of course, dependent upon the packages installed. If sendmail is not initially installed, it will not be an available service or a starting option. You can either run the command /sbin/checkconfig or /usr/sbin/ntsysv from the command line. The latter is a graphics tool that creates a text-based interface where the user can select or deselect which service to start.

If you are just beginning Linux administration, ntsysv is a quick way to control the dameons effectively. It also provides the user with a help option that explains the functions of many of the services. You can run ntsysv either at the console or in an X-Window environment. There are, however, certain terminals that in a GUI environment can cause the characters to display incorrectly. Any additional daemons that are installed later will also be added to the options listed when ntsysv is executed. These too can be configured to start at bootup.

For a better understanding of what services or daemons can or should be started up, Table 2.1 provides a brief overview of several of the available processes.

**Table 2.1 Available Daemons and Services**

| Daemon or Service | Description |
| --- | --- |
| amd | This runs the automount daemon that mounts NFS hosts or drives on demand. Choosing to run this daemon automatically is probably a good idea if you are part of a large network and are using drives located on other machines. |
| apmd | This daemon is used to monitor battery status via the syslog file. apmd logs battery use and depletion of power to the syslog file which can then be displayed or monitored on the desktop. It can also be used for shutting down the machine when battery power gets too low. This option is mostly useful for laptop machines. It is unnecessary to run on desktop or networked Linux servers that have a continuous power supply. |
| arpwatch | This daemon builds a database of Ethernet address/IP address pairings as it sees them on a LAN interface. |
| atd | Similar to the cron daemon, the atd daemon runs commands scheduled by the user at certain times. It will also run batch commands when the load is low enough. |
| autofs | This daemon automatically mounts file systems when needed and unmounts them when finished. |
| crond | The crond daemon is a standard UNIX program that runs programs at scheduled times. |
| dhcpd | This daemon starts a local DHCP server or Dynamic Host Control Protocol and assigns dynamically allocated IP addresses to its client hosts. |
| gated | This gateway routing daemon handles network routing protocols. The gated daemon is not commonly used on today's more dynamic networks. |
| gpm | Adding mouse support to console based applications, this daemon also allows for cut-and-paste operations and pop-up menu applications for console programs. |
| httpd | Under most Linux machines, this daemon is the Apache web server. It serves up HTML and CGI files. |
| inet | Also called the Internet superserver daemon or inetd, this daemon starts up other Internet-based daemons as needed. Some example daemons are telnet, ftp, and rsh. |
| innd | The innd daemon starts up the local Usenet news server or Internet news daemon. You would use this daemon only used if your local box hosted newsgroups. |

**Table 2.1  Available Daemons and Services** *(continued)*

| Daemon or Service | Description |
| --- | --- |
| keytable | This daemon loads the keyboard map as defined in your Linux setup. |
| kudzu | Though not a daemon, kudzu is still listed since it checks for any new hardware upon bootup. It then configures and installs additional software so the new device will be recognized and operate correctly under Red Hat Linux. |
| linuxconf | This daemon will allow you to configure your Linux box using a web browser as an interface. This provides you with the freedom to configure your machine from nearly any location. |
| lpd | The Linux print daemon or lpd is responsible for managing the lpr program. It handles what print jobs are spooled out to the printers. It is required for any sort of print management. |
| mars-nwe | If your machine uses any Novell NetWare compatible systems, this daemon helps manage files and print servers. It allows you to use a Linux machine as a file and print server for NetWare-based clients using NetWare's native IPX protocol. The mars-nwe daemon performs for Netware clients the same sorts of services for Linux users that SAMBA provides for Windows users. |
| mcserv | This is the Midnight Commander server, which allows remote users to manipulate their files on the same machine running this daemon. It authenticates the users against usernames and passwords before allowing them to log on and change files. |
| named | Otherwise known as BIND, the named daemon is the DNS (Domain Name Server) by which IP addresses are resolved to host names, and vice versa. |
| netfs | This program is not a true daemon but simply mounts and unmounts all mount points covered by NFS (Network File System), SMB (SAMBA), and NetWare (NCP). It occurs only during the startup and shutdown processes. |
| network | If your machine uses any sort of network interface cards (NICs) to communicate with other computers, this program activates and deactivates all network interfaces to start at boot time. This is not a true daemon but it can be managed like a daemon and started and stopped via the command-line. |
| nfs | NFS (Network File System) allows for the sharing of directories across TCP/IP networks. You can mount a directory structure on a machine and have that remote file system appear as a local directory. This provides NFS server functionality and is configured by the /etc/exports file. When mounted it will appear as an additional partition when a df command is executed. |

**Table 2.1  Available Daemons and Services (continued)**

| Daemon or Service | Description |
| --- | --- |
| pcmcia | This daemon supports Ethernet and modem connections in laptops. If you are using a desktop machine, you probably will not need this daemon. |
| portmap | Portmap manages servers that make use of RPC (Remote Procedure Calls) connections. These are used by protocols such as NFS (Network File System) and NIS (Network Information Service). Any service that uses the RPC mechanism must have this daemon running. This is one of the more exploited daemons and could compromise your machine's security. Decide whether this is really necessary before granting this daemon permission to run. |
| postgresql | This is a local SQL server daemon. If you are doing any developmental work, postgresql is one of the most dynamic of the free database servers available. |
| random | This program generates high-quality random numbers. Several programs make use of this program for unique figures. It is not a true daemon but starts only on startup and shutdown. |
| routed | Reserved for networking issues, the routed daemon allows for the IP router table to be automatically updated by RIP (Routing Information Protocol). RIP is mostly used for smaller networks, while larger networks require a more complex routing scheme. |
| rstatd | This protocol allows users on a network to receive remote kernel performance statistics for any machine on that network. |
| ruserd | This daemon allows any user on a network to locate any other given user on the same network. |
| rwhod | Similar to the finger command, the rwho command allows a user logged in remotely to determine who else is logged in. |
| sendmail | Probably the most important daemon that helped to shape the Internet, sendmail is an MTA (Mail Transport Agent) that moves electronic mail from one machine to another. |
| smb | This daemon controls all SMB network services. This is the protocol that runs on Linux. SAMBA is the implementation of the protocol and is a very useful tool in that it allows transparency of Linux clients on Windows-based networks. Linux can then function as a file and print server for various Windows machines. |
| snmpd | SNMP (Simple Network Management Protocol) responds to SNMP requests. It binds itself to a port and awaits requests, processes incoming queries, collects information, and then returns the data to the user. |

**Table 2.1  Available Daemons and Services *(continued)***

| Daemon or Service | Description |
| --- | --- |
| sound | The sound program saves and restores the sound card mixer setting at boot time. For some of the newer Plug and Play (PnP) audio cards, this program greatly facilitates the performance of audio under Linux. Again, it is not a true daemon but is found under the ntsysv program for startup and shutdown processes. |
| syslog | This daemon is the means by which many daemons log messages to various system logs. It is recommended that syslog always run for purposes of debugging and troubleshooting performance issues. |
| xfs | XFS is the daemon that controls the X Font server which allows a variety of font types to be used with X Windows. |
| ypbind | This daemon runs on NIS/YP (Name Information Service/Yellow Pages) clients and binds them to an NIS domain. This should not be running on clients that are not using NIS. |

Though these daemons do start automatically if installed and configured for a Linux system, it is also simple either to shut them down via a command line or to restart them after making changes to their configuration files. The normal options used with each of these programs or daemons is status, start, stop, or restart. For example, if I wanted to restart the named daemon after editing the DNS files, I would use the following command: /etc/rc.d/init.d/named restart.

**TIP**

You can manage daemons manually by using the command line or by using various GUI-based administrative tools. It is a good idea to become familiar with the command line first.

These daemons do have a GUI by which they can be administered. Linuxconf is a utility normally run under X-Window that allows for administration of system-specific daemons. It also has a text- and web-based interface for easier administration. See Chapter 12, "Performing Day-to-Day Tasks," for additional information on the Linuxconf tool.

Understanding the command line is imperative to accomplishing complex tasks under Linux. X-Window tools are useful in some instances, but for remote administration or when logging in via a console or Telnet connection, you must know how to use the command line. The next section explains how you can stop or start each of these daemons manually when a GUI is not available.

# Working with Startup Scripts

*Run control,* or rc files, are also known as *startup scripts* and are the actual files that control daemons. Generally, all Linux installs come with their own particular set of scripts that can be customized or altered to suit each administrator's purposes. Many of the default scripts have several options and some highly specialized calls, but that does not limit users from creating their own simple scripts for starting specific programs from within their own directories.

There are two basic locations for bootup scripts; one is the /etc/rc.d directory, which is a global directory for initiating programs for the entire system, and the other location is in the user's own directory where, upon login, certain programs can be started automatically. The first is designed for starting daemons or programs when the run level is changed. For instance when booting up the system or when changing from a command-line interface to the X-Window environment.

Some of the types of files located in the /etc/rc.d directories are as follows:

- ◆ rc0.d/, rc1.d/, ..., rc6.d/ These are directories that contain symbolic links to startup and shutdown scripts, which are executed when the corresponding runlevel is entered. The rc3.d/ directory, for example, controls the command-line interface while the rc5.d/ directory contains the scripts for starting programs integral to the X-Window environments.

- ◆ init.d/ This directory contains the actual scripts as they are executed. Any administrator modifications can be done here and are then carried throughout the other rc*n*.d directories.

- ◆ rc  Script that is called when the run level changes. It then executes the scripts in the appropriate rc*n*.d directory.

- ◆ rc.sysinit  The script that is run when the system is first started.

- ◆ rc.local  The script that is run after all other scripts during booting. This is a convenient place to add simple startup customizations.

The second types of bootup scripts are designed for the individual users and share similarities only in file naming and not so much in function. These user-specific files are generally *hidden files,* meaning they are preceded by a dot or period and are not visible when using a normal ls command. These files are also known as *dot files*. They may also have an .rc extension. One example is the .bashrc file that starts programs at the bash prompt. However, hidden files are not limited to files with an .rc extension. Some other well-known startup files are .profile, .bash_profile, and .bash_login. These are the more standard startup files in each user's directories under Red Hat Linux.

## Defining Run Command Scripts

As an example of run command scripts, the sendmail file in the /etc/rc.d/init.d/ directory is actually a longer script that controls the manner in which sendmail operates. A quick look through the script shows that it has certain arguments for starting up the sendmail daemon. These flags and options can be modified to accommodate the user. Whenever you make changes to default settings, be sure to create a backup copy of the file just in case something goes wrong, such as a typing or misspelling error that leads to the script failing to execute correctly. Before you edit a file, you should copy it and give it another extension. I usually place a .dist extension at the end of my copied file. In this manner you will remember that the .dist extension stands for the *distribution* file that came pre-installed. For example, if you were about to make changes to the sendmail script in the /etc/rc.d/init.d/ directory, you would type the following:

```
cp /etc/rc.d/init.d/sendmail /etc/rc.d/init.d/sendmail.dist
```

This way you can always fix any mistakes or restore the distribution configuration without reinstalling the package. Backing up the file first can save many a headache.

After you copy the file using an alternative filename, you can begin editing it without fear. Looking through the sendmail script, it is clear that the script cleans up several different sendmail options before actually starting the daemon itself.

The daemon first reinitializes the aliases file and then rebuilds the virtual user table, or virtusertable, database. The options associated with sendmail will be examined in greater detail later on. The script handles many of the mundane tasks automatically so that the user does not need to input all the commands by hand. This is fairly typical of most daemons spawned in the /etc/rc.d/init.d directory. See Chapter 18, "Sounding Off on Linux," for a more complete overview of the options associated with sendmail.

Lastly, when executing the script, the user is given several options for checking the handling of the sendmail daemon. This particular daemon can be queried with one of four commands: *start, stop, restart,* and *status.* If you are currently within the /etc/rc.d/init.d/ directory, the command ./sendmail restart will stop and then restart the sendmail daemon. The following is an example followed by the options associated with the sendmail daemon:

```
/etc/rc.d/init.d/sendmail start | stop | restart | status
```

> ### TIP
>
> The period and forward slash are required for commands located in the current directory. Sometimes, simply typing the command by itself produces an error, but placing the period and forward slash before it tells the computer that the program to be executed is located in the same directory. This applies only if the program is also not located in the user's path.
>
> Likewise, you could give the entire path to the script, as in /etc/rc.d/init.d/sendmail restart, but it is sometimes easier simply to change directories into the same location and then place the two characters, a period and a forward slash, ahead of the command.
>
> It is normally not a good idea to add the "." or single period to the PATH variable even though it makes command executions easier. This is a gaping security hole and should be avoided. Suppose I as an untrusted user make a script called "ks" in /tmp and then somehow entice root to "cd /tmp" as I know he, the administrator, often mistypes "ls" as "ks". And supposing "ks" is a script that trashes the system. In other words, "." in the path allows untrusted executables to be accidentally executed.

## Restarting Daemons

Restarting a daemon is required any time changes have been made either to the script itself or to any variables required by the program, such as configuration files. Using sendmail again as an example, if you add any new domain to your machine's virtusertable or add a domain that has permission to relay through your machine, the sendmail daemon will need to be restarted. The daemon must reread its configuration files and then incorporate the new settings into the daemon when it is restarted.

Another method of reinitializing the daemon is to use one of the several signals to the process. The process ID number is sent a HUP signal (short for *hangup*), which causes the program to reread its files. The daemon then parses through all the necessary information as changed by the user without actually stopping and restarting. Red Hat recommends restarting daemons using the previously mentioned start, stop, and restart commands together with the /etc/rc.d/init.d daemons. To reinitialize a daemon after changing its configuration, send daemon *foo* the following command: /etc/rc.d/init/d/foo restart. This will gracefully bring down the process or daemon and start it back up with all options intact. See Chapter VII) for a more complete discussion on sending signals to system processes.

If the previous method is too verbose or if you want to have the configuration files re-read without shutting down the process, send the daemon process a HUP signal. You must first determine what the process ID number is for that daemon. This is done by using a ps command to list the processes and then using grep to single out the daemon in question.

```
[root@pluto init.d]# ps aux | grep sendmail
```

This generates the following output:

```
root    15219   0.0   1.7   1884 1100   ?   S   16:16   0:00
sendmail
```

The process identification number (PID) is the second field in the line. That is the process ID given to that daemon when it was first started. Sending a simple HUP or `kill -1` will cause the daemon to restart. In some cases this is recommended since you will be able to tell if your configuration changes were effective or if they ended up killing the daemon altogether. In the case of the named daemon, you may want to only send it a hangup signal rather than stopping and restarting it over.

```
[root@pluto init.d]# kill -1 15219
[root@pluto init.d]# kill -HUP 15219
```

Another query to see the current state of the sendmail daemon shows that the process ID has now increased, but the daemon is still running:

```
root    15440   1.0   1.7   1884   1100   ?   S   00:00   0:00
sendmail
```

The daemon has reread the information required to run and has been restarted without any interruption to the users using that daemon to transmit mail. With other daemons, the process ID number does not increment when it receives a -HUP command. This is true of the syslogd daemon, which logs information about system processes. The same applies to the named daemon, which controls the Domain Name Services under Linux.

Not all programs or daemons respond to a hangup signal in the same way. Some increment the PID, whereas others do not, and still others require the brute force method—the daemon itself must be killed and then manually restarted. This can be the case with daemons that you write yourself or that spawn multiple child processes. The entire set of parents and children must be eliminated before a new parent process will start. This method involves sending the parent process a kill -9 signal. This signal kills the parent, and then tells the system allows the children to die off gradually.

## Comparing Run Levels

There might be circumstances when users will want to use Linux without other users being able to access the files as well, or when the superuser might want to boot up directly into the X-Window environment without having to log in directly at the command line. In cases such as these, Linux uses different *run levels*. A run level is the current system state as it relates to networking, single-user mode, or a graphical environment.

At any given time a Linux box can be in one of three states: shutdown with no power, single-user mode, and multiuser mode. However, in addition to these three states, there are six distinct run levels—seven if you count 0, which signifies a powered-down state or condition in which it is safe to shut down the machine. However, you cannot or should not boot into some of these modes. The only modes you will probably need to use are run levels 3 and 5 and single-user mode or run level 1. In each of these states, certain protocols are either active or not enabled. These "states of being" are referred to as *System V run levels*. It is useful to understand these conditions since there may come a time that you need to bring the machine down to a lower level or lower run state to accomplish administrative tasks or take the machine to a higher level to circumvent logging into the console by booting directly into X-Window.

If you look at the /etc/rc.d/ directory you will see the various run levels. There are seven in all, rc0.d through rc6.d. When changing run levels, Linux calls the scripts from each of these respective directories and changes the system's state. Table 2.2 briefly outlines each state of the eight possible levels in which a Linux box can run.

**Table 2.2 A Short Description of the Various Run Levels**

| Run Level | Description |
| --- | --- |
| 0 | This is a powered-down state. When in this run level, it is safe to turn off the machine. |
| 1 | This is commonly referred to as the system administration state or single-user mode. In this state, it is safe to perform backups without any interference and to modify the system. |
| S or s | This is nearly the same as run level 1 but is classified as single-user mode. |
| 2 | This is a multiuser mode. This is the normal state of operations for most UNIX machines except Linux. In this level, Linux runs without networking capability. |
| 3 | This is the default boot state for Linux. It is the file-sharing mode and allows Linux to swap files across a network either via NFS or TCP/IP or some other networking protocol. When booting into this state, the user normally receives a console login prompt. |
| 4 | This is a currently unused state that the system administrator can define. |
| 5 | This mode is currently gaining more popularity as users wish simply to boot into a graphical mode running X-Window. Rather than logging into the console prompt and then giving the command to start X-Window manually, this run level automatically gives the user a GUI. Red Hat allows this level to be the default state after running graphical tools such as Xconfigurator. |
| 6 | This is the reboot mode. Moving to this run level takes the machine down to run level 0 and then reboots it into its default mode. |

You can reach each of these run levels via the command line when running as root. To change the default run level, open the /etc/inittab file and locate the line that says id:3:initdefault. This code identifies the default run state as level 3. The file contains enough commented notes to clarify most lines. The suggested states are 2, 3, and 5. You can change run levels by calling the init executable. For example, to move from run level 3 or the command-line interface to the X Window environment, execute the following command at the command-line /sbin/init 5. This will bring up the Red Hat graphical login display. The same can be done for switching to the other levels. To power down the machine, simply type: /sbin/init 0 and to reboot, type: /sbin/init 6. The former command is equivalent to issuing a "shutdown" command while the latter is equal to a "reboot".

# Running Program Specific Scripts

Sometimes you will want to install programs that will need to boot up automatically in case of a reboot or power failure. You might not always have access to the machine when it first comes back up, so you want to make sure that your program starts up by itself. In cases like these where there is no RPM or binary version of the program and you are compiling the executable from source, you will need to create a customized script.

If you lack a broad understanding of how to create a bootup script, you can usually copy an existing script and then modify it for your own use. This, however, is not a foolproof method, especially if you lack experience in programming languages. Another way is to create a very simple script that accomplishes the same means of starting up but without all the extraneous options or commands typical of other scripts.

For an example this time, let's use the Apache Web server. You can install the RPM version of Apache on most any Linux box running Red Hat, which in turn installs all the startup scripts. However, you might want to compile the source code yourself to optimize some of the more advanced modules or simply to try your hand at compiling source. There are advantages to both methods, which won't be examined here, but both also have their disadvantages. For more information on compiling programs from source, see Chapter 11, "Installing Additional Programs." This chapter also discusses the difference between using both source and binary programs under Linux.

After successfully compiling and executing the program you will want confirm that should the machine lose power and need to be rebooted or if for some other reason it needs assistance in restarting, the web daemon will restart as well.

Here is a sample script that you can place in the /etc/rc.d/rc3.d/ directory. It is called S99apache. The initial character needs to be capitalized so that the bootup will recognize it. If you want to disable this function yet keep the script, merely change the capital *S* to a lowercase *s*. The letter *S* signifies *start*, while the other initial letter, *K*, denotes *kill* and is used to shut down certain daemons. Listing 2.5 shows how this simple script starts the web daemon.

**Listing 2.5  A Sample Script for Starting a Release
of Apache that Was Compiled from Source**

```
# Start http daemon - Apache
#
if [ -f /usr/local/etc/httpd/src/httpd ]; then
    /usr/local/etc/httpd/src/httpd -f/
usr/local/etc/httpd/conf/httpd.conf;
echo "Starting Apache"
fi
```

This script simply checks for the Apache binary located in /usr/local/etc/httpd/src/. If the binary file is present, the program starts the daemon with the appropriate configuration file. It also prints out a simple statement informing the user that the web daemon is starting.

Apache is a fairly standard program and is used by most Linux boxes. However, if you want to use other less familiar programs, such as Big Brother, a network monitoring program that informs administrators of the status of all machines on the network, you would use a customized script.

Listing 2.6 shows a sample script, named bb, that you would include in a file that you would first create in the /etc/rc.d/init.d/ directory. You would need to change the permissions to make this script executable. Also, Big Brother requires that the bb user, here referred to as bbuser, be the only user able to execute the script. It is yet another security hole if you allow root to execute this script. Notice on the last line how root changes to the user, bbuser, to then execute the script.

**Listing 2.6  A Sample Script that Executes the Big Brother Daemon,
which Monitors Machines on a Network**

```
#
# Start the BigBrother daemon
#
if [ -x /usr/local/gnu/bb/runbb.sh ]
then
    #
    # Make sure BB is shut down
    #
    sh /usr/local/gnu/bb/runbb.sh stop > /dev/null 2>&1
```

```
     #
     # Initialize a new logfile
     #
     > /usr/local/gnu/bb/BBOUT

     echo "Starting up Big Brother ..."
     su - bbuser /usr/local/gnu/bb/runbb.sh start
   fi
# EOF
```

After creating the main file, you would copy the same scripts created by the default Red Hat Linux install and place symbolic links in each of the different run states. For example, in the /etc/rc.d/rc3.d/ and /etc/rc.d/rc5.d/ directories, you would place a link pointing back to the original script and name the new file S99bb. You create this file by typing the following:

```
[root@pluto init.d]# cd /etc/rc.d/rc3.d/
[root@pluto rc3.d]]# ln -s ../init.d/bb S99bb
[root@pluto rc3.d]# ls -la S99bb
lrwxrwxrwx   1 root    root    12 May  3 12:07 S99bb -> ../init.d/bb
```

You can do the same for nearly any script. If the run level is not important, then another location to place startup scripts is the /etc/rc.d/rc.local or /etc/rc.d/rc.sysinit file. These files can be optimal locations for various utilities such as one that sets the hardware clock to another time clock. The following is an example script that you could place in the /etc/rc.d/rc.local file. This file simply updates the system clock by executing the ntpdate command and logging into a server that has the correct time.

```
# Update the time upon bootup
/usr/sbin/ntpdate -b 129.237.32.1
```

It is up to the administrator to determine what needs to be started upon bootup. Only by testing the various scripts and modes in different directories will you be able to see what formats works best for you.

# Changing the State of Linux Operations

Linux operates on many levels. While a client is logged in, working on certain tasks, the system itself might also be running various routines and programs.

Changing the state of the system without saving information to the disk can be disastrous, both for the operating system and for your own files. A Linux administrator should be familiar with the methods of properly bringing a system down so that it is safe to power off. An administrator should also know how to change the system's current *run level*, or state of performance, whether it is in single- or multiuser mode, before executing anything that might alter the status quo.

This section will look at some methods to shut down Linux properly without damaging file systems as well as to change its run level state so that administrative tasks can be carried out.

## Shutting Down

It is unwise simply to press the power button on a Linux box when you want to shut down the system. This can result in the corruption of files and loss of data. Constant mismanagement of the system and repeated shutdowns in this manner over time can cause serious damage to the software, both the operating system and any programs you may have installed. Linux constantly accesses files while in all run level modes (except for that of run level 0) and keeps the hardware in a ready state of alert. Cutting power to the system renders files unable to write back to the disk and can physically damage the hardware. Linux is not like MS-DOS or other non-multitasking operating systems, which encourage the user to shut down the machine once it has returned to a command-line prompt. MS-DOS is the only system on which the user can suddenly kill the power with assurance that all the files will remain safe. Every other operating system, from Windows 9x to NT to Novell NetWare to all flavors of UNIX, must be shut down in an orderly and safe manner. In the case of Linux, special commands must be given to bring the system down to a safe state so that power can be turned off. Also, only root has this privilege, to prevent any other user from shutting down the machine.

### NOTE

This is no longer true with the latest Red Hat Linux release. A regular user can shut down a Linux box down after logging into the GUI. The GNOME environment, for example, provides the option to halt or shut down the system after logging out. The only stipulation is that you provide the password of the user currently logged in.

Shutting down a Linux box is best done from the command line. While logged in as root, type the following command to bring the machine to a halt or powered-down state where it is safe to hit the power switch. Using the shutdown command with the -h or halt option will bring the system to a reduced state with all data written back to the hard drive. The last two options are interchangeable. The -h option can precede the option now, or vice versa. Most other commands also allow you to place flags either before or after the options.

```
# shutdown now -h
# shutdown -h now
```

The command can also be done remotely. You might need to do so in instances where you must shut down the machine while at a remote location or if you know that the power is to be turned off at some time. In such an instance, you could use either telnet or ssh to access the machine and effectively give the preceding command.

Because the shutdown command is actually located in the /sbin/ directory, which may or may not be in your path you may have to state the entire path to execute the shutdown command. As superuser, you would type the following:

```
# /sbin/shutdown now -h
```

The now option informs the machine that there is no grace period or time to wait for other users to log off. The login command is blocked and no additional users are allowed to connect to the system. The system proceeds to shut down gracefully almost immediately after the shutdown command is issued. However, the command will fail if illegal options are used instead of valid ones.

Red Hat is verbose in describing the shutdown sequence. It will print out to the console each daemon as it successfully terminates. Again, a successful shutdown will result in a green "OK" message being printed to the right side of the respective daemon, and a red "FAILED" notification if the daemon has already been shut down previous to the shutdown command being issued.

As the system sends out, via a TERM, notification that the machine is shutting down, other processes still have time to write out information to the drive. That means that editors can still write out the information stored in the buffer without a loss in data. The -h flag also informs the system that all operations need to be halted and files written to the drive. Failure to use the -h command and then *power-cycling* the box, or cutting power to the machine and then powering it back on when not in a halted state, will result in errors the next time the machine boots up.

The actual shutdown process is accomplished by sending a signal to the init daemon requesting a change in run level. With the -h, or halt command, the shutdown process changes the run level to 0, where it becomes safe to power down.

## Using Additional Shutdown Options

Another option for shutting down a Linux machine is to have a delay in the shutdown period. This is especially useful when multiple users are logged in. A default message is printed to each user's screen specifying when the machine will be shut down.

Issuing the shutdown command with the -k flag does not actually shut down the system, but will send the warning message to all the users who are logged in. This is useful if you want to shut down the machine for a certain period of time, without exactly being sure when the process will occur. The flag is also useful if you simply want to inform the users that the machine will be shut down shortly and that they need to log off.

If you are sure what time the machine will be shut down, you can issue the shutdown command with the -t option and then the number of seconds later when it will be powered down. Here is an example telling the init process to shut down the machine in five minutes:

```
# shutdown -t 300 -h
```

The shutdown option has a couple other flags that make shutting down the machine easier on both the administrator and clients. Instead of sending the default warning message, you can send a customized message informing all the users at all remote login terminals why the machines will be shut down. Here is an example telling all currently logged-in users that this particular Linux box will be shut down at 11:00 p.m. for a hardware upgrade: No particular flag is needed to send users a specific message.

```
# shutdown -h 23:00 Performing a hardware upgrade at midnight
```

Similar to a cron job or at command, the signal sent to init will tell it to wait until 11:00 p.m. before changing the run level to 0.

As is the case with most commands, and as will be the trend throughout the remainder of this book, consulting the man (manual) pages is always a good option for finding out more information about specific commands. Issuing a simple man shutdown query on any command line is a good idea before consulting the newsgroups or before asking others. The man pages can be cryptic, but they all strive to conform to an open standard. With a minimal amount of practice or reading, even the least experienced user can quickly decipher the most intricate commands and their related options.

# Rebooting the Operating System

Sometimes it is necessary simply to restart a Linux machine by rebooting. Unlike Windows, which requires a complete shutdown and reinitialization after installing many programs, Linux tends to avoid any sort of shutdown. It can easily accommodate the installation of new programs without rebooting at all. Processes are also easy enough to stop or restart in order for changes to take effect. Most Linux users tend to disapprove of any sort of program that requires a system reboot. They consider this method of system maintenance a by-product of the Windows operating system and not in keeping with server needs. The only time that you should consider a reboot is when installing a new kernel. Only by shutting the machine down and starting it up again can the new kernel take effect.

Linux does share some similarities with other operating systems in that it provides the user with several different ways to accomplish the same task. Restarting the machine is actually a very simple thing to do, if you have root access. If you are not the superuser, you will get an error message saying that you "must be superuser" to execute this command.

One of the quickest and easiest ways to reboot is to issue the reboot command:

```
# reboot
```

This binary is located in the location as that of the shutdown command and is located in the /sbin/ directory. Like the shutdown command, the reboot command takes various options. You can force a quick and dirty reboot without synchronizing the files to the file system, or you can issue a poweroff option at the end. In any case, the deed is quickly accomplished and the machine changes state and restarts from run level 0.

Like the shutdown command mentioned earlier, the reboot command can do the same to reboot the machine. For example, if you were often the only one working on your Linux box at odd hours, or if you were configuring the kernel, you might want to send the following command to reboot the machine:

```
# shutdown now -r
```

The -r option stands for *reboot*. This command shuts down the system and then issues a soft power-cycle command.

Another quick way to reboot is to use what Windows users call the "three-finger salute" or "Vulcan nerve pinch"—otherwise known as pressing the Ctrl, Alt, and Del keys at the same time. This sends a signal to the init daemon to begin the shutdown process. Once again, however, not all users are authorized to issue this command and only those who have physical access to the console keyboard can effectively start the shutdown process in this manner. If there are non-trusted users accessing the machine physically, this feature can be disabled in the /etc/inittab file. Comment out the last line of this excerpt from the /etc/inittab file.

```
# Trap CTRL-ALT-DELETE
ca::ctrlaltdel:/sbin/shutdown -t3 -r now
```

One of the ways that Linux prevents unauthorized users from rebooting the machine—if in fact they have physical access to the Linux box—is to check for a file called /etc/shutdown.allow. If this file exists and if an authorized user is logged in to one of the virtual terminals, that user can start the shutdown process. The format of this file is one username per line. The file allows for com-mented-out lines to explain who has access. If this file does not exist, the system sends the following message:

```
shutdown: no authorized users logged in
```

Linux is much more secure than some of the other proprietary operating systems. It will prevents unauthorized users not only from gaining access because of the login prompts, but will also try to thwart users from rebooting the machine. Sometimes nothing can stop an unauthorized user from pulling the power or hitting the reset switch, but commenting out the Ctrl-Alt-Del option in /etc/inittab and other inadvertent keystrokes that might be carried over from force of habit from Windows will discourage some users from attempting to gain access. Even if an unwanted intruder did reboot the system, he would return to where he started—at a login prompt. Once there the intruder would still need to provide a valid username and password to access files.

I have found rebooting to be useful only when doing remote work on my system. While configuring some of the older 2.0.x kernels on my Linux box at work, I often had to log in remotely from home and configure the kernel by hand. When done, I was often anxious to see whether I had made any improvement. But for the machine to run the newer kernel, I had to reboot the machine. Simply sending it a reboot command after completing my work and letting the new kernel be installed was simple enough to do from home. I would log back in after a few moments to see whether the machine had come back up. Seldom if ever was I unable to log back in and have to wait until the next day to gain physical access to the machine.

One very welcome change to the Linux kernel with the advent of the stable 2.2.x kernel is the ability to log into the machine via a console connection via a serial cable. The latest kernel supports a serial connection from one machine to the system. If the system were to crash or reboot, you could still monitor the system output remotely just as you would if the output were being sent to a monitor. This is especially useful if you are attempting to monitor several Linux machines. There is not always enough room for seven monitors for seven computers, nor does a switch box help when you are trying to access a downed system from a remote location. Instead, using a product such as a Livingston Portmaster allows you to connect into the Portmaster via a telnet session, and from there to connect via the various serial ports on the Linux boxes. A portmaster works much like a Linux box in that it has an IP address and provides connectivity to any connected machines. Many Portmasters support as many as 30 serial connections or more. This can prove invaluable if you need instant access to a box and if the telnet daemon has died or if the machine is not responding to network queries.

## Using telinit to Change the Run Level

Another method for changing the run level or state of the computer without rebooting is to issue the *telinit* command. As mentioned earlier, init spawns all other daemons and processes. The telinit command manages the different run levels. This command is somewhat similar to init in that when issued as a command it too will cause the Linux machine to change its current run level. When a superuser or root issues the telinit command along with the corresponding run level into which the user wants to change, the init daemon examines the file /etc/inittab to determine where to proceed. This file looks at the relative scripts in each of the /etc/rc.d/ directories and changes the computer's current state to conform with the respective processes. Each level has a certain degree of network connectivity available. Only run levels 0, 1, and 6 are reserved, while the rest are viable states in which Linux can run.

One instance where you might want to change the run level is when backing up of the entire system. The superuser would send a request to the init daemon to change the state to single-user mode. If other users are currently logged in, the root user could also give these users a grace period of a few minutes to a half hour in which to log out, much like the shutdown command would do. If /sbin/ were not in the path, the superuser would also need to issue the full path command to execute it successfully. Here is how the machine might be brought down to run level 1 or single-user mode while granting other users a five-minute grace period:

```
# /sbin/telinit -t 300 1
```

Once the backup is accomplished successfully, the superuser can bring the machine back to a normal multiuser state by sending the following similar command:

```
# /sbin/telinit 3
```

This would enable remote users to log back in again and would also allow networking and file-sharing capabilities. For additional perspectives and information on accomplishing backups of the Linux system, see Chapter 9, "Fixing Mistakes."

> **CAUTION**
>
> You should be careful when using any commands that change the run level or system state of Linux. Such commands can interfere with the needs of other users, particularly if the machine is a system-critical one, such as one that serves up files to local users or that functions as a Web or mail server. In addition, any error in judgment can quickly bring the system to a grinding halt, thus preventing any productive use of the system. You should test new kernels late at night or, if possible, avoid anything that might prevent users from accomplishing their tasks. Certain issues must be addressed, but informing users ahead of time can avoid ill feelings.

# Testing for Problems

When testing new programs or kernels, you should expect to encounter errors when booting up or run into other issues that prevent a successful restart. This does not happen often but it can occur. In some cases, the system may hang or you might encounter a kernel panic. These can be very worrisome errors. However, Linux provides some measures for checking the system and making sure that the system can successfully boot back up.

In my own experience, the vast majority of errors during the bootup process have either been caused by myself or by something that I changed during the last session. Simply retracing my steps and undoing what I had done usually solved the problem. In cases such as these, it was always useful to have some sort of media backup from which to grab an uncorrupted copy, or to have backed up of the file that I was changing. Seldom have I been unable to at least boot into a simple version of Linux and then make changes.

Even with the case of forgetting something as simple as the root password, rebooting and then typing **linux single** or **linux init=/bin/sh** at the LILO: prompt will still succeed in bringing Linux up in superuser mode with root access. Here you can issue a simple passwd command and change the password for the root user.

# Fixing Corrupted File Systems

Be sure you know what you are doing before making any serious changes to the system. Anything you do can have serious consequences once the machine is rebooted. Oftentimes changes you make will not show up until the machine has been rebooted. I had a Linux box with an uptime of over 355 days with no problems. A co-worker accidentally pulled the plug and shut down the machine just a few days short of the one-year mark. It was only then that I discovered some changes made several months earlier prevented a hard drive from booting. If you are still unsure about any changes you make to system files, at least take the precaution of verifying you have some way to gain access to the system again should things go wrong. If you followed the advice outlined in the previous chapter regarding disk partitioning, you can at least reinstall your system with very little loss of data. If not and your system still fails to reboot even after attempting to correct the problems, then your system probably needed to be reinstalled anyway.

One of the most common errors reported by new users of Linux is that the file system had not been cleanly unmounted. This is usually caused by improper shutdown. In cases such as these, Linux uses a utility called *fsck* or file system check (sometimes pronounced "ef es check") which does a file system check on the partitions to make sure there are no corrupt systems or to fix bad blocks or inodes. Usually the default fsck option that comes with Linux is enough to repair any bad file systems. But sometimes it may be necessary to run the fsck command manually to clean up or repair damaged file systems.

When running fsck manually, you first need to know the location of either the device or the directory to be checked. As pointed out in the first chapter, it is always good to keep a hard copy of the partitioning scheme and/or the directory layout with the different partitions. This can come in handy when trying to determine where a particular directory may have been placed or which device contains a specific directory. fsck can also check multiple file systems at one time. Running them in parallel mode eliminates the extra time required to input repetitive commands.

The fsck command requires root access. The following is an example command: Here fsck check the root filesystem on /dev/hda1, a common location for the root partition. If doing a dual boot with Windows or some other operating system, your root partition may be located elsewhere. The -r option is not necessary but allows for more interaction between the user and the command.

```
fsck -V -t ext2 -r /dev/hda1
```

A command such as this verbosely checks the root file system as defined by your system setup (hence the -v) or / and corrects the errors. This command uses the default file system type of ext2 (the -t flag sets the file system type).

By the same token, the command fsck by itself and the file system name will accomplish the same purpose without the flags or options.

```
fsck /dev/hda1
```

The fsck command exists on other systems as well and can be used for a variety of other file system types. Consulting the man pages before executing any command involving fsck is always a good idea.

## Understanding Kernel Panics

In the case of a kernel panic, or when the boot sequence fails to load the kernel correctly and the machine cannot start correctly, you cannot do much to get the computer operative without making changes to the kernel. Upon bootup, an error message saying "Kernel Panic" will usually be followed by additional information stating what might have caused the system to halt. An error such as this indicates a bad kernel or one that cannot read the available options on the system or cannot read them as they are set up in the kernel.

Several things can cause a kernel panic. Often such a panic results from a customized kernel that was built without some necessary options set. When building any sort of custom kernel, it is best to have a backup kernel in case things go wrong. A reboot to the previous kernel will usually solve the problem until a properly configured kernel can be compiled.

Improperly loaded kernel modules can also cause a kernel panic, whether they are for a SCSI device, an improper file system type, or loss of disk partitions. It is always wise to keep some sort of backup handy for cases when the system goes down or when the system does not reboot normally. The best thing to do in these instances is to attempt to reboot the machine with another kernel, whether it be the default or a backup. You can also use the Red Hat boot disk to gain a root prompt or create a Linux rescue disk during the installation routine. If you can get to a root prompt in any manner, then you should be able to correct the problem. I suggest taking enough precautions by adding *golden kernels*, or kernels that have proven trustworthy, and by editing the /etc/lilo.conf file to allow for backup options. If none of these alternatives are available, a most unlikely scenario, a reinstall may be your only choice. I have found it easier in the long run to attempt to resuscitate a bad box than try to reconstruct one via a reinstall. Not much can be done, however, in the event of a bad kernel and no backups except to create a new one or use an older, stable kernel release.

## Checking for Hardware Errors

In the case of damaged hardware, before you start tearing your machine apart and replacing components looking for the source of the error, make sure the error is hardware-related. If you consistently get an error message pertaining to memory or related signal 11 errors, it is a safe bet that the fault in fact lies with the hardware. But check through some of the possible options before tinkering with the hardware. You might just end up making a bad problem worse, especially if you are unsure about what you are doing.

Here are some possible solutions to try before replacing what you may think are defective parts:

◆ Make sure that all the computer parts are receiving power. This may be an obvious solution, but it is surprising how often you forget to plug power into the various drives. As embarrassing as it may be, I have forgotten to plug in hard drives and then been unable to power them up.

◆ Verify that the cables are plugged properly. It is easy on some of the older ribbon cables to place the one-pin or the colored stripe on the cable improperly. Most cables now have a corresponding tab on the end that fits into a similar notch on the drive.

◆ When installing new parts, first make sure they are compatible—that is, make sure that Linux supports this type of hardware. USB and DVD support is still under development for Linux, so don't plug in a USB scanner or WinModem and then get frustrated when it doesn't work immediately.

◆ If some of the installed cards are jumpered, try changing the jumpered settings so there are no conflicts. This was true with an old Adaptec SCSI card I recently came across and installed on my system. Fortunately, the different settings for setting the jumpers or by shorting the pins on the card were printed on the device itself. Also, it never hurts to take a look on the Internet for a more detailed printout of the card's settings. In this particular instance, I needed to turn off a certain jumper so that it would not conflict with the floppy drive.

♦ Check the lights on the equipment. If the network card, for example, is not lit, the card itself may be either defective or conflicting with another card.

♦ Try shutting the machine down completely and then restarting it. This clears any random errors from RAM and resets the machine to a known default state. This whole procedure is a bit too reminiscent of working with Windows, but it sometimes proves effective.

♦ If the machine booted correctly once before, be sure to note the place in which the current boot procedure now hangs. A simple comparison between the two can usually determine what piece of hardware is causing the error.

♦ Linux provides various diagnostic tools in case of hardware failure. Using one of the available boot disks and then mounting the Linux CD will give you a shell in which you can then start probing the hardware.

♦ At the LILO: prompt, try typing **linux single** to boot into single-user mode. This will grant you a root shell and allow access to the system without network interference.

If after trying these options are you still cannot locate or diagnose the problem, then try installing either different hardware or swapping out the existing parts with known functional hardware. The worst-case scenario is to purchase either older parts or purchase newer compatible equipment. As more and more manufacturers cater to the Linux crowd, hardware will soon become standardized on the Linux platform.

## Testing the System

If you succeed in reaching a login prompt, either by resetting some of the hardware or by using one of the boot CDs, it is a good idea to make sure the system is indeed functioning correctly. One of the directories on the system that keeps track of hardware is the /proc/ directory. Here you can usually see what the settings are for various items installed on the machine. For instance, to test for available memory, try using this command:

```
cat /proc/meminfo
```

The cat command is very useful for printing out the contents of a certain file without having to open the file with a text editor. The /proc/ directory is also very unique in that the contents are in a dynamic state and are created on demand by the kernel depending upon the state of the system. None of the files here are static, but only exist in a temporary state while the machine is operational. Several other files in this directory also give additional information about various items. Some worth noting are cpuinfo, interrupts, ioports, and partitions. A thorough perusal of this directory will reveal additional items of interest.

Another directory to be aware of is the /dev/ directory. Here you can find not only information about the different hardware devices, but also a nifty utility called sndstat. This utility reports the status of the sound card. To use this utility, type the following:

```
cat /dev/sndstat
```

This utility identifies the installed sound drivers and the IRQ assigned to the sound card. It also lists the card's configuration and all the audio, synthesizer, midi, mixer, and timer devices. Listing 2.7 shows sample output.

### Listing 2.7 Sample Output from the sndstat Utility Listing Sound Card Information

```
# cat /dev/sndstat
OSS/Free:3.8s2++-971130
Load type: Driver loaded as a module
Kernel: Linux Linux pluto 2.2.16 #1 Wed Jun 14 00:01:53 MDT 2000 i586
Config options: 0

Installed drivers:

Card config:

Audio devices:
0: Sound Blaster Pro (8 BIT ONLY) (3.02)

Synth devices:
0: Yamaha OPL3

Midi devices:
0: Sound Blaster
```

```
Timers:
0: System clock

Mixers:
0: Sound Blaster
```

Checking the dynamic files in the /dev/ and /proc/ directories can prove useful in diagnosing hardware errors. Check any log files in the /var/log/ directory for any errors that may have been logged during the startup routine.

## Identifying Errors in Startup Scripts

Any startup script errors that you encounter will most likely be due to an error on your part, such as a mistake in one of the editing changes that you made. If you made a backup of the script before changing it, you should have no problem. Simply replace the new script with the original and try again. Running a diff command against the two files should tell you where the error lies. Diff is a utility that lists line-by-line discrepancies between the two files. If you have made several changes in the original document and cannot remember all the minor alterations made, running diff against the two files can save hours of trying to get back to the previous state.

If you do lots of file editing, you may want to consider using programs such as RCS or SCCS. These utilities track all changes made by multiple users to critical files. They also allow quick restores from previous use.

Here is an example of two files I used recently when testing my sendmail configuration:

```
diff /etc/sendmail.cf /etc/sendmail.cf.golden
```

The output showed me where I had made a minor change that was preventing users from sending files over 3 megabytes. I had changed the option earlier and had assumed that it was still the default value of only 1 megabyte.

If you are trying to track down the error in your own startup script, you may need either to base it on an existing script or to consult other users. All the possible combinations of scripts and ways in which they can be approached are beyond the scope of this book.

◆ ◆ ◆

A peer of mine was troubleshooting a script she had written. She was trying to get a remote login procedure written in Perl to work. She had already spent several hours trying to determine the error and why the script was not working. Her resolution was set very high, and I was having a hard time discerning exactly what each character was. Finally, I pointed out a colon that should have been a semicolon. It is usually simple typing mistakes such as this one that will cause things to fail. Before blaming anyone, including yourself, make sure you can read all the characters clearly and easily.

◆ ◆ ◆

# Conclusion

Understanding the rudimentary principles of starting and stopping your Linux box prepares you for the next chapter, understanding directories and files types. In this chapter, you have already learned about some preliminary commands and worked within different directories. In the next chapter, you will examine the syntax associated with command-line navigation, learn some simple Linux commands, and look at the many types of Linux files.

# Chapter 3

## Directories

**L**inux files and directories share many common elements with UNIX. Understanding the principles of navigation via the command line is crucial to comprehending how Linux stores files and how the Linux user can access and manipulate these same files. Each file has its own set of rules and methodology.

In this chapter, you will learn about the following:

- ◆ Linux directory structures
- ◆ Files types
- ◆ Basic Linux commands
- ◆ Setting permissions on both files and directories
- ◆ Editing user space

# Linux Directory Structures

Linux organizes its directories using a diverging file structure, where each category branches off from the main directory. It utilizes directories within directories, ever splintering outward to contain the scope of files contained on the system. It is not limited to a preset range of directories but can be expanded or cut back as the need arises. Each Linux distribution must contain some required directories to operate correctly, but each user can expand the most basic system to fit his or her needs.

## Understanding the Basics

Like most other operating systems, Linux also grants access to specific directories for differing purposes. Within each directory, you can create additional subdirectories for classifying and storing files. Linux was initially developed to operate on a command-line basis for directory browsing. Navigating the directory structures from the command line is useful when you are remotely accessing the machine or when a GUI is unavailable. The command line also is the basis for Linux use and continues to provide the most functionality.

The entire hierarchical structure of directories is predetermined before any Linux installation. A standard set of directories must be created to which Linux then refers and uses for storing specific files. These files are necessary for basic Linux operation and must be placed in a static location. Any alteration to these directory structures should be done with the utmost caution. It is acceptable to create new directories not installed by default, but removing directories needed by the system could result in system failure.

The basis for all directories is the root directory, or /. From root, all other directories branch down in an inverted treelike structure. Navigating downward like roots and branching off from each other, these directories form the basis for organizing system data. Because the term *root* is used as the basis for all succeeding directories, the entire file system is viewed as a downward-branching subsystem. The term *root directory* will hereafter refer to the top-level directory from which all other directories and subdirectories originate.

## Navigating with Pathnames

If you understand how Red Hat organizes its file systems, you should find it easier to determine where files are located and where to store or place your own files. This is also handy when attempting to find an elusive binary file either recently installed or located on the system. After the partitioning and formatting phase of the install process, Linux creates a standard set of directories, each within a large centralized partition or located in its own partition. This section looks at how to move through the different directory levels.

To navigate through the directory structures, you need to understand certain terms such as *pathnames* and *paths*. A *pathname* is the full location of a certain file or directory as it stands in reference to other files. The paths are those directories normally accessible by the user. For example, you would use the pathname to tell the system which directory or subdirectories you need either to locate or access. Therefore, if you want to move to a certain directory containing a particular file, you need to know its location or path. Paths are basically the address or location of files. For example, /usr/bin/ is the location or path into which Red Hat Linux installs most of its binary files. These files run most applications under Red Hat.

To refer to a specific file or data set within a directory, you need to know the *filename*. A *file* is the unique block of data contained within a directory; so the term *file* refers to the file's contents rather than the name of the file itself. For example, /usr/bin/gunzip refers to the binary file or executable gunzip located in the /usr/bin directory. In this example, the *filename* is gunzip, which is a compiled file located in a unique *pathname*, /usr/bin/gunzip. The distinction between files and filenames will become clearer as you grow accustomed to using Linux. Files are handled differently depending upon their properties.

Pathnames can be either *absolute* or *relative*. An *absolute pathname* is the entire sequence of directories in relation to the root directory. For instance, the absolute path for the file temp.txt might be /usr/local/bin/temp.txt. *Relative paths* refer to the subdirectories in relationship to the current directory. For example, if the current directory is /usr/local, the relative path to temp.txt would be bin/temp.txt. Notice the absence of the preceding forward slash. This indicates the relative path. Using relative or absolute paths is a matter of taste. It is also a matter of convenience, since the file in question can sometimes be several levels deep within the file structure, depending on where it was placed and depending on the current directory.

Certain restrictions govern the use of filenames and pathnames. Though the two terms are nearly interchangeable, filenames focus on the location of directories or file locations, whereas pathnames emphasize the file contents. No filename can be more than 256 characters long. You may use spaces in a filename, but only if you place quotation marks around the filename. The Linux shell or command-line regards all letters, numbers, and spaces as characters. Also, a single pathname cannot be more than 1,023 characters long, meaning you cannot use extremely long pathnames for files deeply embedded within the file structure unless you are willing first to execute the change directory command, or cd, to switch to an intermediary directory and then change directories to the directory that you want.

## Changing Directories

Changing directories is a simple matter. If you are familiar with UNIX commands or even if you are a former DOS user, the syntax is nearly the same. Beginning at the root directory, you can easily move to any other directory. The root directory is the most fundamental location on the system. From here you can see all available partitions and directories from which the subdirectories branch. You change directories by using the *cd* (*change directories*) command.

Entering the request **cd /usr/bin** will take you to that directory. Likewise, you can move up one directory tree by typing **cd ../**. This takes you to the /usr directory. From there you can change to any other directory found in that location, such as local/ (note that the absence of the forward slash preceding the directory name indicates that this is the relative pathname). You can accomplish this long process of moving up a directory and then back down another with one simple command, **cd ../local**. This will take you out of /usr/bin and place you in /usr/local. Experimentation with these few simple commands can help you navigate throughout the entire structure.

If you ever lose your way or forget where you are, the simple command pwd prints out the current working directory and allows you to gain your bearing. *Pwd* stands for *print working directory*. Many Linux programs, based on the original UNIX commands, are intuitive in this manner.

If you need to return to a primary location, entering a simple **cd /** will place you back in the root directory. This technique is useful if you need to return to a starting place but want to avoid entering a series of cd commands to return to root. Also useful for navigating through the maze of directories is the command **cd -**, which places you in the previous directory.

Suppose that you are in /home/test, performed a change directory command to /usr/local/etc, then wanted to return to /home/test. Rather than retyping the absolute or relative path back to /home/test, you could simply enter **cd -**. Many of these commands are sometimes learned through trial and error. The simple tips in this chapter should make the process less arduous and simpler to understand.

If you want to return to your own home directory, entering the command **cd** by itself will also take you there. For example, if you were performing these actions as root and wanted to return to root's home directory, or /root, you could enter **cd** without any additional options. Your location would then be the home directory for that user. This command examines the current HOME environmental variable or it looks at what is in the /etc/passwd file is this variable has not been changed by either the system or the user. The /etc/passwd file contains additional information about each user, including that user's home directory. This file initially sets the home directory for each user and when the cd command is given changes to that home location.

To read more about user directories, see Chapter 4, "Terminal Shells," and Chapter 6, "Managing Users." These chapters closely examine the /etc/passwd file and explain how home directories can be set for each user.

In addition to changing working directories, the cd command allows you to remain in the current directory. For example, entering the command **cd ./** is the same as moving to the current directory. In other words, you move neither up nor down relative to the working directory. The use of this syntax will prove useful later when you attempt to run executables from a working directory. Entering the command **cd ./bin** from within the directory /usr/local/ has the same effect as entering **cd bin/** from that same directory. Two periods preceding a forward slash, or **cd ../**, indicates a move to a higher directory. The difference is that the single dot and forward slash is more reminiscent of an absolute pathname, whereas the two dots and a forward slash is distinctly a relative path.

If verbose commands are more your style and you enjoy doing lots of typing, a combination of all the preceding choices might be easier to grasp. Thus using the double periods along with forward slashes can take you several directories back. If you were currently in /usr/local/bin, you could return to the root directory by entering **cd ../../../**. It is a bit redundant but accomplishes the same thing as entering **cd /**.

Here is a simple exercise in navigating through several directories. There are three different directories in which you need to change files: /usr/local/bin, /home/test, and /. To navigate through these directories respectively, you can either use absolute paths, or relative paths, or a combination of both:

- cd /usr/local/bin
- cd ../../../home/test
- cd /
- cd /usr

- cd local/bin
- cd /home/test
- cd -
- cd ./

The question is, what is the current working directory? Entering **pwd** reveals what working directory? The correct answer is /usr/local/bin.

Though this system may seem a bit confusing at first, it soon becomes almost second nature as you learn to maneuver through the twisty mazes of the Linux file structure.

◆ ◆ ◆

# Copying and Moving Files

Other useful Linux commands that every user should be aware of are *cp* and *mv*. These stand for *copy* and *move*, respectively. These are the commands that enable you to redistribute files among the different directories.

The cp command makes an exact copy of the file requested and then places it in the destination directory. If, for example, you wanted to place a copy of /usr/local/bin/temp.txt in /home/test/, you would first either change your working directory into the directory where the source file is located or use an absolute path to that file. Then you would copy the file to the destination directory using the cp command. Here is an example using absolute pathnames:

```
cp /usr/local/bin/temp.txt /home/test/
```

If you wanted to rename the file temp.txt to something more unambiguous, you could move that same file from its original source directory and give it a new name. This command applies not only to moving files from one location to another but also to renaming files. Here are a couple of examples:

```
mv /usr/local/bin/temp.txt /home/test/readme.txt
```

In this instance, the file named temp.txt was not only moved to a new location but was renamed readme.txt. Renaming a file in its same directory is just as easy:

```
cd /home/test/
mv readme.txt readme_old.txt
```

In this latter instance, the new file readme.txt is renamed as readme_old.txt.

The mv and cp commands are useful when making backups of files. They can also relocate files into new partitions where the information is safe or they can

---

**CAUTION**

Any commands issued under Linux on the command line will be executed quickly and thoroughly. You will not be asked whether you are sure you want to perform the command, but the shell will do so without question, whereas other operating systems will query repeatedly whether or not you are sure a specific task should be performed. Once a file has been changed, there is little or no way of recovering the previously unmodified file. You can modify the shell to query you before removing a file by aliasing the rm command to "rm -i". In your /etc/bashrc file enter the line, `alias rm='rm -i'`. You will then be prompted as to whether or not you wish to remove a file permanently.

rename other files so that there are no accidental overwrites when re-creating the same file.

## Creating Directories

In addition to copying and moving files, it is possible to copy and move directories. It is advisable to learn first how to make and remove the directories themselves. Creating a directory is simple, so long as you have the permissions to create a file in the desired location. File permissions is discussed in the section, "File Permissions," later in this chapter.

If you are in your home directory or one that you have permission to write to, you will also have the necessary permissions to create a new directory. The mkdir command allows any user with the proper permissions to make a new directory in which to place files. Taking an example from one of my own Linux machines, I would create a directory called docs/ in my home directory, /home/kerry. I would first change to /home/kerry or simply enter **cd**. This command takes any user back to his or her own home directory. I would then issue the mkdir command and give the new directory a name. Here are the steps laid out:

```
cd /home/kerry
```

or

```
cd
mkdir docs/
cd /home/kerry/docs
```

Once the directory /home/kerry/docs is created, I have full use of this new directory and can place any files that I want within it. I can also create additional subdirectories within that directory. To keep files organized, it is a good idea to separate them into their own locations.

## Removing Directories

A similar command, rmdir, will delete any directory that you have the permission to write to and which you also own. It is important to understand that though you may own a directory, if you cannot write to it, you are not able to create or delete files from within that location. The same rules for removing directories applies to removing files. Like rmdir, the rm command removes files but can also be used for removing directories as well. While rmdir is directory-specific, rm can apply to both files and directories.

The following are some of the available options to the rm command. When using rm, place the following flags after the command and before the file in question.

◆ An *-f* or *--force* flag ignores nonexistent files and forces the deletion of any and all files. It also suppresses any error messages that you might otherwise see.

◆ An *-i* or *--interactive* flag prompts users as to whether they really want to delete the file. This is handy if you often second-guess yourself or are prone to performing tasks without thinking.

◆ An *-r, -R,* or *--recursive* flag will remove the contents of any and all directories recursively. Normal removal deletes only files and not directories.

◆ A *-v* or *--verbose* flag will cause the system to print out the actions as they are performed. This is a good command to use if you want to know exactly what the shell is doing as it carries out the command.

You have the option of either using a single letter with a dash preceding it, or using a double dash followed by the verbose wording itself. This is standard operating procedure in Linux and you will see features like this often in use with other Linux commands. The preceding options also apply to the rmdir command. Many standard commands have related executables that perform similar functions but which share nearly the same options.

These options or flags can be used jointly. For example, one way to remove an entire directory and all its contents, including all sub-directories in that location (after first considering carefully whether that is absolutely what you want), is to issue the following command:

```
rm -rf /home/test
```

Notice that this command deletes the subdirectory test/ within the /home directory. The /home directory remains intact, but the absolute path is used to remove the subdirectory test/. Using the -r and -f options allows for recursive deletion and removal of all files, those you own but may not have write permission to within that location. The command recursively probes through that directory and sub-directories and attempts to remove all files. Any files within a directory, once they have been removed, are unrecoverable, as are any directories that you delete.

These are but few text-based commands that you can use to manipulate files and directories. Throughout the remainder of the book there will be others. As each command is introduced, it is a good idea to read the man pages, which give more detailed instructions for each command, as well as to practice using the command with real-life examples. Copy some unimportant files to temporary locations or create new directories in which to place them. Try moving and copying these as well. Once you feel secure in your mastery of these different options, you can start manipulating more important files. However, use restraint; don't move or delete anything integral to the Linux operating system.

---

### NOTE

There are man pages for nearly every command under Linux. If you have any question concerning a specific executable, consult the man page. On the command line, type **man &lt;command&gt;**, replacing &lt;command&gt; with the expression in question.

---

## Understanding the Linux Hierarchical Structure

A graphical representation of the many of the possible directories puts things in perspective and lays out the structure more clearly. Listing 3.1 shows a typical layout for a default Red Hat Linux directory structure.

**Listing 3.1  Typical Directory Structures under Red Hat Linux**

```
/-----bin/
    |--boot/
    |--dev/
    |--etc/
    |--home/----kerry/
    |           |--test/
    |--lib/
    |--lost+found/
    |--mnt/-----cdrom/
    |           |--floppy/
    |--opt/
    |--proc/
    |--root/
```

```
|--sbin/
|--tmp/
|--usr/-----X11R6/
|          |--bin/
|          |--dict/
|          |--etc/
|          |--games/
|          |--include/
|          |--info/
|          |--lib/
|          |--local/-----bin/
|          |            |--doc/
|          |            |--etc/
|          |            |--games/
|          |            |--include/
|          |            |--info/
|          |            |--lib/
|          |            |--man/
|          |            |--sbin/
|          |            |--share/-----man/
|          |            |--src/
|          |--man/
|          |--sbin/
|          |--share/
|          |--src/-----linux/
|--var/-----log/
          |--spool/
```

Listing 3.1 does not show all possible directories, but does show a rough approximation of a standard installation. Nor does this layout show any directories that can be created by a regular user. The possibilities are unlimited in this case.

As shown in Listing 3.1, several subdirectories are repeated in two distinct directories. The directories /usr and /usr/local both have bin/, etc/, games/, include/, lib/, man/, sbin/, share/, and src/ subdirectories. The reason for this is that the /usr directory defines global programs installed by default through the installation program, whereas the /usr/local directory is designed for local users to install their own customized binaries. Often, a self-installed program requires the same directories, so these file types will be repeated in the /usr/local directories.

# Explaining the Directories

For a clarification of standard directories, Table 3.1 briefly lists what each directory does and what types of files might be placed within it.

**Table 3.1  Description of Standard Directories**

| Directory | Description |
|---|---|
| /bin | *Bin* is short for binaries. Binary files are compiled programs that the computer can easily understand and execute. The contents are not normally readable by human eyes. This directory holds all standard files that are needed for essential maintenance. Files such as cp and ls are placed here. |
| /dev | This directory contains all the system devices. From here you can access system hardware such as CD-ROMs, disk drives, modems, and memory. There are also utilities here such as MAKEDEV creates device files. Some installations make links from the cryptic device drivers to more understandable devices. The device linked to the PS/2 mouse is listed as /dev/mouse but is actually /dev/psaux. Here are some additional explanations about files contained in this directory. |
| | The file /dev/console is the device driver associated with the monitor connected to your machine. |
| | The files /dev/ttyS*n* and on are devices to access serial ports. An example is /dev/ttyS0, which is the same as COM1 under DOS. When setting up the modem, ttyS0 or ttyS1 or ttyS2 are the ports for creating a linked /dev/modem device. |
| | The file /dev/hda and the succeeding /dev/hdb, /dev/hdc and /dev/hdd devices are the hard drives themselves. While /dev/hda is the entire hard drive, hda1 is the first partition on that same hard drive. The /dev/hda file holds a single hard drive located in the IDE controller. |
| | The same is true of /dev/sda, which refers to SCSI hard drives. SCSI tape drives are /dev/st devices. |
| | /dev/lp refers to parallel or printer ports. If you were connecting a parallel printer cable to your LPT1 port under DOS, you would enable the /dev/lp0 port. |
| | /dev/null is perhaps the most infamous device of all since it is the garbage device into which all unwanted files disappear. Directing any sort of output or information to /dev/null is the same as removing it from your system. It functions as a "black hole," swallowing up any unwanted output directed to it. |

**Table 3.1  Description of Standard Directories *(continued)***

| Directory | Description |
|---|---|
| | /dev/tty is a virtual console. Under Linux you can have multiple screens on which several different terminals can reside. While logged in and performing a certain task on one console, you can log in a second time by pressing Alt-F2. Once the secondary function is complete, you can return to the original console by pressing Alt-F1. You can have as many as 12 virtual consoles under Linux. |
| | /dev/pty refers to pseudo-terminals. These are the terminals created dynamically whenever a user logs in remotely to the machine either via the network or through a remote Telnet connection. |
| /etc | This directory contains system configuration files. Those files needed for setting up utilities such as the init daemon, run command files, SAMBA, and other programs are found here. |
| /home | The /home directory is the default location for all user files. Under distributions such as Red Hat, the directory also holds all HTML and FTP files by default. The personal directories contain all initialization scripts for user logins. |
| /lib | This directory contains shared library images. These are bits of code that are used by many programs in tandem. Rather than having each program store its own libraries, which would result in increased disk space, Linux makes a set of files available to all programs. This directory also contains static libraries needed for the bootstrap process. |
| lost+found/ | This directory stores lost files. Improper shutdowns and disk errors can cause files to become lost, meaning they are marked as in use but are not listed in the data structures on the disk. The fsck program that normally runs during bootup finds these files. There is a lost+found/ directory on every partition in addition to this one found on the / partition. |
| mnt/ | The mnt/ directory is the default location for mounting CD-ROMs and floppies. To access these types of media, the device needs to be mounted in a temporary location where the user can then access the files located on either device. When this process is complete, the device is then unmounted and successfully ejected. |
| opt/ | This directory does not normally come with the default Linux installation. This is the default location of newer programs such as KDE and Netscape. If this directory does not exist, such programs will create it upon installation. |

**Table 3.1  Description of Standard Directories *(continued)***

| Directory | Description |
| --- | --- |
| proc/ | This is not a directory per se, but a "virtual file system;" the files in this directory are actually stored in memory and not on the drive. This directory contains *dynamically created files*, or files that are in a state of flux and are constantly being generated by the system. These files do not exist as regular text files but are generated upon request. These files provide information about running processes on the system. |
| root/ | This is the home directory for the user root, where startup scripts for the user are stored. Much like the directories in home/ reserved for individual users, this directory contains items pertinent only to the root user. It is kept separate to avoid confusion and to safeguard the system so that even if the /home directory were lost, there would still be a user that could restore that directory or partition. This is done primarily for safety reasons. New users should do as little system maintenance as possible while acting as root, since any error can damage the system. |
| sbin/ | This directory is used for storing essential system binaries. Commands such as fsck, reboot, shutdown, telinit, and update are located here. For a remote user, this directory may not be in the user's path, so if the user needs to use any of these commands, he or she must use the absolute or full path. |
| tmp/ | This directory is intended for temporary file storage only. All users have write access to this location. Mail programs use the directory to store files needed only for that open session, then delete the files when the session is complete. The tmp/ directory has unique permissions that allow users also to start executable files from this location. |
| usr/ | The usr/ directory is by far one of the most comprehensive directories. You should allot ample space to usr/ since this directory stores most default binaries, depending upon the Linux distribution. This directory also stores programs other than those needed for necessary system use. |
| usr/X11R6/ | This directory houses those files needed for running X-Window. It contains the configuration files and binaries for running the GUI. |
| usr/bin/ | This is where Red Hat and other distributions store all their binary executables. Since usr/bin/ is often the dumping ground for so many programs, you should make this directory its own partition. |
| usr/dict/ | This is where Linux stores its list of words. Various spelling and code-cracking programs use this directory and its contents. |
| usr/etc/ | This directory contains miscellaneous configuration files not necessary for system use, unlike those found in the etc/ directory, which are needed to run the operating system properly. |

**Table 3.1  Description of Standard Directories** *(continued)*

| Directory | Description |
| --- | --- |
| usr/games/ | By default, games are kept in this directory. In this directory, Red Hat keeps programs such as Fortune, which prints out sayings and quotes similar to those of fortune cookies. (This program is a particular favorite of mine.) |
| usr/include/ | This directory contains include files needed for the C compiler. These are the header files (those that end in .h) and contain the names, subroutines, and constants for writing programs in C. |
| usr/info/ | This directory has compressed files that contain information about various system-dependent programs. It is intended for users needing additional information about the purpose and use of these files. The directory stores textinfo files in compressed format. |
| usr/lib/ | Here is where libraries equivalent to those found in /lib are kept. This directory is not as vital to the system as those libraries found in /lib. Normally a compile program is linked to the libraries found in /usr/lib, which then directs the program to /lib when the actual code is needed. Other configuration files are also kept here. As you might notice when perusing the contents of these files, there are many symbolically linked files. Any files not needed for the bootstrapping process otherwise located in /lib are contained in this directory. |
| usr/local/ | This directory also requires its own partition due to the potential for users to place their own programs in this location. By default only root may place programs in this directory and it is where the superuser may compile all programs from source. Much like the /usr directory, /usr/local has many of the same subdirectory structures, such as bin/ and src/. Any program that is not included with the default install can and should be placed here to keep it separate. Programs in this partition are easily accessible in case of a reinstall or a system crash. Reinstalling the default programs is simple, but reinstalling your own programs might not be as easy. |
| usr/man/ | This is the default location for installing the manual, or man, pages. The system looks in this directory first for information about a particular program when a man command is given. |
| usr/sbin/ | Other essential programs are kept here for use by the system. These include the various network daemons and other tools needed for managing disk space and use. It is here that you would find system binaries such as usermod and quota management programs. |
| usr/share/ | This directory holds many other directories needed by programs subsequently installed by other users. It is intended for all users. |

**Table 3.1  Description of Standard Directories *(continued)***

| Directory | Description |
| --- | --- |
| usr/src/ | This is one of the more important directories when compiling the Linux kernel from source code. This is where the newer kernel is unpacked and compiled. The directory also contains the source code for all the drivers for running Linux. |
| var/ | This directory holds dynamic files, which are constantly updated. Such files include log files, DNS records, and newsgroups, if any. The average life span for files in this directory is shorter than that of files elsewhere on the system. |
| var/log/ | This is where programs such as syslogd, cron, and wtmp store their messages. Depending upon the Linux release, these messages are rotated on a scheduled basis so that they don't occupy too much space on the system. Red Hat offers a default file rotation method that works well for keeping these files' size manageable. |
| var/spool/ | This directory holds jobs awaiting completion. These include at, cron, mail, and print jobs. |

Each of these directories includes various subdirectories. The variance and number of these are too great to list, but with this standard format you can determine the function of most any file on Linux based on its relative location.

# Commands to List Files

As might be evident from the aforementioned examples, several file types can be found on a standard installation. Each has its own characteristics and is treated differently under Linux. To view the distinct qualities of each type of file, you normally use the ls command. It lists files and directories along with the directory in which the command is issued.

For example, if I were logging into my own directory, /home/kerry, and I wanted to see what files I had stored there, I would enter **ls** at the command line. This command would print out the contents of the directory. Along with this command there are several options available that will list additional information about the file aside from the filename.

For a simple listing of the visible files and directories, entering **ls -F** is sufficient to view the files, the directories with a trailing slash, and even symbolic links defined by the @ sign at the end.

For a more complete listing of the files along with their permissions, ownership, size, and time stamp, enter **ls -l** to display a complete overview. In some directories with more entries than will fit on your screen, the listing will scroll past the files at the beginning. To paginate through all the items within the directory, try piping the files with the *more* and *less* commands. Similar in purpose to the /p option in DOS, these commands allow the user to scroll through the contents of the entire page:

```
ls -1 | more
```

## Determining File Types

Another very functional command is *file <filename>*. If you want to find out the file type of a particular file—that is, whether it is a simple text, zipped, or binary file—you can query its type by simply entering **file** followed by the filename.

For example, if a friend sent me a file and I was unsure what it was or did, I could enter **file** and then the file's name. This is what I would see if I were curious about the file rc.firewall.test:

```
[kerry@pluto kerry]$ file rc.firewall.test
rc.firewall.test: Bourne shell script text
```

The output tells me that the file in question is a text file that is based on the Bourne shell. The file contains a script that I can run to initiate a firewall.

## Understanding Hidden Files

Linux provides certain types of files that are considered hidden; these files have filenames that begin with a period. Entering an **ls -l** command will normally not display these types of files. Hidden files can function as startup scripts, such as .bash_profile, and as configuration files for initiating certain programs. Because different users may not want to have a certain program start up the same way, they can customize the startup script in their own directory. Good examples of this are the .pinerc and .netscape files. While the former is a configuration file specifying information about the user's e-mail client, pine, the latter is a hidden directory that holds files and data for starting up the Netscape browser.

It is usually not necessary to view these files because you can configure them within the program itself. They simply hide any configuration settings or directories so that they do not clutter up the contents of directories or confuse the user as to what files he or she may have created and those created by the system or individual programs.

## Viewing All Files

To view all the files within a given location, including hidden files or directories, use the option -a with the ls command. This will show the visible and hidden files, but will not provide file size or additional information. Like the rm command described previously, ls provides various options that you can specify to gather the most information from the fewest keystrokes. A fairly typical command among Linux users who want to list a directory's contents is the following:

```
ls -la | more
```

Listing 3.2 shows sample output from my own directory.

**Listing 3.2  A Typical ls Command Output with Additional Options Showing All Files, Both Hidden and Visible, and Descriptions of Each File**

```
drwx------    6 kerry    kerry      1024 Sep 11 23:06 .gnome
drwxrwxr-x    2 kerry    kerry      1024 Sep 11 11:55 .gnome-desktop
drwxr-xr-x    2 kerry    kerry      1024 Aug 16 22:37 .gnome-help-browser
drwx------    2 kerry    kerry      1024 Aug 16 22:30 .gnome_private
drwxr-xr-x    3 kerry    kerry      1024 Aug 17 22:18 .kde
drwxrwxr-x    2 kerry    kerry      1024 Sep 11 23:05 .mc
drwx------    5 kerry    kerry      1024 Oct  4 21:26 .netscape
-rw-rw-r--    1 kerry    kerry     11567 Sep 28 20:01 .pinerc
-rw-rw-r--    1 kerry    kerry      3505 Aug 16 22:29 .screenrc
-rw-rw-r--    1 kerry    kerry       349 Aug 22 11:34 .signature
```

```
drwx------    3 kerry    kerry     1024 Aug 16 22:35 .xauth
-rwxrwxr-x    1 kerry    kerry      246 Aug 17 18:50 .xinitrc
drwxrwxr-x    5 kerry    kerry     1024 Aug 17 18:50 GNUstep
drwxr-xr-x    7 kerry    kerry     1024 Oct  4 20:42 GNUware
drwx------    2 kerry    kerry     1024 Aug 26 20:58 Mail
drwxrwxr-x    4 kerry    kerry     1024 Aug 24 22:40 Projects
drwxr-xr-x    2 kerry    kerry     1024 Oct  5 10:39 backgrounds
drwxr-xr-x    4 kerry    kerry     1024 Oct  5 10:41 database
drwxr-xr-x   14 kerry    kerry     1024 Oct  5 11:18 docs
drwxr-xr-x    2 kerry    kerry     7168 Sep  3 21:54 fonts
lrwxrwxrwx    1 kerry    kerry       11 Aug 17 22:34 local -> /usr/local/
drwx------    2 kerry    kerry     1024 Sep 28 20:01 mail
drwx------    2 kerry    kerry     1024 Oct  5 11:34 nsmail
lrwxrwxrwx    1 kerry    kerry       16 Aug 19 22:17 rpms -> /usr/local/
rpms/
-rw-r--r--    1 root     root      1169 Oct  1 21:08 rules
-rw-rw-r--    1 kerry    kerry    12571 Aug 26 20:06 template.html
drwxrwxr-x    3 kerry    kerry     5120 Oct  4 20:40 updates
```

Using the same command in your own directory will produce similar results, although the files and directories will differ. As you can see, there is a large variety ranging in ownership, size, permissions, and date last accessed. For more information about the ls command and all the available options for viewing files, entering **man ls** will answer most questions not covered here.

## Exploring Linux File Types

Now that you can view the different files, let's look at what types of files are available under Linux. Generally, there are eight different types of files under Linux. Table 3.2 examines each in closer detail.

For the most part, the only types of files that most users need to be concerned with are regular files and directories. Though symbolic links are very useful and do provide shortcuts to files or directories elsewhere on the computer, they are reserved for more experienced Linux users. The rest of these file types are implemented for novice Linux users and programmers. A short synopsis of linked files follows in the next section.

**Table 3.2  Linux File Types**

| File Type | Description |
| --- | --- |
| Regular files | These are simple data files that contain anything from text to graphic images to binary executables. This type of file is classified as that which can be stored on the hard drive and later retrieved while the contents can be examined by some type of editor or viewer. |
| Directories | A directory can be thought of as a file folder that contains any sort of information in any combination imaginable. Under Linux there are two unique entries that need to be explained. There are "." and ".." entries at the beginning of every directory listing. The former refers to the directory itself while the latter refers to the parent directory or the directory containing the current directory. Directories are also files that list the contents or files they contain. These can be thought of as *metafiles*. |
| Character devices | These are device files that are actually links or methods of communication between the software and the hardware or peripherals. They process input/output one byte or character at a time. The Linux kernel then creates the interface that allows modules to communicate back and forth between the system and the hardware. An example of a character device is /dev/tty, which is listed in the /dev directory. These are files that actually talk with the system hardware and pass information back and forth. |
| Block devices | Device drivers handle the communications process by processing input/output in streams that are multiples of bytes. They read and write information in blocks of data, not in bytes, as is the case with character devices. Drivers use block devices for specific purposes such as handling swap space. You can use the mknod command to create this type of file as well as character devices. |
| Sockets | According to the definition of Berkeley sockets, which are used by Linux, a socket can also be viewed as a port to which a call or request is made and then plugged in. It is a communications end point and is tied to a particular port on the system. Additional processes can then connect to the system via this port. One example is the socket /dev/printer, which sends messages to the program lpd informing it of jobs waiting to be processed. |
| Named pipes | Like sockets, named pipes allow two processes to communicate with each other. They are created with the mknod command, which generates special files containing both block- and character-specific information. Under Linux there exists a script in the /dev/ directory called MAKEDEV that automates the running of mknod and thus the creation of these types of files. Some FTP programs use named pipes for communicating. |

**Table 3.2  Linux File Types** *(continued)*

| File Type | Description |
| --- | --- |
| Hard links | There are two types of links: hard links and symbolic links. A hard link is a type of alias for a file, and thus is not so much a file type as another name for an existing file. All files have at least one link that points to a data bit with a particular inode. A hard link is an additional link to that same file, only it shares the same inode as the original file. |
| Symbolic links | A symbolic link is much the same as a hard link, except that it has its own *inode,* or descriptive block on the drive for referencing files. It is a file unto itself and merely points to the other file in question. Symbolic links are useful for referencing files outside a given directory without having to change directory. In this way, symbolic links function much like shortcuts. The command to create a hard link is ln, while a symbolic link requires the -s option after it. Links can be made for either files or directories. Symbolic links can also be created to files that do not actually exist, whereas hard links can only be made to real files. |

# Linking Files

As you saw in Listing 3.2, a symbolic link, called local/, pointed to the actual directory of /usr/local. Changing the directory to local/ from within my directory would have actually placed me in /usr/local. If you are sharing directories with others, creating too many symbolic links outside your home directory can create security risks in that users may have access to other directories they may not normally have the right to use. Also be wary of changing any permissions to those locations. For many directories, only root should have permission to write or read the contents. Use both hard and symbolic links with care.

Here is an example that creates a symbolic link to a file. To access the file /usr/local/backup/scripts/dumpfiles from within the directory /home/kerry, I would type the following:

```
ln -s /usr/local/backup/scripts/dumpfiles dumpfiles
```

I first use the command ln to create a link, then the -s flag to state that it is to be a symbolic link. After that I give the absolute path to the file to link and finally state the name of the link as it would appear in the home directory.

In much the same manner as I created the file link, I can also make a directory link. To make a link from the /etc directory the same home directory, I enter the following command:

```
ln -s /etc etc
```

By entering **ls –la**, I can take a quick look at the files in that directory now, and see the link and the directory to which it points:

```
lrwxrwxrwx    1 kerry     kerry     4 Oct  5 14:20 etc -> /etc
```

## Using Symbolic Link Commands

You can also create symbolic links by using relative paths. For example, consider the following command:

```
ln -s ../../../backmeup /usr/local/bin/backmeup
```

This command links a customized executable file created for backing up the files, located in the / directory, to a symbolic link now in /usr/local/bin. Because /usr/local/bin is also in most users' default path, you can execute this script from the command line without having to change directories or copy the script to another location.

Using symbolic links reduces the amount of disk space used and makes routine tasks quicker and easier to perform. It reduces the amount of time spent looking for obscure programs and makes it easier for multiple users to share a program provided they have the correct permissions. Each user can create a link in his or her own directory, whereas before the user may not have had access to execute the program. Once again, this can pose security risks if the permissions are changed to accommodate other users. The system administrator must evaluate the trustworthiness of the users and the power of the program itself before granting such access.

# File Permissions

Many beginning users consider file permissions to be the most confusing aspect of understanding Linux. It can be disconcerting at first, but taking the time to comprehend file permissions will pay off later and will quickly become second nature. As you have seen previously, each file is granted certain permissions. In other words, only certain users can access a particular file or directory, and each file or directory is granted varying levels of permission to perform specific functions.

File permissions are specified a series of nine permission bits that appear at the beginning of every line when you perform an **ls -la** query. There are three sets or groups of three bits: r, w, and x. These stand for *read, write,* and *execute,* respectively. The first set is assigned to the owner of the file, the second to the group owners of the file, and the last to everyone else. These three groupings are sometimes defined as *user, group,* and *other.*

Each character is assigned a value. *Read* or *r* is given an octal value of 4, *write* or *w* is 2, and *execute* or *x* is 1. Each notation or value of a particular group is the sum of that group's value. For example, a file with the string -rwxr-xr-x preceding it would be given a value of 755—the sum of the *user* group equaling 7, and the sum of both *group* and *other* equaling 5 each, or 755 for the entire file.

If a user has permission to read a file—that is, if the file has a value of 4—that user can open and view the file's contents. If the user has write permission, or a value of 2, the owner can change the file's contents or save changes. If a user has a value of 1, or execute permission, that file's owner can execute the file to perform a specified function. Unlike DOS, a file in Linux doesn't need a particular extension to be executable. It requires only the permissions to be altered in order to execute scripts or programs.

The permissions assigned to each file also affect how a file will act. For example, setting the permissions of a file to 777 is not a very good idea. This means that not only the user and the group can read and write the file's contents and also execute the file as a binary, but also that everyone else can do the same. Anyone with access to your directory or to your file could alter its function or use it for not-so-benign purposes.

## Changing Permissions

Changing the permissions on files or directories involves using the command chmod. The chmod command is multifunctional in that there are several ways that the command enables you to change a file's attributes. The most common way is to use the standard nine-bit permission settings—that is, manually changing the octal value of a file or directory. For example, if you own the file readme.txt and want to allow yourself to read, write, and execute the file, yet allow the group only to read and execute it, and allow others only to read it, you would use the following command:

```
chmod 754 readme.txt
```

Now you, as the owner or user, can read, write, and execute the file, while those in the group to whom this file belongs can only read and execute the file. Everyone else can only read the file.

There are several other aspects to chmod. First, only the owner of the file can change the permissions. Root, naturally, can change the permissions of any file. Knowing the other syntax associated with chmod can assist in making global changes to certain files. The letters a, u, g, and o are also used together (a,u,g,o) with a plus or minus sign (+,-). The letters again stand for *all, user, group,* and *other.* The signs add or take away permissions. Used together with the letters r, w, and x, the signs enable you to make the same changes as with the octal values.

Here are some other examples of how you can modify files:

◆ chmod a+w readme.txt allows all users write access

◆ chmod og-x readme.txt takes away execute rights for the group and others

◆ chmod u-rwx readme.txt denies the user read, write, or execute access to the file

◆ chmod a+rwx readme.txt gives all permissions to all users. This is the same as the setting chmod 777

Practice using these commands, along with using **ls -la** to see the results, will give you a better understanding of the power of chmod.

The same rules for setting the permissions for files apply to directories. Even stricter rules are enforced in this case, since allowing all read, write, and execute access to a specific directory can open large security holes and enable unwanted guests access to restricted locations. Take extra care when changing permissions for a directory, particularly if that directory sits in your own home directory or in a sensitive part of the Linux file system.

# Figuring Out Ownerships

Changing the ownerships of files is just as simple as changing the permissions. The command chown changes the user ownership of a certain file, while chgrp changes the group ownership. Files can be owned by a group to allow multiple people access to work on a given file. To change these settings, you must first either own the file directly or have root permission to do so. Also, to change a file's owner, that owner must actually exist, as must the group name. You can verify whether these names actually exist by looking in the /etc/passwd file for the user and the /etc/group file for the group name. Otherwise, Linux will protest and inform you that an invalid user is selected.

The syntax for changing file ownership is simple. If I wanted to change the ownership of a particular file from myself to someone else such as "nobody," a user assigned to specific daemons, I would need not only permission for myself but for that user as well. It is simplest to perform this as root by typing the following:

```
chown nobody readme.txt
```

Changing the ownership back to its former owner would require a similar command:

```
chown kerry readme.txt
```

Changing group ownership is very similar. Some Linux distributions simply set both user and group ownership to the same user. This is generally the case with Red Hat Linux. This kind of setting is useful in that you do not need to worry about additional group names. However, creating a new group is just as easy as setting up a new user. To do this manually, you edit the /etc/group file, creating the group name and then placing the users who belong to the group at the end. Here is a sample output of my own /etc/group file:

```
kerry:x:500:
karen:x:501:
cox::502:kerry,karen
```

Because the user kerry is both a valid username and group name, it appears here as well as in the /etc/passwd file. Karen, my wife, also has an account on my system. The group cox has both kerry and karen, the users, as members. If chgrp is used to change any file to the group name cox, my wife and I have permission to edit or modify the file in any way.

If you wish to change both the user and group ownership of a particular file without executing two separate commands, use a colon after the user's name. For example, to set a specific file to be owned both by the user kerry and the group kerry, I would type the following command; `chown kerry: readme.txt`. The colon following kerry sets both variables.

## Setting *Setuid* Permissions

As mentioned previously, each file is given an octal value that denotes the permissions that users, groups, and all others have for that particular file. Also, only certain users can access specific programs that otherwise could only be run by root. The octal values of 4000 and 2000 bypass this limitation. They are the *setuid* and *setgid* bits. Normally, they apply only to executable files, but they can also apply to directories. Care should be taken when using both setuid and setgid on files.

Identifying setuid (or SUID) and setgid (or SGID) files is simple. When doing an `ls -la` command, you will see at the end of the first string of letters relating to the user permissions an *s* instead of an *x*. This means the file is a setuid. The file is setgid if there is an *s* instead of an *x* in the group permission location. Here are some examples of setting a simple Perl script to setuid and setgid:

```
-r-sr-xr-x     simple.pl          # setuid
-r-xr-sr-x     simple.pl          # setgid
```

You can set these permissions in one of two ways. The first is to set the permission by entering the command **chmod 4555**, and the second is to enter **chmod 2555**. The command **chmod u+s simple.pl** also works. Likewise, **chmod g+s simple.pl** accomplishes the same.

The purpose of setuid and setgid is to ensure that the processes that run the program are granted access to system resources based on the file's user or group owner, rather than on the user who executed the file or created the process. Thus, any user can start a root-owned process and have access to the resources available to the process. setuid and setgid bypass several security restrictions normally in place. If you must change the permissions on a file and enable setuid, do so in moderation. Many distributions tend to avoid setting any programs with setuid enabled. Many security sites frown upon these types of enabled programs as well and will advise users to remove these types of permissions.

The concept of a sticky bit is similar to that of setuid and setgid. These types of files have an octal value of 1000 and are identified by the letter *t* at the end of the file permissions. The purpose of a sticky bit is to keep the executable in memory after the program exits. It is also intended for a user to delete only those files that he or she owns or to delete those files for which the user may have direct write access. The sticky bit feature is designed primarily for a directory such as /tmp which allows any user to execute files from that location owned by that user. The sticky bit limits the user from indiscriminately deleting any files at will, whether the user owns them or not.

The way in which the sticky bit is set on a file or directory is much like that of setuid or setgid. You can enter **chmod 1777 readme.txt** to grant a file or directory full read/write/execute access and to set the sticky bit at the end. A directory such as /tmp will have the following file permission:

```
drwxrwxrwt   6 root      root          1024 Oct  5 16:20 tmp
```

Liberal use of the sticky bit is not recommended. But knowing how it is applied and used is highly suggested. Using the sticky bit helps in cases where former system administrators have deleted the /tmp directory and then tried to re-create it. This happened to me. Strange errors began appearing in the system logs and users were unable to use the Pine e-mail client to read their e-mail. A quick look through the system showed me that the sticky bit had been left off of the /tmp directory. Pine uses /tmp to store mail temporarily. As users were attempting to read mail, Pine would tell them that their session was read-only and that they could neither save nor delete old messages. Once I replaced the sticky bit on the /tmp directory, Pine began to function correctly.

# Disk Usage Limits

When dealing with a large system and with hundreds of users, a very real threat can be the abuse of the system and the accumulation of hundreds of megabytes of data. One way to limit this stockpiling is to institute quotas on the system.

Normally this feature must be enabled in the kernel since it is a feature of the file system. Most Linux systems, however, do ship with this feature enabled. If not, a new kernel will need to be compiled with quotas installed.

Quotas allow you to predetermine how much space each user is allowed to use. Once a user surpasses his or her quota limit, the user receives a warning the next time he or she logs in, and is given a grace period to remove files before the account is locked. This is useful for those users you feel use your system for their personal dumping ground or view your server as a backup system for data files. It encourages users to minimize use to only absolutely necessary files.

## Assigning Quotas

Once quotas are enabled within the kernel, configuring them for each user proceeds quickly. You first want to check to see what quota is set for each user. You can do so with the following command:

```
quota -v kerry
```

This prints out the allowance of space for that user. To edit the quotas for any user, invoke the command edquota. This brings up a text file using the *vi editor*, or the Visual Editor that comes standard with most Linux installs as the default editor unless another editor is chosen in the settings. You not only can set quotas for individual users but also for groups of users. In addition, once you have set up a quota correctly for one user, you can apply the same settings to an entire set of users, thereby avoiding editing the settings for hundreds of users.

You can change the default editor for either yourself or for all users by editing one of two files. To change the default editor for all users to another dynamic text editor such as joe, vim, or elvis, edit the file /etc/profile and place the following lines within the body of the text:

```
EDITOR=joe
export EDITOR
```

The same applies for making local changes. If you want to change the editor for only a specific user, such as yourself, edit the file .bash_profile in that user's home directory and install the same lines as in the preceding example. This works only if the user is using the bashshell as the default command-line shell. Under Red Hat, bash is the default shell.

You may be surprised that simply editing the file will not make the changes immediately. You must either log out and then log back in or call the file in question and have it reread its configuration. The best way to do this is to enter one of the following commands, depending upon what file you edited:

```
source /etc/profile
source ~/.bash_profile
```

The ~/ is referential to that user's own home directory. Rather than typing out the entire absolute path to your home directory, you can simply type a tilde and a forward slash.

The command quotacheck maintains the file system and debugs the level of user space consumption. This command should run when the computer boots up. Often this program is automatically set up with a default install. If not, then it should be set up as a cron job. Along with these commands are a series of related programs that check the system. The commands quotaon and quotaoff initialize the quota system for various file systems. The standard procedure for turning quotas on is as follows:

```
quotaon -uv /home
```

Once quotas have been enabled, you can have the quota system report to you the total disk usage for all the file systems listed in /etc/fstab. The command repquota -a prints out the disk usage of the directories and users.

## Monitoring Disk Use

For less intensive monitoring of directories and simple reporting of disk usage, the command *du* accomplishes much the same thing. Depending upon your location and the directory that you are currently in, running du will show you the amount of hard drive space that each file occupies.

Again, because the output will probably exceed the number of lines that your terminal window can show, it is a good idea to pipe the result through the more and less commands. The du command checks not only your visible directories and files but also hidden file systems or those whose names are preceded by a period. Be forewarned that the output is extremely verbose and that you should implement some options if you want to see a limited result. You can also apply du to just one directory. Entering **du docs/ | more** prints out the size of each file found within that directory structure. If the output appears too cryptic, try using some options such as –k, which then prints out the result in kilobytes. This gives a better real-world definition of space used. I prefer the du -h option, which prints out the end result in human readable format, in kilobytes and megabytes. Though the -k option is the default variable when displaying file sizes, some file systems might be set up differently. Using the -a option will also show you the file size of individual files and not just the directory sizes. This option is more verbose in its tabulating. You can consult the man page for du for additional information.

## Checking Partition Use

If you want to see the disk use for each partition, the command df is recommended. This command lists the amount of disk space consumed and the amount available for each partition. The df command can be viewed as the counterpart to the du command since df views the amount of space used and available for each partition whereas du examines directories.

The standard format for df is first to show the device name for each partition. The next few variables display how much space each partition can hold, the amount used, the remaining space available, and the percentage occupied by files. At the end of each line, the output shows the partition name assigned to the device name.

Like most commands, df takes different options so that you can refine the additional bits of information that the output displays. One of the most commonly used options is –h, which displays the output in a format that humans can understand—that is, in terms of kilobytes, megabytes, and gigabytes. In Listing 3.3, the default df command shows the space in terms of 1 kilobyte blocks. Listing 3.4 shows the df output with the -h option. Here the result is more understandable.

**Listing 3.3  A Sample Printout of Disk Use Showing Disk Space Consumption in Terms of 1 Kilobyte Blocks**

```
      $ df
Filesystem        1k-blocks       Used    Available   Use%    Mounted on
/dev/hda1           497829        38185       433942     8%    /
/dev/hda5          3470648      1230469      2060655    37%    /home
```

```
/dev/hda8          746387    378208    329625   53%   /opt
/dev/hda7         2016016   1341784    571820   70%   /usr
/dev/hda6         2478138   1563570    786452   67%   /usr/local
/dev/hda10         388693     34010    334604    9%   /var
```

**Listing 3.4  A Printout of Disk Space in Terms of Megabyte Blocks**

```
  $ df -h
Filesystem        Size   Used   Avail   Use%   Mounted on
/dev/hda1         486M    37M    424M     8%   /
/dev/hda5         3.3G   1.2G    2.0G    37%   /home
/dev/hda8         729M   369M    322M    53%   /opt
/dev/hda7         1.9G   1.3G    558M    70%   /usr
/dev/hda6         2.4G   1.5G    768M    67%   /usr/local
/dev/hda10        380M    33M    327M     9%   /var
```

Properly monitoring the amount of space used by each partition will help regulate the amount of space that can be allocated to each user. This also helps to prevent one partition from becoming overburdened. If you know that a partition is quickly approaching maximum capacity, you can take preventative action such as further reducing disk use, adding additional hard drives, or repartitioning existing drives. Knowledge of what your users are doing on your system is the key to keeping it operating at its optimal level.

# Conclusion

This chapter covered the most basic commands associated with viewing files and directories as well as moving and copying those files within differing locations. This chapter also highlighted how Red Hat Linux lays out certain file structures and what types of files each separate directory contains. You also learned what types of files exist under Linux and how you can modify file permissions and ownerships. Lastly, you examined how you can control and monitor the amount of disk space on a Linux drive.

This chapter covered the basics for initial navigation and preliminary system administration. It was designed for beginning users who need to understand how files function under the Linux operating system.

Once you have grasped the fundamentals of files and directories, including the setting of permissions for unique files, you can begin interacting with the command line. The next chapter will look at shells that allow the user to input additional commands to the system. Because Linux provides several different possible shells with which to operate, Chapter 4 will outline some of the advantages of each and provide examples of the pros and cons that each shell offers the average user.

# Chapter 4

## Terminal Shells

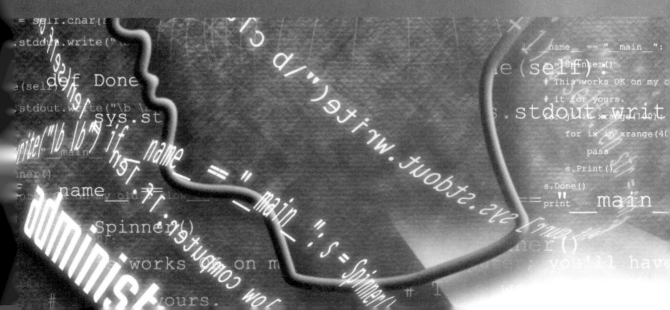

The shell provides the interface between the user and the system. It is here that the user inputs commands, queries, or instructions. The shell is identified by either the prompt that appears at a console connection after logging in or the prompt that appears in any of the terminals via remote login or an X-Window session. There are different ways a shell can facilitate navigation and tasks under Linux. Though considered arcane by newer users, the shell still provides the most dynamic method of accessing and editing Linux files.

This chapter will cover the following topics:

◆ Examining the types of shells available
◆ Editing user files under the shell
◆ Creating shell scripts
◆ Customizing the shell prompt
◆ Understanding paths
◆ Specifying variables under the shell

## Prompts or Shells

Any experience that you have with Linux up to now has been in some type of shell or command-line interpreter. A *shell* can be identified by the prompt immediately preceding the input field under the command-line environment, but it is also much more. It is the entire program that enables you to navigate through the Linux structure and provides you with the means to send commands to the kernel and receive responses.

Like earlier versions of PCs, and UNIX machines, early Linux boxes enabled any user to type a particular command and have the system respond or perform an action. Users entered all these commands on the command line. These early versions involved nothing more than a bracket or >, after which users could input data. However, Linux has become, unlike DOS and some of the other text-only environments, extremely customizable. Under Linux there are several shells from which to choose, each offering a wide range of options. Within the UNIX field there are two major shell types: the Bourne shell and the C shell. The Bourne shell, which is still the default on many UNIX-based operating systems, employs a syntax based on the early shell of UNIX. This program is usually defined as /bin/sh. The C shell utilizes a different syntax that closely resembles the syntax of the C programming language. It also comes installed by default on other UNIX systems and is located in /bin/csh. These shells have made it easier for UNIX users to migrate to a Linux environment, and are still quite popular and readily available under Red Hat Linux. Because Linux was originally designed from the UNIX base, it caters to many previous and current UNIX users. The syntax is still the same, yet operable under a different platform.

# Bash and C Shells

In addition to these two UNIX shells, two other shells are commonly used under Linux. The first is the Bourne Again Shell, or *bash,* which is located in /bin/bash. Under Red Hat bash is commonly soft-linked to /bin/sh so bash is used as the default shell. The other is tcsh and is located in /bin/tcsh. These two shells are enhanced versions of the original shells, sh and csh. They share many of the same traits, but now have additional features that make programming and scripting even easier. One of the most notable features of the bash shell, and one reason that it has become the standard shell under most Linux distributions, is its ability to save a history of previously executed commands. Unlike tcsh/csh, you can recall previous commands. With bash, you can execute a series of commands, close the shell, and then reopen the shell later and use previous commands from an earlier session. bash stores all commands in a temporary directory for later retrieval. Another bash feature is that it enables users to press the Tab key to finish commands. No longer do users have to type out the entire pathname; the bash shell will finish directories and commands based upon available options.

---

## NOTE

The bash shell is the most common shell found on Linux distributions and is the default shell for Red Hat. This chapter will focus mainly on the bash shell. It is the most actively maintained shell and provides users with a stable environment in which to perform system tasks.

## Available Shells under Linux

The file /etc/shells lists the shells available under Linux. This file shows all the installed valid shells and those accessible by any user. They are listed in order of preference, with the first being the default. Listing 4.1 shows the contents of a typical /etc/shells file.

### Listing 4.1  The /etc/shells File under Red Hat.

```
/bin/bash
/bin/sh
/bin/ksh
/bin/zsh
/bin/tcsh
/bin/csh
```

> **TIP**
>
> It is best to stick with a shell that you feel comfortable with. The Red Hat Linux distribution's default shell is probably your best choice if you are just starting to learn Linux.

## Different Shell Features

Table 4.1 lists many of the possible features associated with each shell. The table contains a fairly definitive list and includes nearly every possible feature. This table provides a broad perspective on some of the advantages that each shell might or might not have over the other.

Some of these shell features may need to be recompiled from source code and may not be implemented in a standard RPM release. To enable all features that are possible under each shell, you will have to first *compile the program from source code*, meaning you first will have to obtain the source code from the host site, edit specific variables, and then create the binary program yourself using a code compiler. After creating the executable, you can then add specific flags to the command to insert new features. See Chapter 11 to learn about compiling programs from source.

**TIP**

For additional information about shells and the latest developments for each, consult the FAQ postings on the USENET newsgroups, such as comp.unix.shell, comp.unix.questions, news.answers, and comp.answers. These postings are updated monthly on the preceding newsgroups and can be referenced from any of the USENET archival sites such as http://www.deja.com/.

**Table 4.1  A Comparison of the Available Shells**

| Criterion | sh | csh | ksh | bash | tcsh | zsh |
|---|---|---|---|---|---|---|
| Job control | N | Y | Y | Y | Y | Y |
| Aliases | N | Y | Y | Y | Y | Y |
| Shell functions | Y(1) | N | Y | Y | N | Y |
| "Sensible" I/O redirection | Y | N | Y | Y | N | Y |
| Directory stack | N | Y | Y | Y | Y | Y |
| Command history | N | Y | Y | Y | Y | Y |
| Command-line editing | N | N | Y | Y | Y | Y |
| Vi command-line editing | N | N | Y | Y | Y(3) | Y |
| Emacs command-line editing | N | N | Y | Y | Y | Y |
| Rebindable command-line editing | N | N | N | Y | Y | Y |
| Username lookup | N | Y | Y | Y | Y | Y |
| Login/logout watching | N | N | N | N | Y | Y |
| Filename completion | N | Y(1) | Y | Y | Y | Y |
| Username completion | N | Y(2) | Y | Y | Y | Y |
| Hostname completion | N | Y(2) | Y | Y | Y | Y |
| History completion | N | N | N | Y | Y | Y |
| Fully programmable completion | N | N | N | N | Y | Y |
| MH mailbox completion | N | N | N | N(4) | N(6) | N(6) |
| Coprocesses | N | N | Y | N | N | Y |
| Built-in arithmetic evaluation | N | Y | Y | Y | Y | Y |

**Table 4.1** **A Comparison of the Available Shells** *(continued)*

| Criterion | sh | csh | ksh | bash | tcsh | zsh |
|---|---|---|---|---|---|---|
| Ability to follow symbolic links invisibly | N | N | Y | Y | Y | Y |
| Periodic command execution | N | N | N | N | Y | Y |
| Custom prompt (easily configurable) | N | N | Y | Y | Y | Y |
| Sun Keyboard Hack | N | N | N | N | N | Y |
| Spelling correction | N | N | N | N | Y | Y |
| Process substitution | N | N | N | Y(2) | N | Y |
| Underlying syntax | sh | csh | sh | sh | csh | sh |
| Available for free | N | N | N(5) | Y | Y | Y |
| Checks mailbox | N | Y | Y | Y | Y | Y |
| Tty sanity checking | N | N | N | N | Y | Y |
| Ability to cope with large argument lists | Y | N | Y | Y | Y | Y |
| Noninteractive startup file | N | Y | Y(7) | Y(7) | Y | Y |
| Nonlogin startup file | N | Y | Y(7) | Y | Y | Y |
| Ability to avoid user startup files | N | Y | N | Y | N | Y |
| Ability to specify startup files | N | N | Y | Y | N | N |
| Low-level command redefinition | N | N | N | N | N | N |
| Anonymous functions | N | N | N | N | N | N |
| Variable lists | N | Y | Y | N | Y | Y |
| Full signal trap handling | Y | N | Y | Y | N | Y |
| File no-clobber ability | N | Y | Y | Y | Y | Y |
| Local variables | N | N | Y | Y | N | Y |
| Lexically scoped variables | N | N | N | N | N | N |
| Exceptions | N | N | N | N | N | N |

There are additional numbers added to either the Yes or No options. These indicate the following notes, which explain crucial elements and their presence or development within that shell:

1. Shell functions and filename completions were not in the original versions of either sh and csh, but have since become almost standard.

2. User and hostname completion under csh as well as process substitution under bash are both fairly new and so are often not found on many versions of these shells. However, they are gradually making their way into standard distribution. They may, at the time of this printing, be found in the either shells.

3. Many consider the *vi* (a mnemonic for *visual editor*, a simple text editor) emulation of this shell to be incomplete.

4. The mailbox completion option is not standard, but unofficial patches exist to provide this functionality.

5. A version called *pdksh* is available for free, but does not have the full functionality of the AT&T version.

6. This can be done via the shell's programmable completion mechanism.

7. Certain startup files can be specified only via the ENV environment variable.

## Shell Cautions

When first starting with Linux, pick a shell with which you are comfortable and stay with it. That is not to say that you should exclude others, but until you are comfortable with the Linux environment, do not change shells until you feel the need for additional features. Nothing is more frustrating than fully expecting a function of a shell and then realizing the current shell—that is, sh, tcsh, or bash—does not support the features to which you are accustomed. This happens occasionally when switching between Linux, Solaris, and other operating systems. Be sure you know what the default shell is and where you are before initiating any commands. Otherwise, your commands might provide unexpected results.

The quickest way to verify the default shell is to enter **echo $SHELL**. This command will not only display the shell you are using, but will also show the pathname to that shell.

Similarly, to verify which machine you are currently working on, in case you may be working on another similar machine with a like shell, enter **uname −a**. This prints out the name of the local machine, the kernel version, and date of the last kernel recompilation.

> **TIP**
>
> You can always start a new shell simply by invoking it from the command line. If you are working under the bash shell and want to change to tcsh, simply enter the name of the new shell. To leave that shell, enter **exit**.

## Criteria for Choosing a Shell

Which of the many shells you choose depends on many different issues. Here are some questions you should ask yourself when choosing a shell. Though many users simply accept the default bash shell that comes standard on Red Hat Linux, there are other options that you should also consider. Remember, that even the simplest commands, such as rm, ls, cp, and mv, all function the same no matter what shell is used. Here are a few important points:

♦ *How much time do I have to learn a new shell?* There is no point in using a shell with a different syntax or a completely different alias system if you do not have the time to learn it. If you have the time and are presently using csh or tcsh, it is worth considering a switch to a Bourne shell variant.

♦ *What do I want to be able to do with my new shell?* The main reason for switching shells is to gain extra functionality; so it is vital that you know what you are gaining from the move.

♦ *Will I be able to switch back to my original shell?* If you have to switch back to a standard shell, it is fairly important that you don't become so dependent on extra features that moving back to an older or less functional shell is problematic.

♦ *How much extra load can the system cope with?* Newer, advanced shells tend to be more memory-intensive, requiring more of the system's physical as well as swap memory. If you are on an overloaded machine, you should probably avoid such shells. This is especially applicable if you are using older 386 or 486 machines.

◆ *What support is given for my new shell?* If your new shell is not supported, make sure you have someone you can ask for help if you encounter problems or that you have the time to sort them out yourself. I dabbled in learning tcsh for some time, and was fortunate enough to have a friend I could ask questions when I encountered problems.

◆ *What shell am I using already?* Switching between certain shells of the same syntax is a lot easier than switching between shells of a different syntax. So if you haven't much time, a simple upgrade (from sh to bash, for example) may be a good idea.

◆ *Must you use more than one shell?* If you use more than one machine, you may discover that you need to use more than one shell regularly. How different are these shells and can you cope with having to switch between shells on a regular basis? It may be to your advantage to choose shells that are similar to each other.

## Shell Setups for Users

When setting up or modifying an existing user, it is imperative that the administrator or whoever creates the account defines a shell for that person. Without a shell it is nearly impossible to gain access to the system. Though the process of configuring a new user's account is extremely automated under Red Hat Linux, it is important to realize where certain options are placed that define how the user will interact with the system. For information on setting up individual accounts and configuring the parameters for each, see Chapter 6.

Most aspects of a user's shell along with other variables needed for a user to log in and accomplish tasks via the command line are located in the /etc/passwd file. As its name indicates, this file is originally where a user's password is kept in an encrypted format. In addition to keeping passwords, this file also stores information on the user's home directory and default shell. Normally, the shell assigned the user is sufficient. If, however, the user wants to change his or her shell, the user must be able to use the *chsh,* or *change shell,* command. Otherwise, the user is stuck with the shell assigned when the account was created.

**NOTE**

In the most recent versions of Red Hat Linux, the encrypted passwords are kept in the /etc/shadow file. They can be read only by root since its permissions are set to 400. This helps keep the passwords secure while allowing the system access to the other variables in /etc/passwd.

The file also keeps the user's full name or identifying title along with the type of shell that the user prefers. Here is a sample output from my own account:

```
kjcox:x:500:500:Kerry Cox:/home/kjcox:/bin/bash
```

A colon separates each field. The first field identifies the username, while the second usually is the encrypted password. However, in this example, the password field is simply denoted by an *x*. The encrypted password is stored in /etc/shadow. If shadow passwords were not enabled, then only a jumble of numbers and characters signifying the encrypted password would be visible. Shadow passwords inhibit password-cracking programs from deciphering the encryption and cracking user accounts. Typically, to crack a password a user must first be able to view the encrypted passwords. If the passwords are in encrypted format in /etc/passwd, then a brute force method is taken. A cracking program will run various passwords through its own encryption, and then compare them to the ones in the passwd file. If the passwords can't be viewed, they are harder to decipher.

The next two fields of the /etc/passwd file contain identifying user ID (UID) and group ID (GID) numbers. These are unique incremental numbers that Linux portions out as each new user is added to the system. Red Hat Linux UID and GID numbers begin at 500. My own entry in the preceding /etc/passwd file has the number 500 in both fields because I was first user installed on the system.

**NOTE**

Even though root is the first account created on any Linux system, it receives its own special UID of 0.

The next field contains a comment identifying the user's full name, title, job description, or some other text clarifying that user's function. The next field identifies each user's home directory. This is the default location or directory that the user is sent to after logging on the system. It is here that the user keeps and edits startup files particular to his or her needs. The last field defines the user's shell. See Chapter 6 for more information about customizing the separate fields found in the /etc/passwd file.

Linux also has users on the system who do not generally log in and do not require a shell. These are users who perform system tasks, but who do not exist as valid users with login capability. Examples of such users are nobody and xfs. The system requires a user account under which certain processes run, such as the web daemon or the X font server. The aforementioned "nonexistent" users run these two processes respectively. In such cases, the default shell is set to /bin/false. This setting is to prevent any other user on the system from logging in as that user, procuring a shell, and gaining permissions over the directories and files run by these system users.

### CAUTION

Be careful when changing any user's shell. You can inadvertently disable a user from logging in if the shell doesn't exist. You should take extra caution when modifying root's variables in any way.

Another method of preventing regular users from gaining access to certain daemons and other off-limits system processes is to create an unique user who owns the specific directories containing scripts and HTML files or unique daemons such as the httpd daemon. By using this method, you can avoid using the default nobody user by creating another dedicated system user with only limited permissions. Accounts such as webuser or www are good examples of users who should be given a default shell when used by other processes. This helps discourage users or intruders from exploiting weaknesses in the system.

# Shell Scripts

The shell itself is highly interactive. It can be used as a platform for creating unique scripts of commands to accomplish specific system tasks. The shell provides the environment for users to create these scripts and then run them from the command line. These scripts can either be initiated at the command prompt or can be placed in a simple text file and then started elsewhere, either manually by the user or by an automated system command.

## Understanding the Purpose of Shell Scripts

A user creates shell scripts to avoid repetition. Scripts can handle many mundane tasks and free the user from extra typing by monitoring disk functions. A shell script can execute in one line what would normally take hours of typing to accomplish. It is a simple program that can be automated and executed at times when users are not normally logged in and the system's use is minimal.

Many programmers choose to write scripts for use under the shell in programming languages such as *Perl* (Practical Extraction and Report Language). Though not considered a shell script, Perl scripts share similar features. The Perl language is fairly standard for Internet use and, in the words of Larry Wall, its creator, "it is the glue that holds the Internet together." It is only reasonable, then, that Perl, which contains many of the best features of C, is often used for Internet-related programs or on Web servers such as Linux to perform specific Internet-related tasks.

Writing scripts for increased functionality is largely the role of the administrator of the Linux system. This book does not go into the details of programming, but does point users to solutions and give examples on how to accomplish specific tasks. Many scripts are available on the Internet. Many Linux distributions make scripts accessible for free either on the CD or after installation is complete. Red Hat does so as well, and many system maintenance scripts can be found in diverse locations throughout a typical install. The most common place to find scripts is in the /etc/ directory. A simple search for scripts using any search engine will bring up many possibilities. The most common scripts either end in a .pl or a .sh extension or simply have a name that defines their function.

These are but a few of the many sites with scripts available for users to download and use. Usually instructions are provided along with the scripts. Some sites even offer assistance to beginning users. Because members of the open-source community contributed most of the scripts, a simple request to the script's author is often the best way to get help if, after following directions, you are still unable to get the script to function correctly. Be advised that free scripts often are subject to security holes, but again, the developers are quick to make patches or corrections available.

# Writing and Storing Scripts

It is best to use a simple text editor for composing your scripts. vi is the default text editor with Red Hat, but other editors, such as emacs, developed by Richard Stallman, work just as well. vim, a modified version of vi, is just as powerful but requires less of a learning curve. Elvis and pico are simple-to-use editors designed for beginning Linux users. My personal favorite is joe, a very functional editor based on the old WordStar program. Each of these editors is shipped with the latest Red Hat release. I recommend trying out a few and opting for the one that both best suits your needs and is most comfortable to use.

Give the file any name you want. It is best to name the file by the script's function. For example, one script I wrote to back up all the files on one machine to another using the dump program is called, quite simply, dodump. Its name leaves little doubt as to what the program does. In order to identify this script as a customized program, give it a more descriptive name, perhaps with your initials. For example, I might rename this file to dodump_kjc.sh to identify it as a script written by myself.

I prefer saving scripts in a central location. I usually create a /usr/local/scripts/ directory where I place all executable files or scripts that do not come installed with the Red Hat Linux distribution. You can make symbolic links that point to real files in other locations, from the files in /usr/local/scripts/ to shortcut files located in the default path, such as /usr/local/bin/ or /usr/bin/.

After creating a script called dodump in the directory /usr/local/scripts/, I can make a linked file of the same name in /usr/local/bin/. Thus the dodump program is located in my path. Rather than simply placing them in /usr/local/bin to begin with I can separate those program created by other applications from my won scripts. This is mostly an organizational feature. Some users may choose otherwise and simply clump all programs in one standard location. I edit the permissions so that only I or the root user can read, write, or execute the file:

```
ln -s /usr/local/scripts/dodump /usr/local/bin/dodump
```

Thus when executing the script, the system pulls the dodump program out of my path while preserving the file in its default location.

> **CAUTION**
>
> Keep in mind, however, the directories listed in your default path. When making a symbolic link, remember which directories your path will search first. When users compile a new binary file and place it in their /usr/local/bin/ directory and leave an older binary in /usr/bin, they sometimes forget which directory their default path consults first. Your system checks /usr/bin before /usr/local/bin and thus the newer binary file is ignored. Remember that the search stops at the first match.

Before making scripts available to all users on the system, make certain that the users cannot abuse your scripts. Many users might question my choice on where to place these files, but many people using Linux will not be sharing their system with others. Or if they do, in fact, share their system, they will do so only with trusted users. If a script were used in a larger commercial setting, there would be cause for concern that some users might misuse the script and precautions would have to be taken.

When files are placed in publicly accessible directories, such as /tmp/, anyone can access, modify, and run them. Be certain to place any files you create either in a directory owned by yourself that no one else can access, or in a directory that is owned by a group and thus allows limited access. Do not place executable files in directories anyone can access, as this may have dire consequences for the system. Some users even consider their home directory too much of a security risk. The best way to minimize risks or keep files secure is simply not to store them in public locations and to verify that the permissions are set correctly so that not just anyone can execute the scripts. Or even better, store sensitive data on your own machine and not in a multiuser environment.

Scripts that are publicly accessible should be checked for correct permissions. If you will be making your scripts readable and executable by others, make sure that they are not writable as well. It is not the scripts that present the security risk but the commands within the script. Should anyone be able to alter those commands, they can pose a hazard to the system. In cases where I have backup scripts that require root permissions, I make sure they are owned only by root and that the permissions are set to 500, so that only root can read and execute the file. To set file and directory permissions properly, see Chapter 3.

The syntax of shell scripts should agree with the shell for which it was written. When defining a script or a simple ASCII text file that will perform a specific set of commands, the first line must include a header that points to the script to be used. Table 4.2 shows a couple of examples of shell script headers. A regular script normally uses either sh or csh, although any of the other shells perform just as well.

**Table 4.2  The Headers Associated with Each Shell**

| Shell | Header |
|-------|--------|
| Bourne | !/bin/sh |
| C: | !/bin/csh |
| bash | !/bin/bash |
| tcsh: | !/bin/tcsh |
| ksh | !/bin/ksh |

If you decide to install these shells yourself, you may find Perl in another directory. When installing from source, Perl often places the binary in /usr/local/bin/. However, you can still choose a different default directory or place the binary elsewhere.

**TIP**

To verify the location of any shell binary, enter the following command or a similar one at the command line, either as root or as a local user. Again, what shells you are able to locate depends on each user's path.

```
$ which bash
```

The command which checks the search path and attempts to find the executable of the file in question.

## Executing Scripts

There are two ways to execute a shell script. One is to invoke an interpreter such as sh to execute a file of commands. This means placing the command for the shell, or stating the shell filename, directly before the shell script. You would execute a sample script by entering one of the following commands:

```
    sh script_filename
orcsh script_filename
```

The command calls up the shell, which then reads through the script's contents, executing each line as it parses through it. If you wanted to run a script named runwebstats that you had created for updating the statistics of your Web pages, you would execute the script by entering the following at the prompt:

```
sh runwebstats
```

Another method of executing the script is to change the permissions so that it is executable by the author and then calling it from the command line. In such instances, the *chmod* (*change mode*) command comes in handy. Here is how you would change the file properties:

```
chmod u+x script_filename
```

or

```
chmod 500 script_filename
```

The first instance makes the file executable by the user. The second example not only makes the file executable by the user, but it changes the file so that no one, other than the file's owner, can do anything to it. Setting the permissions to 544 would allow others to view the contents, but they would not be able to alter or execute the file. Also make sure that the directories are tight enough that an undesirable user cannot simply delete the contents of the directory. They should be able to read and execute the files, provided you are in agreement with this, but they should not have write permission to edit or delete the files in this directory. You can review the file permissions settings in Chapter 3.

To run the script, you can either call it from its absolute or relative path. If I were in any directory on the system, I could run a program from my home directory by entering the following:

```
/home/kerry/script_filename
```

Or, if I were in a directory that contained my shell script but was *not* in my search path, I would enter the following:

```
./script_filename
```

But if the directory with the shell script were not in my search path, and my current location were that same directory, I could still invoke it by entering the preceding command.

After writing your script, test it in a way that will not change any crucial system files. Setting the script to run verbosely, printing out any superfluous commands, will assist in debugging it if necessary. Here is how I would run my script:

```
sh -v runwebstats
```

You should play with the different options to verify that the script runs correctly and that you have debugged any problems that might exist. The *-v* or, *verbose,* command works well with the /bin/sh type shells as well as with the /bin/csh derivative shells.

# Dissecting a Shell Script

As an example of how a shell script operates, Listing 4.2 shows a fairly straight-forward script that I wrote for backing up files located on a computer running Linux. The script is merely a collection of commands that the shell reads completely through and then runs it until complete. It is important to note that once the command is executed to run this script, it will read the entire script through before executing it. So even if you do change the file contents before it is run, the shell will still execute the original file. For example, if I ran the script run_me.sh as follows: sleep 10m; run_me.sh and then while it was sleeping I changed the run_me.sh file to change_me.sh. When the shell was done sleeping after 10 minutes, it would still execute the run_me.sh script.

The first line sets the shell type. There can be no spaces in this line, and the pound sign (#) along with the bang or exclamation point (!) must immediately precede the full path to the shell. Because you never know who might use your script later, you should explain what the script does by adding comments with general observations about the script. Create comments by including the pound sign directly before the text commenting on the script. The tar command on each line is the initial command. The script reads through each line until the task is completed and then moves to the next line.

### Listing 4.2  A Sample Backup Script Using the tar Command

```
#!/bin/sh
# This is a script that backs up my files
# It backs up only those directories that cannot easily be
# restored in case of a reinstall.
```

```
# foo.bar.com is the name of a local networked Linux box
# with a tape backup.
#

tar -cvf foo.bar.com:/dev/st0n      /home
tar -cvf foo.bar.com:/dev/st0n               /usr/local
tar -cvf foo.bar.com:/dev/st0n               /var
tar -cvf foo.bar.com:/dev/st0n               /opt
tar -cvf foo.bar.com:/dev/st0n               /etc
tar -cvf foo.bar.com:/dev/st0                 /usr/src

# Now create a Table of Contents that lists the files backed up.
today='date +%d%b%y'
tar -cv /home > /usr/local/backup/home_backup_$today.toc
tar -cv /usr/local > /usr/local/backup/usr_local_backup_$today.toc
tar -cv /var > /usr/local/backup/var_backup_$today.toc
tar -cv /opt > /usr/local/backup/opt_backup_$today.toc
tar -cv /etc > /usr/local/backup/etc_backup_$today.toc
tar -cv /usr/src > /usr/local/backup/usr_src_backup_$today.toc
#
# End of file
```

Listing 4.3 shows another shell script example that does a local backup of logs that store details about user dial-up connections. This script might be used by a dial-up Linux box that receives incoming calls and provides Internet connectivity. Since these log files can quickly become extremely large, they need to be rotated. *Rotating files* involves either moving the existing files to a backup file and then creating the default file anew or simply deleting larger files and allowing the system to create a new file of the same name. Frequent rotation will prevent large log files and will not waste hard drive space. This script was set up on a cron job, or automated process, that ran bimonthly. See Chapter 8 for clarification concerning the cron and at commands.

Though many shell scripts simply call up the /bin/sh shell as the interpreter for a most commands, you can just as easily use /bin/bash to invoke a series of commands. This argument is typically moot under Red Hat since the /bin/sh file is a symbolic link to /bin/bash. What you choose depends on your preference and ease of use. Listing 4.3 is another sample script that rotates certain logs saved by the Radius (Remote Authentication Dial-In User Service) program, created by Lucent InterNetworking Systems, that functions as a client/server security protocol. It logs all the dial-up connections made to a specific machine. With heavy traffic, these logs can quickly grow big and unmanageable.

**Listing 4.3  Another Example Shell Script that Rotates Cumbersome Log Files**

```
#!/bin/bash
# This is a script that will rotate the Radius log files.
# The detail files are found at
# /var/log/radacct/$ip_nums/detail
mv /var/log/radacct/192.168.0.10/detail \
   /var/log/radacct/192.168.0.10/detail.bak
touch /var/log/radacct/192.168.0.10/detail
echo "Starting afresh" > /var/log/radacct/192.168.0.10/detail
# End of file
```

More complicated scripts that use other programs and involve more complex routines perform just as well. It is not feasible for this book to cover all the available options that can be written into scripts. It is important, however, to understand the syntax behind writing shell scripts. The best method of understanding how shell scripts function is to try your hand at writing your own or to beg, borrow, or steal someone else's. As noted earlier, several sites offer functional scripts written in nearly every language for every conceivable operating system. A preliminary search on the Internet will quickly find other files as well.

# Customizing the Shell Prompt

It is not just the shell itself that is so useful; the prompt can also be very informative. What appears in the field just before the prompt can provide the location, the username, and the name of the machine. This information can be invaluable if you have accounts on several machines. Performing a Telnet session back and forth among different Linux servers can quickly cause disorientation. It is easy to forget what machine is your current host. To provide more information in a limited amount of space, the prompt of most shells gives added information about location and user.

The standard shell under Red Hat, as mentioned earlier, is bash. The Red Hat developers have made sure that the prompt provides the user with the name of the user controlling the shell, the name of the Linux box, and the current directory. Here are two typical examples of bash prompts. The first example shows a regular user logged in to a machine called pluto. His current location is the /etc directory. The second example shows the root user logged in to a machine called goofy while in his home directory.

```
 [kerry@pluto /etc]$
[root@goofy /root]#
```

Notice the character just outside the brackets. The dollar sign ($) is reserved for regular users. The pound sign (#) is assigned only to root or superuser. Setting these symbols at the shell prompt is fairly standard practice on all Linux machines.

The latest version of Red Hat provides even more functionality and is far more descriptive in defining where a user is located. The shell prompt still appears the same. However, when a user is logged in to an *xterm* (or one of the many terminal window emulators such as rxvt, aterm, or Eterm), the title bar above the terminal window displays not only the user's name and the machine he or she is logged in to, but also the full path name of the user's current working directory.

Customizing the shell prompt can prove entertaining as well as functional. You can specify exactly what variable you want visible and just how much information to provide. Besides specifying that the prompt display local information, you can also have the prompt print out messages such as who is logged in to the machine or have it print one of the many quotes found in the fortune program. To keep things fairly standard, bash provides the user with some arguments that he or she can be then incorporate into the user's profile. Normally, bash reads the user's own profile for customized settings. This file is one of the dot, or hidden, files.. It is usually called .bash_profile, but on some machines that do not use bash as their default, its name is .profile. If there is no .bash_profile or .profile file located in the user's home directory, then the shell looks to /etc/profile for the global settings and uses the standards there. Users using other shells, such as sh, can find a .sh_profile hidden file. The line in this file that determines the appearance and functionality of the prompt begins with PS1. There is also sometimes a PS2 line that provides additional information that is needed to serve a request. For example, if you do not complete a shell command or split a command across lines, such as hitting the Enter button before a closing quote, you will be given a secondary prompt. PS2 defines the appearance of that prompt. Table 4.3 describes the available settings in the prompt string; you can find more detail in the man page for bash.

**Table 4.3  A Brief Summary of Available Settings that Can Be Used to Define the bash Prompt**

| Variable | Definition |
| --- | --- |
| \t | The current time in HH:MM:SS format. |
| \d | The date in "weekday month date" format (eg., "Tue May 26"). |
| \n | Newline. |
| \s | The name of the shell, (the portion following the final slash). |
| \w | The current working directory. |
| \W | The basename of the current working directory. |
| \u | The username of the user currently logged in. |
| \h | The hostname. |
| \# | The command number of this command. |
| \! | The history number of this command. |
| \$ | The user type. If the effective UID is 0, a pound sign (#)will appear after the prompt; otherwise a dollar sign ($)is used. The former indicates a root user, the latter a normal user without root powers. |
| \nnn | The character corresponding to the octal number *nnn*. |
| \\ | A backslash. |
| \[ | The beginning of a sequence of nonprinting characters, which could be used to embed a terminal control sequence into the prompt. |
| \] | The end of a sequence of nonprinting characters. |

The following example, which draws from many of the commands described in Table 4.2, is one of the more standard methods that Linux uses to create a customized prompt string:

```
PS1="[\u@\h \W]\\$ "
```

The preceding example creates the following prompt:

```
[kerry@pluto /etc]$
```

Setting the variable foo=bar makes foo available to users. It does not need to be exported. Exporting the variable PS1 also makes it available to the children of the shell. It is then a variable or component of that shell and as such exercises certain control over shell features, such as the default editor, path, or, in this case, prompt.

> **NOTE**
>
> Putting these variables together in different combinations is a good method of becoming familiar with their use. By including the path in your prompt, you can become more familiar with the directory structures and where files are located.

Other users might want to create a more unique prompt that still provides information and functionality. Listing 4.4 shows a customized setup that I used to enable multiple users to log in under the shell of their choice. After setting up a user, this file, called .profile, was created in every user's directory by default. Here each user could define what prompt to use depending upon the environment settings. If a user has a certain shell defined in his or her dot file, then the prompt would be modified to provide additional information while allowing the user to retain the shell of his or her choice.

### Listing 4.4  A Sample Profile that Caters to Each User's Choice of Shells

```
# This is the default standard profile provided to users.
# They are expected to modify this file to meet their own needs.
    if [ "$SHELL" = "/bin/pdksh" -o "$SHELL" = "/bin/ksh" ]; then
PS1="! $ "
    elif [ "$SHELL" = "/bin/zsh" ]; then
PS1="%m:%~%# "
    elif [ "$SHELL" = "/bin/ash" ]; then
PS1="$ "
else
PS1='\h:\w\$ '
fi
PS2='> '
export PS1 PS2


#
# End of file
```

Note the presence of both a PS1 and a PS2 option in Listing 4.4's configuration. Though not often used, these options can be set to provide additional settings. Again, the PS2 setting is the line continuation option and displays a simple '>' sign when the command extends beyond the range of the command. The default bash prompt would now appear as follows if a normal user were logged in to the Linux box called pluto and had a current working directory of /usr/local:

```
pluto:/usr/local$
```

This method is more verbose and shows the absolute path. However, when the working directory is several directories deep, the prompt can take up much of the line. Choosing your customized prompt requires some experimentation to determine  what works best for your own needs.

# Additional Bash-ful Traits

The bash shell has many additional features aside from the customizable prompt that make it currently the most popular Linux shell. Again, because most everything under Linux is classified as open-source, anyone can add new and improved functions to the program. If something does not operate correctly, the source is available for all to see and thus correct. Such is the power of making code accessible for all.

## Tracking the Shell's Command History

One of bash's most popular features is its ability to keep track of commands entered at the command line. Essentially, every command entered at the prompt is stored in a file within the user's home directory. This gives bash a distinct advantage over other shells. Knowing the commands last typed allows you not only to track the most recent entries, but also to redo commonly used commands.

If, during one bash session, you enter several commands and then want to reissue the same commands later, you do not have to enter in the same string of words or characters. You can selectively peruse your earlier commands by pressing the up-arrow key until you find the previously entered command. Each time that you press the up-arrow key, the prompt displays the commands that were entered just before the currently displayed ones.

> **TIP**
>
> Using default emacs keys under the bash shell, Ctrl+R performs a reverse search through old commands. Start typing any part of the command and it will complete the command, locating the most recent command that matches your inquiry.

For example, rather than retyping the entire command to move to a new directory or the entire absolute path, you can simply press the up-arrow key until you find that same command entered earlier under that same shell. Once the correct command is displayed at the prompt, you press Enter to execute it again. This feature can save you much typing and guesswork.

The bash shell also remembers past keystrokes in between shell sessions. This means all commands I execute during one bash session are stored and then retrievable when I next log in at a bash shell. All commands under bash are stored in the user's home directory under the filename .bash_history. If you forget where a certain file is located, but remember having been there before or having previously issued the correct command, you can use any text editor and view the contents of the file. Any search command should quickly locate the line in question. Using Ctrl+R will also help find earlier commands. This makes switching between directories with long pathnames easy.

---

### TIP

The cat command works also very well. This command prints out the contents of a file without invoking a text editor. Piping the cat command through the more and less commands will also help to paginate through a file's contents. Entering **cat &lt;filename&gt; | less** is quicker and easier than using a text editor. You can also simply type **less &lt;filename&gt;** and scroll through the contents as well. The more option also works well. Less is more, as Linux users say.

---

## Completing Filenames

The bash shell also helps reduce repetitious typing in other ways. It has an option that allows you to complete file or directory names by simply pressing the Tab key. Rather than typing every filename to its completion, you need only type the first few letters of the file and then press Tab. The bash shell then attempts to complete the file or directory's name. If there is more than one file that has the same initial letters as you entered, bash signals an error with an audible beep and will attempt to complete the word. Two Tab strokes will display all the potential files that share those same beginning letters.

While in the /usr/X11R6/lib/X11/fvwm2, an obscure directory whose location I frequently forget, I wish to edit the file FvwmConsoleC.pl. Because this directory has over 30 files that all begin with *Fvwm*, I need to be specific as to which file I want to edit. The bash shell reduces the amount of typing that I need to do. I can then enter the name of the text editor in which I wish to open the file, type **Fvw,** then press the Tab key. The bash shell finishes the filename that begins with *Fvwm*, then signals that there are more choices. Pressing the Tab key again displays all the other possible files with the same initial letters. I continue typing **FvwmCo** and again press the Tab key. The bash shell again gives an audible alert that there are more choices available. Type in the next few characters and allow bash to complete the end of the file, press Enter, then open the file.

# Paths

Paths help list directories to which you have immediate access from the command line. When executing a file, you can either type its absolute path or the relative directory in which it is located. Verify first that the file's directory is accessible in your path and then simply enter the executable's name. The latter option is by far the better choice.

If /usr/local/bin is not in my path, I would have to enter **/usr/local/bin/runme** to start the program runme. However, if that pathname is in your path, from anywhere on the system you would need only enter **runme** to execute that program.

**CAUTION**

Make sure that the filename you are looking for is unique. As your shell's path goes through the directories, it will stop at the first match it encounters. Be sure to check the listing of your paths by typing **echo $PATH**.

Understanding how paths work and making them accessible is crucial to simplifying your own duties as a Linux administrator. Keep in mind the order your system uses to search the available paths. By placing often-used executables or scripts in a common and early path, you can access them more readily.

## Exporting Paths

Knowing the path to a file can be extremely useful, but when you cannot find a file, there remains a lot of hard drive to search. Linux needs to know where to look first when searching for a particular file. By setting up the correct paths at the beginning, you tell Linux where to look initially and thus save the system time and effort by enabling it to avoid futile searches in remote, obscure directories.

Like other most operating systems, Linux sets up some standard default search paths. These paths are defined in a couple of areas, either for global users or for individual users. When setting up global paths or when making a directory path that all users can quickly reference, you add the path to /etc/profile. When you are editing an individual user's path, the standard file to change under Red Hat is .bash_profile or the file specific to the default shell.

The standard practice for most administrators when installing a program such as Netscape on the system is to place the file somewhere accessible to all users. You will want to provide all users with fast and easy access. You can do so by placing the default install directory within their path.

For a program such as Netscape, you would add /opt/netscape to the path or create a link from the executable to the /usr/local/bin directory. Either way, users on the system can now find the Netscape executable. Now when the system searches for a particular file, it will look in this directory as well for any executables. Any user on the system could quickly find and execute the program Netscape, which would be located in this directory as well.

Here is an example /etc/profile file with additional entries to the default path, allowing all users to access both the Netscape and Star Office directories:

```
PATH="$PATH:/usr/X11R6/bin:/opt/netscape:/usr/local/Office51/bin"
export PATH PS1 HOSTNAME HISTSIZE HISTFILESIZE USER LOGNAME MAIL
INPUTRC
```

Here I have added the absolute paths to the directories containing the Netscape and Star Office executables, or /opt/netscape and /usr/local/Office51/bin. I also need to verify that I am exporting the variable names, such as PATH and PS1. After I add the new path, the shell needs to reread /etc/profile and update its path. You accomplish this by entering the following command:

```
source /etc/profile
```

The system then reads through the /etc/profile file once more and adds the additional directories to its default list of files to which it has immediate access.

## Locating Additional Files

The which command helps to locate files within the available paths. However, this command is only good for locating files found in exported paths. If the directory is not in your path, the system will be unable to find the file in question. Once your shell has reread the contents of /etc/profile, you should be able to see the newly exported files. Had I executed a which command on Netscape before adding it to /etc/profile, it would not have been able to inform me that the executable is located in /opt/netscape/netscape.

To see all the directories currently read by bash and that are in the current path, enter **echo $PATH**. Do not forget the dollar sign before PATH or forget to type the command in all capital letters. PATH is a variable and as such has several unique features. If you type it without the dollar sign, then the word PATH will be printed to the screen.

## Temporarily Changing Your $PATH

To add more directories to your path, at least temporarily, you would issue the following command:

```
export PATH="$PATH:/usr/local/bin:/sbin"
```

For the duration of the session that you are logged in, you will be able to see not only the executable files found in your previously defined $PATH, but also the binaries located in /usr/local/bin and /sbin. If you are trying to keep the system secure and limit access to certain files, this feature can be useful for those instances where typing the entire pathname is long and tedious. By combining the export feature with bash's history file, you can potentially cut the amount of required typing in half.

If you want to make these paths a permanent feature for your own use and not allow others access to the same directories, customizing the ./bash_profile file will produce the same results, except only on a user-specific basis.

This local file sets the paths only for needed files, however. To start up files automatically upon login or to execute them without manually calling them, you would need to add their paths, or just their binary name if their path is already listed, to the .bashrc file. It is here that files start up automatically. It can also be added to $HOME/.profile or $HOME/.bash_profile as required by each user's default shell.

## Miscellaneous Items to Place in Shell Startups

When logging in to a Linux box, it is nice to have something light-hearted to start off the session. A program such as /usr/games/fortune helps by printing out a thought or quote to the shell. This occurs only when the user first logs in to either a terminal session or starts a new bash session. To run the program again, you would need to issue a command for the absolute filename. You could enter the following at the end of a .bashrc file:

```
/usr/games/fortune
```

You can just as easily enter any one of a number of other commands for other programs, including games or even additional Telnet sessions. These all execute upon the initial login.

## Setting Supplementary Environmental Variables

In addition to $PATH, there are other variables that the user can set up in any of the possible shells. These variables allow the user to customize the environment in which he or she operates. These are a series of reserved words written in a high-level language. The user can modify defaults and set standards for any one of the possible shells available. Some come preset by the operating system while others are not predetermined but can be altered with input from the user. Most shells understand these environmental variables. They are not limited to only the bash shell.

In addition to the environment variables, which set standards for global changes and modifications to the system, there are also local variables that, though they change the settings for one session, do not propagate through the system and thus do not alter the settings for another terminal session. (The term *terminal session* refers to the terminal window or console that is brought up for each login.)

Technically, a user can log in to the system myriad times and make changes or export variables for each particular session that do not affect the other sessions. This is true multitasking. To Linux, each login is unique and individualized no matter how many times the same user logs in to the system. Figure 4.1 illustrates this feature.

As indicated by the date shown in the lower screen of Figure 4.1, I changed the variable for $HOME from my own $HOME directory, which is set by default to /usr/local, which is not a true value. After making the change, I also entered an **echo $HOME** command that showed the true value. Had this been a global change, the top screen would show the alteration, but because these are exported variables and can be set or reset, all changes remain until logout. As mentioned earlier, the user can edit the variable for $PATH to suit the session. Upon logout, the variables revert to their original state.

Table 4.4 briefly describes some of the shell environmental variables, explaining which are set by the user and which are set by the shell as it operates under Linux. The user can set these variables under each shell to suit.

You can alter most of these settings to your specifications. As you gain more familiarity with the system, you will find that understanding these variables can work for you rather than against you. Editing them to taste will help improve security and make the system operate in your favor and not work against you.

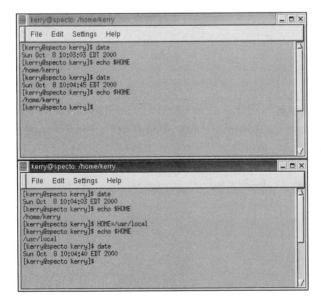

**FIGURE 4.1**

*Environment variables are session-dependent. Though the variable for $HOME is changed in one session, it remains constant for the same user in another terminal window. Changing a variable in one terminal does not affect another terminal's variables.*

**Table 4.4  Configurable Environmental Variables**

| Name | Source of setting | Description |
| --- | --- | --- |
| CDPATH | User | Directory search path |
| COLUMNS | Shell | Width of the window |
| EDITOR | User | Default editor |
| HOME | Login | Default CD location |
| LOGNAME | Login | Login name for the user |
| LPDEST | User | Printer destination |
| OLDPWD | Shell | Previous directory |
| PATH | Login | Search path for binaries |
| PPID | Shell | ID of the parent process |
| PS1 | Shell | Primary shell prompt |
| PS2 | Shell | Secondary shell prompt |
| PWD | Shell | Current location |
| RANDOM | Shell | Random number |
| SECONDS | Shell | Seconds since login |
| SHELL | Login | Path to the shell |
| TERM | User | Terminal type |

# Conclusion

Now that you understand how the shell operates under Linux, you are ready to exercise more control over the command line. The root user is the most powerful user under Linux and has absolute control over every file, program, or directory on the system. The next chapter will explain many of the features of root and what it can and cannot do as well as caution you of the dangers inherent with such power.

# Chapter 5

## The Powers of Root

Unlike other operating systems—where nearly every user has the ability to change system configuration files, modify settings, and shut down the computer—Linux grants permissions to conduct these actions to only one user, root. Only root can make changes to the system that affect how Linux operates. Root oversees all the other users and has the power to modify their settings as well.

This chapter will cover the following topics:

- The role that the root user plays in Linux
- Tips for safeguarding your root password
- File ownerships
- Passwords
- Pseudo-root functions

# The Powers Associated with Root

Many Linux functions can be accomplished only by root or superuser. A superuser maintains total control over accounts and files so that a system is not at risk from multiple users having the same access to a root account. There are also files that should be maintained by only one individual or one account. These are normally restricted to only the root user. To understand why the root account is so important, it is first necessary to look at regular accounts and what they are able to do.

Each user is given his or her own private account with the permission to control the files located within the user's home account and those files specifically owned by the user. Normally, only that user will own the files located in the user's home directory. Unless the administrator or root user changes permissions to be otherwise, regular users will not have the ability to modify or create or delete files elsewhere in the system. Similarly, other users usually cannot change or alter files within personal accounts. Only if they are granted limited permissions or share in ownership can they make editing changes. Files needed by the system are controlled by or reserved for the operating system itself. Generally, unique users own those files, which are not normally in contact with regular accounts. Files such as those found in /usr/bin and /sbin are owned by the root or superuser, which has control over all system files.

Root also controls the creation of normal user accounts. The command /usr/sbin/useradd not only creates a new user on the local system, but creates a home directory, grants a shell, and assigns a UID and GID number to that new user. Other functions, such as assigning new passwords, can also be done only by root. Though each user can change his or her own password after he or she successfully logs on to the system, only root has the power to change separate user passwords globally.

The root account has a unique feature that distinguishes it from other accounts. This is the root password. If lost, forgotten, or shared, its importance is diminished or completely forfeited. The system can continue to function but only for a limited time. As files require either resetting or editing, loss of superuser privileges will prevent needed changes. The system will continue but will start to stagnate. No one will be able to edit important files or to kill and restart processes. Regular users may still be able to shut down the system via the kdm or gdm login window or if they are granted in the correct permissions in the /etc/shutdown.allow file, but they will still be unable to make important editing changes. If something breaks, it will remain broken.

---

**TIP**

If the root password is lost or forgotten, you can only reset it; you cannot recover the original password. The standard practice of encrypting user passwords prevents even root from figuring out what the original text string may have been. In addition, with the correct permissions in place on both the /etc/passwd and /etc/shadow files, only root can view those files' contents.

To reset any lost password, you must first have physical access to the Linux machine. While it is booting up, type, at the LILO: prompt, **linux single**. This command brings up the operating system in single-user mode. Once the operating system is loaded, depending upon your Linux distribution, you will have a root prompt. Booting into single-user mode with a Red Hat distribution displays a root prompt. Once you have booted into single-user mode, you can change the password for root by entering the standard **passwd** command. You do not need to specify a user since you are already at a root prompt. Once the system boots again normally, you should have root access.

---

**NOTE**

Throughout this chapter, the terms *root* and *superuser* will be used interchangeably. *Root* is normally the term assigned to the particular user with a home directory of /home/root. When the `su` or `su` - command without any arguments is issued, short for *switch user*, the user changes to root. Due to the common use of `su` to become root, it has become a misnomer for *superuser*. Both terms, *root* and *superuser*, are nearly identical except for default paths and environment settings.

## Safeguarding the Root Password

Properly protecting root's password guarantees that not only will your system remain safe but so will the personal user accounts. Here are some rules to follow when given root authority and when administering any file system, whether it is on a single-user system or a large multiuser network:

◆ Do not write the root password down anywhere. It is too easy to find and can easily be copied. Once you lose root authority, someone else can take over and change or delete files. Without root authority, you can easily be locked out of your own system. Unless you have physical access, your only choice may be to have someone else reformat and start over. Be sure to have a clean backup from which to start over, if you find yourself in this situation.

◆ Think twice before becoming superuser. Once you do something as superuser, it is difficult to undo the changes. It is hard (if not impossible) to retract any commands given as root.

◆ Check the syntax of every command you give as root. It is easy to think you are in one directory and issue a simple statement wiping out the directory's entire contents. You might even delete an entire /etc or /usr/bin directory, in which case you can no longer run Linux. In cases such as these, either hope for a recent backup or plan on reinstalling.

◆ Plan on doing most of your work either as yourself or while logged in under a regular account. It is better to try to delete a file as yourself and realize you do not have the authority than to purge a needed file while as root, only to realize later that you should not have touched the file you deleted. A simple whoami command will, in most cases, let you know the guise under which you are working.

- At the command line, make sure you remind yourself of who you currently are. Verify that the bash or shell prompt changes to a pound sign (#) when becoming root and that when you relinquish control your prompt returns to a dollar sign ($). If you do alter the .bashrc or .login file, make sure you do so wisely and that the shell will still indicate the status change. Default settings are usually the best. You should reserve the pound sign for root.

- Too much power can lead to abuse or neglect. Become root only when necessary. So often it appears much simpler to issue all commands as root since they accomplish their tasks cleanly and efficiently. But if you fail to remember the extent of root's power, you can easily make a mistake that can damage the system. I know of cases in which users have forgotten that they were operating as root and then altered the ownership of entire directories. When that happens, it is sometimes necessary to reconfigure each file carefully by hand. The less you do as root, the less damage you can do to the system.

- Be sure to create backup copies of any key files you might edit or be unable to restore if you corrupt their contents.

**CAUTION**

When you are given root access, you must guard this power carefully. Do not disclose your password to anyone unless you feel that person can be trusted. If that person either changes employment or loses your trust, you should change the root password immediately.

# Abusing Root Privileges

If you need to edit another user's personal account as root, such as changing the user's password or clearing out files, be mindful that you can just as easily delete the user's files as well as your own. You should make a point of changing individual accounts only with the owner's knowledge and permission. It is important that users trust that you will not probe around in their files and peer at personal documents or alter their contents. If they don't trust you, they will leave, seeking out a better system administrator whom they can trust. Exercise self-control.

Sometimes it is necessary to be authoritarian in your dealings with users. For example, users can either knowingly or unknowingly bring files onto the system that can sully either the reputation of the company or organization to which the system belongs or damage the files that others need and use. Such files include, specifically, pornography, illegal audio recordings (such as MP3s), password-cracking programs, virus-contaminated files, and other malicious files. If you suspect that files such as these are residing on your system, then it is your duty as a system administrator to search out and remove those files when necessary. The locate and find commands are particularly useful if you are doing a routine sweep of the system.

Both commands are fairly simple and straightforward. The find command is rather hard drive intensive as well as incurring a larger share of CPU cycles, but can be used to detect nearly any file. Whereas the locate command relies upon a self-generated database of files that either the user must initialize or the system must perform automatically on a regular basis. Red Hat automatically updates this database as a weekly or nightly cron job. The locate command operates quicker and is less hard drive and CPU-intensive, but if files are changed since the last database rotation, the command will not find the file in question.

The following is a fairly typical example of the use of the find command:

```
find /usr/local -name <filename*> -print
```

First, execute the find command, then state the directory you wish to search. In this case it is the /usr/local/ directory and all its subdirectories. If you wished to search the entire system, a simple forward slash, /, would suffice. Next, use one of the many available options, in this case, the name option to find the name of the file in question. Now state the filename you are seeking. Wildcard options such as an asterisk will search for any file beginning with that sequence of letters. You can also apply the same wildcard options to the word's prefix. If an asterisk is used in both the prefix and suffix position, you may locate any file containing that range of characters somewhere within its name. Last, you specify the print option to output the results to your console.

To execute the locate command, simply type the following:

```
locate <filename>
```

The locate command queries the locate database, or the locatedb file, for the requested term and prints out the results. (Under certain distributions, the locate command is also known as slocate for *secure locate*.) To update the database with the latest file, issue the command **locate -u** to generate a default database in the root directory, if this has not already been done by the default installation. This command includes all files on the system including NFS mounts, mounted CDs and the like within the database. If you absolutely must create a database immediately after installing Red Hat, this is the command to use, otherwise the automated cron job will create the database for you within a short period of time and will do a much better job by skipping unnecessary directories. This database is highly configurable and desired directories can later be dismissed or used exclusively.

While doing a verbose backup of the system, I happened to notice some files in a user's directory whose extension identified them as graphic images. The names associated with those files were also questionable. Further investigation revealed that they were in fact files that went against the acceptable use policy as outlined by the company. For the company's protection, the user was contacted and the files removed.

You might think of the redistribution and proliferation of files such as graphic images or illegally copied MP3s as innocent fun, but the legal ramifications are actually quite great. For any system over which you have direct authority to determine what is hosted, or which you personally administer, you also bear the responsibility over all files that appear on your system. If you do encounter questionable files, consult that particular user's .bash_history file or a comparable shell history file. You can usually determine whether any questionable commands have been executed. Such files, however, are usually the first things that malicious users will attempt to delete to cover their tracks.

Often, such attempts to abuse the system to gain root access are nothing more than weak attempts by so-called "script-kiddies," or users running simple hacks. Possessing no real knowledge of the system itself, script-kiddies run known scripts or perform security exploits to gain root access or access to another user's account. If successful, they will usually try to hide any traces of their hack or will attempt to set up certain unattended processes. Unmonitored processes are usually benign and only consume CPU usage, but if allowed to spread they can quickly become malignant cancers that can consume files and other processes.

Though security concerns will be covered in a later chapter, it is never too early to start honing your skills in Linux defense. If you think your box may have been compromised, start looking for unauthorized connections from other machines or networks. The netstat command is a useful tool for displaying the status of all

TCP/IP network services. By itself it lists all connected sockets. Using the -a option lists just those sockets that are open or listening and not just those with connections. The normal display will show what protocol is being used, the bytes in the send and receive queue, the addresses of remote hosts, and the socket state.

You can expand the regular information to include the user currently using the socket by adding the -e option. If you are interested in viewing the routing tables, use the -r option. The -i flag will list the network interfaces and statistics on each interface. The information it displays is similar to the output of the ifconfig command. Finally, rather than resolving DNS for each connected machine, you can simply view its IP address by using the -n option.

If you do find a machine that is connected or traffic either entering or leaving your box, take note of the protocol, the port, and the utility being run. Check your Linux release against the Red Hat security vulnerabilities page and procure the latest updates immediately. If you prefer doing some proactive investigation for your Red Hat release, check the BugTraq records page at http://www.securityfocus.com/. You can locate any exploits common to your system and take the needed steps to shore up the holes. For more information on securing your Linux machine or checking for security holes, see Chapter 19.

### CAUTION

If you encounter any suspicious activity on your system such as unattended processes, it is best to move quickly to eliminate that the responsible user from the system. Allowing users to run processes without restraint is an open invitation for system abuse.

Not only do you need to check yourself against the system and ensure that you do not make any errors or cause security breaches by leaving unattended ports open, but you also need to monitor the safety of all users from the attack from other users. This can quickly become an overwhelming duty if you do not set the proper controls in place. For a more detailed explanation on system security, see Chapter 19.

How an administrator governs a Linux box is his or her own call. There is no fixed set of guidelines. Some might think it fine to let all users have a copy of the root password and run any processes at their own discretion. Others might rule with a fascist air and not let any file be uploaded without proper authorization. Each administrator must do what works best from him or her as well as what is best for the system. If the purpose of the system is simply to provide web content or run a simple program, then there should be no problem. If, however, sensitive information or mission-critical data are stored on the system, then the administrator must do whatever is necessary to protect those files.

## Establishing Acceptable Use Policies

Make sure that all users are aware of the rules laid out by the administrator before granting them an account. Ignorance of what is acceptable or unacceptable should not be an excuse. Before allowing any user onto the system, he or she should read and sign an Acceptable Use policy. This document should state what is allowable on the machine and the things for which the user will be held accountable. Administrators usually abdicate responsibility for any power outages, system maintenance issues, file corruption errors, natural disasters, or any and all acts of God over which they have no control. The user should also understand that the administrator cannot be held liable for any issue over which he or she does not have power.

Administrators should also it clear that they reserve the right to manage all files and to lock any account or delete any file they feel might harm either the system or other accounts. Basically, an Acceptable Use document is a legal contract protecting those who run the system from the users while ensuring that users do not also harm each other. Not all systems need to be so protective. Administrators, however, should know where their responsibilities lie and where those of other users end. To quote a common saying among system administrators, "That which is not expressly permitted is prohibited."

# File Ownerships

Each file under Linux has certain distinct permissions. Linux assigns ownership for every existing file to either root, a regular user, or a system-specific user. Only these users have control over files belonging to them and to which the permissions have been properly set. Users may share files or make their contents readable, writeable, and executable to others by using the chmod command, but by default files created or owned by a regular will only be under that particular user's authority. Root is the only user who has jurisdiction over every file on the system, so you must be careful when dealing with the root password. This section will look at how Linux portions ownership of each file and how the system then recognizes these files.

## Setting Identification Numbers

Each file has both a user and group owner. Each owner can either set the permissions on that file or directory so that all can see, modify, or execute whatever they want, or set permissions so restrictive that only a file's owner can read the file. An owner accomplishes modifications to the permission settings by using both the chmod and the chgrp commands. For additional information about using the chmod command to change read, write, and execute capability, see Chapter 3.

Each owner, whether he or she is the user or a member of the group, is assigned a specific number. Linux does not so much track ownership by the user or group name as by the *user identification number (UID)* and the *group identification number (GID)*. These are system-assigned numbers that Linux associates with a user name and a group name, respectively. These numbers are specific to each new user and group created. The Red Hat Linux distribution begins all UID and GID numbering at 500. This purpose of this numbering scheme is to help Linux manage who has what control over which file.

To demonstrate this idea, I created a new user on the system. The username is joe. joe has been assigned the UID of 504 and a GID of 505. That means that all files that joe creates will automatically receive this same UID. However, when I execute an ls -l command on the files created by joe, they will show up as belonging to joe in both the user and group fields. However, if I delete that same user and then look at the files that he created, they will no longer have his name but rather the UID and GID number as their owner. Figure 5.1 shows the files created by joe in the /tmp directory. The /tmp directory is unique in that it allows to create and store files in it temporarily. The files are owned by joe, both as user and group. Once I delete the user joe, the files revert back to their UID and GID assigned them, because joe no longer exists in the /etc/passwd file. If you wish to simply view the UID for each user rather than the unique username, use the command ls -nl to display the UID and GID for each file.

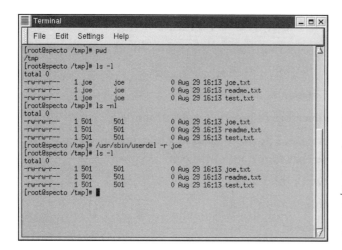

**FIGURE 5.1**

*A sample xterm window showing files created by a unique user. Note that the files return ownership to the unique UID and GID when the user is deleted from the system.*

For most Linux distributions, Red Hat included, the UIDs and GIDs for new users start at 500. This can vary for other Linux flavors and is strictly a convention of each Linux distribution. Users who run certain programs or processes are given UID and GID numbers below or above 500 depending upon the distribution. Because of root's importance, it takes a UID of zero. Thus, any file that shares this UID is both owned and controlled by root and has root permissions.

If you suspect that your Linux machine has been compromised, you should look for new user files in /etc/passwd that also share the UID of zero. If a cracker does succeed in creating a new user and setting that UID, he or she has just succeeded in gaining root access as well.

---

## NOTE

There are still some common misconceptions today regarding the use of the terms hacker and cracker. A hacker is a clever programmer who solves computer-related problems with innovative code. Whereas a cracker is someone who breaks into others' computers for profit, to further a malicious purpose, for an altruistic purpose or cause, or to simply challenge one's skills. In other words, a hacker wears a white hat, while a cracker is viewed as a black hat. Eric S. Raymond, compiler of "The New Hacker's Dictionary" clarifies these terms in greater detail in his online essay, located at http://www.tuxedo.org/~esr/jargon/

## Understanding the Powers of Root

Root can perform any of a multitude of functions on a Linux box. Here are just a few of the functions that only root can do:

- Adjust system resources and quotas
- Change the ownership of any file or directory
- Create directories and device files in any location on the machine, including those that root does not specifically own
- Configure network interfaces
- Manage all configuration files
- Mount and unmount file systems
- Set the system clock
- Shut down the system cleanly

The last function mentioned is one of the most crucial. Anyone with physical access to your machine can bring the system down by unplugging the power. However, root can do this from anywhere in the world if remote access is possible. Only root can change the machine's init state and shut down the system. If the machine is physically accessible and if it starts in run level 5, any user can power down the box thanks to certain SUID programs such as kdm and gdm. Again, these are only allowable if the regular user has physical access to both the console and the machine itself and is given a GUI startup interface.

If it does happen that the machine is shut down by someone other than yourself or the administrator, you will have to start it back up again by either flipping the power switch or performing a hard power-cycle and plugging back in the power supply. You may not want to, however, depending upon how badly your machine has been compromised. It is best to avoid the situation altogether and make your box as secure as possible.

## Assuming Other Identities as Root

An example of the superuser power is typified in the program /bin/login. This program prompts you for a password and subsequently allows all users to log in to Linux. The login program initially begins life as root. After verifying that the username and password entered by a new user are correct, the login program changes its UID and GID to those of the user and launches a shell for that individual. Only a root process can change its own UID and GID. A regular user or any other user on the system that has a UID or GID greater than 500 cannot do the same. Such is the power of root.

---

**TIP**

Once the /bin/login process has changed its UID to that of a regular user, the process is entirely one-sided. In other words, a regular user cannot go back to being root.

---

One of the unique advantages of being root is that you can easily become another user when logged in with superuser privileges. Normally, you cannot become another user without first knowing his or her password. However, root can become user $X$ or user $Y$ without needing to know that user's password simply due to the privileges granted to the root account.

There are three separate ways to become root and/or another user. Normally, you assume root status by simply entering **su**. This will give you root authority in the same working directory, but *without* the same paths and environments normally granted to the root account. You retain the same environment variables as those of the original user.

You can also become root with *all* the necessary paths and permissions by entering **su -**. This command allows you access to the same accounts normally granted only to users who log in initially as root. Your working directory will also change to the root user's home directory. This is useful if you want to access any hidden files owned by root. It also provides easy access to files located in directories such as /sbin, which is part of root's environment by default, but not located in other accounts.

The last method of becoming another user while assuming the same permissions, paths, and default locations as that user is to enter **su - <username>**, replacing the username in brackets with the regular account's username. You can use this method either as root or as yourself. If you use the latter method, you must know that account's password. If you are executing this command as root, no password is necessary. While logged in as user $X$ or user $Y$, you are, for all practical purposes, *that* user and have rights only to files owned by that individual. It is just as easy to delete a regular user's file as it is to do so as root.

Administrators who use the su command as either themselves or when logged in as other users often are counseled to use the absolute path /bin/su rather than simply typing **su**. There is good reason for this advice. If using another user's own login or after having switched to the identity of a user other than yourself or root, any user could easily modify their own path and substitute the su executable with his or her own version. This new compromised su command could then accomplish whatever the user or cracker wanted. By entering **su** without the entire path, you would then execute the user's modified su executable. This could be set up to capture the string of characters that you entered as your password and email them to the user. That way he or she would get an updated version of the root password every time that you became superuser. Using the absolute path /bin/su helps avoid this problem.

## Changing Directory Ownerships

The rules that apply to files also apply to directories. They, too, have user and group ownerships. Correct permissions are especially crucial when you want to create directories or place files within a directory that you do not own. The implications of directory permissions are two-fold. You, as a regular user, are limited in where you can place your files; normally, you can place them only in your home directory. But, at the same time, Linux also prevents other users from peering into your directory and viewing your files. By default, permissions are usually set to allow other users to list your directories, though not to view their contents or modify your files. So Linux's directory ownership rules restrict the user somewhat, but can also give the user's directories greater security.

If you need to place files somewhere other than your home directory, you need to create a directory in its new location as root and then change ownership over to yourself—assuming, of course, that you are the administrator. If not, then the administrator will have to do this for you, but you will have to justify the need. If you have dire need for some location to run or compile programs and cannot locate the administrator to create a new directory, the /tmp directory is available for general users. As an administrator, it is advisable to check periodically on the contents of /tmp and delete files as needed. Red Hat normally clears out older files from the /tmp after a certain period of time via cron jobs. Check the /etc/cron.daily directory for the tmpwatch file, which specifies what files are to be removed.

One reason for which you might need to create a new directory is to designate a location for HTML files. Rather than forcing a user to create a public_html/

directory in his or her own home directory and using the ~<username>/ extension in the user's URL, you can create a directory for the user in the /home/httpd/html or /usr/local/apache directory, depending upon the location of your root Web pages. If you then name this new directory design/, you could use both the chmod and chgrp commands to change the directory's name to reflect the username of the regular user. You can even go one step further. If this user will not be using his or her home directory for mail or storage, but would only be uploading files to this HTML directory, you can use the /usr/sbin/usermod command to modify the location of the user's home directory, as follows:

```
/usr/sbin/usermod -d /home/httpd/html/design <username>
```

Now, whenever that user logs in to the system, the system will automatically take the user to the directory that he or she owns, and will not need to change locations to upload new files. This does make any files within this directory available for perusal by anyone stopping by the site. Best to include either a index.html or home.html file, depending upon what is specified as the Directory Index name. This will hide any dotfiles or other files the user does not wish to share. I usually make a sub-directory within that home directory to then store all HTML files and thus separate any prying eyes even further.

# Recognizing the Users Needed for System Maintenance

Linux has a host of non-existent users that perform system functions only. A quick perusal through both the /etc/passwd and /etc/group files shows the variety of users needed by the system. These users exist for security purposes and to run processes that regular users do not normally allow. These users themselves are unique in that they have no home directory nor do they serve any purpose except to run specific daemons or processes. The user bin, for example, has /bin as its home directory. This directory contains all system binaries that are required for routine maintenance and operational checks. Though owned by root, these binaries can be sent to the bin user to perform whatever function needs to be done. The same is true for the user daemon. For further discussion of daemons and how they can run background processes, see Chapter 2.

Most daemons have a low user ID (UID), sometimes one or two different UIDs, and often a value under 100. One of the processes owned by the user daemon is the at program. Because it will perform root-like commands, the at program needs to be fairly secure and tamper-proof. The user daemon fits that need. Because a daemon is not run by root, but has powers similar to root's, it can execute scripts or programs at the appropriate time. Though it has root-like powers, it is very limited in its scope and function. There are actually few files that it can modify or delete.

Nobody is an important nonuser. The default install of Red Hat Linux assigns nobody a UID of 99, whereas other UNIX systems give nobody a UID of −1 or −2. Solaris chose 60,001 as the default UID for nobody. This user is the catchall user for software that doesn't need or shouldn't have special permissions. For example, the Apache Web server uses nobody as the user to run all the *HTTPD processes*, or the Web daemon processes that serve HTML documents to Internet users. Nobody is also used by the NFS daemon for secure file servers on a network. Because the nobody user does not have any special permissions, even if someone were to gain access to this user, he or she cold do very little with it.

Another daemon that operates as the nobody user is fingerd. The purpose of this daemon is to locate and identify unique users on each separate Linux system. Again, due to its lack of permissions, fingerd has little appeal to crackers, but serves its purpose well.

# Password Files

For users not familiar with Linux, the idea of needing a password in order to log in to the system might seem a bit foreign. Though other systems now call for passwords, they can usually be circumvented. Linux, however, requires that each user set a unique password for him or herself, if only to secure the system. Passwords can be duplicated from user to user, but the password itself should contain a character string that is different from the username. With a bit of time and practice, using passwords soon becomes not only an accepted practice but also a very prudent method of securing your system. Though you may not have any classified or sensitive data on your system, you can take some comfort in the fact that not everyone can access your home directory or files readily due to the implementation of password checking. The topic of passwords may seem dull compared to other Linux concepts. However, with a little care and patience in creating secure passwords for your system, you can avoid headaches resulting from users cracking your system.

# Choosing Unique Passwords

Because Linux security is foremost in the minds of many administrators, the topic of passwords deserves its own section. The first choice you will have to make after installing Linux is that of a password for root. Choose wisely, making sure that your password is easy for you to remember, yet difficult enough that others will not guess it and so that any password-cracking programs will not break it. It is customary to pick something between six to eight characters long, including both letters and numbers. It is acceptable to choose a word or combination of words totaling more than eight characters, but the system will recognize only the first eight. It will disregard all the characters after the first eight.

Many recommendations are available as to the best method to choose a password. Try choosing a combination of words, then either separating them with a number or replacing the letters of the words with numbers. Use the number *1* (one) in place of the letter *l* or the letter *i,* use a *0* (zero) in place of the letter *o,* and substitute *3* for the letter *e.* Yet even this system is not foolproof. Most password-cracking programs take these substitutions into account and will still be quite successful if the word is fairly simple or based on a dictionary term.

Be liberal with your use of special characters such the at sign (@), the ampersand (&), and the other symbols that you find above the numbers on your keyboard. Place several of these characters throughout the password. Use fabricated words or acronyms in place of real words. For example, you could shorten the rhyme, "snakes and snails and puppy-dog tails," to $as&Pdt, which makes an excellent password. You will always remember how the saying goes. The hard part is remembering what to substitute for each initial character.

> **TIP**
>
> Using foreign words combined with special characters is also a fairly secure method for choosing a root password. I often use either German or Portuguese words along with additional characters for my own passwords. This method may not work for user accounts, unless the users are also fluent in the same languages.

Linux assists users in choosing responsible passwords. If the password chosen is too short, Red Hat Linux will respond, BAD PASSWORD: it's WAY too short. If the password contains too few different characters, Linux will give this reprimand: BAD PASSWORD: it does not contain enough DIFFERENT characters. If the password is too recognizable to the system as an average word, Linux will respond, BAD PASSWORD: it is based on a dictionary word. If root changes this password, the system will still accept the new password no matter what the user inputs, but it will have given the user fair warning. If a regular user, however, attempts to input a bad password or one that the system deems unacceptable, he or she will be unable to continue until an acceptable password is chosen.

## Expiring and Locking Passwords

Linux also offers a feature that expires a user's password after a certain date. This feature of the usermod command allows you to modify variables in the /etc/passwd file. If you want to disable a certain account's password on a specific date, using usermod with the -e option will expire that account on that specific day.

If I wanted to expire the password for the user karen on the October 31, 2000, and then issue her a new password, I would type the following command:

```
usermod -e 10/31/00 karen
```

### NOTE

To function, this feature must have shadow passwords enabled. Information regarding the expiration of a user's password is not normally stored in the /etc/passwd file, but in the /etc/shadow file instead. Shadow passwords are the system passwords that are encrypted elsewhere and which no one other than root has access to read. Because the /etc/passwd file must be readable by different system processes, such as bash for determining a user's home directory, the encrypted password text is also readable and thus decipherable. By placing the encrypted text in another file, i.e. /etc/shadow, and changing the permission to 400, only root can then see what the encrypted password text might be.

The usermode e- feature is useful for users who are prone to reset their passwords to something easy. Expiring the passwords at a given time or after a certain number of days forces users to change their password again.

Along with using the -e option, you can also lock or disable an account by using -L with the usermod command to lock an account, or use this option's counterpart, the -U option, to unlock the same account. The -L option places an exclamation point (!) in front of the encrypted text of the password. This disables the password entirely so that the user cannot log in.

Here is how you would lock and then unlock the account of the user joe:

```
usermod -L joe
usermod -U joe
```

Naturally, you can use the usermod command only when acting as root. Because this command actually modifies the /etc/passwd file, which controls all user settings (or modifies the /etc/shadow file, depending on which function is enabled), strict limits are in place to prevent anyone other than root from changing user settings. Normal users do not have the proper permissions to modify their own accounts. The only exception to this rule is the ability to change their password

## Encrypting Passwords

I often receive calls from users requesting that I reset or change their passwords. Either they had forgotten the existing password or they had entered a password into their modem connection box and someone else had changed the asterisks so that their connection no longer worked. Many had difficulty believing that their passwords were encrypted. The best anyone can do in such a case is reset the password either to something similar or to something entirely different if it had been shared or compromised.

The fact that Linux encrypts all the passwords is an extremely good thing. It used to be that the encrypted text was kept in the /etc/passwd file along with other user information. This was not good. The permissions on /etc/passwd are set at 644 and, as such, the entire file can be read with any text editor such as vi, or the cat command can be used against it and the file contents piped over into a separate file, as in cat /etc/passwd > passwords.txt. If a password-cracking program is run against that new file, before long the usernames along with their respective passwords are simple text once again. Realizing that this was not a good thing, the Linux developers took their cue from other more mature UNIX systems such as Solaris and created an /etc/shadow file. The permissions here are set at 400, meaning that only root (as the owner of the file) could read the contents. The /etc/shadow file stores all encrypted passwords. This affords the Linux system a double layer of security. Along with more restrictive file permissions, Red Hat provides MD5 hashing of the passwords within the /etc/passwd file, which adds another level of security, after which it is encrypted with libc's crypt() function. Once a password has been hashed with MD5, you can no longer convert it back to a simple text file. This helps to prevent spying eyes from gaining easier access to the original file, but does not eliminate the possibility that the password could still be guessed using brute force cracking methods.

> **NOTE**
>
> Shadow passwords originally began on such UNIX-based systems as Solaris, but they have since been adopted by nearly all Linux distributions, including Red Hat. On the latest Red Hat release you have the option to install shadow passwords and enable MD5 hashing. These are selected by default and it is a wise decision to allow them to remain so.

Unique system users such as nobody and bin do not normally allow a password to be affixed to them. To ensure that these types of files are not misused, it is a good idea to verify that no password is kept in the field that normally stores the encrypted passwords. An asterisk, or star, should appear instead of the password. This ensures that no one can physically log in under that assumed username. The same can be done on a regular file. By replacing the gibberish of encrypted text with an asterisk, you ensure that the user is no longer validated to log on with a password.

Listing 5.1 shows sample output from an /etc/shadow file. Notice the difference between the users with UIDs under 500 and the five valid users—four normal users and root.

**Listing 5.1  A Selection Taken from a Sample /etc/shadow File**

```
root:$1$xYQciqzI$UrHm3xc3IRpMgJWy4RL.E0:10873:0:99999:7:-1:-1:134538460
bin:*:10819:0:99999:7:::
daemon:*:10819:0:99999:7:::
adm:*:10819:0:99999:7:::
lp:*:10819:0:99999:7:::
sync:*:10819:0:99999:7:::
shutdown:*:10819:0:99999:7:::
halt:*:10819:0:99999:7:::
mail:*:10819:0:99999:7:::
news:*:10819:0:99999:7:::
uucp:*:10819:0:99999:7:::
```

```
operator:*:10819:0:99999:7:::
games:*:10819:0:99999:7:::
gopher:*:10819:0:99999:7:::
ftp:*:10819:0:99999:7:::
nobody:*:10819:0:99999:7:::
xfs:!!:10819:0:99999:7:::
gdm:!!:10819:0:99999:7:::
kerry:$1$rpufM.76$3mGeSA8MW7/.NIVWGZH4q.:10873:0:99999:7:-1:-1:134538460
karen:$1$0dhioOd/$q.XxvVqwv9rjWWGygdL/N1:10821:0:99999:7::11261:134537332
calvin:$1$XAfJDUQ3$XI/QwwIu67ywvm36jtTTF/:10873:0:99999:7:-1:-1:134538436
andrew:$1$H3bNmuQZ$bR22NEMi6sFeIIhkd7d.0/:10873:0:99999:7:-1:-1:134538436
```

The regular logins have a string of nonsensical characters and numbers, whereas the system users possess an asterisk in their password field.

# Pseudoroot Management via sudo

Like all great superpowers, root also has its Achilles' heel. Root's drawbacks lie in its overwhelming power. When you become superuser, there are technically no logs kept other than those for the bash_history or the respective shell history as implemented by that root user. This means that once any actions are committed, they can just as easily be erased from the any shell history files. Since root is also a GID (group ID), anyone who compromises the group file can still gain access to root owned files. Because its power is so overwhelming, root can wipe out all the users and gain control of the box for whoever becomes root. As is often stated in Linux newsgroups, "God, root, what's the difference?" On a Linux machine, this is very much the case. The only way to combat someone gaining root access or corrupting your files is to reformat and start over or to restore from a clean backup. These also are not great solutions.

The ability to perform maintenance on Linux is crucial. One person cannot do everything that needs to be done, especially if the system has a large contingent of users. But tasks such as adding new users, performing backups, and changing passwords all require root access. If you do grant root access to another user for performing maintenance tasks, make certain you trust that person implicitly and that he or she will not do anything prejudicial to your system. Sharing the responsibility of root carries with it the burden of taking blame should anything be corrupted due to negligence or carelessness.

In response to the problem of sharing root-owned tasks, the UNIX community developed sudo. By using the program sudo (or *superuser*), a system administrator can enable certain users (or groups of users) to run some (or all) commands as root while also logging all commands and arguments. This feature takes care of the logging issue as posed by the regular superuser. The sudo program operates on a per-command basis and is not a replacement for the shell. In other words, only certain root-owned commands can be delegated to other users. The root password need not be shared with multiple users. Nor when executing sudo commands does the user gain a root-owned shell or have any more root-like power, except for that which has been allotted him or her.

The sudo program operates by checking a configuration file called /etc/sudoers. A list of users and commands defines who can perform what command with root permissions. This file is created by root and can be edited only by root. The users listed can carry out only those functions to which this file gives them access.

## Configuring the sudo Program

You can find the sudo program in several locations on the Internet. The default location is http://www.courtesan.com/sudo/, yet a simple Internet query will turn up several mirror sites. After downloading and installing sudo properly on the system, you need to configure the /etc/sudoers file and determine who will have permission to perform what action. You can edit this file by hand, but it is recommended that you use the special binary, visudo, that comes installed with the package. The visudo command brings up a text editor; vi is the default editor, hence the binary program's name. This text editor enables you to modify the settings while constructing a database file in a format understood by sudo.

Listing 5.2 shows a potential /etc/sudoers file.

### Listing 5.2  An Example /etc/sudoers File

```
# Host alias specification
Host_Alias              LAN=quasi,sequitur,nihilo
Host_Alias              WAN=k2,lonepeak,olympus,granite,nebo

# User alias specification
User_Alias              IT=kerry,brad,john,dan
```

```
User_Alias                 SALES=bill,greg,dave
User_Alias                 BOSS=mark
User_Alias                 OFFICE=rox,andrea

# Command alias specification
Cmnd_Alias                 DUMP=/usr/sbin/tcpdump,/sbin/rdump
Cmnd_Alias                 BACKUP=/usr/sbin/ufsbackup
Cmnd_Alias                 SHELLS=/bin/sh,/bin/csh,/bin/tcsh,/bin/ksh
Cmnd_Alias                 SU=/bin/su
Cmnd_Alias                 MISC=/bin/rm,/bin/cat
Cmnd_Alias                 SHUTDOWN=/usr/bin/shutdown
Cmnd_Alias                 USERS=/usr/scripts/adu,usr/scripts/dlu

# User specification
IT              ALL=ALL
kerry           WAN=ALL,LAN=quasi,sequitur
brad            WAN=ALL,LAN=nihilo
john            WAN=SHUTDOWN,/usr/scripts/adu
rox             quasi=/usr/bin/shutdown -[hr] now,MISC
andrea          lonepeak=USERS
mark            WAN=SHELLS
dave            nebo=BACKUP,granite=DUMP
greg            LAN=SHELLS

# End of file
```

# Clarifying sudo Options

This section describes the several categories of options configured in Listing 5.2.

## Host Alias Specifications

There are only two categories here, LAN and WAN. LAN defines the Linux boxes currently located within your internal network. They are running Red Hat and Solaris respectively. WAN specifies the servers that handle all accounts and perform different functions such as DNS, mail, news, Web, and virtual Web accounts. They are all running Red Hat.

## User Alias Specifications

There are four user aliases: IT, SALES, OFFICE, and BOSS. IT includes all technical staff, SALES consists of the sales staff who need access to limited items, OFFICE handles all the billing requirements and needs only to add and delete users, and BOSS, or the user mark, should only be using different shells. Even though BOSS has only one entry, other entries are foreseeable. For this reason, you temporarily give BOSS only one entry, but optimize the user mark in the "User specification" category.

## Command Alias Specifications

Command aliases are lists of commands with or without associated command-line arguments. The entries in Listing 5.2 should be self-explanatory.

## User Specifications

The users listed in Listing 5.2 are as follows:

| User | Description |
| --- | --- |
| IT | All staff included under the IT User Aliases specification may run any of the commands as defined by the Host Aliases specifications. |
| kerry | This user may run all commands on the WAN, but may run commands on only two or three of the machines listed in the LAN category. |
| brad | Likewise, the user brad may run all commands on machines listed in the WAN portion of Host specifications, but may only run commands on nihilo, one of the machines in the LAN category. |
| john | On all the machines in the WAN category, the user john may run the shutdown command and may only run the adu script. The adu script is a simple script that adds users to Solaris machines, while the dlu script deletes users. |
| rox | The user rox may run only the shutdown command on one machine, quasi, and also the two additional commands listed under the MISC section. |
| Andrea | This user may only run system maintenance commands as defined by the USERS category and only on one machine, lonepeak. |
| mark | I want to limit this user's access to the system as much as possible. However, because he is management, he does require some access to important files. He may run only those commands listed under the SHELLS category and only on WAN machines. |

| User | Description |
| --- | --- |
| dave | This user handles all the tape backups and may only run the BACKUP commands on the machine nebo and the DUMP commands on the machine granite. |
| greg | He can only run the SHELLS commands on machines situated on the LAN. |

## Understanding sudo's Advantages over Root Access

Using the sudo program offers distinct advantages over simply giving out root access. As you can see from the preceding example, each user's needs are tailored to their specifications and classifications. Users can be added to categories and removed when they leave. There is room for growth and leniency for making modifications to the file. Removing a person's privileges is simply a matter of commenting out a line.

The sudo program also provides other features, such as the timeout option, which will prompt a user for a password again if he or she allows a certain time to elapse with no input. Normally, you can issue any and all sudo commands without having to type a password after logging in, but if you allow a certain length of time to lapse without typing in any more commands, the password check feature will reassert itself. This prevents unauthorized users from logging in to unattended terminals.

You can also track user activity by logging commands to syslog. This lets the administrator see exactly what was done when a user has made a mistake. This option not only tells the administrator which users are to blame, but can exonerate users as well. In addition, if users issue a sudo command that they are not authorized to invoke, a warning message appears and sudo sends an email message alerting the administrator of an illegal attempt to use a nonvalid sudo command.

The advantages that using sudo has over sharing root are as follows:

♦ A single file controls all access to systems on and off the network.

♦ The timeout option can decrease the chances of a user leaving root unattended.

♦ The program maintains a list all users and their privileges, tracking who can do what.

- A variety of users can perform maintenance tasks without sharing one password.

- The administrator can grant or revoke privileges without constantly changing the root password.

- Only one or two users need to share the root password.

- Using the sudo program is faster than logging in and out as root.

- System logging increases accountability for each user's actions.

Just as you must be certain that a user doesn't abuse the privileges that root allows, you must also take care that users do not abuse sudo. Given the permissions granted, sudo can be just as harmful if used unwisely. The program can, however, relieve the administrator of some of the responsibility for care and maintenance of the system. This can be a good thing depending upon the administrator's workload. If your duties are anything like mine, anything that makes it possible to have other users shoulder some of your burdens safely is welcome.

The sudo program has weaknesses that administrators must be aware of. If you allow sudo to run any program that enables a user to generate a shell, that user can gain root access via the shell. Many consider this a large security hole. Be aware of the programs that you allow your regular users to run via sudo. Simply installing sudo does not give the administrator license to abdicate responsibility or control of the system.

# Conclusion

Understanding the importance of root is vital to administering any Linux system properly. The next chapter will look at managing regular users under Linux. It will explain how you can add new users to the system, either via the command line or by using any of the many GUI tools available. It will also explain how to remove defunct users from the system and to customize variables for individual users.

# PART II

## Administering the System

# Chapter 6

## Managing Users

**B**ecause Linux is a true multitasking environment, more than one user can be logged in to the system at one time. Over time, Linux can quickly become congested with additional users. Properly managing each user's account and creating distinct variables for each person logging in to your system will greatly assist in administering the growth of your user base.

This chapter will cover the following items:

- ◆ Adding new users to the system
- ◆ Using the command line for editing user variables
- ◆ Removing users from the system
- ◆ Using GUI configuration tools for editing user settings

## Managing New Users

Now that you have reviewed the basic powers of root and have an operational Linux box, you can begin either to add yourself as a user or add additional users to the system. During the Red Hat installation phase, you were given the option to add yourself as a regular user. You will already have a root login, and because incessantly changing files as root is a recipe for disaster, it is best to create a regular user account. If you have not already done so, use the /usr/sbin/adduser command to set up an account under your own name for periodic login use. Linux is designed as a multitasking server, meaning that more than one user can use the capabilities built in to its design. You can accomplish different tasks under different login aliases. Also, varying users can share files and use the installed programs to carry out any tasks they need to execute. Using a networked Linux machine provides for a range of file sharing and serving.

Linux provides myriad ways to manage each user on the system. Like its proprietary counterparts, such as Solaris and the many versions of UNIX currently on the market, Linux offers several text-based methods of editing user accounts in addition to several GUI tools that can be executed in the X Window environment. Whether textual or graphical, each tool can add, modify, and edit new accounts. Many of these commands and programs allow the administrator to change any of the possible settings available for each user's account. Not only can you determine the user's home directory, but you can also set quotas, permit access to network interfaces, and determine other variables of the user's profile. This chapter will offer several examples. What you choose should be based upon how you interact with the system.

## Using the Command Line

The command line offers perhaps the most efficient method of adding new users. It is the best method of accessing the system if you are logging in from remote locations or need to edit user files quickly. It does not require a high-quality video card; if the machine is *headless* (that is, if it has no monitor), you can later forego using the video card altogether once the operating system is installed. If you use only the command line, you can save disk space by not installing the X Window files. Because Linux will not have to generate the GUI, this method minimizes CPU usage and leaves more of the machine's resources available to perform the networking tasks rather than running desktop applications.

X Window interfaces vary considerably depending upon the type of window manager or customized GUI environment running. It is often easier simply to locate a terminal window or command line to edit users' data. Also, many of the GUI tools used for configuring users are not compliant with differing releases of the GUI. For that reason alone, many novice Linux administrators do not rely upon many of the tools that require merely pointing and clicking. Too much dependence upon utilities that do the configuring for you can be disastrous if the X Window interface fails to come up or if you are presented with an unfamiliar system. Knowledge of the console-based programs rather than GUI tools can mitigate many of the difficulties when problems occur or when you are changing settings.

Knowing how to use the functions of the command line is also useful when you are performing repetitive tasks. When you are using a GUI tool, you still must click every time you need to accomplish a function. Under the command line, a simple script will allow you to execute that same function many times over. You can only accomplish as many functions as the designer built in to the interface. With access to the files themselves, you are free to do what you need without having to use the GUI tools to rewrite any configuration files.

> **NOTE**
>
> Many of the GUI tools are also available in command-line form. These tools enable you to customize the interface, making you less dependent on the designer's conception of what the interface needs to accomplish. Clickable interfaces work well; character-based programs work just as well, only differently.

## Manually Configuring Accounts

Setting up users on a system can be rather mundane and repetitious. Linux has added several additional tools to make the task much easier. It is possible to do it all by hand, but the steps involved can take more time than is necessary. UNIX users believe it is more worthwhile to spend a few more minutes creating a script or shortcut than spending several more minutes typing all the instructions. The script-based method saves time and effort over the long run.

The most basic of all commands in creating new user accounts is the useradd command. Because it creates new files and directories and accesses files owned only by root, useradd must be a root-owned process as well. This file is generally located in /usr/sbin, though some distributions may place it elsewhere. However, if you are logged in as root, this command should be within your path, so simply entering the command should execute its function. To help others migrating from other proprietary UNIX systems, such as Sun Solaris, where the command is sometimes adduser, Linux creates a symbolic link from useradd to adduser so that either command will accomplish the same task.

The following listing is from the /usr/sbin directory. It shows the two commands that you can use for adding new users via the command line.

```
[root@pluto sbin]# pwd
/usr/sbin
[root@pluto sbin]# ls -la useradd adduser
lrwxrwxrwx     1 root     root      7 Aug 16 16:02 adduser -> useradd
-rwxr-xr-x     1 root     root  47592 Apr 15 18:03 useradd
```

To avoid confusion, this book will use the Linux convention and discuss the useradd command exclusively.

# Adding New Users with useradd

When you use useradd, the command does more than simply add a new user to the system. It goes through a series of steps in creating files, adding directories, and modifying other items. This section explains what you will see when adding a new user and describes how the machine actually performs the task so that you don't have to do it step by step. However, understanding the process is always a good idea. Even when adding users via the automated method, you may sometimes have to go back and clean out users in case of file backups or restorations.

When first adding a new user, you might want to use the absolute path to execute the command. Based on the permissions that you currently have as root, and whether you used the su or su - command or logged in directly as root, /usr/sbin may or may not be in your path. It is good practice to use the absolute path, as follows:

```
# /usr/sbin/useradd joe
```

Using the absolute path not only helps you to familiarize yourself with each program's location, but also helps you avoid using any older or replaced files by the same name that come earlier in your search path.

---

**TIP**

You can always add a directory to your path temporarily so that you do not need to type the absolute path each time you invoke the command. Enter the following to modify your $PATH and add /usr/sbin to your default search:

```
export PATH=$PATH:/usr/sbin"
```

---

The useradd command creates a /home/joe directory and installs joe in the /etc/passwd (and /etc/shadow if shadowed passwords were enabled during the install) and in the /etc/group files. It also places specific dotfiles within that user's home directory based on the contents of the /etc/skel directory. Although this command creates the necessary files and directories, you still have not set the password. The user joe will still be unable to log in until the password is set. Once again, to set the password, simply type **passwd** and the username. For instruction on setting user-specific passwords, see Chapter 5.

## Removing Users with userdel

Deleting users from the system is just as simple as adding them. The userdel command, which is located in the same directory as useradd, will search through the /etc/passwd and the /etc/group files and remove any references to the user you are removing. To remove all the files and directories owned by that same user, you must also set the -r option. To remove the user joe from the system quickly and thoroughly, simply execute the following command:

```
/usr/sbin/userdel -r joe
```

Both commands, useradd and userdel, are much faster and simpler ways of creating and removing user directories than were available on older UNIX systems, where nearly everything had to be created or deleted by hand. Now, nearly all Linux distributions provide both the command line and at least one of the many GUI tools that make creating a new user account a much simpler process.

**CAUTION**

After deleting a user and his or her files and directories, userdel also removes any files contained in that user's home directory. The userdel command does not normally grant you a second chance to change your mind. Once the files and directories are gone, they are gone permanently.

## Manually Adding a New User

The steps involved in manually creating an account are more rigorous than simply typing a one-word command. If you were to forego using the command-line tools, here are the necessary steps:

1. Create the user's home directory.
2. Edit the /etc/passwd file to suit, making sure that it has the correct number of fields and that the information is also correct.
3. Add the user to the /etc/group file as well. Either add that user to an existing group or create one specifically for the user.
4. Set the proper permissions on all directories. Do this by using the chown and chgrp commands. To set permissions recursively throughout all subdirectories as well, use the -R option.

5.  Create a unique password for that user using the passwd command.

6.  Copy over files located in the /etc/skel directory. Each user's directory must include these files, as they enable the user to log in with specific customization to the home directory and to work on the system. You do not necessarily need a valid home directory in order to log into the system. These files can include a public_html/ subdirectory for HTML files as well as a mail account.

7.  Copy over any startup files needed to run upon login. You can add the files to be run upon startup either to the .bashrc file when executing a bash shell or to the .xinitrc file if you are launching a GUI. Much depends upon each user's needs and wants.

8.  Create a mail account with the user's name in /var/spool/mail and create any additional mail aliases.

9.  Edit any quota information for that user with the /usr/sbin/edquota command. This is necessary only if quotas are enabled on the system itself.

10. Configure any additional account information such as customized shell prompts or which window managers you wish to start immediately upon login.

11. Verify that the new account is properly set up. Do this by logging in as that user and testing the available features just installed.

---

### NOTE

Quotas are being instituted more often on Linux systems as users store their mail and text files on the server. Quotas help prevent users from dumping masses of frivolous information on the server, by limiting the amount of data a user can store on the server.

---

Using command-line tools, such as useradd and userdel, is much simpler than configuring each feature by hand. Plus, if you do manually configure a feature, you might edit one of the options incorrectly. These console commands take care of most of these issues from the onset. Certain tasks, such as setting up quotas, do require some manual tweaking initially, but once complete these can be added to an automated process, which then is free from constant supervision. It is easy enough to create a script that will accomplish much of what the useradd and userdel commands achieve.

Listing 6.1 shows a simple routine that I used to modify the useradd scheme on an older Linux box. If you do not wish to be stuck with a precompiled command such as useradd, you can edit the following script to taste or adapt it to any Linux configuration. The script adds some extra features for a more specialized system, such as allocating different types of users to a certain type of group. For example, an email-only account would be added to the group 500 while a free account would be assigned to the group 5000.

**Listing 6.1  A Sample Script for Adding Users to a Linux System with Supplementary Features**

```
#!/bin/bash
# adu - a simple script for adding users
if [ -z "$1" ]; then
echo "usage: adu <username>"
echo
exit
fi
# first check and see if the username already exists
grep "^$1:" /etc/passwd
if [ "$?" = "0" ]; then
echo "Sorry, user $1 already exits"
echo
exit
fi
echo "Adding user $1 ... "

FL='echo "$1" | cut -c1'
if [ -z "$2" ]; then
echo
echo -n "Please enter full name: "
read FULLNAME
else
    FULLNAME="$2"
fi
# Set up the type of account to be created
if [ -z "$3" ]; then
echo
```

```
    echo -n "Please enter type of account (e,p,b,v,i,f,d): "
    read ATYPE
    else
        ATYPE="$3"
    fi
    QNAME=""
    GRP=0
    if [ "$ATYPE" = "p" ]; then    QNAME=personal;     GRP=2000;   fi
    if [ "$ATYPE" = "b" ]; then    QNAME=business;     GRP=3000;   fi
    if [ "$ATYPE" = "e" ]; then    QNAME=e-mail;       GRP=500;    fi
    if [ "$ATYPE" = "v" ]; then    QNAME=virtual;      GRP=4000;   fi
    if [ "$ATYPE" = "i" ]; then    QNAME=isdn;         GRP=1000;   fi
    if [ "$ATYPE" = "f" ]; then    QNAME=free;         GRP=5000;   fi
    if [ "$ATYPE" = "d" ]; then    QNAME=dsl;          GRP=6000;   fi
    if [ "$GRP" = "0" ]; then
    echo
    echo "Invalid account type: $ATYPE"
    echo
    exit
    fi
  # Use the useradd command and set quotas
    echo ".. useradd -d \"/home/$FL/$1\" -s /bin/bash -c \"$FULLNAME\" -
m \"$1\""
    useradd -d "/export/home/$FL/$1" -s /bin/bash -c "$FULLNAME" -m "$1"
    echo ".. passwd \"$1\""
    passwd "$1"
    echo ".. edquota -p \"$QNAME\" \"$1\""
    edquota -p "$QNAME" "$1"
    echo ".. usermod -g \"$GRP\" \"$1\""
    usermod -g "$GRP" "$1"
    echo ".. chmod 711 "/export/home/$FL/$1""
    chmod 711 "/export/home/$FL/$1"
    echo ".. chown "$1" "/export/home/$FL/$1""
    chown "$1" "/home/$FL/$1"
  # Send the new user instructions on how to dial in
    if [ "$ATYPE" = "p" ]; then    mail $1 < /usr/sbin/guide_dial-up.txt
;fi
```

```
   if [ "$ATYPE" = "b" ]; then    mail $1 < /usr/sbin/guide_dial-
up.txt    ;fi
   if [ "$ATYPE" = "v" ]; then    mail $1 < /usr/sbin/guide_virtual.txt
;fi
   echo
   echo "Setup complete."
   echo


   # End of file
```

You will recognize many of the useradd options from the previous chapters. This script creates an account for the user. It prompts the administrator for input, such as a username, which it then checks against the /etc/passwd file to see whether another user has already taken that name. If the username is available, the script then prompts for the user's full name and finally the group to which to assign that user. After gathering the necessary information, the script employs the useradd command and enters all the information gathered. Finally, the script assigns quotas to the user's account and sends the user a text e-mail explaining some basic functions.

A script like this takes care of some of the features that that you would ordinarily have to handle manually. It also showcases other distinctive innovations in Linux such as allocating the users to a particular group based on the type of account they requested and sending them an email with appropriate instructions.

The script in Listing 6.2 assists in manually deleting any rogue accounts. It is much shorter since, as you will discover when using Linux, it is much easier to delete files than to create them. Like the script in Listing 6.1, this script also has a short name that briefly describes its function. The name, however, is the script's least important aspect. You can change the name to whatever best describes it or suits its purpose.

### Listing 6.2  A Simple Script for Removing Users from the System

```
#!/bin/bash
# dlu - a simple script for deleting users.
#Print out the info for the user editing the account
if [ -z "$1" ]; then
echo "usage: dlu <username>"
```

```
echo
exit
fi
# Check to see if the account exists
# If so, remove the directories
grep "^$1:" /etc/passwd
if [ "$?" = "0" ]; then
echo
echo "Deleting user $1 ... "
FL='echo "$1" | cut -c1'
userdel "$1"
echo
echo "Removing directory /home/$FL/$1"
rm -r /home/$FL/$1
echo
echo "Removing /var/spool/mail/$1"
rm /var/spool/mail/$1
echo
echo "User $1 deleted."
echo
exit
else
echo "Sorry, user $1 does not exist"
echo
exit
fi
```

Remember, the /usr/sbin/usermod command allows root users to modify existing accounts. Proper use of the flags associated with this command will enable changes in the user's shell, directory, and identifying name. But, as mentioned previously, you can also edit the /etc/passwd file manually, although such editing is usually not a good idea unless you deem it necessary.

# Using GUI Tools

The command-line tools that come preinstalled with Red Hat should suffice for most administrative tasks. However, because Linux is a developing OS and because each administrator wishes to accomplish his or her own tasks in his or her own manner, many developers are coming up with new clickable interfaces that offer a graphic format for accomplishing the same tasks as the command-line tools. A quick perusal through the Freshmeat (http://www.freshmeat.net/) or Linuxberg (http://www.linuxberg.com) home pages, each a hosting a wide range of developers' tools, quickly shows the variety of programs currently on the market. Most of the programs are available for download.

Fortunately, Red Hat makes available a very versatile and robust client with the default install. Linuxconf is now considered the default tool for most all configuration tasks. Most Linux distributions, Red Hat included, provide older tools for modifying configuration files, but with the growing numbers of new Linux users demanding user-friendlier interfaces, these GUI programs are a welcome relief for those still struggling to grasp the intricacies of Linux.

## Editing Accounts with Linuxconf

One of the more recent advances made in Linux administrative tools is a utility called Linuxconf. Linuxconf was first included with Red Hat 5.1 and has proved to be a boon for users desiring to tweak and manage tools and utilities better on the system. It not only helps configure nearly every aspect of the Linux OS, but is easy to use and helpful for beginners just learning about Linux. The management of user accounts is just one small aspect of all that Linuxconf is capable of manipulating.

If you are familiar with older versions of Red Hat or you cut your teeth on the older Red Hat releases, you will recognize parts of the Red Hat control panel within Linuxconf. Though still available on Red Hat and other distributions, the control panel has limited scope. It was, and still is, an excellent tool for setting up printers, enabling modems and dial-up accounts, and editing the network configuration, but it is limited in changing or modifying user accounts.

The Linuxconf program comes in a variety of versions. The most common one is the GNOME-based Linuxconf, which is the version that this section will examine. It is quickly setting the standard for configuring most aspects of the Linux system. Because it is under constant and active development, users can expect to see many upgrades in the very near future. The screenshots that have been included in this book are based on the latest Red Hat release. You can expect more options and features to be added with each new release.

# Understanding Linuxconf Versions

Linuxconf is more than just a GUI tool for editing files and user variables. It can be used for these purposes, of course, but can also be used to control various aspects of the system. You can also use the Linuxconf utility to configure daemons and processes such as SAMBA and sendmail. It is a highly versatile tool for managing many features of your system.

You can invoke Linuxconf to run in one of four different ways:

◆ **Command line.** The command-line mode enables you to view scripts so that you can edit them properly. If you do not like GUI environments, this is the preferable mode. Plus, familiarity with the scripts and their location helps when you are attempting to change settings remotely or without an X Window interface. The command-line method is the quickest way to access a remote system and edit settings. You usually access a remote system using an xterm window within X Window environment or on the system console.

◆ **Character cell.** Much like the older Red Hat installation program resembling a DOS or WordPerfect 5.1 environment, this mode lets you access the settings without running X Window but still offers you the ease and simplicity of the editor. This approach of using Linuxconf is also resolved within a console terminal or within an xterm or a related terminal window.

◆ **GNOME-Linuxconf.** This is perhaps the most recognizable interface, and also the easiest to use. You will examine this interface in closer detail in this section. The interface uses the libraries of one of the better window managers, GNOME. For more information on using window managers, see Chapter 12.

◆ **Web-Based.** Both Netscape, which is a graphic web browser, or Lynx, which is a text-based browser, work equally well in editing the configurations.

Depending upon how the $DISPLAY variable is set on your machine, Linuxconf will normally start as GNOME-Linuxconf or as the character-cell format. Changing this option can help in determining how you can access the program. The Web-based method will also display an informative screen presenting you with the alternative methods of accessing the program. Note these alternatives carefully, as this screen will be displayed only once.

## Configuring User Settings under Linuxconf

With the inclusion of Linuxconf into the Red Hat release, even the most naïve administrator can effectively configure the networking, set up multiple users, fix system files, and change passwords. As seen in Figure 6.1, there are three main categories that can be edited under the main Linuxconf window; Config, Control, and Status.

The first section handles networking, user accounts, file systems, miscellaneous services and the manner in which you want Linux to boot. This is probably the main section that you, as an administrator, will be using for setting up clients or accounts. It is also useful for editing the network configuration.

The next section, Control, as shown in Figure 6.2 contains entries for the Control-panel, Control files and systems, date and time and Features. These sections allow you to manipulate aspects of Linux operation.

The first section, Control-panel, does not allow you to configure files or settings, but to change active processes. These include shutting down the system, mounting and unmounting partitions, as well as configuring superuser tasks. The second subdirectory edits configuration files, changes permissions on files, and edits

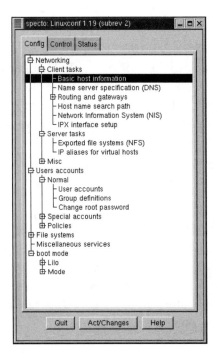

**FIGURE 6.1**

*Linuxconf is divided into three main categories for easy modification of files. The main Config window handles most tasks needed by administrators.*

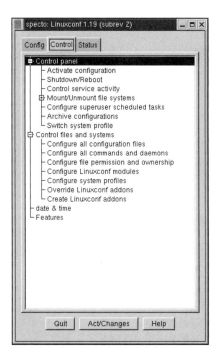

**FIGURE 6.2**

*The second category in the Linuxconf menu, Control, allows you to change running Linux utilities and to modify system settings.*

Linuxconf addons. The third section allows you to edit the date and time on the box, including your time zone. You can even use this section to retrieve the correct time from an atomic clock server elsewhere on the Internet. The last section defines special Linuxconf behavior, such as setting up the keyboard map.

In this last, and undoubtedly extremely short, section as shown in Figure 6.3, you can view the kernel boot messages, any additional boot messages and review previous Linxuconf messages. This is especially useful when wanting to verify any changes made by someone else to the file systems.

For the next few sections you will examine the first category, Config, and look at setting up user accounts. Under the Config tab in the main Linuxconf menu, select the User Accounts option. You will be presented with three separate tabs for configuring differing accounts: Normal, Special accounts, and Policies. For simple user account setup, the first option under the Normal heading is sufficient. See Figure 6.4 for a display of the differing account types.

Not only can you modify the normal accounts, but you can change group definitions as well as the root password. Restricting access to the Linuxconf program is essential if you do not wish others to be altering your root password. It is prudent

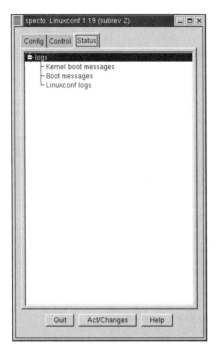

**FIGURE 6.3**

*The third category in the Linuxconf menu, Status, checks the Linux logs.*

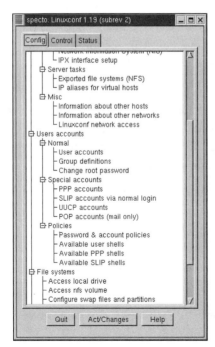

**FIGURE 6.4**

*The User account configurator menu, which sets up various account types on the Linux operating system.*

to always log off once you are through with Linuxconf in order to prevent anyone from tampering with your settings. Much like you would never leave a root shell open on your desktop, the same holds true with the Linxuconf program.

After selecting the Normal accounts button, you will be presented with a window much like the one in Figure 6.5. Here you can set all the variables for every user account on your system.

You may modify each account by highlighting the respective username. Normally you will see only the account login name, a more verbose name describing in greater detail the account type, the UID of that user and the group to which he, she, or it belongs. You can add an individual account with minimal effort and with little knowledge of the command-line options. The Quit, Add, and Help buttons below the user information window will assist in configuring a new account.

When you select a user, a dialog box will appear that contains more information regarding that user. As shown in Figure 6.6, you will see the regular Base info tab describing basic user info as well as the Params tab and the Privileges tab.

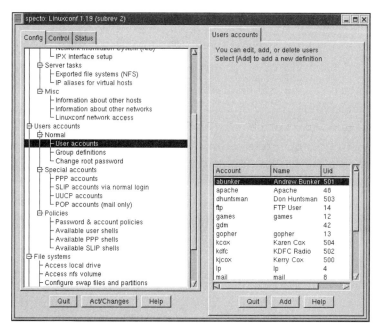

**FIGURE 6.5**

*The User accounts menu allows you to add, edit, or delete users from off you system.*

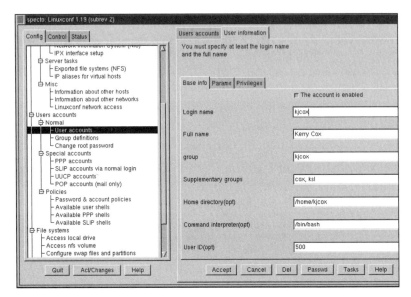

**FIGURE 6.6**

*The User information dialog box allows you to define the variables associated with the user. This window saves the information in the /etc/passwd file.*

Here you can specify any information you may wish to set for a particular user. Normally, you need only enter the login name and then click Accept to create the new account. The other fields, such as group, Home directory, Command interpreter, and User ID will be completed by the Linuxconf program for you. If you like, you may return later and modify the preselected settings and add or modify any fields you wish.

You will also be prompted automatically to enter a new password for that user. Again, like the command-line options, if Linux determines the password you selected to be unsafe, you will be warned but allowed to continue if you wish. If you are unsure as to the group with which you wish to associate a particular user, you are given a drop-down menu and can choose any of the pre-defined groups. If you create another group later on, you can return to this menu and change the selection. The same is true for the Command interpreter option. Though optional, Red Hat will assign bash to the user as the default shell. If that user desires another shell you can select from the list of installed shells on your system.

In the next tab under the User information section, Params (see Figure 6.7), the administrator can enter information about the life of the account or the life of the user's password.

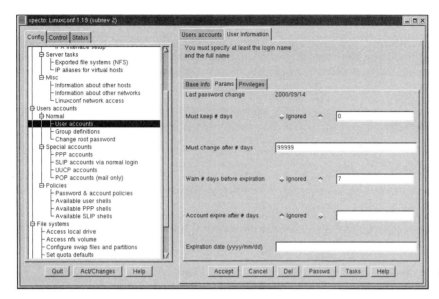

**FIGURE 6.7**

*The Params tab under the User information window sets account and password variables for each user account.*

You can set the minimum number of days to maintain the password, or the number of days after which it must be changed. You can also specify that the system prompt the user to change his or her password a specified number of days before it expires, after which that user will no longer be able to log on to the system. Unlike the Base info tab, the Params tab, which stores information in the /etc/passwd file, stores the entered information in the /etc/shadow file.

Linuxconf goes beyond much of the regular command-line input. In other words, you are not required to know exactly which configuration file requires editing or where in the system directories that file is located. The last tab, Privileges, is placed elsewhere in the system than in the /etc/passwd or /etc/shadow files where the previous options are edited. The GUI configuration makes the process much easier than editing specific files by hand.

The Privileges tab (see Figure 6.8) makes it simple to set user permissions. It is so simple that improper use or ignorance of what this utility can do could result in security problems.

If you wish to allow a certain user control over the Linuxconf program, you may define his or her privileges in this window. He or she may use not only Linuxconf, but can also exercise control over other various system settings if you so desire.

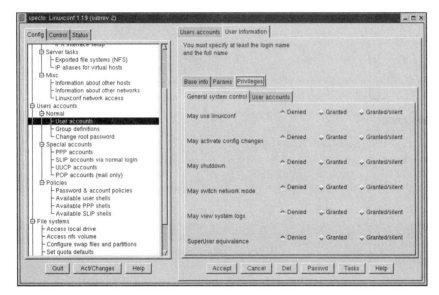

**FIGURE 6.8**

*The Privileges tab does not so much set directory and file permissions as grant the user access to control and execute certain root-privileged tasks. These are privileges over general system utilities.*

The Linuxconf program contains so many options that explaining them all would require an entire book. However, each tab offers a Help option that attempts to explain many of the terms and uses associated with each option.

In addition to offering user configuration options, Linuxconf also provides a User definitions option. Figure 6.9 shows the User definitions screen, which displays each group and its respective members. The screen also offers the option of adding additional groups and configuring their settings.

In most Linux distributions, there are more groups available in the Group file than there are users listed in the standard User file. Many of these groups should be left alone, as they perform specific tasks relative to the system. Unless you are sure what function each group performs, do not change or delete their settings.

To add a new group, you click the Add button. Linuxconf then displays the Group specification window (see Figure 6.10).

Here you need to enter integral user information regarding multiple or group accounts, comprising items such as the group name, the group ID (GID), and the members who will belong to the new group. Creating groups under linuxconf is a useful feature when you want to share a certain directory with only specific users.

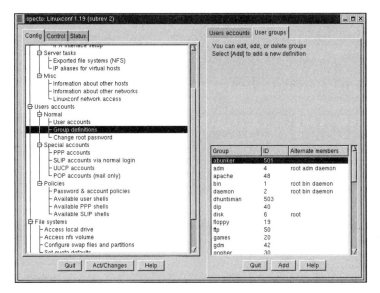

**FIGURE 6.9**

*Similar to the User accounts screen, the User groups screen provides the group name and group ID and also lists the members of the group.*

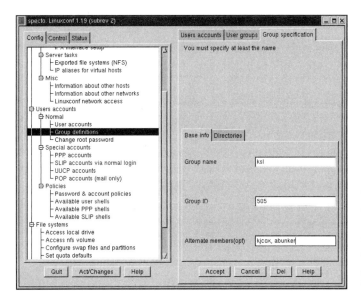

**FIGURE 6.10**

*Linuxconf will usually assign the next GID available. You can, however, change the group ID to almost any number you wish.*

The Directories tab lists the home base directory, which this group will then share. This window also establishes the permissions that each user has over shared files. The default value of 700 allows only the group members access to read, write, and execute while excluding all other users who do not belong to the group.

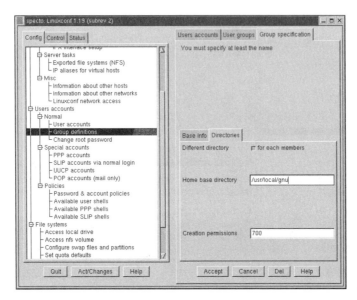

**FIGURE 6.11**

*You can define the home base directory for groups as well as set the permissions.*

The permissions on any home base directory, which is shared by group member, can be adjusted to be highly exclusionary, allowing no one to read or write to a particular location, or be very permissive by setting the permissions to 777, thus granting everyone the ability to read, write, and execute files from the shared group location.

Since Linuxconf is such a powerful program, granting other users the rights to Linuxconf is equal to granting root access. Resetting or changing the root password is a very simple procedure under Linuxconf (see Figure 6.12), so you should grant access to this program with as much prudence as you would when giving out the root password. All administrators should be extra cautious if they are leaving a running version of this program on their desktop at any time. Treat it as you would an open terminal window with root access granted.

**FIGURE 6.12**

*Linuxconf will also allow you to change the password for root.*

After typing in your choice, the program will admonish you just as you would be warned on the command line if your root password were too short, too easy to guess, or based on a dictionary word.

## Setting Shells under Linuxconf

Although the past few sections have covered most of the many features of Linuxconf that deal with managing users, there remains a plethora of other attributes to this program. Some of the other tasks that this configuration tool can handle include setting the default shell and listing all other available shells. Linuxconf's Available user shells tab (see Figure 6.13), located under the Policies tab in the User account Configurator, allows the administrator to edit the /etc/shells file without invoking a text editor and editing the file directly. As is typical for many of the tabs under Linuxconf, system files are easily edited without having to know their location or editing the file by hand.

This tab is helpful when you need to know which shell can be used for each user account. It is sometimes wise to make several shells available for any user. I sometimes like to have several accounts on the same system, each using a different shell.

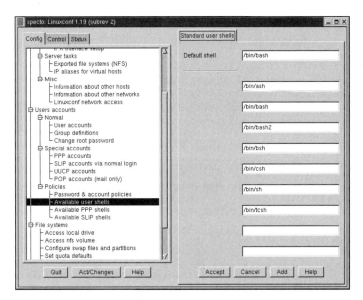

**FIGURE 6.13**

*Unlike /etc/shells, which lists your shells by preference, the Standard user shells tab lists the available shells alphabetically.*

**NOTE**

Setting multiple accounts with different shells can be a lifesaver. Once, a Linux server crashed and I could not immediately bring up the external hard drives that housed partitions such as /usr/local and /home. I discovered to my horror that the previous administrator had deleted /usr/bin/bash and had replaced it with a symbolic link to /usr/local/bin/bash. Though the partition /usr was on the internal drive, the partition /usr/local was not and also was not readable by the system. I was effectively cut off from logging in because both my regular account and root required some sort of shell upon login. Now, because that shell was missing, I could not gain access to the system either as root or as myself. Fortunately, I had another account that used tcsh as its default shell. With that account, I was able to regain control of the system, mount the external drives, and fix the broken link. I thus quickly corrected the misdeed of the previous administrator.

## Using Linuxconf for Partitioning

Knowing the available partitions, their mount points, and their sizes is very handy if your system suffers a partition crash or faulty reboot. Linuxconf also provides this information along with a method of editing it to suit. Much like the fdisk utility used during the installation, Linuxconf enables you to edit and modify existing partitions.

**CAUTION**

This is a very sensitive task of Red Hat Linux administration; you should be careful when modifying anything related to partitions. This section is recommended for informative purposes only.

Under the main Config window of Linuxconf, the File systems button will bring up several options for accessing other partitions or file system types. The sections allow for reconfiguring or partitions and network volumes.

Figure 6.14 shows the Linuxconf Filesystem configurator window that lists the various partitions and drives that can be accessed. Here is a listing of each option that can be edited by Linuxconf.

Linuxconf handles many other tasks aside from user management. The next few chapters will often refer to the Linuxconf program as an alternative means for

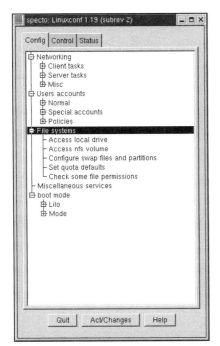

**FIGURE 6.14**

*The latest version of Linuxconf displays the various partition types accessible for editing.*

**NOTE**

You can find more information about the Linuxconf program at the Linuxconf Project home page (http://www.solucorp.qc.ca/linuxconf/).

accomplishing networking tasks, configuring sendmail, managing virtual domains, and setting a host of other configuration options. However, before using Linuxconf, it is crucial that you first learn the command-line options and be capable of configuring files by hand without the use of clickable interfaces that distance the user from the files. Nothing is worse than becoming dependent on a GUI tool and then either no longer having access to an X Window display or attempting to complete related tasks on a headless server, whether from a remote console or after a system failure. Familiarity with the console, in this case, does not breed contempt.

# Conclusion

Once you have begun to manage the users on your system properly, you can begin looking at the system itself. The next chapter will examine system processes. That discussion will help you to identify what is currently running on your system and will explain how to start, stop, and change the value of each process through the use of signals sent to each process. You should then be able to recognize how your system operates and how much of the hardware each program requires.

# Chapter 7

## Identifying Processes

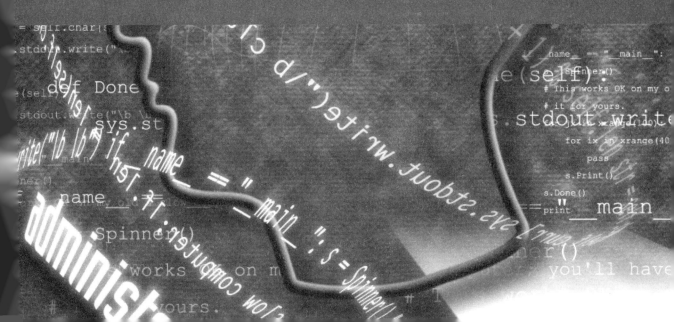

**W**ith Linux, you can identify and track every process that is running on your system. A *process* is a single program running in its own virtual space on the operating system. It is separate from a job or command, which can be several distinct processes working in tandem to complete a specific task. Each individual command is executed as a single process. A process has a wide range of uses and can be one of many things; anything from a daemon to an application currently running on the display, or a system program executing a planned or needed function. Linux assigns to each of these processes a number that can then be used to change the process's function or state. Manipulating a process's attributes grants the user more freedom in determining how Linux operates and what type of priority each program is given. Sending commands to the processes themselves also grants both the user and the system a large amount of flexibility in tailoring the system's operation.

This chapter will cover the following topics:

◆ Process ID numbers

◆ ID numbers assigned to users and groups

◆ The priority and nice value of processes

◆ The life cycle of a process

◆ The commands and signals used to manipulate a process

# Understanding Processes

Linux is extremely dynamic in how it allows users to track each and every program running on the system. Along with the ability to view each and every process, administrators can also change the manner in which it operates. Individual processes can be stopped, started, killed and modified. Nearly every function or operation executed under Linux can be monitored. With that monitoring comes the ability to change the program's priority or to kill it altogether. Though users should leave many operations alone—such as those that the system requires in order to run—others, especially those initiated by normal users on the system, can be customized.

Each of these operations is called a *process* and as such can be any of the following:

◆ A daemon that starts up at boot time

◆ A command issued by a regular user

◆ A program, such as a cron job, that begins at a specific time

◆ A call to the system from an outside source, such as a request to view a Web document or an FTP request either to upload or download a file

Linux allows several processes to work in tandem or to execute simultaneously. Such is the nature of true multitasking operating systems such as Linux. For many of these processes, such as those that the system requires in order for Linux to function properly, each process quickly accomplishes its task, leaving hardly a trace once it is done. Each task can be logged and its progress tracked, but the process itself leaves little of a residual memory footprint.

## Identifying Processes with PIDs

Linux offers control over each of these processes. As each process starts, Linux assigns it a *process ID (PID)*. This is a unique number not shared by any other process on the system.

### NOTE

Though this number is exclusive when it is first assigned, Linux can assign the same process ID to another process later. However, before relinquishing its process ID, the process first must either complete its task or be killed. No two processes can have the same PID at the same time.

By assigning a PID to every active, sleeping, or zombie process, both the system and the user can track the progress of each system action, monitor its progression, and modify its condition.

### NOTE

Zombie processes are those processes whose parent has died, but which remain alive as child processes, although they are not actively doing anything. The init daemon will eventually reap these processes. Zombies do not normally affect the system adversely.

Although the number value assigned to each process does not mean anything in and of itself, it facilitates the method by which Linux tracks the items currently running on the system. When Linux first boots up, it begins to incrementally assign PIDs to each process, beginning at 1. The init daemon, which starts all other processes, receives this primary number. The system considers init to be the parent process, and all other succeeding processes, either spawned or generated by init, to be child processes.

Once these PIDs reach the maximum value of their numeric type (which is a 16-bit value on Linux and can reach up to 65536), they "rotate" and begin reassigning new values to new processes. Depending on the purpose and load placed on the machine, this can occur either hourly on a heavily taxed machine or weekly on Linux boxes seeing little or no use.

Sending a unique signal to a specific process can change its status and the way that the process interacts with other configuration files or system files. For example, you can coerce Linux into handling the many processes currently running on the system differently; you might compel the OS to take notice of a relatively unimportant process, force it to carry out its task more speedily, or kill any processes hogging too many CPU cycles. Understanding that each process receives its own ID number is crucial to modifying the manner in which Linux handles its many tasks. To view the PID of each process, see " Using *ps* to Display Running Processes," later in this chapter.

When a process completes the task assigned it, it releases that number and dies gracefully. That process ID number can then be given to another process either when the system reboots or when Linux has completed a certain number of tasks, and then begins reassigning the new PIDs when it starts its set of 65536 processes anew.

A user cannot change the PID of a process, nor can any two processes share an existing PID. The only way a user can change the value is either to slay the process and start it again or, in some cases, cause the process to reread its configuration file. However, unless you are absolutely sure you need to kill a process, do not attempt simply to change its PID.

Certain tasks never release their PID. The init daemon, for example, always has the initial PID value of 1. If you kill this process or try to change it, your Red Hat Linux machine will either reboot or fail. It is important to recognize which processes are necessary to routine system functions and which are generated by users and thus can be manipulated. Depending upon your Linux version, you should be careful with processes that have low PIDs .

A parent PID (*PPID*) is the PID of the process's parent process. In some instances, a process will spawn a copy of itself when the need arises or when there are multiple requests for that process to serve. If you kill the PPID, the system will also kill all of the parent process's child processes. In this manner, Linux links processes and their functions.

## Identifying Users and Groups by UIDs and GIDs

When created, each user under Linux receives a user ID (UID) number. This number is also added to the filename of each file created by that user so that the machine recognizes file ownership. You can edit or change user ID numbers under the /etc/passwd file, but doing so is not a good idea. Such changes can result in confusion as to what files are owned by whom, especially if an existing UID is given to another user. It is best to let the system assign you a UID. To review UIDs and how the system assigns unique numbers to each user, see Chapter 5.

The same holds true for group ID numbers (GIDs). Under Red Hat Linux, the same name can apply both to the user and the group ID. For example, the username joe can identify both the user owning certain files and the name of the group to which these files also belong. This does not necessarily mean that joe is both a username *and* a groupname, but that this string of characters is used to identify both the name of the user and the name of the group. The group joe can contain additional users aside form the user joe. The method of affixing the same name to both users and groups makes assigning users to different groups easier since a user can also be a group and thus share files with others more readily.

**CAUTION**

The UID and the GID can share the same name, so be careful not to confuse them. They can have different numbers. If you need to find out a file's use or group ownership, check both the /etc/passwd and /etc/group files for their numeric values.

If you access or view a file by entering the ls -l command, the output will show you both the usernames and group names of the files and directories within that location. Usually, the first column states the file's permissions, and the second displays the username. The group name is in the third column. If a user changes his or her UID, the files also lose their username and group name affiliation and assume of the UID number previously associated with that user.

Suppose that your username and group name is joe and that you own several files on your Linux system in various directories. This username also has a UID of 510 and the groupname also has a GID of 510. Though they both share the same numbers they are the same, since a username is not also a groupname in spite of the similarity in numbering. If you were to remove this user from the system by executing the /usr/sbin/userdel -r joe command, all files outside the /home/joe directory and were originally owned by joe, would no longer list joe as their owner, but would  instead retain their former UID and GID.

The same is true when you download Linux programs from the Internet. Once you have unzipped and untarred the files, they are usually assigned a specific number. Because the user who created them normally does not exist on your system, Linux assigns the files the number or UID and GID previously associated with that user. If the groupname is the same as that of a system group, then sometimes the system will assign that same groupname to the new files. For example, certain developmental programs are often given the groupname wheel. Though the user fred who first created this program is not on your system, the system group wheel probably is, in which case the files would then have a generic UID number assigned them and also have a groupname of wheel. Pay attention to the usernames and group names the next time you download a file or test another program from another system.

## Applying UIDs and GIDs to Processes

In addition assigning to UIDs to files and directories, Linux also assigns UIDs to processes. When indicating processes, the UID is the user identification number of the person who initiated the process, except in the case of setuid (SUID) or setgid (SGID) programs which can then take on another ID number. Only the person who created or started the process or the superuser or root user can make any changes to that process's functions. This method of allocating user and group IDs can quickly become confusing when the process is run with SUID and SGID processes. This discussion is limited to regular processes. For more information on SUID and SGID processes, see Chapter 3.

For example, if I start a process as myself, that process will continue until one of the following occurs:

◆ The process completes its cycle and exits gracefully.

◆ I kill the process prematurely.

◆ The superuser or a user running as root decides that the process needs to be terminated. Either type of user has the permissions necessary to stop or kill the process.

If none of the preceding occurs and the process continues, it can either run indefinitely or it can enter a zombie state. If the process becomes a zombie, it will run until the init daemon reaps exit statuses, those zombie processes, orphaned programs, and dead states, or until the system is rebooted.

How much of the system's CPU and memory is allocated to a specific process depends upon the user and the type of process running. For example, suppose that you start a process as yourself using the vi editor to open a file, by entering **vi dmesg.txt**. The system will give this process the next available PID and UID number and will have less processor time available to it. This is due to the simple fact that a regular user is running the process and its operation is not integral to system performance. The process will receive a lower *priority* or the availability of processor time relative to other processes awaiting completion. Less processor time will be granted to that process to accomplish its task.

A process initiated by a system user, a daemon, or by the superuser, however, will receive a higher priority. By setting a higher priority to that process, the system will devote more CPU cycles to the process's completion.

The group ID (GID) number is much like the UID number. It is based on the group numbers located in /etc/group. Here, too, the system allots the processor time to the process based on the owners within the group. If that group contains system users or daemons, they will, in turn, receive a higher priority. Because several members can belong to the same group, Linux must first check the list of users in the /etc/group file and verify their ownerships over the processes running. The same is true if you are trying to modify a process. If you do not belong to the group that started that particular process, the system will deny you access to modify or change the process's priority.

## Modifying a Process's Priority

A process's priority establishes the conditions under which it will run until the kernel determines the CPU time that is needed to be allocated to another process. If the priority is high, as determined by its *nice value,* or its value in scheduling priority, the process will continue to run until it has exhausted its allotted CPU time. When that occurs, the system can then devote remaining CPU time or cycles to completing other process tasks. Depending upon its priority, a process is then either preempted by another process with a higher priority or allowed to complete its task without interruption.

In a nutshell, then, the Linux kernel or the operating system's core chooses what process to run by evaluating which process has the highest "internal priority" based upon the user who executes the process and the importance of the function to the system. Once that priority is set, the system runs each process in a prioritized manner until all the tasks are accomplished.

Although you cannot change the priority of a process directly, you can change the nice value of a process, or the level at which it runs. Then other processes with higher nice values can complete their tasks while allowing tasks that have been waiting longer in the queue to complete their function without stressing the system.

Other factors not influenced by the priority of a process are the amount of CPU time that the process has already consumed and the length of time that it has been waiting to run. To set these values, you instead use the ulimit command. This command determines resource limit settings. It is normally a built-in command with the bash or ksh shell and can be used to set limits on the number of system resources.

Consider the following illustration of the priority of a process. Suppose that an httpd process has been running for some time. Because the process has been running so long, the system gives it a higher priority and grants the process more processor time so that it can complete its life cycle and then exit gracefully. In addition, if a remote user has placed a request to connect to a local server via a Telnet session and the local system is busy completing other tasks, the user may have to wait until the current process's priority drops low enough that it loses the CPU. The longer the user waits, the higher the priority assigned to that task. In this manner, Linux can complete most tasks quickly and succinctly.

# Setting the Nice Value of a Process

The nice value of a process is the amount of CPU or processor time allotted to a process as it competes with other processes for those same resources. Each process receives its nice value from the kernel. The term "nice" derives from the priority's "niceness," or how well it cooperates with other users on the system. The nicer the value, the more accommodating it is to other processes competing for the same system resources. The *lower* the nice value of a process, the *higher* the priority it receives.

If you want to place a process or command ahead of other processes or want to have the system deal with that process first before all others, you set the nice value extremely high. The possible ranges for nice values are −20 to 20. The default value for most processes is 0.

If multiple processes all have the same priority, they are placed in a run queue. When the CPU is free and is able to process jobs, it takes the first process in the lowest non-empty queue. The CPU executes that process until it is preempted by another request or the CPU time is taken away forcefully, at which point the CPU starts up the next lowest process. Due to the speed of most processors today, these tie slices are executed rapidly. In the early days of UNIX, when processor speed was much slower and CPU time was a precious commodity, if a process took up more time than anticipated and was considered crucial to the system, the process's priority would continue to increase. Measures were taken to ensure that one process could not dominate an entire system.

Regular users can increase the nice value only of processes that they own. They cannot, however, decrease the value. That is, a normal user can only make a process less important and place it further back in the scheduling queue. Only root can make a process more important by lowering its nice value. Thus the system handles the scheduling of processes with the least amount of user intervention.

By using the nice command, a user can change the nice value of any given process that he or she owns. The command is located in /bin/nice. Any user can change the level of a process that only he or she owns by using the following command:

```
nice +5 mytask
```

This command changes the nice value for the process mytask. If mytask were taking up too much of the CPU and thus slowing down the system, the process's owner can assign it a higher nice value so that the system reassigns the process less CPU time.

One instance where you would definitely want to set the nice value high so that it would use the minimal amount of the system resources is for a process that runs constantly using spare CPU cycles.

One example of this is the seti@home project. Any user can download radio signals received by the SETI (Search for Extra-Terrestrial Intelligence) Project. These blocks of signals can then be analyzed on any user's system, whether the system is running Linux or any other OS, as it searches for some coherent signal in the midst of space noise. A process like this takes up much of the system's resources and can significantly increase the load on the CPU. The best way to keep Linux functional while also running an intensive program such as this is to set the nice value of the process as high as possible. A command such as the following is advisable:

```
nice +20 setiathome
```

With a nice value set at its highest, the load would be minimal since other more important processes on a busy system would preempt this process frequently. Thus, Linux would continue to function well while accomplishing other rigorous demands.

If you want to dedicate more of the computer's resources to accomplishing certain jobs such as compiling a new kernel, the same nice command with a lower setting would finish the job quicker:

```
nice -20 make
```

However, setting the nice value too low can cause undue strain on the system and also make other processes inoperable. If all the system's resources are taken up with the one command, there might not be enough left to finish necessary tasks or system programs needed for Linux to remain operational.

**CAUTION**

Use discretion in changing the nice value on processes. If you are sharing the system with other users, be mindful of their requirements as well.

In addition to using the nice command to set and initial nice-value on a process, you can modify its usage by running the command renice. Be aware that only root can change the nice value on any process. The influence of the renice command exceeds that of the nice command, in that the command can force all processes owned by a single user to have their ID changed and/or force the PIDs and ownership of all processes to be altered, thus also causing their placement in the CPU queue to change.

For example, the following renice command would change the processes 11894 and 257 to receive a lower priority so that the kernel can devote more time and resources to other programs. It would also change all processes owned by both kerry and root to receive the same nice value as the other two processes.

```
renice +10 11894 -u kerry root -p 257
```

Using the renice command is sometimes considered a much simpler way to change a process's value than using the nice command. However, much depends on you, the user or administrator, and which command you prefer to use.

## Understanding the Life Cycle of a Process

Knowing how a process operates is also useful. By better understanding how your machine creates and manages processes, you will be better able to control the operation of your Linux machine. Parent processes spawn child processes which are off-shoots of the main process. A process cannot just spontaneously generate itself, but must be initiated either by the init daemon or by another running process. To create a process, the parent process, or the initial process, initiates a fork. Here the term *fork* suggests that the process creates a copy of itself. This child process then is identical to the parent except for a few differences, the most important being that the forked process has a new and unique PID and that the child PPID is equal to that of the parent PID. Each child process also inherits the open file descriptors after a fork() call.

The fork command, which creates the new process, also resets all accounting information of the new process so that it will be distinguished from the parent process. If this information were not reset, then the system could become confused between the parent and child processes. The fork() call that tracks the new PID within the file descriptor table that tracks open files per process. The fork command tells the kernel that a new PID number needs to be assigned to the child process. These descriptors are small tables that the kernel uses to keep track of all processes. If these tables are not kept current, how the child process is created can have direct bearing on the parent process.

# Sending Processes Commands and Signals

This section examines how you can view each process under Linux. Being able to see what the system is doing at any given moment is useful in determining not only how your own processes are affecting system performance but how others may be imposing a strain on the system as well. Because Linux is so transparent, each process can be manipulated. If a certain process is taking up too much of the resources, it can be killed, or if the system seems to be handling the load well, more processes can be initiated.

Similar to other proprietary systems, Linux enables the user to distinguish just where his or her programs might be affecting the system's speed, performance, and allocation of resources. Linux grants the user control over each and every process and allows the administrator to adjust the system load and resources based on need. Other operating systems allow you to list running processes, CPU and memory use, but Linux is very flexible in that you can directly affect performance to meet your own needs. Once the processes are visible to the administrator, they can be altered to suit the situation.

## Using ps to Display Running Processes

One of the most versatile tools for monitoring the state of the processes on any given system is the ps command. Of all the commands used daily, ps is perhaps the most functional and widely used by any administrator. This command displays all the running processes. It gives detailed information about each process's PID, its load on the CPU and memory, as well as other important statistics. The command's output is basically a snapshot of the system at the time that the command is issued. Any commands initiated after the execution of the ps command will not be present in this snapshot. The ps command looks only at the processes running at a specific moment in time.

Interpreting the output of ps is an important administrative skill. At times you may be called upon to locate and identify errant or zombie processes. Or, you might discover a process that is out of control, in which case you will have to kill that process entirely to avoid harming the system's performance. You can also use ps to determine who is running what processes on the system. This command is an important tool when you are checking for culprits exploiting the CPU for their own purposes or who exceed the acceptable and fair use policy of the system. Determining the UIDs of these processes makes tracking down their owners much easier.

Several options are associated with the ps command. The following are some of the more common flags used with ps (Listing 7.1 shows the output of these commands):

```
ps aux
```

or

```
ps -aux
```

The hyphen is optional. It was used in the earlier days of UNIX and is still an acceptable feature. Generally, the command is issued without the hyphen.

### Listing 7.1 The Output of ps on a Typical Linux Machine

```
USER        PID %CPU %MEM   VSZ   RSS TTY     STAT START     TIME COMMAND
root          1  0.0  0.1  1120    68 ?       S    Aug17     0:07 init
root          2  0.0  0.0     0     0 ?       SW   Aug17     0:27 [kflushd]
root          3  0.0  0.0     0     0 ?       SW   Aug17     0:15 [kupdate]
root          4  0.0  0.0     0     0 ?       SW   Aug17     0:00 [kpiod]
root          5  0.0  0.0     0     0 ?       SW   Aug17     4:59 [kswapd]
root        361  0.0  0.0  1208    44 ?       S    Aug17     0:00
/usr/sbin/automount -timeout 60 /misc file /etc/auto.misc
root        388  0.0  0.2  1172   160 ?       S    Aug17     0:28 syslogd -m 0
root        397  0.0  0.0  1452     0 ?       SW   Aug17     0:00 [klogd]
daemon      411  0.0  0.1  1144   104 ?       S    Aug17     0:00 /usr/sbin/atd
root        425  0.0  0.1  1328   112 ?       S    Aug17     0:00 crond
root        439  0.0  0.3  1156   212 ?       S    Aug17     0:08 inetd
```

```
    named   453  0.0  0.6   2424   420 ?      S    Aug17  0:00 named -u
named
    root    467  0.0  0.0   1204     0 ?      SW   Aug17  0:00 [lpd]
    root    495  0.0  0.4   2128   320 ?      S    Aug17  0:05 sendmail:
accepting connections on port 25
    root    520  0.0  0.0   1660     0 ?      SW   Aug17  0:00 [safe_mysqld]
    mysql   541  0.0  0.0  10836    44 ?      SN   Aug17  0:00 [mysqld]
    xfs     609  0.0  0.0   3044    60 ?      S    Aug17  0:00 xfs -droppriv
-daemon -port -1
    root    623  0.0  0.0   2452     0 ?      SW   Aug17  0:00 [smbd]
    root    632  0.0  0.6   2032   396 ?      S    Aug17  0:18 nmbd -D
    root    737  0.0  0.0   1696     0 ?      SW   Aug17  0:00 [sh]
    root    868  0.0  0.0   2396     0 ?      SW   Aug17  0:00 [sshd]
    root    882  0.0  0.0   1092     0 tty2   SW   Aug17  0:00 [mingetty]
    root    917  0.0  0.0   2596    60 ?      S    Aug17  0:02
/usr/local/etc/apache-ssl/httpsd -f /usr/local/etc/apache-ssl/conf/httpsd.conf
    nobody  918  0.0  0.0   1412    64 ?      S    Aug17  0:00 gcache 99
/usr/local/etc/apache-ssl/logs/gcache_port
    nobody  920  0.0  0.0   3192     0 ?      SW   Aug17  0:08 [httpsd]
    nobody  921  0.0  1.9   3192  1252 ?      S    Aug17  0:13
/usr/local/etc/apache-ssl/httpsd -f /usr/local/etc/apache-ssl/conf/httpsd.conf
    bb      2814 0.0  0.0   1692     0 ?      SW   Aug17  0:00 [runbb.sh]
    bb      2815 0.0  0.4   1676   288 ?      SN   Aug17  0:19 [bbrun]
    root    4519 0.0  0.1   3832    68 ?      S    Aug17  0:02
/usr/local/etc/apache/bin/httpd
    kjcox   2765 0.0  0.1   1680   112 ?      S    Aug21  0:00
/opt/wp8/shbin10/wpexc
    root   13590 0.0  0.0   1148    52 ?      S    Aug23  0:11 gpm -t ps/2
    root    5430 0.0  0.0   2236     0 tty    SW   Aug24  0:00 [login]
    kjcox   5431 0.0  0.0   1740     0 tty    SW   Aug24  0:00 [bash]
    nobody  4180 0.0  1.4   4204   904 ?      S    Aug27  0:01
/usr/local/etc/apache/bin/httpd
    kjcox  26677 0.0  0.0   1652     0 tty    SW   Aug29  0:00 [startx]
    kjcox  26684 0.0  0.0   2304     0 tty1   SW   Aug29  0:00 [xinit]
    root   26685 0.6 19.6  69664 12556 ?      S    Aug29 19:58 /etc/X11/X :0
-auth /home/kjcox/.Xauthority
```

```
   kjcox   26689   0.0   2.2    4328   1440  tty1   S    Aug29   0:35  wmaker
   kjcox   26693   0.0   1.8    9448   1192  tty1   S    Aug29   0:12  gmc
   kjcox   26696   0.0   0.4    1944    300  tty1   S    Aug29   1:03  wmmon
   kjcox   26702   0.0   0.0    1348      0  ?      SW   Aug29   0:00  [esd]
   kjcox   26704   0.0   0.0    2636      0  ?      SW   Aug29   0:00  [gnome-name-
serv]
   kjcox   26739   0.0   0.0    2088      0  pts/1  SW   Aug29   0:00  [telnet]
   kjcox   28284   0.0   1.6    5160   1048  tty1   S    Aug29   0:01  ical
-calendar /home/kjcox/.calendar
   kjcox   28286   0.0   0.0    2284      0  pts/5  SW   Aug29   0:00  [telnet]
   kjcox   28751   0.0   3.5   10496   2264  tty1   S    Aug29   0:00  licq
   kjcox   31430   0.0   0.0    2592      0  pts/8  SW   Aug29   0:00  [ssh]
   kjcox   21355   0.0   3.8   45548   2468  tty1   S    Aug30   0:36
/usr/local/office51/bin/soffice.bin
   root    25514   0.0   0.3    1380    248  ?      S    07:00   0:00  /sbin/mgetty
-n 1 ttyS0
   kjcox   29527   0.0   0.7    1752    512  pts/3  S    09:52   0:00  bash
   kjcox   32082   0.0   1.5    1744    984  pts/6  S    11:38   0:00  bash
   kjcox   32336   0.3  25.2   27256  16156  tty1   S    11:49   0:29
/opt/netscape/netscape
   kjcox   32337   0.0   5.7   16668   3656  tty1   S    11:49   0:00  (dns helper)
   bb       3345   0.0   0.6    1240    444  ?      SN   14:09   0:00  sleep 300
   root     3359   0.1   1.9    2320   1228  pts/7  S    14:13   0:00  login — kjcox
   kjcox    3360   0.2   1.5    1732    976  pts/   S    14:13   0:00  -bash
   kjcox    3384   0.0   1.1    2360    732  pts/7  R    14:14   0:00  ps auxww
```

As you can see on the last line, the ps auxww command also lists itself since it too is a process.

---

**TIP**

As you can see in the last column, the output cuts off part of the pathname for some of the programs. To view the entire pathname or execution of a specific program, enter the ps aux command with an extra ww at the end which stands for wide output. Each w allows an additional line for the filename. Thus, entering **ps auxww** will display the entire command as it was issued to start the program.

The first line of the output shows the headings for the columns. The following table defines each field:

| Field | Description |
|---|---|
| USER | The username of the process's owner. |
| PID | The process ID number. |
| %CPU | The percentage of CPU time the process has recently used. |
| %MEM | The percentage of memory the process is using. |
| VSZ | The virtual size of the process in kilobytes. |
| RSS | Resident set size (the amount of physical memory used). |
| TTY | The terminal ID number. |
| STAT | The current status of the process. This field has additional flags that better describe the process. Below are the explanations for the flags found under this section: |

| | |
|---|---|
| D | Signifies the process is in disk for a short-term wait |
| I | States the process is Idle |
| R | States the process is currently running |
| S | States the process is currently Sleeping |
| T | The process is stopped or traced |
| Z | The process is a zombie or defunct process |

Other flags can be used jointly with the ones used in the previous example:

| Flag | Description |
|---|---|
| L | States that the pages locked in memory |
| N | Signifies the process as a low-priority task |
| W | A process with no resident pages |
| < | Signifies the process as a high-priority process |
| START | States the process start time |
| TIME | The amount of CPU time the process has taken up |
| COMMAND | The command itself, its name, and its arguments |

# Defining ps variables

The preceding definitions are based on the sample output in Listing 7.1. In the last line of Listing 7.1, you can see that the ps auxww command listed in the last field is the command that requested the process that generated the output. The process was executed by the user kjcox and was given a PID of 3384. It took up 0 percent of the CPU but consumed 1.1 percent of the available physical memory. The virtual size of the process was 2360 kilobytes. The resident set size, or amount of physical memory used, was 732. The process was run from a pseudoterminal located on another machine from which the command was issued. It had the identifying number of pts/7. The other terminals, or ttys, as listed in the ps output were issued locally on the Linux machine itself. The start time for the process was 14:14 hours, or 2:14 p.m. It used up 0:00 time on the CPU at the time that the snapshot was taken. It obviously did use some CPU time earlier, but when the ps aux command was executed, the process had already completed its required CPU time.

A quick glance through the other processes in Listing 7.1 finds that the main system processes all begin with a PID less than 10. The output also shows what day the machine was started. Once a process has been alive for more than 24 hours, the output simply states the day that the process began rather than the hours it has been alive. Most of the processes are also in a sleep state. This is the default state when processes are not executing instructions. All the processes required to operate a Linux system do not need to run continuously and there can be lag times. During these periods of inactivity, they enter a sleep state until they are called again to perform their task.

# Narrowing Down Process Searches

Because each Linux box can run more processes than a single terminal window can display, the method of displaying all the processes and then scrolling through all the entries is to invoke the pipe (|) command along with the more or less options. Here's an example command:

```
ps aux | more
```

This command enables you to press either the space bar or the Enter key to paginate through all the entries. The pipe command is very versatile and allows you to use other functions as well for locating specific processes.

If you want to verify that your Web server is in fact running, you can use the ps command along with the grep command in conjunction with the process in question. You would input the ps command along with any options and then pipe it through the grep command, which then looks for any httpd processes. httpd is the Web daemon that runs most Web servers.

---

**NOTE**

The grep command is a very handy tool to learn and use. This search feature matches the input following it to a specific directory or file. It can locate a specific instance of the word following it. Red Hat Linux also comes with a related program called rgrep, or *recursive grep,* that will sift through a directory and subdirectories to find the file or string of words in question. For now, you need only understand that you can use grep to find a particular process.

---

```
# ps aux | grep http
    root     32094  3.5  1.9  2384 1220 ?        S    22:03   0:00 httpd
    nobody   32097  1.0  2.0  2556 1296 ?        S    22:03   0:00 httpd
    nobody   32098  0.0  2.0  2556 1296 ?        S    22:03   0:00 httpd
    nobody   32099  0.5  2.0  2556 1296 ?        S    22:03   0:00 httpd
    nobody   32100  1.5  2.0  2556 1296 ?        S    22:03   0:00 httpd
    nobody   32101  0.0  2.0  2556 1296 ?        S    22:03   0:00 httpd
    nobody   32102  1.0  2.0  2556 1296 ?        S    22:03   0:00 httpd
    nobody   32103  0.0  2.0  2556 1296 ?        S    22:03   0:00 httpd
    nobody   32104  0.0  2.0  2556 1296 ?        S    22:03   0:00 httpd
    nobody   32105  0.5  2.0  2556 1296 ?        S    22:03   0:00 httpd
    nobody   32106  0.5  2.0  2556 1296 ?        S    22:03   0:00 httpd
    root     32108  0.0  0.6  1148  400 pts/3    S    22:03   0:00 grep
http
```

The output is verbose. It lists the parent process of httpd as owned by root and then all child processes as owned by nobody. You can use ps again to narrow down the list of processes to just that of the parent process:

```
ps aux | grep http | grep root
```

Now you are looking for only those http processes that are owned by root. The output will be much more limited:

```
# ps aux | grep http | grep root
```

```
root    32094   0.0   1.9   2384 1220 ?      S   22:03    0:00 httpd
root    32125   0.0   0.6   1148  400 pts/3  S   22:11    0:00 grep http
```

In addition to listing just the parent process, which you can now manipulate as needed, the output also lists the grep command. Because the grep command also listed httpd as one of the components to its search, the command itself was included in the output. Knowing how to locate specific processes by using ps will come in handy later when you look at the possible signals that you can send to each process.

If you replace the aux option with the -ef option, the ps command lists the UID of each process. The output is a full listing of all the current processes, including the UID, PID, and PPID numbers. The following is sample output after running this command on a current system:

```
# ps -ef | more
UID         PID   PPID  C STIME TTY       TIME CMD
root          1      0  0 Sep10 ?     00:00:03 init
root          2      1  0 Sep10 ?     00:02:58 [kflushd]
root          3      1  0 Sep10 ?     00:00:30 [kupdate]
root          4      1  0 Sep10 ?     00:00:00 [kpiod]
root          5      1  0 Sep10 ?     00:01:26 [kswapd]
bin         240      1  0 Sep10 ?     00:00:00 [portmap]
root        287      1  0 Sep10 ?     00:00:02 syslogd -m 0
root        298      1  0 Sep10 ?     00:00:00 [klogd]
daemon      312      1  0 Sep10 ?     00:00:00 /usr/sbin/atd
root        326      1  0 Sep10 ?     00:00:00 crond
root        340      1  0 Sep10 ?     00:00:00 inetd
root        354      1  0 Sep10 ?     00:00:00 [snmpd]
root        368      1  0 Sep10 ?     00:00:01 named
```

Here the UID column shows the username of the process's owner. The PID field is the process ID, and the PPID column lists the PID of the parent process. The C field shows CPU scheduling information. Though this field is all zeros due to the lack of active processes on my own system, Linux will allot varying amounts of CPU activity to each process based on its importance. Again, the STIME column states the time the process was started, and the TTY field shows the name of the control terminal. In this sample output, the TTY field lists a question mark either because the program is not associated with a specific control terminal or because the process does not require a terminal to start. The latter is the more likely scenario since no user intervention within a terminal was required to start the process. The TIME column displays the amount of time that the process has been running, while the last field, COMD, is the command that runs the process along with any options entered with the command.

A variation on this same theme would be to add the -1 option to the ps -ef command. This option also displays the process flags and the process status. Here is a sample of the same command with the -1 flag included:

```
# ps -efl | more
      F S UID      PID    PPID    C  PRI  NI ADDR   SZ WCHAN  TIME      CMD
    100 S root     1      0       0  60   0   -    274 do_sel 00:00:03  init
    040 S root     2      1       0  60   0   -      0 bdflus 00:02:58  [kflushd]
    040 S root     3      1       0  60   0   -      0 kupdat 00:00:30  [kupdate]
    040 S root     4      1       0  60   0   -      0 kpiod  00:00:00  [kpiod]
    040 S root     5      1       0  60   0   -      0 kswapd 00:01:26  [kswapd]
    140 S bin      240    1       0  60   0   -    272 do_sel 00:00:00  [portmap]
    040 S root     287    1       0  60   0   -    318 do_sel 00:00:02  syslogd
-m 0
    140 S root     298    1       0  60   0   -    346 do_sys 00:00:00  [klogd]
    040 S daemon   312    1       0  60   0   -    278 nanosl 00:00:00
/usr/sbin/atd
    040 S root     326    1       0  60   0   -    321 nanosl 00:00:00  crond
    140 S nobody   32105  32094   0  60   0   -    639 posix_ 00:00:00  [httpd]
    140 S nobody   32106  32094   0  60   0   -    639 posix_ 00:00:00  [httpd]
    140 S root     371    5456    0  60   0   -    910 do_sel 00:00:00  smbd -D
```

To fit the newer fields on the screen, the output omits the STIME and TTY columns. Now the F field, listing the process flags, is visible in the first column. The second column, S, holds the process status. In this case, all the processes are sleeping. Because you included the extra flag at the command line, the output also lists the UID, PID, PPID, and C fields as before, but adds a couple of extra fields. The PRI field shows the scheduling priority, while NI shows the nice value for each process. As is the default, zero is standard for nearly all processes for the NI field. As mentioned earlier, 0 is the middle or neutral value for all processes. The ADDR column is the memory address of each process. The SZ field lists the size in pages of the process in the main memory. The WCHAN column shows the address of the object that the process is awaiting. The last two fields are fairly explicit; TIME and CMD show the time that the process has consumed and the command in its entirety.

Possibly the most important aspect of each of these commands is that the output enables you to identify the running process and its PID. After ascertaining the PID, you can then send that running program a signal and either change its value or cause the process to reread its configuration or slay the process altogether.

# Controlling Rampant Processes

Generally, a process runs amok because the parent process did not create the child process correctly or the child creation process got out of hand. Take, for instance, an incorrectly spawned child process that does not receive a kill signal after the parent dies. If left to its own means, the child process can sometimes start to take up more memory and then quickly consume all available memory. Although I have seldom seen it happen under system processes, an improperly written program sometimes will allow the parent to die but not the children. Some of the consequences can be an out-of-control process that prevents any other programs from starting and that thwarts any user interaction with current programs or causes the system to lock up completely. (Such processes rarely if ever cause the system to lock up completely; if this occurs, you can usually address the problem by logging in and then quickly slaying the process. Only once in the six years I have used Linux have I ever locked up my box so badly that it required a reboot, and that was due to my own ignorance and a poorly written program.)

One real-life example of a rampant process that does not adversely affect the system, but that can cause minor inconvenience, is the sendmail daemon. When initiated properly, this can be the most stable of all programs. Sometimes, however, users can surpass the limits of slow hardware and make excessive requests of the process. The sendmail daemon creates child processes that handle individual mail requests. If the forking process gets out of hand or if the parent process does not create child processes properly, each child process will continue to run and not die after completing its task. This happens when the daemon receives repeated requests to send mail faster than the daemon can initiate the child processes. The system can quickly become bogged down with older processes that have completed their tasks but have not died.

When this happens, it is best to slay all pertinent processes and start over. Issuing **killall** or the **kill -9** command only for those processes identified as belonging to a certain parent process will cause all programs or functions with that name to be killed. For example, the following command would kill any sendmail processes if a parent or child process got out of hand. All jobs with the sendmail name are deleted from the system.

```
kill -9 'ps aux | grep sendmail | awk '{print $2}''
```

### NOTE

The character preceding the ps command is called a back-tick or grave accent mark. This character appears most commonly under the tilde (~) character in the upper-left corner of a keyboard. It is not to be confused with the single quotation mark.

This command is actually a series of commands using grep and awk. As the command parses through the list of all running processes, grep and awk extract all processes that are identifiable as those belonging to sendmail. These include both the parent and child processes. All these identifiable processes are then killed. To restart sendmail, you must restart the parent process.

## Determining System Use and Users

Another useful command to be aware of is uptime, which prints out the time Linux has been up, the system load, and the number of users logged in. The following is sample output from a system at work. This system is the office mail server, so it must run for long periods of time without crashing.

```
[kjcox@mail kjcox]$ uptime
 8:40pm  up 46 days, 5:27, 2 users, load average: 0.25, 0.11, 0.03
```

The uptime command will become a familiar feature to Linux users as they each compete for the maximal amount of extended use on one system. Linux users pride themselves on the amount of time they can keep a Linux system operational without a reboot. How long it will run without requiring a shutdown command depends largely on the programs running and the type of user. I have heard of several Linux machines that have had uptimes exceeding a year. Some administrators who use Linux as a print or file server disable the power switch so that uneducated users will not mistakenly power off the machine, as they have become accustomed to doing with other systems.

Though the uptime command's output does display the number of users on that particular machine, it does not give any additional information about who specifically is logged in. For information regarding whom is logged in, use the commands who or w. The latter command, w, generally produces more verbose output. It displays the terminal number, the login time, the machine on which the user logged in, the amount of time the user's session has been idle, and the currently running command. The command who's output will show the user-name and the terminal number.

The commands who and w can assist you in determining how many remote users are using the system as well. This helps when you need either to reboot the machine or power it down for an upgrade. If there are many users logged on, you might want to wait and power it down later. If you are in a hurry to power it down, then consider using the wall command, which sends a quick broadcast message to all users logged in. Simply enter **wall** followed by the message, and that text will appear in their terminal window.

If I wanted to let everyone know I was shutting down the system in five minutes, I would use wall as follows. The message would appear in my terminal window as well as the terminal window of the other users on the system.

```
[kerry@pluto kerry]$
Broadcast message from root (7) Sat Aug 26 14:50:53 2000...
The system will be shut down in 5 minutes.
```

If a user does not have a terminal window running, (a distinct possibility as newer users are increasingly moving to X Window environments) he or she will still receive the message but it will be at a console window they may not normally see. If this is the case, you may want either to reschedule the time or simply take the more abrupt route and kill that user's connection. Sometimes it is better to ask forgiveness than permission.

## CAUTION

I do not condone simply pulling the plug on anyone's session, as the user might be in the process of editing some important file. However, if you are facing an emergency, killing the connection might be the only alternative. Try either to talk to the user in person or to send that user a talk request, if the talk feature is enabled on your system. Administrators who simply kill users' connections will not be highly regarded.

I have had to kill user connections in the past, especially when an uninvited user had logged in to one of our less guarded machines. In such situations, the ps command comes in handy. If the ps command's output uncovers a process that appears to be running either by an unknown user or by an unidentified process, the UID is the best way to track down the culprit.

If I have proven that joe is an unwelcome guest or that the user is running an undesirable process, here is how I would look for user joe on the system, locate his login shell's PID number, and then simply kill it:

```
ps aux | grep joe
```

Make certain it is the login shell's PID you kill and not simply a PID of that user's programs.

Depending upon the output I receive, I could then send the kill signal to the PID. This would terminate that user's connection. When caught doing things on the system that they should not be doing, most users simply go away. However, others may come back with a vengeance. Know what processes should and should not be running on your system. For further discussion of Linux security, see Chapter 19.

Each system behaves differently under different loads. On slower systems running X Window, the entire system may slow down, while other machines might be able to handle the GUI much better than others, even though they are only slightly more powerful. Also, some programs leak memory and can quickly fill up the swap space on any given machine. Older versions of Netscape are notorious for doing just that.

---

**TIP**

You can monitor the load placed on a system by using uptime. However, this command's output provides a poor indication of the present load since the loads displayed state only certain periods of time and do not accurately reflect the current status. A command such as top displays the ever-changing status of the system load.

---

Once the swap space on a Linux machine is filled, the machine's performance will deteriorate. Hunt down and terminate any programs that are consuming the swap space. Lack of space can affect your machine's speed and substantially increase the load on the resources. Careful monitoring of running programs will keep you informed as to what is acceptable to run and what should be avoided. For example, prolonged use of the Netscape Communicator program will result in increased swap space consumption. Once the Netscape program is shut down swap space returns to normal levels.

## Monitoring a System's Load Using top

The top command does not show the current system state in a static format. Unlike ps, which simply takes a snapshot of your system at the moment the command is issued; top gives you a real-time analysis of all processes running at any given moment. The default refresh time is five seconds, but you can modify this setting depending upon how often you need updates. You change the refresh time as follows:

```
top d10
```

The *d* sets the next number as the interval between refresh screens in seconds.

While top can be considered more memory-intensive than ps on systems with limited physical memory, you may use it as a secondary process to better track down rampant processes. This can further bog down the system if too many too many processes are running or if one process is already out of control. Its primary purpose is for debugging the system. The top command can also quickly show you what process might be out of control along with the necessary PID in order to shut the process down.

A nice feature of top is that it automatically updates itself. You can have a version of top running continuously in the background if constant supervision of the system is preferred or required. Be mindful that top is more CPU-intensive than that of ps. If you require an updated display of all processes on the system every few seconds, you may want to either lengthen the refresh times or run it periodically. This is yet another instance where you can set the nice value of a program quite low.

Figure 7.1 shows sample output of top as seen in a regular term window.

Like other commands, such as uptime and ps, top displays processes, system load, and the amount of time the system has been running. In fact, the very first line of top's output is identical to that of uptime. But the output also displays information not seen elsewhere. The top command's output states the exact number of processes and breaks them down in terms of those sleeping, actively running, zombied, and stopped. These figures are subject to change depending upon the number of programs running or the power of the CPU.

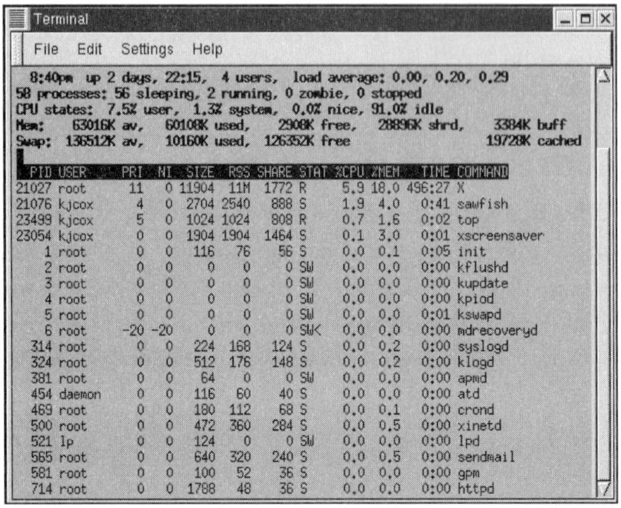

**FIGURE 7.1**

*The top command's output lets you view not only the amount of time a system has been up, but also a running total of processes and their load on the system.*

Next, top's output displays the amount of CPU usage in the kernel. The output displays this as the percentage of the CPU that is in use by both the user and the kernel; the output also indicates the percentage of the CPU that is idle. This information can be useful if you are determining whether a problem lies with a user's configuration or with the system itself. In the case of a daemon run amok, the system load would be much greater than that of the user's utilization of the CPU.

The last few lines show the memory usage. Memory is normally divided between physical memory and swap memory. These lines show how much is normally available, how much is used, and how much is free. They also state the amount of shared and buffered memory on the system's physical memory and the cached amount of physical memory currently being used by the buffer cache, i.e. caching disks.

The top command is a very practical utility to use when you are monitoring the processes currently running on a Linux machine. It provides ample information for determining the cause of system problems and can also render details about other processes that may need to be managed. The program will continue to run until you press the q key to quit.

Normally, top will sort the processes in order, with the most CPU-intensive process placed at the top. But you can also sort by memory and/or CPU use. The program automatically refreshes the screen every few seconds. A couple of the more frequently used options associated with top are sorting the output by either memory, typing M in the top display, or sorting by processor use, by typing P in the window. If you need to know the additional options that top accepts as input, entering a simple help query or pressing the h key will bring up a display that shows the various possibilities.

# Recognizing Commonly Used Signals

Signals are used to manipulate the processes either running or sleeping on the system. They enable users to tell the process to either drop what it is currently doing and do something else, or to reread a currently running file or process. The kernel handles some signals, such as kill -9, while others are managed by the program that first initiated the process. Most often the SIGHUP or HUP signal will make a daemon re-read its configuration files, but that is not always the case for some daemons. In either case, there are many types of signals. Each is used with the kill command.

You can use one of two methods to send signals to the system: either as a numeric value such as a -1 or a -9, or as a written request such as the hangup signal or -HUP command. This book will explore only a few signals closely. Most users need to know only a couple of signals FOR normal daily use, the -1 and -9 signals being the most frequently used.

Table 7.1 lists some of the more generic signals, along with their numeric value, their names, and their actions. The numbers in boldface do not apply to every system, including the various distributions of Linux, so it is possible that these signals will have different numbers than those listed.

A kill signal sent as -1 can also be sent as a -HUP command. As shown in the table, above every numbered kill command also is a name that can be used in lieu of the numbered command. When sending a signal to a process there are two elements that are needed to properly modify the process: the order (here the kill command), and the action (either a number or a signal name). A -1 or -HUP command will cause the program to reread its configuration files. It sends a hangup command, signaling the process to restart. This command is useful when you are changing configuration files such as httpd.conf for the web server and then want the server to reread the new configuration without stopping and restarting the daemon itself.

You can also slay any pesky process that is disrupting the system or that has stopped. To do so, you issue the **kill -9** command with the process's PID

**Table 7.1  A Brief Summary of Signals Used by the kill Command and Their Purpose**

| Number | Name | Description | Default Action |
|---|---|---|---|
| 1 | SIGHUP | Hangup | Terminate |
| 2 | SIGINT | Interrupt | Terminate |
| 3 | SIGQUIT | Quit | Terminate |
| 4 | SIGILL | Illegal instruction | Terminate |
| 5 | SIGTRAP | Trace trap | Terminate |
| 6 | SIGIOT | IOT trap | Terminate |
| 7 | SIGEMT | EMT trap | Terminate |
| 8 | SIGFPE | Arithmetic exception | Terminate |
| 9 | SIGKILL | Kill | Terminate |
| 10 | SIGBUS | Bus error | Terminate |
| 11 | SIGSEGV | Segmentation fault | Terminate |
| 12 | SIGSYS | Bad system call | Terminate |
| 13 | SIGPIPE | Broken pipe | Terminate |
| 14 | SIGALRM | Alarm clock | Terminate |
| 15 | SIGTERM | Program termination | Terminate |
| 16 | SIGURG | Socket in extremis | Ignore |
| 17 | SIGSTOP | Stop | Stop |
| 18 | SIGTSTP | Keyboard stop | Stop |
| 19 | SIGCONT | Continue after stop | Ignore |
| 20 | SIGCHLD | Child status changed | Ignore |
| 21 | SIGTTIN | Invalid read | Stop |
| 22 | SIGTTOU | Invalid write | Stop |
| 23 | SIGIO | I/O possible on floppy | Ignore |
| 24 | SIGXCPU | CPU time limit up | Terminate |
| 25 | SIGXFSZ | File size limit up | Terminate |
| 26 | SIGVTALRM | Virtual time alarm | Terminate |
| 27 | SIGPROF | Profiling timer alarm | Terminate |
| 28 | SIGWINCH | Window changed | Ignore |
| 29 | SIGLOST | Resource lost | Terminate |
| 30 | SIGUSR1 | User-defined | Terminate |
| 31 | SIGUSR2 | User-defined | Terminate |

number. For example, if Netscape gets bogged down or appears to hang as it sometimes does, you simply take the following steps to shut it down.

As shown in Figure 7.2, the ps command lists all the processes that carry the name associated with netscape. You can use either auxww or simply ax to list the processes. After the program prints out the necessary information, you can take the PID number of the process and kill it using signal 9. This closes any instances of netscape that may still be running.

## Running Commands Using nohup

One of the best ways to keep processes running, even after the shell or user who started the initial process is terminated, is to use the nohup command. Short for *no hangup*, nohup initiates the process and then keeps it running even after the shell is closed. Normally, when a shell is killed, it sends a hangup signal to all its descendants. Everything initiated by that shell or by a child process of children shells is also sent a hangup signal. If you start a program under shell A, for instance, once you log out or close shell A and initiate shell B, the process started under shell A will also be killed.

You can start a program and free up a shell simply by placing an ampersand (&) at the end of the input entered at the command-line. That tells the program to run only while the initial shell is kept open. If the terminal window is closed, then the program will also be killed. This is not true of cases where a shell initiates a daemon process, which then is independent of any shells. It applies only to programs that are started under the command line and are shell-dependent.

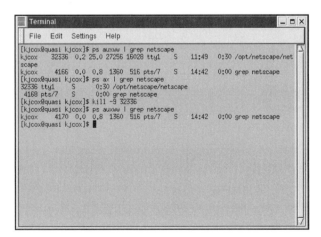

**FIGURE 7.2**

*This screenshot shows two different methods used to display the active Netscape process. Once I identified the PID, I killed it using the -9 signal.*

Suppose that I want to start bigprogram from a terminal window. The best way to start the program and still have control over the terminal—that is, to keep bigprogram from controlling the command line so that I can run additional commands—is to start the program with an ampersand at the end. For example:

```
[kerry@pluto kerry]$ ./bigprogram &
```

If the program is located in the current directory, this command initiates the program. This command returns control of the command line to me so that I can continue entering information or executing additional commands. But, if I then close this window or exit this terminal, the program would also stop.

If I first enter the command nohup, as follows, the program continues running even after exiting:

```
nohup bigprogram &
```

Any output that the program generates would be placed in a file called nohup.out located in the same directory. In that file, you can verify that the program started cleanly and is fully functional. Running a tail command on the nohup.out file will show any additional output that the program might otherwise display to the command line as if it were running from a shell. Lastly, to confirm that the program is functional, run a ps command and then use the grep function to single out the program. As many Linux administrators would say, "you *grep* out the program" in order locate the item in question. Then you can verify that the program started cleanly and is still running.

I use the nohup command with programs such as monitoring tools that must always run, yet must be initiated from the command line. I may not always be able to keep that terminal open or be logged in as myself. Thus enters the functionality of the nohup command. The nohup command is especially useful when I need to log on to the server at work either to check on a process or to restart another process after making changes to the configuration.

# Conclusion

Now that you can see the processes running under Linux and can also manage them all either by killing them outright or by restarting them, you can next start looking at scheduling tasks and cleaning up remnants for older processes. The next chapter will examine cron jobs and how they can automate much of the system operations. You can also use tools such as cron to organize and save files for later use.

# Chapter 8

## Cleaning Up

**L**inux is designed primarily to function as a server, and as such, there are many tasks a Linux system must perform throughout the day. Even the best administrators cannot always remember to perform these tasks or have the time to accomplish them. Linux provides a way to complete such jobs automatically. The cron daemon provides not only the administrator but also every user on the system with a utility to automate chores and duties. These jobs include updating lists, rotating logs, and clearing out unnecessary or obsolete files.

This chapter will cover the following topics:

◆ Understanding what cron does

◆ Executing the crontab editor

◆ Clarifying the syntax for scheduling events

◆ Cleaning up the system

◆ Saving files for later use

# Scheduling Maintenance with cron

*Cron jobs*, or background processes that perform automated tasks silently without user intervention, are one of the many benefits that Linux users enjoy. A cron job frees the administrator from daily, weekly, and even monthly mundane tasks. Any task that performs system maintenance or requires any undue amount of typing or is repetitious in nature can be transferred to the cron daemon, which will perform that operation at the required time. This is especially useful for non-interactive duties that do not require the user to input commands or monitor the system interactively. This daemon is especially useful for late night tasks or jobs where the user does not need to be present, whether physically connected at the terminal or logged in remotely.

Red Hat Linux uses the cron program as refined by Paul Vixie. Now commonly known as the *Vixie Cron* package, it offers more security features and greater functionality than older UNIX cron programs. Here are just a few of the options that Vixie has added to this program:

- ◆ You can specify months and days of the week as names and not just as numbers.

- ◆ You can shorten these names to an abbreviated form, such as mon, tue, jan, and feb.

- ◆ You can add *step values,* or specific time frames, to amounts by using a /*n* suffix. Thus, 6-22/2 means that it will run the program from 6 A.M. until 10 P.M. every two hours.

- ◆ You can also define environment variables in the crontab file. You can place the MAILTO command in any user's crontab file so that the results of the crontab run can either be mailed to a specific user or suppressed.

It is important that you send the results of a crontab run only to the user responsible for the task that cron handled. If others receive the mail, they can gain added insight into how certain root processes function or how others use the system. Though this is not necessarily dangerous, it is best to let users work independently of each other. The less they know about the other users, including root, the better.

## Defining cron's Purpose

Because the average user does not manage a computer 24 hours a day, seven days a week, and because there are tasks that need to be carried out at inopportune times, there is a distinct need for cron jobs. Without user intervention, aside from setting up the initial syntax and scheduling of events, the cron daemon will manage all routine checks, system maintenance runs, and backups when called upon at certain periods of time. (Because the daemon handles its tasks according to specific scheduled times, the word *cron* finds its basis in the word *chronological.*) You can set up cron to handle most requests that can be input on the command line. Any type of command that requires an sh shell and can be started manually can just as easily be started from a cron job.

When you are setting up any sort of cron job, whether it be system-intensive or a simple script that executes in a fraction of a second, you should schedule cron to perform standard routines in the evening or early in the morning, when user load is at its lightest. This is recommended in part to avoid conflicts with any programs to which users might need access during the day and because most system resources will be free to accomplish the scheduled task quickly. If a cron job is to delete older files or rotate log files, it is best to accomplish such tasks when no user is actively accessing the system or changing files while cron is manipulating them.

The cron daemon itself takes up few of the system's resources. However, depending on the type of program it executes, cron can either place a heavy load on the system or run silently without any user noticing its presence. Some routines can be run at any time of the day without causing any problems or slowdowns. If the routines handle simple backup and maintenance tasks that do not affect user files, you can schedule them for most any time without dire consequences. Tasks such as incremental or differential backups are safe to execute in early evening hours, whereas full backups are best left to a late night run. Try to avoid doing any automated tasks at peak hours. Any program that changes or updates system or user files during the day runs the risk of conflicting with user tasks. You can find more information on backups in Chapter 9, "Fixing Mistakes."

## Managing crontab Files

The file that controls the cron daemon is called the crontab, or *cron table*, file. It is a simple binary in the same location as most other binary files in Red Hat Linux, /usr/bin/. This executable creates the ASCII text file in which tasks are subsequently saved. These can be unique pathnames to other files, which are executable or files that contain multiple scripts which the system then runs. To execute the crontab command and edit your selection of files to run, you usually type the following:

```
crontab -e
```

The -e flag launches crontab into edit mode. The crontab file will apply only to the files associated with the user who started up the file; these files include not only those that the user owns but those to which he or she has access. The default editor is defined by the system. Red Hat Linux uses vi as its default editor.

If I execute this command as myself or under the username kerry, I will create a cron table for my own use. However, root or superuser can create or edit a crontab file for any other user, including root, by simply placing a -u flag followed by the username. If I, as root, still wanted to edit my crontab file, I would type the following command:

```
crontab -u kerry -e
```

This would bring up the crontab file created by the user kerry.

Though root can edit anyone else's file, regular users can only edit their own file. The fields and programs executed within the crontab file vary from user to user, but all users still must adhere to the same syntax that govern normal usage on any Linux machine. They can work only with files and directories that they either own directly or for which they share group ownership.

The file created by the crontab command is a simple text file thatis kept in the /var/spool/cron directory. Each respective crontab file is both owned and named after the user who created it.

If the users kerry and root both create a crontab file, a quick glance in the /var/spool/cron directory will show that there are now two files, one for each user. However, Red Hat Linux prohibits regular users from viewing the contents of these files. Only superuser can view the contents of its own and others' files.

As the following output shows, root can view the contents of the /var/spool/cron directory. Though the file kerry is owned by the group kerry, it allows only read and write permissions to the user, which is root. The same applies to the contents of the entire directory. Only root has read, write, and execute permissions.

```
# pwd
/var/spool/cron
# ls -la
total 16k
drwx------     2 root      root        4.0k Sep  2 14:05 .
drwxr-xr-x    19 root      root        4.0k Jun  8 13:49 ..
-rw-------     1 root      kerry        216 Sep  2 14:05 kerry
-rw-------     1 root      root         498 Aug 16 09:17 root
```

Though you can view each file with any text editor, it is recommended that you use the crontab command to edit the file and not do so manually. If you were to use vi and open the file manually, a warning message will state that you should configure the file only by using the `crontab -e` command. The crontab command creates the simple text file in /var/spool/cron, named after the same user who issued the command. In addition, the temporary file that is produced when you initially create the crontab file is kept in the /tmp directory until you save the crontab file. When you use the command, `crontab -e`, to open up the text file, you will also notice that at the same time a temporary file named crontab.xxxx is inserted in the /tmp directory. There is little chance any other users will be able to view the file's contents since the permissions are set at 600 and is owned exclusively by that user executing the file.

### NOTE

The crontab program operates much like sudo. You can technically open the /etc/sudoers file much like the /var/spool/cron/root file, but you are advised not to do so. Much as the configuration file should only be opened with the visudo command, the crontab file should only be opened with the crontab command.

Usually each user gets one cron file. If allowed, each user on the system can create his or her own crontab file and use it to manage tasks. The corresponding text file carries the owner's username. If you are migrating users from one Linux machine to another, you should also transfer the respective crontab files because much of the user's functionality on the new system will be based in its ability to run automated tasks via cron.

The best way to move a crontab file is simply to use ftp to send those files from the /var/spool/cron directory into the same location on a new machine. Be sure to set the permissions for each file to those of the previous owner. If FTP is not set up yet, you can alternatively use the tar command to back up the files into one large file and then manually move it to the new system. For more information on using the tar command and backing up files, see Chapter 9.

In addition to those crontab files used by regular users, there are also crontab files that the system uses. These are predetermined by each Linux release, since each version adds utilities that require automated maintenance. The file that lists what jobs are normally executed by the system on a regular basis is usually /etc/crontab. Here you edit the tasks the system performs and specify when cron will execute those duties. Listing 8.1 shows sample output from a standard Red Hat Linux install.

## Listing 8.1  A Typical /etc/crontab File Used by the System for Regular Maintenance

```
SHELL=/bin/bash
PATH=/sbin:/bin:/usr/sbin:/usr/bin
MAILTO=root
HOME=/


# run-parts
01 * * * * root run-parts /etc/cron.hourly
02 4 * * * root run-parts /etc/cron.daily
22 4 * * 0 root run-parts /etc/cron.weekly
42 4 1 * * root run-parts /etc/cron.monthly
```

The list of environment variables that appears at the beginning of the output is one of the added features that come with the Vixie Cron package. You specify the shell, path, and home directory for each of these tasks, and stipulate who receives via e-mail the results of the crontab run after the task is either successfully or unsuccessfully carried out. Each entry as listed in the /etc/crontab file points to a certain file that contains additional scripts. If you want the system to run a definitive task at a specified time, here is where you can also enter the script or modify an existing one to your liking. Users who prefer to rotate their log files at shorter intervals can find this specific system task in this location as well.

### CAUTION

Bear in mind that any additions to these files will affect the system globally, whereas each user's crontab entries affect only the individual's files. Exercise caution when changing system files. If you break something, certain logs and files may stop working. As a precautionary measure, always make a backup before changing any system file.

# Editing crontab Files

If you need to remove the cron files of a particular user, simply deleting the user's file from the /var/spool/cron directory is normally sufficient. This is useful if the user is no longer present on the system of if you need to lock his or her account.

Renaming the file also prevents the user from accessing his or her cron jobs. Usually, entering the `/usr/sbin/userdel -r` command is enough to remove any leftover files. It does not hurt, though, to check this directory after removing a user.

A good administrator should run a periodic check on the cron files used by regular users. This not only ensures the well-being of the system, but also verifies that the users are abiding by the terms of the fair-use agreement—a simple contract, whether written or oral, that the system will not be abused or used inappropriately. The best way to check up on what users are running is by logging cron use. Under Red Hat this is a fairly standard procedure. The cron log files are generally kept in the file /var/log/cron. Any text editor will print out the results of the past few days' or weeks' worth of cron files. These are also rotated periodically so you may have to consult renamed files such as cron.1, cron.2, and so on for older cron entries. A regular check to make sure the backups and routines are running correctly is also not a bad idea.

Administrators desiring to take a more proactive approach and be notified about the system's routines can also receive an e-mail from the cron daemon when the tasks it performs are complete. As mentioned previously, you insert a MAILTO value into the crontab file. Root is generally the catchall account for normal system cron jobs. But, as root, you can also insert the MAILTO variable into any user's crontab file and have the results mailed to yourself or someone else. Any empty MAILTO variable inserted into the crontab file will suppress all mail from cron. Though this suggestion may smack of despotism and not be condoned by the users themselves, I have found that some users will quickly abuse any freedom granted them on a system. As an administrator, you must be willing to play hardball when necessary.

If I wanted to have all the crontab results of the user `calvin` mailed to me, I would simply insert the following into the crontab file of /var/spool/cron/calvin:

```
MAILTO=kerry
```

Remember, to edit another user's crontab file, you must be root. To invoke the crontab file, I must enter the following:

```
crontab -u calvin -e
```

To suppress all mail from a particular user such as root, insert an empty MAILTO variable in that user's crontab file as follows:

```
MAILTO=
```

Red Hat, like many of the other Linux releases, runs cron jobs that rotate log files every week or so. These files can quickly become oversized and occupy more hard drive space than they are worth. The cron daemon rotates these files out by renaming them and then creating a new log file. After a certain time period, cron deletes these older logs. Log files will be kept long enough that any pertinent errors or tasks can be tracked. You can specify elsewhere just how long you want to keep certain log files. To find out more about how the system logs certain files, see Chapter 10, "Logging Errors."

## Customizing Specific crontab Entries

Linux has other system cron entries. These cron jobs are set up by default during the installation process and are best left alone. The location of these files is the /etc/cron.d directory. Much like the root cron jobs, which are user-defined, the jobs in this directory are system-defined. They deal mostly with the rotation of log files and a routine cleanup procedure to clear out stale files or crashed programs. If programs need to be run continually or transitionally to monitor files or programs, they might be placed in this directory. However, this directory is normally reserved for programs that install their own series of cron jobs.

Another cause for caution that might be encountered under older versions of Red Hat, but less frequently with later releases, is the use of the default text editor to edit cron entries. The crontab command defaults to vi as the standard editor for changing the cron files. This text editor is not recommended for newer users, as its learning curve is rather steep. Beginning Linux users prefer a more functional and familiar editor like joe or pico, which are considered user-friendly to new beginners and can be used like most any word processor. The text editor joe is a throwback to the old WordStar days, whereas pico runs like the Windows Notepad text editor and can be considered a simple word processor. Each editor has its own set of commands for saving and editing files, but the commands are simple compared to those of vi. Though more difficult to grasp for neophytes, vi is extremely versatile and has a myriad of editing commands and can be called upon to perform most any function.

To use another text editor such as joe or pico, you must export another editor to the terminal variables. You can do so by entering the following command at the command line of the terminal at which you want to edit the crontab file:

```
export EDITOR=joe
```

At the end of this command, you input the name of the default editor you want—whether joe, pico, jed, or another editor. To make the change permanent, you will need either to edit your own .profile text file or to make the change global for all users by editing the /etc/profile file. You can accomplish this quite easily. Simply place the following lines within either of the two aforementioned files:

```
EDITOR=joe
export EDITOR
```

The changes will not take effect for that terminal session until after the source files have been reread. To change the variables, enter one of the following possible commands. Although the correct choice may depend upon your system's configuration, reviewing each of these choices should help give you an overview of the process. Each of the following commands will update your terminal session and will utilize the editor you selected.

```
source /etc/profile
source ~<username>/.profile
source /home/<username>/.bash_profile
```

Changing the default editor can mean the difference between making a successful cron entry and quickly becoming discouraged and giving up. I have seen too many beginning Linux users turn away from reaching their full potential with Linux due to frustration with a text editor.

**NOTE**

One important item to be aware of with cron files is that cron jobs will be performed only while the system is up and running. The same is true for the cron daemon. If it does not start up correctly or is shut down sometime during operation, the cron jobs scheduled for that interval will not be carried out. If the system is brought down for routine maintenance or because of an error, be mindful that those jobs will not be performed during that time period, but will pick up the next time after it is brought up.

Once you have made an entry in the crontab file, the system will immediately start consulting that particular file. The time at which a program, script, or file needs to be run depends on your scheduling. You can either have it start immediately after entering you task or schedule the execution of the task for a later date, as much as a month later.

> **TIP**
>
> Be mindful of changes in time, such as daylight savings time, that might play havoc with some scheduling and can cause programs to run either twice or not at all. Red Hat Linux compensates for such changes if you specify them during the install, but it is best to double-check that your computer's time is in sync with standard time.

# Setting Correct crontab Syntax

The manner in which cron jobs are implemented is important. Even though jobs are unique to each user, they still share the same syntax. The cron daemon recognizes a specific set of instructions and uses them to run the jobs as needed. The basic format is first to lay out the time in which the job needs to be performed and then give the command. It is customary also to explain the function of each cron job by placing a commented-out line at either the beginning or end of the job. Comments are lines that you don't want the program to read, but which serve as explanatory statements for other users. You usually indicate that a line is a comment by marking it with a pound sign (#). When reading the crontab file, the cron daemon will usually ignore these lines or the words following any pound sign on the same line.

The standard syntax for creating a crontab entry is as follows:

```
minute     hour     day     month     weekday     command
0-59       0-23     1-31    1-12      0-7         /usr/local/bin/runme
```

Some older UNIX systems provide an additional field that inputs the username for a particular function. Generally Red Hat doesn't provide such a field, but instead confines itself to the six-field format. The user field is sometimes found in the system's own crontab file, /etc/crontab.

Only certain numbers can be used for each field. Fields are separated by a single space, whereas multiple numbers in a field are grouped together with commas. As is customary with most UNIX systems, counting begins with zero. The only exception, in this instance, is in the weekday field, where both 0 and 7 equal Sunday and 1 equals Monday.

Generally, a tab separates the time fields from the command field. If the desired scheduling is for every day, then an asterisk is placed in the field instead of a number. Similar to a wildcard feature, the asterisk represents all possible numbers.

Among other possibilities, a single digit is an exact match with a certain time or day, whereas numbers separated by a comma and having no space between them represent two different times or days in that single field. It is possible to have a wide range of hours or minutes in a cron job, each separated by a comma. Here is a cron job that runs every 10 minutes, every day:

```
0,10,20,30,40,50 * * * *          /usr/bin/backup_run
```

The backup_run script is executed every 10 minutes according to the computer's time clock. This execution occurs every hour, every day of the week, and every month of the year.

## Tailoring Tasks to Unique Times

Another possibility is to have a job run every hour at certain hours of the day. For instance, the same job could be run every three hours, and then only on Monday through Friday. This is how such a job looks when customized:

```
30 0,3,6,9,12,15,18,21 * * 1-5          /usr/bin/backup_run
```

The first field states that at the half hour, or thirty minutes past the hours specified in the second field, the cron job will execute the command. Linux typically uses military time instead of the standard a.m./p.m. separation, which can result in confusion on international systems. Thus, the command /usr/bin/backup_run executes at 3:30 a.m., 6:30 a.m., 9:30 a.m., 12:30 p.m., 3:30 p.m., and so on.

This example also demonstrates that instead of placing a comma for several integers, you can include a range of days by using the hyphen. The expression 1-5 covers Monday through Friday. You can also use a range of values along with a comma in a single field. Thus 1,3,5-7 is also a valid expression that specifies Monday, Wednesday, and Friday through Sunday.

You can also manipulate the crontab file by using the flags -l and -r. The -l flag prints out the contents of the specified user's crontab file. It is a quick and effective way to see exactly what a user's crontab file contains. Again, the root user can check any regular user's file by prefacing the -l flag with a -u and the username. For example, to see the contents of joe's crontab file, a superuser would enter the following:

```
crontab -u joe -l
```

Such usage is not a condoned practice, but when it comes to system administration, few things can or should be kept secret from the administrator.

The -r flag is a removal option. Rather than manually removing the user's cron entry in the /var/spool/cron directory, root can execute the following command to wipe out joe's entire crontab file quickly and easily:

```
crontab -u joe -r
```

This is a quick way to clean up files left over by a defunct or malicious user.

The command field does not always need to include the absolute path to a unique binary command. It can, along with the binary, also have several flags working together. You can create various commands and string them together by using the pipe character (|). Here, for example, is a sample crontab line that might be used to kill any stray instances of sendmail running at a late hour:

```
0 2 * * *     kill -9 'ps aux | grep sendmail | awk '{print $2}''
```

This cron job is run at 2 a.m. every morning and will kill any sendmail daemons it finds. The user can then have the sendmail daemon start up the next morning by entering the following crontab line right below the preceding one:

```
0 6 * * *     /etc/rc.d/init.d/sendmail start
```

This statement calls upon the sendmail daemon to start up promptly at 6 A.M. and to continue for the next 20 hours until it is killed again at 2 A.M.

If you want to be verbose in the method of starting the sendmail daemon, you could also type the following, which better demonstrates the use of flags and options in a cron entry:

```
0 6 * * *     /usr/lib/sendmail -bd -q1h
```

This statement also starts up sendmail at 6 A.M. as a daemon process and queues up the mail every hour.

The syntax and use of sendmail are covered in more detail in Chapter 18, "Sounding Off on Linux."

# Filtering Users

The cron program also provides a way to filter out those users who should be denied the use of cron files. This is a useful capability for administrators seeking to limit the amount of personalized jobs on a busy or congested system. The cron.allow and the cron.deny files specify who may or who may not use cron. In the Red Hat Linux distribution you may have to create them since they are not installed by default. The standard location for each is /etc/cron.allow or /etc/cron.deny. Either one or both of these files can be created depending on how you wish to manage your cron files. If you want to keep certain users from creating their own crontab files, create an /etc/cron.deny file and insert the names of those who should not be allowed to use or create crontab files. The same is true of those users you want to allow crontab file use. Insert their names into an /etc/cron.allow file.

> **CAUTION**
>
> Be aware that if the cron.deny file exists, you should not deny access to either yourself or root if you want to be able to edit the file later. If only the cron.allow file exists, you should allow access to your username and root.

The syntax for creating one of these files is simple. If you are using cron.allow, place the usernames of those users who may use the crontab command on one line, each separated by a comma. Certain catchalls may also be used, such as ALL to allow all users to use the file. In the cron.deny file, place those users you wish to deny access to the crontab command. Placing an ALL variable in /etc/cron.allow file in order to allow all users use of crontab may seem a bit redundant since everyone can use crontab by default. It is, however, a good habit to start since there are other files that rely upon both a *.deny and a *.allow file to know whom to allow and whom to deny access.

The order in which these files are read is also pertinent. The cron.allow file is read first and the cron.deny is read last. This is unlike the hosts.deny and hosts.allow files, which deny users first. Also, unlike the hosts.* files, the cron files can exist separately or jointly on a Red Hat box.

# Cleaning Up the System

One of the more useful tasks that cron jobs can perform is to clear out older files and delete unessential core dumps and the like. *Core dumps* are snapshots of the memory address of programs that have crashed. If a program dies, rather than simply giving the user a cryptic General Protection Fault or the ubiquitous "Blue Screen of Death," as many programs do under other proprietary operating systems, crashed programs under Linux leave a *core dump* or *core file* in the user's directory or the directory from which they were initiated. Core files are mainly useful for developers who are writing their own programs and who need to understand what went wrong. But for administrators, core dumps can fill up hard drive space and are not always needed. Running a cron job periodically that locates and removes core files can help keep the system clean and free of congestion.

Here is a sample command that you can place in your cron job in one of two ways. It takes care of removing old core files from your own directory.

```
find /home/joe -name core -exec rm -f {} ';'
```

This command looks only through the user `joe`'s home directory and locates and removes core files by running the find command. It looks for any file named core. It then launches the exec command and attempts to remove the file. The last few items are flags and options that are necessary to remove the file. The command is rather simple in its function but it accomplishes its purposes quickly and cleanly.

You can place this command in the crontab file using two different methods. You can first place the entire command with all its flags and options in the crontab file itself. Here's how it might look if you wanted the command to run at 2 A.M. nightly:

```
0 2 * * *        find /home/joe -name core -exec rm -f {} ';'
```

Another option is to place the command into a plain text file and give it a name. You might call the file core_remove and change its permissions to 755 so that you could edit it while allowing others to execute it. How you set the permissions is entirely up to you, but the file does need to be executable in some manner. Entering a simple `chmod u+x core_remove` command will also do the trick nicely.

When creating this file, be sure to use the proper syntax at the beginning. Usually entering `#!/bin/sh` on the first line is sufficient for any script. This tells the machine that the script can be run from the command line. If you do not specify this option within the file itself, the cron daemon executes scripts using /bin/sh by default.

# Removing Unwanted Files

Some text editors create backup files automatically. Such backup files have an extension at the end to distinguish the older file from the newly created one. The text editor `joe` does this by default by adding a tilde (~) to the end of every file altered. These temporary files help users who are prone to saving files incorrectly and who constantly need older versions for backup or restoration purposes. However, they also tend to fill up the hard drive, much like core files. Rather than having backup copies of every text file on your system, it is advisable to remove all editor-created backup files once a week. Running this job late on a Sunday night or very early Monday morning still gives you a window of opportunity to locate a backup file over the weekend or if you suddenly remember on Sunday morning an important file that you had deleted on Friday.

Here is one method of clearing out the older backups early Monday morning:

```
30 3 * * 1    find / -name *.bak -exec rm -vf {} ';'
```

This method adds the -v option to the rm command to make the results more verbose. Everything that the cron job does and all the results that it generates are saved and emailed to the cron job's owner. In this manner, the user can see exactly where and what files were deleted. Though restoring them may prove more difficult than deleting them, such an option is useful for tracking the files edited.

Where you place this file is also up to you. One possibility is to place it in a distinct directory that you can recognize, but which no other user can access. Not allowing other users to execute your scripts by setting the permissions correctly, such as changing ownerships and executing the chmod command correctly, is a preferable security option versus hiding the scripts. Placing scripts in a certain location is useful mostly for keeping track of custom files. As mentioned in Chapter 4, I like to create a /usr/local/scripts directory where I keep all my cron scripts. That way I can edit my crontab file and point to the script but not have the complete command visible to any other users. Here is how the second possible configuration might look:

```
0 2 * * *          /usr/local/scripts/core_remove
```

This configuration does the exact same thing as the first example, except the entire command is restricted to one file. With a script such as this, you can also have the program execute multiple commands, each following the other.

Here is another example script I use to monitor the progress of the news server I maintain. This script cleans up all the files every night and sends me an e-mail informing me that the task was completed. Here is how the script might look within the crontab entry:

```
# These are the cron jobs used to maintain the news server.
```

```
    0  0 * * *           /var/news/bin/news.daily dalayrm expireover
lowmark flags='-s -q -v1'
   43 7,12,17,22 * * *           /var/news/bin/ctlinnd -s reload
incoming.conf crontab
    0,10,20,30,40,50 * * * *           /var/news/bin/nntpsend
```

The first command processes all the old articles at midnight, while the second reloads all the incoming files. The last command sends out the new articles to all the feeder sites every 10 minutes daily. You could just as simply place all three of these commands within a file and run them as a single crontab entry.

## Saving Wanted Files

You can also use cron to create backups of important files. Depending upon how you perform your backups, they can either copy important files to a local partition on your hard drive or they can be run as a nightly cron job and back up data to another media source located on a remote machine. Consult Chapter 9 for more information on setting up backup routines.

For now, let's examine how cron can store files locally. Such a backup plan is especially useful in that it can be executed on a nightly basis to prevent a user from accidentally deleting an important file or corrupting their own data. Unless that user has root access it is unlikely he or she can damage system data. Measures such as those mentioned are implemented to protect novice Linux users from themselves. When you are running a machine that has many users logging in, it is always a good idea to have some sort of backup plan and manage the data that users share or access separately.

If only personal files need to be backed up nightly, the following example is one possibility for backing up the files. I like to place the backup copies on a separate partition in case one fails or gets reformatted in an unfortunate (and extremely unlikely) scenario. I usually copy the files themselves from my home directory and then store the backup files in another directory to which I have permission. Here's one example:

```
    0 3 * * *           cp /home/kerry/docs/* /usr/local/backup/docs/
```

This cron entry copies all the files located in my ~kerry/docs/ directory and stores the backup files in the /usr/local/backup/ directory. It overwrites the older files every night.

If you need to back up system files, the following routine will set up a hierarchy of backed up files. These are the virtusertables required by sendmail. These tables list all the virtual e-mail addresses of virtual domains hosted on the system. It really doesn't matter what type of files these are, though, as long as they make a daily backup and allow you to retrieve versions from several days ago in case a mistake was made prior to the last few backups.

```
 0 23 * * *    cp vmail.txt.4 vmail.txt.5; cp vmail.txt.3
vmail.txt.4; cp vmail.txt.2 vmail.txt.3; cp vmail.txt.1 vmail.txt.2; cp
vmail.txt.0 vmail.txt.1; cp vmail.txt vmail.txt.0
```

This routine copies the next-to-last (penultimate) backup of vmail.txt to create the most recent copy. In other words, version 4 copies over version 5. The older the file, the larger the number. Version number 5 is the oldest backup copy then. The same method of backup then happens in ascending order, where one version copies over a later version; for example, version 3 then copies over version 4. Version 0 is then the most recent backup of the primary file, vmail.txt. In this manner, you can have nearly a six-day backup of the file. This helps greatly if you discover a few days too late that an important entry was removed from the vmail.txt file; rather than exploring the backup media, you can quickly grab the correct entry and replace the appropriate line in the current file.

How you use the crontab file depends mostly on what you normally execute at the command line. Whatever you can do there can just as easily be accomplished in a script and carried out whenever you choose. By experimenting with different scripts, you will soon discover the best methods for carrying out tasks.

# Conclusion

Now that you can set up crontab files and automate simple tasks, you should be able to reduce some of your work load by allowing the system to pick up the more mundane, repetitious chores associated with system administration. You can start automating different tasks and configuring cron to perform these duties at varying intervals. The next chapter will deal with issues related to backing up needed files. An effective backup plan proves invaluable when you need to restore a file either lost or corrupted. You will learn what types of media are recommended for performing backups as well as easy methods of saving and restoring data.

# Chapter 9

## Fixing Mistakes

No administrator can be perfect and configure a Linux machine to do everything he or she wants or needs it to do. Add to this situation multiple users, each wanting to add his or her own files and performing different tasks on the system. Sooner or later someone is bound to make a mistake and either delete, overwrite, or lose an integral file. In cases like this, it is essential to have a standby plan for restoring or fixing the mistakes. As the saying goes, "an ounce of prevention is worth a pound of cure." However, with Linux you cannot always foresee what users or crackers will do to your system. Certain things are beyond any administrator's control. Therefore, knowing how to fix mistakes and perform restores is essential.

This chapter will cover the following topics:

◆ What to do to prepare for a backup

◆ What type of media you should use

◆ How to organize backups coherently

◆ What security issues to be concerned with when backing up data

◆ How to perform a successful backup

# Understanding the Need for Backups

Many people do not feel the need to back up data. These are usually regular users, not administrators. However, your job as a good Linux administrator is to guarantee the safety and dependability of your users' or customers' data. In instances where management does not heed the warnings of administrators, minimal effort or expense is granted towards preventive maintenance or investing in data backup and recovery until a crisis hits. Preemptive measures can prove a boon. Not taking any steps can be a recipe for disaster.

The true measure of a good administrator is one who is hardly ever thought of or needed. It's like most machines—you can tell it is a successful and dependable one if you set it up and never worry about it again. A Linux administrator is reflective of those boxes he administers. Always backing up data at regular intervals will ensure that you remain out of the limelight and consigned to uneventful obligations. This is actually a good thing. Nine times out of 10, people remember you when things go wrong, not when everything is functioning correctly.

## Worst-Case Scenarios

One thing that anyone who manages a Linux box dreads most is having to restore files that have either been compromised, altered, or deleted from the system. Such tasks can involve painful hours of attempting to relocate the original files or doing a reinstall in order to bring the system back up to previous specifications. However, you can avoid much of the pain of fixing these types of errors if you take proper precautions.

When I was at the University of Wisconsin–Madison, handling complaints or problems by faculty and staff, I quickly learned six important words in dealing with the most common issues: "Do you have a recent backup?" More often than not, the answer was "no." There is no excuse for not having a backup of all important files on any system. There is no magic to this, and a degree in rocket science is not needed. Even regular users should be aware of the steps needed to perform system backups. Understanding how things get lost is the first step to restoring data.

There are myriad ways that data can be lost or corrupted. Hardware glitches can cause directories to become inaccessible. A friend once had a coworker change ownership recursively on an entire partition so that suddenly all the files were then owned by the coworker. A simple -R flag wiped clean all previous ownerships of more than a thousand customers. The employee's mistake was not malicious, but simply the result of a simple typo. Former employees, though, are not above committing acts of grievance. With a few simple keystrokes, they can wipe out an entire disk. Such is the power of root. When incidents such as these happen, then it is time to recover data through the use of backups.

## Preparing for a Backup

Planning some sort of strategy before saving files is not only recommended but is also required. How you back up files will determine server performance. You do not want to increase server backups to the point of jeopardizing user accessibility. Not only that, but performing backups when others are utilizing the resources can result in corrupt backups and incomplete file saves. Depending on usage of files, some may require daily, weekly, or monthly backup. While you are writing data from the hard drive to some form of media, another user might be modifying that data. This happens all too frequently, resulting in corrupted data or the inability to read the data in the event of a restore.

You must ask yourself several questions when deciding what kind of backup to perform and how best to accomplish it:

◆ *What files do you need to back up?* Distinguishing between files that are only temporary, such as log files and files that are pertinent to only the customer or you, can make all the difference in creating an effective backup. You do not want to waste space on the backup media with files that would not be restored anyway, or that would be moot to all users if the files were restored. Most system files fall under the latter category since you can just as easily restore them by using the installation CD. If space, CPU cycles, and hardware resources are no object, then you may choose to back up all personal files and directories created by the users. This is yet another reason to place the system files in their own partition. If you do need to perform a complete restore you can simply reformat the partition with the system files and reinstall the operating system. Now you need only restore the files in users' home directories.

The file size should not be a concern. Sometimes even the smaller files are just as important as the larger ones, especially if they are keys or license validations for commercial software. If you are running Linux, you should opt for the open-source solution as well, but we recognize that the GNU community has not yet caught up with many programs available commercially. Still, even the smallest configuration file can be as integral to system performance as a several gigabyte database.

◆ *How often will the files that you are backing up change?* Do users make daily updates? If you are saving logs, how often are those logs rotated? Do you have a database that changes only periodically or does it undergo modifications continuously? If so, decide what would be the longest time frame between backups, or how much change will occur if a restore is needed. Would the users suffer from potentially losing all changes made since the last backup? If the files are changed only once a month, such as those found on a web page or static HTML files, there is no need for a daily backup. In fact, creating a daily backup might even cause more harm than good. If you keep a daily backup, you might soon have all the older media rotated before the user notices that he or she needs something restored from the previous month. Decide what can and can't wait.

◆ *Where are the files that you need to back up?* If you need to back up all the files in a certain partition, simply copying the entire partition to the media is far easier than attempting to cut and paste certain directories. With Red Hat Linux, which supports and encourages partitioning your drive for different directories, backing up a partition can be the easier chore. If your partitioning scheme selected many partitions—such as /usr, /usr/local, /home, and /opt—choosing only a couple of the partitions that contain important data is rather simple. You can omit a partition such as /usr/bin entirely since it contains mostly files installed from the install CD.

◆ *Who on staff is responsible for performing backups?* A tool such as sudo can grant limited powers to certain staffers so that the security of the entire system is not compromised. Having just one person manage a larger system can prove an impossible task. You can distribute the workload by allowing several people to control certain computers. Once the files are backed up, whether they are placed in a central location or kept in individual cubicles can also make the difference in how quickly the files can be restored. This leads to the next question.

◆ *How quickly can the files be restored to their original state?* If a problem is discovered and users need to access their files as soon as possible, decide how quickly the needed files can be located and placed back in their original location. Tape drives can sometimes take a while to locate all the necessary files, so users need to be aware of the limitations of the system. Other mirroring tools or RAID devices might provide immediate results. In cases such as these, it is best to make the restorative process as transparent as possible. Ideally, the end user should not even be aware that any changes have been made on the system.

◆ *Where will the data be restored?* It is generally not a good idea to place the files being restored back in the same directory from which they came. You might inadvertently overwrite some other files that did not need to be restored. If, for example, you were restoring the contents of the /etc directory, you would definitely not want to restore the files back into that same directory. An alternative might be to place them in the /tmp directory and then move the needed file(s) as necessary.

## Backing Up to Magnetic Tape

One of the most commonly used types of media for storing data is magnetic tape. Tape is commonly used for external storage. Keeping the data offsite after it is backed up is a good way to prevent loss of data in case of theft, fire, vandalism, or random acts of God. Restoring data becomes a simple matter if you keep good backups external from the computers themselves. If kept onsite, they can quickly suffer the same fate as that of the original equipment.

The recommended type of drive to use with Linux is a SCSI tape drive. Both external and internal drives work fine. It is important to consider using SCSI since the file transfer rate needs to be fast to back up the necessary data with the least amount of down time if you decide to perform backups or restores in single-user mode. Otherwise, performing backups while the system is running and users are logged in is called a *hot backup*—not the most effective method of saving data because users may change data while the system is writing it out to the backup media. Still, this may be the best choice for most administrators, and using the fastest media available is advised. Red Hat Linux recognizes and configures most SCSI cards currently on the market. If you are using the new configuring device, kudzu, Red Hat will detect your card and tape drive upon bootup. Nearly all tape drives are assigned the designations /dev/st0, /dev/st1, and so on, depending on the number of drives. The *st* stands for *SCSI tape,* and the numbers following it indicate the drive number assigned to the drive. When you are backing up to tape, you will refer to the device name /dev/st0, /dev/st1, and so on as the location for saving and restoring files.

Tape media is cost efficient. A 12-gigabyte tape currently costs about $20.00 U.S. There are several new distributors appearing on the market advertising large 50-plus gigabyte storage devices that easily interface with most systems. For a couple hundred dollars you can have enough tape to complete several days worth of backups for all servers. These tapes are also very easy to transport. The most common 8 millimeter or 4 millimeter tapes are relatively compact and can easily be transported from location to location. Their compact size also makes them easy to store in small, secure locations such as fireproof safes and lock boxes.

At my current workplace, I use 4-millimeter magnetic tape to back up data. Management needed an economical, yet reliable, solution. Several DDS2 Hewlett-Packard tape drives were available for use, so I commandeered them for use on the Linux machines. For only a few hundred dollars, I was able to deliver full backups for more than 20 Red Hat Linux machines. In the first month alone we executed three or four restores, which saved us countless hours of work after a couple of users mistakenly deleted important data from the web server.

However, magnetic tapes are vulnerable not only to users but to the elements. Due to their sensitivity, tapes should be kept away from strong magnetic fields. Even audio speakers contain magnets and can quickly affect a tape's quality. Placing backup tapes near speakers is just as damaging as storing them on top of the monitor. Tapes are also sensitive to strong heat and humidity. Keeping magnetic tapes in some sort of reserved box or container is probably the best solution. Store the tapes together in a secure location. They should be easily accessible, but away from the view of clients and visitors.

Another thing to consider when using magnetic tapes is that they have a limited life span. A tape has moving parts and as such can wear out more quickly than a CD-ROM or some other disk used for storage purposes. Not only do the parts wear out on a tape—that is, the gears become stuck or the case breaks—the tape itself is also rather fragile. You probably know of an instance where a cassette audiotape got stuck in a car's tape player. The crumpled and stretched tape did not improve its audio quality. The same happens to 8 millimeter DAT tapes and the like. If stretched or broken, the data on them are about as useful as data sent to /dev/null (which is referred to by Linux and UNIX developers as the black hole into which any input disappears). Any data sent to /dev/null is eliminated entirely from the system. /dev/null is the bit bucket that receives unwanted data. Unlike the Recycle Bin and Trashcan under Windows and Macintosh respectively, /dev/null offers no way to retrieve data sent to it. Keep in mind that tapes do not last forever but that the writing process and heat from the machine will eventually take their toll. Rotate new tapes in as needed. The average life span for a typical 4 millimeter tape is 50 to 100 backups or 2-3 years. After that the tape begins to stretch and lose its cohesion. Consider replacing tapes after this amount of use or time has exceeded, whichever comes first.

Also keep in mind is that it is possible to compress data onto a regular magnetic tape. Standard compression methods can double the storage capacity of most tapes. However, the retention rate for compressed data often leaves something to be desired. Compressed data are easily corrupted during the restoring portion of files, rendering those saved files worthless. For instance, accessing or reading the data will take longer since there is more information physically situated on the same length of tape; depending upon the software, corruption is a possible side effect. It is usually best to go with standard backup methodology and save the data in uncompressed format. Compressing data might prove frugal now, but in the end, frugality does cost.

## Backing Up to Removable Drives

*Removable drives* are disks that can be hot-swapped or removed from an operating system and replaced with other disks while the system is operational. These are standard hard drives or media that connect to a server prior to bootup and can be removed after the backup is complete. SCSI drives, for instance, can be connected while the system is running, the drivers then unloaded or reloaded, and the SCSI drive detected. Some of the newer RAID arrays accommodate swapping out IDE drives internally and then allowing the parity drive to reload the same data onto the newer disk. The transfer rate is extremely fast, and restoring can prove to be just as quick. However, most systems do not have the means of accommodating removable disks, and they are also expensive. The per-megabyte cost is much higher for removable disks than for that of tape media. While a smaller SCSI hard drive holding several gigabytes of data can run into the hundreds of dollars depending upon disk speed, the same amount of data can be placed on just a portion of a $10 magnetic tape.

## Backing Up to Zip Disks

Although not competitive in terms of storage capacity, disks such as the Iomega Zip and SyQuest disks have seen some use among Linux users. Generally these types of disks, resembling larger and thicker floppy disks, hold somewhere between 100 and 1,000 megabytes. Their cost ranges between $10 and $50 per unit. For most users who need to save only a limited amount of information, these types of disks are economical. Most use the Zip disks to shuttle the larger files back and forth between computers. Under Linux, you first must mount the Zip disks to access the contents as well as write to the disks.

Some people now argue that Zip drives and floppy drives, unlike CD-ROMS, and even tape drives, are now obsolete. They require special hardware and drivers and are still too expensive for the amount of data they can feasibly back up. But in their defense, Zip disks do have fewer movable parts and are less inclined to wear out than tape drives. They are built of much the same components as floppy disks and as such have a relatively long life span depending upon the care granted them. For smaller systems or where Linux is used in a workstation environment, Zip disks are a cheap and effective means of accomplishing minor backups. The hardware and disks now come standard on some prebuilt PCs.

## Backing Up to Floppies

As with Zip disks, newer types of floppies are appearing on the market. These new floppies hold between 120 and 200 megabytes per disk. If they catch on and the Linux community accepts these drives as a means to temporarily archive data, then perhaps floppies will survive as a storage medium. The latest kernel provides support for these types of floppies. They still have a few drawbacks; the media is slow to read and write input, they are costly, and their shelf life is less than a few years. You should probably not consider floppy disks, whether they are 1.44 or 100 megabytes, as viable long-term storage media.

## Backing Up to Writable and Rewritable CDs

Another backup medium is writable and rewritable CDs. In the past couple of years, these types of CD players along with the media itself have become much less expensive. Quickly approaching regular CD-ROMs in terms of both cost and speed, a good rewritable CD player can be purchased for under $200. The average unit can now run at four times or eight times when writing or burning to the disk, and most can now read information off a standard CD-ROM at about 20 times. The difference between a CD-R and a CD-RW lies both in the type of CD it uses as well as in the manner that it stores data.

CD-Rs are cheap and plentiful. You can purchase a blank CD-R for less than one dollar and can literally burn the data onto the CD. The laser within the player carves out notches in the surface of the CD, which then become a permanent record of the data. Once the data are etched on the CD, they cannot be changed or altered. The data create a lasting record for periods up to 20 years or more, though it is doubtful that any data would still be accessed in the same format that far in the future. This medium is good for keeping records of web pages, programs, or files that you anticipate keeping in a static state or not updating frequently.

CD-R quality also varies. Three standard colors represent the degree of quality of the CD-R. At the lowest end is the blue CD-R, then the silver CD-R, and finally the gold version. The difference in these CD-Rs lies in their quality, life expectancy, and performance under burners with higher speeds. The gold

CD-Rs supposedly have longer life and are more resistant to scratches and errors. They also hold data better and are not as prone to bad burns and thus becoming "coasters." If the data to be backed up require a long shelf life, then the gold CD-Rs might be the media of choice. Since most data are continuously updated, opting for the cheaper media is definitely more economical. Chances are the data will expire before the CD-R.

If the amount of data to be backed up is minimal, a CD-R can be used repeatedly, closing out each session after a backup and then opening a new session the next time. Eventually the entire 650 possible megabytes will be consumed; subsequently, the CD-R is good for retrieval methods only. Also, storing data that require certain read, write, or execute permissions on a CD-R is also not a good idea. As with the CD-R's counterpart, the CD-ROM, the data burned on a CD-R become read-only. Write and execute privileges are lost. You can recover or reset previous privileges on a disk drive, but the process can be tedious. If you wish to archive the data into a tarred and zipped file, the entire file can then be placed onto a CD-R disk, and when later uncompressed, it will retain earlier permissions. This does require that you back up all the files locally into a tarred, zipped file and then save them to the medium. Also, they cannot be larger than 650 megabytes in size. For backing up systems with a great deal of data, however, CD-Rs are not the best method.

CD-RW disks are somewhat more versatile. Because of the formatting involved in making CD-RW disks accessible, they can store about 500 megabytes of data and can also keep the same permissions as the original data. The disks themselves are slightly more expensive, ranging from $2 to $10 per disk, but they can be reused many times. Like a floppy disk, they can be wiped clean if after a certain period of time you would like to start fresh. The newer CD-RW technology appears far superior to that of zip disks as the latter is considered stalled both in development and in performance. Linux is quickly adding greater software and hardware support for CD-RW players and the technology used both to burn and save data. As CD-RW burners become more popular and as Linux continues to make strides toward better supporting CD-RW burners, look for them to also become standards in backup protocols for home and office use due to their ease in mobility between one computer and another, and in the cost-effectiveness of the CD-R media.

One of the problems with CD-RWs is that they are rather slow. Because their write speed does not approach that of a hard drive, you might sometimes have to back up the data onto the local machine using the CD-RW. Or, if the CD-RW is already attached to the machine that you are backing up, you might need to spend more time and system resources for the CD-RW to accomplish its task. SCSI CD-RWs are quicker and more reliable, whereas external CD-RW burners utilize the parallel port for transmitting data, and are cheaper and more prone to making coasters. The newer USB CD-RWs are also dependable, but until the 2.4.x kernel is stabilized and USB driver support is fully integrated, your best bet is an internal SCSI CD-RWs.

Another item to consider is that the software needed to operate CD-RW burners is still under development for Linux. There are already more mature programs available for Windows. However, I personally use mkisofs and cdrecord to create burnable images and then to burn the data onto a CD. They accomplish the task quite well, though the learning curve may be rather steep for some. It is all command-line based, though a quick perusal through such Linux software sites as http://freshmeat.net should turn up several GUI front-ends for both of these utilities. For more information on using mkisofs and cdrecord to burn data onto CD-Rs, see "Burning Data or Audio Files to CDs" later in this chapter.

Some people prefer to map their Linux machine to their Windows machine and back up the files this way. Samba accomplishes this task very well. NFS will also perform remote mounts when mounting Linux partitions to other Linux machines. Or, simply using an FTP utility will accomplish the same task just as well. However, if you use FTP, you will either need to run some sort of ftp daemon on the Windows box or sit directly in front of the Windows machine and perform your download there. Both of these alternatives are unattractive to the regular Linux user who professes some dislike for other systems. Samba and NFS are covered in more detail in Chapter 15, "Networking Linux," and Chapter 16, "Internet Connectivity."

## Backing Up to Internal Hard Drives

As mentioned previously, data can be written to or read from hard drives, whether they are local or external. If a hard drive is situated on the server itself, you should be careful that in the event of hardware failure you can still retrieve the data. Verifying the drives are interchangeable with other machines might be a worthwhile consideration since Linux will normally protest if it encounters a new piece of hardware when booting up in a different configuration than that to which it is accustomed. You can install an additional hard drive in the machine and use that drive for storage purposes. If the primary hard drive fails, you might still be able to mount the secondary backup disk on another system or within the same computer with a new hard drive. As the first two chapters explained, spreading the partitions over several physical hard drives is a worthwhile precaution.

## Using RAID Arrays

A RAID Array, though still costly for most uses, is the business preference. With RAID, depending upon the level you decide to use, you can organize multiple hard drives to perform mirroring tasks and can instantaneously take over the primary functions of the main drives if a drive crashes or if traffic increases. One of the reasons that a RAID Array is expensive is the hardware required. Most RAID Array require SCSI hard drives that normally are twice as expensive as a regular IDE drive. If you use proprietary hardware, that cost can easily triple or quadruple. But many consider a RAID Array worth the expense.

There are some newer technologies that can deliver RAID performance using IDE drives, such as what's offered by Promise Technologies. Also, the latest Linux kernel also supports software-based RAID so you can configure IDE drives to deliver nearly the same performance as that of SCSI. The cost here is much lower than that of SCSI when using regular IDE drive and optimizing kernel-based software.

Newer systems are on the market that support Linux and offer you speed approaching that of a SCSI drive, but do not require SCSI drives. Products such as Can of RAID and those made by RAIDZONE feature hardware such as Ultra DMA-66 IDE drives that run at 7,200 rpm, nearly equal to that of older SCSI devices, as well as the ability to stripe information across several hard drives. If a piece of hardware fails, you can quickly replace the part with one purchased at a local computer store. No data are lost, since the information is stored across the other drives as well. I use the Can of RAID device for databases at my office, and it works exceptionally well with Linux.

With RAID-5, it is not necessary to perform backups manually, though the same cannot be said of RAID levels 0, 1 and 2. Most of the archival work is done automatically and is transparent to both the administrator and the user. The system can be configured with a few simple scripts to perform any additional tasks or system specific tasks such as backups, mirroring drives, restoring files, and performing searches.

# Organizing Backups

Backups can be performed in varying degrees. One of the most comprehensive types of backups is a *complete backup*. This is exactly what the name implies: a complete backup onto the storage media of every file. Regardless of any changes or modifications since the last backup, a complete backup copies all files regardless of any changes or modifications made since the last backup.

There are some pros and cons to complete backups. They can be time-consuming and are difficult to manage when attempting restores. To restore just a single file, the administrator must look through the entire backup, which can be several gigabytes. Spending so much time reviewing a backup might not be worthwhile. Likewise, if the files remain relatively unchanged from backup to backup, you might waste system resources by archiving redundant files continuously. However, if users are extremely dynamic in their modifications and the files are constantly changing, and if a full backup does not take too much time, it might be worth the effort to perform backups often, if not daily. This is best left up to the administrator, who can best judge the utilization of the system.

## Alternating Strategies

If complete backups are overkill or if the contents on the system seldom change, then an incremental backup is recommended. The difference between these two types of backups is that whereas a complete backup writes all files regardless of their size or change date, an incremental backup backs up only those files whose contents have changed or whose time stamp is later than that of the last backup. The option of an incremental backup is valuable to users concerned with system performance and those who simply cannot afford to have the system down for extended periods. It is also a useful option for those who have limited backup resources. An incremental backup takes up much less space than a full backup requires and is appreciably quicker.

The basic syntax for incremental backups allots a backup level to differentiate between each backup. Although a full backup is given an assignment, designation, or backup level of 0, an incremental backup performed after a full backup would receive a designation of 1. This designation informs the system that all files changed since the previous full backup or level 1 backup should be saved. Likewise, performing a level 2 backup will save all files changed since the level 1 backup. A level 3 backup does the same and saves those files changed since the level 2. It is a common practice among many administrators to perform a full backup routinely at least once a week and then to execute incremental backups periodically during the week. The full backup is best done on the weekend, whereas maintenance backups or incremental backups can be done late during weekdays or early mornings. I often come in early in the morning and begin the incremental backups before many users come online. By the time most users are ready to check their first email, I have saved all changed files.

## Working with the at Command and cron Files

In addition to the incremental backups, another time-saving device is an automated or unattended backup routine. It cannot be stressed enough that with Linux, many of the more mind-numbing tasks can be automated and carried out with little or no intervention on the part of the administrator. Nothing is worse than being stuck at the office or in an equipment room waiting for a backup to complete. For many of the complete backups I had to perform, I found that one tape was enough to back up an entire server. Late in the evening on a Friday I would place a magnetic tape in the drive and would start an at job.

Like the cron command, the at command uses plain-text config files and thus is more dynamic and can be executed from the command line. This process waits until the user-specified time and then begins. The at command has its advantages over the crontab file in that it does not need to be edited every time a backup command is needed and that any administrator can quickly issue a command to start the process later and then simply head out the door. The typical syntax for an at command consists of at followed by the time at which the service needs to be performed. Then you input the command to be executed. You launch the at command by pressing Ctrl+D.

If I wanted to execute the script backmeup located in my scripts/ directory at 11 P.M., I could set up the following at command before leaving for home:

```
# at 2300 /usr/local/scripts/backmeup
# ^D
```

The at command is very useful for periodic use or when a single request needs to be executed. For more repetitious commands or redundant backups, the cron command is probably preferable.

One of the disadvantages to automated backups is that they leave the machines unattended and, if access to the servers is still fairly unrestricted, anyone with the proper clearance can seize the backup tape when it is completed. Though it seems juvenile or paranoid to suggest that you might not be able to trust your own coworkers, abuses have been known to happen. Someone might not have direct access to certain files on the system but could easily gain them if he or she grabs a backup tape or other backup media. Treat the media the same as you would the servers. Just because they are on tape, CD, or some other media source, that does not mean someone cannot extract the information just as easily or quickly.

Once you have decided how and when to perform backups, set up a schedule specifying when it is best to do the complete backup first and then the incremental backups.

Here is a sample schedule from my own routine that might be used as a template for others:

Sunday evening
Full Backup (Level 0)
Automated at 11 P.M.

Tuesday morning
Incremental Backup
at job at 6 A.M.

Wednesday morning
Incremental Backup (Level 1)
at job at 6 A.M.

Thursday morning
Incremental Backup (Level 1)
at job at 6 A.M.

Friday morning
Incremental Backup (Level 1)
at job at 6 A.M.

This routine works well for me since it does not require my presence to replace the tape manually. Though I do sometimes come in early to monitor the progress and make sure that the tape does not hang or stop midway through the backup, I usually can place the tape in the night before and set the at command to carry out its task the next morning. Because one of the main servers I back up requires about 4 gigabytes for a complete backup, it would take approximately two and a half to three hours for it to complete its entire process. That is why I do the complete backup on Sunday evening to Monday morning. Depending upon the number of users, I also sometimes bring the Linux box down to the single-user level to carry out the entire backup to ensure that no other users write back information. Normally Sunday evenings are quiet enough that I can complete the full backup automatically and do not have to be present to adjust the system.

The incremental backups usually take less than an hour and sometimes complete in just a half an hour. The duration also depends upon your computer's speed, the amount of data, and the system load. When I arrived in the morning, the backup would be complete, and the tape fully rewound and ejected. As mentioned, I sometimes arrive early in the morning to carry out the task manually and bring the server into single-user mode, but often a *hot backup*, or one that is performed when others are still logged in and while the machine is in multiuser mode, works just as well. The preferable choice is to execute a backup when all users are logged off and when there is no network traffic to or out of the machine. However, this may not always be feasible. Use your discretion when performing backups or attempting to perform a backup both ways. Restoring some sample files to check their integrity after the archive is a good method for confirming that the backup was a success.

How you set up your schedule will depend upon the previously discussed factors regarding the type of backups performed and the kinds of files that you need to back up. You should carefully monitor the system during the first few backups.

# Comparing Archival Programs

Currently a wide range of backup programs is available for Linux. More are being added to the collection each day. This section looks at just a few of the more established and popular ones. You should try several and decide which one best suits your purposes. What works for one administrator may not work for your company or network.

## Using the tar Command

When it comes to popular archival programs, open-source is probably the best known and most used. These types of programs form the standard against which most programs are judged.

One example of the open-source model is the archival program called tar. *Tar* is an abbreviation of *tape archival*. This method of saving files to tape is one of the oldest and most common ones. The tar program was developed to accommodate the efficient transference of files to tape and to other machines. The program stores files and directories in one single large file. It parses through directories recursively and pipes all the information into a single, "tarred" file. This is a highly effective way of saving tree structures and preserving ownerships of individual files. Most Linux users use tar not only for backing up files but also for creating one large file for redistribution.

One drawback to tar is that it does not preserve symbolic links by default. However, you can address this problem with a single additional flag or option when tarring directories or files. Such flags and options prove useful when you are attempting to move large directory structures from one partition to another or from one machine to another. Because the cp command does not by default move files recursively from a subdirectory to a directory, it is prudent to wrap up that entire branch of the tree limb into what is called a single "tarball." Then the cp command can easily move the new tarred file to another location, where it is untarred and creates the new directory structures.

◆ ◆ ◆

The best method I have found for using tar is as follows. Suppose, for example, that my home directory, /home/kerry, includes a subdirectory called docs/ and I want to share that directory and all its contents with a user on another system. The easiest way to accomplish this is to tar up all of the directory and its contents and then either email it or use ftp to send the file to the user. I would first use the cd command to change to the directory that contains the files or subdirectories:

```
cd /home/kerry
```

Next, I would execute the tar command first, then the flags or options, and tell the file the name and location of the new tar file and finally the directory or file that I wanted to tar. Here is an example of how I would execute the script:

```
tar -cvf /usr/local/backups/docs.tar docs/
```

The -c flag tells tar to *create* the file. In this case, the flag tells tar to create /usr/local/backups/docs.tar by reading through the directory structure docs/. The -f flag provides the name of the file to create. The -v option is a request to create the file in verbose mode so that as the program executes the command it will also print out the subdirectories within the docs/ directory as it reads through the contents. Next, I need to name the newly tarred file's location and give it a .tar extension so that both the system and users will recognize the file type.

---

**NOTE**

Be aware also of the –u or –update option, which appends to the archive file only those files that are newer than those already in an older archival file. This means that if you are overwriting an existing tar file, you need only update those files that are newer. I don't often use the –u option, but you might find it useful if you are tarring larger files or perform backups frequently.

◆ ◆ ◆

Another flag option that you should consider when using the tar command is the -p or --preserve ownerships feature attempts to retain all file attributes. The -p option will doubly ensure that all the files tarred will keep the same permissions and ownerships that they had originally.

If you forget to place the correct extension at the end of the tarred file, you can always rename the newly created file later and give it the correct extension. To verify that you did in fact create a tar file, use the file command against the file in question. The file command prints out the type of file that you will examine. If, at the command line, I entered **file docs.tar**, the output would be as follows:

```
docs.tar: GNU tar archive
```

The file command is extremely useful for verifying other people's files and making sure they are, in fact, tar and not executable files. It also checks files whose identity is not certain. Some people simply forget to place the .tar extension at the end, or call it a .gz file when in fact it is both a tarred and gzipped file. Whenever an error occurs when you execute the tar command, use the file command to determine the file's correct file type.

The preceding was a rather simplistic example of tarring up directories. You can do the same with files just as readily. The same commands apply, only at the end of the command you type the names of all the files to be tarred. Remember that when you restore these files they will be placed within the directory in which they are untarred, exactly as they were saved. It is good etiquette among users to tar multiple files within a directory; then, when the files are untarred, they will be stored in a new directory rather than strewn about in a user's home directory or temporary location.

The tar command is also extremely important when you are backing up files onto tape drives or other backup devices. The tar command is often used with tape drives. In my own experience with tape backups and Linux, I have used tar heavily as an archival method. The syntax is simple and backing files up remotely onto a backup device on another machine involves the same methodology as does using tar to back up files to local backup directories. Because I did not have a tape backup on my Linux box but instead used a tape backup that sat on another Linux box, I was able to move many of my files offsite and thus make the data more secure. Here is an example of the syntax I used when tarring up files from my Linux machine onto another Red Hat machine that had a tape backup device. In this example, I call the remote machine nihilo.

### Listing 9.1 A Sample Script That tars Up Files on a Local Box to a Remote Tape Backup Box

```
#!/bin/bash
# This is a simple backup method to save files.
# It saves files from my Linux box, quasi,
# to the remote box, nihilo.
# It backs up only those files I cannot easily replace.
tar -cvf nihilo:/dev/nst0 /home
tar -cvf nihilo:/dev/nst0 /usr/local
tar -cvf nihilo:/dev/nst0 /var
tar -cvf nihilo:/dev/nst0 /etc
tar -cvf nihilo:/dev/st0 /root
```

The option nst0 on the remote tape device tells it not to rewind the tape when it finishes backing up. This option enables you to place many partitions at the end of each partition backup. For the last partition, you omit the n option and the tape rewinds itself.

## Optimizing cpio for Older Backups

Similar to GNU tar, cpio is also a common method of backup by Linux users. Based on the cpio command of ATT's version of UNIX, this version of cpio can be used for transmitting files to older UNIX systems, some of which may not have tar. I often have been frustrated with older versions of Red Hat Linux, some from the 4.2 and even the 3.0.3 era, running limited programs or older kernels. I still use one of the first Red Hat releases running kernel 1.2.13, which does not support any of the new archival programs, but does have a stable version of cpio. It backs up the data well.

The cpio command handles files and directories much the same as tar does. Unlike tar, the cpio command does not copy files into one large file, but pipes the files into the remote tape location or to the other backup media. One of the more common practices with cpio is to copy entire file directories to other locations. You can do so using one long command rather than creating a single tar file and then moving it elsewhere and untarring it. The cpio command is often used with the find option.

Many different options and flags are available for cpio; the three main ones are -i, -o, and -p. The -i option copies files that match certain patterns and extracts them into a remote location. If you specify no pattern, then cpio copies all the files. You can use several other options with `cpio` and the -i flag. They are relatively standard and are similar to those used by tar.

The following expression is an example of cpio with the -i option:

```
cpio -i "*.bak" < backup.mydomain.com:/dev/st0
```

This expression grabs all the files from the remote tape drive that end with a .bak extension that are backup files. You can also use the following flags with -i:

◆ -d, which creates directories rather than placing the files into existing directories

◆ -f, which reverses the method in which cpio searches for files; that is, it grabs all the files not matching the expression.

◆ -v, which is verbose mode and prints out the progress of the command

The next flag is -o. Using the cpio command combined with the find command helps to save all the files that the `find` option locates and then pipes them out to the remote backup device on the machine named backup.mydomain.com. The -o option runs the program in copy-out mode or it pipes the output into a file rather than displaying it on the screen. The list of filenames is gathered from stdin. Here is another example:

```
find /home/kerry -name ".bak" -print | cpio -o >
backup.mydomain.com:/dev/st0
```

Here `find` looks in my own home directory and locates all the files with the .bak extension. After locating these files, the expression saves them onto the remote tape backup, or backup.mydomain.com:/dev/st0.

The last of the three options is the -p option. This flag preserves the files and their attributes from one location on the local machine to another directory also on the local machine. Again, this bypasses the creation of tar files and exceeds the old UNIX cp command's capabilities in that it recursively creates subdirectories. The latest incarnation of the cp command can now perform the same task and can also recursively create subdirectories. Using the `find` option once again, I move my /home/kerry/docs directory to another location the same system:

```
cd /home/kerry
find  docs/* -print | cpio -pdm /usr/local/backups/docs
```

This last expression includes some additional options. The -p option preserves the ownerships of the files, whereas -d creates the new directory in /usr/local/backups, and the -m option retains the previous modification times on the files so that they will appear never to have been touched or moved. Normally, without the -m option specified, all the files would receive a new modification time.

The cpio command has some advantages over tar, yet it is also limited in its use. Employing this program along with the others will help an administrator better determine which backup strategy best fits his or her needs. Rather than using one exclusively, you should use several together.

## Backing Up Mobile Media Using dd

The handy dd program is useful for copying smaller files from a hard drive to a device such as a floppy drive. It copies sector-by-sector to the device you specify, destroying any file system or data present on the target device. One such use is with boot images associated with the Red Hat Linux distributions. By copying the boot.img image as supplied on the Red Hat CD to a floppy, nearly any machine that can first read from the floppy device can also boot up Linux. Rather than first having to copy images to a Windows machine and then using rawrite on that machine, you can simply use the dd command to perform the same function on a Linux floppy drive.

The syntax for the dd command is very straightforward. For most dd commands, you need only give the command and then tell it what file to copy and where to place it. Here is an example for placing the default boot.img file onto a floppy:

```
dd if=/mnt/cdrom/boot.img of=/dev/fd0H1440
```

You can accomplish the same when saving files onto a floppy disk for redistribution. You can also use the dd command to copy any range of bytes, by specifying the offset to start at the length to copy. This helps when you require only a specific range of data and not the entire file.

## Dumping Data to Backup Media

The dump and restore commands are favorites for archiving data. The dump command is based on the Solaris ufsdump command, which dumps or pipes all specified files onto tape. Rather than creating a large file that holds the directory structure and its contents, the dump command literally "dumps" or sends all the raw data from the directory's contents onto a tape, to a remote location, or even back onto the local hard drive. Much like cpio, the dump command does not create a separate file before saving a file to tape. Unlike the tar and cpio commands, which can print the standard output to the screen while also writing those same files to the archive, the dump command writes the table of contents to the beginning of the archive. For this reason, dump's archive is more likely to list a file that does not appear on the tape. Likewise, if the file is modified during the backup process, the changes may not appear on the tape. This is one instance where tar and cpio have a distinct advantage over dump.

However, dump also has several advantages over tar. The dump command can span several tapes, whereas tar can only write to one tape. If dump's output exceeds the length of the backup media, it will stop the procedure and prompt the user to replace the first tape with a second, where it can continue the backup procedure. Dump can also back up files in the /dev directory and other files of every imaginable type. Symbolic links and devices files can also be restored as easily as any file created by a local user. The dump command performs incremental backups. To perform incremental backups for entire partitions, dump is the preferred utility.

The dump command reads the inode of each file and then determines when it was last changed. In this manner, it spans multiple tapes and offers incremental backup routines. The command does not necessarily look for the files themselves, but examines the locations on the disk that each file occupies and then determines the file's size and its archival method. This activity limits dump's performance. The dump command cannot span multiple partitions for backup purposes. To back up a specific directory, it will perform a dump only on the directory's partition. Thus, if you have created two partitions, one holding /usr and the other /usr/local, running the dump command on /usr will back up everything in this directory with the exception of /usr/local since that directory resides on a separate partition. Also, you may dump only those files found on the local machine. You cannot use this method to dump partitions located elsewhere, such as on NFS-mounted partitions, which do not reside locally on the physical hard drive but are only temporarily mounted. However, dump's hybrid counterpart, rdump (*remote dump*) can accomplish this task.

The dump command determines how far back the incremental backups go by using the /etc/dumpdates file. Usually when the command dump is issued, it is given together with the -u option, which updates the /etc/dumpdates files once the backup is complete. This file is readable by root and is found in ASCII text format. You can modify the file manually so that restores will read only those files that you want to back up. No special commands are needed to edit this file.

Because both dump and restore require access to the partition's device, root permission is usually required. For example, if performing a dump of the root directory in /dev/hda1, normally you only would have permission to that particular partition. Therefore, the dump and restore binary files are located in the /sbin directory, a location similar to that of the shutdown command and other high-level commands that are not normally found in root's path. I make it a practice simply to state the full pathname to these commands when executing a dump or restore routine in order to minimize the directories located in root's path.

You can run dump locally or remotely. In other words, you can dump files from the hard drive to an attached tape drive, or you can just as easily dump them to a backup machine with a tape drive. However, to dump files remotely, you need root access to the other machine as well. Linux provides a method for achieving root access on the backup machine. Years ago when most networked machines were run by trusted individuals and security concerns were minimal, developers created the .rhosts file. In this file you can enter the names of trusted machines that can have remote access to your machine. By placing the name of machine requiring backup in the /root/.rhosts file of the backup machine, you can grant a remote user root access remotely.

---

**CAUTION**

If you want to allow the machine quasi.mydomain.com access to backup.mydomain .com, you would enter the names of each respective machine—in this case, quasi.mydomain.com—that will be backed up into the /root/.rhosts file, thus allowing root read/write access to the tape drive device on the backup machine. You would also need to enable rsh and rlogin in the /etc/inetd.conf file on the remote backup machine. These programs are normally considered security holes and are disabled if internal security is an issue.

You should replace rsh with ssh and thus eliminate many of these security issues. However, rsh and rlogin will operate adequately if you are on a secure network— that is, if your system is protected by a firewall or you otherwise feel confident in your system's security.

> **NOTE**
>
> To keep all servers that require periodic backup onto the archival machine relatively secure, you can use the chmod command to set the /root/.rhosts file on the backup server to 600, thus enabling only the root user to read and write to the file. Both rsh and rlogin still represent a serious security hole, but only to the backup servers themselves.

You can specify several options for the dump command when setting the type of backup procedure. You must first indicate what level of backup you want to execute. Full backups usually take the -0 option. (Remember, Linux begins its counting with the number 0.) Once a full or primary backup is completed, dump will write to the /etc/dumpdates file, and when a sequential -1 backup is performed, dump will search through /etc/dumpdates and compare the files requested for this backup procedure. You can also change the block size, density, and feet of any type of tape when backing up.

Listing 9.2 shows the syntax that I normally use for a standard dump that backs up the entire contents of my Linux box. You can place similar coding into a simple executable script much as I have done in this example.

### Listing 9.2 A Sample Script Used for Backing Up Multiple Partitions onto a Single Magnetic Tape

```
#!/bin/bash
# Back up all the partitions
#
/sbin/dump -0uf /dev/nst0 -b 64 -B 4000000 -L "/" /dev/hda1 &&
/sbin/dump -0uf /dev/nst0 -b 64 -B 4000000 -L "/home" /dev/hda7 &&
/sbin/dump -0uf /dev/nst0 -b 64 -B 4000000 -L "/opt" /dev/hda8 &&
/sbin/dump -0uf /dev/nst0 -b 64 -B 4000000 -L "/usr" /dev/hda5 &&
/sbin/dump -0uf /dev/nst0 -b 64 -B 4000000 -L "/usr/local" /dev/
hda6 &&
/sbin/dump -0uf /dev/st0 -b 64 -B 4000000 -L "/var" /dev/hda10
# End of file
```

The -f option tells dump where to place the files. In this case, it is the remote tape otherwise known as device /dev/nst0 or /dev/st0. The n prefix simply informs the system not to rewind the tape once the backup is complete, but to continue with the next partition.

In this instance, I am using DDS-2 4.0 gigabyte tapes, which are more than sufficient for an entire backup of all pertinent data. If all the partitions are more than 4 gigabytes, you can limit the directories in a given backup routine. Or, you can allow the backup to span more than one tape. The dump command will prompt you for an additional tape once it has reached the physical end of the media and will continue its backup on the second, third, and fourth tape as necessary.

## Remotely Dumping Files

Performing backups to a remote machine is a simple matter of prefacing the device name with the remote machine name and a colon. The following example shows how to back up the directories of a domain name server or DNS server onto the remote backup machine:

```
#!/bin/bash
# Back up all the partitions on ns1.mydomain.com.
/sbin/dump -0uf backup.mydomain.com:/dev/nst0 -b 64 -B 4000000 -L
"/" /dev/hda1 &&
/sbin/dump -0uf backup.mydomain.com:/dev/st0 -b 64 -B 4000000 -L
"/var" /dev/hda5
```

I call the preceding script /dodump and have made it an executable file—that is, I used chmod to set it to 700, and have placed it in the / (root) partition of each machine that I want to back up.

Now let's closely examine each section of the previous script:

◆ The first section is the absolute path for the dump command. Normally, dump is not located in root's path. Hence, it helps to define the absolute path.

◆ This section is where you define the types of backups to be performed— that is, whether it is to be a full backup or an incremental backup. Because each full backup usually requires less than an hour to be completed, I like to do a full backup, or a 0 backup, each time. If time and CPU cycles are of the essence, you can do a level 1–9 backup, which will back up only those files that have changed since the previous backup.

The -u option instructs dump to update the /etc/dumpdates file after a successful backup. You can check this file to see when the last backup was completed. The -f option tells dump the name of the device to which it should transmit the data. From this device the dump command passes the dump data to the backup machine and then onto device nst0/ or st0/.

◆ The next series of options indicate the blocking factor. The -b 64 option specifies that the data should be backed up in blocks of 64 kilobytes. This is fairly standard and is required for larger tapes.

◆ The next option, -B 4000000, specifies the size of the tape. Normal 120 meter DDS-2 tapes hold 4 gigabytes of data uncompressed.

◆ The -L option allows you to affix a label to the partition you are backing up, hence the / suffix. This option is limited to only 16 characters, so I like to use only the partition name. This feature is a new addition to the latest release of dump. It came standard with the Solaris ufsdump program and has just now found its way to Linux dump/restore.

◆ You must next define the partition that you want to back up. You can feasibly give this option the name of the partition itself such as /usr/local or /var, but I prefer to define the device name of the partition. This ensures that the backup will be done correctly.

◆ You may also need to place a double ampersand at the end of each line to make certain that the program does not overwrite the directory that you just finished backing up. Normally you would use a semicolon (;) to differentiate between each backup command and prevent it from overwriting the previous dump execution. Dump dictates that the double ampersand be used between multiple backup calls when saving to a single tape.

Now look at the sample output of a backup routine. The dump command's output tends to be verbose to ensure that the backup is done correctly. You can just as easily pipe this output to a file if you want to save it for future reference. Redirecting the output to an appropriately named log file by adding a redirect symbol to the end of the expressions, for example, > my_saved_file.txt, accomplishes this same task and allows you to peruse the output at a later time.

```
 /sbin/dump -0uf backup.ksl.com:/dev/st0 -b 64 -B 4000000 -L "/var"
/dev/hda5 >> /tmp/backup.log.000508
```

Listing 9.3 shows a log of backup.mydomain.com when the dodump command was last executed.

**Listing 9.3  Sample Output from a Dump Request**

```
# /usr/local/scripts/dodump
  DUMP: Date of this level 0 dump: Tue May  2 09:19:11 2000
  DUMP: Date of last level 0 dump: the epoch
  DUMP: Dumping /dev/hda1 (/) to /dev/nst1
  DUMP: Label: /
  DUMP: mapping (Pass I) [regular files]
  DUMP: mapping (Pass II) [directories]
  DUMP: estimated 79612 tape blocks on 0.02 tape(s).
  DUMP: Volume 1 started at: Tue May  2 09:19:15 2000
  DUMP: dumping (Pass III) [directories]
  DUMP: dumping (Pass IV) [regular files]
  DUMP: Closing /dev/nst1
  DUMP: Volume 1 completed at: Tue May  2 09:24:14 2000
  DUMP: Volume 1 took 0:04:59
  DUMP: Volume 1 transfer rate: 278 KB/s
  DUMP: DUMP: 83299 tape blocks on 1 volumes(s)
  DUMP: finished in 298 seconds, throughput 279 KBytes/sec
  DUMP: level 0 dump on Tue May  2 09:19:11 2000
  DUMP: DUMP: Date of this level 0 dump: Tue May  2 09:19:11 2000
  DUMP: DUMP: Date this dump completed:  Tue May  2 09:24:14 2000
  DUMP: DUMP: Average transfer rate: 278 KB/s
  DUMP: DUMP IS DONE
  DUMP: Date of this level 0 dump: Tue May  2 09:24:14 2000
  DUMP: Date of last level 0 dump: the epoch
  DUMP: Dumping /dev/hda6 (/home) to /dev/nst1
  DUMP: Label: /home
  DUMP: mapping (Pass I) [regular files]
  DUMP: mapping (Pass II) [directories]
  DUMP: estimated 13763 tape blocks on 0.00 tape(s).
  DUMP: Volume 1 started at: Tue May  2 09:24:31 2000
  DUMP: dumping (Pass III) [directories]
  DUMP: dumping (Pass IV) [regular files]
  DUMP: Closing /dev/nst1
```

This actual output would continue far beyond this listing. The dump command first passes through the entire directory structures to be archived and takes note of all files. It maps all files and then begins the dumping pass. If between the mapping and the dumping pass a file is changed or deleted, dump will not catch the modified file and the archived data will not accurately represent the hard drive's state. Files can actually be missed or incorrectly saved on the backup pass if file modifications occur during the actual backup session. This will result in an erroneous representation of the data stored on the backup media. This is the reason that it is crucial to reduce or limit user operations when performing a backup.

Table 9.1 is a more complete overview of how dump backs up data as it parses through the file contents.

**Table 9.1  An Explanation of What Each Dump Pass Accomplishes**

| Pass | Action |
| --- | --- |
| Pass I | Creates a list of all the files on the drive to be archived |
| Pass II | Scans the hard drive multiple times to build a list of directories that require backing up |
| Pre-Pass III | Creates a dump header and tow inode maps |
| Pass III | Writes the header, the directory inode, and the directory data blocks for each directory in the backup list |
| Pass IV | Writes the header, the file inode, and the file data blocks for each file in the list |
| Past-Pass IV | Writes a header at the end of the dump to signify where it ends on the tape |

# Burning Data or Audio Files to CDs

One of the easiest methods for saving large datasets or ISO images less than 650 megabytes is to burn the file onto a blank CD. Due to the relative low cost of blank CDs, larger files, including Linux distribution CDs, can be stored onto durable media that can withstand magnetic fields and fluctuation in temperature. Like magnetic tapes, though, CDs are not impervious to high stress and temperatures and should be handled cautiously as well.

Normally, when burning data onto a CD, you will first want to create a manageable file containing all the data in one lump sum. This file or image is known as an *ISO image*. Much like a tar file stores a variety of files in one single location, an ISO image also stores files and directories. If using the ISO 9660 filesystem, file permissions and symbolic links are not preserved with the burn. The files generated from that image are saved in read-only format. Most burn processes under Linux are designed to use ISO images for creating unique CDs with accessible files.

To burn a CD, you are required to have installed either an internal or external CD burner. These can be one of four different types of burners: parallel, SCSI, USB, or IDE. The last option is still under development, although it is anticipated that within the year the latest Linux kernel will support USB CD burners.

The first choice, a burner connected via a parallel port or connected internally via a regular ribbon cable, is not recommended. Though these types of burners are cheaper than most, they cannot always keep a continuous flow of data from the hard drive to the CD burner. This produces buffer overflow errors and results in nonfunctional CDs ("coasters").

The next option, a CD burner connected via SCSI, is the preferable choice. SCSI burners normally cost more and require some form of SCSI card interface, whether internal or external, but the results are worth the price. Under Linux, SCSI burners result in fewer buffer overflows and most varieties are well supported by both the kernel and the software used to run the burning sequence. If using an IDE-based CD burner for saving the image, you should also enable SCSI emulation in the Linux kernel. Programs such as cdrecord still talk SCSI, but the kernel translates that data into IDE for the drive.

To create an image that can then be burned onto a CD, the Linux machine must have two files installed: cdrecord and mkisofs. Download the latest copies and then install them using the RPM utility:

```
# rpm -ivh cdrecord.xxx.i386.rpm
# rpm -ivh mkisofs.xxx.i386.rpm
```

You can place the latter file either on the server with the CD burner attached or on any other machine on which you wish to save files. The former file, cdrecord, must be placed on the Linux box with the burner. I normally use mkisofs on my own machine to create the single image file or ISO image. Once this file is created, I use ftp to send it to the server with the SCSI burner attached.

When creating an ISO image, decide first where to place all the files that you wish to burn. For example, if you had several mp3 files in the /home/kjcox/mp3/ directory, you would create an ISO image from that directory. The current contents of the mp3/ directory would show up on your burned CD. To create an ISO image from the files in /home/kjcox/mp3/, you would first follow these steps:

1. Change directories into the subdirectory directly below the one from which you want to create an image; in this example, you would enter **cd /home/kjcox/**.

2. Now create the raw image in that same directory. Make sure that you have enough space within that partition to hold the entire contents of the directory twice: once for the files themselves, and once for the raw image.

```
# mkisofs -r -o image.raw mp3/
```

This creates a large raw image in your /home/kjcox/ directory. This is the simplest way to create a large file that can then be burned onto a CD.

Another way of accomplishing this is to create an iso image. This works well both using the Windows system and using mkisofs under Linux. Check the man pages on mkisofs for additional information on the flags.

Here is an example of generating an iso image:

```
# cd /home/kjcox
# mkisofs -o /opt/GNUware/SourceIT_disk1.iso -J -r -V SourceIT -p
GNUware -P GNUware -v SourceITdisk1/
```

Once you have made your image.raw or SourceIT_disk1.iso file, you can either use FTP to send them to the server with the CD burner or begin burning the images on your own system. Be sure to place them in a directory or partition with sufficient space, depending upon the size of your file.

If you are using a SCSI burner, check the SCSI bus on the machine with the burner by executing the following command:

```
# cdrecord -scanbus
```

Now, make sure the CD drive itself is free of any extra CDs. You can substitute the device /dev/sgd with the device name of the SCSI CD burner:

```
# cdrecord -eject /dev/sgd
```

Mount the iso or raw image you created earlier to make sure that it looks the same when mounted as when burned onto the CD:

```
# mount -t iso9660 -o lo,loop=/dev/loop0 /home/kjcox/image.raw
/mnt/cdrom
```

Now change to the /mnt/cdrom/ directory and verify that all looks fine. Change directories and check the files and their permissions. If everything looks all right, you can now begin burning the CD. Insert a blank CD and change to the directory that contains your image:

```
# cd /usr/local
# cdrecord -v speed=4 dev=/dev/sg2 image.raw
```

The entire burning process requires some time depending on the speed of your drive. In this example, the software speed in the expression is set the same as that of the drive, or four x. When the process is complete, you can unmount the image from the /mnt/cdrom directory either prior to or after ejecting the CD:

```
# umount /mnt/cdrom
```

You can now eject the CD manually. Check the CD's quality by mounting it on another Linux machine or on another CD-ROM and verifying that the files you created have the same permissions and are accessible.

If you are burning smaller files at different periods and want to use the remaining space on the blank CD later, you will need to use cdrecord's -multi option.

For example, here is a very stripped down routine demonstrating how you would write multiple files to a single blank CD:

```
# cdrecord -multi -v datafile1.iso
```

This routine writes the first iso image to the CD. It will take a few moments to complete this task, and after a short while you will again receive control of the command prompt and can then issue the next command for the second data file that you want to burn on the CD:

```
# mkisofs -r -M /dev/scd0 -C 'cdrecord -msinfo dev=/dev/sg2' -o
datafile2.iso /path/to/directory/tree
```

```
# cdrecord -multi -v datafile2.iso
```

Repeat these steps for as many datafiles as can fit on the CD. The command for burning the last datafile and closing the CD for any further burns is as follows:

```
# cdrecord -v datafileX.iso
```

The $X$ represents the incremented number associated with the last burn. For more information on burning CDs a single time or multiple times, check the following file on your local hard drive or on the machine which performs the CD burning.

/usr/doc/cdrecord-1.8/README.multi

# Choosing Commercial Archival Programs

Although you can choose from the many open-source programs for performing backups, several commercial companies offer more dynamic backup programs. Some of the more popular ones are NovaNET, BRU, Veritas, and ARKEIA. Each has its pros and cons.

One of the best interfaces on a Linux desktop is that of NovaStor's NovaNET program. In addition to providing a point-and-click interface, NovaNET stores all the backup data as specified by each remote server in a database. This makes for very quick restores. NovaNET is one of the best-looking programs now on the market and has a lot of Windows-like features that appeal to new Linux users. In fact, many of the icons used by NovaNET are taken directly from the Windows set. It also has one of the best plug-and-play features yet seen. It recognizes the SCSI card type and the tape drive make and model.

When you first log in to NovaNET, it connects either to the local NovaNET database server created during the installation process or to another NovaNET server on the same subnet. Each additional machine you wish to back up must also be running the NovaNET client. This client in turn talks to the main server and parses information regarding the files stored on its drives. Once you are logged in to the main server, the interface offers several different tabbed selections, including any additional machines running similar clients and any SCSI backup devices detected. You may also set up security options and allow certain users administrative rights to perform various backup duties. NovaNET looks and acts much like a Windows NT server, but in spite of that is still a fairly robust and easy-to-use program.

However, as stated earlier, because NovaNET stores all the data in a common database, if that database file becomes lost or corrupted, all backup data are also lost. These databases also have the potential to become larger than the backup files themselves. As each remote machine is accessed and the list of files is compiled into this database, with frequent changes or large storage drives, the databases can quickly use up the available space on the backup machine. If you are using NovaNET on a backup machine, be certain to devote a fair amount of hard drive space to the unique databases it creates. NovaStor recommends that you devote at least several hundred megabytes of free drive space to each remote machine to be backed up. Another drawback to this program is that you cannot connect to NovaNET servers on other subnets. You can attempt to bypass this restriction by creating NFS-mounted file systems and then back up data locally.

One of the most popular commercial applications for backing up files is BRU. With the Professional release of the latest Red Hat Linux, you receive on the Linux Applications Library an evaluation copy of the latest BRU program. You can use this copy for free for 30 days, but you can purchase the program at any time thereafter at a reasonable cost. The BRU support team is extremely helpful. When I was evaluating several open-source and commercial products for my company's in-house use and for the purposes of this book, I sent several questions to the BRU team. The team responded instantly and was very straightforward about BRU's pros and cons.

The interface for BRU comes in both a command-line and X Window format. The latter is invoked by the xbru command. The GUI is not as flashy as NovaNET's but it does provide a lot of the same functionality. It requires the latest Samba release on the Linux server to mount and back up Windows machines. BRU is very dynamic in its GUI configuration and nearly all the command-line options are also available in the X Window format. You need little or no knowledge of the command-line flags to operate the GUI version properly. The buttons are large and friendly and can be easily navigated for backing up most servers. Like nearly all fast commercial programs, BRU also requires a client installed on the remote machines in order to access the files not located on the local machine.

You can find more documentation on the BRU home page than this overview can provide. The BRU home page is at http://www.estinc.com/.

Another product that has a large following among Windows users is Veritas. This program's developers have partnered with Red Hat in releasing its product to the Linux community. Veritas requires either the Motif libraries, which are proprietary and costly, or the lesstiff libraries, which are free and open to public development. I recommend using the latter. Installing the program itself using the RPM format is simple. The binaries, both the command-line and the X Window versions, are installed in /usr/openv/netbackup/bin/. The two files are bp and xbp, respectively. The latter file launches the GUI.

One very important feature of the Veritas program is its ability to back up SQL, Sybase DB2, Informix, and Oracle databases. Normally, high-end databases provide their own method of backup. Veritas is able to mimic many of these same proprietary tools and archive dynamic database files. Most backup routines for databases require file locking before they can back files up. Veritas is able to accomplish the same sort of file locking on databases and other files in order to prevent those files from being written to while a backup is in progress. As more commercial database programs are ported to Linux, there will be an ever-increasing need for robust backup programs that can handle the commercial needs.

ARKEIA is also a very versatile backup program that has received glowing endorsements from many of its users. It has a more dynamic interface that includes many customized icons and buttons. It appears simple to use, though I experienced a few more aches and pains in getting it operational.

Another backup utility, AMANDA, which is not a commercial product but has many commercial features (that is, it can be used in a commercial setting due to its quality and attributes), is worth mentioning. Developed originally by James da Silva at the University of Maryland Computer Science Department around 1992, AMANDA has since been modified by other enthusiasts. Its goal is to back up a large number of client workstations to a single backup server machine. It now supports nearly all platforms and can back up Windows machines, using tools such as Samba to access their data.

Like most open-source products, AMANDA is still under development. It has many features that make it easy to manage but is still limited in some aspects. AMANDA is easily supported using cron jobs, but is limited to one tape per run. It cannot yet support runs that are spread across more than one physical tape. Here is one instance where a simple dump or tar file exceeds the capabilities of a fancier program.

The aspects of setting up and configuring AMANDA properly far exceed the scope of this book and would require an entire chapter to do them any justice. Instead, you should consult the AMANDA home page to download, install, and set up AMANDA correctly. You can find out more information about AMANDA at http://www.amanda.org/. At this site, you can view and compile the source code or grab the RPMs from a mirrored site. The RPMs are by far the easier method for beginning administrators to get AMANDA properly running.

Each of these programs is available for a free evaluation period and can be purchased once the evaluation period expires. Red Hat Professional version offers many of these programs on a third-party disk. Each of these directories includes a readme file that explains how to install and configure the respective program properly. There are also detailed instructions for ordering the full version or obtaining a license key. Red Hat demonstrates its forward thinking by partnering with other companies that support the Linux cause or offering evaluation versions of commercial programs.

# Using Compression Utilities

With the advent of worldwide networks and the proliferation of data, the compression of data becomes increasingly important. The size of data becomes critical in determining speed of transmissions and the retention of data in backup strategies. Using a dependable compression utility will assist in both sending and receiving useful data in a manageable form. This section looks at a couple of compression tools that will assist in reducing file size, whether for storage purposes or for the sharing of data across networks.

## Zipping Up Files

The GNU zip utility is used to compress files. For example, suppose that the tarred file docs.tar is roughly 4.5 megabytes. It can contain several hundred files that can occupy a copious amount of space, but which all are now wrapped into one file. However, this file still does not fit onto one standard high-density floppy so that you can either give the floppy to someone else or transfer it to another machine not connected to a network. Here is where the GNU zip command comes into play.

After you type **gzip** and then the filename, GNU zip uses a compression algorithm and reduces the file's size. It also affixes an additional extension to the end of the file on which you are executing the command. Here is an example of how you can make the docs.tar file smaller:

```
# ls -la docs.tar
rw-r--r--     1 root     root     4587520 Oct 23 20:22 docs.tar
gzip docs.tar
ls -la docs.*
rw-r--r--     1 root     root     1058335 Oct 23 20:32 docs.tar.gz
```

The file as a tarred archive file was considerably larger than it is after you apply the gzip utility. Although originally the file was more than 4 megabytes, it is now a little more than 1 megabyte, small enough to fit onto one floppy disk. This compression also saves bandwidth and allows smaller files to be transmitted quicker over the Internet.

You can enable the highest mode of compression by adding a -9 option to the gzip command. However, increasing the compression rate reduces the chances of successfully retrieving the data in the event the data becomes corrupted. Some users prefer simply to use the default and not place any compression degree in the command. There is the opposing argument that increasing the compression creates fewer bytes to backup, thus fewer sectors that could fail, and fewer transmission errors during the backup process. Similar to compressing files onto a tape backup or using any additional compression methods with tapes, making a file even smaller can make it slower to extract.

Older administrators remember when the default compression command was compress, but that command is slowly being phased out. Many also think that gzip is much more efficient and better at compressing the file size. The compress command still makes its appearance in the form of filenames that have the extension .z. At one time in its history, gzip saved files with a .z extension, but in order to avoid confusion between it and compress, the extension was changed to .gz. You can still find vestiges of these extensions throughout the Internet. Some of the older programmers still use the more antiquated extensions for compatibility reasons.

In addition to including the gzip command, Linux includes a couple of other similar commands, zip and unzip. These are used mainly for MS-DOS files and function similarly to the popular DOS/Windows utility, PKZIP. Under Linux you can still manipulate DOS files readily using these two commands. You may also save files or zip them up for redirection back to DOS or Windows platforms. Such is the versatility of Linux and open-source.

Be sure to distinguish between gzip and zip. Though they appear to function in the same manner, they do have different options. Most Windows zip and unzip programs treat a gzipped file just as they would a zipped file; however, the converse might not be true under Linux. For example, when unzipping a zipped file, Linux renames DOS files in all uppercase letters. Because Linux prefers filenames all in lowercase letters, it might be advantageous to keep the system uniform and use the -L option with unzip so that all the files, once unzipped, have all lowercase filenames. If the -L option is not used, the filenames revert back to the way they were saved under DOS and appear in an uppercase, eight-character filename format. Linux does not rename the files to be uppercase, but instead allows them to revert back to the way they were saved. This is a CR/LF issue. This is how the files were saved on the DOS system. Linux merely changes them to a more user-friendly format.

> **NOTE**
>
> Gzip, or GNU zip, is not the same as the zip/unzip utilities. The former deals with Linux file compression while the latter handles DOS-zipped files.

For additional information about all the possible settings for zip and unzip as well as gzip, refer to the man pages for each command. A full examination of each command's available options is beyond the scope of this book.

## Using a More Complete Compression Utility, bzip2

A relative newcomer to the scene of compression utilities, bzip or bzip2 goes a few steps beyond the gzip utility. It compresses the file size even further. The bzip utility is very similar to gzip, sporting only a fancy new algorithm that shrinks the files even further. The utility is being used with files larger than 10–15 megabytes. The algorithm helps reduce the size an additional megabyte or two, which over the long run makes file transfers quicker for users who are still using the slower 28.8 and 33.6 modems. The syntax for bzip2 is much the same as that for gzip.

Depending on the type of files, the bzip2 utility can compress larger files down to a smaller ratio than that of gzip. There is no way to effectively calculate the exact ratio of compression for all files, but overall bzip2 appears to employ the most effective compression method. Larger programs can be made smaller and transmitted securely over the Internet, often via e-mail, whereas uncompressed versions might require a considerable amount of time to send. Many users sharing larger files are advocating that bzip2 become the standard compression format.

One place you can see bzip2 being used to great effect is with the latest kernel downloads. The most recent 2.4.x kernels are well over 20 megabytes. The bzip utility reduces the file to under 20 megabytes and saves 4–5 megabytes.

The following is an example on how to unzip and untar a bzipped kernel:

```
bunzip2 -c linux-2.2.17.tar.bz2 | tar xvf -
```

The kernel source archive remains intact while creating a new linux/ directory and uncompressing the files. The directory itself is exactly the same size as any directory created by a gzipped file. It is only the compressed and tarred file that is smaller using bzip2.

tar also supports bunzip2 and, like gunzip, you can incorporate the bunzip2 command into a single tar execution. The flag used by tar to bunzip2 the file while installing is I. This option is similar to the z option used by tar when wanting to unzip tarred and zipped files in a single command. If I wanted to untar and bunzip the same kernel file using only tar, I would type out the following command:

```
tar xvIf linux-2.2.17.tar.bz2
```

The I flag tells tar to bunzip2 the file before untarring. Rather than type out two separate commands connected by a pipe (|), bunzip2 is now incorporated into the tar command. You must also have bzip2 installed on your computer for this to work. This option also functions in reverse when tarring up multiple files into one large tarred and bzipped file.

# Restoring Backups

Once you have performed the necessary backups of all your Linux servers, all the data are now safely stored. It is only a matter of time, however, before you will need to restore either corrupted or lost data. If you have followed the preceding instructions, the tape should automatically rewind once all the partitions have been backed up. However, if you need to rewind the tape, you should use the *mt* (for *magnetic tape*) command. You can use mt either to rewind or retension the tape or to forward or reverse the tape to a new location based on which partition you want to examine.

## Restoring tarred Files

Restoring tarred files is just as easy as tarring them up. You are not obliged to untar them immediately to see their contents; rather, tar gives you the option of printing out the tar file's contents verbosely so that you can see exactly what the single tar file contains. Using this option is a recommended practice for Linux users, if you do not entirely trust the owner of the file or have some doubt about where the files might be untarred upon execution of the untarring command.

To check the tar file's contents first, enter the following on the command line. This example uses the docs.tar file created from the docs/ directory.

```
tar -tvf docs.tar
```

The -t or --list option prints out the files within the tar file exactly as if they were being written out to the directory. You can either use the full or abbreviated version of this option when adding the flags. -t and --list are the same command; the latter is simply the more verbose method of telling the command what sort of additional option to perform. When you use -t, no files will be written out to the hard disk.

If the output is agreeable and appears to be what you expected, you can extract the data and save them onto a disk. You can do so by using the -x or --extract option instead of the -t option. In addition, you can still place other flags, such as -p for retaining the original permissions. A sample restore from a tar file would look like this:

```
tar -xvfp docs.tar
```

Often files are both tarred and gzipped using GNU zip. For example, if you zip the docs.tar file, make it docs.tar.gz, and then moved the file to another directory, restoring is a simple matter of first unzipping and then untarring the file.

You can accomplish this in either one of three ways. You can first unzip the tar file, then untar the data file that remains tarred after the unzipping process. This requires two separate steps and usually leaves you with the tar file only when completed. You will need to execute the gzip command in order to compress the file again to its previous state.

```
gunzip docs.tar.gz
tar -xvf docs.tar
```

The second method incorporates the gzip utility directly into the tar command. By simply adding a -z option to the tar command, it will both unzip and untar the file, creating the new directory. This is one of the recommended ways to handle such files.

```
tar -xvzf docs.tar.gz
```

The last method is the one that I prefer since it will also work with bzip and other compression programs. It also leaves the tarred and zipped file intact in case it needs to be moved or the directory it creates needs to be redone. Basically, the method involves combining both the gunzip command and the tar command with a simple pipe. Here is how extracting a sample file might look:

```
gunzip -c docs.tar.gz | tar xvf -
```

The -c option is essentially the zcat command that prints out the compressed contents of the file. Following the pipe, the tar command untars the file contents while printing the files, all in one fell swoop. Linux proves again that it can accomplish in one single line what might normally take a couple of commands or several individual commands.

## Bringing Dumps Back to Life

Restoring data if necessary is one of the most important capabilities that you need for successful backups. All your effort is in vain if you cannot produce the data stored on the backup media. It is good practice to restore data periodically from selected tapes or other media to verify that the dumps are being carried out successfully.

To access the tape media, it is also a good practice to be familiar with the commands used to control tapes in tape drives. The most common command is mt, which allows you to rewind, erase, or re-tension the tape in the event it fails midway through the process or if you wish to make a fresh backup and do not have any leftover data that may corrupt the newer data.

If you make a mistake and choose the wrong partition during a restore session, you would rewind the tape to access the first backup partition. The following are two different ways you can access the tape; the former is executed locally, whereas the latter is executed remotely:

```
mt -f /dev/nst0 rewind
mt -f backup.ksl.com:/dev/nst0 rewind
```

To restore files from a dump session, you use the restore command. The restore command is slightly more interactive than tar, in that it enables you to do more than read and restore an entire directory or partition. For example, after you complete a restore, the command enables you to read through several later interactive backups and restore those as well all by using the -r (read) option. This is a very powerful feature. If you need great flexibility when dealing with dynamic backups and restores, the restore command can accomplish nearly any necessary task.

Another advantage restore has over other commercial applications is that it keeps track of the data or files on the tape media itself. On other commercial applications, the database, which records the file and its location on the tape, is kept locally on the hard drive. If the backup machine becomes corrupted and the database is lost, all backups are considered lost as well. This is not the case with the restore command. You can restore files from any machine onto any other machine without accessing a database. Of course, doing so would make the entire restore procedure longer and more arduous, but the stability offered more than offsets the disadvantage of longer restore sessions.

Also, restore can replace any older file with a backup file on demand. If you specify the -x (*extract*) option, restore places all the requested files into the current working directory. This process is highly interactive and enables you to replace a file located several directories below the root directory. To accomplish this, you need to specify the complete pathname, not just the relative pathname.

◆ ◆ ◆

For example, if I want to restore the file /home/kerry/docs/research/ linux/backup.txt from a dump of the /home directory, I need to specify the file as kerry/docs/research/linux/backup.txt, because I am already in the /home directory. Since /home is the default directory or partition I used when performing the backup, dump/restore uses this location when printing out the directory's contents. It is a good practice to restore files to a temporary working directory so that the existing files are not mixed with the restored ones. The /tmp directory is a commonly used location for provisionally locating restored files.

◆ ◆ ◆

The restore command when used with the -t or --type option will also parse through the entire contents of a tape to locate a specific file. This option is useful if a dump backup spans several tapes. Rather than restore multiple files from of multiple tapes, you can instead print out the contents and find the file you need. You can also use the -s option. When followed by a particular tape number, the -s option will immediately prompt the administrator for that volume number or the partition number of the backup series. Thus the command restore -s 4 requests that backup number four of a specific series be placed in the machine; then restore will find the requested file.

By using the -f option with the restore command, you can specify a particular file. This is a highly effective option when used together with -i, which places restore into interactive mode. In this manner you not only can specify certain files but can also respond to queries by the program.

The syntax all comes together in the following example, which pulls up the aforementioned backup.txt file from an earlier dump routine:

```
/sbin/restore -iv -b 64 -f backup.mydomain.com:/dev/nst0 -s 2
```

The second series of files to be backed up were those located in the /home directory. Because backup.txt is located in this partition, you request the file from this series. This command creates an interactive restore, as specified by the -i option, which is probably the best choice if you are restoring only a few files. You will then be given an older sh shell prompt display in which you can choose which files to restore. You use simple UNIX commands such as ls and cd to navigate through this directory structure. Here is a simple example of what you will then need to do to restore a specific file:

```
home> ls
home> cd docs/research/linux
home/kerry/docs/research/linux> add backup.txt
home/kerry/docs/research/linux> extract
volume #: 1
```

You would want to list all the files and verify that you are actually in the partition containing the /home files. Next, change directories to the appropriate location. Once you have located the file(s) you wish to restore, type **add** and the filename(s). You may also use wildcard characters such as the asterisk. For example, <filename*> would select multiple files of the same name. Another ls command will show that the files you selected with the add command now have an asterisk next to them. If a file is selected that you do not wish to restore, you may unselect it using the delete <filename> command. This does not delete the file from the tape media, but merely unselects it for the restore process.

Next, begin extracting those files by entering **extract**. This command creates a restore directory in your current location. You will also be prompted to specify the volume number. This is almost always 1 unless the partition spans more than one tape. You should always try to avoid making multiple tapes, but in some instances it cannot be avoided.

Finally, you will be prompted as to whether you want to set the owner for these new files. I nearly always choose the "yes" option, although for some files this may not be a good idea. This setting establishes the ownerships for the files to belong to that person doing the restore. In most cases this is harmless enough, but if system files require restoration, you may not want to give root or some other user ownership of them.

As the process begins, you will see that it restores each file selected verbosely. Though the feature that indicates the progress of the restoration is not like a progress meter, it does help to confirm when each file is complete. Once a particular file is displayed, you can move it back to its original location.

Once the restore process is complete (depending on the file size and location, this process can last anywhere from 15 seconds to a couple of minutes to several hours), you should exit the interactive restoration by entering **quit** or **exit**.

Now if you invoke an ls command in your current directory (which should still be /tmp), you will see a new directory labeled /home or whatever directory it is that you restored. Simply ascend through those directories until you locate the file(s) you restored. Once that is done, you can move them to their new or permanent locations. You can delete all the files in the /tmp directory after the older archived files have replaced any damaged or missing files.

## Remotely Controlling Multiple Backup Tapes

One very useful utility I recently discovered is mtx. This open-source program allows an administrator to swap multiple tapes remotely in certain SCSI drives. For instance, I have an older SCSI HP C1533A autoloader tape drive that contains a cartridge, which holds six separate DDS2 tapes. From the comfort of home, as a cron job, at another terminal in the building I work, or even while away on vacation, I can swap tapes back and forth remotely as each completes its task.

You can obtain mtx either by compiling the source code yourself or by installing the RPM. The mtx program is included with the latest Red Hat release and can be selected during the installation process. The binary is usually installed in /usr/local/bin if compiled from scratch and should be only accessible by root. The syntax is simple. Listing 9.4 shows a sample command that queries the status of the drive.

**Listing 9.4  An Overview of a Multiple-Tape Autoloader Using mtx**

```
# mtx -f /dev/sg0 status
  Storage Changer /dev/sg0:1 Drives, 6 Slots ( 0 Import/Export )
Data Transfer Element 0:Full (Storage Element 2 Loaded)
      Storage Element 1:Full
      Storage Element 2:Empty
      Storage Element 3:Full
      Storage Element 4:Empty
      Storage Element 5:Empty
      Storage Element 6:Empty
```

The output displays the tape number of the tape currently loaded and the status of the other tape slots. Here only two of the six available slots are full. Element number two of the tape container is currently loaded in the data transfer element for backup purposes. When complete it will be rotated back out to Storage Element number 2, and the tape in Storage Element number 3 will be placed in the Data Transfer Element.

Changing tapes is also simple. The syntax requires the command, the device name, and the source and target slots. Listing 9.5 shows a request to use the next sequential tape, or to exchange tape two for tape three. The number at the end is also not necessary; a simple next request will accomplish the same task and rotate the next available tape into place.

### Listing 9.5   A Request to Load the Next Available Tape Using mtx

```
# mtx -f /dev/sg0 next 3
Unloading Data Transfer Element into Storage Element 2...done
```

You mainly need to be concerned about knowing exactly what tape is assigned to each slot. Here the status option is very useful. Be sure to write notes on which tape is where if you are doing backups on multiple servers. If you wish to perform a backup on only one server and then rotate the tapes after each session, you can attach these commands to the end of a cron job or script that backs up the server nightly. That way a fresh tape will be installed for the next night's backup. Listing 9.6 shows the status of the tapes after a change tape command is completed.

### Listing 9.6   The Current Status of Multiple Tapes after Changing Tapes

```
# mtx -f /dev/sg0 status
  Storage Changer /dev/sg0:1 Drives, 6 Slots ( 0 Import/Export )
Data Transfer Element 0:Full (Storage Element 3 Loaded)
      Storage Element 1:Full
      Storage Element 2:Full
      Storage Element 3:Empty
      Storage Element 4:Empty
      Storage Element 5:Empty
      Storage Element 6:Empty
```

The first set of commands queries the status of the tapes. Here the tape from slot 2 was loaded into the read/write position within the drive itself. On the next line is the command to unload the current tape and load the next one. Finally, the tape from drive 3 is loaded in the machine for a new backup.

If you want to unload the current tape and free the cartridge so that it may be ejected, you state the source drive number and then the target drive. In Listing 9.7, the script unloads the tape from position 0 and places it in the cartridge at position 3, or the third tape in the sequence of six.

### Listing 9.7  A Request to Unload the Backup Tape from the Read/Write Position and Ready the Cartridge for Ejection

```
# mtx -f /dev/sg0 unload [0] [3]
Unloading Data Transfer Element into Storage Element 3...done
```

After unloading the tapes from the main (0) drive, you can then load them out of sequence by giving a command similar to the preceding one. Again, you state the source drive number and then the target by using the following command. This command loads the tape from slot 3 in the cartridge into the main (0) drive. Notice the lack of brackets around the source drive number.

```
# mtx -f /dev/sg0 load 3 [0]
```

As is the case with nearly every Linux utility, there are several methods of accomplishing the same task. Also, for nearly any job, there are several different tools available to perform the same function.

# Conclusion

This chapter examined the various reasons that an administrator should make weekly, if not daily, backups. You looked at the various media involved and some of the software solutions available to create an effective archival system. In the next chapter, you will explore how Red Hat Linux logs information. You will learn about what the various message files are, what information is logged to them, how to interpret the log files, and how you can customize your own logs. You will also examine when log files should be rotated, how Red Hat accomplishes this rotation, and how important it is to keep up-to-date logs for security reasons.

# Chapter 10

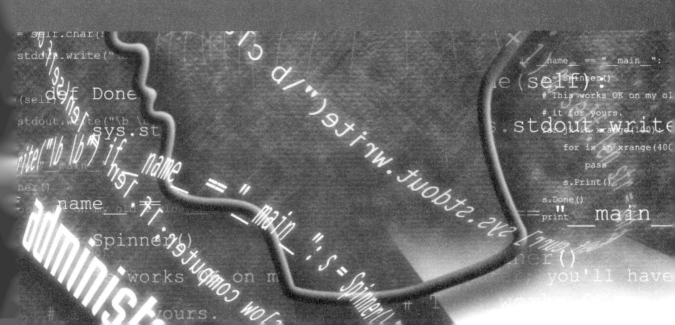

### Logging Errors

One of the most essential aspects to correct system administration is properly diagnosing any ills or problems with the system. Linux provides logging of most all system processes for later evaluation. These log files are kept in several reserved locations to separate them from other system and user files. During the initial partitioning of the drive or drives, it is customary to set aside a /var partition to store all log files. Because they have a shorter life span than most other partitions, this partition sees more activity than other files. Learning to interpret these files will assist in fixing errors and problems under Linux.

This chapter will examine the following subjects:

◆ Tracking normal system logging procedures

◆ Understanding the different levels of logging

◆ Discarding and rotating log files

◆ Saving log files for later examination

◆ Using syslog to improve logging capabilities

# Monitoring System Use

When you are managing a larger Linux system, or even a relatively small one, there are times when certain processes require monitoring. This monitoring is needed for fixing errors, tracking user needs, managing security settings, determining system use, or simply finding out how the system is processing certain programs. All of these processes can be monitored and logged or configured in such a way that the system can save all messages to the hard drive.

Nearly all daemons generate some sort of message for the administrator to examine later. These daemons can include anything from the Web daemon or httpd (which in the case of Red Hat is by default the Apache Web server) to the sendmail daemon, which tracks every e-mail either received or sent through the machine to even the named daemon which provides dynamic name service and translates IP addresses to human-readable domains. Each of these daemons and others like them will generate output that is, in turn, logged by the system. There are other programs that can be installed by hand that will produce messages that will be logged by the system. Though these are less frequent than daemons, scanning the log files and parsing information created by custom programs can prove just as beneficial for debugging programs. Firewall scripts, for example, can send any and all messages directly to the local drive where it may be later examined for security exploits.

The system also performs more specific functions integral to the safety of the operating system itself. It will log all users who use telnet to access the box, track those users who either become or attempt to become superuser, and keep a record for all files transferred to or from the local host. Though these types of records may not seem important at first glance, as you become more familiar with Linux and how it operates, they will provide clues to better understanding many issues.

## Tracking Logging Levels

Log files are necessary for many administrative uses. Their primary purpose is to help you check for errors when you are either installing new programs or debugging running systems. Most programs, whether they are proprietary executables, CGI scripts, or open-sourced programs, either print out errors to standard log files in their own directory or some other predetermined location or save them to the system log directory. Much depends upon what type of program is run or to what degree you wish to monitor the messages that the program generates. This type of monitoring is useful when dealing with multiple users who are not quite as familiar with the Linux operating system or who are attempting to run new or obscure programs on the system. By periodically consulting the log files when you notice something strange on the system, you can often learn what types of programs are being run or why the system is behaving as it is.

Suppose that you notice the system load increase from its normal levels of 0.05 or 0.10 to something outrageous such as 2.50 or over 3.00 system load. In such instances, you can check the log files over the past few minutes and see what types of programs or utilities were run. On our mail server, for example, when the system seems sluggish or when the mail appears to spool for longer periods, I check the /var/log/maillog file and determine whether a user was sending a large amount of mail, or I can look to see who last logged in by using the last command and then check the bash_history log file common to nearly every user's directory. In one of myriad locations, depending upon the situation, I can trace the cause of the error to either a user or the system.

There are also varying levels of logging. Most system logs are configurable and can be set to generate a minimal number of files. If you need more information, you can set system logs to the debug level, and thus generate extremely verbose logs. The syntax for the Red Hat Linux syslog.conf file, which determines the logging level, is fairly standard across most all Linux distributions. How those options listed under this configuration file are implemented varies. Some programs suggest an extremely high debug level whereas others require only the most minimal of logging information. However, I suggest allowing all programs to generate at least a minimal number of logs if only to ensure that the system files are operating correctly.

Table 10.1 lists examples of fairly standard abbreviations of logging levels used for most system files. The levels range from the fewest files generated to the most effusive.

These levels are program-specific and can be set or reset depending upon the program in question. Often, when changing these values, you must either restart the processes or send their PID a hangup or -HUP signal. This restart causes the process to reread the system configuration and effect the logging level.

You can read more descriptive explanations for each of these different levels in the syslog and syslog.conf man pages.

**Table 10.1 The Different Logging Levels Available**

| Level | Description |
| --- | --- |
| emerg | Sends emergency messages for panic situations |
| alert | Posts an alert if the situation is urgent |
| crit | Notifies the administrator if critical errors are detected |
| err | Sends general error messages |
| warn | Warns of unusual conditions |
| notice | Informs of system notices |
| info | Sends verbose informative messages |
| debug | Generates extremely verbose messages for debugging purposes |

The  messages generated in these logs can either be kept at a minimal number that you allow to grow slowly or they can grow quickly like a cancer and overwhelm the directory until the specified partition is full. Once data are saved to a file, the way that the influx of information is handled is entirely up to the administrator. Because logs can grow rapidly, unbounded in size, and because a finite amount of disk space is available on any given computer, certain management options need to be exercised.

The administrator can manage his or her log files in several ways:

◆ Discard all the generated data created from the logged processes

◆ Periodically clear all the log files and restart the processes

◆ Rotate the log files into backup files and start afresh

◆ Save the log files onto backup media

If you hardly ever consult your own log files or even care about them, the last option is probably the least efficient use of your computer resources. But if log files have a high priority for debugging and security purposes, you will want either to cache them for later examination or save them to backup media.

As mentioned in Chapter 9, saving log files is not a recommended procedure. The only exception is if you often must deal with severe security-related issues. In such a case, you would need a longer and more detailed list of logged data to be accessible for later perusal.

The following section breaks down the possibilities for the first two scenarios—how they are handled, or what the best choice for each might be. The topic of rotating log files requires a large section of its own. Managing backup log files also requires a more thorough explanation.

## Discarding All Logs

You might find that log files are more of a nuisance than a tool. This might be the case, for example, if you are not a programmer and do not need to debug any developmental software or you do not normally experience any sorts of system problems. If so, then you might prefer to clear out the log files. This method is mostly for users who are on single-user, nonnetworked systems who do not need to check their system for security errors and who might not be concerned with most logs.

Because clearing the log files is not standard practice, some modification of the system might be necessary. The output as created by the system can just as easily be piped to /dev/null and deleted immediately from the system. The crontab file would be the first place to modify the settings.

You can limit nearly all system log files to their minimum number by editing your syslog.conf file. Setting the default level to emerg requires the system to log only those messages that warrant immediate attention. Normal system maintenance messages are dropped and the contents of the /var directory are kept to a healthy minimum. The only other reason that someone would want to edit this file would be if his or her system handled a high volume of traffic and if it also had very limited space available. Log files can very quickly eat all free disk space and can bring a server down when a partition runs low.

Some system administrators keep the files for a short time and then discard them all. This is recommended since some hardware and software issues should be checked for errors. Some simply prefer to clear the files out from their directories and let the system start logging messages again from scratch. Again, even this method is not recommended since some daemons require the process itself to be restarted in order for the log files to continue saving messages. It may be necessary to *touch* or create new log files after the daemon process is restarted. In most cases, there is no difference between empty 0 byte files and text files with text. The daemon will concatenate new text to the file as it restarts. Otherwise, the daemon is holding onto the inode of the old log file rather than the inode of the new log file.

## Periodically Clearing and Restarting Logs

Some administrators prefer to allow the log files to grow until they reach critical mass. The administrator can determine how long he or she wants to keep the files, rather than just sending all logs to the bit bucket or "black hole" commonly known as /dev/null. Keeping the log files is especially useful for later examination; for example, you can use the grep command to locate certain files or commands executed by users on the system. By hanging on to the log files, administrators possess better histories of system performance, which can help them evaluate performance more accurately.

There are several different tools for perusing log files. For just examining regular system logs, you might want to try a log-colorizing program, which color-codes your logs on the fly. Based on the color scheme, you can tell whether your box is all right from across the room. Depending on which log file you wish to view, you can continuously pipe the tail portion of your /var/log/messages file to a terminal window or console display.

To view new messages as they arrive in a certain log file, use the -f option with the tail command:

```
# tail -f /var/log/messages
```

You can quickly determine whether your system is logging too much or not enough.

For checking your FTP or Web daemon log files, you can try some Apache log filters of xferlog analyzers, which produce useful information for evaluation. You can customize any sort of log scanner program to suit your particular situation. A wide range of log filters and parsers are available on Linux software pages such as Freshmeat or IceWalkers. I am reluctant to recommend a specific log filter since tastes vary. However, one of the more highly recommended and used log-watching programs is swatch. You can always consult the GNUware CD that came with this book and look up the Administration portion for a variety of different tools.

Red Hat is designed to periodically rotate all log files. If you wish to do this yourself, disable the configuration files or edit them to your taste. Keep the files for longer periods of time indefinitely, or clear them out more often than before. If you do insist on periodically cleaning out your log directories, it is better to restart the daemons if any modifications are executed on the logs. For example, if the /var/log/messages file is removed or simply deleted altogether, it is prudent to invoke the touch command to re-create an empty messages file and restart the inetd daemon process. The touch command creates an empty file with the same name. Linux will sometimes work if the file is empty, but it is prudent to enter some text if only to let yourself know that the file was created by hand. Under Red Hat this file cannot be empty, as some text must first be entered or piped into the file. After creating the new file, you must edit it by entering a single line of text.

Here is how some administrators might clear out older log files:

```
# cd /var/log
# rm messages
# touch messages
# echo Creating a new log file > messages
# ps aux | grep syslog
# kill -HUP <syslog process PID>
```

Once the process has been successfully restarted, be sure to execute an `ls -la` or `tail/var/log/messages` command to verify that new data are being logged to that file. Again, using the `-f` option with tail will help ensure that the data are being written to the file. The `-f` option will continue feeding information to the screen as more data are logged to the /var/log/messages file. Rather than simply capturing a single snapshot of the file, you can see the messages as the computer generates them. Running the tail command with `-f` is useful in debugging a system that has other users who either run their own programs, generate a lot of e-mail traffic, or who tend to fiddle with settings or poke around in secure location. Tailing messages is also useful when cleaning up DNS records. In this manner you can see error messages as they occur.

## CAUTION

If you manually clear out a log file, such as /var/log/syslog, or attempt to create a new one in its stead, always verify that the new log file is collecting data. Be sure to verify that the daemon process that controls the logging is also running after it receives a hangup or –HUP signal. All too often, novice administrators kill a daemon process or create a new log file and either they forget to restart the daemon or they consult the logs days later only to discover that the file was not collecting data. Always check your work.

# Rotating Log Files

A standard practice among system administrators is to rotate the log files after a certain length of time. Rather than discarding the data immediately, administrators save the data to a new filename in an uncompressed format. If space is a concern, you may also compress the files into a gzipped file and then unzip them at your leisure or simply view the compressed contents by using the -c option along with the gzip command.

To view the contents of a zipped file without opening it, you can use the -c option piped through the more and less programs:

```
# gzip -c messages.1.gz | more
```

This command displays the head of the file and enables you to paginate through the remainder of the text by pressing the Enter or space bar key.

## Using grep to Locate Errors

Rotating the log files allows for later perusal in a static format when viewing larger dynamic files. Piping the files through more or less will allow you to view the contents line by line, but locating the proper entry can be tedious. Once the log files are in static form—that is, when the system is not writing to them—the grep command helps in locating troublesome or flagged notices. After a period of time, the older files are rotated out and deleted and are replaced by younger saved files. This is the preferable method for systems with sufficient disk space and is the default standard under Red Hat Linux. For systems with less drive space, a shorter rotation time is normally implemented or fewer files are saved.

To locate questionable entries in sensitive log files, such as failed SU requests or attempts by regular users to become superuser, simply use grep or egrep to identify botched or successful attempts:

```
# grep su /var/log/messages.1 | more
# grep failed /var/log/secure.3 | less
```

Either of these commands will display the line that matches the grep query. Any other string of text can be matched against other log files.

◆ ◆ ◆

By default, most systems rotate their log files to a similar name after one week and append a numeric value to the end. With Red Hat and other Linux distributions, files are kept for an additional four weeks. This means that besides the log file itself, four other files are given incremental numbers. Usually they are assigned a number beginning at either 0 or 1, but letters can just as easily be affixed. There is no limit to the number of rotated logs. You can keep as many logs as your system can afford to store. The lower the number, the more recent the file.

Some administrators like to use the day of rotation as a suffix to their log files. This is a useful method but it can prove confusing to novice users. It is a bit more difficult to set up and run, but if older files are archived for later use, this is the preferred method to implement. Listing 10.1 shows the output from a typical Red Hat log directory displaying the rotated messages files.

**Listing 10.1 The Output from a Typical Red Hat Log Directory Displaying the Rotated Messages Files**

```
[root@pluto log]# ls -la messages*
    rw——-    1 root    root       18167   Oct 25 19:30  messages
    rw——-    1 root    root       75291   Oct 24 04:00  messages.1
    rw——-    1 root    root      111379   Oct 17 00:27  messages.2
    rw——-    1 root    root      103811   Oct 10 03:50  messages.3
    rw——-    1 root    root       86921   Oct  3 03:09  messages.4
```

# Customizing the Rotation

How Linux rotates the files is based in part upon the logrotate command, which determines which files are rotated and which are removed. The basic configuration settings for rotating logs are set up in the /etc/logrotate.conf file (Listing 10.2 shows an example of a logrotate.conf file). Here you can decide how long you want to keep certain files or how soon you want to delete them. The syntax of logrotate.conf is relatively easy to grasp. Red Hat assists by including comments where appropriate so that most users can edit the file themselves.

**Listing 10.2  A Sample Red Hat logrotate.conf File**

```
# see "man logrotate" for details
# rotate log files weekly
weekly

# keep 4 weeks worth of backlogs
rotate 4

# send errors to root
errors root

# create new (empty) log files after rotating old ones
create

# uncomment this if you want your log files compressed
#compress

# RPM packages drop log rotation information into this directory
include /etc/logrotate.d

# no packages own lastlog or wtmp — we'll rotate them here
/var/log/wtmp {
    monthly
    create 0664 root utmp
    rotate 1
}

# system-specific logs may be configured here
```

The example shown in Listing 10.2 is from a fairly standard vanilla install. All logs within the /var/log directory are rotated automatically whether or not they contain information or are empty. According to the period of time specified by the /etc/logrotate.conf file, the older files will be replaced by the newer log files. You can specify exact times and dates you wish to rotate the logs. In the first section, you can specify whether you want the files rotated daily, weekly, or monthly. If you choose the weekly option, files will be rotated every seven days. If you choose the monthly option, then the files will normally be rotated on the first on the month.

The second section specifies how many levels of logs you wish to store. The default is four rotations. You can increase or decrease this default number as your needs change. Next, you specify who receives notification via email once the logs either succeed or fail to rotate. Root is the catchall user for system notification. You may specify other users as well if they require an email informing them whether the logs were successful.

The next section creates a new or empty log after the older one is rotated. You can leave the field commented if you would rather not create any new files for an extended period. The following section within this file specifies whether to conserve more space by compressing the files using gzip. Next, within the /etc/logrotate.conf file it mentions how specific RPM packages place additional information about their logs in the /etc/logrotate.d directory. This directory must be included so that those files can be rotated as well. In this directory, daemons such as Apache, FTP, squid, and others keep their information about how often their files should be rotated and so on. This directory is part of the RPM package and is not directly connected to the system files. In other words, the directory itself is not part of the operating system, but is for setting up other utilities. Each file tells the system where to place its own specific log files and how often they each must be rotated.

◆ ◆ ◆

As an example, look at the Apache log file located in the /etc/logrotate.d directory. The first section of this file defines where to look for the access_log or the file that records who referenced a particular local Web page:

```
/var/log/httpd/access_log {
    missingok
```

```
postrotate
        /usr/bin/killall -HUP httpd 2> /dev/null || true
endscript
}
```

The most important thing about this file is defining where the log file is stored. If you decide to compile your own release of Apache and not use the RPM program, you can easily substitute your new directory in place of the RPM directory and let the system rotate your newer logs as well. This is a hybrid solution for using system-automated tasks along with your own source code.

The next-to-last section consists of the system-handling tasks, which are best left alone by users. Here the file /var/log/wtmp is rotated and certain permissions are altered for the purpose of limiting users from seeing or altering the contents of this file. In the last section, root can define any additional rotational schemes. Any custom-installed programs that use log files can also be rotated in this section. This is for those additional files that you have either defined or are installed later and require rotation. For example, any firewall log files or tracking software that outputs to a static file can be defined in this last section of the /etc/logrotate.conf file and thus allow the system to handle the task of rotating the files.

## Manually Rotating Logs

Other files require manual setup. This is best applied to log files or files that see frequent modifications. For example, at a previous place of employment I kept a copious /etc/mail/access list for handling virtual domains and their users. These are lists of specialized email users who belong to a virtual domain or one of many domains that can exist on a single Linux box. This list saw much use and many of the help desk employees frequently needed to add new users or modify existing users. With so many hands changing the record, there was always a chance that something could be mistakenly deleted or corrupted.

I created a simple script that would rotate out the log file and keep backup copies. This script provided me with five additional days of backup, which I could use to discover any errors. Though I also took preventive measures of making tape backups, having a rotated file on hand helped for instant recovery. The access file does not grow as quickly as a log file might. However, it is also used for reducing the amount of *spam,* or unwanted mail coming from bad sites. After you enter the name of the unwanted domain, any mail from that site can be either dropped or rejected altogether. Over time, entering these domain names can cause the access file to grow larger. More about the access file and using sendmail to virtual domains will be covered in Chapter 18, "Sounding Off on Linux."

This script is not intended to replace the default Red Hat method of rotating logs, but you can apply it to other file types or logs you might wish to rotate. This particular script is usually run as a cron job since the log file rotation happens early in the morning when traffic is the lightest.

The following example shows how to rotate the /etc/mail/access file manually for backup purposes:

```
#!/bin/sh
cp /etcmail/access.3 / etcmail/access.4,cp /
etcmail/access.2 / etcmail/access.3,cp / etcmail/access.1 /
etcmail/access.2,cp / etcmail/access / etcmail/access.1
/etc/mail/make
/etc/rc.d/init.d/sendmail restart
```

The last two lines are not entirely necessary, but I have added them for good measure. The second-to-last line rehashes the database used by the access file, whereas the last line restarts the sendmail daemon. As with the log files that you examined earlier, it is sometimes best to have the daemon reread their configuration files. Restarting the daemon here ensures that sendmail will read the latest access list.

You can run this simple script daily, weekly, or even monthly depending upon the amount of data generated. If you apply this script to other log files and set your logging level for debug or info, you will probably want to rotate the files more frequently. Logs that are set for warn or crit can continue generating data for longer periods.

# Recognizing Untouchable Log Files

Two files should never be rotated or manipulated by a regular user: /var/log/last-log and /var/log/wtmp. The former is a sparse file that records the UID of all users who have previously logged in to the system. The latter file tracks the users who are currently logged into the system. This is not a totally accurate file since sometimes a user's shell is killed with an incorrect signal or is canceled prematurely, before the system has cleaned up the parent shell. Do not rotate these files manually. Red Hat takes care of this rotation via the logrotate.conf file.

Another important item to consider when creating other log files or modifying their settings is ownership. Only root should have read and write permissions to the log files in the /var/log directory. You should use chmod to set these permissions to 600 so that regular users cannot view the contents of these files. Files such as messages, secure, and maillog sometimes contain passwords or other sensitive data that could assist regular users in gaining root access. They also reveal much about other users on the system and the processes or actions they are taking. Close examination of the various configuration files in the /etc directory shows that the setting is usually 600 by default. Some of these files do allow a setting of 644 or even 640, but the setting depends on the types of log files. No one but the owner, usually root, should be allowed to modify a log file.

# Saving Log Files to Backup

For some systems, you must save all data to some form of media, whether for financial or security reasons. If this is the case, archiving log files is a reasonable method for clearing out room on the drive for additional logs. This is a particularly effective method when you are tracking logged firewall data. On larger systems where it is crucial to store all hack, spoofing, or malicious attempts to enter your system, you may need to refer to older files. The logs generated in a single day by firewalls in larger companies can fill up an entire disk. At my current company, we log megabytes of hack attempts on a daily basis. No one person can sift through all the data logged by the firewall. In situations such as these, you can create alternative scripts to parse through the larger files and look for malicious users. Such files are already available on sites such as Freshmeat, a good reference point for locating programs designed specifically for Linux users.

It is preferable to rotate out the older log file first, so that information is no longer written to the active log file, and *then* save those static logs to a backup media. In other words, copy the current log file to a new name so that it is static and no longer being altered by active daemons or processes. Now copy the newly created file to your preferred backup media. The best way to accomplish this is to set up a cron job to run late at night that first moves the files and then appends them with either the date or a numeric value. Once you are sure that the newly created log files are working and again logging new data, back up the older files onto tape or tar them up for storage.

For purposes of organization, it is best to keep your regular backups separate from the log backups. In case of a system failure, a rule of thumb is that log files do not get restored to the disk. Their transient nature does not guarantee any serious benefit if they are restored.

# Finding Logs

Linux tends to keep log files scattered among several different directories. For a neophyte attempting to diagnose a problem on his or her machine, it can be intimidating finding the correct file that might hint at the problem's source. Even the files in /var/log are rather cryptic, with names such as secure, spooler, xferlog, cron, and netconf. These files can also multiply if additional RPM-based programs are installed that place their default log files in the same location. Even so, many programs scatter their logs throughout the system.

## Locating Standard Log Files

Though older Linux distributions spread log files among many different locations, the more recent release has standardized and localized most logs into one unique directory. You can find almost all system log files in /var/log. This is a vast improvement over other systems, such as Solaris, that scatter files throughout the entire drive and among partitions. Under Red Hat Linux it is recommended that the /var directory is set aside as its own partition. This is one of the available partition options available when initially partitioning the drive. The /var partition can also be set to be smaller than other partitions since its files are more subject to change, are of varying sizes, and can easily be reformatted without any great loss of data.

To locate all the files that might be of use, reading first through all the configuration files provides a good indicator of where to look for any stragglers or misplaced logs. Most configuration files are located in the /etc directory. Like the logrotate.conf file also situated there, these configuration files point to the directories where most logs are stored. The initial startup files or run command files can also be useful for locating additional logs. You can find these files in the /etc/rc.d directory. For more specific programs, also peruse the /etc/rc.d/init.d files, which control the startup of separate daemons.

For general system configuration under Linux, probably the most crucial file for determining the type and amount of logging for individual processes is the /etc/syslog.conf file. Listing 10.3 shows a sample syslog.conf file. As this listing indicates, Linux provides short explanations to assist you in configuring the file for more specific purposes. These comments provide the logging level for each type of file as well as its respective location.

### Listing 10.3 A Sample syslog.conf File

```
# Log all kernel messages to the console.
# Logging much else clutters up the screen.
#kern.*                                 /dev/console


# Log anything (except mail) of level info or higher.
# Don't log private authentication messages!
*.info;mail.none;news.none;authpriv.none    /var/log/messages


# The authpriv file has restricted access.
authpriv.*                              /var/log/secure


# Log all the mail messages in one place.
mail.*                                  /var/log/maillog


# Everybody gets emergency messages
*.emerg                                         *


# Save mail and news errors of level err and higher in a
# special file.
```

```
uucp,news.crit                                /var/log/spooler

# Save boot messages also to boot.log
local7.*                                      /var/log/boot.log

#
# INN
#
news.=crit                                    /var/log/news/news.crit
news.=err                                     /var/log/news/news.err
news.notice                                   /var/log/news/news.notice
```

The first section in the above configuration file normally prints out default messages to the console. However, if it is commented out, the messages do not appear. You do not want the syslog daemon continuously interrupting your terminal session with notification errors, hence the first rule defining messages to /dev/console does not normally apply. These default messages are not stored or filed away in any manner, but they include messages generated by the kernel as it comes online.

The messages file in /var/log/messages tracks the use of daemons such as inetd, ftpd, bind, DNS, and syslogd. Any other message that handles system settings and daemon processes will also be written to this file.

The /var/log/secure file saves messages sent to the system as determined by outside connections, such as requests made by users outside the system or logins and/or telnet sessions made from remote locations or users on other machines. The file is named secure because the files logged are associated with maintaining security on the system. The file does not record unauthorized attempts to access the system, but does monitor other regular login requests.

The messages file monitors users and their requests to become superuser. On other older systems, the /var/log/sulog file used to track these sorts of logins. Red Hat has consolidated these requests into one file. Like the access_log file, which records nearly every access request for local Web pages, the messages file is becoming the default location for most security and user-related issues. The file logs unsuccessful, or worse, successful attempts by unauthorized users to become superuser. If you ever feel a cracker may have compromised your root password, this file might be the first place to investigate. It is also the first place that crackers would go to clean up after themselves and cover their tracks. If this file is missing or changed, you have cause to worry.

The next file, /var/log/maillog, tracks the e-mail sent through the system. On very busy systems with many users, this file can quickly grow out of control. It lists the origin and destination of each e-mail request and tracks it until it leaves the system. For security purposes, this file is very useful in determining whether your system is open to relaying by *spammers*, or those users who seek to abuse open systems by sending unwanted mass e-mails to any viable e-mail address. Spamming happens when uninvited users from outside your domain or control use your box to relay or pass on unsolicited e-mails. These e-mails range from the most offensive pornographic solicitations to the standard junk e-mails that promise to generate large amounts of money with very little effort. The maillog file is useful for monitoring the amount and types of e-mail moving through your Linux box. Unfortunately, if you do not consult this file often, you may become aware of your breach in security after the fact. Fortunately, the latest release of sendmail that comes installed by default with Red Hat denies relaying, so those outside your domain cannot hijack your box for their own purposes.

One of the other informative log files also available in this directory is the xfer-log file. This file tracks the files that users have been either uploading to or downloading from your system via FTP. This helps indicate what sorts of files — that is, their names and sizes — are being moved to and from your Linux machine. This file is especially useful for finding out whether users are trying to gain access to sensitive regions of your system. Such users will first attempt to copy a susceptible file from your system to their own where they can better glean any valuable information from the system. Careful checks of this file can better inform you of which users are potentially malicious and will assist you in better staving off any attacks from them.

Most files in the /var/log directory are simple text files that not only can be read but also modified. You can parse and save specific lines of text when supervising system usage. Some of the files, however, cannot be edited or modified. Their contents are generally in binary form and are not easily read except when used as a command. For example, one file, lastlog, can be read only when the last command is used. This file records the most recent users to log in to the system, the length of time that they were on, and the terminal from which they logged in. This file cannot be modified, nor should it be copied or moved to another location.

Another file in this directory is the wtmp file, which attempts to keep track of who is currently logged in to the system. It too stores its information in binary format and cannot be accessed through a typical text editor. You can view its contents only by using the w or who command.

If it does become necessary to parse through one of the binary log files, I recommend using the command strings with the file and then use the grep command to isolate any specific characters. This will display any specific entries in a file not normally accessible by a text editor or by using the more or less command.

Both the lastlog and wtmp files may not be writable by other daemons but only by a specific group since users who set other users' permissions to be writable can compromise Red in order to ensure only certain system users may write to this file. This increases security and the accuracy of the dependable logs by defining only system users as both owner and group and disallows regular users from modifying log files.

## Working with Nonsystem Log Files

Other crucial log files that administrators should be aware of are the log files generated by the Web server. On most Linux servers, Apache comes preinstalled. Since Apache and Linux servers serve much of the Web content now on the Internet, it is likely that your Linux system will also come with Apache running by default. If you do not wish to run a Web server, you may have to turn off Apache manually by executing the program such as /usr/sbin/ntsysv or by manually shutting down the daemon by entering **/etc/rc.d/init.d/httpd stop**.

Where the standard files are located depends upon the distribution. The default location for the Apache log files in Red Hat is /etc/httpd/logs. Apache usually keeps three standard log files, though some configurations provide the option of one large common file that stores all information. The three most common files are access_log, error_log, and referer_log.

The first log file, access_log, displays either the IP address or domain of the users from outside the system who attempt to access any publicly available HTML files. The second file, error_log, stores error messages generated by Apache as users attempt to access the HTML documents or programs. These can include CGI scripts or other modules stored in the Apache HTML documents directory. The last file, referer_log, lists where the URL the browser or Web-crawler was at prior to viewing your page.

Several programs available for Linux can parse through the information found within these logs and can generate dynamic HTML content so that you and others can see exactly what pages are being accessed by whom.

One program that I use on nearly all my Web servers is Webalizer. I prefer compiling it from source and editing certain variables, but Red Hat makes an RPM version available with its Professional release. Red Hat recommends Webalizer as well for tracking user Web requests and for monitoring your Web page traffic. Similar to the commercial WebTrends program, which costs thousands of dollars, Webalizer does much the same thing for free.

You can download the latest Webalizer release from its home page at http://www.mrunix.net/webalizer/. Webalizer's developers, like the developers of other open-source projects, are very responsive to questions and provide a FAQ page for answering many of the questions and solving many of the problems that users encounter.

Log files are easily manipulated and can generate raw data sheets, giving administrators a broad overview of their system. Better understanding the purpose of each log file and the information it stores will assist you in upgrading the security and efficiency of your Linux system.

# Conclusion

Now that you have learned how Linux logs to static files errors and messages, including problems encountered when testing out new or developmental software, you can begin installing additional programs of software packages not included with the standard Red Hat Linux installation CD. Part III, "Customizing the System," will examine how you can start optimizing the system beyond what is included with a default install. Chapter 11 explains how you can configure, compile, and install programs from source code. It will also explain how you can install RPM packages on Red Hat and what the difference is between using source code and RPMs. Finally, you will examine some other methods by which you can install programs on the system, including simple binary files. You will also learn how to convert .deb packages to .rpm files. The chapter will explore some of the pros and cons of both source code and RPM packages in closer detail.

# PART III

## III

### Customizing the System

# Chapter 11

## Installing Additional Programs

**N**ow that you are familiar with basic Linux operations and commands, and can add new users, manage accounts, and navigate the myriad file systems found under Linux, you are ready to build upon this knowledge base and expand the default Red Hat Linux installation. Until now, you have been using tools that loaded with the regular install or were available on the distribution CDs. However, a wealth of other programs is available for Linux that does not come with the standard Red Hat Linux release. Understanding how to install the additional programs, libraries, and utilities and properly configuring them is the focus of this chapter.

This chapter will not explain how each individual program is configured, since that would far exceed the scope of this book. Instead this chapter will acquaint you with what types of programs are available and how to install the most frequently used as well as the most basic programs.

The chapter will cover the following topics:

◆ Understanding how open-sourcing code works

◆ Locating executable programs under Linux

◆ Compiling your own code from source

◆ Installing Red Hat Packages (RPMs)

◆ Briefly exploring some GUI RPM tools

# Compiling Source

Of all the many tasks and duties that I perform on Linux, I take the most satisfaction in compiling my own source code. You can either write your own source code or, more likely, simply download source from the Internet and then compile it on your Linux machine. Few computer-related tasks are more rewarding than compiling simple ASCII text files written in a distinct programming language such as C or C++, and then using a compiler to change them into a binary form. Compiled code or text that has been converted into a more computer-recognizable form is a standard method for distributing software among other operating systems.

If viewed in a text editor, binary code is a meaningless jumble of characters, but to the Linux operating system, it is a much faster way of executing commands. Linux reads compiled code much faster than plain executable text files. Compiled code is also much more compact than plain text and as such is easily transferable. Once compiled, the text changes from being readable by human standards to a binary format readable only by computers.

# Open-Sourcing the Code

There are some drawbacks to working with binary code. Once a program is compiled, there is no way to see how the code was written except to try to disassemble the code back into readable format. Also, many people who write code are not eager to share with others what they have written because writing code is how they earn their livelihood. Most Linux coders, however, write their programs on the side and share what they have written for the benefit of others.

To understand how Linux operates and how it can afford to distribute the source code, let us first look at the different types of code available. There are four distinct categories into which most programming code falls (see Table 11.1). Some of programs are released in different forms and fall under more than one category.

Because many of the proprietary programmers and systems distributors deal with the code only in binary form, users are unable to see how the program was created. This is typical of larger companies that hoard their code under lock and key. Users cannot make editing changes or correct bugs within the program, but are forced to wait until either a patch is released or until a new version comes out. There is also the hidden danger of viruses or malicious commands being embedded within the code itself. Hence, one of the chief arguments against proprietary and closed-source code is that not only is the corrective and developmental process long and often arduous, but users risk exposing their machines to software glitches or even attack by unscrupulous users willing to exploit the latest security holes. This problem is not limited only to software for non-UNIX systems; Linux also is also vulnerable to the risks of poorly written code.

**Table 11.1  Brief Descriptions of the Different Types of Code Available for Public Use**

| Code Type | Description |
| --- | --- |
| Proprietary | Code belonging to a company that makes money off the code's sale and licensing. This source code is available only to the programmers and is never seen by the general populace. |
| Closed-source | Code that is either sold or distributed freely to the public. The source is not made available for individuals to peruse. Members of the Linux and Open Source community liken this type of free code to "free beer" —free in price only, but not in liberty to know the contents or for later use. |
| Binary-only | Code that is generally given away as freeware; no licensing restrictions apply. However, the code is compiled source only. Some open-source developers make parts of their code available for viewing but do not charge for the code. They also restrict any sort of modification stating that the code itself is theirs to modify as they see fit. It can be open to public viewing, but this type of code falls under more restrictive licenses and *not* the GNU or General Public License (GPL). |
| Open-source | Code that falls under the GPL, where all source is made public and any changes must also be open for public review. Developers may charge for their product, but all source must be available for peer review. |

Linux, more often than not, attempts to bypass most of the hidden pitfalls of closed-source or proprietary code by making the source code for its operating system and for much of the software that runs on it available to the public. Developers find this an extremely useful practice since their users can edit the source code, share that information with others, and then contribute it to the community. This speeds up the process of fixing bugs and releasing new versions with additional features.

Like the Linux operating system itself, many of the programs now available to run under Linux also fall under what is known as the GNU General Public License (GPL). Simply stated, anyone has the freedom to modify existing code and even sell the modified code so long as those changes are made available to the community at large. Linux's participation in GPL has contributed to an explosion in the amount of software now being generated for Linux consumers. Not only are there more programs available for public download from the Internet, distributors are packaging ever-increasing amounts of software with the basic Linux kernel. Nearly all software included with the Red Hat Linux distribution falls under the GPL. Red Hat also offers a Powertools package which includes other software packages not authoritatively recognized as being GPL but which are extremely useful.

## Finding the Local Binaries

Because most Linux distributions are released on one to three CDs, depending on the types of code they offer, there is only a limited amount of software that can be distributed at one time. The standard Red Hat release offers everything on just one CD. However, the commercial releases include the source code for all the RPMs along with other third-party applications that can take several additional CDs. Due to size restrictions, the most common release of Red Hat distributes only the binary forms of the packaged programs on a single CD. Red Hat also offers the source code for all their packages at its Web site should users wish to create their own packages or customize the software more to their liking. Red Hat is a trusted source, and the danger of getting any sort of nonfunctional or malicious software that can actually be disruptive to the operating system is minimal. Users who are not entirely trusting or who simply want to modify the code for their own use can modify the programs, as well as the source code that comes with the commercial release, as they see fit.

With the release of 4.2, Red Hat chose the /usr/bin directory as the default location for nearly all binary programs. This directory is where all utilities and programs not integral to system operations are placed. Such programs include window managers, some games, networking tools, and graphics programs. For this reason, either the /usr or /usr/bin directory is placed in its own partition. As the administrator installs more precompiled programs or packages developed by Red Hat, this directory continues to fill up. Because the directory is kept separate in its own partition, any user can quickly determine the limited capacity of that directory.

One of my own Linux boxes shows the distinction between my /usr partition and the others that I have set aside. Because all the working programs are now located in one distinct area, I can better allocate data to other areas.

Here is a quick printout of what a df -h command reveals about the space on one of my many Linux systems:

```
$ df -h
Filesystem          Size   Used   Avail   Use%  Mounted on
/dev/hda1           486M    35M    426M    8%  /
/dev/hda5           3.3G   909M    2.3G   28%  /home
/dev/hda8           729M    82M    609M   12%  /opt
/dev/hda7           1.9G   838M    997M   46%  /usr
/dev/hda6           2.4G   817M    1.4G   36%  /usr/local
/dev/hda10          379M    30M    330M    8%  /var
```

The -h (*human-readable*) option prints out the used and available disk space in megabytes for clarification rather than printing out the number of occupied kilobyte blocks, which is the default option of the df command.

As the preceding example shows, the /usr partition is one of the larger partitions and it consumes nearly as much file space as the other directories even though it contains only binary files. Depending upon how you use your system—for storage purposes or for trying out new programs—you will want to adjust your directory sizes accordingly.

If you think you will use only Red Hat packages or RPMs for additional program installations, adjust the size of your /usr partition to occupy more space. If you would like to compile your own programs, make the /usr/local directory large enough to accommodate several hundred megabytes or gigabytes of data. If your machine will be devoted to being a Domain Name Service (DNS) or newsgroup server, the /var partition will need to be several times larger than that of either /usr or /usr/local. New users should try different partition sizes and see what layout works the best. Much depends on what function that your Linux box will serve. For additional information on how to lay out your partitions, refer to Chapter 1.

## Running the Latest Versions

When installing most binary programs or RPM packages, you will want to look for the final product in the /usr/bin directory. Programs you compile yourself will probably go elsewhere, such as /usr/local/bin. Make sure that your path has this directory installed by default. This is usually done for you during installation, but you can verify your path with a few simple commands.

> **NOTE**
>
> Red Hat Linux installs many of the system binaries in /bin, /usr/bin, /sbin, /usr/sbin and /usr/X11R6/bin. These binaries are used for system maintenance issues or for programs normally run by root. They will not always be available for regular users in their path.

To test your path, either as a regular user or as root, and verify that the binaries are accessible from anywhere on your system, type the following:

```
echo $PATH
```

Here is how the system responds to a regular user's request to view his or her default path:

```
$ echo $PATH
/usr/local/bin:/bin:/usr/bin:/usr/X11R6/bin:/home/kerry/bin
```

As mentioned in Chapter 4, the echo command prints out the value of the path variable. In nearly all cases, Linux makes sure you can access those programs necessary for regular use.

You may want to access other files from the command line without having to type the absolute path to run the program. If this is the case, you can easily add another directory to your path by editing the variable:

```
export PATH="$PATH:/usr/sbin:/usr/games"
```

You retain the original path or the $PATH variable as stated above by including $PATH in your export statement. Those directories listed behind it are appended to the original path:

```
$ export PATH="$PATH:/usr/sbin:/usr/games"
$ echo $PATH
/bin:/usr/bin:/usr/X11R6/bin:/home/kerry/bin:/usr/sbin:/
usr/local/bin:/usr/games
```

When Linux looks for a particular program, it processes all the directories as defined by the user's path, querying each to see whether the program is located there. Beginning with the first directory listed in the path, Linux moves down the line until it finds the file. If you have a binary in /usr/bin and yet have another by the same name in /usr/local/bin, Linux will take the first one found in its path. If you are installing precompiled binaries, RPMs, or your own executables, be sure to check your path so that the system locates the newer files first. It is recommended that customized directories be placed toward the end of the path so that the system checks its own directories first. Placing /usr/local/bin before the system directories is regarded as a security hole because other users can place their own customized binaries in the /usr/local/bin directory, (provided you have granted them this privilege) and thereby bypass a system program.

Be aware of where your programs are when you install subsequent binaries or compile your own. It is good practice to query the programs you are running to find out their exact release number. Though you may have installed a more up-to-date version of the same program by hand, the system may still be running the older version.

The best way to verify your program's version is to execute the program at the command line. Simply enter the program's command with a -v or --version flag following it. This is the generic method of printing out the version release. Some commands require an uppercase *V* or some other flag. Most, however, will print out additional information if you specify a --help option. Also, if the command requires supplementary flags, you can display a list of available options, including one that prints out the release number, by entering the command by itself.

The same practice applies to querying the RPM database and determining the version of a particular package. Although the --version flag will not always work with each program, you can always check the RPM release number. Use the queryformat option or -qf flag along with a 'which' request and the package name surrounded by back-ticks. For example, the following statement queries the RPM database regarding which emacs release is installed.

```
rpm -qf 'which emacs'
```

Most GUI programs that run under X Window will also have an About... drop-down menu that displays its release version. If you are unsure whether you have installed the latest version on your system, check your paths, make sure that the directory in question is located in the first position in your path, and verify that the install procedure places the binary in the correct location. You can check to verify the location of the installed program or to certify that it is in your current path by issuing a 'which' command. 'which' searches through the directories in your path and attempts to match the program with a binary by the same name.

Usually source code provides a makefile that lists where compiled binaries are placed. Even a novice Linux user can interpret these simple text files and decipher the context of the code. Consult the programmer's home page or e-mail the developer if you are still uncertain.

If you wish to place the programs in a location other than that which is stated in the Makefile, you can change the default direction by appending a `--prefix=` suffix to the end of your ./configure script. The Apache Web server program, for example, is highly configurable and users are allowed to state the default Apache location. To change the root directory for Apache you would issue a command similar to this:

```
# ./configure --prefix=/usr/local/etc/apache
```

Using a `--prefix=` addendum is much more convenient than editing a Makefile. Tinkering with Makefiles, especially if unsure as to which other files are dependent on the root directory location, can be a recipe for causing the program to fail in its compilation.

## Obtaining the Source Code

Once you have decided which program version to install on your system, the most preferable choice for some is to download the source code and compile it yourself. Some might argue that grabbing a precompiled binary or an .rpm file is simpler and quicker, but the very latest code is not always immediately available in compiled form. If you like to live on the cutting edge, as many Linux users do, grabbing the source and doing it yourself is the best method. This is especially true of programs such as the Linux kernel, which is available for all Linux flavors only in source code. Though some distributions release updates of the kernel in binary form or through patches, you should compile the kernel code manually on the destination server. Red Hat will make the latest kernel version available in RPM format if the current release requires an important security update. However, few computer-related accomplishments are more gratifying than transforming several megabytes of text into a functioning program that performs to your specifications.

Obtaining the code is one of the more difficult tasks. Only recently has an effort been made to bring together in one of several locations the programs of developers worldwide and organize their software in some cohesive format. Sites such as Freshmeat (http://freshmeat.net/) make an impressive attempt at distributing

Linux code to all Linux users. Basically, developers themselves post information about their programs to the site and inform others of newer releases. The information includes a description of their program, its home page, access to the source and/or binary, a *changelog* (a summary of items improved or fixed since the last release), and an overview of what the program does. The site categorizes and arranges these pieces of information within a database that can be browsed.

Other sites include Linuxberg (http://linux.tucows.com/), which was recently purchased by Tucows. Another popular site for Windows programs, Linuxberg sports an impressive collection. The Linuxberg site provides links to the software itself as well as more in-depth descriptions. Other sites take the distribution of the code one step further and make the software available for purchase in CD format. An example of such a site is GNUware (http://www.gnuware.com/). A site of my own making that helps in the distribution of Linux source code, GNUware provides the convenience of over 1,300 Linux programs all on one or two CDs. Any user can copy, compile, and install these programs onto his or her hard drive. This sort of utility is designed for Linux users who have either slow or nonexistent connections to the Internet, but still want the option of trying out Linux programs. This site helps such users bypass the tedious download time and gives them a chance to edit the code and also contribute back to the Linux community.

Several other sites throughout the Internet also provide source code along with documentation. The Metalab site (http://metalab.unc.edu/), located in North Carolina near the home of Red Hat Linux, provides a unique repository for nearly all Linux programs, including distributions, software and different applications. Here you not only may obtain the majority of free and open GNU Linux programs, but many of the larger distributions themselves. Linux code is freely available, and though you can purchase your favorite flavor, you can just as easily download the entire program onto your computer as well, provided your connection to the Internet is fast and reliable. Metalab is home to much Linux code, both for the operating system and for different utilities. In addition to the source code, Metalab also makes available reams of documentation that can help you better understand how Linux works. Linux programmers realize that it takes time to understand the intricacies of Linux and to make their programs functional. But getting something to work and getting it to work correctly and as you want it to function can be two entirely different learning processes.

Besides the Metalab site, many Linux users, whether they are professional consultants or simply enthusiasts, create their own "how to" pages that accompany their software development. Hundreds of HowTo pages and explanations are available at http://www.linux.com. One major resource is the Linux Documentation Project, which keeps not only nearly every man page imaginable, but also dozens of white papers or more technical explanations of how Linux operates. It also serves as a repository for more sophisticated clarifications. Often these pages include gems of knowledge that can help beginning Linux users. It is not necessarily true that the writers of code can best explain how something works. It is often the users who provide the best documentation.

# Creating Directories for New Code

After downloading the source code into a temporary directory on your machine, you can begin uncompressing the files into the directory of your choice. Where you unzip and untar the files is not so important since their location will only hold all the source code and the newly created binaries. You may not necessarily choose to keep the executables in this location but place them instead into a common location where other binaries are stored, such as /usr/local/bin. Where you place the binary itself on the system is the more crucial factor. For now, you should place the source code used for compilation purposes within a reserved directory—someplace where the partition has sufficient room for extra files. Several administrators prefer using the /usr/local/src as a temporary directory for installing and compiling source code. I prefer creating my own directory in the /usr/local directory. Something such as /usr/local/gnu works just as well as any default location. You can change or modify this site to suit your own tastes.

Some programs need to be installed in a specific directory. The Linux kernel, for example, should always be unzipped and untarred in the /usr/src directory. When fully expanded, the kernel creates its own linux/ directory, overwriting the older one. If you are creating a new Linux kernel, be sure to move or rename the older linux/ directory in /usr/src; otherwise you may encounter problems when it comes time to compile and install the new kernel. Also check for symbolic links such as a Linux link pointing to the older Linux source directory. Remove any links before uncompressing the newer source code. You can find more information about compiling a new Linux kernel from source in Chapter 14.

Some people like to unzip all their files within their own /home/ directory. For instance, I might like to place all the source code for every new program that I download into /home/kerry and have unique directories for each program.

Though this makes the new code easily accessible, it also creates a jumbled mess in your home directory. I prefer instead reserving this space for my own text documents and not for program source code. Sometimes a program directory might share the same name as a data directory that you are using in your home location.

To keep things separate and to avoid any confusion, do not compile in your /home location. If you must compile in your home directory, due to permission issues or for convenience, it is a good idea either to create a subdirectory to keep things organized or to delete the raw source code once the program is installed.

Usually new users should create a unique directory just for source code. Here you can install and compile to your heart's content. Placing this directory in /usr/local is often a good choice since the data are kept on a distinct partition, away from other data. Most programs that you compile from source usually install the binaries in /usr/local/bin, also on the same directory tree. Some Linux users prefer placing everything in /usr/local/etc, but this directory can also get clogged up with miscellaneous files from other installs. If the programs that you are installing are part of the GNU project for free software, you might create your own directory location, such as /usr/local/gnu. Then you will know this directory's locations and can grant yourself the correct permissions to place and compile source code there.

To create your own directory for compiling code, you can follow these steps:

1. Decide where you want to place a temp directory.
2. Change directories to the default location, by entering **cd /usr/local**.
3. Make the new directory of your choice, by entering **mkdir gnu/**.
4. Grant ownership to the correct user and group. Under Red Hat, these will most likely be your own username for both variables. For example, I would enter **chown -R kerry gnu/** and **chgrp -R kerry gnu/**.
5. Change to your new directory and place the tarred and zipped file there.

Once you have decided where to place your source, you are now ready to unzip and untar the code. Most programs are archived by using the tar command; however, there are varying methods of compressing the files. Some might be tarred only or have just the .tar extension. As Chapter 9, "Fixing Mistakes," explained, most programmers opt to use the GNU zip utility. This gives the file a .gz extension along with the .tar extension.

### NOTE

Over time, some of the files might become antiquated and you may want either to update their directories or delete them altogether. Most good programmers plan to place their updates in the same location as their earlier releases. Before removing any source directory, be sure to check the README or INSTALL files and verify what the changes are between the two releases. If the latest release or the changelog file has no special comments, you should be able to delete the older directory without much difficulty. Once you unzip, untar, compile, then install the new release, the most recent release overwrites all the older binaries in their default location.

The following example shows how a programmer might tar and compress a developmental program, in this case a window manager package:

```
WindowMaker-0.63.0.tar.gz
```

You are not limited to using all lowercase or all uppercase letters, nor must you use only one period in the entire expression. You can use a mixture of upper- and lowercase letters, combined with numbers, punctuation marks and other non-alphanumeric characters. The only limit is keeping the filename to 256 characters.

Other programmers might choose to use the compress command with their finished product, which would give the filename a .Z extension. Others might combine both tar and zip utilities and give the file a .tgz extension. Though the compression routines differ, uncompressing them and untarring them is done with gunzip.

When you untar most compressed programs, the untar and unzip routine will create a unique directory, usually with the same name and release number as the compressed program. Issuing a generic untar and unzip command should be create a new directory with the relevant files located inside. Sloppy programmers will simply unzip all the files into the current directory without creating a new, distinctive directory. As a result, such programmers ultimately will waste a lot of time and effort cleaning up. Check the contents of a file before uncompressing by using the t option. This lists the contents of an archive before the files are extracted. There are several ways this option can be applied.

```
tar -ztvf <filename> | less
gunzip -c <filename> | tar tvf - | more
```

Either of these commands or a variation on each will display the archived contents of a tarred and zipped file before uncompressing.

A standardized command for both untarring and unzipping the source is as follows:

```
gunzip -c WindowMaker-0.63.0.tar.gz | tar xvf -
```

Some of the more recent programs are compressed with the bzip2 command. To untar and unzip such source, you must substitute the gunzip command with bunzip2:

```
bunzip2 -c WindowMaker-0.63.0.tar.gz | tar xvf -
```

You can substitute any other *.tar.gz, *.tar.bz2, *.tgz, or *.Z filename in place of Window Maker. This window manager is just one that I chose to use as an example.

For more information regarding compression utilities, consult Chapter 9.

These types of commands are not required to unzip the program. There are several other ways to open a similar file. You can gunzip it first, then untar the file. This is sometimes a more roundabout method, but it accomplishes the same thing.

```
unzip WindowMaker-0.63.0.tar.gz
tar -xvf Windowmaker-0.63.0.tar
```

A distinct disadvantage of this method is that when the file becomes uncompressed, it occupies more space on the system while extracting the files and it is no longer zipped. A gzip command is required to recompress it.

Another method frequently used is simply to add the -z option to the tar command. This unzips the file at the same time it is untarred.

```
tar -xvzf WindowMaker-0.63.0.tar.gz
```

Many people prefer this option since it is a shorter, fairly straightforward command. One option used with this command is -v, which prints out the results of the decompression in verbose mode. This option allows you to see the directories exactly as they are created and the location of the files. The -x option simply stands for *extract* rather than *create*. You use this option when archiving the files. The -p option is used to retain the same permissions after extraction as before compression.

I chose Window Maker as an example since it is a fairly large file and has several unique parameters to its name. In chapter 12, you will examine GUIs under X Window. Window Maker offers an interface with many functions, and is useful for demonstrating many unique features of the Linux X Window system.

After issuing the appropriate untar and/or gunzip commands, you should now see a new directory in /usr/local/gnu or wherever else you have chosen to install these files. Entering an **ls -la** command will show the new WindowMaker-0.63.0/ directory along with the archived program source. The nice thing about the standard uncompress commands using gunzip and then piping the tar command afterwards is that it does not unzip or compromise the integrity of the archived program file. Rather it merely parses out the information and as it does so it untars the files and creates a new directory. After opening the file, you can just as easily redistribute the same tarred and zipped file to someone else.

Another fairly common practice is to create symbolic links to the new directories. For example, if the new directory just created has a release number at the end, such as WindowMaker-0.63.0/, you might want to make it more standardized and create a symbolic link to a simple WindowMaker/ directory. This way you always know where to go and do not have to constantly affix a release number to the end of the directory name. Here is how you would create a link:

```
ln -s WindowMaker-0.63.0/ WindowMaker/
```

When upgrading to a later version, delete only the symbolic link, untar the newer version, then create a new symbolic link.

## Compiling Code

Once the correct archive directory has been fully untarred and gunzipped, you can then change location by using the cd command and moving down into the new directory:

```
cd WindowMaker-0.63.0/
```

The first thing to do with any program is to look for a file called README or INSTALL. Most programmers insert these files within their code to assist those using their programs. The README file usually explains more about what the program does and perhaps how to use it. Use any text editor to read the file's contents and find out more about the program. The README file should also contain the release name, the author's name, and his or her e-mail address or some other method of contacting the author in case you absolutely cannot get the program to work. Poorly written programs do not provide all this information. Try to make sure that the programs you obtain either include such documentation or provide the author's contact information.

The INSTALL file explains how to compile the program correctly and also lists other programs needed for this program to work. Usually the INSTALL file also lists all the types of machines on which this program has been tested and has been proven to work. Some other notes included in the INSTALL file explain the various types of flags or options that can be listed with the `./configure` command that the system might require to compile the program correctly. For example, rather than editing the Makefile and changing the default installation location you can add a `--prefix=/usr/local/etc` or other variable to change the default location. Or should the system require a particular type of C compiler and its location, or if it allows you to enable a certain feature such as sound or compatibility with other libraries, these options would normally be listed in the INSTALL file. Also, most programs grant you the option of linking to other libraries if necessary. Basically, the INSTALL file describes most of the steps needed to install and compile your new program correctly.

When you install Window Maker or any other program that depends upon other programs to function, you will discover that to compile the program correctly, you must install additional libraries beforehand. One of those libraries that was previously included with the program is now listed separately to avoid forking the project or causing unnecessary splits and divergences in program development. The INSTALL file lists exactly those files upon which Window Maker relies. One of those files is libPropList.

## Configuring Dependent Libraries Beforehand

The following is a quick and easy method to perform an initial install before compiling Window Maker:

1. Change directories one level up so that when you issue a pwd command you can see that your current location is /usr/local/gnu.

2. Untar and gunzip the libPropList-0.10.1.tar.gz file, which creates a directory with the same name.

3. Change to the new directory and read the INSTALL file there just as you did with the WindowMaker file. The instructions are very simple

and easy to follow, as are most INSTALL files.

4. Execute each of the following commands, separately and in order, and things should install without complication. Be aware that most `make` `install` commands are usually the last step and should normally be performed as the root user.

```
./configure
make
make install
```

Make sure that you issue each command separately. If you get any error messages, write them down and see whether you have carried out the directions correctly. Often simple misspellings cause the worse errors. It can be easy to confuse a period with a comma, especially if your video resolution is set high.

If you have successfully compiled the program in the past and the preceding routine is "old hat," you may execute the commands all in succession or as one single command:

```
./configure ; make ; make install
```

Once you have successfully installed the libPropList binary, you'll notice that the source directory is still in /usr/local/gnu. Don't be too eager to delete this directory quite yet. You may still want to refer to its contents for reference or recompile the program if you ever suspect that the binary has become corrupted—an unlikely but possible occurrence.

After verifying that all the needed files are installed, you should be ready to compile and install Window Maker. You can move to the older directory location in one command—that is, move up one directory structure and then back down into the new one. If you are still in the libPropList-0.10.1/ directory, you can change to the WindowMaker-0.63.0/ directory by entering the following:

```
cd ../WindowMaker-0.63.0/
```

Enter **pwd** to verify that you are in the right directory. Once again, read through the INSTALL file to make sure you understand what files are needed and what you need to do. Fortunately, the authors of Window Maker realize that many beginners start learning Linux by first compiling a GUI such as theirs, and so they have written the instructions very carefully and in a manner that does not patronize novices.

# Running the Configure Routine

As with the libPropList installation, you first need to enter the following to begin the configure routine:

```
./configure
```

However, unlike libPropList, the configure routine lets you specify additional options. To enable sound and compatibility with other window managers, simply enter the following:

```
./configure --enable-sound --enable-gnome --enable-kde
```

The purpose of the configure script is to check the programs required for the binary against the programs already installed on the machine. If it finds the Linux install lacking a certain binary or library, the configure script will either stop and print an error message explaining why it was unable to continue at a given step. Most configure scripts are now standardized, in that a specific set of libraries and programs is necessary to run the newer program. Not so long ago, many of the variables had to be checked by hand and the proper options correctly placed in the command line so that each program knew where to find the dependent files. The configure script makes much of that handwork obsolete.

Its function is to create a makefile. This file is generated dynamically based on the available options loaded on the system. You can either accept the makefile based upon what the script has determined are installed components or you can edit the makefile later by hand. You can edit the makefile so that it does what you need it to do. For example, you might need to edit the file if you need to include additional libraries or if a path is wrong (that is, if it points to a binary located in a directory that occurs earlier in your path than the one you want it to use). Some programmers advise against tinkering with the generated makefile, reasoning that it can cause their own programs perhaps to fail. All too often, novice programmers mess with the code and fail to compile the code cleanly. Then they point the finger at the authors rather than at themselves.

The following is a small sample of the output generated by the ./configure command. You can see how each individual package is queried and what the response is, whether the correct version of the program is located or not. In this instance, the configure routine ran successfully.

```
# pwd
/usr/local/gnu/WindowMaker-0.63.0/
```

```
# ./configure --enable-sound --enable-gnome --enable-kde
loading cache ./config.cache
checking for a BSD compatible install... (cached) /usr/bin/install -c
checking whether build environment is sane... yes
checking whether make sets ${MAKE}... (cached) yes
checking for working aclocal... found
checking for working autoconf... found
checking for working automake... found
checking for working autoheader... found
checking for working makeinfo... found
checking host system type... i586-pc-linux-gnu
checking for ranlib... (cached) ranlib
checking for gcc... (cached) gcc
checking whether the C compiler (gcc  ) works... yes
checking whether the C compiler (gcc  ) is a cross-compiler... no
checking whether we are using GNU C... (cached) yes
checking whether gcc accepts -g... (cached) yes
checking for ld used by GCC... (cached) /usr/bin/ld
checking if the linker (/usr/bin/ld) is GNU ld... (cached) yes
checking for BSD-compatible nm... (cached) /usr/bin/nm -B
checking whether ln -s works... (cached) yes
checking for object suffix... o
checking for executable suffix... no
checking for gcc option to produce PIC... -fPIC
checking if gcc PIC flag -fPIC works... yes
checking if gcc supports -c -o file.o... yes
checking if gcc supports -c -o file.lo... yes
checking if gcc supports -fno-rtti -fno-exceptions ... yes
checking if gcc static flag -static works... -static
checking if the linker (/usr/bin/ld) is GNU ld... yes
checking whether the linker (/usr/bin/ld) supports shared libraries... yes
checking command to parse /usr/bin/nm -B output... ok
checking how to hardcode library paths into programs... immediate
checking for /usr/bin/ld option to reload object files... -r
checking dynamic linker characteristics... Linux ld.so
checking if libtool supports shared libraries... yes
checking whether to build shared libraries... yes
checking whether to build static libraries... yes
```

```
checking for objdir... .libs
creating libtool
Fixing libtool for -rpath problems.
checking host system type... i586-pc-linux-gnu
checking for POSIXized ISC... no
checking for gcc... (cached) gcc
checking whether the C compiler (gcc -g -O2 ) works... yes
```

The total output of ./configure would run for several pages, but the preceding example shows how many of the necessary programs are searched for and subsequently found. If you have any questions as to the proper syntax or flags that can be affixed to the configure script, type ./**configure --help** for a list of available options associated with configure.

## Running the make Command

Depending upon the location of the source code and who owns the files and directory, more likely than not you can run the configure and make commands as yourself. It is not always necessary to perform this task as root. You can also invoke the make install command as yourself, but it will be effective for only root. The new binary or binaries must also be in a directory for which that regular user has read and execute permission.

The next step in compiling is issuing the make command:

```
make
```

What follows is perhaps one of the most rewarding parts of the entire process. Some might consider this strange, but it is rather enjoyable sitting back and relaxing while the computer now does its job. Usually the process runs verbosely so that you can watch as each compile command takes a part of the code or a file.c and compiles it into a file.o piece of code. The ASCII text files are converted into binary or executable format. Many programmers would advise you to grab a snack or a drink while their code compiles.

How long the make command runs depends upon the code's size and complexity, as well as the speed of the computer. On my 200 megahertz Pentium box with 64 megabytes of RAM, compiling Window Maker takes about 10–15 minutes. Compiling a new Linux kernel can take as long as 20–30 minutes depending on what else I am running concurrently on the system. Though my machine may seem slow compared to the newer machines on the market, it is still much faster than when I compiled my first 2.0.31 kernel on an older 486 with 8 megabytes of RAM. It took about four and a half hours for the make command to finish compiling. I would usually start it up at my office in the evening, log in later that night from home, then finish the last few steps.

With some programs, after the make command has done its task, you have an option of entering **make test** or **make check**. Each command runs a series of pre-defined scripts that test the new binary for stability. If the script passes all the tests, the program informs you and recommends that you continue the install process. Programs such as the latest Perl will usually prompt you to execute a `make test` before installing. This is to ensure that you install a fully functional binary.

## Installing the Compiled Source

When the make command is done compiling the source, you can usually enter the following:

```
make install
```

You will probably need to invoke this command as root since you will not have permission to install some files in sensitive areas. The script installs all the binaries in their designated areas as defined by the program's author. For the most part, these areas will include /usr/local/bin and perhaps /usr/local/lib or other libraries. Most programs will not attempt to fool around much with system directories or to share system libraries. They will usually install their own or request that you install supplementary files. You can usually rest assured that most binaries will be placed somewhere in the /usr/local directory.

Users who do not have root access and share a machine with others while using their own X Window display may want to try using the `--prefix` option. This option is not specific to only to Window Maker, but the same general rules apply to other programs configured via the GNU autoconf program. Check the INSTALL file to validate its use with other programs. For Window Maker, if you can't get superuser privileges or cannot become root, you may install the required files in your own home directory. To do so, supply the `--prefix` option when running configure while building Window Maker. You will also need to supply the --with-appspath option, to specify the path for additional configuration files needed to run Window Maker. Here's an example:

```
./configure --prefix=/home/<username>--with-appspath=/home/
<username>/GNUstep/Apps
```

Be sure to place the expression /home/kerry/bin in your search path so that your system will know where to find the executable. To add this location to your path, first enter **echo $PATH**. Red Hat normally adds a bin/ directory to your home path for cases such as these. You may need to add /home/kerry/lib to your LD_LIBRARY_PATH environment variable located in /etc/profile. Once all that is done, you can run the installation script that copies over various configuration files for Window Maker into your home directory. (Of course, you should replace /home/kerry with your actual home directory path.)

## Checking for Debugging Symbols

If you want to make the binaries smaller without the debugging symbols, enter the following:

```
make install-strip
```

Sometimes developers want to see what causes a program to crash when they are first attempting to get it to run. If you strip off the debugging symbols, you will be unable to use such tools as gdb, otherwise known as the GNU debugger, to figure out exactly what section of the code caused the program to fail. But if you are interested only in getting the program to run cleanly and fast and are not concerned with tweaking the code much, then strip out the symbols. This makes the binaries smaller and less CPU-intensive.

This option is generally available with other programs and their debugging symbols can also be removed from off their binaries if this option is available. If, after installation, you decide you would like to strip the binaries and make them smaller due to their stability or need for more speed, use the strip command to make the compiled programs smaller. Execute the strip command with the binary name. For more information on removing debugging symbols consult the strip man page or man strip.

Binary installation usually goes quite fast. As is the case with several programs, you will need to tell Window Maker where your new libraries are located. First, be sure that the following line is in your /etc/ld.so.conf file:

```
/usr/local/lib
```

Your /etc/ld.so.conf file is where Linux looks for libraries on your system. Red Hat normally does not include this line in this file, so you will have to add it yourself. You then make the system fully aware of these new locations by entering the following:

```
/sbin/ldconfig
```

This command rereads all your libraries and their respective locations.

If you do not have root access and cannot modify the /etc/ld.so.conf file for system files, you may modify the LD_LIBRARY_PATH variable under your profile and have the same functionality, i.e. the system libraries will be accessible to the regular user.

To start the actual program and run the GUI, you need to become yourself again or exit superuser mode. If you are still at the root or pound sign (#), enter **exit** and make sure that your prompt displays the dollar sign ($) and that the shell now belongs to you. A simple whoami command should identify your shell ownership. Now enter the following:

```
wmaker.inst
```

This command is distinctive to the Window Maker program. Many programs have additional requirements or commands that need to be executed after the binaries are installed. Window Maker is no exception. The preceding command copies into your home directory certain required files containing configurations and graphics. If everything completes successfully up to this point, the rest should function well and you should be ready to run Window Maker. More about starting up the X Window environment is covered in Chapter 12.

If things do not work, return to the INSTALL file and check out the section on troubleshooting. Most INSTALL files should have either a troubleshooting section or a frequently asked questions (FAQ) file somewhere in their documentation.

## Installing Binaries

If you do not enjoy compiling source or feel that it takes too much effort or time, many programmers have made it possible to bypass the entire process altogether and simply install the binary file. For many programs, this alternative is preferable and easily accomplished. Normally the programmer compiles the source himself, tars and zips up the binary, then offers it to all via the Internet or from his or her Web site. If the binary depends on additional libraries or programs, these can either be compiled into the source or included in the zipped file. In such cases, most programmers include a detailed README file indicating the location of each file. Many programmers consider this the easy way out, and users can quickly install a program in this manner.

Although some users might find that installing programs from binary files is easy, it has its perils. Not all programs can be distributed as binaries. Some might require linking to additional libraries, but this is usually accomplished by the Makefile. Also, some unscrupulous Linux users might take advantage of users' trust and include malicious data in their files. Such devious behavior is uncommon; most programs undergo careful study before they land on the Internet, and any such culprit who is caught would face the scorn and ridicule of his or her peers. Nevertheless, some people crave recognition, even if it is negative.

Before attempting to install a binary file, try to compile the source yourself. The more you know, the better off you are. You can then begin to understand how source code and the Linux community operate.

# Defining RPM Packages

One of the most exciting developments from the Linux community in the past few years is the *RPM Package Manager* (RPM). Many new and innovative concepts are emerging in the open-source community, and Red Hat is one of the major contributors offering new designs and programs that facilitate Linux use. The RPM is a prime example as it was written by Marc Ewing and Eric Troan, the original founders of Red Hat. Red Hat's developers recognized the challenges involved in correctly and uniformly installing many sourced programs. Each user has his or her own preferences when it comes to compiling the binary, and this has resulted in several different binary versions of the same program. In response to requests for a standardized version of each program, Red Hat designed a method of simply installing a precompiled binary of the program along with documentation and libraries all in one package.

With RPMs you need no longer worry about options or libraries; in most cases, when you run the install for the RPM, your program is installed simultaneously. RPMs work on other Linux machines and even on some different UNIX distributions as well as they do on a Red Hat Linux release.

# Differences between RPMs and Source

As the name indicates, RPMs are designed to manage the program packages. Though binaries are spread across several partitions, depending upon your configuration, all the files and their respective locations are tracked in a single database. This makes installing, uninstalling, and upgrading new programs extremely simple. All commands are issued on the command line as root. The user needn't bother with any messy details or learn any instructions. Because the database that the main RPM program manages is extremely detailed, you can query the system about exactly what program is installed on the system. You need not hunt around older directories or use the find or locate commands to delete a defunct binary. The RPM program handles all the configurations automatically so that you never lose your customizations, something that is impossible with sourced programs generated from tarred and zipped files.

RPMs not only benefit end users, but also code developers. Red Hat provides you with the commercial releases of the source RPMs from which you can create your own customized RPM versions. RPM code developers also provide the source RPM code so that other users can verify the correctness of the code and check for any malicious line of syntax. Using the RPMs that contain the source code, and from which normal binary RPMs can be created, users can also create a binary RPM.

Do not confuse RPMs with patches. RPMs are not just binaries, but the program itself and all its attachments rolled into one. This makes the process of installing and updating older versions quite simple.

The major goals of the RPM project are fourfold. RPMs are to offer Linux users the following advantages over previous code installations:

◆ Upgradability      ◆ System verification

◆ Powerful querying     ◆ Pristine source

## Advantages of Using RPMs

With RPMs you no longer need to wipe out a complete directory to upgrade your machine to a newer release. Even Microsoft requires that you rename or even overwrite an older Windows directory for the upgrade to function correctly. All the previous settings and programs are lost if anything goes wrong. RPMs, however, retain your partitioning schemes and your original data files. You lose nothing when upgrading to newer RPM packages. All cross-referenced and linked files remain intact, and older RPM packages not included in the upgrade also continue to function.

One of the best features of the RPM packaging is that you can still query the RPM database as to exactly what file is installed and from where it came. You can verify any dependent packages and view the package header, which contains a brief summary of the package's contents. This summary shows you exactly where each file is stored within your directory structure.

Another powerful feature associated with RPMs is the capability to verify the integrity of a particular package. If you feel you may have accidentally deleted a crucial component or file associated with an RPM package, you can ask the database whether that file still exists. If it is lost, a simple reinstall or upgrade will fix the problem. The RPM program also saves previous configuration files for certain programs such as Samba, Apache BIND, PHP and sendmail so that they are never lost when you upgrade programs whose configuration files may be crucial to continued productivity of the system. In the case of other programs, the previous configuration file is merged with that of the newer file. Such is the case with several system files found in the /etc directory.

Probably one of the more important features of the RPM program is that the same source code used to build an RPM is available to other developers. Rather than creating a binary file that no one can look at or modify later, anyone can use the source code to create both a sourced RPM file and an RPM binary. Most programmers who work with RPMs make their source available so that anyone with the RPM program installed on his or her machine can create his or her own binary RPM file to use or distribute.

Most commercial releases of Red Hat and other Linux flavors enclose an additional CD that contains all the source code for the RPMs. In this manner, the source code stays fresh and the binaries can be easily re-created. Many users opt to build their own binary RPMs rather than simply trusting the distribution.

Though such precaution might seem almost paranoid, it is also handy in that the user can configure any additional options into the code rather than accepting the default options that come with the install.

# Using RPMs

The RPM program is used to accomplish five basic functions:

◆ Installing

◆ Uninstalling

◆ Upgrading

◆ Querying

◆ Verifying

Each of these functions is available from the command line or with one of the several GUIs available with the installation or from additional downloads.

For purposes of demonstration, you will first examine the command-line options for each function and then look at the most widely used RPM, Gnome-RPM. Though other RPMs are available, such as Glint and Xrpm, Gnome-RPM is currently the default manager for the Red Hat release. It is anticipated that in the next few years most other distributions that rely upon RPMs will use this GUI.

## The Composition of an RPM File

Before examining the different methods of utilizing RPM files, you should first examine the makeup of an RPM file. Using the RPM package that installs the zip command, you can see the elements that make up a distinct RPM file. A normal RPM filename is composed of five distinct entities. Some may have additional or alternative components, but for the most part, each RPM adheres to this basic structure. Here is how the zip RPM looks if downloaded from the Internet or from a Linux CD:

```
MySQL-3.22.25-1.i386.rpm
```

The first section is the name of the file. In this example, it is simply named *MySQL*. To query the RPM database or remove or upgrade the file properly, you must know this part of the file.

The second section is the version number. For this particular RPM, the version is 3.22. The version numbers are usually indicated by a period. This period sets them apart from the release number, which follows immediately afterward and is separated by a hyphen. This particular version of MySQL is release number 22 of version 3 thus indicating it is stable by its even number. Most developmental programs adhere to the same standard set by the Linux kernel, where the first number is the main version number, and the second indicates whether the version is stable or developmental. Stable programs are indicated by even numbers whereas odd numbers signify developmental versions. The third or last number is the release version. Some program developers do not adhere strictly to this rule. Version 2.3 of some programs can also be classified as stable. However, the general trend in numbering programs is to categorize releases as stable or developmental based on their version number. The last set of numbers, 25-1, is the number of times that release has been patched or recompiled since its official stable release. Chapter 14 explains the numbering scheme for Linux kernels in more detail.

The fourth section is the architecture type. Because most Linux versions are designed for the PC using Intel architecture, an i386 is placed in this fourth field, indicating the file's architecture type. For other hardware types, such as an Alpha chip or Sparc box, this field would contain an alpha or sparc signature, respectively. Red Hat develops its programs from these types of architecture as well and their versions are released as often as the Intel-crafted packages. Some of Red Hat's more recent RPMs releases use an i586 or i686 to separate them from other older versions. These releases are geared to higher-end boxes.

The last field is the RPM identifier. This is a suffix appended to RPM files to indicate their file type. Even without the RPM suffix you can still install the file. Using the file command on any RPM file will still point to its true nature as that of an RPM file. The RPM suffix is used mainly for clarification as opposed to .deb or .slp formats. If you are downloading onto a Windows machine, these RPM files are sometimes renamed and the periods are substituted with underscores. When downloading onto a different platform, make sure you keep the same naming scheme as was originally intended. If the file is renamed or changed, you can always use the file command to identify the file type properly.

Now that you are familiar with how an RPM file looks, let us examine how it works and acts.

# Dynamic Package Installation

The standard method of installing an RPM file is to invoke the rpm command first, then the requested options, and then the filename. Here is an example of how to install the zip RPM from a superuser prompt. Remember that all install and update commands executed with the rpm command must be done as root or superuser.

```
# rpm -ivh zip-2.2-1.i386.rpm
zip                       ###################################
#
```

Because the rpm command is located in /bin/rpm, it should already be included in root's path. There is usually no problem invoking it from wherever you might be on the system. This means that you can download an RPM file to any directory and still install it without a hitch. Once the binary has been successfully installed from the RPM package, you can safely delete the downloaded file. As the preceding example shows, the program installed with no problem. You could now delete the file, zip-2.2-1.i386.rpm, without any problems. The binary is installed in /usr/bin/zip. The RPM file also installed additional files that you will look at momentarily.

This command uses several options. The -i option is used to install the program. The other two letters are installation options. The -v option runs the command in verbose mode, whereas the -h option prints out a row of hash marks representing the install progress. It is a good practice to implement the last option. In the unlikely case that something should hang or not install, you can at least determine whether anything was installed or whether it failed in its execution. If the hash marks fail to increment, you should reevaluate the validity of the RPM file.

If the package is already installed and you are attempting to reinstall, RPM notifies you that the package in question is already installed:

```
# rpm -ivh zip-2.2-1.i386.rpm
package zip-2.2.-1 is already installed
#
```

If you are determined to reinstall the package or to force an overwrite of the same binary, you can use the `--force` option. Using this option is the same as using the `--replacepkgs`, `--replacefiles`, or `--oldpackage` options; it forces a reinstall of the specified package.

Sometimes the package you are attempting to install conflicts with some previously installed package. This is the case if you try to install an older package over a later version. The error you receive tells you that your file conflicts with another file:

```
# rpm -ivh zip-2.1-5cl.i386.rpm
package zip-2.2-1 (which is newer then zip-2.1-5cl) is already
installed
file /usr/bin/zip from install of zip-2.1-5cl conflicts with file
from package zip-2.2-1
#
```

If you choose to ignore the error message and install the older file, you can do so by using the `--oldpackage` option or the `--force` option mentioned previously:

```
# rpm -ivh --oldpackage --force zip-2.1-5cl.i386.rpm
```

Using this option is not recommended, but works if you want to go back to an older release. A preferred option is to remove the existing RPM file, perhaps using the `--nodeps` flag if other packages depend on the file, and then reinstalling the older file.

## Uninstalling RPMs

There may come a time that you might want to remove an RPM file, either because you were only trying it out or because you want to place a more recent version on the system. (In the latter case, some would advocate that you upgrade rather than remove the file.) In either case, removing an RPM file is much simpler and quicker to accomplish than removing sourced programs. With source programs, you need either to read the makefiles and determine exactly where all the files were placed or pay close attention while installing them and note their locations. In either case, it is easy to overlook a file placed in an obscure directory or forget to delete a library. With the latest autoconf-generated source packages, you can invoke a similar uninstall command as used by the rpm program and do a "make uninstall" with standard compiled sources. This will generally do a thorough job in removing all the installed programs.

RPMs handle all the tracking and monitoring of the installation files for you. When you remove an RPM file, all instances of that particular program are erased from your drive. No registries are changed or modified in the process. No telltale signs bog down the computer and no remnant files keep records of older, defunct programs. This is yet another advantage of open-source software over proprietary closed-source software.

To remove an RPM file from your system, the command requires only one option:

```
# rpm -e zip
```

Notice that you do not need to type the version or release number of the file when uninstalling. If you know the exact name of the file, you can remove it without any problems. If you are unsure as to the exact name of the file, you can run the query `rpm -qf 'which <filename>'` to determine the exact RPM file-name and it version number. Using the GUI, Gnome-RPM, is also helpful in locating the exact spelling of the file you are attempting to locate. If you misspell or add an extra ending to any file that you are attempting to remove, the program responds with an error and states that the file is not installed. This is true, since Linux is case-sensitive and requires the exact spelling to uninstall the package successfully.

At times, removing certain files can break dependencies. If the file that you are trying to remove is required by another program in order to run, the RPM program will let you know and will not complete the request:

```
# rpm -e zip
error: removing these packages would break dependencies:
    foobar-1.2 is needed by zip-2.2-1
```

The RPM file foobar does not exist and is a typical filename used for imaginary files. But if that file did exist and depended upon the zip file, RPM would not allow the uninstall process to continue as the command currently stands.

You can force an uninstall of RPM files if you feel it is absolutely necessary or have a good reason for doing so. Though the developers of the RPM program do not recommend forcing an uninstall, in some instances you need to remove a particular file in order to install additional files. You can force an uninstall by using the `--nodeps` option with the `-e` flag. This tells the RPM program not to look for dependent files when uninstalling.

```
# rpm -e zip --nodeps
```

There is no hash option to view the progress of the removal. In this instance, you have to take RPM's word for it that the file has been successfully removed. To determine whether the package has been successfully uninstalled, run a second query after the removal process to see whether the package is still installed.

## Performing RPM Upgrades

It takes only a few months following the initial install of Linux to discover that several of your installed packages are no longer the latest version available. At this point, you might consider upgrading them. This is simple enough to do with the RPM utility. Upgrading RPM files is similar to performing the initial install. If you try simply to install the latest file over the existing package, RPM will notify you that there is a conflict in package dependencies. You will need to use the -U option to update the file instead. As with the initial install, only root can execute this command.

Here is a sample upgrade of zip-2.2-1 to zip-2.3-7:

```
# rpm -Uvh zip-2.3-7.i386.rpm
zip                        ####################################
#
```

This is the same process that most Linux versions use when updating the previous Linux version to a newer one. The valued configuration files are either left alone, or if the update is relatively major and requires a new configuration, RPM will save the older file with an .rpmsave extension.

## Querying the Package Database

To find out what version of the RPM file you have installed on your system, you can query the database by specifying the -q, or *query,* option. The following query determines the version of zip:

```
# rpm -q zip
zip-2.3-7
#
```

Any user on the system may query the database as to the latest RPM package version. You do not need superuser permission to execute this command.

You can also use the -q option with other variables to gather additional information on the installed RPM package files. If you want to print out a list of all the packages on your system, you use -q along with -a. For example, you can use the following command to pipe the information into a text file that you can then bring up with any editor:

```
# rpm -qa > list.txt
```

For a more complete briefing of all the features included in a specific installed package, you can apply several other variables that the -q option features. For example, you can use -i to print out not only the version number, but also a summary of the version's history and a description of what the RPM file accomplishes. This information is similar to that supplied with the README file in most sourced programs. Figure 11.1 shows an example from the latest zip file.

For more information on exactly what additional files are installed with the zip program and where they are placed, you use the -ql option. Here is an example of output generated after this option was specified:

```
# rpm -ql zip
/usr/bin/zip
/usr/bin/zipcloak
/usr/bin/zipnote
/usr/bin/zipsplit
/usr/share/doc/zip-2.3
/usr/share/doc/zip-2.3/BUGS
/usr/share/doc/zip-2.3/CHANGES
/usr/share/doc/zip-2.3/MANUAL
/usr/share/doc/zip-2.3/README
/usr/share/doc/zip-2.3/TODO
/usr/share/doc/zip-2.3/WHATSNEW
/usr/share/doc/zip-2.3/WHERE
/usr/share/doc/zip-2.3/algorith.txt
/usr/share/man/man1/zip.1.gz
```

The -q option is very useful for printing out additional information about uninstalled packages instead of packages already contained in the local rpm database. Rather than determining what files were placed in which directories *after* the installation, you can use the -q option to print out where the files would be placed before actually installing the package.

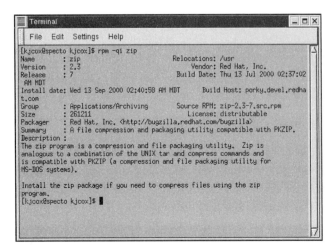

```
Terminal                                            _ □ X
 File  Edit  Settings  Help
[kjcox@specto kjcox]$ rpm -qi zip
Name       : zip                  Relocations: /usr
Version    : 2.3                      Vendor: Red Hat, Inc.
Release    : 7                     Build Date: Thu 13 Jul 2000 02:37:02
 AM MDT
Install date: Wed 13 Sep 2000 02:40:58 AM MDT    Build Host: porky.devel.redha
t.com
Group      : Applications/Archiving   Source RPM: zip-2.3-7.src.rpm
Size       : 261211                    License: distributable
Packager   : Red Hat, Inc. <http://bugzilla.redhat.com/bugzilla>
Summary    : A file compression and packaging utility compatible with PKZIP.
Description :
The zip program is a compression and file packaging utility.  Zip is
analogous to a combination of the UNIX tar and compress commands and
is compatible with PKZIP (a compression and file packaging utility for
MS-DOS systems).

Install the zip package if you need to compress files using the zip
program.
[kjcox@specto kjcox]$ █
```

**FIGURE 11.1**

*A -qi query to the RPM program results in a summary that shows who built the RPM, when it was built, from what source it came, and more.*

For example, the command `rpm -qpl zip-2.3-7.i386.rpm` lists the contents of the file without actually installing the files. A similar command `rpm -qpi zip-2.3-7.i386.rpm` prints out information about the zip program before it installs. This way it is not necessary to install every file in order to see what files were placed on your system.

Some of the other options associated with the query command are as follows:

| Option | Description |
| --- | --- |
| -d | Shows those files marked as documentation files, such as man pages and doc files. |
| -s | Displays the state of the files in a certain package. |
| -c | Lists those files marked as configuration files. The option is applicable to programs such as Apache or Samba that require these types of files. |

## Verifying the Integrity of Installed Packages

The last step in testing the integrity of an installed RPM package is to verify it. To do so, you use a command that checks the information that is installed from the packages against information from the original package. The command tests such things as the size, MD5 sum, permissions, type, owner, and group of each file.

You run the verification of the RPM file by using the -v or *verify* option. To verify the program file zip, for example, you would enter the following command:

```
# rpm -Vf /usr/bin/zip
```

If everything is verified correctly and there are no complications, then RPM will not print out any output. If you suspect that your databases are corrupt, you can verify the installed file against a newly downloaded RPM file, as follows:

```
rpm -Vp zip-2.3-7.i386.rpm
```

You may want to rebuild the database if you find that the database is corrupt. You can either rebuild the existing database or create a new one. You should do so only if the situation appears drastic. Whenever you rebuild the database you run the risk of corrupting the data further. But if things already look bleak, rebuilding may just fix things.

To re-create the existing database, use the following command:

```
rpm --rebuilddb
```

To create a new database, enter the following:

```
rpm --initdb
```

This command creates a new RPM database on your system. It completely removes all information about the installed RPM packages from off your machine. This should be the very last option considered.

## Creating RPM Packages from Source

If you want the freedom of the RPM format, yet want or need to view the source code, you can create binary RPMs from source RPMs. Many developers make their source code available in a *.src.rpm format so that users can then create their own binaries for easy installation. Some users prefer compiling their own RPMs along with their own variables or options. Red Hat provides a unique location near the source kernel for compiling your own RPMs.

To create a binary RPM from the source RPM and install it, follow these steps:

1. Become superuser or root by entering **su -**.
2. In the directory where the source RPM is located, enter **rpm -ivh** <packagename>.src.rpm.

3. Change directories to Red Hat's SPECS directory by entering **cd /usr/src/redhat/SPECS.**

4. Issue the following RPM build command to create the i386 formatted RPM: **rpm -bb <packagename>.spec.**

5. Enter the following to change to the new directory where the binary RPM is now located: **cd ../RPMS/i386.** (When using a Sun- or Alpha-based system, this directory will have a different name.)

6. To install your binary RPM, enter **rpm -ivh <packagename>.i386.rpm.**

Once you have installed the RPM package, you may safely delete the binary in this directory and re-create it later. Often developers will make only the source RPM available to guarantee the integrity of the binary RPM. This places the burden of successfully building the package in the hands of the users.

## Staying Current with Update Agent

A good way to keep your RPM packages current or to ensure your machine's security is to download and update the packages periodically. However, if your system needs to stay current on *all* RPMs or if you wish to stay up to date on only selected RPMs, then locating the required packages on your own or visiting that program's web page may not be as productive as automatically downloading the RPMs from off the Red Hat site or by using the Red Hat Update Agent, which keeps your system current on all installed RPMs.

Red Hat's latest release provides a useful tool, Update Agent, which retrieves the most current packages from the Red Hat download site. The program does require you to register on the Red Hat web page to access its FTP site. To register, go to http://www.redhat.com/now. Once you register, you can select a username and password, which you should use to configure Update Agent.

After you finish registering, you can launch your Update Agent from within the desktop and then connect to the Red Hat site, providing the newly created account name and password. You can initiate this same program within any other window manager by typing **/usr/bin/up2date** at any root command line. Only root can start up this program.

To operate the Update Agent, locate the main startup by first opening up the Gnome desktop. Click the main Gnome logo icon or the Main Menu button on the Gnome panel in the bottom-left corner, then choose System, Update Agent.

If you are using KDE as your default window manager, choose Panel, Red Hat, System, Update Agent. Each time you start this program as yourself from within Gnome or KDE, you will be prompted to enter root's password (see Figure 11.2).

Now you will be able to configure Update Agent to grant you access to Red Hat's inventory of updated programs.

### NOTE

If using another window manager, you must start the program as root. Gnome and KDE act as wrappers for this particular program and thus they will prompt you for root's password when attempting to run root-owned programs.

Once the main Update Agent window launches (see Figure 11.3), choose the Configure button to set up your connection. The Configuration dialog box appears. (The Abort button applies only when downloading or installing programs and closes the program.)

**FIGURE 11.2**

*Under Gnome and KDE you will be prompted for root's password when attempting to start the program as a regular user. Under other window managers you will need to be root in order to launch this application.*

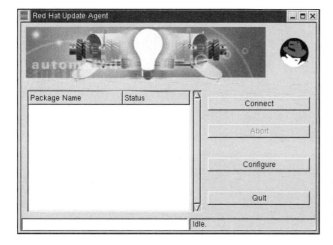

**FIGURE 11.3**

*The main Update Agent window, which enables the user to configure or connect to the main Red Hat RPM site.*

The Configuration dialog box displays three tabs. Under each you can enter information that will enable you to connect to the main RPM site and download information:

- *User.* In this tab, you enter the username and password that you chose after registering at the Red Hat site. You also need to provide a valid email address.
- *Retrieval.* Use this tab to specify the name of the server and grant the program instructions for installing and updating downloaded programs.
- *Exceptions.* In this tab, you can select specific files or packages that you wish to exclude from your search.

Figure 11.4 displays the User tab. Fill in the username or password you chose after registering at the Red Hat site. You should also place your email address in the space provided.

Figure 11.5 shows the Retrieval tab. This tab requires that you enter much more detail about your configuration and the names of the download servers. You must enter a server name from which you will download the updates. This can be either a Red Hat server or a mirrored box. The tab also enables you to pick the program that will download and install the new packages.

**FIGURE 11.4**

*The User tab of the Configuration dialog box is where you enter your username and password.*

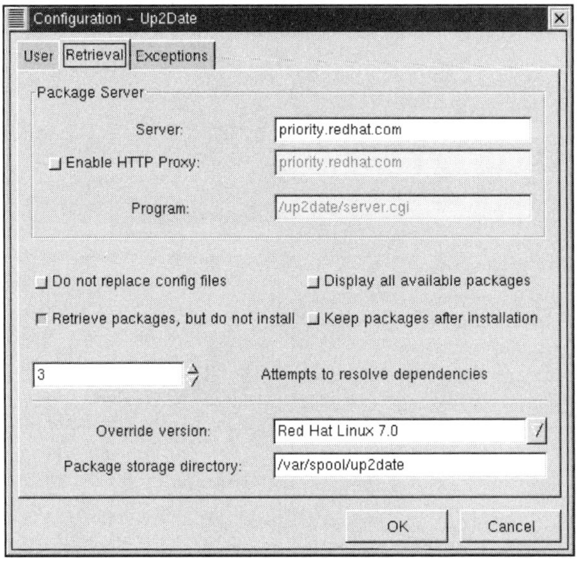

**FIGURE 11.5**

*The Retrieval tab of the Configuration dialog box. Here you input information regarding the download servers.*

Below the server fields are check boxes and other fields that enable you to optimize the methods of downloading and installing the new packages. As with the Gnome-RPM program, you can choose exactly how the newer packages will be handled. You can back up older configuration files or simply overwrite them, have the program display all the available files, retrieve the packages without installing them, and install downloaded packages elsewhere.

You can also decide whether or not the program should attempt to resolve dependencies. You can choose the number of times the program should check for dependencies with other programs. This number can be between one and 10. You can also opt to override the Linux version that the program is currently updating and the default location at which you will store downloaded programs either before updating or for archival purposes.

Figure 11.6 is a screenshot of the Exceptions tab, which enables you to specify packages and files that you normally will not wish to download, search for, or modify. You can use the wildcard options: the asterisk (*) and the question mark (?). The asterisk when used at the end of a file will disregard all packages that begin with the characters preceding the asterisk (*). For example, the RPM packages kernel, kernel-headers, kernel-source, kernel-utils, and kernelcfg will all be ignored because of the wildcard option. If you are unsure of the package name, use the question mark (?) to locate packages with similar spelling.

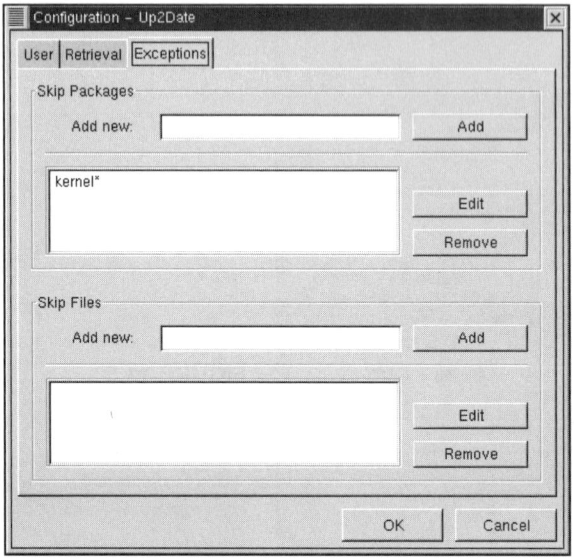

**FIGURE 11.6**

*The Exceptions tab of the Configuration dialog box. Here you place those package or filenames you do not wish to update.*

In the lower part of the dialog box, you can ignore certain files in addition to packages. If you are aware of a particular file type or name that you will not be updating, select its name here along with any wildcard options, and that particular file will not be downloaded.

## Running Update Agent in an X Window Environment

After filling out all the pertinent information, you can now connect to a server and download the needed files. If you have a LAN connection, you will not need to set up a Point-to-Point Protocol (PPP) connection. If you are updating the machine from a box at home, you will first need to be connected to an Internet service provider (ISP) and establish a viable connection. To review setting up PPP connections, see Chapter 16.

On the main Update Agent screen, click the Connect button. A status bar appears in the bottom-left corner of the main page and indicates that the application is connecting and retrieving information from the referenced FTP site. If you have selected any files to be excluded, you will see a dialog box such as the one shown in Figure 11.7. In this particular example, the kernel* packages were selected to be excluded from downloading. Additional status information

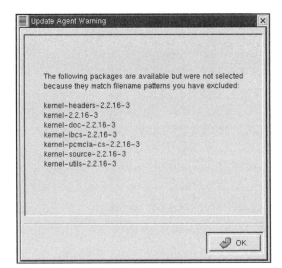

**FIGURE 11.7**

*A dialog box displaying the exceptions you choose not to download.*

will appear in the bottom-right corner of the main Red Hat Update Agent window.

The Update Agent next creates an HTML page that is viewable in your browser. This page provides additional information about each package you choose to update. If you chose to install the Netscape Communicator package, the Update Agent will then launch this browser for you. You may access the page from within any browser that renders HTML pages.

Based upon your needs, you may select the package you wish to install by checking a box next to the package. You should see a web page such as the one shown in Figure 11.8, which was generated by the Update Agent.

After you finish selecting those packages to download and install, click the Request selected packages button next to the package name. If you prefer to update your system with all the available packages, click the Request ALL packages button; you will not be required to make individual selections beside each package. After you have made your request for the packages, the browser window closes.

Next, the main Update Agent dialog box lists the packages selected for downloading (see Figure 11.9). The column Package Name lists each package, whereas the Status column inserts a small button next to each package. Below this window is a small status bar that displays the download and dependency

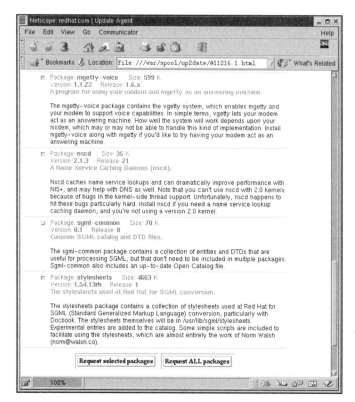

**FIGURE 11.8**

*A Web page displaying the packages available for downloading. Select those packages for updating by clicking the check box next to each package name.*

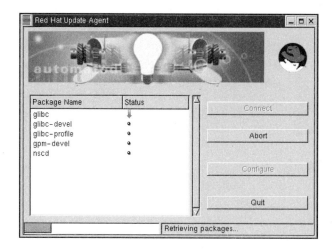

**FIGURE 11.9**

*The main Update Agent dialog box displaying the progress of each downloaded and installed program.*

check status. When the packages finish downloading, the button in the Status column changes to a red arrow. The arrow then becomes a check mark when each package has been successfully installed. The progress bar in the lower-left corner of the dialog box reflects the work remaining before all updates have been downloaded and installed.

After all the packages have been retrieved and/or installed on your system, a window opens informing you of the procedure's success. You also receive an e-mail verification that the requested procedure has been completed. The verification will be sent to the address that you specified as your user ID.

## Updating Packages from the Command Line

If you do not wish to run Update Agent from within a window manager or from an xterm or GUI desktop, you can also choose to run the program from the command line (see Figure 11.10). At a root shell prompt, enter **/usr/sbin/up2date -l** to retrieve a list of available packages that you can update. Remember again that depending on the speed of your machine and the packages available, the list may scroll by too quickly for you to read each one. You can pipe the output to a pager, using an option such as `less`, or redirect the output to a text file, which you can read with a pager or any text editor.

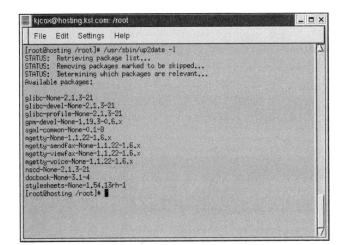

**FIGURE 11.10**

*Displaying the packages available for updating using Update Agent from the command line.*

To download and install the packages you want, use the *batch mode* option, which consists of a -b or --batch flag following the main command. To download the latest rpm program, for example, issue the following command:

```
# /usr/sbin/up2date -b rpm
```

Or, if you wish to download multiple updates, follow the batch option with each package name:

```
# /usr/sbin/up2date -b glibc gpm mgetty nscd
```

This command enables you to download and install each package listed on the command line.

## Using alien to Convert Packages

If you want to test packages under other formats such as the Debian .deb, the Slackware .tgz, and the Linux Stampede .slp formats, you can use a Linux utility that converts RPMs into these other formats and back again. The alien program is a Perl script that provides interoperability between the different package managers available on other distributions. Often developers accustomed to a certain distribution such as Debian create packages for their distribution only, leaving Red Hat users unable to load their utility without completely removing their specific distribution such as Red Hat, and then installing the new distribution that supports the new package type. The same goes for many Linux users who are not using Red Hat. Though the RPM package is simple to install, many feel a particular affinity for their own distribution. The alien program bypasses many of the hurdles by enabling users to convert these packages into any other binary package format. Though a Debian user can install the rpm program and maintain two separate databases, RPM and DEB, it is far easier to use alien to convert packages between these two binary packages.

---

**CAUTION**

In general, though, you should not use alien to convert certain packages such as init, libc, and other system-specific files into other formats. Doing so can break your system. Downloading the Stampede version of the latest kernel, converting it to RPM format, and then installing it on a Red Hat box is definitely *not* advised. Differing distributions install system programs in variable locations. The alien program is intended primarily for unique programs that provide added functionality and which are not integral to system performance.

The alien program is available from the alien home page at http://kitenet.net/ programs/alien/, but can be downloaded from any of the many Linux mirror sites or from clearinghouse sites such as Freshmeat or Linuxberg. There is also a current release available on the GNUware CD.

Once you have placed the tarred and zipped program in a temporary location, uncompress it by issuing the following command:

```
gunzip -c alien_x.x.tar.gz | tar xvf -
```

Replace the *x*'s with the latest release number. This will create a unique directory named alien/. Change directories into this new location and read the README and INSTALL files. These provide basic instructions for installing and running the program. If you are anxious begin using the program, simply enter the following line to set up, make, and install the program:

```
# perl Makefile.PL; make; make install
```

Rather than typing in the individual commands separately, you can splice them all together onto one line with semicolons.

Next, either download or procure a copy of the package you would like to convert. If you have a friend who is a confirmed Debian user who likes his or her format exclusively, you can share many of your favorite RPM packages by using alien to convert the very latest zip RPM file to a .deb file. Here is the most basic syntax for using alien:

```
# alien --to-deb zip-2.3-4.i386.rpm
```

If you have all the necessary libraries and dependent files installed, alien will create a .deb file, which is then ready for redistribution. The same applies to .slp and .tgz files. The Slackware .tgz format is probably the most versatile since it provides the standard binaries independent of the platform that you are using.

```
# alien --to-tgz zip-2.3-4.i386.rpm
```

This command creates a zip-2.3.tgz file. Once you uncompress and untar the file, the program also creates the normal directories in which these files are installed.

Copy the *.tgz file to a location such as /tmp and then unzip them. You may then replace the binaries in the standard locations. This program is not intended exclusively for use with system files, but can be very useful for obtaining the binaries and then installing those files by hand.

The alien program is also capable of installing the newly created packages imme-diately after their creation. When converting programs from their .deb extension to .rpm format or reversed on a Debian system, once the conversion is done it will begin installing the binary onto the system. Simply add the -i option and the package will install after its conversion:

```
# alien --to-deb -i zip-2.3-4.i386.rpm
```

You can also provide a description of what the program does by adding a --description= option followed immediately by a short string that explains the function of the program.

```
# alien --to-rpm --description="A utility for compressing files"
zip-2.3.tgz
   zip-2.3-2.noarch.rpm generated
```

As always, the best way to determine additional options or to find answers for more syntactical questions is to consult the man pages.

## Running Gnome-RPM

One of the more functional tools to be released for Linux is Gnome-RPM. It provides a GUI for browsing the contents of the RPM database and allows for quick installation and uninstallation of the various files. It is also customizable in that users can set up their own directories into which they can then place their own RPM files for organizational purposes.

Modeled after the typical collapsible directory tree structure, Gnome-RPM also provides several tools for searching for a lost RPM file or for procuring the lat-est version from the Internet at one of the many mirrored RPM sites.

The Gnome-RPM program is executed with the gnorpm command. Much like its predecessor, glint, gnorpm also provides users with a visual representation of each RPM file (see Figure 11.11). But unlike glint, gnorpm accepts several com-mand-line options that reflect the same capabilities that the rpm command offers at the command line.

The basic commands available from the command line are quite evident here as well. You can install, uninstall, query, and verify. In addition to providing these very basic commands, gnorpm adds a few other options. You can also select your choice of packages to be uninstalled by simply clicking on the package and adding a check mark to its respective icon. The gnorpm program also has a Find

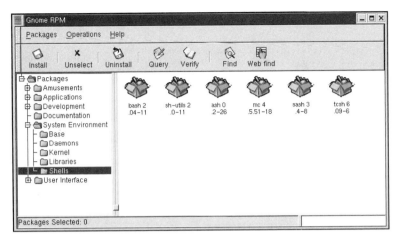

**FIGURE 11.11**

*An initial image of the Gnome-RPM window displaying the packages in the right-hand box available for each category shown in the left-hand column.*

feature for locating RPM files directly on the system and a Web Find feature that is tied into the external program rpmfind. With this latter utility, if you are connected to the Internet, you can locate the file of your choice as well as choose from a large assortment of files elsewhere.

In the main interface window's lower-left corner, you can browse through the many categories or RPM files available, most of which come preinstalled. On the right side are the packages themselves. Only by clicking within one of the folders on the left can you see each individual option.

Among the icons that appear across the top of the screen, the first is perhaps the most important. More often than not, users wish to download new RPMs rather than delete the existing ones. Clicking on the Install button brings up the Install window shown in Figure 11.12.

In this Install window, you can opt to install additional RPMs from your distribution CD or unselect those already installed. The Filter drop-down menu at the top provides options to display all packages, all but the installed packages, only uninstalled packages, only newer packages (this option is available only if you are upgrading to a later version), and only uninstalled or newer packages. Below the Filter control is a tree structure window that lists the packages. This list consists of the categories found on the mounted distribution CD. Like the Gnome-RPM window, the Install window enables you to begin selecting and unselecting the packages you wish to add. If you select the option All Packages from the Filter drop-down menu, you can see those packages already installed, highlighted in green, and those not installed, shown in black (see Figure 11.13).

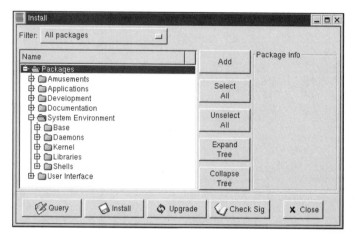

**FIGURE 11.12**

*The Install window for Gnome-RPM, where you can select specific packages for installation.*

In Figure 11.13, all Desktop applications have been installed and thus show up in green. The Window Maker desktop is still uninstalled and thus shows up as black. Checking the box next to the application name and then clicking the Install button on the bottom of the window will then install the program from off the Red Hat Linux installation CD.

You can also select one of the other options from the Filter drop-down menu. By doing so, you change the display in the tree structure window. Selecting the Only Uninstalled Packages option displays just those packages not already installed on your system (see Figure 11.14).

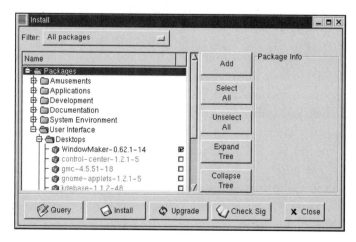

**FIGURE 11.13**

*If you choose the All Packages option, Gnome-RPM displays all packages—those that are installed and those that are not but are available on the installation CD.*

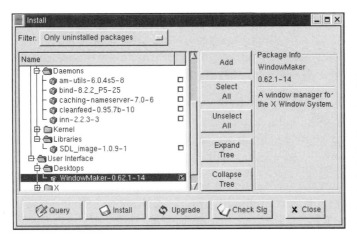

**FIGURE 11.14**

*If you choose the Only Uninstalled Packages option, the program lists those packages that are not already installed but which are available for installation. You may select or unselect each listed package as you wish.*

Now you can use the buttons to the right of the directory tree structure either to select all, unselect all, expand, or collapse the tree structure. To the right of these buttons are short summaries of each package's function. If you want to install only a few additional files, you should choose the Unselect All button and then collapse the tree structure. Then you can work your way through all the available packages and select only those that you want.

The buttons across the bottom of the screen enable you to query the packages on the CD. After selecting your packages, you can then choose the Install button either to reinstall a previously uninstalled package or upgrade to a newer release. If you are installing a new package, gnorpm launches the install process.

The program then displays a small progress window that indicates the number of packages selected, their size, and the time remaining in the installation process (see Figure 11.15). You might recognize a similar window from the initial install process of Linux. After the install process is complete, the selected packages are ready to be accessed.

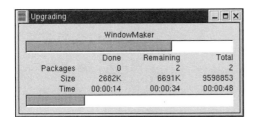

**FIGURE 11.15**

*The progress meter as the program downloads and installs new packages.*

You can also choose to uninstall selected packages from the main Gnome-RPM. Choose the directory with the package you wish to remove. After you highlight the package(s) that you wish to uninstall, a confirmation window appears asking you to confirm your decision (see Figure 11.16).

If you reply affirmatively, the program uninstalls your selected RPM package. As with the console command, the program does not display any sort of visual progress indicator showing the progress of the uninstall procedure, but after a few moments the selected package will disappear from the window.

The next option on the main gnorpm window is the Query button. Before you use this tool, you must first highlight a single package to be queried. Functioning much like the RPM command-line options -qi and -ql, the Query tool provides a description of the RPM package, details about its build, and a display of all the files installed and their respective locations (see Figure 11.17).

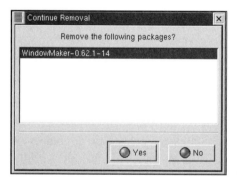

**FIGURE 11.16**

*Gnome-RPM prompts you for confirmation when removing unwanted or obsolete packages.*

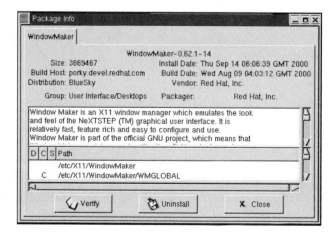

**FIGURE 11.17**

*The Query tool provides a more verbose description of the package information.*

The Query button brings all the additional command-line traits together in one simple interface. In addition, you can verify the individual packages and confirm that they correspond to the original packages as they were installed (see Figure 11.18).

The last two features on the main gnorpm window, Find and Web Find, provide additional functionality and leave gnorpm's predecessors far behind in performance. The Find option allows you to locate a specific package (see Figure 11.19). Several additional options for locating that file can assist you in defining your search. You might select the Match Label option if you know the name of the file that you want to find. You can also look for a file in a particular group or category such as Applications, Development or System Environment or in a group that requires that file. The options are fairly generic and far-reaching. After the program finds the file, you can also query, uninstall, and verify it.

The last option is perhaps the most versatile. With it, you can now locate RPM files from nearly anyplace in the world. Make sure you are first connected to the Internet, either by a LAN or modem connection, then click the Web Find button to bring up a list of nearly all the possible RPM packages available. The gnorpm program executes the rpmfind program and then first queries a database at a remote site and downloads the list of all available programs. As each individual

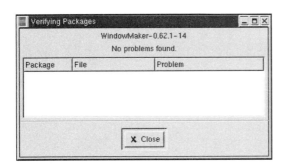

**FIGURE 11.18**

*When gnorpm verifies that no problems occurred during installation, the program displays a verification window.*

**FIGURE 11.19**

*The Find tool locating new packages for installation.*

package is examined, the rpmfind program queries the remote site and downloads further information. This information is displayed under gnorpm.

As shown in Figure 11.20, the window to the left displays all the possible programs available; their names appear on the far left, and then their status and distribution on the local system. The example in Figure 11.20, joe, a simple text editor, is currently not installed on the local machine.

To install joe, you can do either one of two things, both of which will allow you to install the text editor later. If you click the Download button, rpmfind prompts you to confirm that you want to download the selected packages (see Figure 11.21). Next, an indicator will appear that displays the progress as it is downloaded.

You can then install the packages later. The Install tool does all the work for you. You are prompted to download the package, but once it is on the local system, the program automatically installs it for you.

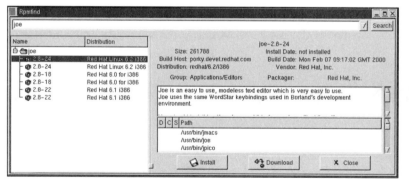

**FIGURE 11.20**

*The rpmfind utility provides a verbose display consisting of the package's name, the release to which the package belongs, and a description of the file.*

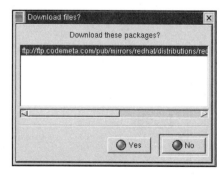

**FIGURE 11.21**

*A window confirming the download of the new package.*

The dynamism of the gnorpm program makes it extremely easy to install a plethora of programs on your system. And because the software is open-sourced and free to the public, there are no hidden costs. The only obvious disadvantage to this program is the lack of available mirrors. If one of the selected sites' FTP access is full or unavailable, the program gives no response. However, once the program locates a valid site and confirms the presence of the requested file, it quickly starts downloading.

Once the file is completely downloaded, gnorpm again prompts you to verify the installation of the new file. It brings up the Install window once more and even chooses the appropriate directory in which to install the file.

If you are unable to establish an Internet connection, other options are available. Many sites make RPMs available for purchase on a CD. As with the distribution CD, you can quickly access the files located there by mounting the CD on your machine and perusing the contents (see Figure 11.22).

The Gnome-RPM program makes the entire installation process using RPMs a painless procedure for even the most novice of users. Although being capable of installing source is a tried-and-true measure of an administrator's worth, RPMs make it possible for the average user to perform the same task. Though compiling code from source might be considered enjoyable to the novice, RPMs have made it possible for all source code and the finished product to go out to the masses.

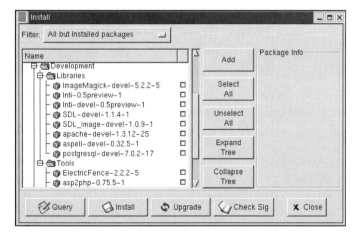

**FIGURE 11.22**

*Loading additional packages from a CD.*

# Conclusion

Now that you are familiar with the rudimentary steps for installing and upgrading additional Linux programs available not only on the distribution CD but from the Internet, you can begin customizing the X Window interface that forms the basis for many of the Linux operations. Configuring a default window manager will help you decide which type of environment you would like to work in when using GUI tools. You can choose from more than 20 major window managers, each of which has its pros and cons. You are limited only by your taste and the look and feel of the environment that you wish to use. Within X Window, you can also begin to use one of the many Office suites now available for Linux as well as database servers, financial or personal accounting managers, and task managing programs. If you configure Linux properly, the variety of programs that you can now run is limited only by your imagination and by the number of people developing for this unique platform.

# Chapter 12

## Configuring Applications under the X Window System

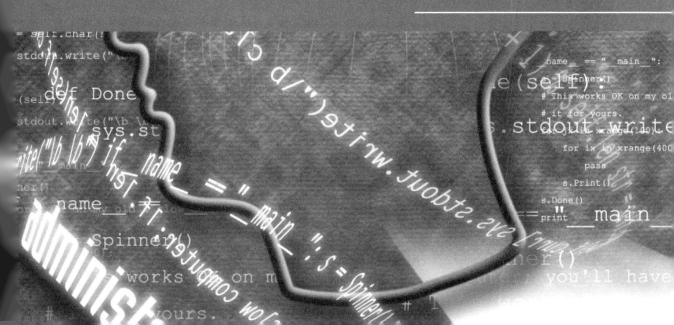

Once you understand how to install additional programs onto your machine via the command line or by using specific GUI tools, you can begin to customize your X Window System interface. X is the *de facto* standard for new installations. Red Hat boots into an X Window System environment for the default install process if the machine has a video card that is new enough and if the machine can also start up directly into X upon bootup so that you need not use the command line. This default process gives users direct access to X terminal emulators, which provide command-line functionality but also allow for the use of GUI programs.

This chapter covers the following topics:

- ◆ Setting up XFree86, the most common implementation of the X protocol
- ◆ Using automated configuration utilities
- ◆ Installing custom window managers
- ◆ Theming your interface
- ◆ Installing major software packages for office, graphics, and database programs
- ◆ Configuring fonts for use under X Window

# Customization of the X Window Interface

Perhaps the most customizable feature under Linux is the window manager. The window managers control the windows and terminals within your X session. With different managers you can tweak the appearance and feel of your GUI. Using themes and plugins that are available for each manager you can even make your desktop appear and function just like a Windows or Apple desktop, or it can be personalized it to appear like something never before seen. Each window manager offers a wide variety of icons, graphics and textures to assist users in creating their own unique desktop display.

After working with the command line under Linux, you might find the use of GUI clients liberating. Though many consider the command line the strength of Linux, and thus give it a significant advantage over other operating systems, others are accustomed to the point-and-click interface. In fact, it is fast becoming commonplace among novice users to rely upon a GUI to accomplish most day-to-day tasks. Most users have grown used to interfaces such as Windows, the Apple desktop, and the newcomer, BeOS. When converting to a new operating system such as Linux, they tend to expect more user-friendliness. Moving back to a command-line interface seems for most to be a regression.

Though it may be more powerful and dynamic, as pointed out several times in earlier chapters, the command line is reputed to be more difficult to learn. Users must practice and use it frequently to master all the commands and the options associated with them. For this purpose, the general move among Linux developers has been to create a point-and-click interface without compromising the viability of the command line. It is not so much a move to "dumb down" the method of interaction between the user and the system, but to become more user-friendly and attract more developers. As the Linux user base grows, more work will go into integrating the flexibility of the command line toward a more dynamic clickable interface, one that still retains the vitality and customizability for which Linux is known. Linux already offers over 20 major interfaces or window managers for use on any of the countless Linux distributions.

## Distinguishing GUIs

To understand a window manager's purpose, you first must understand how Linux renders a GUI. Before loading any GUI clients, Linux uses an X Window System interface. The long history of GUIs and their development is beyond the scope of this book. However, the X Window System, or *X* as many enthusiasts refer to it, is what generates the interface between mouse and screen and enables the rendering of windows with text, graphics, and the like.

Currently, the most popular X Window server is XFree86. In addition to its versatility and developmental support, XFree86 sports the lowest price of all X Window servers—it is free. XFree86 is the program that holds all drivers for unique video cards and their chipsets. It also contains a database of many of the monitors currently on the market. XFree86 allows you to adjust the horizontal and vertical refresh rates. Many card and monitor manufacturers are seeing the wisdom in releasing drivers for their products for use under Linux. The XFree86 people incorporate this information into their knowledge base and make the Linux GUI better with each passing month. With the release of XFree86 4.0, Linux will have even quicker response times in refreshing your display and displaying graphic information. With the release of 4.0, the video drivers now tap directly into your hardware, enabling a faster transfer of data to the card itself. This means that 4.0 will have direct-rendering capabilities, which is a boon for users with 3-D cards. Already, I have read reports of games and X terminal emulators showing a much faster response time to redraw requests. As progress continues, you will see XFree86 4.0 setting the standard for faster video responses. The tarfiles and RPM releases for 4.0 are already available for the latest Red Hat release. Those with faster cards should see a marked improvement in X's rendering of images and redrawing of windows.

Several other GUI servers are available—several of which have been commercially released. It is reported that they provide better support for a limited number of cards. If you are fortunate enough to have a supported card, then the video resolution can be excellent. However, most consumers purchase their card first and worry about the software later. For this reason, XFree86 tries to provide support for all cards, whether they are capable of an excellent rendering or a somewhat lower resolution image. Much depends upon the drivers released by the card's manufacturer and the level of resolution to which you set your card. If you experience problems with the rendering, try to set your card to a lower bit-per-pixel setting. As time passes, it is foreseeable that XFree86 will provide support for rendering images that is as good or better than that of its commercial counterparts.

## Specifying Video Settings

On the latest Red Hat release, the initial install routine walks you through the most tedious part of the X Window setup process. Very little manual tweaking of configuration files is needed. You should be familiar, however, with some of the basics of your video card and monitor. You should also consult the back of the monitor manual for the different settings such as the refresh rate used for the display. These are good bits of information to have close at hand when you are executing the install process. It is also good sense to know the exact model and make of the video card. Some of the newer ones may not be supported in the very latest XFree86 release, so it is better, if you are buying the hardware first, to go with a more established name and part.

During the install process, most distributions will prompt you for some specific settings. The latest version of Red Hat will even go so far as to detect automatically the type of video card that is installed and load the drivers specific to that make. Some commercial UNIX systems do not have this feature, so you must load the drivers manually instead.

After determining the type of video card installed on your machine and checking that the proper XFree86 RPM packages are installed, Red Hat then attempts to resolve the type of monitor connected to your system. Properly configuring this option is essential, though Red Hat will usually do a fine job of determining the correct make. If your monitor is not included in the provided list, choose Generic Monitor if your monitor is an older noninterlaced make, or Generic Multisync if it is a newer SVGA display. (I usually opt for the latter choice since the brand names I have available at work are usually not included in the provided list.) The horizontal and vertical sync rates as fixed by the installation are usually sufficient to achieve a limited display. Consult the owner's manual for more specific settings. For my own desktop Linux machine, I wished to set the resolution at 1,280 × 1,024, knowing that my monitor was able to achieve this resolution. Red Hat, however, wanted to set the rate lower. After testing a few similar makes, I finally found one that achieved my purposes. Be careful in setting radically different monitor types as the default. Again, this can lead to problems with the display.

Next, the install routine will detect your video card and its *chipset*, or the hardware drivers used by the video card's manufacturer. On my test machine, Red Hat chose the S3 Virge (generic) drivers as those for my video card, even though they are a newer brand of card. The generic chipsets for this card sometimes work just as well for newer cards as for older ones. If you cannot find the exact make and model of your card, choose one that supports the same chipset. In some cases, you might need to refer to the card's home page for additional information.

Below the section on video hardware are some buttons for selecting the amount of memory on your video card. This can range anywhere between 256 kilobytes to 32 megabytes. Red Hat will usually choose the correct figure, but you can modify this setting as needed. Below these options is the Test Configuration button. You may either opt for the generic install configuration or the Customize X Configuration button below it. I recommend customizing your X configuration since you can then set the bits-per-pixel rate as well as test your new settings to verify that they do indeed work. An added feature on this same page enables you to use the graphical login upon bootup rather than logging in at the command line. Or you can choose to skip configuring X altogether if the box is too slow, does not have enough memory or drive space, or will not require X for the tasks it will perform.

I prefer customizing X to my own specifications while skipping the graphical login. The Customize page allows for varying levels of resolution and pixel bits. Depending on the make of your video card and the model of your monitor, the settings shown in the following table can vary somewhat. With the latest Red Hat Linux release, all the options are already selected, and when you test the configuration it will attempt to display the highest range. Here is a break down of the settings for a generic 4 megabyte video card:

| 8 Bits per Pixel | 16 Bits per Pixel | 32 Bits per Pixel |
| --- | --- | --- |
| 640 × 480 | 640 × 480 | 640 × 480 |
| 800 × 600 | 800 × 600 | 800 × 600 |
| 1,024 × 768 | 1,024 × 768 | 1,024 × 768 |
| 1,152 × 864 | 1,152 × 864 | 1,152 × 864 |
| 1,280 × 1,024 | 1,280 × 1,024 | 1,280 × 1,024 |
| 1,600 × 1,200 | 1,600 × 1,200 | |

I have found that the 16 bits-per-pixel rate set at 1,024 × 768 suffices on most all video cards to provide the needed color and resolution. This setting is also the recommended setting for 15-inch monitors and greater. These higher settings are recommended only if you have a monitor of 17 inches or greater; otherwise the fonts might be too small to be easily readable. Also, higher pixel settings will require more time to render the image. Higher resolutions will lower the color depth, and so it becomes a trade-off between higher resolution or increased color depth. Eight-bit settings will allow only as many as 256 colors. This is fine for simple console usage, but when you are running a higher-end monitor with graphics-intensive programs, usually 16 bits is the preferred setting. You can use 32-bit resolution for high-end graphics work or for gaming on Linux.

While still in the Red Hat install routine, you can test the settings chosen to verify their correctness and to see whether the monitor and card will display images correctly. If an image or graphic does not appear in the test, you will be informed that the settings are incorrect and will be prompted to return to the configuration routine. Here you can either test a different setting or delay X configuration until after Linux is installed. The Xconfigurator program does a fine job in organizing the most optimal setting for your display under the command line.

The latest X installation routine works better than earlier Red Hat releases where you had to choose the default settings sight unseen and no opportunity was given to verify their correctness. Only after you installed Linux could you test to see if X started up properly. Any additional tweaking was done after Linux was installed. Now with Red Hat 7.x you can set up XFree86 correctly before logging in the first time.

Another option with X is to boot directly into the X Window System and avoid the initial command line login. Before confirming that the graphical display shows up under X while still in the testing phase, you may also specify whether you would like to boot directly into X Window the next time that you start up the computer. In this manner, you can avoid booting directly into the command line. For some beginning Linux users, booting right into X Window might be the preferred option. You will still be able to get to a command line using an Xterm or X-Terminal window. But some users might prefer starting from the command line. When starting out at a console connection, you can start X Window differently simply by using the command prompt rather than having it boot up with the earlier settings. The matter is left up to you.

This graphical login screen, the GNOME Display Manager (GDM), boots the machine directly in run level 5 or the graphical environment. Based on xdm, GDM features much of the versatility as xdm, which has been around nearly as long as X. Users are still required to enter a username and password, but GDM provides an additional display feature that makes the login process more aesthetically appealing. GDM also provides several other options for setting the Session, Language, and System variables:

◆ From the Session drop-down menu, you can choose to log in to either the GNOME or KDE desktop environments, or else choose one of the older window managers, including AnotherLevel, and a manager called FVWM95, both of which are based on the fvwm2 window manager, only with different settings. There is also a Default option called Failsafe, which should allow you to start a generic X session if no other window managers are installed.

◆ The Language option allows international users to pick from one of several available languages. This is especially helpful to those users not intimately familiar with English but who still wish to use Linux.

◆ The System option allows you either to reboot or halt the system. You don't need a password to execute these commands if physical access to the machine is allowed. Anyone sitting at the terminal login screen can thus either cause the machine to reboot or stop all processes, unmount the partitions, and power down the machine without corrupting files.

To read more about run levels and the default settings used by Red Hat, see Chapter 2.

If you wish to return to run level 3 or boot into a command-line interface, try running the Xconfigurator command again and not choosing the option of booting into X initially. If you do return to the GDM screen again and you wish access to the command line, you can always bring up another virtual terminal by pressing the Ctrl+Alt+F2 key combinations. For additional virtual desktops, try hitting any of the other F keys. To return to the GDM window from a command-line prompt, press Ctrl+Alt+F7, which is the default X virtual desktop.

## Running Xconfigurator

If you later decide to make changes to the manner in which you bring up the X server, several options are available. The easiest is a Red Hat utility, Xconfigurator. This program must run as root and you should run it at the console rather than in an X terminal session. Xconfigurator must test your video card's capability, and cannot do so effectively while in X. This program brings up a text-based session that walks you through the various settings for the video and monitor. First, the program determines the make of your video card, shows the results from the video test, and then offers you some possibilities to choose from as to the make and model of your monitor.

### CAUTION

Be sure to choose a monitor that best matches yours in terms of vertical and horizontal refresh rates. Setting your rates above that which your monitor can handle will overclock the display and might cause irreparable damage.

Xconfigurator now edits your settings for XF86Config, which is a simple text file that stores all your video settings. This files resides in the /etc/X11 directory. There is a symbolic link to the same file in the /usr/X11R6/lib/X11 directory and this file could be manually edited there as well. Once you run Xconfigurator, it creates a new XF86Config file for you. If you decide to run this utility, be sure to back up the original file beforehand. You could make a change and then be unable to boot back into the X Window System, especially if you have made some custom changes to the file by hand.

The monitor will blink several times as Xconfigurator attempts to determine the refresh rates, which it then stores once complete. You can also choose the color rate and resolution as described previously. Try a lower resolution before attempting a higher setting with new or familiar video cards or monitors. Xconfigurator will hang or fail if the monitor or card cannot support the requested frequency or when probing unsupported cards. You can run the Xconfigurator program as many times as you need to get the settings just right.

## Editing the XF86Config File

Another method of configuring your X Window System is to edit the XF86Config file by hand. As mentioned earlier, this file is generated automatically by the Xconfigurator program or comes preinstalled if you chose a full install of all XFree86 programs and configuration files. You may edit this file as much as you like, but if you wish to save your changes, create a backup beforehand and understand that any later attempt to run Xconfigurator will undo your changes. This file is not only where you change the settings for your monitor and video card, but is also where you edit the options for your mouse, fonts, and keyboard.

If you are unable to get a certain option to run using the Xconfigurator, you can make the changes in the XF86Config file by hand. This is useful in cases where you may want to add another entry to your font path or undo any additional flags not normally defined by Xconfigurator. A bit of experimentation will help in getting certain options functional.

## Setting Up the Mouse

Listing 12.1 is an excerpt taken from a generic XF86Config file. The section Pointer is where the mouse configuration is set.

### Listing 12.1  An Excerpt from a Generic XF86Config File for Setting Up the Mouse Options

```
Section "Pointer"
    Protocol     "Microsoft"
    Device       "/dev/mouse"


# When using XQUEUE, comment out the above two lines, and uncomment
# the following line.


#    Protocol    "Xqueue"


# Baudrate and SampleRate are only for some Logitech mice


#    BaudRate    9600
#    SampleRate 150


# Emulate3Buttons is an option for 2-button Microsoft mice
# Emulate3Timeout is the timeout in milliseconds (default is 50ms)

    Emulate3Buttons
    Emulate3Timeout     50


# ChordMiddle is an option for some 3-button Logitech mice
#    ChordMiddle


EndSection
```

The syntax of the file is as follows. Typical for the XF86Config file, the Section/EndSection pairs the mouse settings or similar device variables under X. In other parts of the XF86Config file, there are Subsection/EndSubsection pairs as well, as used in the section that defines the screen resolution. The Protocol option defines the make of the mouse. The Device option tells how to handle the unique device file that is normally a symbolic link to the true device name, in this case /dev/ttyS0 (otherwise known as COM1 under the DOS environment). A couple of sections in this example are commented out since they are not required for this type of configuration file.

One of the most important segments when defining the mouse type is the one that enables you to emulate three buttons for a regular two-button mouse. During the setup routine, as the system creates the configuration files for the keyboard and mice, you can define the mouse type and choose whether you want three-button emulation. With three-button emulation, the user can press both left- and right-mouse buttons simultaneously to achieve a third button's functionality. The third button is good for pasting selected text in other terminal windows. With those types of mice with scrolling wheels, such as the Microsoft IntelliMouse as one example, the middle wheel is already configured to be the third button, so no changes are necessary to configure this feature. Red Hat detects this type of mouse by default. By pressing the wheel, you can paste highlighted text into other windows.

To configure the three-button emulation feature, download the latest imwheel program from the imwheel home page at http://jcatki.dhs.org/imwheel/. You may choose either to compile the program yourself or use the Red Hat RPM package and allow the system to make the necessary changes. I recommend installing the latest version by hand. This way you have more control over what files the program installs or changes. After compiling and installing the binary, you will need to make some adjustments to your XF86Config file. Simply comment out the two sections regarding ChordMiddle and Emulate3Buttons. Then affix this line to the end of the file:

```
ZAxisMapping    4 5
```

Be aware that earlier imwheel releases exhibited some security holes. Consult the imwheel home page for the latest source code or check the RPM Repository page to download the latest RPM release. If you are only concerned about programs released under Red Hat Linux that may have security flaws, check the Red Hat Errata page for any bug fixes provided by the distributor.

> **NOTE**
>
> The Red Hat Errata page is a prime source for information regarding the latest code and debugging and security fixes. Here you can download the most recent patches for RPMs that come with the distribution CDs:
>
>     http://www.redhat.com/support/errata/
>
> The main Red Hat page is usually busy, so consult one of the mirror sites first before giving up:
>
>     http://www.redhat.com/download/mirror.html

## Manually Editing the Default Resolution

Two important sections in the XF86Config file are the Device and Screen sections near the bottom of the file. Here you can edit the resolution settings by hand. On my own system at work, I use a Voodoo 3 2000 card with 16 megabytes of RAM. To test some of the 3DFX settings or test programs I must first set the resolution at 640 × 480. Should I wish to run some of the Linux programs that optimize this accelerated card, they can only be run at the minimum resolution. Later, when running standard programs, I can move to a higher resolution. Hence I can log in at one depth but quickly change to another. The XF86Config file must be able to determine the card type both for a generic setting when configuring the installation and by the card's make and model. Listing 12.2 shows the Device section from the XF86Config file.

**Listing 12.2 An Excerpt Taken from the XF86Config File Displaying the Graphic Device in Use on the System**

```
    #
********************************************************************
    # Graphics device section
    #
********************************************************************
```

```
# Any number of graphics device sections may be present

Section "Device"
    Identifier        "Generic VGA"
    VendorName        "Unknown"
    BoardName  "Unknown"
    Chipset    "generic"


#     VideoRam 256


#     Clocks    25.2 28.3


EndSection


# Device configured by Xconfigurator:


Section "Device"
    Identifier   "3Dfx Interactive, Inc.|Voodoo 3 2000"
    VendorName   "Unknown"
    BoardName    "Unknown"
    #VideoRam    16384
    # Insert Clocks lines here if appropriate
EndSection
```

Below the Device section, you can determine the default resolution. I have chosen as a default color depth 16-bit and the resolution to start at 640 × 480 but I can manually change it to 1,024 × 768. There are two major sections: one for the regular SVGA server and the other for accelerated servers that optimize 3DFX cards. You can configure both to boot into any resolution supported by the monitor. Listing 12.3 shows how you might do so. If, however, you want to boot initially into X using an 800 × 600 resolution or also have 1,024 × 768 as an available resolution, you would simply add them to the Modes section in the order in which you wished to view the settings.

**Listing 12.3 Configuring the Default Resolution for the X Window Environment**

```
#
***********************************************************************
# Screen sections
#
***********************************************************************


# The Colour SVGA server

Section "Screen"
    Driver        "svga"
    # Use Device "Generic VGA" for Standard VGA 320x200x256
    #Device        "Generic VGA"
    Device        "3Dfx Interactive, Inc.|Voodoo 3 2000"
    Monitor       "My Monitor"
    Subsection "Display"
        Depth         16
        Modes         "1640x480" "1280x1024"
        ViewPort      0 0
    EndSubsection
EndSection


# The accelerated servers (S3, Mach32, Mach8, 8514, P9000, AGX, W32,
Mach64
# I128, and S3V)
Section "Screen"
    Driver        "accel"
    Device        "3Dfx Interactive, Inc.|Voodoo 3 2000"
    Monitor       "My Monitor"
    Subsection "Display"
        Depth         16
        Modes         "640x480" "1280x1024"
        ViewPort      0 0
    EndSubsection
EndSection
```

By pressing Ctrl-Alt-+ (for higher resolution) or Ctrl-Alt-- (for lower resolution), you can alternate modes and switch from a 640 × 480 display to a higher resolution on the fly from within X Window. This will move the display to a higher resolution and then rotate back through the lower settings. For systems with better video cards or larger monitors, you can set up a host of different resolutions and change settings at will.

# Starting X

After properly configuring X Window, you can boot into the X Window environment. The standard method of bringing up the GUI is to enter the following on the command line if you are not already at a GDM display:

```
startx
```

This is the method for users who normally log in to the system at run level 3.

Several additional options are available with the initial command. If you configured your XFree86 settings correctly—that is, if you added more than one resolution setting and color depth—you should be able to start in different color modes. For instance, if you had the default depth set for 8-bit mode and wanted to boot instead into 16-bit mode, you would use the following options with startx:

```
startx -- -bpp 16
```

This brings up the color depth as 16-bit rather than 8-bit. Because you are passing a different argument to the server, the statement must be prefixed with two dashes and the bits-per-pixel setting must also have a single hyphen affixed before it. Rotating through the resolution options again requires pressing Ctrl-Alt-+ or Ctrl-Alt--.

The startx command first looks for an .xinitrc file in that user's home directory. This is where you can set the default window manager type. If there is no .xinitrc file, the default Red Hat Linux install creates an .Xauthority file in which it stores information about the default window manager and the setup. As of the most current Red Hat release, the window manager launched by default, if no specific one is chosen during the installation, is the sawfish window manager. GNOME provides additional utilities such as the panel as well as GNOME-based programs. GNOME is actually a collection of daemons, protocols and utilities that make up the desktop environment. Sawfish controls the window functions and appearances.

# Window Managers versus Desktop Environments

A window manager compromises a portion of a customized GUI. If no default window manager is defined, either by yourself or by the Linux distribution (a most unlikely possibility), you may only see a mouse cursor and an X terminal window. Much of the basic functionality of the window such as the resize portions of the window and titlebars will also be missing. Fortunately, nearly all Linux distributions come with a default window manager or desktop environment that not only provides several GUI programs but also a customization routine and a look and feel similar to that of most commercial releases.

In a nutshell, a window manager provides a standardized appearance and functionality for the X Window session. A window manager defines myriad aspects of the desktop's operation, including the following:

◆ The manner in which windows are opened

◆ The appearance of all aspects of the window, such as the titlebar and the frames around each window

◆ The way in which the manager handles virtual desktops

◆ The manner in which keyboard shortcut keys function

In short, a window manager manages the GUI environment and determines how the user controls the operations of the desktop.

Currently, more than 20 different major types of window managers are available for the Linux operating system. Some lesser known and used managers are based on the more popular ones, but these simply customize and tweak the features of the more established ones. These managers range from those that resemble the Windows 95/98 environment or the Macintosh interface to several that look and operate like the NeXT operating system. The managers that mimic the NeXT operating system are undoubtedly among the less popular ones, but even these have many advocates, each desiring to preserve the functionality provided by NeXT while incorporating it into the Linux operating system. Such is the attraction of Linux: Users can resurrect an obscure OS and restructure it to suit their new environment.

Several of these managers contain configuration files, otherwise known as *themes*, that enable you to customize the general appearance of the window manager further. In some cases, you can make your machine appear almost exactly like a Windows95/98 or Macintosh machine. The greatest advantage that these managers have over their proprietary counterparts is that they are extremely customizable and can be made to appear however you like. You can edit either the appearance of your own window manager when you log in or that of one of your user's.

This section explores two examples of major desktop environments and one window manager: GNOME, KDE, and Window Maker. The first option, GNOME, is installed by default in the Red Hat Linux release. KDE is also available for installation, though it requires additional files to be selected and installed. The last manager comes as an RPM file on the latest CD. The source code is also available for download from the Window Maker site, and it is recommended by the developers that any RPMs be removed before installing from source. Due to the size of the two desktop environments and the complexity in setting some of the variables, Red Hat recommends using the RPMs. Both GNOME and KDE have their own internal window managers; kwm is the window manager for KDE and Sawfish, and Enlightenment is now the default window manager for GNOME. Although this section will mention several of the other window managers currently available and discuss a few of their features, only the three major ones will be examined closely.

It is important to differentiate between a window manager and a desktop environment. A window manager operates more like a shell on top of the X Window System. It relies upon separate libraries that come with Red Hat and controls the look, feel, and function of its terminals and windows. A desktop environment is more autonomous and sets up its own window managers, building upon custom libraries to create a unique appearance. A desktop environment also boasts its own sets of programs developed specifically for use under its environment. Like Windows, both KDE and GNOME sport a startup button from which the user can launch a variety of applications.

According to its developers, only KDE is a true desktop environment. KDE is considered a desktop environment because it not only controls the look and feel of the entire desktop but also handles the libraries that support the GUI, controls the X environment to some degree, and provides a host of programs that are specifically written for use under KDE. GNOME also operates much like a desktop environment, because it uses the GTK libraries, whereas KDE uses the Qt libraries. However, GNOME differs slightly as a desktop environment because it relies upon a separate window manager such as sawfish to manage the windows, color schemes, virtual desktops, and audio files. Though GNOME does offer a large selection of programs created for it as well, it can also operate under several different default managers. Window Maker is a simple window manager. It is smaller, quicker to operate, and very customizable. It has its own windowed appearance that can be altered to suit most any need. No specialized programs have been designed specifically for Window Maker, but it does offer dockable applications that you can attach to the docking toolbar. Because its code is so streamlined, it is the manager of choice for those users running a GUI on slower machines. The other two are more memory- and CPU-intensive.

## Examining the Default Manager for Red Hat

The Red Hat Linux distribution's default desktop environment is the latest GNOME release. GNOME and KDE share similarities in appearances, and both function similarly and even include a wide variety of dependent programs with the installation. However, GNOME differs from KDE in one important aspect: The entire GNOME release is built upon a different set of libraries, namely GTK, along with several other libraries such GLIB available at the GNOME home page, http://www.gnome.org/.

GTK (GIMP Tool Kit) is a unique set of libraries developed specifically for the GIMP (Graphics Image Manipulation Program). This program was originally developed as a graphics utility similar to Adobe Photoshop. Because the available libraries at the time were not sufficient for their purposes, the GIMP developers decided to create their own set of libraries, GTK. GTK has been popularized among many Linux programmers and the majority of programs now being created for Linux use GTK as their base. For many, GTK is the developer's building blocks for Linux.

The standard GNOME package that comes with a vanilla install is independent of window managers. You can still use the tools associated with GNOME, such as the panel that holds the applets and programs that run under most any window manager. Red Hat installs the latest version of Sawfish, formerly known as Sawmill, as the default window manager for GNOME. Together they comprise Red Hat's desktop environment. Earlier Red Hat releases used Enlightenment, an extremely dynamic window manager that was further developed at the Red Hat Labs. In addition to using the configuration options available for GNOME that allow you to change the icons and display settings, you can also access the window manager of your choice and change to any of the other installed managers as well.

For example, right-clicking anywhere on the GNOME toolbar brings up its configuration options. In the screen that appears, you can edit the appearance of nearly any feature, including the framework of each window, the titlebar associated with those windows, and the various themes that come preinstalled. These themes are entirely separate from the themes included in or downloadable for KDE. Because the images for each theme must be custom-tailored for that particular window manager, the same theme will not always operate under other window managers.

You can select or create any theme of your choice from off the Themes.org page, http://www.themes.org/. Here you can select themes for GNOME and KDE as well as Window Maker, Blackbox, Sawfish, and others. The site provides detailed instructions for installing any of the themes featured on the site, along with plans for creating your own themes for the WM of your choice.

Using a configuration tool that looks similar to that of KDE, GNOME lets you choose your window manager and then enter in additional configuration settings for that particular manager. Enlightenment allows for the greatest degree of editing and can hold as many as 32 virtual desktops, each having 64 virtual windows. This capacity accounts for 2,048 virtual windows for a single user account. Most default window managers allow as many as eight default virtual desktops within a console environment. Some allow more than eight under the X session, but most do not offer that capability.

GNOME is under active development. It not only has a large developer base but also has a major distribution supporting its progress. The latest release under Red Hat 7 has a polished finished and has shown a marked improvement over its initial 1.0 release. As shown in Figure 12.1, GNOME has many similar features to that of other commercial GUIs but is uniquely Linux with the applications it runs. Both KDE and GNOME are anticipating a 2.0 release late in 2000. GNOME has recently received a major boost from other commercial developers who have decided to adopt GNOME as its default GUI. Sun recently announced that it would abandon CDE and adopt instead GNOME as its interface. IBM has also released plans to adopt GNOME in its own Linux releases.

Like Windows and KDE, GNOME offers a start button that launches a list of applications. This button is located on the GNOME panel, which is the heart of the GNOME system. GNOME is not so much a desktop environment as a

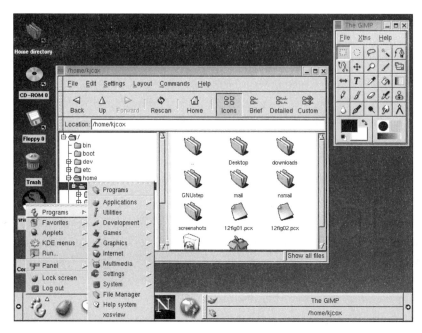

**FIGURE 12.1**

*A quick look at the GNOME desktop reveals that GNOME shares many of the same features as KDE.*

user utility that resides within a window manger. GNOME utilizes the recognizable GNOME footprint on the GNOME panel that identifies it and the location for startup utilities.

The GNOME home page briefly describes the components of the GNOME panel, which includes the following:

◆ *Menus.* Menus are lists of items, each of which starts an application, executes a command, or opens a submenu. The leftmost icon normally seen after installation is a stylized footprint icon (the GNOME logo). This is the main menu, one of the most important objects in the panel. This menu provides access to almost all the applications, commands, and configuration options available in GNOME. GNOME sometimes provides a folder icon on the panel that links to a specific directory. This icon is also part of the menu feature set. GNOME enables users to create their own menus with personalized contents to use in addition to the main menu. To open a menu, just click the icon with the left mouse button.

◆ *Launchers.* Launchers are buttons that either start an application or execute a command when you left-click them. You can place launchers on the panel to execute an often-used program such as Netscape or the Gnumeric spreadsheet.

◆ *Applets.* Applets are applications that run within the GNOME panel itself. You may choose from a variety of applets to run as they are listed under the main menu. Some of the most commonly used applets are clocks, mounting devices, weather tools, and the GNOME desktop applet, which allows you to choose from among the many virtual desktops. Another well-used applet is the tasklist, which allows you to control your application windows in various ways, including changing the focus, iconifying windows, closing windows, and killing applications.

◆ *Drawers.* Drawers are much like panels in that they can hold additional applications and can be opened or closed. A drawer can hold anything that a panel can though it is fully customizable. You may choose any sort of icon for your drawers in order to distinguish customized drawers from the default system drawer. Left-click the Drawer icon to open or close the drawer.

◆ *Special Objects.* Special objects are items that you can add to a panel. They perform functions generally not available through the other panel objects. For example, you can create a logout button, which begins the logout sequence to end your GNOME session.

When you perform a full install of both desktop environments, both KDE and the latest release of GNOME allow you to use applications from both environments within the other.

---

**TIP**

As Figure 12.1 shows, GNOME offers menus not only for Red Hat GTK-based applications but also KDE-specific applications. KDE provides links to Red Hat GNOME programs in their own environment.

---

GNOME comes with a very detailed manual that assists in clarifying most questions put forth by beginning Linux and GNOME users. This manual is usually installed by default when the GNOME workstation option is chosen for an install. Otherwise, it is available separately on the CD release and can be installed later if needed. Due to GNOME's similarity to better-known commercial operating systems, new users should not have difficulty making the transition to Linux or to either of these desktop environments.

# Installing and Upgrading GNOME

Due to the large volume of libraries and programs needed to run GNOME, the developers encourage beginning users to use the RPM releases of GNOME. You may download the source and compile each package individually. The latter method requires much more effort than is necessary and is discouraged unless you are a developer or you want to review the source code.

The main GNOME home page, http://www.gnome.org/, lists other mirror sites that contain the same files in case the main site is congested with traffic. With the most recent release of GNOME, 1.1.2, GNOME's developers have partnered with Helix to produce an even more dynamic release. Helix GNOME is touted to be the user-friendliest version yet available. It also sports a look and feel that elevates it to a level of sophistication that rivals that of commercial products. When locating the binary source for the Red Hat release, the GNOME site redirects you to the Helix GNOME home page, http://www.helixcode.com/.

There are two choices for downloading and/or upgrading to the latest version. You may opt either to download all the files to a temporary directory on your hard drive and then run a simple RPM command, or to use the new auto-installer feature. Because Helix GNOME is an open-source company, it makes all source code available. To fund much of its work, Helix GNOME also sells the entire suite of programs on a CD, which bypasses much of the time and bandwidth issues and supports the GNOME cause. However, the recommended option is to download the very latest releases using the auto-installer option. You can do this in one of two ways: Either use a text-based browser such as Lynx and have the installer automatically configure the necessary settings, or download the installer and execute it yourself.

To install the latest Helix GNOME version automatically, you call the go-gnome script remotely from the browser. The following steps start the install process:

1. Open a terminal window.

2. Using the su command, become superuser. Only with root privileges can you install all the packages successfully.

3. Start go-gnome by entering the following command. Make sure you have the Lynx browser installed on your machine and a fast, dependable connection to the Internet.

```
lynx -source http://go-gnome.com | sh
```

The script automatically starts the easiest installation method for your system. You can choose which packages you want to install. After you make your selections, the script fetches the packages from the Internet and installs them automatically. This is the reason that you need a root console.

However, it should be mentioned that a cracker could theoretically exploit this script. My recommendation is to download the packages to your drive and verify their authenticity before running the command to upgrade or install the packages.

If you wish to run the install script yourself, the steps are nearly the same:

1. Download the file installer-latest-intel.gz from the off the helixcode.com homepage and place it in a temporary directory. This directory can be one of your making in your home directory or a unique directory in /tmp. Keep the files separate from others.
2. Unzip the file by entering **gunzip installer-latest-intel.gz**.
3. Make the file executable by entering **chmod u+x installer-latest-intel**.
4. Now run the installer by entering **./installer-latest-intel**.

After making sure that you have a viable Internet connection, the installer program begins connecting to the respective Helix GNOME site. The program tests your system for the latest software and then lets you choose the packages to install.

Once the most current Helix GNOME files are loaded, you will have an autoloader function so that you can later upgrade to newer releases. The temporary directory stores the downloaded files until they are installed; afterward they are deleted. You may copy these files to a separate directory for use elsewhere or for selected upgrades on machines not connected to the network. However, because of the library dependencies, it is best to save all the files and install them at once.

Helix GNOME has a much cleaner interface than the standard GNOME desktop. It also provides several additional utilities that do not normally come with GNOME, including extra window managers such as the new Sawfish (formerly Sawmill) program. Helix GNOME demonstrates just how dynamic the Linux platform is becoming.

# Discussing the Features of KDE

KDE is currently considered by some to be the forerunner in the quest for easy-to-use Linux interfaces. Although it has not been that long since the Linux community split between the two camps of GNOME and KDE, they have since resolved many of their differences and now are cooperating in their separate developments in order to appeal to both sets of users. The GNOME developers took the open-source stance, stating that only GNOME conformed to the higher standards required by the GPL. Meanwhile the KDE project managers and enthusiasts pointed to the stability of KDE and its user-friendly interface. They also held the position that KDE was quickly becoming accepted by many in the Linux community despite of the stipulations of the Qt license. But as the Qt developers saw the wisdom in making their source code free and open, both camps of thought have reached an understanding. Recently the Qt developers have decided to release the Qt libraries under the GPL, thus removing any limitations that purist Linux enthusiasts may have had concerning its use.

According to the developers of KDE, their project is not just a window manager, though it does technically use a manager for its interface. Rather, KDE is considered by its makers to be a *desktop environment*, which is reflected in its name, the *K Desktop Environment* (*KDE*).

KDE relies upon many applications built with the Qt libraries. That does not limit it, however, from running programs based on non-Qt libraries. Netscape and GIMP, which are built with a different set of libraries, can still be run under KDE. The external appearance and framework match that of the KDE window build, whereas the internal buttons and links still use their own libraries and retain their own appearance. KDE and the KDE window manager (kwm) look alike because they both are built on the Qt libraries. GNOME and its window manager may not necessarily both use GTK and thus can appear different. Window Maker, for example, which does not depend on GTK, can be run jointly with the GNOME panel.

KDE's appearance is very much a hybrid combination of the Windows and Macintosh desktops (see Figure 12.2). The K Application Starter button on the lower panel, which provides a complete listing of the KDE utilities, is reminiscent of Windows. Yet some of the other icons resemble the Macintosh OS. With KDE Themes, you can make the desktop seem even more like its proprietary counterparts or give it an entirely different look, one truly unique in its own right.

The lines and framework of the windows are clean and defined. Though it may appear at first glance to operate like Windows, there are distinct differences. First, a panel appears at the bottom of the screen, which like a Windows panel can be positioned elsewhere on the page and resized. However, the upper portion of the

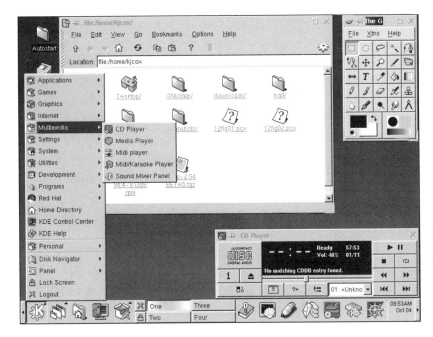

**FIGURE 12.2**

*A vanilla KDE install, displaying its basic features and window appearance.*

screen features a taskbar that displays currently running programs, similar to an Apple utility. By clicking the large "K" icon on the lower left, much like to the Start button under Windows, you can see the various types of programs that run under KDE. It too is fully configurable; you can add additional Start buttons to the panel to create your own set of icons and preset programs. You can also minimize this entire panel to either side or corner of the desktop and place the running programs in a drop-down menu located on the top of the screen. This configuration provides yet more space on the desktop and still keeps visible the programs running under the GUI.

KDE also provides information about the other virtual desktops used under KDE. For example, you can run an application on one virtual desktop and then switch to a different virtual desktop, where you can run another, unrelated program. This clears up much of the clutter associated with the limitations of having just one screen in which to accomplish all the tasks. Nor do all the programs clutter up the panel. Each program, when minimized, is associated with its own virtual desktop. Switching to another virtual desktop provides a new pristine space to store running programs.

A vanilla KDE configuration provides just four default virtual desktops, each with its own window number as a name. Under older window managers, these windows were called *pagers*, which you could use to bring up or page a new workspace. Clicking on each panel's respective link brings up the new virtual desktop. KDE can hold as many as eight virtual desktops, each of which you can rename with a specific identity.

When using KDE, I like to identify each desktop with a specific task. One virtual desktop is titled "Internet," and holds all the Internet-related programs, such as the browser, links to URLs, and so on. Another is termed "Mail" and holds all mail clients. Yet another is called "Network" and has open terminal windows to other machines on the internal network or LAN. Such a naming scheme helps in organizing a desktop. No longer must you hunt through the various minimized icons for the running application. Simply switching to the correctly named virtual desktop will provide all associated programs in its category. Nearly all window managers provide this type of functionality.

## Theming the Desktop

As is the case with nearly all window managers, KDE allows you to customize the desktop appearance to whatever size, shape, or color you wish. KDE also encourages those more adventurous to tweak the source code to advanced levels of customization. For those who lack the knowledge to undertake such tweaking, or who simply like the general design, KDE offers different *themes* or visual patterns for users to use to configure the appearance even more. A theme allows users to change the default window borders, fonts, background, and icons to a more customized appearance.

Some themes are based on other operating systems or television shows and movies. Figure 12.3 shows another example, a theme called DrawingBoard. The basic premise is to relate all the graphics to a specific subject matter. For example, a theme might set a particular tone by using a distinct background image such as cartoon characters and then having the other images reflect the same feel as used in that cartoon. Thus the themes that KDE offers are similar to those used on both Windows and Apple operating systems, except that KDE makes it easier for the average user to choose them.

Themes for whatever window manager you are using are available on the Internet. One of the most popular sites for the exchange and creation of new themes for nearly all window managers is http://www.themes.org/. You may either download or contribute your own design to the database for others to use. The site provides explicit instructions for designing your own theme and for sharing the information. Many themes come preinstalled with the manager, but you can add hundreds of themes later from the Internet as they become available.

To add a theme to the KDE desktop, locate the KDE Control Center under the KDE Start button. Under the second or Desktop item, look for the Theme Manager item. KDE installs a few themes by default but you can quickly add more. Sites such as http://www.themes.org/ or one of the themes.org subdomains, http://kde.themes.org/, host a wide range of themes for all desktops. Simply download one that looks interesting, save it to a temporary location or one that you can use for storing additional themes, and then click the Add... button under the Theme Manager. You may also change existing themes by

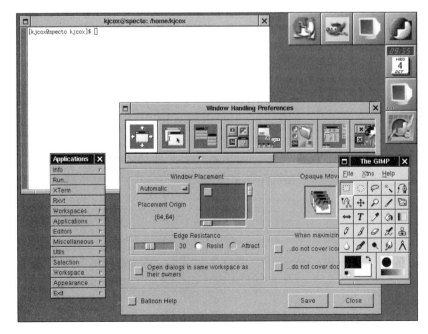

**FIGURE 12.3**

*A themed desktop under the KDE environment.*

giving them a new name or even create your own theme. The same page offers detailed instruction for theming both the KDE desktop and nearly all other window managers. Under the page of your choice, choose the Creating themes link to see how a sample theme is made. Naturally, the site promoters encourage Linux for all uses and suggest using the GIMP to create each image within the customized theme.

As with the themes available under the Windows operating system, the user can customize a multitude of KDE items to suit. You can change or configure a theme's colors, wallpaper, panel, sounds, icons, window border, window titlebar, window gimmick, window button layout, file manager, and console. Whether you create you own theme or choose to use an existing one, KDE and other managers enable you to customize your interface to *your* liking, rather than restricting you to an appearance determined by a commercial developer.

## Discussing the KDE Packages

Because it requires few programs, KDE installs quickly and easily on any Linux box, no matter the distribution. Red Hat has provided nearly as much support for this environment as it has for GNOME, so you can either install KDE initially or upgrade later using RPMs from the Red Hat site. KDE also provides Red Hat-specific RPMs from its own FTP site, ftp://ftp.kde.org/.

As with any program, there are two major methods of installing KDE: *source* or *RPMs*. For many, compiling the source from scratch is the only way to install a manifold program such as KDE. Source code is usually released prior to the RPMs, so to ensure that you have the very latest updates, patches, and features, installing from source is the optimal method. Just as GNOME requires the GTK libraries, KDE first mandates that you install the Qt libraries. These are available from the main Qt site at http://www.troll.no/ or from the main KDE site as well. They are also available in either source or RPM format. Be sure to read their instructions before attempting any sort of install. There is still some discrepancy between installing the 1.x and 2.x versions of Qt. By the time this book is in print, the latest release of KDE will have adopted the 2.x libraries as its standard.

If you are using RPMs to upgrade, you install the Qt libraries by issuing the simple RPM command in the same directory that the RPM libraries are located:

```
rpm -Uvh *.rpm
```

You can find all the documentation needed for compiling and installing at the main KDE home page, http://www.kde.org/. To avoid increasing the already congested traffic at this site, try one of the many mirrored sites. These locations carry all the same source code, documentation, and information as the main KDE site. Using a mirror site will most likely also increase your download speed, which, considering the size of many of these files downloaded via a modem, can be quite tedious.

The documentation includes explicit instructions on how to compile and install each program on your hard drive. Generally you can install as many as 10 packages, although only two are required and a third is recommended. The others merely complement the core KDE files with a wide assortment of utilities. Sequence is also important in successfully installing the programs. Here is the recommended order as shown on the main KDE installation page:

◆ *kdesupport* (recommended). This package contains support libraries that have not been written as part of the KDE project, but which are needed nevertheless. If the libraries in this package (libgif, libjpeg, libmime, libuu, and libgdbm) are already installed on your system, you may not need to install kdesupport. You should probably install it if only to standardize on the release.

◆ *kdelibs* (required). This package contains shared libraries that all KDE applications need.

◆ *kdebase* (required). This package contains the base applications that form the core of the K Desktop Environment: the window manager, the terminal emulator, the control center, the file manager, and the panel.

◆ *kdegames* (optional). This package includes games such as *Mahjongg, Snake, Asteroids,* and *Tetris,* to name a few.

◆ *kdegraphics* (optional). This package includes various graphics-related programs such as PostScript Previewer, DVI Previewer, and a drawing program.

◆ *kdeutils* (optional). This package includes various desktop tools, including a calculator, an editor, and other nifty utilities also found on a default Red Hat install but using the Qt libraries and optimized for KDE.

◆ *kdemultimedia* (optional). This package contains multimedia applications such as a CD player, a mixer, and an MP3 player.

◆ *kdenetwork* (optional). This package includes Internet applications. Currently the package contains the mail program, the news reader, and several other network-related programs.

◆ *kdeadmin* (optional). This collection of system administration programs includes the user manager and the System V run-level editor among others.

◆ *kdetoys* (optional). This package includes toys.

◆ *korganizer* (optional). This package completes your desktop with an organizer.

You are not required to install the optional programs in this order, but you might experience problems if you do not install the first three programs—kdesupport, kdelibs, and kdebase—correctly or in the order indicated in this list. After you have installed the packages and verified that they defaulted to the /opt/kde directory (you may choose another directory in which to install KDE, but it's best to comply with the program defaults), you may then edit the .xinitrc file in your home directory so that KDE starts automatically when you boot into the X Window system. If there is no .xinitrc file in your home directory, create one at the terminal window. Using your favorite text editor, such as vi, pico, joe or jed, add the command startkde to your .xinitrc file. This command authorizes KDE to be the default X interface on subsequent bootups as well.

If you are booting into run level 5 of the default Red Hat desktop or you are bypassing the command line and logging in at the GUI, you can choose KDE as your default window manager. Otherwise, after logging in to GNOME manually, you may reconfigure your default environment to KDE by executing the switchdesk command. This command enables you to choose between GNOME, KDE, or the most basic GUI.

The next time you enter **startx** at the command line, KDE will automatically create additional directories in your home directory where it will store information. The latest version of Red Hat creates a Desktop directory automatically in case you choose KDE as your default interface. You may bypass this function by removing the Desktop directory from the /etc/skel/ directory. Subsequent users will not receive a KDE directory unless they manually choose KDE as their startup.

KDE provides a detailed help manual to help you learn more about its functions and accessories. For the purposes of this chapter, it is sufficient to cover some of the base install routines. Comprehensive coverage of the entire scope of KDE or any other window manager or environment is beyond the scope of this book.

# Installing KDE RPMs

Installing KDE through the use of RPMs is a preferable choice for novice users. You might have to wait longer for the latest RPMs to become available, but if you are still uncomfortable with source or want to install everything in one fell swoop, waiting might be the preferable choice.

Before attempting any install, verify that KDE is not installed by default with your release of Red Hat. Or, if you want to upgrade, either choose the upgrade option under the RPM command or completely uninstall the older release before installing again. Beware, though, that if you uninstall, you might lose certain configuration settings for various programs such as Kppp, the dial-up networking utility. Back up any configuration files up that you might need later.

Install both the Qt and Qt-devel files first by using the standard RPM command. The quickest way to install multiple files sharing similar prefixes is to enter the following command:

```
# rpm -ivh qt*.rpm
```

This command generates output similar to the following:

```
qt-1.44                     ##############################
qt-1.44-devel               ##############################
```

Be careful when applying this same principle to the KDE files. Make sure that you first install the support files (kdesupport), then the kdelibs package, and finally the kdebase package. Once these three packages are successfully installed, you may execute the following command to finish installing the rest of the files:

```
# rpm -ivh kde*.rpm
```

Hash marks appear as each package is installed. If you encounter any errors installing a particular package, try first to install the package individually or wait until all the other packages have been installed. The package may require a library from another package before it can be installed. If neither of these solutions work, you can attempt to uninstall the package and then try a new installation. However, chances are good that you will install it correctly without any complications.

> **CAUTION**
>
> Additional related files rely upon Qt-developmental files in order to run. Though the RPM version does install the necessary headers for Qt, these may not be located in the same place as would the compiled version of Qt. If you are installing Qt from source, the install program might place them elsewhere. This is sometimes the case with the Red Hat version of the Qt libraries. Programs that rely on the Qt headers may look for them in one location and not find them.

## Compiling KDE Source Code

For enthusiasts or purists who still insist on compiling code, KDE provides the full KDE source for inspection and modification. As with the installation of most any source code, there are just a few steps to follow to compile and install the newly created binaries.

The files you will want to download will have either a .tar.gz or a .tar.bz2 extension. These extensions identify the files as being tarred and zipped for archival purposes. There may also be files with different extensions, and these tar files can be uncompressed in the same manner.

Files archived as tar source files normally install into /usr/local/kde by default. You can override this setting by using the --prefix option of the configure script. If you prefer setting the default directory to /opt/kde, you may do so when configuring. The following are some simple steps to follow when installing the source code of KDE. You must repeat each of these steps for every tarred and zipped package:

1. Unpack the packages by entering **tar -xvzf <packagename>.tar.gz**. If the packages end with a different extension, use the appropriate command. You may also unpack the packages by entering **bunzip2 -c <packagename>.tar.bz2 | tar xvf -**. Both methods work equally well. The choice is a matter of preference.

2. Change directories to the newly created package directory by entering **cd <packagename>**.

3. Configure the package by entering **./configure**. This command is where you add any extra flags or options. To define a new default directory, enter **./configure --prefix=/opt/kde**.

4. Some packages (notably kdebase) have special configuration options that might be applicable to your installation. Enter ./**configure --help** to see the available options.

5. Build the package by entering **make**.

6. Install the package as superuser by entering **make install**.

If all goes well, the binary will install in the new location either as you specified or as the program's makefile previously defined. Again, you must perform these steps for each package file.

# Performing Postinstallation Procedures

Once all the new binaries are installed, make sure that you have added KDE's binary installation directory, /opt/kde/bin, to your path and KDE's library installation directory to your LD_LIBRARY_PATH. To do so, you add the new directory either to the /etc/profile file where the system's path is stated or to the user's own .bash_profile file. The library path is added to the EXPORT line.

> ## CAUTION
>
> It is unwise to set LD_LIBRARY_PATH blindly. In the vast majority of cases, setting this variable is unnecessary and can do more harm than good. A web page at http://www.cis.ohio-state.edu/~barr/ldpath.html, written by Dave Barr, explains the evils of LD_LIBRARY_PATH.

Even though you can use most of the KDE applications simply by calling them, you can benefit fully from KDE's advanced features only if you use the KDE window manager, KWM, and its helper programs.

To make running KDE easy, the developers provide a simple script called startkde that is installed in $KDEDIR/bin and is therefore in your path.

Edit the file .xinitrc in your home directory in order to call the new window manager or desktop environment when X first starts, making sure first to create a backup in case things go wrong. Remove all other entries or comment out those lines that might call a window manager, and then insert startkde instead. Restart the X Window session. If you use kdm/xdm, you will have to edit the file .xsession instead of .xinitrc. Like gdm (GNOME Display Manager), kdm/xdm (KDE Display Manager or X Display Manager) is a bootup screen that you can use for systems hosting multiple users. Rather than going to a command line, users will have a pleasant background from which to log in.

If your home directory has no .xinitrc or .xsession, simply create a new one with just one line containing the word *startkde*.

> **NOTE**
>
> Some systems, notably Red Hat Linux, use an .Xclients instead. Check your own configuration to see how you call a window manager.

This process should result in a pristine KDE desktop. If you had previously opted not to install KDE during your initial Linux install, KDE creates a new directory called Desktop in which to store everything that appears on your KDE desktop—template files, as well as a .kde directory in which to store additional files. The rest of the desktop is very intuitive. It will look and feel much like a commercially available proprietary interface.

## Using Window Maker

The Window Maker window manager was originally based on the AfterStep window manager, which is a knock-off of the NeXT operating system pioneered by Steve Jobs of Apple fame. AfterStep's developer, Alfredo K. Kojima, left the AfterStep company and created his own release, Window Maker. This manager uses $64 \times 64$ pixel-sized icons, each with its own label and graphic to identify it when minimized. It also employs the window shade feature common on all Macintosh releases. When you double-click the titlebar, it rolls up the window beneath it like a window shade, leaving only the name of the window within the titlebar visible. If you double-click again, the program window rolls back down. This is a very effective way to conserve space within the desktop.

The desktop itself is also has a very clean and intuitive appearance (see Figure 12.4). You can customize everything visible, including the background and menus, to suit your own tastes. The desktop also supports themes and can be tailored to sport myriad images and looks.

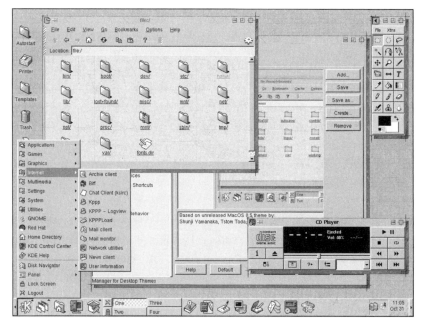

**FIGURE 12.4**

*A very vanilla install of Window Maker on a typical Linux desktop.*

Window Maker does not use any sort of toolbar or panel, but the GNOME toolbar can just as effectively be run in this environment. Because Window Maker is fully GNOME-compliant, it supports many of the same commands for GNOME under its own interface and allows the same programs to be run as well. The GNOME panel will run on Window Maker as well. The easiest way to run the GNOME panel under Window Maker is to run GNOME first and then change managers from within the GNOME environment.

Rather than providing a panel by default when starting only Window Maker, this manager provides access to the programs through a fully customizable, clickable drop-down menu. Left-click (or right-click, depending upon how you set your configuration file under the WindowMaker Preferences Utility) anywhere on the desktop. A drop-down menu appears. You can either configure this menu by hand by editing a simple text file or by inserting your own variables into the Preferences Utility program. Rather than having to click in a predetermined location to access the files you want, you can simply click anywhere on the desktop to display all the available options.

Window Maker also supports virtual desktops, though they are referred to as *workspaces*, which aptly describes their function. You can both create and delete these virtual workspaces in the drop-down menu display or in the Preferences Utility. Window Maker comes with a default configuration file called a *menu*, which is a simple text file that lays out the different tree structures available under the clickable interface. Again, editing this file by hand might prove the simplest way to add or delete available programs. After installing Window Maker on the Linux system, the window manager also places a GNUstep/ directory in your home directory. For example, you would find the configuration files pertinent to Window Maker in the following location:

```
~/GNUstep/Library/WindowMaker/menu
```

The *tilde* (~) represents a user's home directory. In the preceding directory, you can edit nearly every configuration option by hand and customize your own manager's appearance. You do not use these options to configure global preferences. Those are usually placed in /usr/local/GNUstep/ or the default directory that you defined during the install phase.

One of the first changes you will want to make to your menu file is to insert a configuration option so that you can edit the menu later. Here is an excerpt from a typical menu file that allows for later modifications:

```
"Configure" MENU
        "Window Maker Configuration" EXEC xterm -T "Window Maker
Configuration" -e vi ~/GNUstep/Library/WindowMaker/menu
    "Configure" END
```

The words in quotation marks are what appear in the drop-down menus. The preceding example tells the program to execute an X terminal with the titlebar saying "Window Maker Configuration." The script then executes the vi editor, which opens the menu file in the xterm window. The Configure MENU and END options create a clickable submenu in the desktop interface.

Window Maker is not as point-and-click-based as the previous two window managers. It can, however, run any of the same programs used elsewhere within its own interface. Window Maker is designed for the user who likes to edit basic text files and configure items by hand rather than rely on a wizard or walk-through menu.

Another Window Maker feature that makes it recognizable to many is the Dock feature on the far-right side. Under AfterStep, this feature was called the Wharf. Icons linking frequently used programs are placed in the Dock. Instead of bringing up the drop-down menu, double-clicking the respective icon launches the program just as readily. Many Window Maker enthusiasts also place icon-based applets on the Dock. These are small programs that run continuously and either display system performance or audio utilities. In my own scheme, I have an applet that runs a clock, a CPU meter, and an applet that checks all processes and users on the system concurrently. A plethora of applets is available for Window Maker on the Internet, with an applet fitting most any user's needs.

For a closer view of Window Maker's potential, Figure 12.5 shows my own desktop display.

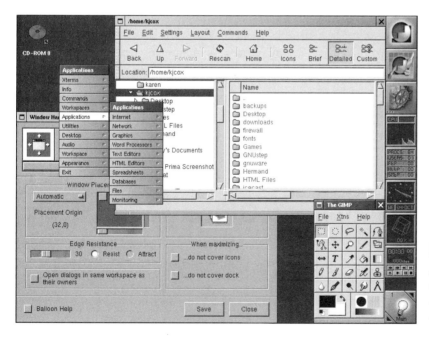

**FIGURE 12.5**

*A more customized view showing off some of Window Maker's features.*

## Installing Window Maker

Window Maker has fewer system and software requirements than GNOME or KDE. You can run it on a slower machine with less RAM and CPU power yet still achieve fast response times. As always, if you are using any sort of GUI under X Window, the better the video card, the quicker the refresh rate and visual performance. A thorough description of the steps required to install Window Maker is provided in Chapter 11.

Once you have the source code downloaded onto your machine, carefully reading through the documentation files and the other readme and install files should answer any particular questions about the system on which you are installing the program. Remember that you must also run the wmaker.inst utility to place the customized GNUstep/ files in your home directory. Only in your own GNUstep directory can you begin editing the system.

The Window Maker developers are also prompt with releasing the RPM version of their product. If they do not release it immediately along with the source, it takes only a few extra days for someone else to create his or her own RPM version of the latest release. This version also is easy to install, but as with the sourced version, you must run wmaker.inst to generate the needed files.

One of the many positive elements about each of these window managers is that on systems with many accounts and people logging in, each user can have a customized interface adapted to his or her own taste. Larger systems can even have a customized pop-up menu that prompts each user for his or her choice in window managers.

# Suites for Home and Office

One of the biggest complaints against Linux by new users has been the absence of viable office suites. As Linux becomes more mainstream, it is rallying some major developers behind it who are porting their applications to the Linux platform. Currently, Linux is still seen more as a server platform than as a workstation. Servers rarely require a word processor, spreadsheet, or presentation program. These are easier run on a workstation not running critical applications. Thanks to the stability of Linux, users can run a system as both a server and workstation, or configure their system to be a workstation only, disabling many of the server features and conserving CPU cycles for their own use. For a more comprehensive explanation on how to turn a server and networking application on or off, refer to Chapter 15.

This section examines some of the more popular office suites and word processor programs now available for Linux. Nearly all are still proprietary, and the source code is not available. However, the binaries or the programs themselves are free for all to download and install. The functionality of these Linux programs is nearly equal to that of the Windows and Apple platforms.

# Using StarOffice

Among the many killer apps that have come along for Linux, perhaps one of the foremost available is the StarOffice Suite recently purchased by Sun Microsystems. Only a few years ago, IBM had considered purchasing StarOffice for use on its own operating system, OS/2. Instead the company opted for purchasing the Lotus Suite, thus leaving StarOffice open for Linux development.

The StarOffice interface closely resembles that of the Microsoft Office Suite. It too has many of the same features, and the look and feel are quite similar to that of Microsoft Office. It quickly imports and exports documents from and to Microsoft Word, Excel, and PowerPoint. StarOffice also utilizes many of the same commands for editing text. The format variables are also nearly the same. Any novice Microsoft user will quickly feel at home with this interface. Moving from the Windows platform to Linux StarOffice requires less effort on the part of the user than learning a new office suite under Windows, such as WordPerfect Office.

Besides providing the word processor, StarOffice also provides a web browser, an email client, and all the tools necessary to work on the Internet. Much like the Netscape Communicator package, StarOffice also provides all the functionality needed to compose and send email using either a POP3 or IMAP server, browse web pages, read threaded newsgroups, and design HTML content. To design HTML content, you can either import a new text document into HTML format or create the content using an HTML editor also included with the suite.

StarOffice includes a spreadsheet program that imports the latest Excel documents and customizes them to suit. Again, many of the same features that come with Excel are also available under StarCalc, which is the StarOffice spreadsheet program. Virtually any utility found with the Microsoft Office Suite will also be available for the Linux port of StarOffice. The most recent release of StarOffice 5.2 enables users to create databases much like Microsoft Access does.

StarOffice compromises some of its features to slim down the package. The entire suite, tarred and zipped, can be downloaded from the Internet. Rather than the 500+ megabytes of data that the latest Microsoft Office Suite requires for a complete install, StarOffice is only slightly more than 90 megabytes fully compressed and when installed occupies less than 200 megabytes. It is also self-contained, meaning it does not change any of the configuration files, but runs within its own directory. StarOffice loads its own set of libraries and configuration files to retain the same appearance and feel on all platforms, whether Windows or Linux. This contributes to one of the few disadvantages that I discovered with the latest release: Speed is not one of its greatest features. If you start up the program after a fresh reboot on a 500 megahertz Athlon with 128 megabytes of RAM, it takes 30–45 seconds until StarOffice is fully operational. But the features provided by the program, bringing office management to the Linux platform, far outweigh the speed issues.

## Downloading and Installing StarOffice

You may obtain StarOffice from a subdirectory on the Sun site, http://www.sun.com/staroffice/. Sun requires you to register before downloading, but in turn will inform you about upgrades and additional Sun programs. After registering, you can either opt to download the entire program, a sizable feat even for fast machines with bandwidth to spare, or to purchase a copy of the program on a CD. I recommend spending the few dollars (approximately under $10.00 U.S.) and having Sun mail you a copy. This way you will have a single copy for installing on as many machines as needed. Also, you won't need to use FTP to send the large tarred file to different servers.

The best method of installing StarOffice is first to create the default directory into which you wish to install the program. Make sure you or the person running the program owns that directory so that the install routine does not encounter any major permission problems and abort the install. I chose to create a directory in a larger partition:

```
# mkdir /usr/local/office52
# chown -R <username> /usr/local/office52
# chgrp -R <username> /usr/local/office52
```

Next, untar the downloaded file into a temporary directory, such as /tmp, or another directory over which you have the correct permissions. StarOffice should create an additional installation directory called so52inst/. Look for a file called setup:

```
# cd /tmp/so52inst/
# ./setup
```

Running this command as yourself or the appropriate user launches a graphical installation window. You will be prompted to fill out several forms that will include information about yourself as well as the configuration of your Internet connection. After you complete all the fields, StarOffice begins the install routine, a task that lasts only a few minutes depending on the speed of your computer. You should not need to tweak your system any further.

If you add StarOffice's directory path either to the global /etc/profile file or to each user's individual .bash_profile, you can start StarOffice from a single entry on a command line:

```
PATH="$PATH:/usr/X11R6/bin:/usr/local/Office52/"
```

Run the command `source /etc/profile` to enable the settings. StarOffice starts up with the simple command, soffice. To get your system fully functional on the Internet, StarOffice prompts you to fill out a few forms regarding your POP3 server, usernames, and the names of the servers that you frequent for connectivity. Filling out these forms is still a relatively minor task considering the ease and freedom that StarOffice grants in interfacing and exchanging information with other Microsoft systems and Microsoft-centric users.

Figure 12.6 shows how a regular text document appears along with the various menus that assist in choosing additional options. StarOffice emulates Microsoft to a high degree, so much so that it, too, along with the Start button, allows you to integrate the entire Linux desktop under the StarOffice display. This creates a Windows-like display. You may actually browse through the programs and directories under the StarOffice integrated desktop by pointing and clicking. Additionally, if KDE is already installed on the system, StarOffice detects this window manager and places a link on the KDE desktop, and also returns the favor and incorporates all KDE programs into its own Start button. The smooth integration of these two systems can in part be credited to StarOffice's own background as a German company, much like that of KDE's own history with German developers.

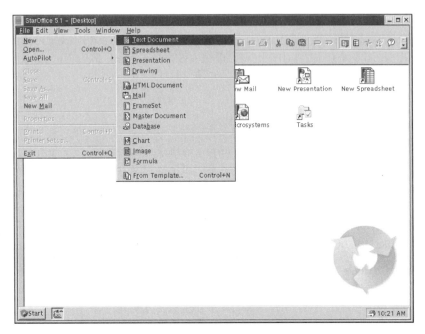

**FIGURE 12.6**

*The StarOffice
program running
under Linux.*

## Perfecting WordPerfect for Linux

The process of installing WordPerfect for the Linux operating system is a bit more convoluted than that of StarOffice, if only because WordPerfect's tarred and zipped file does not resemble that of regular Linux files. Weighing in at less than 25 megabytes does help in its attractiveness for downloads. Though it is named GUILG00.GZ, it is not only gzipped, but also tarred.

> **NOTE**
>
> The Personal Edition of WordPerfect Office 2000 for Linux users is available for free download. It should be mentioned that a commercial version of WordPerfect Office 2000 is also available for Linux. It has all the same features and applications that were released under the Windows version. Because of its cost and the affinity most Linux users have for free software, I will focus on the Personal Edition of WordPerfect that can be downloaded from the Internet.

Before doing the standard install, place the file in its own directory and then run the standard command:

```
# gunzip -c GUILG00.GZ |tar xvf -
```

Once all the files are uncompressed, simply execute the Runme file as follows:

```
# ./Runme
```

Make sure that you are also within an X Window environment because the Runme file then will launch a graphical installation menu. Once the WordPerfect program has been fully installed, you can launch it by entering the command **$HOME/wpbin/xwp**, where $HOME is the location where you installed WordPerfect.

---

### NOTE

Shortly after Corel announced its support of Linux and subsequently placed WordPerfect on the Internet for download, thousands of requests for this program were placed in the first 24 hours. To date there have been over one million downloads of WordPerfect for Linux.

---

The interface for WordPerfect is very similar to that of the Windows version. Though the display relies upon the older Motif libraries (hence its unique appearance and use of different radio buttons and drop-down menu items), it still has many of the same options found on the commercial release. Figure 12.7 shows WordPerfect displaying a default text document. Notice the separation of the program window and the text window.

The WordPerfect for Linux Personal Edition, which is the version available for download, is missing a few items, including templates and additional macros, that you can get only with the commercial release. Therefore, purchasing the full version might be worthwhile. The very latest Corel Office Suite for Linux shows great promise and provides Linux users not only with the full release of WordPerfect but also Presentations and QuattroPro.

WordPerfect provides added functionality for multiple users on your system. Although you can achieve the same with the Personal Edition, the commercial release allows multiple users to log in from *dumb terminals,* or machines that have little to no hard drive space and rely upon the network for their programs. On networked Linux boxes or dumb terminals, WordPerfect can run on all versions of Linux, each under its own session. The full-fledged WordPerfect Office 200 Suite is the recommended program if you want to retain some standardization on a networked system, such as that of a large corporate office or educational setting.

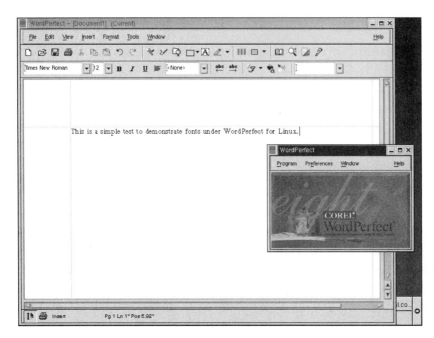

**FIGURE 12.7**

*The WordPerfect program as it appears under Linux.*

Though WordPerfect's appearance may not match that of StarOffice, it more than makes up for it in speed. WP8 is a quick and efficient word processor that handles larger documents quickly and easily. It too can both save and export into the majority of other document types, including the Microsoft Word format. It also includes the Publish to HTML option that comes with the Windows version. WordPerfect is an excellent choice for users who need to accomplish simple text editing and document publishing.

## Exploring Newcomers to the Linux Scene

A newcomer to the scene of Linux word processors is the AbiWord suite. Although AbiWord provides its source code, it is relatively immature in its development. AbiWord is available with the latest Helix GNOME release, though not by default. You may choose to install it as part of the desktop or download the code yourself and compile it for your own use. AbiWord requires an additional set of libraries and graphical support, so choosing the RPM version is the recommended method.

Another word processor that has come of age for Linux is KOffice, designed for and with the assistance of KDE developers. Though still in its preliminary stages, it demonstrates much potential. With the release of KDE 2.0 late in 2000, KOffice is expected due out at the same time. This suite of utilities should be available soon for the average user in RPM format. Currently, some bugs still need to be worked out and additional features need to be incorporated. When KOffice was first released, it still required supporting libraries and manual configuration.

There are also ongoing plans to improve upon many of the simple Notepad-type programs that run under Linux. These programs are very useful for simple messages or text files and can be found under both GNOME and Linux. They do not have or require many of the bells and whistles touted by the larger, commercial varieties, but they are useful for quick messages and instructions. One of my personal favorites that fall into the category of text editors is NEdit. NEdit now uses the GTK libraries and as such has greatly improved it stability and performance. Though it is classified as a text editor, it offers many dynamic features such as color coding of HTML tags or programming symbols. This feature helps greatly in keeping track of the many cryptic codes and symbols that Linux programmers use. NEdit can accomplish many of the same tasks as its larger counterparts without hogging memory or CPU cycles.

# Graphics

Undoubtedly, the original killer app for the Linux operating system was the GNU Image Manipulation Program (GIMP). The GIMP was a watershed program for people using Linux. Suddenly, they were no longer beholden to an extremely expensive program such as Adobe Photoshop to create dynamic images or edit existing pictures. The GIMP also provided the Linux community with a set of libraries now being used to develop additional programs, including the GNOME window manager.

## Designing with the GIMP

The GIMP has both drop-down menus and icons that allow you to select different graphical features when manipulating the images. One of the major strengths of the GIMP is its ability both to import and export images in and out of different formats. Much of this book was written under StarOffice and exported to Microsoft Word format, whereas the graphic images were all captured with the GIMP. The GIMP saves images in many differing formats, including the .pcx format. The fact that a book about Linux can be written on a Linux operating system while all the screenshots and images that better clarify the OS's function were also captured under the same system speaks volumes about this dynamic operating system.

For users interested in using a scanning program or scanner under Linux, the GIMP provides an interface to Scanner Access Now Easy (SANE). SANE interfaces with nearly any scanner, whether it is a parallel port or SCSI connection. Once the picture is scanned in, the GIMP can then process and save the image in the desired format.

**NOTE**

Most Linux distributions include the GIMP on the install CD, so you should require much information regarding the process of installing the GIMP. Updates appear regularly and can be downloaded via the GIMP Web page, at http://www.gimp.org/. From this page you can also download the GTK libraries. Unless a major update is needed, the existing libraries will usually suffice. The GIMP promotes the use of the RPM install, but source code generally appears sooner than the RPMs do. Both methods are easily installable.

GIMP continues to make headway with Linux developers and enthusiasts. It is not uncommon for Web page graphics to be developed entirely using GIMP. In addition, most GIMP installations come with preloaded *extensions* or *filters* that equal Photoshop in quality and versatility. These are also called *plug-ins* and can render unique colorations or textures on any image. Simply testing a few of these features will demonstrate the high degree of quality now available under Linux.

You can install GIMP by using either the RPM or source code version. Generally, the RPM release is the preferred format because the install is so easy and fast. The source code can be compiled in a matter of minutes and is well documented. For complete instructions on compiling and installing source code, refer to Chapter 11.

Installing additional plug-ins is just as simple. After downloading the appropriate plug-ins from the GIMP site, simply place them in your plug-ins directory, whether it is the global GIMP directory or in the user's ~/.gimp/plug-ins/ directory. The next time you start up the GIMP, these plug-ins will be available.

## Viewing through Electric Eyes

The GIMP is to Linux graphic utilities as a Porsche is to sports cars. If, however, you do not require a lot of thrills and extras, then you might want to look at the all-purpose vehicle of graphics programs known as Electric Eyes. Developed by the creator of Enlightenment, Electric Eyes is installed by default with GNOME.

You can start up Electric Eyes by typing **ee** at any command line. The program has several features that allow you to change the hue and blending of most images. It also includes a slide show feature that flips through a series of photos, much like flipping the pages of a photo album. This feature works well when presenting slides or a series of pictures at meetings or conferences.

For any need under Linux, there is usually a tool, either available on some site or under development. Such is the case with graphics. Even the older versions of Linux still have tools that can accomplish most graphical editing tasks.

## Using TrueType and Adobe Fonts under Linux

One of the biggest complaints voiced by new Linux users is the lack of quality fonts available for the GIMP and other text or graphics programs. Though the X Window interface is very useful, it does not yet support, by default, the abundance of TrueType fonts found under Windows and Macintosh. However, there is a quick and easy way to install these fonts under Linux.

### NOTE

Thanks to Zach Beane (xach@mint.net), the developer of the GIMP News page (http://www.xach.com/gimp/news/index.html), this section presents just a few easy steps that you can follow to download a wealth of fonts that will install and work under Linux.

Everyone loves to see great fonts incorporated into graphics. Unfortunately, the only fonts that work well at large sizes with the GIMP are Adobe Type 1 fonts, and Red Hat Linux and other distributions install only a few fonts by default. Red Hat does provide certain font servers such as xfs and xfstt, which display TrueType fonts. However, these font servers can be difficult to setup. The following are some simple instructions for getting alternative fonts to operate under a vanilla Red Hat install.

Finding the necessary fonts is the easy part. The FTP archive site, ftp.cdrom.com, offers hundreds of Type 1 fonts that can be plugged directly into X. You may have to hunt around the site to locate the latest fonts. Many similar sites abound on the Internet.

The Dragonwick font appears in the font archive as dragonwi.zip. (An unfortunate side effect of fonts intended for DOS is that their names often are not reasonably descriptive.) To plug this font directly into X, follow these steps:

**0**  Download the zip file to a directory on your system.

**1**  Unzip the dragonwi.zip file using the following unzip command:

```
# unzip -L dragonwi.zip
```

It produces this output:

```
Archive:   dragonwi.zip
   exploding: dragonwi.afm
   exploding: dragonwi.pfb
   exploding: dragonwi.pfm
   exploding: dragonwi.txt
```

The -L option keeps the fonts lowercase while unzipping. Without the flag, the unzip command changes them back to their uppercase DOS format.

**0**  The only file you need and should care about is the dragonwi.pfb file. Copy it into your /usr/share/fonts/default/Type1/ directory. This is where your system stores the Type 1 font files.

**1**  You must also let X know where the new fonts are located. Edit the fonts.scale file located in the Type1 directory. Here are a few lines from mine:

```
thomas.pfb -adobe-thomas-medium-r-normal—0-0-0-0-m-0-
iso8859-1
   tiempo.pfb -adobe-tiempo-medium-r-normal—0-0-0-0-m-0-
iso8859-1
```

```
    tif_b.pfb -adobe-tif_b-medium-r-normal—0-0-0-0-m-0-
iso8859-1
    tif_e.pfb -adobe-tif_e-medium-r-normal—0-0-0-0-m-0-
iso8859-1
    tiffhevy.pfb -adobe-tiffhevy-medium-r-normal—0-0-0-0-
m-0-iso8859-1
    tiffthin.pfb -adobe-tiffthin-medium-r-normal—0-0-0-0-
m-0-iso8859-1
    title.pfb -adobe-title-medium-r-normal—0-0-0-0-m-0-
iso8859-1
    tribe.pfb -adobe-tribe-medium-r-normal—0-0-0-0-m-0-
iso8859-1
```

**0** To enable the font servers to recognize dragonwi.pfb, add a line that resembles the following:

```
    dragonwi.pfb -adobe-dragonwick-medium-r-normal--0-0-
0-0-m-0-iso8859-1
```

The only two critical variables in the line are the first entry, which tells the name of the font file, and the third entry, which tells X what to present to the user as the name of the font.

The third entry is useful if your font file is named something like shtoo.pfb. That type of filename is not very descriptive. You should change the third entry to SharkTooth to give you a better idea what the font is.

**0** Save your fonts.scale, then run the following programs:

```
    # cd /usr/share/fonts/default/Type1/
    # mkfontdir
    # xset fp rehash
```

These commands create an index file for your fonts and rehash the font server to use the new index, respectively. Now when you go to use the Text tool in the GIMP, a new font, dragonwick, will be available in all your graphics programs.

An excellent program, typelinst, automates this whole process. It is available from the type1inst home page (ftp://sunsite.unc.edu/pub/Linux/X11/xutils). It is much easier to configure and install all the downloaded fonts than to tweak them by hand.

# Dynamic Linux Databases

Databases are proving to be a powerful driving force in creating dynamic web sites, for storing home and office data, and for archiving unique information for a variety of purposes. Linux offers several free database programs, each with its own pros and cons. The biggest draw of databases for Linux is not only the stability that Linux offers, but also the dynamism of the databases themselves. Though they do not provide file locking like some of the more robust commercial database programs, MySQL and other databases for Linux can handle a tens of thousand database entries with no problem.

## Setting the Standard for Free Databases

One of the more popular free database programs currently available, MySQL (pronounced *my sequel* or *my S Q L*) can handle large databases. Developed from its predecessor, msql, MySQL has grown to become the accepted standard for many databases programs. MySQL is not designed to process databases over a several thousand entries, and thus cannot yet compete with many of the industry powerhouses such as Oracle or Sybase. It is instead designed to work with smaller, more dynamic databases. It interfaces well with HTML front ends, such as PHP3 and PHP4. These can be compiled into the source code as modules. PHP provides a dynamic interface for users to access those databases via a web browser. MySQL is quick and powerful and, best of all, free.

The source code for MySQL as well as the RPM and binary versions of code is available at the MySQL home page, http://www.mysql.org/. The recommended procedure for installing MySQL is to use the RPMs, though many users favor compiling the source themselves. The easiest way to install the RPM release of MySQL is first to download the latest release. One prime location for downloading the latest Red Hat RPMs is http://w3.rufus.org/. The three needed files are the core MySQL, MySQL-devel, and the MySQL-client RPMs. Red Hat's latest commercial release provides the RPMs for MySQL. These are not usually found on the main installation disk, but are instead located on the Powertools disk. To verify which files you may install, enter the following command:

```
# ls MySQL*
```

This command generates output similar to the following:

```
MySQL-3.22.32-1.i386.rpm
MySQL-client-3.22.32-1.i386.rpm
MySQL-devel-3.22.32-1.i386.rpm
```

To install the database and start the server, use the standard RPM install command:

```
# rpm -ivh MySQL*
```

This command installs all the necessary files, including the run command file, which initiates the server when your machine is rebooted.

## Making MySQL Your SQL Database

To install MySQL via source code, you need only one single file that in turn creates the client and all needed developmental files. Copy the tarred and zipped file to a centralized location and then uncompress the directory, as follows:

```
# cp ~/downloads/mysql-3.22.32.tar.gz /usr/local/gnu/
# gunzip -c mysql-3.22.32.tar.gz | tar xvf -
```

Next, make a symbolic link from the new directory to a generic mysql directory and change to the new directory, as follows:

```
# ln -s mysql-3.22.32 mysql
# cd mysql
```

Now run the install script in the following location:

```
# scripts/mysql_install_db
```

Yet another way to install MySQL is to execute the generic configure and make commands either separately or jointly. The following example shows how to execute the commands jointly:

```
# cd mysql
# ./configure ; make ; make install
```

After you have compiled and installed the program completely, you can start up the database server from the command line:

```
# bin/safe_mysqld &
```

You can automate the startup of the program using the Red Hat run commands. Create a new script in the /etc/rc.d/init.d/ directory, name it mysql, and then insert the preceding command on the first line. Make the script itself executable, as chmod 755 mysql, and then create symbolic links in the ../rc3.d/ directory:

```
# cd /etc/rc.d/rc3.d/
# ln -s /etc/rc.d/init.d/mysql S99mysql
```

Add other symbolic links to the other run levels that require the MySQL daemon to start up.

### NOTE

If you install MySQL using the RPMs, Red Hat will automatically provide the run commands in their respective directories. You will not have to create the links as described in this section.

### CAUTION

Once MySQL is installed, it will remind you to change the MySQL root password. This is a must. Users who allow programs to run with the default passwords or who leave empty passwords create security holes. Be sure to change the MySQL password before doing anything with MySQL.

Once it is installed, MySQL runs a daemon process in the background that monitors SQL requests and provides the information upon demand. But if you still flinch at the idea of customizing source code and editing run command files, the RPM version of MySQL will also work fine.

One prime example of a Internet site that incorporates MySQL along with a Web front end is http://freshmeat.net/. This sites stores a database of information concerning the latest Linux programs available. It also lists the location, the developer, a brief summary, and the version number of most Linux programs.

This site receives tens of thousands of hits a day, yet it remains one of the quickest sources of information available on the latest Linux products.

Rather than entering all the commands by hand in a command-line environment, you can call upon several programs that are available to assist in this process. These programs provide a graphical environment in which the data can simply be plugged into the different fields. Gmysql is based on the GTK libraries, whereas Kmysql runs under the Qt libraries just as KDE does. These are just a couple of the many programs emerging for use with MySQL.

## Using PostgreSQL

PostgreSQL is available on the Red Hat installation disk. You may choose to install it along with MySQL and use it for creating dynamic databases. Though not as well known as MySQL, PostgreSQL nonetheless enjoys a large following and has several features not found on MySQL. It too is available in both source and RPM format. Red Hat uses RPMs to install the program, create the database logs, and automate the server startup with each reboot of the system.

Though it employs syntax similar to that of MySQL, PostgreSQL's syntax has some differences. Still, both use the main SQL commands, and moving from one to the other is not that great a leap. Explaining every command and how to use PostgreSQL is beyond the scope of this book. Suffice it to say that the install routine creates a default user named postgres who owns the PostgreSQL databases. To install the PostgreSQL source code, you use the same commands as you would with most any source code: configure, make, and make install. The database files are kept in a standard location; usually this location is /usr/local/psql. Before starting up the interface you must first start the PostgreSQL daemon. Much like the other system daemons, you can start up the PostgreSQL daemon initially by entering the command /etc/rc.d/init.d/postgresql start. This will initialize the databases and also set up the postgre user who will then own the databases. If you wish for the daemon to start automatically upon bootup, run the /usr/sbin/ntsysv command and select the postgresql option to start up at boot.

Executing the command-line interface in which you can then enter queries and commands requires typing **psql** at any command line. This can be done either as a regular user or as root. PostgreSQL also provides a convenient GUI interface for creating databases and tables. The pgaccess command will launch a utility to create new databases, tables, queries, etc. It also comes with a Help Index file for looking for more specific commands.

If you require or are considering using a commercial database to store company information, consider first the benefits that come with using a program like MySQL or PostgreSQL. Though the learning curve may be somewhat steep at first, there are ample sources of support. Both are constantly being refined and improved upon by an entire community of developers. Plus, various commercial organizations are providing support at low cost. This way you have resources available that are beneficial for smaller companies or organizations. Because the source code is free, there is little monetary risk to your company or organization. The only necessary investment is to spend some time learning its intricacies.

# Conclusion

Now that you have configured the X Window server and are familiar with many of the window managers, text editors, and databases, you are now ready to start using what you have learned in a real-life situation. The next chapter deals with printing under Linux. Because of Linux's stability, many users feel comfortable setting up Linux as a print server and then simply walking away. If left undisturbed to do its job, Linux will perform flawlessly for hundreds of days without a reboot. Many users actually forget that Linux is even there until someone pulls the plug. The next chapter examines how you can set Linux to act as a print server for other Linux machines, for a network, or for a group of Windows workstations. The reverse also applies; you can print from your Linux box through any sort of Windows workstation.

# Chapter 13

## Linux Print
## Serving

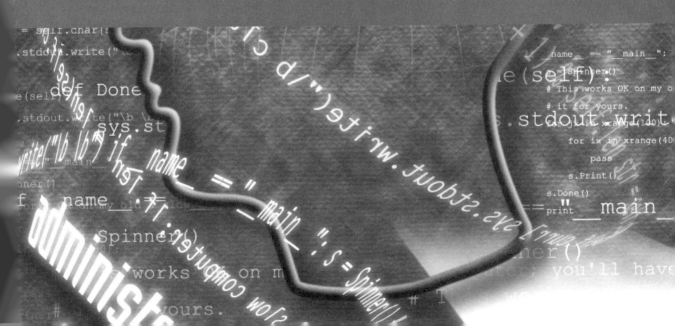

N ow that you are familiar with the task of configuring and installing new programs and have used some of the text editors and word processors, from the more generic to most complex, you will probably want to optimize these tools and print out text from the system. This text can range from documents created yourself or articles downloaded from the Internet. Most people still prefer paper copies of e-mails or memos for archival purposes or for redistribution. Properly setting up printing under Linux is integral to making Linux a functional tool for everyday use.

This chapter will cover the following topics:

◆ Setting up printing services on your local machine

◆ Understanding serial devices

◆ Using the Red Hat PrintTool

◆ Configuring the lpd daemon

# Printing on the Local Linux Box

Though saving information in a digital format is useful and cost-effective, in some instances you will need to generate a *hard copy* of your data—to print onto paper information stored on the computer. The much-heralded "paperless society" has been somewhat slow in developing, and in many instances computer technology has resulted in the opposite effect. Many people print the volumes of data churned out by the Internet along with the voluminous supply of daily emails. This has actually increased the demand for paper rather than reducing consumption. Still, paper remains an assured method for saving data in tangible form. While the bits and bytes of data stored on a hard drive are indecipherable to most people, a printed sheet with neatly formatted information enables you to present stored data in a concrete, legible form.

As Linux continues to make headway in the field of desktop publishing and word processing, there will continue to be the need for some method of processing data and information into a hard copy format. Linux supports a wide range of printers and has several methods for transmitting processed data and information either to printers physically connected to the machine or to other printers connected via a network. In either case, Linux is robust in spooling out data to a printer. In cases where the machine and the printer are mission-critical and require uptime 24 hours a day, seven days a week, many choose Linux for their choice in print servers.

The printer that many users employ is not always the one that they choose initially. Often, printers are passed from one department to another or handed down from fellow co-workers, friends, or family members. In a similar sense, Linux users don't necessarily buy a printer because they think it will work well with Linux; rather they consider each printer's reputed quality or economy. It is expected of the printers themselves that they will function well under most any operating system. Users fully expect their printer to fulfill their printing requirements. Getting their chosen printer to work under Linux may not be as easy as deciding upon a brand name. Nothing can be more frustrating than buying a printer that functions poorly with your system. However, if you invest a bit of time and effort, setting up Linux for printing can be a rewarding experience.

## Connecting via Serial Devices

Installing a printer under Linux is a relatively simple process. For the most part, installing a printer under Linux only involves connecting the printer to the parallel port on the back of the machine and then configuring the software. Linux provides the most basic of drivers that will work with even the most advanced printers. Nearly 95 percent of all printers currently in use are simple parallel port printers that plug into any 25-pin serial port. Most any parallel port cable works. Because the majority of printers currently on the market are ink jet and laser jet printers that interface with serial ports, it should not be too difficult to connect the printer to the computer physically.

However, a new printer's package usually does not include a printer cable. You have many options when choosing a printer cable. Printer cables are graded and priced based on shielding and length. Most computers today have *EPP/ECP parallel ports*, whose performance is vastly superior to that of the original standard parallel port. To get the higher performance touted by many of the current printers, you need to use *IEEE-1284-1994* standard cables.

Contrary to popular belief, there is no such thing as a "standard" parallel printer cable. Usually people think of a "standard" printer cable as one with a DB25 connector to connect the PC's parallel port, and a Centronics 36-pin connector to connect the printer. The end that connects to the printer is a common connector for that end of the cable. Known as a Centronics connector, the male connector on the end has a tonguelike protrusion in the middle that you insert into the printer slot. At its opposite end is the male DB25 connector, which fits into the female parallel port receptor.

Regular printer cables may work adequately for printing to older, slower dot-matrix printers. However, for contemporary printers and other parallel port devices like zip drives, scanners, and other devices capable of 2 megabytes-per-second operations at lengths of up to 30 feet, an IEEE-1284-1994 cable is the faster and preferred cable. This performance does not come without a cost. The better performance cables can cost up to $70 or $80 U.S. for a standard length cable. However, the transfer rate and integrity checking of data will only improve system performance. If speed is not of the essence or if you are not printing out reams of paper daily, then regular lower-priced cables should work just as well.

To optimize these newer printer cables, check your machine's BIOS settings. As your PC boots up, enter into the BIOS settings and look at the current printer configuration. You can enter the BIOS settings on your computer's motherboard by pressing either the Delete key, or the F2 key, or the appropriate key combinations before the system starts the OS, but after it completes the memory test. Make sure you have EPP/ECP selected as your standard printer connection. If you find an issue with your printer or if the data do not appear to be transferring correctly or slower than expected, you may try some of the other settings as well.

## Preparing Linux for Print Jobs

If you are setting up your Linux box to serve exclusively as a print server, you need to be aware of a few details. The printer should be physically connected to the box, so that you do not lose print jobs if you lose your connection to the network. Select the Local printer option if the cable physically connects the printer to the Linux machine. The system also needs to know the name of the queue to which to send print jobs. The most recommended name for a print queue is lp. In addition, this queue requires a directory into which to store the jobs until the printer is available or until the preceding jobs have completed their print cycle. Though this directory usually requires very little hard drive space because print jobs do not normally need to exist for very long, it is a good idea to create a separate partition. The default location for the print queue is /var/spool/, but you can change this default setting to /usr/local/spool or some other directory. The configuration file that specifies the location of the default spool is the /etc/print-cap file. Under Red Hat Linux systems the /etc/printcap file normally points to the /var/spool/lpd/lp directory as the default location for the Linux printer. If your system will have only one printer, this location is usually adequate.

Red Hat is more verbose in its printer settings than are other systems, which tend to keep the user ignorant about how the machine operates. Red Hat Linux allows full user interoperability, meaning that the user can manage not only his or her print jobs, but all print jobs sent to the connected printer. Because Linux is a true *multitasking* system and can handle requests from several operators at once, it can also handle several print jobs at the same time. Linux performs *spool-ing*—or receiving print requests, storing them in the order they are received, and then sending them out in a manageable order—so as not to overload the printer. Spooling applies not only to networked printers but also to single-user machines. If you send several print jobs at one time, the *print spool* handles them. They wait in the print spool until it is their turn to be printed.

If you are setting up Linux to be a print server only, be sure to disable many of the superfluous services not needed for that machine. For example, though Linux runs a sendmail and httpd daemon by default, you should disable these services. The only daemons that should be running are the crond, init, lpd, sys-logd and other daemons started by the kernel. You should also disable the FTP and Telnet services and any other services that the server does not require. For more information on securing Linux systems, see Chapter 19.

To set up a Linux box as a print server, you need to know the port to which to connect the printer cable. The latest releases of Linux can usually detect the specific port and to which the printer cable is connected. Power on the printer before allowing Linux to detect the printer connection. Once it determines the active port you can begin interfacing the operating system with the printer. The same naming of ports under alternative operating systems does not necessarily apply to Linux. Under Windows, the standard ECP printer port is LPT1. Under Linux, this port is the device name /dev/lp0. For Linux to detect the printer while installing the drivers, the printer must be physically attached to port. For optimal results, you should connect your printer to the machine before powering up.

After your system detects a viable port, it will show the port number of the detected port. In most instances, this port number will be /dev/lp0 or /dev/lp1. If your system does not detect any viable port or printer, first verify that the cables running from the port to your motherboard are securely connected and attached correctly. Then check to make sure that your printer's cable is properly attached to the machine.

---

**NOTE**

Several years ago, while setting up Red Hat 4.2 on an older 486 to be a print server, I mistakenly attached the printer cable backward to where it fit into the motherboard, placing the 1-pin on the opposite side. Though I had configured the software correctly, I was unable to get the printer to work. I assumed that the fault lay with the software. Later, when I checked the internal settings, I saw my mistake. Do not immediately blame the software if you fail to get the printer to work on the first try.

---

## Configuring the Printer Variables

Once the printer and cable are physically connected, you can begin to set up the software. Older Red Hat installs set up the printer while you installed Linux. One of the initial setup options was to choose your printer type and then configure the printer. With the latest Red Hat release—that is, any version newer than Red Hat 6.0—root configures the printer after the operating system is fully installed.

Before attempting to set up the printer, check the Red Hat Compatibility List to verify that your printer is compatible with the OS. Nearly all printers will work to some degree with Red Hat, but some might not be fully compatible. The pages may print, but the quality of printout might be lacking. Before ripping the machine apart and rechecking hardware settings, consult the Hardware Compatibility List on the Red Hat home page located at http://www.redhat.com/support/hardware/. If the item is not listed, then Red Hat does not support it.

You should be aware of the following printer definitions:

◆ *lpd.* This is the *line printer spooler daemon.* Like other daemons, lpd starts when the machine boots up. Also like other daemons, lpd can be manually started and stopped by the root user. This daemon manages the print jobs as each is spooled.

- *lpr.* The offline print manager submits each print job to the spooler daemon. Users can invoke the lpr command to view the current print jobs.

- *Input filters.* These filters handle printer-specific formatting issues. For example, if you have several printers connected to your machines, the input filters will encode the job depending on the printer device to which you send it.

- *The /etc/printcap file.* This configuration file describes multiple printers supported by your machine, whether they are local or networked, and tells Linux how to handle each job.

- *The /var/spool/lpd directory.* This directory is the physical location of the print spool. If you do not wish to use any of the commands associated with print management, you may look in this directory to see what print jobs are currently in the queue. If you cannot clear out the queue and many large jobs are waiting, you can manually remove all jobs from the print queue by deleting them from this directory.

- *The PrintTool utility.* This tool is commonly associated with setting up and configuring printers on your machine. You can either run this program by itself from the command line as superuser or launch it from within the control panel. You must execute the necessary commands from within an X Window session and under a window manager such as GNOME or KDE.

---

**NOTE**

For each of these variables, you should check the man pages for further information. The manual pages list additional options and related commands for managing printers. The primary page to consult is man lpd, which lists all the variables needed to manage print spools and print jobs.

---

# Using the PrintTool Utility

Because most users will want to configure print jobs from within a GUI, using the PrintTool utility is perhaps the fastest and most reliable way to set up your printer. As mentioned in the preceding section, you can either launch this program from the command line or locate it in the control panel. To do either, you must have root privileges. Within the control panel, the PrintTool program is the third icon from the top.

You will need to be familiar with this utility after starting up the GUI or when you need to configure other network or system interfaces. The PrintTool is installed by default, but you can easily install or update the utility from either RPM code or source code. Rather than customizing the printer configuration setting or editing the /etc/printcap file by hand—both of which are rather intimidating tasks—you can simply use the PrintTool option.

As even a quick perusal of the /etc/printcap file will reveal, you need a strong familiarity of the /etc/printcap syntax before attempting to manually configure the file. The following shows the /etc/printcap file:

```
# /etc/printcap
#
# Please don't edit this file directly unless you know what you are
doing!
# Be warned that the control-panel printtool requires a very strict
format!
# Look at the printcap(5) man page for more info.
#
# This file can be edited with the printtool in the control-panel.
##PRINTTOOL3## SMB laserjet 300x300 letter {} LaserJet Default 1
lp:\
:sd=/var/spool/lpd/lp:\
:mx#0:\
:sh:\
:if=/var/spool/lpd/lp/filter:\
 :af=/var/spool/lpd/lp/acct:\
 :lp=/dev/null:
```

Because the PrintTool alters sensitive files in the /etc directory and creates new entries in /var, only superuser can access any sort of configuration tool that sets up the printers. The typical interface of the PrintTool program appears as shown in Figure 13.1.

The features included with PrintTool are simple. You can edit, add, or delete a printer from your selection using the buttons arranged along the bottom of the screen. The drop-down menus available from the menubar across the top of the

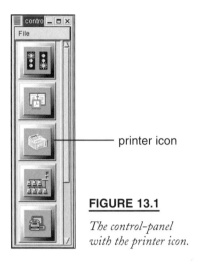

**FIGURE 13.1**

*The control-panel
with the printer icon.*

printer icon

screen allow you to restart the lpd daemon, which controls the entire print process, or perform selected tests and send default test pages to the printer.

After you decide to add a printer to the available list, PrintTool presents a list of options as shown in Figure 13.2.

You can choose among one of four available options. You are not limited in the number of printers that you can host on the PrintTool configuration, but you must set up each individually. The choices are:

◆ *Local Printer.* This option is for printers that are physically attached to your Linux machine via a parallel port or serial cable.

◆ *Remote Unix (lpd) Queue.* These are printers that are on the local LAN and that can be accessed via a TCP/IP network.

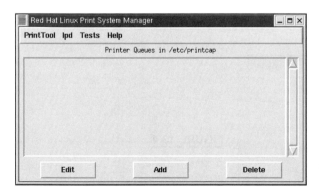

**FIGURE 13.2**

*A typical PrintTool
configuration.*

**FIGURE 13.3**

*You can select the printer type, whether it is local or networked.*

◆ *SMB//Windows95/NT Printer.* These printers are physically attached to a computer running Windows and that are accessible by a Linux machine running either SAMBA or a manager program such as LAN Manager.

◆ *NetWare Printer (NCP).* These are the available printers attached to different machines using Novell NetWare as their operating system.

◆ *Direct to port printer.* If you wish to print to a specific port rather than to a serial connection, use this option. This choice is new under the Red Hat Linux 7 release.

Regardless of the printer types that you select, Linux can either send print jobs to them or receive print requests for them. You must also verify that your machine can communicate with each of these external networks before adding them to your PrintTool configuration.

If you are editing the local printer entry and want to define the local printer, PrintTool displays the Edit Local Printer Entry dialog box shown in Figure 13.4. The first few fields are filled in by default based upon the ports that PrintTool detects.

By choosing the Input Filter option, you bring up the Configure Filter dialog box, as seen in Figure 13.5.

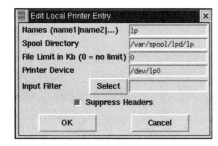

**FIGURE 13.4**

*Editing the local printer fields.*

As mentioned earlier, not all existing printers will be available. Because the listed drivers listed are generic and can provide the same level of printing capability as some of the newer drivers, you can substitute one printer driver for another. Most HP LaserJet printers will take the generic HP LaserJet driver as shown in Figure 13.5 and print just fine. Even though many PostScript printers support unique features, all such printers support a common standard subset of the Post-Script language.

Also known as the *printer filter*, the Configure Filter dialog box provides a brief description of the printer driver, the resolution, and the paper size, along with a color or black and white option. You can also define the different print options for fixing the stairstep effect in certain print jobs. If not configured correctly, the text will indent more and more on each successive line. This can be aggravating for users accustomed to pristine printing on other systems. The Fix stair-stepping text option should normally be selected to prevent the text from shifting on the printed page. The page margins are also definable, which is a necessary option for odd-sized paper.

After defining the correct printer driver, you can start editing the external options or adding the correct syntax so that your Linux box can speak to other machines. These items are normally configured only if setting up the Linux box to function as a server and not as a client. If you are running SAMBA, an implementation of a protocol that allows Linux and Windows machines to talk to each other over a TCP/IP network, you can also print to a Windows machine.

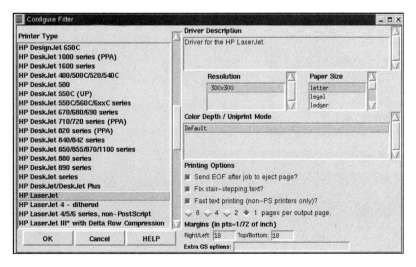

**FIGURE 13.5**

*The Configure Filter dialog box lists the filters available for your printer type.*

(Chapter 15 covers setting up SAMBA in more detail.) Printing through a Windows machine is as simple as editing your Windows machine so that the printer is shared with other machines on the Network then placing the computer's name in the Printer Entry dialog box as shown in Figure 13.6.

Once again, the name or names of the printer appear in the first field, and the print queue appears just below that. You can choose to limit the size of print jobs so that you do not fill up the available space in the queue or lock up memory on the print server. The two most important features here are the name of the computer to which the printer is attached and the name given to the printer. Adding the IP address of the computer is optional and is needed only for the client. On LANs that share accounts, you can also set up a username and password to send print jobs to any available printer. This helps to curtail large or unauthorized print jobs.

Again, you should fill out the filter correctly to make the right drivers available. After completing these entries, you can return to the Print System Manager.

Depending upon the type of install, you should see a list of available printers. Here much depends upon compatibility. For example, older Okidata printers use the HP LaserJet drivers to run. You may need to know more about the printer than what it stated on the device's case. For the most part, the HP LaserJet drivers apply to most HP LaserJet printers, regardless of the model number. Consult the web page of your printer's manufacturer to find out more about its drivers and connectivity. For the newer printers, such as the HP LaserJet 2100 or 3100 series, the standard HP LaserJet drivers work fine. You may want to test your setup later and verify the accuracy. A couple of other options that the install

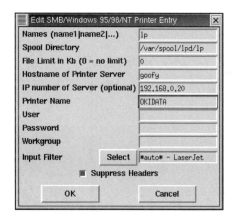

**FIGURE 13.6**

*Editing the fields for a printer connected on a SAMBA, Windows 98, Windows NT or Windows 2000 network.*

program will request are paper size and resolution. Depending upon the type of printer selected, you can keep the default settings for these options.

As shown in Figure 13.7, I have made two printers available on my system. One is an SMB printer connected via an SMB network, and the other a local printer connected to the serial port. I can access these printers through the Linux system by defining the device number, such as /dev/lp0 or /dev/lp2, to which each print job should be directed. Both of these printers are also available to others on the system, depending on the rules that I have set up in the SAMBA configuration file. In this file, you can specify which users can use a printer or have access to it through the system.

# Testing the Printer Configurations

You can now begin testing the setup by opening the Tests drop-down menu from the Print System Manager dialog box. By printing an ASCII or PostScript test page, you can tell whether your system is set up correctly and if you are using the correct filters. Some of the older printer configurations may print out the page, but with garbled characters. If this is the case, try using another printer filter. With older printers that produce garbled output, some require an IRQ be assigned to the lp port; others work fine in polling mode. If the characters do come out muddled or dropped, try loading the lp kernel module and explicitly forcing it to use an IRQ.

If this solution does not work, you can also try printing directly to the port. This is the last option under the Add a Printer Entry dialog box. If you can print to the port, then your physical setup is all right and you should re-examine your software

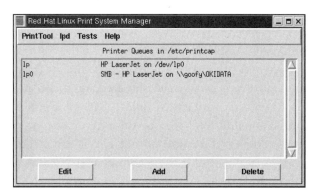

**FIGURE 13.7**

*A list of printers available both for a local machine and for networked boxes.*

setup. In most cases, this should force the system to print any text file. Be sure also to restart the lpd daemon so that it rereads the /etc/printcap file. If both options—testing new filters and printing to the port—fail, check the hardware.

I remember installing a very early version of Red Hat on a machine given to me. No matter what I tried I could not configure the machine to print. Then, I checked the internal cabling and discovered that whomever had built the box had plugged the cable in backwards. This is an unlikely scenario in today's machines, but possible nonetheless in older systems.

## Restarting the lpd Daemon

The lpd daemon runs the entire printer system. Like other daemon processes, lpd sits in the background checking its port, awaiting print requests. The Linux system must run the print daemon before any sort of printing occurs. During the Red Hat Linux installment process, you can set up the daemon to start automatically. Or, if you choose to set it up later upon boot, you can define it using the /usr/sbin/ntsysv command. This utility selects which options should be started upon bootup. You can manually restart the lpd daemon, much like you do under the PrintTool command. Changing the lpd status via the command line gives you more control over the stop and restart options.

The following text is a sample command to restart the Linux printer daemon (lpd). As is the case after modifying any configuration files, you should either send a HUP signal to the PID or stop and restart the daemon.

```
# /etc/rc.d/init.d/lpd restart
Shutting down lpd:          [ OK ]
Starting lpd:               [ OK ]
```

## Printing Directly to the Port

To print files without using any additional GUIs, you can use the command line. To do so, you must first have root permissions and then use the cat (*concatenate*) command. The cat command prints out to the standard input. Be aware that accomplishing this as root is not recommended unless it is not a public queue. In other words, it is fine to forcibly send files to the printer as root provided you are the only person on your machine and no one else is using the printer. However, using the lpr command instead is the recommended method of sending files directly to the printer. In nearly all instances one uses lpr. If this does not work, then the cat method will also work. When using cat, the command prints out the contents of a file while directing the output to the printing device. Here is a simple example:

```
# cat paper.txt > /dev/lp0
```

Several additional commands are used in tandem with the lpd daemon. The simplest method of printing documents to the print server, after configuring all the available printers, is to use the lpr command to send the request directly to the printing device. Here is the command's proper syntax:

```
# lpr [-Pprinter] <filename>
```

For example, rather than defining the paper.txt file to be printed out to /dev/lp0 which can either be the local or networked printer depending on how you set up the printer and filters, you simply use lpr. Here is an example of how to execute this command:

```
# cat paper.txt | lpr
```

The cat command reads the file and outputs it. The data is redirected to the lpr command, which then submits the data to the default print queue. Again, the lpr command is how you submit print jobs to the Linux printer daemon (lpd). A regular user cannot use lpr to force the printer to read the files. However, a regular user can still print to any of the configured printers using most any text editor of word processor.

Several options are available that you can use with the lpr command. You can define the printer with a -P option, and you can also specify the number of copies to print by entering -# followed directly by the number of copies. If you enter a -s before the name of the file, the command sends a symbolic link of that file to the queue instead of the file itself. This option is useful when you are printing large papers. The man pages describe and explain several other useful options in greater detail.

Other commands associated with the lpd daemon are lpq and lprm. The lpq command displays the status of the print jobs currently listed in the print queue. You can execute this command on the command line to display the job and its job number as it awaits processing. The lprm command removes jobs currently sitting in the queue awaiting processing. The following command cancels *all* jobs awaiting processing:

```
# lprm -
```

If you enter this same command followed by a number, you kill the print job that was assigned that particular identification number.

Printing either through or from Linux is extremely stable. As mentioned earlier, Linux is a good choice for print servers due to its stability and robustness in handling and processing incoming jobs. Many people set up a Linux server on older 486 machines. Simply plugging in a printer to the back of the box, booting it up, and then disabling the power switch is not a far-fetched possibility. I have heard stories about Linux print servers that can stay up for over a year, sending print jobs to the printer all the while.

In many cases, I have seen an unmarked Linux box handling the incoming print requests and churning out reams of printed material. A good indicator that a machine is doing its job is that you never have to think about its operations. Often it is only when the machine crashes that people give it serious consideration. I have known administrators who have told their managers they were running Windows- or Novell-based printer servers when they have actually been running Linux. For political reasons, many managers insist on the most popular operating systems, but administrators know better. Using Linux guarantees dependable performance. In any business environment where uptime is crucial, Linux helps to recycle older parts and keep employees content.

# Conclusion

The chapter explained how to use Linux for printing purposes. Because of its stability, Linux is a good choice for reliable printing. However, at times your Linux machine may have additional devices attached that are not printers; these devices may require some tweaking of settings. In such cases, you may wish to recompile your kernel to enable support of newer devices. The next chapter will explain what a kernel is and why it is important to be able to recompile a Linux kernel. Chapter 14 will also walk you through the basic steps of obtaining a current kernel, configuring it for your system, and then installing your custom kernel in place of the operational kernel. The chapter will also look at other features including patching a running kernel, updating kernels using RPMs, and keeping backup kernels in case of an emergency.

# Chapter 14

**Building a
Custom Kernel**

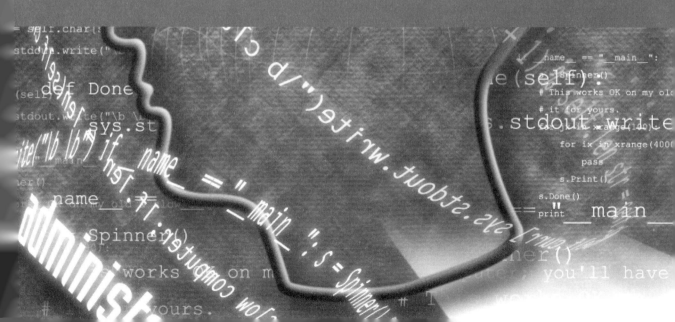

One of the most rewarding experiences that Linux provides is that of creating your own working kernel. Other proprietary systems restrict you to using the kernel or core element of the operating system as it comes installed. However, because the entire Linux system is open-sourced, you can view the text that comprises the foundation of Linux and thus compile it anew and create a new kernel. With each succeeding release of a newer, more stable kernel, the Linux operating system becomes that much more dynamic and responsive.

This chapter covers the steps required to build a new kernel as well as the following subjects:

◆ Understanding the difference between default and customized kernels
◆ Locating the most recent Linux kernel
◆ Distinguishing stable source code from developmental source code
◆ Choosing the right options for your machine
◆ Compiling the actual code
◆ Inserting modules into running kernels
◆ Patching existing kernels
◆ Troubleshooting bad kernel installs

# Defining the Linux Kernel

The Linux kernel is what runs the Linux operating system. Under most Red Hat installs, the kernel itself is located in the /boot directory and is called vmlinuz. Because the core of the Linux kernel is always in memory, the smaller the kernel, the faster your system will run. Rather than booting up the machine with every possible device driver preloaded, Linux loads only those drivers required by your machine. If you are compiling your own kernel, you can state exactly what drivers you want loaded or reduce the number of unnecessary devices recognized by your machine.

The latest kernel provides you with modularized support, meaning you can also insert or remove modules of Linux code that powers individual devices from the running kernel. This modularized support can help make the kernel itself even smaller and thus free up more memory and resources for other applications. Linux takes a conservative and minimalist approach to managing a server by using the least amount of system resources possible. The operating system grants all leftover assets of the system to the running applications. This can cause problems in that poorly written programs can develop memory leaks and thus bog down the entire system. But on the whole, Linux runs well due to its small kernel size and memory management. Optimizing a kernel configuration is will assist in developing a stable and robust system.

## Distinguishing Default Kernels from Customized Kernels

One of the best tests of a Linux administrator's skills is to compile a customized Linux kernel. Normally, rebuilding a kernel is not a regular occurrence, nor is it something that the system requires frequently. Most Linux distributions include a highly modularized or dynamic kernel that can function with most any peripheral device. With the default installation of these distributions, the default kernel immediately meets hardware requirements. This type of standardized core install usually does not require tweaking on the part of the administrator. If new hardware is installed, the kernel can usually detect it and will install the module for that piece of hardware without any recompilation or upgrade of the kernel.

But if an administrator wants to use more cutting-edge technology or if some of the settings are not to his or her liking, he or she can also build a customized kernel from scratch. A modified kernel differs from the default installed kernel, which is based on a configuration determined by the Linux distribution and might include additional source code. Other distributions may also include possible patches or inclusions to the kernel so that additional programs will run as well. In contrast, the customized kernel is usually built on source code downloaded from the Internet and then compiled on the machine to the user's specifications. Red Hat provides the option of installing the kernel source code as well as the headers and libraries so that you can compile the kernel later.

The default kernel release that comes with most Red Hat Linux releases is configured to be as generic as possible. In other words, the kernel is set up to run on all manner of systems, regardless of the different peripheral devices, the make and version of internal cards, or even such features as CPU model and memory type. To create such a flexible kernel, the developers modularized many of the devices. Rather than building the device drivers right into the kernel and making it larger than necessary, they use what are called *modules*. These modules can be incorporated into the kernel as they are needed and then released when done. This keeps the kernel small and sleek, resulting in a quicker and faster machine. Because the kernel is always running, the smaller the memory and CPU footprint the kernel requires, the more resources the kernel frees up for other programs.

Administrators who choose to incorporate modules into their kernel configuration create a *modularized kernel*. This differs from the module-free designs that are called *monolithic kernels*. Today, administrators seldom can build a truly monolithic configuration. Because of all the features required and the additional hardware cards and features included in most computer systems, a monolithic kernel would still function, but it is recommended that you use some modularization to optimize the system on slower or smaller machines. The older the machine, the better to implement modules to improve performance.

A typical compiled kernel under Red Hat can be anywhere from 500 kilobytes to 1.2 megabytes, depending on the configuration and whether or not drivers are compiled or set as modules. Most default kernels that come with a Linux distribution are just a little more than 600 kilobytes. Bear in mind, though, that a modularized kernel results in a smaller overall kernel size, whereas a monolithic kernel is larger. A typical Linux kernel as determined by the distribution usually modularizes all drivers. This allows nearly all systems to recognize all hardware configurations without creating an abysmally huge kernel. If you are compiling your own kernel, do not discount additional drivers in order to minimize kernel size if doing so compromises a machine's performance. Choose instead to select those drivers as modules, if possible.

## Obtaining the Latest Kernel Version

Before discussing a customized kernel compilation, it is important to note that there *will* come a time when you will need to rebuild the default kernel or install a new kernel. This need will arise due either to hardware, performance, security issues, or perhaps bugs in the default kernel and the necessity to upgrade to a better version. At some time you will need to know where you can obtain the latest kernel.

An example of one reason for reinstalling the kernel recently occurred. A bug was detected in both the sendmail program and the latest stable kernel. A local user could exploit this bug to gain root access. The solution was to update to the latest sendmail package and install the latest stable kernel. The kernel developers quickly issued a stable release and patch, and sendmail's developers also released their latest secure version. Many administrators quickly recompiled the latest kernel, replacing the older, insecure one. Red Hat also issued an RPM release of the latest kernel, which quickly upgraded Red Hat's previous default configuration.

Several good sites list information about the Linux kernel, including the latest changes, newest features, and other features under development within the kernel. Plus, even if you do not plan to compile the kernel on your machine, it is interesting to note the source code and the comments that developers have added within the code. If you are curious, take a look through some of the source code of the Linux kernel. Much of it might be indecipherable to the neophyte. But for the curious it does provide a unique insight into the workings of Linux.

Probably the most comprehensive site for gathering information and source code on the Linux kernel is the Linux Kernel Archives (http://www.kernel.org/). Here you may download the very latest Linux kernel source code as well as older releases for compatibility purposes and monitor the changes being made to the code almost daily. If your connection is slow or unable to log in due to the number of ftp users, try a mirrored site. The kernel developers provide mirrored sites in all parts of the world. The Linux Kernel Archive Mirror System is set up so you need only substitute the two-letter designation for each respective country into the main kernel.org hostname.

> **TIP**
>
> If the main kernel.org site is slow to respond, such as on the day of a new major release, use the designated mirrors such as www.<country>.kernel.org or ftp.<country>.kernel.org to reach a mirror supporting that specific country. To access the U.S. kernel archive site, type www.us.kernel.org, or to access the German ftp site, the designation is ftp.de.kernel.org. Each mirror will have a full archive of /pub/linux and /pub/software, although it might not carry both the gzip and bzip2 compression formats.

The only time you might experience any problems accessing the main site is immediately after the release of a new kernel. Often, the other sites are attempting to mirror the information along with the many Linux developers who want to try out the latest and greatest kernel.

Another site worth mentioning is kernelnotes.org (http://www.kernelnotes.org/). Formerly known as LinuxHQ, this site links not only to the latest source code, but also provides information to a host of other sites that document, explain, and give step-by-step instruction in upgrading, compiling, and installing a new Linux kernel. It also explains in detail how to install a kernel release (i.e. the full kernel source), and applying a kernel patch (i.e. the difference in source code between the latest release and the earlier version). Both contain full source code and can be used equally well to update a kernel to a newer version. The latter option, the kernel patch, might be more appealing to Linux users who do not have the time to compile a new kernel from source, yet who require the latest version on their machine. This site provides links to other sites that can assist you in getting past the challenges posed by kernel compilations.

Aside from the many Web sites linked from the kernelnotes.org site, a host of other FTP locations provide immediate access to the latest kernel. Though the Web sites themselves often link to another FTP or http site, going directly to the FTP location might prove quicker in the long run, especially for users who are connected via a slower modem and who must pay connection charges. One of the most popular sites that also provides a plethora of Linux applications and documentation is the Metalab site (ftp://metalab.unc.edu/). This site hosts not only all versions of the Linux kernel, but also most Linux distributions, GNU Open-Source programs, and an excess of applications designed exclusively for Linux. You can also find information about related systems such as Solaris and FreeBSD. This site offers more to download than you can ever hope to use on any given machine.

# Distinguishing Stable Source Code from Developmental Source Code

At any given time, two distinct versions of the Linux source code are available. One is the *stable kernel*, which has been tried and proven to operate without any unexpected crashes or significant glitches. It had been tested on the vast majority of the systems and found to be dependable enough to be classified by developers as stable. Most drivers and features have been tested on several types of Linux boxes and each has operated without any problems.

The other type of kernel is the *developmental kernel*. This kernel is less stable and often prone to crash machines, though its code is nonetheless based on the previous stable release. However, developers use this code to try out new configurations and explore the possibilities for adding new device drivers (including test drivers for such hardware features as DVD and USB devices) and support for additional peripherals and internal devices. Although the development kernel is not recommended for the faint of heart, some Linux users swear by it since it represents the cutting-edge (if not bleeding-edge or extremely alpha test drivers) of Linux development. To run newer hardware devices, you must sometimes install the latest developmental kernel.

It is also in this latest kernel build that you can see the direction in which Linux development is heading and the various features becoming available. If your system has USB devices that require the latest drivers, the developmental release may be your system of choice. If, however, you require an extremely stable system for production use, you may be better off with the stable release. At the current rate of development you will not have to wait long to the latest developmental kernels to quickly become stable.

Linux distinguishes between the two kernels in the following manner: *<major version>.<minor version>.<patch>*. The first item is the version number assigned to a kernel. Currently, the Linux kernel is in version number 2, and the kernel is expected to remain in version 2 for the immediate future. The second or middle field or minor version defines whether the kernel is stable or developmental. Releases with an even-numbered minor version are stable, while odd-numbered one are developmental and sometimes unstable. The odd-numbered developmental kernels are not intended for production or mission-critical servers. The last field is the release or patch number. The number in the last field indicates the patch level and can increment between one to two times a month during slow periods or two to three times a week during periods of rapid development.

Therefore, a kernel marked 2.2.17 is Linux kernel version 2, is stable, and has been preceded by 16 previous kernel patch level since that version was deemed stable. A kernel marked 2.3.46 is version 2 as well, but is developmental, and is patch level 46 of the developmental series. This type of identification is used not only in the Linux kernel but in other Linux application releases as well. With most all Linux distributions, whether Red Hat or others, it is usually only the stable kernel that makes its way into the distribution series. Seldom, if ever, has a developmental kernel been released under a commercial distribution. This is not to say that it is rash to use the developmental releases, but a stable kernel is more desirable if you want to provide stability for the servers that it will operate. Again, the developmental versions are geared mostly toward developers who want to debug and test the newer features and gain support for the top-of-the-line hardware.

# Properly Compiling a Kernel

There are several different approaches to running a compiler against the Linux source code and creating a new functional kernel. The methods described in this section are taken from my own experiences in creating new kernels under Red Hat and are also based on suggestions and information gleaned from the included source documentation. Your own methods may vary over time, but the method outlined in this section should provide enough of a foundation to create new kernels successfully.

## Preparing for the Install

Once you have either downloaded the latest kernel or decided to use the default source already installed, you can begin the process of compiling a new kernel:

1. If you are installing a *vanilla kernel*—that is, pristine source code from a new release—you should place the tarred and zipped file in the /usr/src directory. You can actually place it anywhere, but you will soon discover that it is easier to maintain tradition and place the file in this directory for the purposes of compiling. You should perform this step only as root. If you performed a full install from the distribution CDs, you will also find the existing kernel source on the CDs. The CDs also include all source headers and libraries needed to create a new kernel.

2. Rename your older linux/ directory for backup purposes. Be sure to name it something that will identify it as the older directory, as in the following example:

```
mv /linux /linux-2.2.xx
```

The latest version of Red Hat Linux 7.x provides a symbolic link to the older directory. For example the link linux/ will actually point to linux-2.2.16/ or to the stable kernel release. You can delete the symbolic link since the newer source code will create a directory with the name linux/.

3. Once you have backed up the older directory, you can untar and unzip the newer source code within the /usr/src directory using the following command, where the *xx* at the end of the filename represents the release number:

```
gunzip -c linux-2.2.xx.tar.gz | tar xvf -
```

You can accomplish this same step by typing the following as well:

```
tar -xzvf linux-2.2.xx.tar.gz
```

If you are uncompressing a bzipped file, you can accomplish the same task by substituting the gunzip command with bzip2, as follows:

```
bunzip2 -c linux-2.2.xx.tar.bz2 | tar xvf -
```

4. Next, you will see that a new linux/ directory has been created. You might want to rename this new directory to reflect the release version so that you are always aware of the release number that you are running on the machine.

```
mv linux/ linux-2.2.xx/
ln -s linux-2.2.xx/ linux/
```

These commands ensure that any links pointing to /usr/src/linux can still find the latest version of the Linux source code.

You should also look in the new directory for further information concerning this kernel release. Of special interest is the directory named Documentation/. Here you will find step-by-step instructions on how to compile the source code. This directory also outlines additional procedures and explains further many aspects of the kernel, from networking, to adding support for PPP, to supporting sound. The documentation explains or describes nearly all the kernel features in some manner. If a particular aspect of the kernel requires further clarification, this directory most likely will include a plain text document that will help you.

5. One step that helps with major upgrades, such as moving from the 1.x kernels or even the 2.0 kernel to the 2.2 kernel, is to add symbolic links from your own libraries to libraries located on the kernel. Some might consider this an unnecessary step since there are already symbolic links from the /usr/include directory pointing back to the /usr/src/linux directory. This step is recommended only if you are upgrading from earlier kernel releases numbered 1.x. To add such links, invoke the following commands:

```
cd /usr/include
    rm -rf asm linux scsi
    ln -s /usr/src/linux/include/asm asm
    ln -s /usr/src/linux/include/linux linux
    ln -s /usr/src/linux/include/scsi scsi
```

This last item is not necessarily a default link and may need to be created.

6. Once you have completed making symbolic links from the /usr/include directory to the new linux/ directory, you can return to the source location and begin configuring. To return to the /usr/include directory, enter the following command:

```
cd /usr/src/linux
```

7. If you are compiling an existing distribution kernel, make sure that you leave no stale files or compiled binaries and dependencies remaining from any older kernels. Though this step may not be necessary for a first-time compile, it is best to execute this command in any case. Run the following command from within the /usr/src/linux directory:

```
make mrproper
```

This command removes all files ending in an .o extension. This command helps ensure that no older compiled bits of source code will mistakenly be reinserted into the new kernel. The command recursively probes all directories to make sure that you are left with only clean source code.

# Determining Source Code for the Kernel

In this section, you determine which drivers and parts of the source code will be compiled into the new kernel. Much of this process depends upon your own system. You need to decide which device drivers to load and what type of support to provide the kernel. This can be a rather tedious process, but can be less arduous if you follow a few simple rules:

◆ *Know your system inside and out.* Be aware of the types of cards you placed in your box and the configuration for each. Whether you built the machine yourself or purchased it from a vendor, keep all the necessary documentation that came with the each component. If you do not have some of this documentation, consult your vendor for more information.

◆ *Do not skimp on the drivers you load.* If you are not sure which type of card you have, select several from the same category that may accomplish the task. It is best to load these cards as modules, if they are available as such, to avoid creating too big a kernel. You can always remove some of the drivers later after verifying which driver fits your system's needs. It is better to have too many drivers than to have too few and not have the system reboot properly.

◆ *If you installed the source code from the distribution, bring up the configuration menu for it alongside your own menu.* This way you can compare side by side the settings that your default installation chose and incorporate those same settings into your customized kernel. This process might seem a bit overly cautious, but if you are unsure as to what settings may or may not work, you can consult the default kernel.

◆ *Consult the documentation before attempting any sort of recompilation.* Read the installation instructions provided in the /usr/src/linux directory. Also, look at the kernelotes.org and kernel.org Web pages that explain in more detail the system settings. Do not rely wholly upon a single source for information about your system. In the same vein, do not take only this book's word for how to compile a kernel, but consult listed Internet pages as well.

◆ *Talk with others who have successfully recompiled a Linux kernel.* Get their views on the subject and weigh them against what you have learned. Ask questions on the newsgroups, bulletin boards, and other public media if you are unsure about anything. An extremely productive and often reliable source of information is the comp.os.linux newsgroup. I have received many e-mails and valuable tips from many readers and postings to the comp.os.linux.misc, comp.os.linux.setup, and the comp.os.linux.hardware newsgroups. If you are looking for information regarding a more specific category, perform a search for any newsgroup containing the word *linux*.

After familiarizing yourself with the various conditions and measures needed to protect yourself from a bad compilation, you are ready to begin configuring the settings.

## Initiating the Configuration

There are three different ways to edit the kernel configuration. The first is the command-line configuration, which is a very functional method for simple console editing. If you change your mind about a certain option that you have entered, or simply make mistakes when entering certain options, you ordinarily must start over. However, the command line offers a simpler way to make changes. Linux provides default settings that often achieve the same result that you desire. If the default settings match your objectives, you can apply them simply by pressing the Enter key. Using the command-line is the preferred method of editing the kernel configuration if using a slow modem to connect to a headless or distant machine. This can be useful when installing new kernels on distant or slower machines.

You initiate the command-line configuration either at a console or in an xterminal session. All the options provide a Help menu in case you are unsure about what each of the drivers does or for what type of system each is valid. Here is the command for the command-line editor to be run within /usr/src/linux/:

```
make config
```

Figure 14.1 shows a terminal window under X Window running the kernel make config command. Again, this option is not limited to running under X Window but can also be executed under a single console connection, via a serial connection, or from a remote machine as shown in Figure 14.1.

The next option is somewhat more verbose and provides you with an *ncurses session*, or a display that resembles an older DOS window. You can start this command both within an X Window terminal or in a regular console session. It

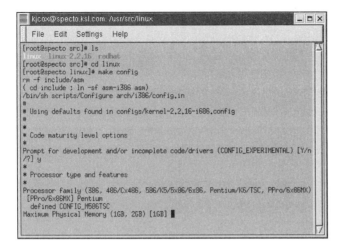

**FIGURE 14.1**

*Running the command* make config *under an X Window session.*

provides a treelike structure that assists in altering previous options or categories. You can collapse and expand the subdirectories and edit each option. As the command's name itself indicates, menuconfig is more a menu-based editor than a command-line editor.

    make menuconfig

Figure 14.2 shows menuconfig running under another xterminal display. As you can see, menuconfig provides a more interactive display that provides a greater number of configurable settings.

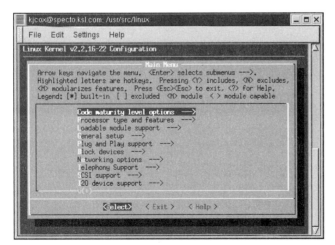

**FIGURE 14.2**

*Running the command* make menuconfig *under an X Window session.*

The last option for editing a menu, xconfig, is perhaps the one most preferred by both new and accomplished users. It is a GUI window that provides a clickable interface that includes radio buttons and various displays for different options. You can start this configuration only under an X Window session. The `make xconfig` command can be a bit more processor-intensive as it requires you to run X. The command to activate this configuration is as follows:

```
make xconfig
```

> **TIP**
>
> You should save the default configuration to a file in case you change a needed setting. You can recall the default file later and make minor adjustments. Give each successive kernel change a name indicative of that session. Before changing the kernel setup, save it to a file called distribution_kernel. Once you have edited the new kernel configuration, save it as test_kernel_1, and then increment the number with each succeeding compilation. Once you have a configuration that operates to your satisfaction, save it with a name such as golden_kernel_config.

Figure 14.3 shows the initial display that this command brings up.

This type of interface makes configuring the kernel much easier. If you have saved a previous configuration from an earlier compilation you can choose now to load that configuration and use those options selected. This facilitates changing only a few options quickly rather than re-entering new kernel options. Choose the Load Configuration from File option and locate the configuration file saved from an earlier compilation. This file is normally located in your /usr/src/linux directory. You can also edit the same simple text file with any text editor and change the "Y," "N,"or "M" options.

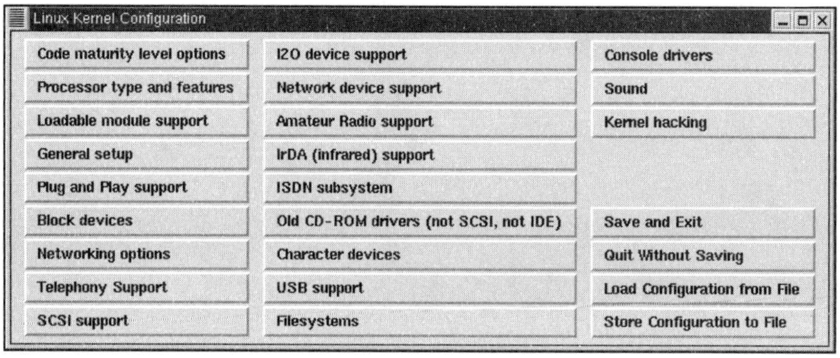

**FIGURE 14.3**

*The display that appears when you run the command* make xconfig *under an X Window session.*

Also, with the `make xconfig` command you can change your selection during the kernel editing process or skip ahead to another section. The xconfig option also allows you to save your settings in case of a mistake. If you want to edit just one setting later, you do not have to start over with the entire procedure again; instead, you can load the configuration from the previous session and make your change.

Each section that you choose to edit brings up another dialog box with various options available. Within the dialog box, you can move to the next series of choices or to the previous dialog box. Or, when you are finished, click the Main Menu button. Each of these dialog boxes is extremely navigable, as shown in Figure 14.4.

If one of the options sounds unfamiliar or if you simply would like to know more about the feature that you are either enabling or disabling, click the Help button. An additional dialog box then appears giving you more information on the subject, as shown in Figure 14.5

If you are unfamiliar with a section or option, read the Help dialog box closely. Chances are you will not require the information, but if you purchase additional hardware later, knowing beforehand what the kernel supports will help you choose hardware compatible with your kernel or with the latest Linux kernel. Also, closely examine the default settings and then adjust them as necessary. It cannot be stressed enough: *Be familiar with your system.*

**FIGURE 14.4**

*A sample xconfig session displaying with an individual dialog box.*

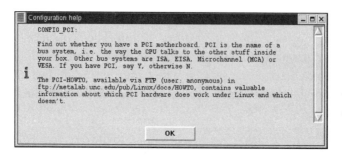

**FIGURE 14.5**

*An xconfig Help dialog box explaining more about the selected option.*

## Choosing the Settings

A number of options are available under the latest kernel set. Table 14.1 lists the major groups of options in the most recent 2.2.17 kernel. Currently, this is the stable kernel release.

Table 14.1 **The Options Under the Linux 2.2 Kernel Configuration**

| Option | Description |
| --- | --- |
| Code maturity level options | Enables prompts for developmental or incomplete drivers. |
| Loadable module support | Indicates whether the modules are loaded automatically, and provides version information. |
| Processor type and features | Provides additional information regarding your system's processor. |
| General setup | Determines networking support, motherboard specifics, power management, and kernel support for different binary types. |
| Memory Technology Devices (MTD) | Provides support for flash, RAM, or memory on chips. |
| Parallel port support | Provides backing for parallel ports. |
| Plug and play configuration | Includes support for PnP devices within the kernel. |
| Block devices | Supports floppy and hard drives that connect as peripheral devices. Also supports RAID devices. |
| Networking options | Prompts for configuration options regarding TCP/IP networking, IP masquerading, and other protocols. |
| Telephony support | Provides support for telephony cards for voice-over-IP connections. |

**Table 14.1** **The Options Under the Linux 2.2 Kernel Configuration (continued)**

| Option | Description |
| --- | --- |
| ATA/IDE/MFM/RLL support | Provides support to faster ATA drives as well as other hard drive issues. |
| SCSI support | Provides support for any SCSI devices. |
| IEEE 1394 (FireWire) support | Connects various devices to your computer. Though still experimental, FireWire is a high-performance serial bus. |
| I2O | Allows your hardware support to be split into OS-specific and hardware-specific modules. |
| Network device support | Includes information about the different network cards or NICs supported by the kernel, along with various networking devices and capabilities. |
| Amateur radio support | Connects your box to an amateur radio. |
| IrDA (infrared) support | Supports wireless communication for laptops. |
| ISDN support | Provides the necessary support for an ISDN connection, which is a fully digital telephone service. |
| Old CD-ROM drivers | Enables you to choose your model if you are still using an antiquated CD-ROM (not SCSI, not IDE) that is not ATAPI or SCSI. |
| Character devices | Supports virtual terminals and console connections on serial ports. Also supports different mice, joystick, video, floppy tape, and PCMCIA configurations. |
| File systems | Specifies the type of file system support that you require for your machine, locally and on the network. |
| Console drivers | Supports the console display. |
| Sound | Compiles support for the options required by your sound card. |
| USB support | Configures Universal Serial Bus Support, one of the last hurdles to bringing Linux to the same level of other operating systems. |
| Kernel hacking | Provides control over the system even if it crashes. This setting is not recommended for novices. |

Once you have selected all the options required by your system, save the configuration to the hard drive. As mentioned previously, you should give the configuration a simple, descriptive name, such as test_kernel, to distinguish it from other compilations, including subsequent compilations.

> **NOTE**
>
> If you forgot to edit an option or need to make as quick change to one of the options, you may edit your test_kernel text file by changing the Y options to N on the necessary item. Be sure to save your file when you are finished. Then continue the compilation process.

## Compiling the Kernel

Once you have made all the changes that you feel are needed and have saved a copy of your settings, you can leave the Main Menu and begin compiling. The next step is to set up any dependencies and remove older compiled bits of source code. The dependency option, dep, checks for the modules and kernel sources that require compilation. Linux will not need to compile every bit of code but will create only binary elements for those items selected.

```
make dep
```

The first part of the command creates all the dependencies, whereas the second removes older compiled source code no longer needed. The second part of the command is necessary only for compilations that you perform after the initial compilation. This process should take only a few minutes to create links and then clear out the older files. After the commands finish executing, you can begin making a new kernel.

Under older 2.0.x kernels, the customary way to compile was to execute a make zImage command. This command creates a smaller kernel image using the GNU zip utility:

```
make zImage
```

However, due to the size of more recent 2.2.*xx* kernels, some administrators advocate using a similar command to compress the kernel even further:

```
make bzImage
```

The make bzImage command has nothing to do with the bzip2 compression utility. This is a common misconception. The "b" preceding the "zImage" option merely stands for "big." The gzip utility is still used to compress the kernel. The cutoff between using the make zImage and the make bzImage commands is approximately 508 kilobytes. If your kernel is larger than 508 kilobytes, then use the make bzImage command, otherwise your system will complain that your kernel size is too big. Invoking the make bzImage command circumvents this error. Though both commands make the same size kernel, how the system loads the kernel will depend upon what command was issued to create the new kernel.

The next part of the process requires the longest amount of time. Depending upon the speed of your computer and the number of devices that are compiled into your settings, total kernel compilations can take anywhere from 10–15 minutes to four hours. Much depends upon what sort of processes are running synchronously on your system, and what sort of load your compiler is placing on the resources.

The first kernel I ever made took over four hours to compile. This was due largely to the speed of the computer, an old 486 33-megahertz model with only 8 megabytes of RAM. If you add more features to the kernel and provide additional support for more devices, you can estimate that it will take even more time for the process to finish. Now sit back and watch the compiler commands roll by. This might be a good time to take a break, grab a soda, or play a game.

## Building and Installing Modules

After the kernel is completely done compiling, you need to make the modules. During the configuration, when using the commands xconfig, menuconfig, or config, you have the option to specify parts of the drivers as modules instead of making them components of the kernel itself, thereby increasing the kernel size. If you chose the module option and selected some drivers to be run as modules—that is, to be inserted in and out of the running kernel based on demand—you need to enter the following two commands:

```
make modules
make modules_install
```

You will notice that as the newer kernels are installed, a new directory with the same release as the kernel is created in /lib/modules. If you did not choose to make any modules during the configuration phase of the kernel process, you can skip this step.

# Editing the lilo Configuration

If this is your first compilation, you will want to edit your /etc/lilo.conf file if you normally use lilo to configure your bootup sequence. Otherwise, you may want a lilo boot sector to a floppy. This is a minor safety precaution in case you do not want someone to be able to reboot the machine into single-user mode and then redo the root password. You can always take the floppy with you and prevent unguarded reboots. Securing the machine physically against any unauthorized access is also a strong recommendation. However, if you place lilo on the Master Boot Record (MBR) or /dev/hda1, and if the machine does indeed reboot, it should come back up after a few moments and will not require that you manually replace the boot floppy.

Also be sure to back up your distribution copy of the lilo.conf file. If you make a change and then realize that your new setting may not work, having this backup copy will enable you to restore the default setting easily. Copy the preinstalled lilo.conf to another filename. Here is one possible suggestion:

```
# cp /etc/lilo.conf /etc/lilo.conf.DIST
```

The .DIST extension identifies this file as a distribution file or one that came with the default install.

This file is quite dependent upon your system. Listing 14.1 shows an example from my own system with comments included. The first section is the default location for the new kernel and is usually the /boot/vmlinuz file. The second section lists the older file that you might currently be using. It is a tried and tested kernel, and so I usually give it the release number as its name. The last kernel version is usually the older distribution kernel. If using a Red Hat 5.x or 6.x release, this can be a 2.0.x or 2.2.x kernel and so it is named linux.old.

### Listing 14.1  A Sample lilo.conf File

```
#
# general section
#
boot=/dev/hda
# install=/boot/boot.b
# message=/boot/message
prompt
```

```
# wait 20 seconds (200 10ths) for user to select
# the entry to load
timeout=200


#
# default entry
#
image=/boot/vmlinuz
    label=linux
    root=/dev/hda1
    read-only


#
# golden entries
#
image=/boot/vmlinuz-2.2.16
    label=linux.golden
    root=/dev/hda1
    read-only


#
# older entries
#
image=/boot/vmlinuz-old
    label=linux.old
    root=/dev/hda1
    read-only


#
# end of file
```

In this file, I have granted myself a couple of options for safety. First, when Linux first boots up, it normally stops at the LILO: prompt. I have given myself 20 seconds in which to choose the type of kernel that I wish to boot. At that prompt, I can press the Tab key to see the available choices: linux, linux.golden, and linux.old. If your machine is a dual- or triple-boot machine, you might also include settings for a particular Windows version or some other operating system. It is in lilo.conf that you can enter settings for alternative boot partitions.

During the initial installation, be sure that any other operating systems are already installed because lilo will overwrite any boot record on the Master Boot Record. Red Hat will also attempt to detect other systems and grant you the options to set one of them up as the default system.

The first entry in lilo.conf is also the default OS. Because the kernel labeled `linux` is the first entry, that kernel will begin booting after 20 seconds, without any interaction on my part. By placing an entry for the Windows partition in the first section, I ensure that Windows is my default boot OS. If something goes wrong with the new kernel, I also have the option to boot back into my older kernel. Be sure to save the System.map and the vmlinuz files in the /boot directory. Their names should correspond to their appropriate entries in lilo.conf.

If you want to boot up other operating systems, Listing 14.2 shows an example of how you can set up Windows as the default OS. Though the Linux partition is not listed first, Linux provides a default option for specifying Windows as the default OS into which the system can boot.

**Listing 14.2  A Default lilo.conf File Generated During the Red Hat Install**

```
boot=/dev/hda
map=/boot/map
install=/boot/boot.b
prompt
timeout=50
linear
default=windows

image=/boot/vmlinuz-2.2.14-5.0
    label=linux
    read-only
    root=/dev/hda2

other=/dev/hda1
    label=windows
```

The user can configure the options specified in the lilo.conf file. You may specify any system you wish. To change the default OS, simply substitute `linux` for `windows` under the `default=` option. As you can see, this drive is separated into two partitions, /dev/hda1 and /dev/hda2. Linux is installed on /dev/hda2, hence the `root=` variable.

For some people, saving the kernel directly back onto the hard drive is an impractical option, or a disagreeable one at best. They like to make absolutely sure that the newly compiled kernel works before changing any configurations or settings to their machine. Making sure that the kernel works usually involves first copying the new kernel directly onto a bootable floppy. After you have stored the kernel on the floppy, you insert the floppy in the floppy drive and reboot the machine. If the machine boots successfully, you can safely load the kernel onto your drive. Once that is complete you can edit the lilo.conf file to point to the new kernel and have it be the default kernel. Make sure to rename or backup the original kernel so that you have something to fall back on if the newer kernel does not boot.

## Placing the New Kernel on Boot Media

Now that both your kernel and the modules have successfully compiled and you have edited your boot configuration, you can place the new kernel and System.map on your boot media. This means either locating them somewhere on the hard drive or placing them on a floppy disk. If you choose to keep the new kernel on the hard drive, you will need to locate the new kernel now called vmlinuz, and place it in your /boot directory or in your / (root) directory. Because the default kernel under Red Hat comes installed on the /boot directory, keeping any newer kernels there can be convenient also.

If you wish to manually copy the new kernel to the /boot directory, use the following two commands to copy the newly created files to their default location.

```
cp /usr/src/linux/arch/i386/boot/bzImage /boot/vmlinuz
   cp /usr/src/linux/System.map /boot/System.map
```

Another option that I like to move as well is the System.map file. It usually is created right in the linux/ directory and can also be placed in the /boot directory as well.

On the latest Red Hat release, there are several symbolic links pointing to the files vmlinuz and/or System.map. You can remove these symbolic links. The files they point to are usually identifiable by their release number.

An even easier method of installing the newly compiled Linux kernel is to issue the following command after running the make modules and make modules_install commands.

```
make install
```

This command copies the correct kernel to the proper location. The preceding example that manually copies the kernel is x86-specific. Using the make install command under Red Hat will locate the correct kernel for your distribution and then copy it to the proper boot directory. It will also move the older kernels and retain the symbolic links to then point to your new kernel. At the end it will also run the /sbin/lilo command and reread your lilo.conf file. This is why you edit the LILO configuration before installing the kernel.

If you wish to place the newly created kernel and the System.map file on a floppy disk, copy them by using the following command.:

```
cp /usr/src/linux/arch/i386/boot/bzImage /dev/fd0
```

Once you have the new kernels in place, you need to let lilo know where everything is situated. Run the following command to make the lilo executable re-read the configuration file and to enable lilo to identify the newly created kernels. The command also informs the system where to look for the older kernels.

If booting a kernel from off the floppy drive, change the /etc/lilo.conf file to point to the proper location. Rather than using the placing the root=/dev/had in your lilo.conf file, replace it with root=/dev/fd0.

Again, if you wish to skip the make install command and run lilo by hand instead use the following command.

```
/sbin/lilo
```

You may also wish to run a similar older command that works well, which does more of the task automatically.

```
make zlilo
```

This command installs the kernel and makes the floppy bootable, but does not do anything with the modules.

After executing all these steps, you can reboot the machines and see how well the new kernel operates, by entering the following command:

```
shutdown -r now
```

If all goes well, you should have a shiny new kernel running your system. Most Linux distributions like to notify you of the kernel version at the login: prompt. If yours does not indicate its kernel release, type the following command after logging in:

```
uname -a
```

You can always find out in this manner whether you are using the latest kernel or not.

# Troubleshooting the Kernel

There is no guarantee that the process will always go this smoothly. You may have selected an option that your system does not support or have forgotten to add another option required by your system. For example, forgetting to support properly the correct SCSI card, which in turns runs your boot SCSI hard drive, may cause bad things to happen. In situations such as these, knowing how to recover from a kernel panic or some other catastrophe is essential to getting your Linux machine operational again.

## Storing Golden Kernels

As you may have noticed in the "Editing the lilo Configuration" section, I like to keep a backup copy of my functional kernel in case anything does go wrong. And, things can frequently go wrong if you are trying out a new developmental kernel or testing a new device. There are many different choices you can make when configuring a kernel and it is all too easy to think you are choosing one option when, in fact, you are choosing something else.

Also, the default settings are easy to overlook. One way to make sure you can recover and boot back into the system if a kernel goes bad is to create *golden kernels*. A golden kernel is one that has been tried and tested and proven to run well under normal situations.

As the "Editing the lilo Configuration File" section demonstrated, you can name the golden kernels anything you want. You can also label them with their release number so that you know just what release you are dealing with. Affix a label to each individual kernel so that when the LILO: prompt appears you are confident that you are choosing the kernel that you want. You can edit this test kernel later with another kernel compilation; then the new, proven kernel can become your next golden kernel while the older one is rotated out to become your linux.old kernel. In this manner, you have two backups in case one does not work with either the correct settings or the hardware configuration. It is also a good idea to keep a backup of the kernel on a floppy drive or some other transferable media.

If a kernel panic occurs, chances are its cause is something in the latest kernel that you either forgot to choose or that you chose incorrectly. Kernel panics can also be caused by bugs in the kernel, but more often than not panics happen due to user misconfigurations. Boot back up into your backup kernel configuration, recompile, and try again. Comparing the new configuration with the old one is also one way to make sure that your newer kernel contains options similar to those of your older kernel. Open another terminal window and start a config or xconfig session elsewhere on the same page and compare the options selected to each other. You will most likely discover the source of your kernel panic in this manner.

## Patching Kernels

If you do not wish to go through the entire process of kernel compilation or if you simply do not have the time or the resources to wait for your machine to compile anew, you can also upgrade between releases by patching the kernel. Patches are distributed in the traditional gzip and the bzip2 format. The latter keeps the file size down and reduces bandwidth usage. To install by patching, download all the newer patch files from the same locations as those of the entire source code and change directories into /usr/src, just as you would when compiling the kernel from source. If you are moving from kernel 2.2.5 to 2.2.16, you will need all 11 patched files between the two releases. Next, uncompress the first patch file or the kernel release that next follows your current running kernel and while doing so use the patch command to apply the patch to the local kernel as shown in the following command:

```
cd linux
gzip -cd ../patch-2.2.xx.gz | patch -p1
```

Patches often seem to not start out with linux/—they're often linux-vanilla/ or something similar. Keep this in mind when looking to patch your current Linux release.

If you are using the bzip2 utility, then you should execute the patch as follows:

```
bzip2 -cd ../patch-2.2.xx.bz2 | patch -p0
```

Apply patches for each of the versions numbered higher than the current kernel you are running until you have reached the latest version. You cannot apply the very latest patch, patch 2.2.16, to kernel 2.2.5, but must move upward through each patch until you reach the latest. Patching does not allow you to tweak each option, but it does allow you to upgrade and resolve any security or hardware concerns regarding a previous version. You are restricted to either the options that you set up with the last complete kernel recompilation or those determined by the release.

You may also want to remove the backup files on your system after each patch completes. These are identified as *xxx~* or *xxx*.orig. A good command to use to search through your directory and purge these older files is as follows:

```
find . -name '*.orig' -exec rm -f {} ';'
```

Also verify that there are not any failed patches. These are identified by the designations *xxx#* or *xxx*.rej. If there are failed patches, then either you or the kernel developer has made a mistake. In cases such as these, you will want to get a complete fresh linux-2.2.17.tar.gz source and install that rather than fighting with patches. Download the latest complete source and compile from scratch. However, chances are good that if you follow the preceding instructions and those that come with the latest patch, you will have no problems. An alternative method of patching is to use the script patch-kernel. It determines your current kernel version and applies any patches found. The latest patch usually includes the patch-kernel script.

Given the different methods available to update or modify your kernel, you should have no cause for trepidation if you find that you need to recompile. Using the latest kernels can only improve system performance. With the ongoing efforts of the Linux community, each subsequent kernel release contains support for more and more hardware configurations. As new hardware and opportunities continue to develop, it is only a matter of time before you will need to compile a kernel, and to improve and hone your Linux skills.

# Conclusion

This chapter discussed configuration issues not covered by the default Red Hat Linux install. You have learned about configuring your machine for more day-to-day issues and making your machine a more productive tool. In the next chapter, you begin thinking outside the box and accomplishing tasks that require communicative skills between computers, including setting up networking tools. Once your machine can exchange information with other machines, you can start using it to function more like a server rather than a personal desktop computer. Chapter 15 explains how to set up basic networking functions, broadcast IP addresses, and resolve hostnames and domain names. The chapter also examines command-line procedures for changing networking configurations and for hosting your own domain. Creating a useful networked Linux machine will prepare you for establishing a productive presence among other networked machines and on the Internet.

# PART IV

## Thinking Outside the Box

# Chapter 15

### Networking
### Linux

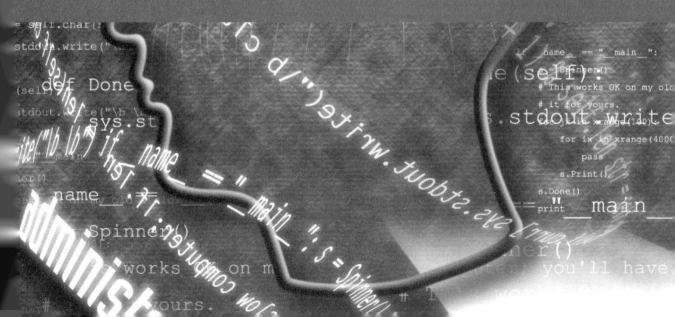

The primary function of Linux is to service networks. This means that Linux is designed to communicate with other networked computers and to exchange data between those systems. Understanding how Linux serves as a platform for exchanging data across either local area networks (LANs) or through the cloud of networked machines now known as the Internet will assist in entering the correct data in the appropriate files on your own Linux machine and establishing communications with other networked machines and devices. Configuring the proper networking protocols under Linux will assist in making Linux a viable asset to either your home or business.

This chapter will cover the following basic topics:

◆ Moving information across networks via routes and packets
◆ Assigning identification numbers or IP addresses to a networked machine
◆ Examining basic configuration files for creating networked devices
◆ Dynamically providing IP addresses and hostnames
◆ Creating domains and giving your machine an identity
◆ Communicating and sharing files with other machines
◆ Creating name servers for hostname lookups
◆ Setting up Apache for secure transactions

# Creating an Internet Presence

Having a presence on the Internet today is crucial to any sort of personal or business-related venture. Even if that presence is only for academic use or for the exchange of ideas and information, knowing how to create a simple Web page or share a file across a network has become a necessary skill. Because Linux has proven to be both a cost-efficient and stable platform for creating network servers, it is recommended that you understand how standard networking protocols under this operating system function.

Because Linux has built-in TCP/IP networking, currently the base protocol for Internet data transmission, it is important to understand how this protocol communicates with other machines. This chapter deals with some of the more basic networking configuration issues such as routing, IP addressing, and domain names. It will not go into great depth for more complex networking and routing issues but instead will look at how Linux handles networked topics and how you can optimize Linux to work on networked systems.

# Understanding Networking Basics

The most basic functions associated with networking use the ISO/OSI model (see Table 15.1). This outline was originally designed to explain the relationship of hardware to software to data and has been adopted by nearly all facets of networking paradigms to explain the varying depths of networking currently available today. To understand how networking works, you must first look at how it is configured to operate. The ISO/OSI model specifies the manner in which information passes from the lowest level, that of hardware or physical structures, to the higher level, that of software, which in turn makes the information accessible to users for processing.

**Table 15.1  The OSI Model in Simple Terms**

| Layer | Name | Purpose |
|-------|------|---------|
| 1 | Physical layer | Provides the cable or physical connection for transmitting information |
| 2 | Data link layer | Sends and receives packets, and identifies hardware addresses |
| 3 | Network layer | Sets up the routing and keeps track of transmissions |
| 4 | Transport layer | Verifies the correct reception of data on both ends |
| 5 | Session layer | Authenticates and authorizes packets transmissions |
| 6 | Presentation layer | Handles data errors and compression |
| 7 | Application layer | Provides user services, such as mail, Telnet, and FTP |

Though the ISO/OSI model is used primarily for network design, the world of networking often refers to the model. Having a basic grasp of its structure and purpose is essential to understanding how the Internet and networking between machines operate.

For most Linux administrators, most networking configurations will be a simple matter of installing an Ethernet card into an internal slot within your Linux box, plugging in an Ethernet cable into the back of the card and then configuring Linux's networking settings. Once these settings are activated, the Linux box can then communicate to other machines.

Linux normally uses TCP/IP when talking to other machines, whether across the Internet or via a LAN connection. The OS can be configured to use other protocols as well, including IPX when communicating on Novell networks, but Linux defaults to the TCP/IP stack. TCP/IP is a method of connecting and linking software from one machine to the other. Several ingredients comprise the entire TCP/IP suite of protocols. These include the following protocols:

◆ *Internet Protocol (IP)* is the protocol that transmits raw data, stripped of any additional information, from one machine to the next.

◆ *Internet Control Message Protocol (ICMP)* is the low-level support function for IP. It transmits error messages, helps in routing packets, and echoes requests. ICMP is normally used with the ping command.

◆ *Address Resolution Protocol (ARP)* translates hardware addresses or MAC addresses to network addresses. A MAC address is an identification number assigned to a network card. The address helps servers recognize individual machines.

◆ *User Datagram Protocol (UDP)* sends data from one program to the next using IP. UDP does not verify the transmission of individual messages.

◆ *Transmission Control Protocol (TCP)* builds on top of UDP and certifies that each message has been received.

Given this basic overview of the networking principles that make up the physical and application layers of data transmission between machines, let us now look at how these individual parts of data or packets are moved back and forth among computers.

## Packaging Data into Packets

Linux supports a variety of physical networking methods; the most common today is that of *Ethernet*. Linux also supports *token ring*, *ARCNet*, and *modem-based* networking protocols, such as SLIP and PPP. For now, this chapter will deal with LAN-based network connections. One of the quickest methods of moving data between two machines is via a network interface that utilizes an

Ethernet connection. Linux machines can support more than one network interface and thus can move data using a variety of methods, Ethernet being the most common one employed in LAN connections. But other protocols can just as quickly be put into place and used with TCP/IP.

Ethernet is dependent upon the types of physical connections that it employs to communicate with hosts within and without a networked group. For example, you can install more than one Ethernet card within a Linux box so that it can communicate and transmit data from one network to another or from one machine to the next. If you send data outside your own internal network, this type of message or data forwarding is called *routing*, or using a gateway interface to transmit the data onward. Understanding how network routing operates is one of the most complex issues at hand when you configure Linux to speak with other machines. For information on setting up PPP connection or using modems to connect Linux machines, see Chapter 16.

The normal method of sending data is to encapsulate them—that is, to break up the larger bits of information into what are called *packets*. Packets are wrapped bits of data broken into two basic parts: the header and the payload. The *header* provides information about the individual packet, such as its source and destination. It also contains instructions explaining what to do with the information when it arrives at its target, certifies its authenticity, and determines any other protocol specific data. The *payload*, meanwhile, is the information itself or the raw data that are carried over the network to the destination host.

As the packets filter down through the stack of information as indicated in the ISO/OSI model, each protocol adds its own information headers to the packet's header. Much like a Russian *Matroishka* or nesting doll, where each doll is placed within a larger doll's shell or nested inside the mother doll, the shells of each layer encapsulate the smaller one within the larger, outer layer. Once the packet arrives at its destination, each shell is unwrapped or opened in the reverse order that it was nested.

How each protocol header wraps the packet before sending it depends largely upon the type of protocol through which the data are being transmitted. Suffice it to say that the amount of data attached to each packet varies with the protocol. Depending upon the packet's destination, each succeeding protocol layer must perform a specific set of routines to unwrap and decode the nested information successfully.

## Routing through Networks

Information is routed through and from its own internal network via a *router*. Unlike a hub or switch, which merely blindly forwards packets to other routers and then onto their destinations, routers track and log arriving and departing packets. These routers then communicate with other routers and transmit the data intelligently. A well-configured router can handle gigabytes of data quickly, sending them to their destination.

Packets are sent from the Linux box to a *gateway* or *break*, which is a router that communicates with the larger wide area networks (WANs). When you configure Linux, you will need to provide a valid IP address for its gateway in order to communicate with other networks.

The topic of router configuration is beyond the scope of this book. Suffice it to say that Linux can assist in sending the packets in a logical manner and can even be configured to function as a router if necessary. Such configuration can help you bypass much of the cost in commercial products, but not any of the headaches. You can find more information about setting up a Linux box to function as a router on the Linux Router home page, http://www.linuxrouter.org/.

## Preparing Linux for Networking

The first step in setting up networking on your Linux box is to install a network interface card (NIC). Several brands and types of NICs are currently available on the market. Linux supports the vast majority of these. Each is based on a different type of *chipset*, or hardware driver specification, which the NIC uses to communicate with the system hardware. Some NICs share the same chipset under a different brand name, so knowing some history about your hardware does help when deciding on the correct driver. Much like video cards, network cards have a certain standard to which each manufacturer adheres to retain uniformity and conformity in drivers. This standardization assists some of the smaller developers in creating their own drivers and spares them from writing new drivers from scratch. It also saves Linux developers from writing superfluous drivers for each card on the market. Many can be carried over for different card manufacturers.

Before purchasing any form of NIC, be sure to check one of the many Linux compatibility pages to make sure that either your card or the card's chipset is currently compatible with Linux. Most cards will have no problem, as the latest kernel should support most cards. Currently most administrators must decide how much they are willing to spend on an NIC, and whether that cost will ultimately translate into performance. You can purchase a reasonably priced NIC ranging anywhere from less than $10 to somewhere more than $60. The cost depends upon the type of NIC (that is, whether it is ISA or PCI) to the method of transmission. Whether it offers a 10 megabyte or 100 megabyte transmission speed or if it is effective for both home or office networking, a good NIC card should not constitute too high a cost.

You normally configure your Linux box for a network connection during the installation process. Depending upon the type of installation you choose, such as an FTP download or network install, or whether you choose the Server or Workstation configuration, the Linux install program prompts you for certain bits of information about the system and the type of connection needed.

You need to provide the necessary information to the computer in order for the networking to function. If you are installing the Linux machine on a viable network with actual IP addresses, be sure to contact your network administrator for a valid IP address or choose an IP address not currently in use if you are responsible for IP addresses. Do not simply choose a random IP address. This will cause problems not only for your own system but also for other networks. Verify that the valid IP address you choose is really available by using the ping command. On another machine also connected to the same network, try pinging the IP address you wish to use. If you do not get a response, chances are good that that IP address is available:

```
ping 192.169.10.35
```

If the ping command returns values, then another machine is already using this address. If the command returns no values, then that address is vacant or the machine using it is currently powered down or not connected to the network. Be certain to confirm this with the network engineer or system administrator before simply grabbing the IP address. You can only use an IP address not already in use by another computer, whether you are using IP numbering for the Internet or for just your local LAN. These, too, require some sort of unique IP address by which each machine identifies itself.

Each machine—whether it is a Linux box, a Windows machine, or one that uses some other type of operating system—must be able to identify itself in some unique fashion if it is connected to a network of other machines. The normal method for ensuring that your machine has a unique identifier is to use IP addresses based on the ipv4 networking protocol. IP addresses are numbers that come in a set of four, as in *xxx.xxx.xxx.xxx,* where each set of *x* numbers represents a value in the range of 0 to 255. Depending upon the machine's basic purpose, its IP address can consist of any number between 0 and 255 within each of the four fields as defined by ipv4 networking. However, if the machine will communicate not only on the local LAN but also on a network of Internet-linked computers, the machine can have only one valid number assigned to it; that is, each machine must have one unique address that no other machine on the same network duplicates. Depending upon the type of business or educational institution in which you work, you may administer only one or two valid IP addresses or you may have control over several hundred.

Several ranges of IP addresses are designated as nonvalid IP addresses. These addresses are designated for *private networks*, or computers within a certain logical domain, either behind a firewall or simply connected to each other either with or without Internet connectivity.

The numbers in the 127.*xxx.xxx.xxx* block are assigned to individual computers that only talk to themselves. These are *localnet* or *localhost* machines, and their numbers not usually assigned for interconnectivity or for server-to-server communication. Normally, the 127.0.0.1 IP address is the standard value for machines that require self-communication, whether they are networked or not.

The 192.168.*xxx.xxx* block is assigned for private networks, which require connectivity among the machines, yet may or may not have Internet access. For example, if you have a network at home or at the office and the machines can talk to each only other via an Ethernet connection, you would assign each of the computers a unique number from within this block. The addresses from this block are not valid outside of the internal network. To enable the machines to talk to computers or networks outside of the internal network, a computer or gateway must perform some sort of name address translation (NAT) that bridges the internal network to the outside world. Each computer on the internal network sends packets through this gateway. When the computer sends a packet, the gateway translates the machine's IP address into a valid IP. The gateway also reverses the incoming packets back to the non-valid IP address so that the internal machine can communicate with the outside world.

You can accomplish the same process by using *IP masquerading*, a valid operation under Linux. It changes the non-viable IP address into the same IP address as that of the gateway, then sends the packet out to the Internet. Packets that return through this gateway are also reconverted into a form that the machine behind the gateway can then understand.

## Starting Network Installation

When you are setting up Linux, most distributions will either attempt to detect a networking card or ask whether you want to set up networking on your system. Red Hat detects the internal NIC from a vast list of supported cards. If it cannot detect the card, it skips the network configuration routine. If your install skips this step, verify that your card is inserted correctly and not conflicting with any other cards.

Recently I was attempting to set up a machine in which I had installed a networking card that I knew was supported by Red Hat. However, after three different installs on the same box, Red Hat had failed to detect the card. Because the machine was an older one that had been used only as a stand-alone workstation previously, the only change I had made was to install the card. It turned out that the motherboard sat lower than the cards could reach. The card was not fully inserted in its PCI slot and therefore was not fully usable by the system. If you have problems getting the system to recognize a card, confirm that the card is physically connected and deal with any hardware issues before attempting multiple installs.

Once the Red Hat network driver configuration has completed successfully, and has verified that a viable NIC is installed, it will begin to ask for more pertinent information. At this point, it doesn't matter whether your card can actually speak to other machines outside the network. Only if you are installing the operating system from outside your network will you need to have the card physically connected and operating.

Linux usually prompts you for a method of identifying your computer to the network. This means assigning your machine a static or permanent IP address that will stay with the machine indefinitely, or assigning it a dynamic IP address that will change each time the computer boots up. These dynamic IP addresses can be assigned either by BOOTP or through a DHCP server. If the address comes from a DHCP server, the network allows only a particular range of IP addresses. Check with your network administrator to see what range your machine will fall under and whether an address is available. Some networks hold valid addresses at a premium. Until ipv6 becomes standardized, IP addresses will become more difficult to procure for private use. If your IP address is assigned via a BOOTP or DHCP server, you need not configure the rest of your network settings since these servers will assign your IP addresses automatically. However, setting your own IP address can be more tailored to your tastes as well as educational.

If you do not have a permanent connection to the Internet but instead rely upon a dial-up connection, Red Hat supplies the necessary drivers for setting up a modem or provides one of several methods for configuring your network connectivity.

---

**NOTE**

The next level of IP addressing is ipv6. This networking protocol should provide not just millions of viable addresses, but tens of trillions of possible addresses for public use. It is conjectured that not just servers or computers will be able to host an IP address, but nearly any sort of electrical appliance will be given a unique number and provide some sort of networking capability.

---

If you have no need for network connectivity, you should remove any network cards from your machine. This will not only free up an internal slot, but also save you from an unneeded step.

Let us configure a machine on its own network—that is, a computer not connected to any outside machine with a discernible IP. The following is a sample network Linux configuration. It may talk to others on its own network, connected via a hub or switch through which the packets are routed. This example is valid for a separated network and should be considered as only an example. How you set up your own network will depend largely on how you wish to configure it to talk to the other connected computers.

| Variable | Setting |
|---|---|
| IP address: | 192.168.0.25 |
| Netmask: | 255.255.255.0 |
| Default gateway: | 192.168.0.1 |
| Primary name server: | 192.168.0.254 |
| Secondary name server: | 192.168.0.253 |
| Domain name: | astronomy.org |
| Hostname: | antares.astronomy.org |

The following is a summary of the variables that you must set for your machine:

◆ The *IP address* is a unique identifier for your system. If you are on a connection that includes a range of valid IP addresses that have been allocated for your use, you may need to ask your network's administrator which address to use. If you are the administrator and are setting up a private network, feel free to choose one of the many available within the 192.168.*xxx.xxx* or 10.*xxx.xxx.xxx* range. If you are using your machine only to talk to itself or if it will need to be in *loopback mode*—that is, to have no physical connection to the outside but just a TCP/IP connection to itself—then use 127.0.0.1. Most machines that are connected to the outside also use this loopback address.

◆ Your *netmask* lists the highest value available for each field within your network class. Given that the majority of networks are class C, or have the first three sets of the four decimal addresses already determined, you should fill in the first three fields with the number 255. If you have a class B address, which has a larger amount of IP addresses to use, you should have only 255 in the first two fields. Again, if you are unsure of your settings, check other machines within your network or talk to your network administrator. If you are using only the loopback address, then your netmask should be 255.0.0.0.

◆ The *default gateway* is the IP address of the machine through which your server talks to the outside world. This address can be either a firewall or a router that broadcasts your packets to the outside world. Some networks set a number with a .1 at the end whereas others prefer a .254 or .253 address. If you administer a smaller network, depending on the range that you manage, the gateway can be any number between 1 and 254. A gateway is simply a machine that lives between two fields of network addresses: one which is the internal band of IP addresses, and the other which is that of the outside world. Some networks have multiple gateways. Talk to your network administrator about which one might be appropriate for you. If you are simply using the loopback address or are isolated from other networks, you will not have a gateway.

◆ The *primary nameserver* is that machine on your network that provides Domain Name Service (DNS) for your network. That service includes translating IP addresses such as 192.168.0.10 into something understandable like www.mydomain.com. The *secondary nameserver* backs up the primary name server in case it goes down or becomes inaccessible.

◆ The *domain name* and *hostname* are the names assigned to your network. Most people prefer not having to recognize long sequences of numbers, particularly if they are attempting to locate an obscure network. Names make it easier to remember locations or servers.

These variables are requested during the initial setup process. You can enter them if you are aware of what each field requires. If you are unsure of your system's IP address or would like to adjust each variable later after the system is operational, Linux provides several methods for adjusting your network settings.

## Configuring Network Settings after Installation

Once you have successfully installed both the hardware and software on your Linux machine and have verified their viability, you can now adjust the settings on your network device, provided they still are functional. Probably the easiest method of making these adjustments is to use one of the several GUIs that come provided to edit the text settings, which control all the networking configurations. Alternatively, you can edit the files by hand, a preferable option for many users who may need to accomplish this task remotely and without an X interface. This section first examines the files themselves and how they set up networking connectivity. Then you will explore the options available with various tools to accomplish the same tasks using a couple of different GUIs. For more information on setting up the X Window System or starting GUIs, see Chapter 12.

The most important files to be aware of are the following:

- ◆ /etc/HOSTNAME gives the system a specific hostname for the computer on which it resides.

- ◆ /etc/hosts lists the various hosts on the networked system. It also maps the different hostnames to various IP addresses. This helps to expedite packet transfers since no hostname lookups are required.

- ◆ /etc/services lists all available ports and the services or processes associated with their use.

- ◆ /etc/inetd.conf tells the system which services should be honored as valid requests and that should be started by the daemon as needed.

- ◆ /etc/resolv.conf tells the system which domains to list under the DNS search order. It normally outlines the domain to search and the order of the name servers.

- ◆ /etc/host.conf specifies the order in which to search the name systems when resolving hostnames.

- ◆ /etc/sysconfig/network lists various items such as hostname, IP address, and gateway. This file is best configured with a GUI but can also be edited by hand.

- ◆ /etc/sysconfig/network-scripts/ holds various device bootup options. In this directory, you can set up the manner in which network devices, such as eth0 or ppp0, boot up.

## Defining Your Computer's Hostname

The first variable, HOSTNAME, is a simple text file that contains the name and domain of the computer. A sample HOSTNAME file might look like the following:

```
antares.astronomy.org
```

In some cases, changes to this setting do not take effect until the network process has been restarted, the current user has logged out, or the computer has been rebooted. Because you can stop and restart anew nearly everything under Linux without ever powering down the computer, you should always attempt to stop and restart the process before attempting a reboot. Only in the most extreme situations should you power down the system.

The normal method for restarting the network process is to use the network script provided by most Linux distributions. Here is how Red Hat encourages users to issue a sample restart:

```
/etc/rc.d/init.d/network restart
```

## Configuring the Hosts File

The second variable, /etc/hosts, is convenient for both large and small networks. You need not type in the full address of each computer on the system or query the name server for each computer and its location. Instead, you can consult the /etc/hosts file, which provides a list of all IP addresses, hostnames, domains, and aliases of all available computers on the network. The last field is perhaps the most significant since it allows you to log in to that computer simply by entering its alias rather than typing out its full path. For example, you need not type **antares.astronomy.org**, as simply typing **antares** will suffice.

Maintaining this file on larger networks can be problematic if you frequently change IP addresses and computer names. If your network is relatively static and does not need reconfiguring often, the /etc/hosts file will reduce some of the load on your name server and provide quick connections to other machines.

Table 15.2 describes an example /etc/hosts file.

**Table 15.2  A Sample /etc/hosts Table Listing Available Networked Computers**

| IP Address | Full Computer Name | Alias |
| --- | --- | --- |
| 127.0.0.1 | localhost.localdomain | localhost |
| 192.168.0.1 | antares.astronomy.org | antares |
| 192.168.0.2 | vega.astronomy.org | vega |
| 192.168.0.3 | deneb.astronomy.org | deneb |
| 192.168.0.254 | polaris.astronomy.org | polaris |
| 192.168.0.253 | regulus.astronomy.org | regulus |
| 142.58.12.213 | sirius.nasa.gov | sirius |

According to the table, the local system consists of several computers, each with a specific astronomical name combined with its domain name. The last row describes an additional computer, located outside of the local domain, to which this server might also have local access. Normally, computers that lay outside the domain are covered under the DNS entries on the system's name servers, but for the sake of illustration, this example lists sirus.nasa.gov to demonstrate how /etc/hosts provides easy access to a host outside the domain.

# Setting Up Services

The third file, /etc/services, provides a longer list of all available processes under Linux. These include the name of the service in the first field, the port number and the type of protocol, an alias for the service, and then usually a commented-out field explaining the service's function.

Here is a brief extract of a sample /etc/services file:

```
www         80/tcp     http              # WorldWideWeb HTTP
www         80/udp                       # HyperText Transfer Protocol
link        87/tcp     ttylink
kerberos    88/tcp     kerberos5 krb5    # Kerberos v5
kerberos    88/udp     kerberos5 krb5    # Kerberos v5
supdup      95/tcp                       # 100 - reserved
hostnames   101/tcp    hostname          # usually from sri-nic
iso-tsap    102/tcp    tsap              # part of ISODE.
csnet-ns    105/tcp    cso-ns            # also used by CSO name server
csnet-ns    105/udp    cso-ns
rtelnet     107/tcp                      # Remote Telnet
rtelnet     107/udp
pop-2       109/tcp    postoffice        # POP version 2
pop-2       109/udp
pop-3       110/tcp    pop3              # POP version 3
pop-3       110/udp
```

Most of the processes accessed use either TCP or UDP. To enable one of these services, you need to verify that you have installed the executable either by using an RPM file or by compiling the source yourself and then installing the daemon in the proper location.

For example, to enable the pop3 daemon on a Linux system, you can either use the simple RPM binary that comes with most installations or download the source from its site at ftp://ftp.cac.washington.edu/pine/. Untar and unzip the source, run the commands necessary to compile the source, and then verify and install the executable in /usr/sbin. In the third field under the port number 110, place the word pop3 or the respective process name. You may wish to add a comment afterward if one is not already there. You can add new daemon processes to ports that are over 1024, but to those ports less than 1024 it is advised to not make any changes. You must conform to standards that have been set for port numbers and the processes affixed to them. If you are installing a new process, such as the Big Brother monitoring system that runs under port 1984, verify the correct settings and then make the correct entry.

## Selecting Entries for the inetd.conf File

The fourth option, /etc/inetd.conf, is closely tied to the previous entries in the /etc/services file. To enable the various daemons when they start up, uncomment the line on which the daemon is located by removing the pound sign preceding the text. Because most Linux distributions have tcp_wrappers installed to add security and to provide added logging to the various processes as they run, you will notice that the /usr/sbin/tcpd daemon is often executed in place of the process itself. The tcpd daemon is a silent port monitor that checks the user's authenticity before executing the process without proper authority.

> **NOTE**
>
> Red Hat Linux installs tcp_wrappers by default during a normal install. Seldom do you find any machine not running tcp_wrappers. Be sure to enable this utility if you choose a customized or limited setup routine.

The syntax for a sample line in the /etc/inetd.conf file is as follows:

```
service      socket-type      protocol      wait/nowait      user
server-program      server-arguments
```

The service option is taken from the /etc/services file. Anything listed in this file can also be started here. Whether you add a new service manually or if its respective RPM adds the service automatically, the new service must conform to the preceding syntax. Here is an example taken from the /etc/inetd.conf file that starts up imap upon boot:

```
#
    # Pop and imap mail services et al
    #
    #pop-2     stream   tcp    nowait    root     /usr/sbin/tcpd ipop2d
    pop-3      stream   tcp    nowait    root     /usr/sbin/tcpd ipop3d
    imap       stream   tcp    nowait    root     /usr/sbin/tcpd imapd
```

After making any changes to the /etc/inetd.conf file, you need to have the inetd process reread the configuration. To accomplish this, send the process a HANGUP signal or a -1 command. First, determine the process ID of inetd:

```
# ps aux | grep inetd
```

The system should return something like the following. The numbers can vary depending upon your system.

```
# ps aux | grep inetd
    root          412  0.0  0.6  1124  436 ?     S    20:32  0:00 inetd
```

Note the PID number and send it a kill command:

```
# kill -HUP 412
```

Verify that the process is still running by repeating the ps command. The process should return the same information as before. If something was amiss with your configuration or syntax, the process might die after it receives the HANGUP signal. If this is the case, check your syntax, particularly the use of tabs, and restart the command from the beginning, executing it from the command line:

```
# /etc/rc.d/init.d/inetd start
```

You may also start up the command in the run command directory.

# Resolving Domains and Name Servers

The fifth configuration file, /etc/resolv.conf, specifies the search domains and name servers within the network. This helps your system locate other servers both inside and outside your domain. If you place the local domain on the first line, you can locate internal servers simply by typing their hostname or alias when using either Telnet or FTP to log in. The syntax for this file is first a keyword to identify what the file needs to do and then an IP address or domain, with each field separated by spaces. The file has four available fields in which you can enter variables.

The first field is `search`. The `search` field defines the domains that will be searched, in order, for a given host. Several internal processes, one of which is mail, use this option. This field tells the system the name to use to address the localhost when sending and receiving mail. The `domain` field identifies the host's local domain. If both the `domain` and `search` field appear in this file, then the last one is used. Red Hat Linux systems prefer the `search` option when setting up default resolv.conf files.

The next field is `nameserver`, which is similar to the `domain` field. This parameter may be the IP address of the local DNS server or it can include several name server addresses, both within and outside of the network. If this field lists multiple name servers, the system will query each in the order they are arranged. If the first does not respond, the next is then queried. Red Hat recognizes as many as three name servers.

The last field is `sortlist`. This feature enables you to sort the returned domain names in a specific order. If one class C domain should take preference over a related class B domain, then the class C is placed first on the list.

Here is a sample /etc/resolv.conf file. In the `sortlist` field, the IP address is connected to the netmask using the typical *IP/netmask* syntax. As you can see, the classes correspond with their netmasks.

```
search astronomy.org nasa.gov
nameserver 10.10.10.254
nameserver 10.10.10.253
sortlist 10.10.10.0/255.255.255.0 10.1.0.0/255.255.0.0
```

## Configuring Hosts

The sixth variable used in networking that you need to be familiar with is /etc/host.conf. This file lists the order in which the different name services will be searched when resolving hostnames. For example, if you wish to have your /etc/hosts file looked at first before querying the name servers or DNS servers, you would place an order query on the first line followed by the command to resolve the hostnames, with the two elements separated by a comma. The line below the order option contains the multi option, allows either single or multiple returns from the queried server if this option's setting is turned on.

Here is another sample file:

```
order hosts,bind
multi on
```

## Setting Up the Main Networking File

The next variable in the fields of needed networking files is /etc/sysconfig/network. The file contains a list of the hostname, domain name, and gateway in addition to a few other variables that the system needs in order to route through the local network. The following is sample network file taken from a Linux box that has a valid connection to other networked machines. As you can see, there are several empty options in the IPX range. Because this sample box does not connect to an IPX network, these variables are set to be empty.

```
NETWORKING=yes
FORWARD_IPV4="yes"
HOSTNAME="antares.astronomy.org"
GATEWAY="192.168.0.1"
GATEWAYDEV="eth0"
NISDOMAIN=""
IPX="no"
IPXINTERNALNETNUM="0"
IPXINTERNALNODENUM="0"
IPXAUTOPRIMARY="on"
```

This particular file holds information about the hostname and gateway along with NIS and IPX information. It also details the basic networking information needed to establish a connection to other networked machines. For most tasks, it is easiest to edit this file directly rather than using a GUI client such as linuxconf.

## Configuring Networking Capabilities from the Command Line

The last file that you can edit by hand is a directory located in /etc/sysconfig/network-scripts/. This directory contains several configuration files and executables. The primary file used for setting up networking capabilities under

Linux is ifcfg-eth0. This file configures the primary Ethernet device, or eth0. You can either edit the variables by hand or use the netcfg command from within the control panel GUI. By setting the values for each networking option manually, you can ensure that only the necessary fields are added to the file. As Linux continues to grow and cater to X users who require clickable configuration tools, more empty fields will be added. This can lead to the bloating of configuration files.

If you are setting up a single Ethernet device, the following sample values create a good template for configuring your device:

```
DEVICE=eth0
USERCTL=no
ONBOOT=yes
BOOTPROTO=none
BROADCAST=192.168.0.255
NETWORK=192.168.0.0
NETMASK=255.255.255.0
IPADDR=192.168.0.25
```

Another important element is the ONBOOT field. If this variable is set to yes, then this device will be turned on and be enabled when the machine is booted. This saves the user the task of enabling the device every time he or she boots up the machine.

If you wish to enable or disable a device manually, use the executable ifup or ifdown located in the same directory. After making any changes to the configuration files, such as ifcfg-eth0, you can then bring down the device and then take it back up. This process will result in a momentary loss of connectivity, but if it is done quickly enough, the loss will hardly be noticeable. It is recommended that you perform this operation directly from the terminal at the computer rather than through a telnet session. Performing the latter will terminate your connection.

To bring the device up or down, use the following commands:

```
# cd /etc/sysconfig/network-scripts/
# ./ifdown ifcfg-eth0
# ./ifup ifcfg-eth0
```

You can apply the same command to the other network devices such as ifcfg-lo or any aliased network devices.

You can more easily edit this file using a GUI. The file can support multiple entries, so you should be careful when making any manual additions or alterations. The next section discusses the use of GUIs for editing network-related files.

## Using a GUI to Edit Network Variables

When you adjust or add additional network variables, two simple programs are readily available for use on most Linux systems. The first is native to the Red Hat system and the other has been more or less adopted by several distributions not only for editing the networking aspect but for adjusting most functions on their system. This section first looks at the former utility, netcfg, which was designed primarily for Red Hat.

As with most Linux utilities, netcfg's name is also the command. Because this program alters many of the most basic networking files, many of which you just finished examining, netcfg requires superuser access to run. You must also be within an X Window System environment. As you may have already discovered in Chapter 12 when setting up X, it does not matter which window manager you use as long as you are in the correct environment—namely X and not the console. You will get an error message if you attempt to start up this file outside of X.

You can start this program from the command line in an xterm window by entering **netcfg** as root or superuser, or you can execute the program from within the control panel program. Clicking the graphical network icon located on the control panel has the same effect as entering **netcfg** on the command line. When the program starts, it displays a dialog box with four main buttons across the top of the screen, each having various fields below for further configuration (see Figure 15.1).

Under the first button, Names, you can assign the Hostname and Domain of your system. The two text fields below are the Search and Nameservers options, which are the same as those discussed previously. Within the Search text field, you can enter the names of the domains that you wish to set as the default domains. These domains are queried in the order that you list them for your own and any respective hosts. The Nameservers text field below the Search field allows you to list the IP addresses of the name servers that contain all DNS information for local and Internet sites. It is strongly recommended that you use IP addresses, since you are configuring a name server. You cannot resolve a hostname to an address without an IP address, unless the name server is listed in /etc/hosts.

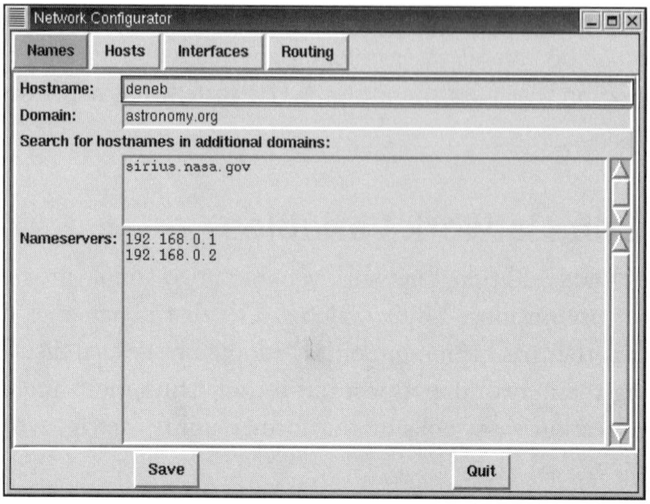

**FIGURE 15.1**

*The initial Network Configurator dialog box that appears after you enter the netcfg command.*

The next button on the Network Configuration dialog box, Hosts, lists the hosts accessible to your machine from within your network. Here you list the IP, name, and nickname or alias of each host as it appears via your network connection. Within the GUI, this display box is equivalent to the /etc/hosts file shown in Figure 15.2.

You can add, edit, and remove the hosts as necessary. Any changes that you make on this screen affect your /etc/hosts file directly.

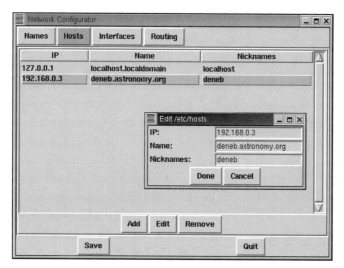

**FIGURE 15.2**

*The Hosts tab of the Network Configurator dialog box lists the machines available on your network.*

The third tab, Interfaces, lists the various types of interfaces available to your Linux box and their current status (see Figure 15.3). This tab can assist novice users when they are setting up new devices and do not feel comfortable yet editing the configuration files by hand. You can also use this tab to bring a device up or down. It is easier to enable or disable a device manually.

The available interface types are PPP, SLIP, PLIP, Ethernet, ARCNet, Token Ring, and Pocket (ATP). For most administrators, the two most used choices are PPP and Ethernet. You will examine the configuration of PPP devices more closely in Chapter 16.

Using the Ethernet interface as an example, when you add a device, you can choose to set the IP address and netmask for that particular interface (see Figure 15.4). The network and broadcast are added automatically based upon your choice of configurations. You can also activate the interface at boot time, in which case the device eth0 will automatically be activated the next time that the system reboots (if this is the first Ethernet interface on the system). You can either enable or disable each interface by clicking a button in the main window.

The last button on the Network Configurator dialog box is Routing (see Figure 15.5). In this tab, you can specify which gateway is the default when routing outside of your network.

In the Routing tab, you can add, edit, or remove static routes through your network. For example, if you have an alternate gateway through which you want to

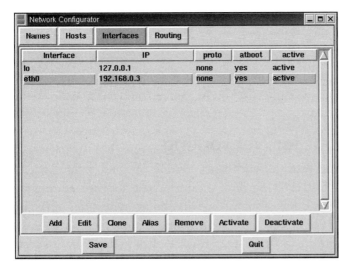

**FIGURE 15.3**

*Configuring the interfaces on a typical Linux box.*

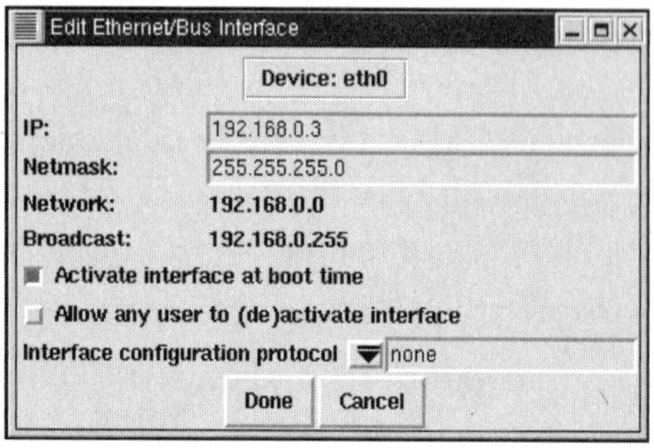

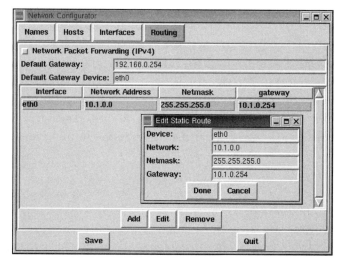

**FIGURE 15.4**

*Editing the primary Ethernet device.*

**FIGURE 15.5**

*Setting up routing in the Network Configurator dialog box's Routing tab.*

connect to other hosts, you could add your alternate gateway's IP address into this tab and create a static route to another network. Most Linux users will seldom use this tab, because most networks do not require a static route. If, however, you find yourself behind a firewall, as is frequently becoming the case on many networks, this tab can assist you in configuring your network settings.

## Running linuxconf for Networking

Another utility that provides added networking options is the linuxconf program. Its GUI is fast evolving into an all-purpose tool for editing most any text file found on the Linux system. You will find many features of the linuxconf utility that assist you in editing system configuration files on your Red Hat Linux system. There are too many features to look at in depth in this section, but carefully perusing and becoming familiar with the many features of linuxconf will help you understand your system even better. The linuxconf utility is constantly being updated and developed further to provide additional functionality.

The network tools for this utility are located within the first major section of the linuxconf tree structure called Config. For specifics regarding the basic host configuration options, look in the following directories: Config, Networking, Client tasks. The section detailing the different Config options is one of the first configurable items of the many sections listed in the tree-like structure. Figure 15.6 is a sample display in which a user can enter basic host networking information.

In the tree-structure file list, click Config, Networking, Client tasks, Basic host information. You can then configure not only the name of your system and its IP addresses but also any network devices. The current version of linuxconf displays four network devices by default, although you can override the default and specify that the utility display additional devices.

Additionally, the next entry within the Client tasks section, the Name server specification file or Resolver configuration file, displays all the name server information needed to allow your system to resolve DNS issues and to speak with other systems locally (see Figure 15.7).

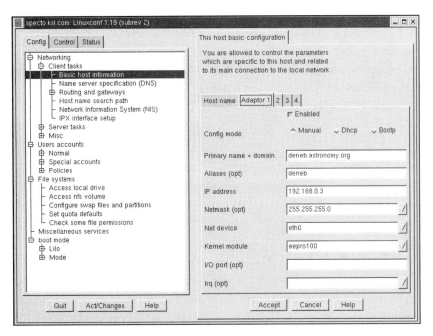

**FIGURE 15.6**

*The basic host configuration section under the Networking tools of linuxconf.*

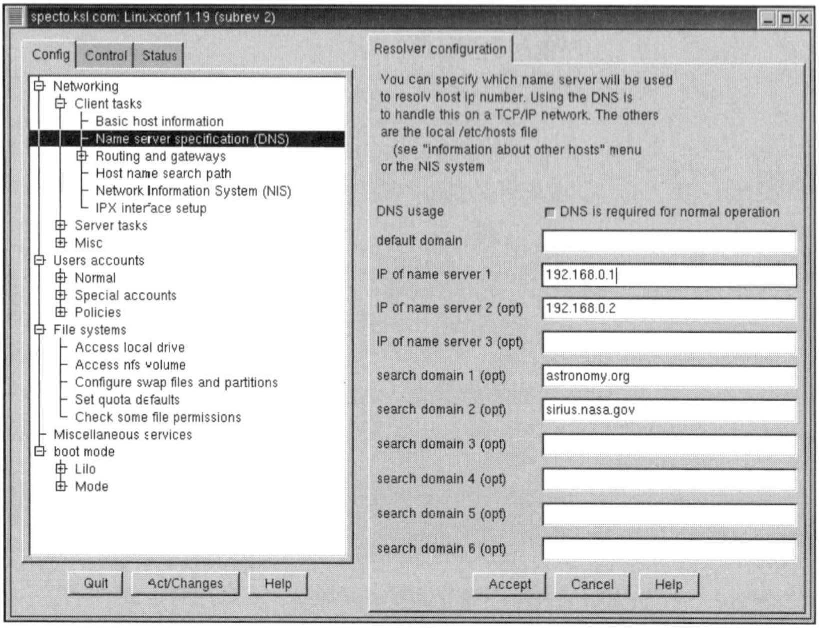

**FIGURE 15.7**

*The resolver configuration settings under the linuxconf program.*

The linuxconf utility offers several options that enable you to tailor the name servers and DNS search patterns just as easily as you could in the simple text file. For this task, some users consider using the GUI even easier than working with the text file. Beginning users should try both alternatives before deciding which one they prefer. Explore linuxconf's other windows, such as the Host Name Search Path or the Name service access window as it is displayed in its dialog box as shown in Figure 15.8, to discover how its GUI makes it easy to configure name servers that provide examples in other menus of alternative possibilities.

Rather than familiarizing yourself with the proper syntax, you need only choose from the available options. Although only a limited number of options are presented, the source code is freely available if you need to modify the options. You can also request modifications from the developers.

# Testing the Connection

Entering the proper data for network settings is fine, but unless you can verify that they are correct you will still be without network connectivity. This section demonstrates a few tools that you may use to ensure that you have the software

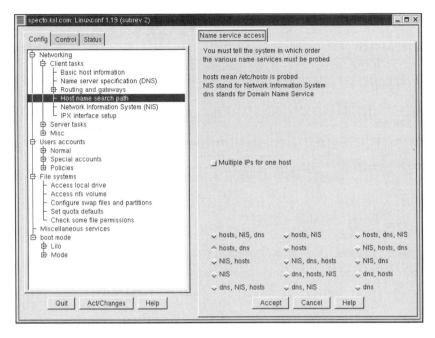

**FIGURE 15.8**

*Name service access settings under linuxconf.*

properly set up. You can also use this section as a troubleshooting guide since these are the same tools that you would use to check for problems with your connectivity. (Note, however, that this section presumes that if you are checking your system for errors, you have already made sure that the hardware is installed properly, that all cables are plugged in correctly, that the network card is seated in the motherboard, that the link lights on the card are lit, and that the interrupts are configured correctly.)

## Using the ifconfig Command

After making all the proper entries, you can start testing the viability of your network settings. The best way to verify that your network devices are working is by using the ifconfig command. Only root can change the settings displayed by this program. Any non-root user can execute the command to see what IP addresses are in use by the system. Depending upon your release, you may have to use the absolute path to the command or make sure that its location is in your path. Otherwise, you may simply want to type in the full path. On my Red Hat Linux box, the full path is /sbin/ifconfig. Listing 15.1 shows sample output for a properly configured system.

## Listing 15.1 The Output Generated by the ifconfig Command

```
# /sbin/ifconfig -a
eth0        Link encap:Ethernet   HWaddr 00:00:C0:83:BC:7C
inet addr:192.168.0.10  Bcast:192.168.0.255  Mask:255.255.255.0
UP BROADCAST RUNNING MULTICAST  MTU:1500  Metric:1
RX packets:14976 errors:0 dropped:0 overruns:0 frame:0
TX packets:5822 errors:0 dropped:0 overruns:0 carrier:0
collisions:0 txqueuelen:100
Interrupt:10 Base address:0x310 Memory:cc000-d0000


lo          Link encap:Local Loopback
inet addr:127.0.0.1  Mask:255.0.0.0
UP LOOPBACK RUNNING  MTU:3924  Metric:1
RX packets:55636 errors:0 dropped:0 overruns:0 frame:0
TX packets:55636 errors:0 dropped:0 overruns:0 carrier:0
collisions:0 txqueuelen:0
```

The data reported by this command show only the IP address of the current machine and whether its network device—in this case, eth0—is up and running. It also displays the MAC address of the network device, its interrupt number, and its base memory address. The ifconfig command is useful for debugging purposes in that it shows the number of errors generated by the network delivery, including the number of collisions. The command also indicates which packets were dropped. If the card were configured incorrectly, the ifconfig command may list a large number of errors, but more than likely would not show the card at all.

Much like the ifup or ifdown commands in the /etc/sysconfig/network-scripts/ directory, the ifconfig command can also be used to bring a particular network device up or down or to enable or disable its functions. In fact, the ifup and ifup commands are nothing more than a set of Perl scripts that utilize ifconfig along with other variables.

You can use ifconfig to accomplish the same tasks by typing **ifconfig**, the interface name, and the **down** or **up** variable. The following examples show how to bring down and then back up on the primary Ethernet interface:

```
# ifconfig eth0 down
# ifconfig eth0 up
```

## Configuring Additional Network Devices

The ifconfig command is also useful if you are on a system that hosts multiple virtual domains or domains that are not identified by a box but are virtual and exist within another machine. For example, the server antares.agronomy.org could also host virtual domains named stars.com and astronomy.net. Any box can host a unique domain that exists only on that machine. Each domain would then have its own unique IP address if you wanted to make certain that it is uniquely identified, provided that the name server responsible for the domain also pointed to this IP address.

You use the ifconfig command to enable the broadcast of each IP address. For example, in the /etc/sysconfig/network-scripts/ directory, you could copy the ifcfg-eth0 file to another file called ifcfg-eth0:0. This new file would then hold the information regarding this new domain name, including the IP address and hostname. Make sure that the new IP address is not the same IP address that your server currently uses, but that it still is valid and falls under a range of IP addresses that you own.

The following command, for example, defines the device eth0:0 to a specific IP address.

```
# ifconfig eth0:0        206.71.77.51
```

After entering the necessary information into that file, you can begin testing to make sure it works. Enter **route -v** to check the current IP addresses. Now enter the following commands:

```
# /sbin/ifconfig eth0:0 up
# /sbin/ifconfig -a
```

The last command prints out the available IP addresses in use by the system. Make sure that the command includes the newly created domain IP. Run a ping test to verify that the IP address or domain assigned to it is alive and that you are currently using the correct IP. Try pinging the box both from the local machine hosting the IP and from another networked machine:

```
# ping 206.71.77.51
```

If the test returns a response, your configuration is correct and complete. You can now begin assigning other virtual domains to the same machine.

> **NOTE**
>
> If you are using the default Apache install, you can also use a name-based virtual hosting method rather than burning an IP address for each virtual domain. Consult the Apache home page, http://www.apache.org/, for more information regarding name-based IP addressing. This type of IP addressing normally requires a couple of additional lines in your httpd.conf file, the default configuration file for setting up the web server.

## Using the Hardware Device Files

Another method of checking your devices and verifying that the hardware portion of the setup is working well is to look in the /proc/ directory. This directory does not contain the static files that are usually found in most Linux directories. These are files that are generated spontaneously to reflect the state of the kernel. Because this directory monitors systems files that are in a state of constant flux, they cannot be rewritten or cleared constantly. It is better to generate their content on the fly.

One of the best methods for checking the IRQ of a network device or monitoring the input/output ports of different devices is to use the cat command and output the results to the console.

If you wanted to see what IRQs were in use by the different devices, you would enter the following command:

```
# cat /proc/interrupts
```

To check the IO ports in use, use this command:

```
# cat /proc/ioports
```

You use the same format to check the current state of memory use:

```
# cat /proc/meminfo
```

This directory contains additional information about your system, and you can output each file to the console and examine the results. This is useful if you are installing a new network card that has a conflict with another device. Such a conflict can happen between older network cards and sound cards, each sharing the same interrupt, such as IRQ_10. Using this command, you can see how your machine defines each card's interrupt.

◆ ◆ ◆

# Connecting across Different Platforms

Though you may now feel confident in your Linux abilities and that you are ready to set up multiple Linux boxes so that they can talk to each other, enabling cross-platform communication may not be as simple as adding certain numbers and editing network files. In particular, enabling Linux and Windows to communicate requires some additional effort. Fortunately, Linux has now become much easier to network to Windows boxes. In fact, many administrators now use Linux as a file server, visible in the Windows Network Neighborhood and as a server to which users can transparently map their drive. The program used to facilitate Linux and Windows communications is called SAMBA, and much of how it operates and how you can configure it under Linux will be looked at closely in this chapter.

This section looks at the SAMBA utility and explains how you can configure Linux and Windows to be transparent to each other.

## Setting Up SAMBA to Communicate with Windows

Though the SAMBA program has nothing to do with the dance by the same name, it does conjure up the image of Linux performing some quick footwork with other systems, namely Windows. (SAMBA's name is actually based on the acronym for Session Message Block (SMB) protocol services.) The program provides a bridge between the two platforms and makes it possible to serve files between the two systems. SAMBA allows you to share Linux file systems with the various incarnations of Windows. In addition to enabling you to share directories and files, SAMBA enables network printing either through a Linux box or printing from a Linux box through a Windows machine.

The various components of this suite of protocols are described comprehensively under the default /etc/smb.conf file. In this file, you can edit the various directories, or *shares,* you wish to make available to other users on the network. Linux provides, as usual, two options to configure this file, either by hand or through the use of a GUI editor. Any changes made to the smb.conf file will not take effect until the SAMBA daemon is restarted.

Most Linux distributions have a version of SAMBA ready for installation. You can install this version either through the RPM version or through the source code release. The RPM version is by far the easier method to install. It places each of the several necessary files in their respective directories and makes it simple to start and stop the daemon.

The typical method of starting, stopping, or restarting SAMBA involves executing the standard command located in the run command directory. As you have seen previously with the other daemons, you can send this daemon a restart signal:

```
# /etc/rc.d/init.d/smb restart
```

Such a command usually restarts two different services. SAMBA is actually composed of both the smbd daemon, which controls file and print services to the various Windows versions and to other Linux and UNIX clients, and nmbd, which provides NetBIOS name-serving and browsing support. RPM installations usually provide for both to be started at the same time, but both are equally customizable using the smb.conf file. The following is sample output from a restart command to the smb daemon:

```
# /etc/rc.d/init.d/smb restart
Shutting down SMB services: [  OK  ]
Shutting down NMB services: [  OK  ]
Starting SMB services: [  OK  ]
Starting NMB services: [  OK  ]
```

This service provides some useful functionality. For example, you can see Linux systems from within the Network Neighborhood icon of any Windows 95/98/2000 machine and subsequently access your own personal directory on that Linux box, if your login name and your Linux directory's name are the same. You can also share certain directories under SAMBA for others in your same workgroup to access, both for downloading and writing purposes.

## Configuring the smb.conf File

The key to making SAMBA work and giving other systems the correct permissions to access your Linux directories is to understand the /etc/smb.conf file. For most uses, editing only the first few lines of the smb.conf file is sufficient to get

Linux and Windows conversing. Be aware that any changes that you make to the configuration file will affect the performance and usability of your network. If things do fail, check your own settings before you blame SAMBA. Also, if the machine does not work properly after you change the files and restart the daemon, make sure that the network is even viable before faulting your editing skills. Windows machines cannot view a Linux box if the connection is not available.

> **CAUTION**
>
> Before attempting to edit this file, be sure to back up the original file. Any changes you make may corrupt the file, so you want to be able to restore the default settings easily.

Before making editing changes, first test the connection between hosts by running the ping command for each machine. Under Windows, click Start, Run, then type **ping <IP address>**. Then do the same on the Linux box, substituting the IP address of the Windows or other Linux box for the original address. Normally, Windows sends only three packets for the purposes of a ping test. Linux will either time out if the connection is unreachable or continue to run ping unless you press Ctrl-C to halt the output.

Most commented-out lines under the smb.conf file begin with a pound sign (#). SAMBA does not read these lines. Also, any line that begins with a semicolon (;) is also a comment. These lines are usually those that can be edited for a particular purpose, either to restrict that function's use or to reserve it for later.

The smb.conf file consists of three main parts: Global, Homes, and Printers. Additional entries are available, but they are usually used only for specific functions. This section focuses on the first three entries, but you can learn about the others by visiting the main SAMBA page (`http://www.samba.org/`), which provides additional support and documentation.

## Editing the Global Section in SAMBA

The first four options in the smb.conf file under the Global section heading—Workgroup, Server String, Hosts Allow, and Printcap—are generally the most important for any SAMBA configuration. Most systems can begin talking soon after these lines are enabled correctly. Listing 15.2 shows a sample taken from a Linux system that sits on a private network. This system is modeled after a network using astronomical names. Here the primary workgroup is called SOL, again using the astronomical terminology. Each of the servers on this network is named after a planet. The Hosts Allow option specifies which servers under that specific IP address can have access to this particular server running SAMBA. Also, this file enables some preliminary settings for networked printers. Hence there is an entry for the /etc/printcap file, which contains the necessary printer information.

### Listing 15.2  A Sample Global Section Under the smb.conf File

```
#
#======================= Global Settings=========================
[global]

# workgroup = NT-Domain-Name or Workgroup-Name
workgroup = SOL
# server string is the equivalent of the NT Description field
server string = Pluto
# This option is important for security.
# It allows you to restrict
# connections to machines that are on your local network. The
# following example restricts access to two C class networks and
# the "loopback" interface. For more examples of the syntax, see
# the smb.conf man page
hosts allow = 192.168. 127.
# if you want to load your printer list automatically rather
# than setting up each print individually, then you'll need this
printcap name = /etc/printcap
load printers = yes
```

After you have created these few entries and restarted the daemon, you should be able to see your Linux box under the networked Windows machines as shown in the Windows icon, Network Neighborhood, that are also on the same workgroup. This means that the workgroup you listed in the Global settings should agree with the workgroup that the Windows machines also use. If you have any questions about the workgroup that you are currently on, under Windows choose, Start, Settings, Control Panel, Network, Identification. Check to make sure that the Workgroup box agrees with that which you have entered in the smb.conf file.

To test your configuration, first click the Network Neighborhood icon under Windows and check whether your computer is visible. If not, right-click the icon again and then click Find Computer. Enter the name of your Linux box as defined by your hostname settings. Once you find your machine and have verified that your configuration settings are correct; you can now begin to add additional components.

To be able to print through a SAMBA-connected Windows machine, return again to your Linux machine and begin configuring the PrintTool program. To use a SAMBA-linked network printer, display your PrintTool dialog box (see Figure 15.9). Click Add, then choose the SMB/Windows 95/NT Printer option.

Next edit the Printer Entry dialog box (see Figure 15.10) with the correct information about the machine to which the printer is connected. This can be either a Windows or Linux box. Several of the fields are optional, including the User and Password fields. If you wish to restrict use, enable these fields both here and

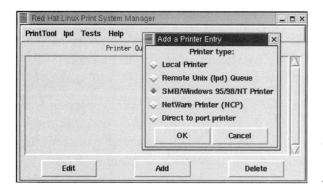

**FIGURE 15.9**

*Selecting the SAMBA printer option.*

**FIGURE 15.10**

*Configuring the printer option to print through a SAMBA-interlinked machine.*

under your smb.conf file. Otherwise, simply naming the host machine and the printer is sufficient.

To check your printer's name on your Windows machine, click the My Computer icon, then the Printers icon. Highlight the printer to which you wish to print and then open the Properties menu. Under the Sharing section, check whether the name is correct as you have it in your setup. You can also insert additional information such as comments and passwords.

After enabling these features under the Print System Manager, restart the lpd printer daemon to ensure that the changes have taken effect. Highlight the printer entry just made and click Tests, Print ASCII Test Page. If all is configured correctly, you should be able to print through the networked machine.

## Enabling and Disabling Encrypted Passwords

If you are still unable to find your box or if you discover that the password settings disable access to your remote machine, check your Windows release number. SAMBA supports both clear and encrypted passwords. Early SAMBA versions defaulted to clear text password configurations. With the release of Windows 95 OEM Service Release 2, Windows began encrypting its passwords. All Windows 98 and 2000 versions do likewise, as does Windows NT with Service Pack 3.

You can clear this hurdle in one of two ways: either enable password encryption on the Linux side or disable the encrypted password option on the Windows client side. With the first method, enable encrypted passwords under the smb.conf file by uncommenting the lines shown in Listing 15.3.

### Listing 15.3 Unencrypting Passwords under the smb.conf File

```
# You may wish to use password encryption. Please read
# ENCRYPTION.txt, Win95.txt and WinNT.txt
# in the Samba documentation.
# Do not enable this option unless you have read those documents
;   encrypt passwords = yes
;   smb passwd file = /etc/smbpasswd
```

On the Windows side, execute the following series of steps, but with the following warning: If you enable plain text password use in Windows 98, all passwords are sent on the network in an unencrypted format. Anyone using a network monitoring program, or packet sniffer, can view these passwords. If security is a concern for your network environment, do not enable plain text passwords. These are the steps used only under the Windows 95/98 CDs.

1. Insert your Windows 95 or 98 CD-ROM into the CD-ROM drive.

2. Click Start, Run.

3. In the Open box, type **<drive>:\tools\mtsutil**, where <drive> is the letter of the CD-ROM drive that contains the Windows CD-ROM. Then click OK.

4. Right-click the ptxt_on.inf file, and then click Install.

5. Restart your Windows machine.

After you have successfully performed these steps, you should be able to see your own directory on the Linux box. You can click and drag files between the two systems now as well as open documents under Windows that are stored on Linux. Other users on your systems sharing accounts on the same Linux box can do likewise and store their personal documents on the networked Linux box, thus keeping their own directory free for other documents. This makes backup routines simpler since all crucial documents are then in one place for nightly backups. Users thus do not have to back up their own system separately.

# Setting Up the Homes Section under SAMBA

The Homes, or Share Definitions, section under the smb.conf file gives users access to user directories on your Linux server even if they do not have a specific login in the smb.conf file (see Listing 15.4). Normally, when a user attempts to log in through SAMBA, it checks for an entry in the smb.conf file. If SAMBA fails to find an entry, it will look under the Homes section for an entry. After finding the correct entry, SAMBA then makes that directory available to users on the network.

**Listing 15.4  A Sample Homes, or Share Directories, Section in smb.conf**

```
#============================ Share Definitions =================
  [homes]
comment = Home Directories
browseable = no
writable = yes
```

The comment option is the same as server string under the Global section in that what you enter in this option will be visible as the comment section under other Windows machines. The SAMBA GUI editor or SWAT (SAMBA Web Administration Tool) offers other options for configuring shared home directories. SWAT allows SAMBA's smb.conf file to be remotely managed using your favorite web browser. SWAT is enabled on TCP port 901 via inetd. But for now, rather than using a GUI client it is usually sufficient to enable other users to browse or write to the files.

## Adding Printers to SAMBA

In the Printers section (see Listing 15.5), you can make additional printer entries available to other users on your system who are using either a Windows or Linux machine. You can enter your printer's identity when connected directly to your Linux machine, using a name by which other Windows users can then identify your printer under their menus.

### Listing 15.5 A Sample Printers Section in smb.conf

```
# NOTE: If you have a BSD-style print system there is no need to
# define each individual printer specifically
  [printers]
comment = All Printers
path = /var/spool/samba
browseable = no
# Set public = yes to allow user 'guest account' to print
guest ok = no
writable = no
printable = yes
```

Like the Printer System Manager under Linux, this section allows you to enable others to use the printer connected to your Linux box.

The Global, Homes, and Printers sections are all that are necessary to enable your Linux machine to communicate with Windows machines. Once you have properly set up the smb.conf file, you can begin adding other Windows users to your Linux system and set up a sharing or file-serving protocol for users to share and redistribute files among themselves from a communal Linux machine.

## Mounting SAMBA Shares

Now that Windows users can see your Linux shares, it is also possible to share Windows files with Linux users. The most common method for accomplishing this is to use the smbmount command to mount a Windows share onto your Linux box. After successfully mounting the directory, you can access the files much as you would any other mounted directory such as the CD-ROM on your own drive or another directory from another Linux machine using something such as NFS.

The usual syntax for mounting shared Windows files and directories is as follows:

```
# /usr/bin/smbmount <Windows server name or IP address/directory
name> <local mount directory> -U <username%password>
```

Of course, the person using the Windows machine must provide a valid username and password for the Linux user under the Sharing option. Once you have finished accessing the files on the mounted SAMBA directory, you may unmount the directory or a share the same way you would unmount any media devices.

The smbumount command followed by the local mount directory or mount point will release your control over the Windows directory. Make sure that you do not have an active prompt in that location or directory; otherwise, you will be unable to unmount the partition. The syntax for unmounting is as follows:

```
# smbumount /mnt/samba
```

**CAUTION**

Some of the older SAMBA versions do not release the partition even after they are unmounted. The only way to release these mounted SAMBA partitions is to reboot the machine. This is a bug under older SAMBA releases and should be resolved in later releases.

Mounting Windows shares is also a quick, useful way to back up Windows files onto a Linux machine. For example, the following script mounts a directory located on a Snap server onto a local Linux machine and then uses the cpio backup routine to back up all the files:

```
#!/bin/sh
# Back up the Snap /aweb directory on the graphic design machine.
```

```
# using cpio
  /usr/bin/smbmount //206.81.148.15/internetwork /mnt/snap -U
backup%backup
  cd /mnt/snap/aweb
  touch level1.0.cpio.timestamp
  find . -print|cpio -oacvB > /dev/st0
```

Within this script, you outline which directories you want to back up and which protocol you wish to use. You then outline the command needed to mount the partition under Linux. Once the partition is mounted, you can run the commands necessary to begin the backup routine.

You can apply the same principle to other protocols. Here is a similar script using the dump command to back up the same mounted partition:

```
#!/bin/sh
# Back up the Snap /aweb directory on the graphic design machine.
/usr/bin/smbmount //206.81.146.17/internetwork /mnt/snap -U
backup%backup
/sbin/dump -0uf /dev/st0 -b 64 -B 4000000 -L "snap server" /mnt/snap
```

Nearly any type of shared file under Windows can now also be seen under Linux. This script can quickly exchange information between both parties without creating an account on the Linux machine to which the Windows user can send files using ftp.

## Using SWAT to Configure SAMBA

A very useful tool that makes it unnecessary to edit the smb.conf file manually is the SWAT utility currently bundled with Red Hat Linux. SWAT provides a quick and easy way to set up the necessary lines in your smb.conf file without having to familiarize yourself with all the syntax.

Enabling this feature involves editing some additional files. First, verify that there is a section in your /etc/services file that resembles the following:

```
# Local services
linuxconf    98/tcp
swat         901/tcp         # Add swat service used via inetd
```

Next, uncomment the line in your /etc/inetd.conf file that allows the linuxconf tool to run under the Web browser. It should look something like the following line:

```
linuxconf stream tcp wait root /bin/linuxconf linuxconf --http
```

Restart the inetd daemon by sending a -HUP signal to its PID. Then verify that inetd is still running by using the ps command.

```
# ps aux | grep inetd
```

You should now be able to access the SWAT tool or the SAMBA Configuration Tool. Open up a Web browser, such as Netscape, then enter either the IP address of your server or its FQDN (Fully Qualified Domain Name) followed by a colon and the number 901:

```
http://192.168.0.10:901/
```

or

```
http://vega.astronomy.org:901/
```

You can also use a text-based browser to edit the files. Lynx provides a handy text-based interface for accessing HTML files. Start lynx in a terminal window, then enter the URL of the SAMBA machine followed by **:901**. This command should bring up a configuration similar to the one described previously. Under both the text-based and graphic browser such as Netscape, you will be prompted to enter root as the username and root's password in the security dialog box. Now, under the Netscape Web browser an interface much like the one in Figure 15.11 will be visible. This is the Web-based tool called the SAMBA Web Administration Tool (SWAT).

The row of buttons in SWAT's opening screen represent the main categories of variables that you can configure. The links listed below the buttons lead you to detailed explanations about each configurable variable under SAMBA. Let's explore the Global values as examples.

**CAUTION**

Before committing to any changes on the system, be sure to back up your smb.conf file. SWAT greatly changes this file, removing any comments and leaving only the most basic parameters.

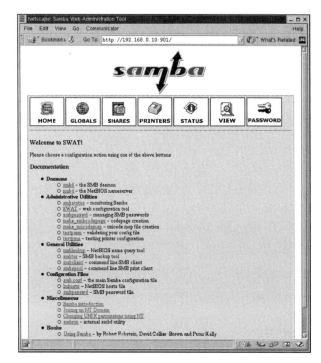

**FIGURE 15.11**

*Opening screen of the SWAT tool under Netscape.*

Figure 15.12 shows how you might enter the most basic information in SWAT for changing entries in the Global section.

Once you have committed these changes to the system, you can stop and start SAMBA manually by clicking the Status button. This brings up the Server Status window that shows all the active connections and shares along with any open files (see Figure 5.13). The buttons in the Server Status section enable you to auto-refresh the screen based on your parameters, as well as stop and start the daemons.

The SWAT feature is extremely useful when you are managing Linux servers remotely or when you want to avoid the headache of editing another text file by hand. SWAT provides users with a functional utility that makes file serving practical and functional between Linux and Windows. Maybe the two platforms can dance after all.

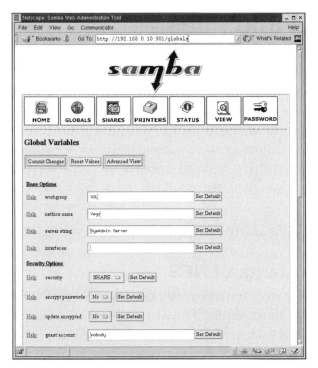

**FIGURE 15.12**

*Editing global variables under SWAT.*

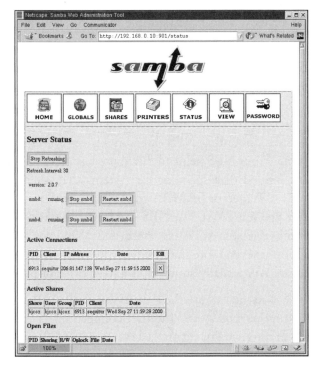

**FIGURE 15.13**

*SAMBA's Server Status window displaying active connections and open files.*

# Sharing Drives and Files

Linux is much more versatile than other systems. You can not only share files and data across a network with Windows computers, but you can also mount partitions and directories from one Linux box to another. In other words, a directory on one machine can be mounted or remotely connected, with all permissions and links intact, to another machine. This is the equivalent of physically removing a hard drive from one machine and placing it in another. Rather than opening machines and changing drives repeatedly, you can have networked Linux machines share information dynamically across a physically linked connection. Mounting a drive or partition is a simple task among trusted Linux machines.

## Understanding the Merits of NFS

One of the most versatile tools available under Linux and other UNIX systems is Network File System (NFS). With NFS you can mount a directory or other partition located elsewhere on a networked system and have it appear as a local directory. In other words, though the directory is physically located elsewhere, it appears as if it were just another directory on your Linux machine. This capability is especially useful for users who have multiple machines and must share disk resources.

Unlike a utility such as SAMBA, which allows cross-platform data transfers among network systems, NFS actually mounts the directory on your system. This mount then allows for true access of remote files including UNIX permissions and links. Similar to using the mounting command used for mounting the CD-ROM and floppy drives, mounting NFS directories gives a user complete access to shared file systems. Thus NFS helps to distribute resources more effectively for machines with limited disk space or for systems that require easier access than through an FTP, Telnet, or SAMBA connection. To draw a parallel between Linux and other operating systems, NFS can be viewed as the UNIX answer to the file sharing available with NetWare and Windows' Network Neighborhood. But NFS offers even more than that. If you use the df command, any mounted NFS partition will actually show up as a local drive or partition.

The default install of NFS does not secure the system very well. Making directories available for mounting purposes over Internet connections is a very bad idea. Unless you want to grant virtually anyone access to your files, you should not run the NFS daemon. As with any sort of file-sharing mechanism, you must be cautious to whom you grant privileges. However, for use within a semi-secure environment, such as a home or office that has no direct connection to the outside world, or within a system with a system with a connection that either is either behind a firewall or that can be temporarily disabled—NFS is optimal for sharing resources over the network. Linux can boot off some of the more limited drives and then mount /home or /usr/local directories from another server. You can even edit the main file that handles this mounting process, /etc/fstab (the *file system table*), and upon bootup have the external partitions mounted for local use.

You can make NFS quite secure (or at least more secure than NIS or even NIS+) by controlling access so only particular users or machines can mount your exports. NFS is extremely useful for Linux installations and when used properly a single Linux box with one CD-ROM can quickly install Linux on a host of other machines without any CD-ROMs but through a simple network connection.

## Mounting and Unmounting Media

Before looking at how NFS operates, let's first examine the process of mounting media, using some examples from local Linux systems. The most basic of any type of mounting is that of local devices onto the Linux system. For example, if you are using a regular PC with a standard ATAPI CD-ROM, Linux requires that you first mount the device before accessing the files contained on the media. When you are done using the device, you must then unmount it. As is the case with floppy drives, failure to unmount the device before extracting the media results in corruption errors the next time you reboot your machine. Use the examples in this section as a template for mounting and unmounting media via the devices.

By default, you can only mount CDs onto your device as root. After you insert the CD onto the drive you can execute the mount command from nearly any location. Enter the following command for standard iso9660 CD drives:

```
# mount -t iso9660 /dev/cdrom /mnt/cdrom
```

You can also abbreviate the process simply by entering the mount command and the source and target destinations:

```
# mount /dev/cdrom /mnt/cdrom
```

The mount command takes the -t option to determine the mounted file system type, which, in this case, is iso9660. On most systems, this flag is optional. Next, you point to the device name, /dev/cdrom, and mount it in a particular location under the file systems. Most Linux distributions provide a /mnt directory in which you can mount a file system. Red Hat provides /mnt/cdrom/ and /mnt/floppy/ directories for mounting those types of files.

This command lends itself easily to script writing, allowing you as root to mount and unmount media easily. Once the system has determined that the CD is correctly mounted, you will usually receive a confirmation that it is in read-only mode, hence the ROM affirmation for the device name:

```
# mount /dev/cdrom /mnt/cdrom/
mount: block device /dev/cdrom is write-protected, mounting read-only
```

## Mounting Directories and Partitions with NFS

Based on Sun's Network File System, the current implementation of NFS is designed to be as user-transparent as possible. You can mount a server running the NFS daemon on virtually any other Linux or UNIX host. You need to pre-configure just a few files so that the daemon allows other users to mount the local file system. It is imperative that you configure these files correctly to ensure that you do not allow users on other systems to abuse the available resources.

The two files that you need to configure are /etc/fstab and /etc/exports. The first file lists the actual device name, the partitions, the file system type, and the manner in which they can be accessed. You can configure the second file manually to allow a specific user to access a particular directory located on the fstab file. It is this second file that configures all allowable directories.

Suppose, for example, that you want to share the CD-ROM drive located on your own machine, quasi, with another Linux box, sequitur, situated within your network but lacking a CD-ROM drive of its own. Using NFS, you log in to sequitur and mount the CD-ROM on quasi onto sequitur's file system. The sequitur machine now appears to have a local CD-ROM. Users of sequitur can use the remote device to extract information from the mounted CD. To accomplish this, follow these steps:

1. Mount the CD on the server running the NFS daemon.

2. Enter the correct information about the host and client systems in your /etc/exports file. The directory or device to be shared goes first, then the

name of the client system that will use the remote file as a local one. The last field defines this export as read-only. Other options include (rw) for read-write. This entry allows only the host sequitur to mount the CD-ROM locally.

```
# example /etc/exports file
/mnt/cdrom          sequitur.fortuna.org(r)
```

3. Start up the NFS daemon on the host system. You can do this from the command line of your Red Hat Linux box:

```
/etc/rc.d/init.d/nfs start
```

4. You can also verify that the NFS daemon starts up automatically by using the /usr/sbin/ntsysv file to configure those processes that start up at boot.

5. After confirming that you have configured NFS properly on the host side, you can switch over to the client side. Use the showmount -e command either on the client or server side to verify that NFS is running and is successfully exporting the requested directory.

6. Become root on the client—in this case, sequitur--. You can execute the mount command from nearly any location on the machine, provided you are using full pathnames. Mount the host device on the client by entering this command:

```
# mount -t nfs sequitur.fortuna.org:/mnt/cdrom /mnt/cdrom
```

7. Execute a df -h command to determine the mounted partitions on the local drive. This command's output should enable you to see the additional NFS-mounted partition. You can accomplish the same by executing a bare mount command.

```
# df -h
Filesystem          Size    Used    Avail   Use%    Mounted on
/dev/hda1           486M    35M     426M    8%      /
/dev/hda5           3.3G    1.0G    2.1G    33%     /home
/dev/hda8           729M    369M    322M    53%     /opt
/dev/hda7           1.9G    1.2G    690M    63%     /usr
/dev/hda6           2.4G    817M    1.4G    36%     /usr/local
sequitur.fortuna.edu:
/mnt/cdrom          642M    642M    0       100%    /mnt/cdrom
```

Change to the /mnt/cdrom directory, where you can then peruse the directory structure on the CD as easily as you can on the host box. If necessary, copy the files from their remote location onto another location on the hard drive.

When you are finished with that particular drive or device, unmounting the host drive from the client side is as simple as unmounting other local devices. Be certain you are not currently accessing any files from the remote location or have a terminal session pointing to any of the files within the mounted location. If that happens, you will be unable to mount the partition.

To unmount the device, simply enter the following:

```
umount /mnt/cdrom
```

For more complex mounting, such as mounting formatted file systems, you can enter the following setting into your host's /etc/exports file:

```
# sample /etc/exports file
   /home                 sequitur(rw) nihilo(rw,no_root_squash)
   /usr/local/gnu        *.fortuna.edu(rw)
```

The first line allows users on the clients sequitur and nihilo to access the /home directory. You can place this directory anywhere on the client computer, but the mounted directory must be located on the local subnet. The no_root_squash option denies access to setuid root commands. This prevents users from executing a command that might be harmful to your system. The next line allows any host from the domain fortuna.org to have read-write access to the /usr/local/gnu directory.

To make sure that a system mounts an NFS file system upon boot, you need only edit the /etc/fstab file. As with the other entries listed in /etc/fstab, you can accomplish an NFS mount automatically simply by adding another entry, as shown in Listing 15.6.

### Listing 15.6  A Sample /etc/fstab File that Provides Automatic Mounting of Directories via NFS

```
/dev/hda1          /             ext2      defaults          1 1
/dev/hda5          /home         ext2      defaults          1 2
/dev/cdrom         /mnt/cdrom    iso9660   noauto,owner,ro   0 0
/dev/hda8          /opt          ext2      defaults          1 2
/dev/hda7          /usr          ext2      defaults          1 2
```

| | | | | | |
|---|---|---|---|---|---|
| /dev/hda6 | /usr/local | ext2 | defaults | 1 2 |
| /dev/hda9 | /var | ext2 | defaults | 1 2 |
| /dev/hda10 | swap | swap | defaults | 0 0 |
| /dev/fd0 | /mnt/floppy | ext2 | noauto,owner | 0 0 |
| none | /proc | proc | defaults | 0 0 |
| none | /dev/pts | devpts | gid=5,mode=620 | 0 0 |
| sequitur.fortuna.org: | | | | |
| /mnt/cdrom | /mnt/cdrom | nfs | ro | 0 0 |

This change to /etc/fstab enables you to mount the remote CD-ROM on the local /mnt/cdrom directory. You can do the same with directories. In fact, you can quickly expand even the most minimal installation of Linux on a 500-megabyte hard drive to several gigabytes worth simply by mounting the drives from other machines on the local system. Ensuring that the mounted drives contain the /home or /usr/local or even the /usr directory can quickly increase the functionality of the most basic system.

Carrying over the same concept to UNIX or Linux distributions other than Red Hat works just as well. It does not matter what type of other UNIX system is running; if you can run NFS on your Linux box, you will be able to mount other devices and directories easily on your local machine as well. The syntax for other UNIX distributions does not follow the exact same specifications as those for Linux. Consult the man pages for other UNIX versions and their required syntax.

## Using xhost to Export Remote Applications

The concept of mounting devices and partitions on other remote systems has been extrapolated even further. This section looks at a very useful Linux function called xhost. Some users either cannot or do not want to mount an entire partition on their system, but wish to use on their own desktop a specific program hosted on another system. The xhost function enables these users to do so. This utility is designed for users of the X Window System since it allows the remote GUI application to run locally.

For example, at my job it is sometimes more useful to run certain GUI applications located on *headless machines*—machines without a monitor—rather than trying to edit the files in text-mode only. Instead of strapping a new monitor onto the remote Linux system or to some other UNIX variant, I simply export the remote GUI application to my own X session by using xhost.

In one case, I needed to use Solaris's metatool remotely to re-create larger disk partitions from separate physical drives on a Sun Microsystems machine. The only problem was that I was located quite some distance from the machines themselves and had to perform this task remotely on a Linux box since I had no other Sun machines from which I could use the same application. Even if I had had access to a monitor, the machine itself would have required traveling to the new location. Using xhost, I was able to do run the metatool program from the convenience of my own home.

The same general situation has occurred with several of the Linux machines that I currently maintain. Recently a large security hole was discovered in a distribution kernel and I needed to install a new kernel on the 15 or more Linux boxes that I maintain. Rather than attaching a monitor to each machine, since all were headless, I used the xhost command to export the xconfig menu to my own X display.

**CAUTION**

Like NFS, xhost does not provide the best security if you decide to make certain features available to others. Any network sharing or exporting is allowed at your own discretion.

Here are some simple steps to export remote applications to your own Linux system. In this example, you export linuxconf from a remote machine to your local machine.

1. Within your own X session, use telnet to switch to the machine that has the application that you want to export to your own local machine.

2. Become superuser by entering **su** on the remote machine.

3. Within the remote machine's terminal window, enter **export DISPLAY=\<your local machine's name\>:0.0**. For example, on my

remote machine, sequitur, I would enter the following to export applications to my own machine, quasi: **export DISPLAY=quasi.fortuna. org:0.0**.

4. As superuser in a window on your local machine, enter **xhost +**.

5. Within the remote machine's window, change directories to one that includes the executable for the application that you wish to run, by entering **cd /sbin**. In this directory you will find linuxconf.

6. Enter **./linuxconf** in the remote machine's window. A new GUI window should pop up on your local machine's display, allowing you to work with linuxconf from the remote machine.

This capability is especially helpful when you are at home and need to configure remote hard drives or when you want to use the xconfig command to recompile a kernel. Any application that uses a GUI or that depends upon X to run can be exported to another display. By using the command xhost +, you open up a large security hole. Any user can then export his or her applications to run on your display. This also means that he or she can also read or change your keystrokes. Use this utility with a large degree of caution.

Another alternative is to run xhost with the name of the host that you wish to connect to the X server:

```
# xhost +sequitur.fortuna.org
```

Be aware that this command still poses a potential security risk. Before you use the command, consider whether you feel that you can trust the users on your system.

## Mapping Linux Directories to Remote Machines

Once you feel comfortable with the various drives and devices that you can load onto Linux, you can go about serving files to other users on the network. Linux lends itself well as a *file server*, or location on which users can store company or educational data. The operating system hardly ever crashes, and can handle large amount of logins. Linux also performs true multitasking—that is, many users can work on the same file or upload or download files from the system simultaneously, while all this activity, thanks to applications such as SAMBA (as explained earlier in this chapter), remains transparent from other users' machines.

A good administrator realizes that not everyone will be as enthusiastic as you might be about Linux. Many are comfortable with the operating system on which they learned computing, which usually is Windows. Therefore, you need to be both diplomatic and flexible in helping those users gain access to the Linux file server. One of the best ways to assist these users is to map their Windows machines to Linux. This does not require a lot of effort, but will greatly assist those users in getting connected.

The first step to mapping your Windows users' machines to the shared Linux file server is to make sure that they have an account on the Linux box. Generally, you should give them the same name as that which they use to log in to their Windows box or, conversely, make sure that they log on to Windows using the same username that they use to log on to the Linux box.

A good practice is to use the first initial of a user's first name and then their full surname. For example, a standard abbreviation of Joe Smith's username would be jsmith. If your system has other users named Smith with the first initial of *J*, add a number to the end of the name. Jason Smith might then have the username jsmith1. You can, however, use middle names as well to differentiate the usernames. Many of these decisions are left to the administrator. Consult other users or administrators to formulate your own strategy.

Make sure that each user can now see his or her account on the Linux box. Click the Network Neighborhood icon and see whether the name of the Linux box along with a description appears in the window. If not, right-click the Network Neighborhood icon and perform a Find Computer search. If you still do not see the Linux box, restart the Windows machine and verify that you are logged in by the same name. Also, try restarting the SAMBA daemon on Linux:

```
# /etc/rc.d/init.d/smb restart
```

Though SAMBA is stable, if other Windows machines are on networks such as NT that are Master Browser–enabled, they can sometimes confuse the configuration.

Next, if the user is using Windows 98 or a more recent Windows release, click Start, Programs, Windows Explorer. Much like the older Program Manager of Windows 3.1, Windows Explorer enables you to peruse the contents of your Windows directories. Click View, Folder Options, then select the View tab and then make sure the option Show Map Network Drive Button in Toolbar is checked. Click OK to save the configuration.

On the toolbar, click the Map Drive button. Choose the drive letter you want to associate with the Linux box, and then under the Path option, enter the name of the Linux box and the username. For the user `joe` to connect to his account `joe` on the Linux box quasi, he would enter the following:

```
\\QUASI\joe
```

Select the Reconnect at Logon option button to ensure that this mapped drive reconnects when the Windows machine reboots. Click OK. You will first be prompted to enter a password to `joe`'s account before viewing the directories contents. If other users who will have access to this same mapped directory will use this machine, make sure that Windows does not save the password. The Save This Password in Your Password List option is best left unchecked each time that you log in. Once you have made the initial login, you will be granted unlimited access to that particular directory until either the Windows or Linux machine is rebooted or disconnected in another fashion. This unlimited access obviously opens a major security hole, but you probably should not store highly sensitive data on a network machine anyway.

This method of connecting Windows to Linux allows even the most distrusting users of Linux quick and easy access to shared files. By setting up a shared folder as well, multiple users can upload and exchange data and documents on a common source.

# Resolving Domain Names and IP Addresses

Two of the more important functions of Linux are name serving and resolving IP addresses. Linux is a popular platform for setting up a name server or DNS server. For most any network, Domain Name Servers are a must. They are the method by which domains convert the static IP addresses assigned to workstations, and servers back into a human-readable format. For example, the IP address 206.81.147.158 does not indicate what that particular server might be, but if you can resolve it to a domain such as www.gnuware.com, you have a better idea of what the server might be. A domain name is also easier to remember and pass along to others. Memorizing sets of IP numbers, each assigned to a domain, is not conducive to a dynamic Internet.

This section looks at setting up a basic name server on the Linux platform. The program used by most Linux servers that serves up the majority of name server inquiries on the Internet is BIND. Red Hat installs this program by default and provides for easy configuration. Though this section will not tackle all the vagaries associated with setting up a name service and configuring all the BIND options, it will explain how to set up BIND on a Linux box and begin hosting name services for your own or for others' domains.

## Registering a Name Service with a Root Server

The first step in performing name service for a domain is registering the name server with a root server. Root servers are those primary name servers that keep track of all DNS entries and domain names on the Internet. When performing a hostname lookup, all name servers eventually check these entries and domain names. Each name server eventually creates a large cache of IP addresses and domain names that allow it to perform quick local lookups. If a name server is stumped by an unfamiliar domain name, it can query name servers authoritative for that domain, i.c. those responsible for the .com, .net, .edu and .org domains, and pull down that information as well.

INTERNIC, now known as Network Solutions, was the first system set up to host DNS entries. This system hosted several root servers throughout the country. These root servers served as the primary location for most Internet addresses. INTERNIC hosted any domain ending in a .com, .net, or .org extension. If an organization wanted to create a new domain name, the managers of the root servers first had to approve the name; then an entry was created in the main database. These entries were then filtered down through localized name servers as requests were made for the new domain name.

Because Network Solutions no longer has exclusive rights to registering domain names, several other primary name servers have sprung up offering the same service. These name servers register domain names and host principal entries in their root servers for a lower cost while providing more attention to their clients. With increased competition from added servers, the cost of creating your own domain name and a presence on the Internet has dropped.

Before you can start your own host, you must first register your primary name server with one of these root servers. You normally register your primary and secondary name server in conjunction with your domain name. Depending on the number of servers your domain is offering and the different services of each, you would register a domain name and then the primary and secondary name servers in conjunction with the domain.

For example, if you were setting up a large domain with mail, Web, and DNS servers and perhaps a secure server and a virtual domain server available for customers, you would want to have separate machines hosting each of these services. Each would then have a unique name within the domain created.

For example, it is customary to name each server by its function. If a specific Linux box's purpose were to serve as a mail server, it would be called mail.domain.com. Likewise, a mail server within the gnuware.com domain would be mail.gnuware.com. The same is true of the Web server, which would be called web.gnuware.com or www.gnuware.com. If the gnuware.com domain provided virtual hosting, then the virtual server could be called hosting.gnuware.com.

However, some administrators feel that simply naming the box by its function is impersonal. It is also a good practice for security reasons to give the box a name for internal identification. Giving the box a name that reflects its function opens it up to security attacks. If you discovered an exploit that abused a security hole in the mail daemon that ran under Linux, the mail server would be open for attack due to its name. Therefore, giving the box an alias or CNAME (which you will learn about in the following sections covering BIND settings) allows others to identify the machine as an entity and not single it out by its use.

Naming Linux machines is entirely up to the administrator. When choosing a naming convention, opt for something that allows for multiple hosts. If you know that your network will have only a limited number of servers, you may choose a convention that has only a finite number of names, such as the planets in the solar system or the number of elements in the periodic table. If you expect the number of servers to grow, choose a paradigm that will grow with it. The Greek or Roman gods are a favorite among system administrators. Other paradigms include mountains, rivers, natural formations, fictional characters, famous people, stellar objects, cities, and any other grouping of people, places, or things.

I prefer Latin names for my personal servers and stellar names for the servers at work. In this manner I can identify my own machines by affixing a Latin term, which also denotes each machine's function, while distinguishing the machine's name from the star name attached to the work servers. The importance of the server correlates to the star's magnitude; for example, because of the Web server's relative importance, I might name it sirius or polaris. Each administrator can choose how he wants to name his or her servers. It is important, however, to keep the naming scheme consistent.

After registering with a root name server and setting up ns1.gnuware.com and ns2.gnuware.com to function as primary and secondary name servers for your domain, you can begin entering into your local name servers the names of the individual servers within your domain.

## Installing BIND

BIND is one of the most popular programs for hosting local DNS service. Established and supported by the Internet Software Consortium (ISC), BIND remains the easiest method for configuring Linux to run as a name server. Installing BIND is the simple part; configuring it to run properly is a bit more difficult. You can download the source code and compile the binary yourself from the main Web page (http://www.isc.org). Along with the code are instructions for setting up different options by which the code can be compiled.

The recommended method for setting up BIND is to download the RPM from the RPM repository home page (http://rufus.w3.org/Linux/RPM/ or http://www.rpmfind.net). Locate the latest BIND version and download the bind, bind-utils, and bind-devel packages. Install all of them by executing the following command as root in the same directory as the packages:

```
# rpm -ivh bind*
```

Once installed, these programs create a /var/named directory with a file containing a list of the root servers called named.ca and a sample localhost configuration file called named.local. You can use the latter file to generate additional configuration files for each of the servers on the local network. The program also installs a file called named.conf in your /etc directory. This file keeps track of all the domains hosted within your network, the primary and secondary name servers, the domains authorized to host and transfer domain name information, and the root servers file, known as named.ca or root.hints. If you are installing the latest BIND code from source, you will be provided with these files and will need to place them in the appropriate directory.

Once the program is fully installed, whether by RPM or by source, you can begin configuring a forwarding and reverse lookup DNS entry. You might create a template file for each and then substitute the necessary information when you add a new server.

## Configuring Forwarding Files

The forwarding file usually has the same name as the domain itself. It can be prefixed with db. or simply carry the name of the domain. Some examples include db.gnuware, gnuware.com, or db.gnuware.com. The *db* stands for *database*. Either method works, though preferences differ in the types of domains hosted by a server. For example, if a machine hosted the gnuware.com and the gnuware.org and gnuware.net domains, the first example would be insufficient for all three domains.

Within the forwarding file are certain abbreviations called *resource records*. These records assist the name server in determining certain file types and entries. Table 15.3 describes some sample resource records.

**Table 15.3  Sample Resource Records**

| Resource Record | Description |
| --- | --- |
| SOA record | Indicates the authority for all zone data |
| NS record | Lists all name servers for the zone |
| A record | Indicates name-to-address mapping |
| PTR record | Indicates address-to-name mapping |
| CNAME record | Provides the canonical name (for aliases) |
| MX record | Lists the mail server address |
| IN class | Provides the Internet address |

The forwarding file tracks all the names listed under a specific domain. For example, all the servers ending with the gnuware.com suffix, such as mail.gnuware.com, www.gnuware.com, and ns1.gnuware.com, would be listed in this directory under the CNAME (canonical names) record. Each entry is case-sensitive. Listing 15.7 shows a forwarding file template, db.gnuware, which I use when creating new entries.

**Listing 15.7  A Sample DNS Forwarding Entry for db.gnuware**

```
; =========================================================================
; NAMED RECORD FOR : gnuware.com
; ─────────────────────────────────────────────────
; Date:         Who:           What:
; ─────────────────────────────────────────────────
; 09/20/00      Kerry Cox    Create Primary db File
; =========================================================================


; ───────────────[ DOMAIN AUTHORITY ]───────────────-
@                 IN      SOA      ns1.gnuware.com.
hostmaster.gnuware.com (
                         2000092001        ; SERIAL  = (YYYYMMDDXX)
                         10800             ; REFRESH = Every 3 Hours
                         3600              ; RETRY   = After 1 Hour
                         604800            ; EXPIRE  = After 1 Week
                         86400             ; MINIMUM = TTL of 1 Day
                         )


; ───────────────[ NAME SERVERS ]───────────────--
IN        NS   ns1.gnuware.com.
IN        NS   ns2.gnuware.com.


; ───────────────[ MAIL SERVERS ]───────────────--
IN        MX 10       mail.gnuware.com.


; ───────────────[ CANONICAL NAMES ]───────────────
              IN      A        205.82.148.20
mail          IN      A        205.82.148.10
hosting       IN      A        205.82.148.15
secure        IN      A        205.82.148.12
ns1           IN      A        205.82.148.254
ns2           IN      A        205.82.148.253
localhost     IN      A        127.0.0.1


; ───────────────[ HOST ALIASES ] ───────────────
www           IN      CNAME        gnuware.com.
web           IN      CNAME        gnuware.com.
```

```
antares        IN       CNAME       ns1
polaris        IN       CNAME       mail
```

Unlike other scripts, which use a pound sign (#) to preface commented lines, this script uses a semicolon,. Each section provides a simple label that indicates the purpose of each record entry. It is a good habit to include a change record at the top of the file so that anyone redoing the record or making an additional entry can see what the preceding person did. Change records are also helpful for troubleshooting purposes in case the named daemon dies or fails to restart after you send it an HUP signal.

Under the Domain Authority section, you should keep the serial number as up-to-date as possible. Some administrators like to use the current date and then increment the last number when a change is made. This way the data are forwarded to other name servers when they do a lookup on your domain. If the serial number is not incremented properly or is done out of order, you will see an error message in the /var/log/messages file. Also, any changes that you have made to the file will not be propagated to other DNS servers. The worst-case scenario is that other hosts throughout the Internet will be unable to see your site. The numbers below the serial number determine how long your domain information will be cached on other DNS servers.

The Name Servers section tracks the name servers and to whom they should look for additional DNS information. The Mail Servers section lists any mail servers and prioritizes each according to importance. You can create backup mail servers by listing them below the main entry and giving them a higher number and thus lessening their priority.

In the Canonical Names section, you list any other servers that use the gnuware.com suffix. As shown in Listing 15.8, the prefix is listed in the first column and the gnuware.com suffix is added to the name when a lookup is performed.

In the Host Aliases section, you can affix additional names to the canonical server names. For instance, if you want to look up www.gnuware.com, you can enter **gnuware.com**. The site ns1.gnuware.com is also known as antares. gnuware.com via the CNAME entry recorded in the db file. Rather than having to type in the full hostname every time when attempting a Telnet session to this machine, the simple command **telnet antares** will also establish a connection to the same box. This only works when on the same network or if the full hostname of the other machine is entered in the /etc/hosts file on the client side.

# Configuring Reverse Entries

Reverse DNS entries provide a means of looking up a domain name by IP address. Rather than looking for a specific domain, if you know the IP address of the box in question, you can then find out the domain name attached to that IP address. These files are usually cataloged by the class IP address. For example, based on the configuration discussed in the preceding section, the name of the reverse file containing gnuware.com would be db.205.82.148. In this manner, the IP address is mapped to the proper domain name.

Another important file in addition to the default reverse IP file resides within the /var/named directory: the db.127.0.0 or localhost lookup file. This file provides the name server with a localhost entry. The syntax is nearly the same as that of the script shown in Listing 15.7, except that this script provides a Reverse Names section instead of a Canonical Names section. Substituting for the hostname is the last number, in this case 1, which then becomes 127.0.0.1. This is usually the first line of the configuration file that specifies specific IP addresses.

Here is the line as it would appear in the db.127.0.0 file:

```
1                       IN      PTR        localhost.
```

Be certain to include a dot or period after the end of `localhost`. This entry maps the address to the name of the server.

The file for your class C domain, such as 205.82.148, might have the entries indicated in Listing 15.8.

**Listing 15.8  A Sample DNS Reverse Entry
for the 206.81.148 Class C Domain**

```
;======================================================================
; REVERSE RECORD FOR :205.82.148
;  ----------------------------------------------------
; Date:          Who:              What:
;  ----------------------------------------------------
; 09/20/00       Kerry Cox         Updated DNS Entries
; 09/25/00       Kerry Cox         Added new servers
;
;======================================================================
```

```
;  ───────────────[ DOMAIN AUTHORITY ]───────────────-
148.82.205.in-addr.arpa.    IN    SOA    ns1.gnuware.com.
hostmaster.gnuware.com. (
                    2000092500         ; SERIAL  = (YYYYMMDDXX)
                    10800              ; REFRESH = Every 3 Hours
                    3600               ; RETRY   = After 1 Hour
                    604800             ; EXPIRE  = After 1 Week
                    86400              ; MINIMUM = TTL of 1 Day
                    )


;  ───────────────-[ NAME SERVERS ]───────────────-
                    IN    NS    ns1.gnuware.com.
IN          NS    ns2.gnuware.com.


;  ───────────────-[ REVERSE NAMES ]───────────────
10            IN    PTR    mail.gnuware.com.
;11           IN    PTR    available
12            IN    PTR    secure.gnuware.com.
;13           IN    PTR    available
;14           IN    PTR    available
15            IN    PTR    hosting.gnuware.com.
20            IN    PTR    www.gnuware.com.
253           IN    PTR    ns2.gnuware.com.
254           IN    PTR    ns1.gnuware.com.
```

Much like the forwarding file, this file simply lists the domain names and their respective IP addresses. However, immediately under the Domain Authority section, the in-addr.arpa entry lists the class C in reverse order. Because DNS lookups start from the end and work their way back to the beginning or largest number, reversing the numbering assists in providing the correct format.

As in the preceding localhost entry, in the db.206.81.148 file, there must be a period at the end of every domain name listed in the Reverse Names section. Any available IP address is commented out for later use.

## Editing the named.conf File

The last important file needed to configure name service successfully is the /etc/named.conf file (see Listing 15.9). The formatting for this file requires specific characters and indentation. Tabs are the best method of ensuring compatibility throughout the file.

**Listing 15.19 A Sample /etc/named.conf File Listing Primary Reverse and Forward Entries**

```
// ——————————————————————————
//                              NAMED.CONF ( BIND VERSION 8 )
// ——————————————————————————


options {
directory "/var/named";
allow-transfer {
205.82.148/24;   //our domain
205.82.149/24;   //our domain
205.82.148.253; //secondary dns server
};
};


// ——————————————————————————
//                              ROOT HINTS
// ——————————————————————————

zone "." {
type hint;
file }root.hints};
};


// ——————————————————————————
//                              REVERSE ENTRIES

zone "148.82.205.in-addr.arpa" {
type master;
file "205.82.148";
};
```

```
zone "149.82.205.in-addr.arpa" {
type master;
file "205.82.148";
};
zone "0.0.127.in-addr.arpa" {
type master;
file "127.0.0";
};


// ————————————————————————
//                         PRIMARY FORWARD ENTRIES
// ————————————————————————


zone "bonneville.com" {
type master;
file "bonneville.com";
};
zone "gnuware.com" {
type master;
file "gnuware.com";
};
zone "ksl.com" {
type master;
file "ksl.com";
};
```

Each of these entries points back to the main directory listed on the top of the file, /var/named. You can separate the files into unique directories by creating a /var/named/zone directory and storing the files there. Just make certain that the directory variable under options points to that same file.

Name servers are sometimes the first machines to get hacked by malicious users. Once you control someone's DNS, you can point their page anywhere. BIND has also had a notorious history for allowing exploits. Be certain that you are running the very latest BIND version and that your options section defines IP ranges that can allow DNS transfers. In the preceding example, the script allows only servers within the two class C ranges and the secondary DNS to have DNS transfers.

You must add to this file every new domain for which you do DNS hosting. The same applies to the secondary DNS server, which has similar listings but points to the primary DNS for all its files (see Listing 15.10).

### Listing 15.10  A Sample /etc/named.conf from the Secondary DNS Server

```
// generated by named-bootconf.pl

options {
directory "/var/named";
allow-transfer {
205.82.148/24;   //our domain
205.82.149/24;   //our domain
205.82.148.254; //primary dns server
};

/*
* If there is a firewall between you and name servers you want
* to talk to, you might need to uncomment the query-source
* directive below.  Previous versions of BIND always asked
* questions using port 53, but BIND 8.1 uses an unprivileged
* port by default.
*/
// query-source address * port 53;
};

// ------------------------------------------------
// ROOT HINTS
// ------------------------------------------------

zone "." {
type hint;
file "root.hints";
}
;// ------------------------------------------------
```

```
// SECONDARY REVERSE ENTRIES
// ————————————————————————————--

zone "148.82.205.in-addr.arpa" {
type slave;
file "205.82.148";
masters {
205.82.148.254;
};
};
zone "149.82.205.in-addr.arpa" {
type slave;
file "205.82.149";
masters {
205.82.148.254;
};
};
zone "0.0.127.in-addr.arpa" {
type slave;
file "127.0.0";
masters {
205.82.148.254;
};
};
// ————————————————————————————-
// SECONDARY FORWARD ENTRIES
// ————————————————————————————-
zone "bonneville.com" {
type slave;
file "bonneville.com";
masters {
205.82.148.254;
};
};
zone "gnuware.com" {
```

```
type slave;
file "gnuware.com";
masters {
205.82.148.254;
};
};
zone "ksl.com" {
type slave;
file "ksl.com";
masters {
205.82.148.254;
};
};
```

Like the /etc/named.conf file on the primary server that points to the secondary server for allowable transfers, the configuration file on ns2.gnuware.com points to the primary DNS server, 205.82.148.254. Each forwarding entry also looks to the primary server for information regarding domain names and IP addresses.

If the primary server becomes unavailable for any reason, the secondary server can then provide the necessary information to any hosts with ns1 and ns2 for their primary and secondary name servers. Name server redundancy is crucial when many networked systems are attempting to resolve IP addresses or look up certain domains.

## Starting the Named Daemon

If you are running the RPM version of BIND, you should start the named daemon, which constantly runs in the background, as an automated process. As with most daemons under the Red Hat release, there is an entry in /etc/rc.d/init.d that is configured to start the named daemon upon bootup. Starting and stopping the named daemon take the same syntax as most other daemons:

```
# /etc/rc.d/init.d/named start|stop|restart
```

If you make any changes to the db files, you not only need to increment the serial number, but also restart the named daemon. A similar option is to issue the ndc reload command. Make sure the ndc executable is in your path.

As always, you can also use the ps command to locate the PID number of the named process and then send it an HUP signal. If you do not wish to use the Red Hat daemon manager to restart the daemon, determine the PID of the named process by entering the following command:

```
# ps aux | grep named
named       789  0.0 10.9  8596 6888 ?           S     Jul20   4:33
named -u named
```

The user named will own the process, and its PID will be in the second column of the output as shown.

Restart the process by sending it the following command as root:

```
# kill -HUP 789
```

You can also send the same kill command to the named.pid file, which contains the PID of the running process. Under Red Hat Linux, this PID is located in the /var/run directory.

```
# kill -HUP 'cat /var/run/named.pid'
```

Both commands send the daemon a hang-up signal and cause the daemon to reread its configuration files.

## Using the nslookup Command

When you are doing any sort of queries regarding domain names or IP addresses, a useful utility that comes with the BIND program is nslookup. Short for *name server lookup*, this command can query name servers on your own system or name servers elsewhere. After you provide the domain name or IP address, the command can help resolve it to the IP address or domain name, depending on the variable that you request.

Any user can invoke the nslookup command. Simply enter **nslookup** at the command line. The display will then show the default name server and its IP address. Type in the IP address or domain name of the server in question. If that domain exists within the name server cache on the local box, you will see the domain name and its respective address.

If the IP address is cached or if the named daemon has not recently queried the server hosting that domain name, the nslookup command will respond with a *nonauthoritative answer*. This means that the time to live (TTL) for the domain has expired and the result pulled from the cache is no longer authoritative. The domain's IP address may have changed in the meantime. However, the IP address the nslookup command returned is what was pulled from that box's cache.

To change to another server and verify that the IP address received is valid elsewhere, enter the following command: **server <server name>**. Here is how a sample nslookup session may look when querying:

```
[kjcox@ns1 kjcox]$ nslookup
Default Server:  ns1.gnuware.com
Address:  205.82.148.254

> 205.82.148.20
Server:  ns1.gnuware.com
Address:  205.82.148.254

Name:     gnuware.com
Address:  205.82.148.20

> server ns1.vii.com
Default Server:  ns1.vii.com
Address:  206.71.77.2

>
```

Any name server queries will now ask ns1.vii.com for IP addresses or additional information rather than the local networked name server, ns1.gnuware.com. This is a viable alternative if your local name server is not correctly caching hostnames. You can use nslookup for troubleshooting your configuration.

To look up the MX or mail server records for a particular domain, enter the following at the nslookup prompt:

```
> set q=mx
> gnuware.com
```

The output of this command will be similar to the following:

```
Server:   ns1.gnuware.com
Address:  205.82.148.10

gnuware.com        preference = 10, mail exchanger = mail.gnuware.com
gnuware.com        nameserver = ns1.gnuware.com
gnuware.com        nameserver = ns2.gnuware.com
ns1.gnuware.com    internet address = 205.82.148.254
ns2.gnuware.com    internet address = 205.82.148.253
```

To set the type to be even more verbose, enter the following to extract more information from the queried name server:

```
> set q=any
```

You will find nslookup to be a useful tool when resolving IP addresses to domain names. To quit nslookup, enter **exit**. Entering **quit** will only return a "nonexistant host/domain" response. The nslookup utility will attempt to resolve the variable `quit` to a host or domain. You can also press Ctrl-D to stop the utility.

# Serving Up Web Pages

One of the most frequently used tools under Linux is Apache. Apache is probably the most popular Web daemon currently available for Linux. In fact, this tool is perhaps the prime reason that many burgeoning administrators even install Linux on a network machine. Apache enables them to try their hand at creating their own unique Web site or to host other *virtual Web sites*—sites that have domain names other than that of the local machine's hostname. Apache comes installed by default under Red Hat Linux, even when the most minimal options are selected. Adding content to the default Web page is both quick and simple with Apache.

This section examines the basics for loading Apache on a Red Hat server and configuring it to meet your most fundamental needs. The section will look at some of the configuration settings for optimizing your machine and also explain how to install a secure server for doing e-commerce across the Internet. Because the topic of Apache could easily fill up an entire chapter covering all the nuances of its system, this chapter will simply cover the most basic settings.

If you wish to run a basic Web site, the standard RPM installation is sufficient to accomplish nearly any task. However, if you want to incorporate additional modules or programs such as PHP or MySQL databases into the setup, installing Apache from source code is the best option. Because so many of the systems at my office require *PHP scripting*, one method of incorporating database files into dynamic Web content, I often opt to install Apache from source. Try both using the RMP install and installing from source at least once to see which method you prefer.

## Installing the Apache RPMs

If the default installation has not already installed or updated the RPM packages, you can do so by locating the latest binaries from the RPM Repository site (http://rufus.w3.org/Linux/RPM/ or as it is now known http://www.rpmfind. net/). The key files are apache, apache-devel, and apache-manual. The last two files are not necessary but provide some valuable functionality if you want to develop the program further or read about Apache's technical aspects.

Installation requires entering the following command as root in the same directory as that of the RPM files:

```
# rpm -ivh apache*
```

Or, if you want to update to the latest Apache release, enter the following:

```
# rpm -Uvh apache*
```

Apache installs the httpd.conf configuration file in the /etc/httpd/conf/ directory. Older Apache releases included two additional files that required editing; srm.conf and access.conf. The latest Apache distribution consolidates these three configuration files into one. Here you can edit Apache's root directory, determine how it handles httpd requests, and tweak a host of other configurable variables. The default variables already installed require little or no tweaking to operate.

The standard RPM install also creates a /home/httpd/ directory containing its respective cgi-bin/ and html/ directories. In the former, you can place CGI scripts that process perl or CGI requests from the Web pages. The html/ directory holds all static HTML Web pages. You place all *.html or *.htm files in this directory.

# Installing the Apache Daemon from Source

If you are installing Apache from source, the method is similar. The following steps are required to set up and configure Apache to run on a standard Linux machine successfully:

1. Download and unzip the Apache source code into a standard directory such as /usr/local or /usr/local/etc. I prefer the latter directory because that is the one in which older Apache releases were customarily installed.

2. Create a symbolic link between the expanded directory, such as apache-1.3.xx/, and a directory named apache/. To do this, change to the directory holding the expanded Apache files, then enter **ln -s apache-1.3.12 apache**.

3. Change to the new Apache directory, then go to the directory titled src/ if you want to do the long manual installation (which is recommended) and then customize the file named Configuration.

4. If you wish to try the latest method, which resembles other source code compilation processes, remain in the same Apache directory and enter the following sequence of commands: **./configure --prefix=<prefix> ; make ; make install ; <prefix>/bin/apachectl start**, replacing <prefix> with the Linux file system path under which Apache should be installed. For example, use /usr/local/apache or /usr/local/etc/apache.

5. There may not be much to change in the Configuration file, but look carefully through the file's contents for any additional modules you may wish to enable.

6. In the same directory, enter **./Configure**

7. Enter **make**.

8. After the make command executes, you will have an executable file called httpd in that same directory. Copy the file down one level into the Apache root directory by entering **cp httpd ../**.

9. Customize the httpd.conf file located in the conf/ directory. You will want to tailor this file to your server's specifications and needs.

10. To start up the server, enter the following (your system might require a different command): **/usr/local/etc/apache/httpd -f /usr/local/etc/apache/conf/httpd.conf**.

11. Test to make sure that the system is running by opening your base URL on a browser. For a machine named quasi.gnuware.com, for example, you would type the following URL in any browser window: **http://quasi.gnuware.com/**.

12. You can also verify that the httpd daemon is running via the command line, by entering the following command: **ps -ef | grep root | grep http**.

Remember that your home html directory will no longer be /home/httpd/html/. If you installed everything as described in the preceding steps, you will find that your root html directory is in /usr/local/etc/apache/htdocs/.

You will also want to modify your /etc/rc.d/init.d/httpd run command file. If you are impatient, copy the apache/bin/apachectl file to /etc/rc.d/init.d/ and rename it httpd. You should back up the original file first in case you later decide to use the older RPM Web daemon.

In the same root Apache directory you will also find the new cgi-bin/, conf/, and logs/ directories. Consult the Apache man pages for any additional information regarding system configuration. By following the preceding steps, you will be able to configure a new Web server from scratch and compile in any other modules or variables as needed.

## Securing the Web Server for E-Commerce

If you want to do any sort of secure transactions via the Internet, such as gathering credit card numbers and protecting them from prying eyes, you will probably need to set up encrypted Web pages using Apache. Though you can purchase various programs that will make your pages *encrypted* or enable the padlock icon on your Netscape Web browser, there are free modules that you can compile into your Apache Web daemon just as easily.

The only cost you might incur for setting up a secure site is the price of a secure certificate from one of two trusted sources: VeriSign and Thawte. Since it recently acquired Thawte, VeriSign now controls over 95 percent of the market for secure certificates. Though the two companies have merged, Thawte still offers certificates of the same quality as that of VeriSign, but at nearly a third of VeriSign's price.

Here are the programs that you will need, in addition to the latest Apache source code, to enable secure Web pages:

◆ OpenSSL-0.9.5 or the latest equivalent version. OpenSSL was based originally on SSLeay, a similar program that will also suffice, but encryption advocates now endorse OpenSSL. It is currently available at http://www.openssl.org/.

◆ Apache-SSL or Apache_1.3.12+ssl_1.xx. This is a series of files and directories that are placed within the main Apache directory after compiling Apache initially. They are available at http://apache-ssl.org/.

## Installing OpenSSL

To install the OpenSSL utility, follow these steps:

1. Download the latest version of OpenSSL. Currently, the latest version is openssl-0.9.6. This is subject to change, as development proceeds rapidly.

2. Unzip the file in the same directory as that of apache/. Although you can choose a different directory, storing the file in this directory is convenient. I placed the file in /usr/local/etc/ since this is where I am accustomed to placing Apache from earlier installs and because I prefer keeping my own /usr/local directory uncluttered. The /usr/local directory is the recommended location for the current Apache release.

3. Change to the new openssl directory just created, then enter the following command: ./**config**.

4. Enter **make**.

5. Before you install your newly created binary, you should always test it to ensure that it will not mess up any files. Enter **make test**.

6. If your binary passes the test, enter **make install**. This command installs all the necessary files and directories into the /usr/local/ssl directory. You can change this option by adding a prefix to the make command, but, as always, you should use the default instead because developers base most of their configuration on the default settings.

7. Generate some keys and test csr files either to generate your own certificate or procure one from a certificate authority such as VeriSign or Thawte. See the following section to learn how to generate keys and csr files.

## Generating Keys and csr Files

After you correctly install OpenSSL, you can begin generating a key and a csr. Either you or a CA will use these files to create a signed certificate.

Save the key file in a safe place, because you will need it later; if you lose it, you will be out money. You should burn the key onto a CD or other permanent storage medium and then store it in a safe place.

To generate the keys and csr files, follow these steps:

1. Enter **cd /usr/local/ssl/private**.
2. To generate the key file, place about five simple text files into the directory. They will assist in making the key. To create the files, enter the following: **/usr/local/ssl/bin/openssl genrsa -des3 -rand file1:file2:file3:file4:file5 1024 > quasi.gnuware.com.key**. This command creates a key file for a server named quasi. You can substitute any filenames that you choose.
3. After generating the key, secure it in a safe place. Again, if you lose the key, you will be out of money.
4. Now create a PEM phrase. This is a personal phrase or character sequence that will identify you to the server. It operates much like any password in that you must type in the correct set of characters in order for the secure server to start up. Keep this phrase safe. It will be required both for filling out the csr and for starting up the secure daemon.
5. Enter **cd ../certs**.
6. Now create a csr that you will use to submit to the CA for a signed certificate. To do so, enter the following command: **/usr/local/ssl/bin/openssl req -new -key ../private/quasi.gnuware.com.key > quasi.gnuware.com.csr**.
7. You are prompted not only to enter your PEM phrase, a unique text string known only to you, but to also enter detailed information about your company, organization, contact person, and e-mail address. Be sure

to keep this information documented as well, since you will need to reproduce it again exactly as you have typed it here if you choose to renew your certificate after the year is over.

# Installing Apache-SSL

To set up the Apache-SSL module, you must recompile the Apache source code. This is yet another reason that you should install Apache from source. You can purchase and install the latest Apache RPM that comes with the Red Hat Professional release, but for administrators with limited budgets or those who download the Red Hat distribution from the Internet, compiling the required programs from source is more economical.

To configure and install the SSL module, follow these steps:

1. Compile OpenSSL correctly as described in the preceding section.
2. Download the latest release of Apache.
3. Unpack Apache into a different directory. For the regular version, enter **/usr/local/etc/apache/**; for the secure version, enter **/usr/local/etc/apache-ssl/**.
4. Enter **cd apache-ssl/**.
5. Unpack the apache+ssl file in the new directory, apache-ssl/.
6. Run the file patch ./FixPatch and choose **y**.
7. Make certain that your version of apache+ssl corresponds to the Apache release that you are running. If not, the FixPatch executable will fail.
8. Enter **cd /usr/local/etc/apache-ssl/src/**.
9. Edit the file named Configuration. You shouldn't need to make too many changes here. My Configuration file looks like the following:

```
EXTRA_CFLAGS=
EXTRA_LDFLAGS=
EXTRA_LIBS=
EXTRA_INCLUDES=
EXTRA_DEPS=

#CC=     gcc
#CPP=
#OPTIM=
```

```
#RANLIB=

TARGET=httpsd

#
# SSL Related stuff. N.B. This is set up to use the SSLeay
source, NOT an
# installed version.
#
#KEYNOTE_BASE=/home/ben/work/KeyNote
SSL_BASE=/usr/local/etc/openssl-0.9.6
SSL_INCLUDE= -I$(SSL_BASE)/include
SSL_CFLAGS= -DAPACHE_SSL
SSL_LIB_DIR= $(SSL_BASE)
SSL_LIBS= -L$(SSL_LIB_DIR) -lssl -lcrypto
SSL_APP_DIR= $(SSL_BASE)/apps
  SSL_APP=/usr/local/etc/openssl-0.9.6/apps/openssl
```

10. Run the ./Configure routine.

11. Enter **make**.

12. After the make command executes, you should copy your binary file to the same location as you copied the httpd file earlier. Enter **cp httpd ../**.

## Editing the httpsd.conf Configuration

Like the httpd.conf file set up previously and used for configuring the regular apache Web daemon, there should be another httpsd.conf file, which determines how the secure Web daemon runs. In the httpsd.conf file you will have to specify a particular port number. Unlike the regular httpd daemon, which runs under port 80, secure Web transactions operate through port 443. It is here in this file that you can make these particular modifications.

The following list explains how to properly install the secure Web daemon configuration.

1. Copy the selected lines as shown below from the sample OpenSSL/httpd.conf file and add them to the httpsd.conf file listed in /usr/local/etc/apache-ssl/conf/.

**2.** Add these lines to the end of the file, since Apache reads things from the beginning to the end with the latter settings overriding the previous:

```
SSLEnable
SSLCacheServerPath          src/modules/ssl/gcache
SSLCacheServerPort          logs/gcache_port

SSLCertificateFile          /usr/local/ssl/certs/thawte_test.cert
SSLCertificateKeyFile       /usr/local/ssl/private/quasi.
                            gnuware.com.key

SSLVerifyClient    0
SSLVerifyDepth     2

SSLSessionCacheTimeout    300
```

**3.** Check the httpsd.conf file on a working server and determine what you need to change. You may have to change the port number to 443 rather than port 80.

**4.** Start up the secure server by issuing the following command: **/usr/local/etc/apache-ssl/httpsd -f /usr/local/etc/apache-ssl/conf/httpsd.conf.**

**5.** Enter your PEM phrase when prompted.

If all seems well after you have completed these steps, you will be able to encode Web pages and transmit the information securely to yourself or others for processing.

# Conclusion

Now that you can set up network connections, you will be eager to create similar dial-up connections using your modem or cable-modem or any other device that connects to an ISP or another Linux box providing Internet connectivity. The next chapter will also look at the various programs used on Linux to connect to the Internet. Much like the many freeware programs that are available to Windows users, a plethora of Linux applications provides the same functionality for users of Linux, whether within an X session or on the console.

# Chapter 16

## Internet Connectivity

The preceding chapter dealt with configuring LAN Internet connections. Setting up valid IP addresses requires both capital and a purpose, and not all Linux users can afford to give themselves a viable static IP address. In cases such as these, there must be some other method to provide a valid address with which to connect to the Internet or to other networks. This chapter will look at setting up a modem connection and establishing links between home and office use. Learning to connect individual machines with limited bandwidth to each other is the precedent here, as well as optimizing the Linux software currently available to establish connectivity from smaller networks to larger ones.

The following topics will be dealt with in this chapter.

◆ Setting up a modem under Linux

◆ Creating a stand-alone PPP server

◆ Allowing multiple machine to optimize one connection using *ipchains*

◆ Selected firewalling issues

◆ Configuring browsers for Internet use

◆ Using basic FTP commands and retrieving information remotely

# Using Dial-Up Connections

Though the popularity of increased bandwidth to the home is increasing and more regular users are setting up DSL (Dedicated Server Line), cable modems, and ISDN lines, there still remains the regular user who can afford only a dial-up modem connection. Modems still comprise the large majority of user connectivity to the Internet as attested by the popularity of free hosting services and commercial ISPs (Internet Service Providers) that rely upon home computers and the standard modem in order to connect to their service.

As Linux grows in popularity and more people replace the default operating system with their own Linux flavor, there will be an increased need for easy modem configurations under Linux. In addition, once those machines are connected they can be used for establishing other networked machines to the Internet via IP masquerading all with one simple modem connection. This boon is not without its perils. As more and more people use their machines to connect to the Internet from their home and as their connectivity time increases, some people will exploit any security hole and compromise unsuspecting machines. This chapter will also deal with keeping out the most intrusive attacks for those with 24/7 connectivity. For more information on enhancing Linux security, see Chapter 19.

## Deciding on a Linux Modem

Now that you have installed Linux and have toyed with the various features included with the system, you will most likely want to gather more information and start sharing what you have learned. One of the best ways to get connected with others, aside from networking with local users, is to use a modem to connect to the Internet. This means you can access e-mail, read and post to newsgroups, use Telnet and FTP to communicate with other servers, and, most importantly for many Linux users, browse Internet sites.

To dispel some myths perpetrated by the competition, Linux provides as many, if not more, Internet access resources as other operating systems do. In fact, the latest statistics place Linux as the Web site provider of choice. The rest use Solaris, another UNIX off-shoot, and then Microsoft's IIS server.

For most purposes, a regular run-of-the-mill modem will work just fine, but you should take a few precautions for Linux. Currently, you are advised not to purchase or use a WinModem. WinModems are designed for use with Windows and these specific types of modems require a proprietary operating system to access the drivers necessary for normal operation.

There are two different types of modems: a hardware-driven modem, and a software-enabled modem. WinModems fall into the latter category. Because most WinModem manufacturers have not released the code necessary to run their specific modems, Linux developers cannot write specific drivers for the modem into the kernel. An effort is under way to port these software driven modems to Linux, but for now users are advised to shy away from installing on a Linux machine any hardware that is designed specifically to run only under Windows.

---

### NOTE

PCTel has written a software driver, specifically an HSP emulator, for WinModem specific chipsets. Lucent has also released a driver for its WinModems, too, but according to its documentation, it is available only for Red Hat Linux and not for any other distributions of Linux. These two companies currently constitute the body of research being done to export WinModems to Linux.

## Comparing External and Internal Modems

It is far easier to buy a hardware-driven modem, which has all the necessary drivers built into the system. Linux queries the modem, sends it the necessary commands, then establishes the handshaking and connections. You can choose two types of hardware-driven modems: the external and the internal. Each has its advantages and disadvantages. Most people seem to prefer the external modem since it is easy to access, it can be powered on and off, and it frees up an ISA or PCI slot on the motherboard. The latter advantage can be crucial if slots are limited and there are several other peripheral devices. An internal modem is appealing for some since it does not require external input or power to turn it on or off, it frees up a COM port, and it is generally cheaper than an external modem.

Linux seems more compatible with external modems, and it is easier to transfer these modems among machines. (The latter issue becomes a moot point after you learn about IP Masquerading and how one Linux modem can be shared among several computers.) Internal modems work just as well. It is important, in some instances, that you are able to configure the IRQ and COM port either by hand or in the BIOS settings. Though Linux now supports a limited version of "Plug and Play," it is always nice to be able to switch the settings on the card itself, if needed. However, most modems already have a reserved range of memory addresses and IRQ numbers dedicated for their use.

The brand or model of modems to purchase is not integral to configuring it to work successfully with Linux. I have several US Robotics or USR 33.6 modems that I use both at home and at work, and all function adequately under Linux. In fact, in my experience, the latest Windows release lacks the basic drivers for installing this particular make and model of modem and identifies it only as a generic modem. On older Windows machines, I must download the specific drivers for the modem to work correctly. Linux, however, has no problem seeing my model modem and assigning it the required settings. Linux also tends to connect at a slightly higher rate than Windows does using the same modem.

If you are looking to purchase a modem for use under Linux, you should consider a brand name. Brand name modems tend to be more reliable, and most recognizable names offer some degree of warranty. Some generic brands have proven to be flaky in my experience. I have personally tried US Robotics, 3Com, Zoom, and Cardinal modems on various Linux machines, and all have worked well. Check the manufacturer's site before making any purchases and verify that they do indeed support Linux.

## Manually Configuring a Modem under Linux

Two accepted methods are currently in use for setting up two-way networking between your machine (the *client*), and the machine at your local Internet service provider (ISP)(the *host*). One is better known as Point-to-Point Protocol (PPP) and the other is Serial Line Internet Protocol (SLIP). PPP has become the preferred method of communication between two computers, because it is faster and works well with other LAN protocols such as TCP/IP. Implementation of multiple protocols is especially useful when allowing your Linux box to talk to other machines on a LAN network while retaining a dial-up connection via PPP to another ISP. SLIP is still used today for dial-up connections, although it has become more common for connecting two computers through a serial connection—hence its name's reference to serial lines.

Setting up PPP is often the most intimidating aspect to configuring Linux properly. Fortunately, many of the default interfaces that come with Red Hat also have simple walkthrough configurations that help set up the Linux connections. You can still accomplish the same task by hand, but Linux provides a couple of other options that make the process extremely simple. It has quickly become as easy as setting up a dial-up connection under Windows.

This section examines three different methods of configuring a PPP connection to an ISP. The first is by editing the files by hand. The second is by using the netcfg utility that comes with the control panel utility under the Red Hat Linux distribution. As shown in Chapter 15, netcfg can configure several different types of network devices, including PPP. The third method is to use one of the many PPP dial-up tools now available. Gnome comes with a Dialup Configuration Tool and a PPP dialer that enables you to create a new Internet connection and then connect to your ISP when you are finished. This section also looks at KPPP, a dial-up tool distributed by the KDE desktop environment. Both utilities by Gnome and KDE are very good examples and will be used in this section's examples. Several other utilities that accomplish the same task and are mentioned in this section as well.

## Verifying PPP

First, make certain that PPP is installed on your system. Most types of installation methods under Red Hat install PPP by default. This includes pppd or the PPP daemon, which controls PPP and runs in the background during your period of connectivity. To verify that the protocol is indeed installed, simply issue the RPM command as follows:

```
# rpm -q ppp
ppp-2.3.11-7
```

The exact version number may vary from release to release. If the program has not been installed, which in the most recent Red Hat version is unlikely, you may either choose the source or binary. You should use the RPM method for purposes of updating and keeping a uniform format throughout your system.

Again, installing the latest version is a simple matter of executing the rpm command as root along with the filename:

```
# rpm -ivh ppp*.rpm
```

You can install PPP using the source code, but doing so is not recommended. There are too many possible configurations and it is easy to foul up the settings and quickly become discouraged.

## Aliasing the Modem to Its Device

To avoid the headaches associated with device names under Linux, Red Hat recommends making a symbolic link from the true device name to a more identifiable designation. For example, under DOS, the modem normally connects to COM2 or COM4, while sometimes reserving COM1 for the mouse. The same is also valid under Linux, except that you connect the modem to /dev/ttyS0 through /dev/ttys3 rather than COM2 or COM4. Remember that under Linux and UNIX, counting begins with zero. Thus, /dev/ttyS0 is saved for the mouse and /dev/ttyS1 can be allocated to the modem. A recommended method of identifying these files is to give the real device a more recognizable name. Creating a symbolic link is the preferred method:

```
# ln -s /dev/ttyS1 /dev/modem
```

This example creates a new filename, /dev/modem, that links to the real device. If you need to change modems later or edit the COM settings, you can replace this file with the correct settings.

Another method of creating this link without having to create the link by hand is to use the modemtool utility found under the control panel. You can either run modemtool separately or execute it from under its parent utility, the control panel. Here you can select the device or serial port to which your modem connects. As stated in the upper section of the screen (see Figure 16.1), the utility simply creates a link from /dev/modem to your actual device.

For many users, this method is the simpler way to identify your modem and configure its settings rather than creating the symbolic links manually.

## Editing Modem Files by Hand

Once you have verified that PPP is installed and your modem is properly configured, you can now begin to edit the necessary files to connect your machine to an outside machine. Be sure to do all editing as root. Take the same precautions as you would when altering any file. Back up a file that you are changing if you feel that that you cannot either quickly recover it or the restore its settings. Backing up simply entails copying over the file with a *.bak or *.dist extension:

```
# cp /etc/resolv.conf /etc/resolv.conf.dist
```

For the most part, these files are relatively small and easy to restore to their former state. Creating backup copies is a good habit to begin. After verifying things still function after you are done making changes, you can replace that backup with a similar file and add a *.golden extension, signifying it is a valid changed file.

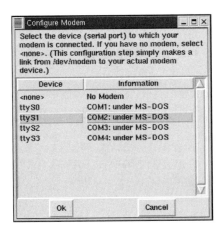

**FIGURE 16.1**

*The modemtool utility, which detects and configures your modem's device name.*

Whenever you connect to the Internet through a dial-up connection, the outside world not only becomes transparent to you—that is, you can now browse and view other sites—but you also become transparent to others. If your ports are not correctly closed or if you do not have the necessary security patches in place, anyone with a functioning packet sniffer or port scanner can quickly compromise your Linux machine. You should take the following precautionary measures:

1. Place the following in your /etc/hosts.deny file. If you do not have this file, create it. You probably already have tcp_wrappers installed, as it installs by default with the latest Red Hat releases, and this file requires tcp_wrappers in order to work.

   ```
   ALL: ALL
   ```

2. Type the following in your /etc/hosts.allow file:

   ```
   ALL: LOCAL
   ```

The first file denies all users from outside your system to all ports and processes on your local machine. The second file allows only the localhost access to the needed ports. You may add any additional IP addresses, hostnames, or services to the latter file and allow other users to access your home machine.

I sometimes add the IP address for my machine at work to my home machine's hosts.allow file. This way I dial up at home and do work on my home machine while at work.

In your /etc/resolv.conf file, add the following lines. You'll have to change them based upon your own ISP and its name servers. Talk to your ISP's support staff if you don't have viable IP addresses of a name server that you can access.

```
search my_isp.com
domain my_isp.com
nameserver 192.168.0.254
nameserver 192.168.0.253
```

Be sure to replace the variables in this example with the correct numbers and names associated with your own Linux connection.

Now in the /etc/hosts file, you can place the following lines.

```
127.0.0.1          localhost.localdomain    localhost
192.168.0.10antares.astronomy.org      antares
```

If you find you need to change your machine's name, you can do so in the /etc/HOSTNAME file.

In the /etc/networks file, place the following lines of text. Again, this file is designed for local configuration settings, and the second line is entirely optional. The localnet feature allows for internal addressing of the network.

```
loopback        127.0.0.0
localnet        0.0.0.0
```

In the file /etc/mailname, type the next few lines. (This step also is optional.)

```
my_isp.com
```

Replace isp.com with the name of your ISP. Some possible examples are aol.com or wisc.edu, if you use your educational institution as an ISP.

In the file /etc/ppp/pap-secrets (or /etc/ppp/chap-secrets if the ISP uses Microsoft), place the following line:

```
my_user_name         *          my_password
```

Replace the two variables as needed. Some ISPs might require additional extensions after their usernames, such as *.ppp or *.slip, to distinguish between users and their types of dial-up connections. Talk to your ISP about how it handles incoming connections.

## Configuring the netcfg GUI

Once you have properly set the security variables as outlined in the previous section, you can finish establishing a PPP connection using a GUI. The two recommended tools that come with Red Hat are netcfg or linuxconf. Both are configurable tools and will also dial the ISP's phone number and establish the proper connection. These tools require that you insert the main access number of the ISP that you are calling along with your username. They also list many of the device connection settings and can help in configuring any dial-up script that you may want to add.

Using the netcfg option, setting up a PPP connection is straightforward. Open the netcfg utility by entering **netcfg** at the command line and then choosing the Add button. You will want to create a new PPP device link. The, Create PPP Interface dialog box should now appear (see Figure 16.2).

The Create PPP Interface dialog box is self-explanatory. Verify that you enter the correct phone numbers, usernames, and passwords, and then choose Customize. This brings up the Edit PPP Interface dialog box (see Figure 16.3). You will want to specify the correct setting for your modem here, including line speed and the device name.

Next you can also choose to set the variables under the Communication tab (see Figure 16.4). Here you specify the actual script that your computer will send to the computer that it is dialing. Most PPP servers or ISP login server into which you dial up receives "login" and recognizes it or matches it against "ogin." The same with the "ord" option, which is matched against "password." Some ISPs may require other variables. Talk to the administrators if you experience any problems.

You may click the Edit button to change the default values and to add the figures needed for your particular connection. The Insert and Append buttons are for adding other commands into the body of the script.

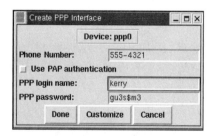

**FIGURE 16.2**

*Choosing a new PPP interface connection under netcfg.*

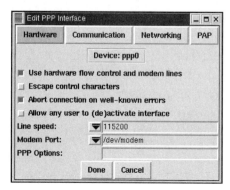

**FIGURE 16.3**

*Editing the hardware options on the PPP interface.*

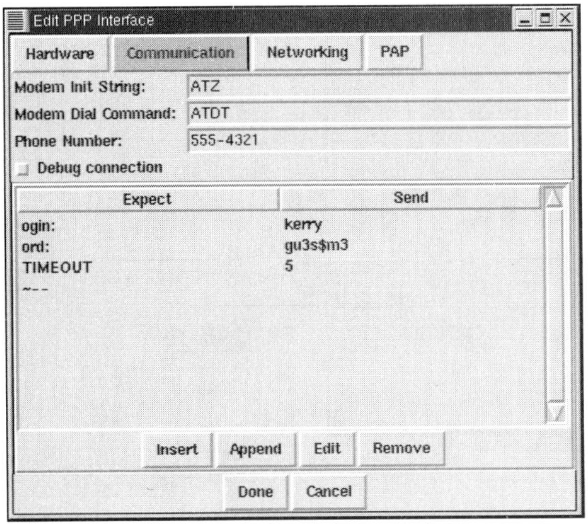

**FIGURE 16.4**

*Editing the Communication options on the PPP interface.*

To place an additional command before the `Timeout` variable, you click on the Timeout line and then click Insert. Fill out the values, then click Done. To append a line to the end of the script, press Append, complete the required field, then click Done.

The Networking tab is for setting the interface connection rate, timeout, packet sizes, and so on (see Figure 16.5). You can use this window to specify additional information for the system and to customize the connection.

The final tab under the Edit PPP Interface dialog box is PAP (see Figure 16.6). In the PAP tab, you enter a username and secret password. Much like the step

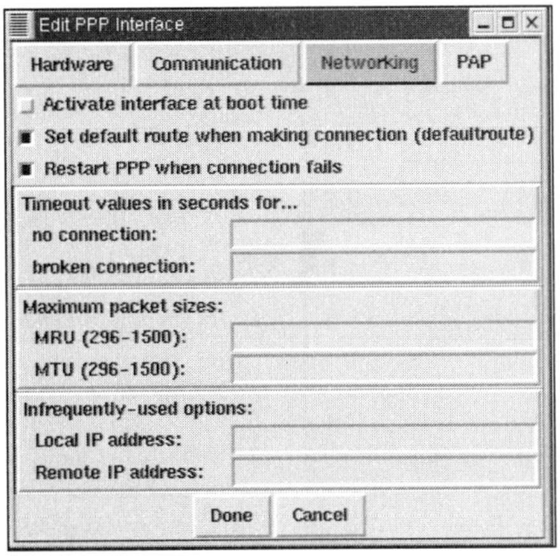

**FIGURE 16.5**

*Changing the Networking values for a PPP connection.*

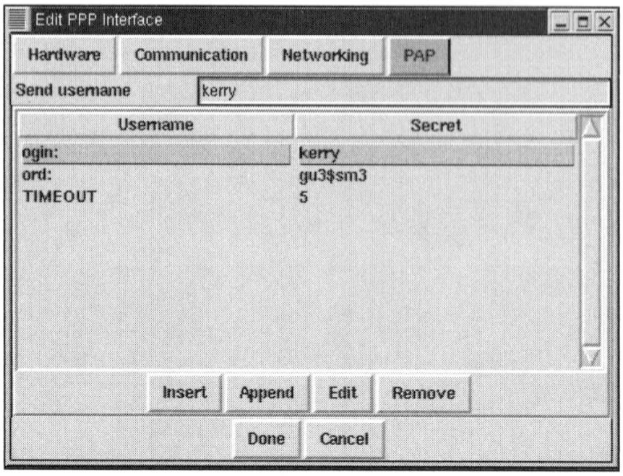

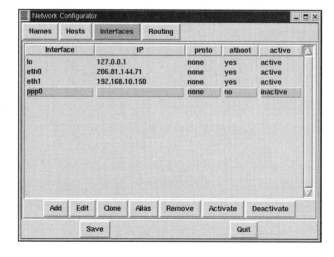

**FIGURE 16.6**

*Configuring the PAP-secrets file under netcfg.*

described previously where you insert the login and password variables, here you can accomplish the same thing. This tab enables you to rewrite the contents of the /etc/ppp/pap-secrets file. You can also use this tab to set up chat expressions to test your modem's connection.

Once all the correct variables are in place, you may return to the netcfg main window. Then click the Interfaces button to enable the connection (see Figure 16.7). Simply highlight the ppp0 connection and then click the Activate button. Your modem should dial, connect, and shake hands with the ISP's modem. After a few moments, you will be able to test your connection by attempting a ping or telnet command to contact a location remote from your network.

**FIGURE 16.7**

*Activating a PPP connection under the main netcfg window.*

Once you click the Activate button, the Network Configurator script will dial in to your Internet provider and begin executing the script you entered previously. With many of the PPP dial-in scripts provided, you will see a Debug button somewhere on the screen. This will assist in tracking down any errors you may encounter when attempting to dial into another provider.

## Enabling a Dial-Up Connection under linuxconf

Setting up a similar connection under the linuxconf program can be just as simple and will also dial up and connect to the ISP. As shown in Figure 16.8, linuxconf's routine is very similar to that of netcfg. The same windows are present along with the same fields. Here also you may activate the connection and edit the variables.

In both the netcfg and linuxconf windows, you can configure your machine so that it will activate the connection upon bootup. This allows you to connect immediately to the ISP as your machine comes on. Depending upon the fair use procedures defined by your ISP, you can remain online for as long as the ISP allows.

Under the very latest release of Red Hat Linux, the PPP/SLIP configuration interface is not available. It is recommended that users wishing to create a dial-up connection to an Internet Service Provider use the Red Hat PPP Dialer,

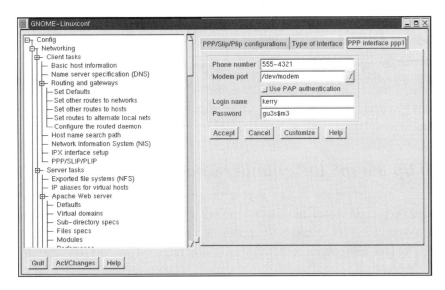

**FIGURE 16.8**

*Configuring the entries under linuxconf for establishing a PPP connection.*

which can be executed from the command line by typing the executable rp3. This replaces the linuxconf PPP dial-up utility.

## Using GNOME and KDE Dial-Up Utilities

One of the easiest methods of creating a dial-up connection is to use a tool such as the GNOME rp3-config and rp3 utility and the KDE kppp program. Both are available with the latest Red Hat release. If you wish to use the KDE kppp program, you must choose to install the KDE programs during the initial Red Hat Linux installation or install them at a later time. Both the KDE dialup tool and the GNOME rp3 program can be used under different window managers. They are not dependant upon their respective window manager or environment in order to run. In other words, you do not have to be running the KDE desktop environment in order to use kppp.

Both rp3 and kppp offer many unique features that make the tools even more versatile than that of the netcfg and linuxconf configuration programs:

◆ They require just one window to connect.

◆ They prompt for a root password rather than forcing you to change the permission of the binary itself.

◆ They monitor your connections and show modem activity.

◆ They measure the bandwidth usage in an easy-to-read graph form.

◆ They can calculate phone costs based on connection time or transfer of bytes.

◆ They can dock into the Gnome or KDE toolbar.

◆ You can set up multiple connections to other ISPs.

You can start either utility at the command line by typing its respective filename. You should run each program as root. Otherwise, the program will prompt you for the root password.

### Setting Up the rp3 Utility under Gnome

A major step in assisting the novice user with Linux is the GNOME desktop's Dialup Connection Wizard. Similar to the wizards used under the Windows operating system, this tool detects your attached modem, sets up the variables, and then provides easy connectivity. You are not required to edit any files by hand, but only provide root's password and some information about the ISP or hosting service that you are calling.

Once kudzu, or the Red Hat hardware detection tool has properly detected and configured the modem attached to your machine, you can begin configuring the software under Linux to establish a dial-up connection to your Internet Service Provider. Both steps are very easy since Red Hat takes much of the guesswork out of your hands and does a fine job in installing the proper settings for your machine.

Setting up your modem under Linux is now a simple task. If you are using an external modem, shut down your machine and then plug the connection into an available COM port with a cable supplied by the manufacturer. If you are using an internal modem, verify that the device is not a WinModem, open the case, and insert the card into the proper available slot. Start up Linux again and wait for kudzu to detect your modem. If kudzu does not detect your modem initially during the bootup sequence, you can still configure it using the rp3-config program.

As root under any X Window terminal, enter **rp3-config**. The program presents the screen shown in Figure 16.9.

Next, the rp3-config program checks your system for any existing modems and verifies whether you have already configured a modem under the control panel or the netcfg utility. You will be simply prompted to allow the system to check all devices for any attached modems as shown in Figure 16.10.

**FIGURE 16.9**

*The splash screen for creating a new Internet connection under the Gnome desktop using the rp3-config command.*

**FIGURE 16.10**

*Allow the system to select your modem.*

The rp3-config utility now checks through all available /dev/ttyS devices and listens for a dial tone. If kudzu did not detect a modem during the bootup sequence or after running kudzu manually, the program prompts you to allow the rp3-config program to detect the modem now. Turn your modem on and make certain that the analog line phone cord is plugged in the correct port on the modem itself. The rp3 utility then checks for a operational modem and tests for a dial tone. As shown in Figure 16.11, it functions much like a Windows Wizard and looks through your system for the proper hardware and then configures it appropriately.

**FIGURE 16.11**

*The rp3-config command examines all ports and devices for any connected modems.*

If you do not already have a modem set up under your Linux settings, the screen shown in Figure 16.12 appears. Here you can enter the settings for you modem manually. This screen often appears if you do not have an active phone line plugged into your machine.

If the program detects no modems on your system, you may still enter the settings manually. If the program detects a modem, a window similar to that shown in Figure 16.11 appears, in which you may either confirm the detected setting, modify the settings, or add an additional modem.

Next the program prompts you to create an account name for this particular account. Hit the Next button and you will be shown a dialog box much like the one in Figure 16.13. You should stay with the same format as used by Linux. If you have a single modem, name the account **ppp0**. This name will create less confusion later if you decide to alter the settings yourself. However, if you wish to identify your connection by a less cryptic name, you may name the connection whatever you wish. Most users choose the name of the ISP to whom they are connecting.

If the phone from which you are dialing requires a prefix to reach a dial tone, such as a 9 or pound sign (#), enter that number or character in the Prefix field. If you are dialing from a home computer or you do not require an escape character, leave this field empty. Now enter the area code and phone number of your ISP. As the screen in Figure 16.13 shows, the prefix and area-code are optional.

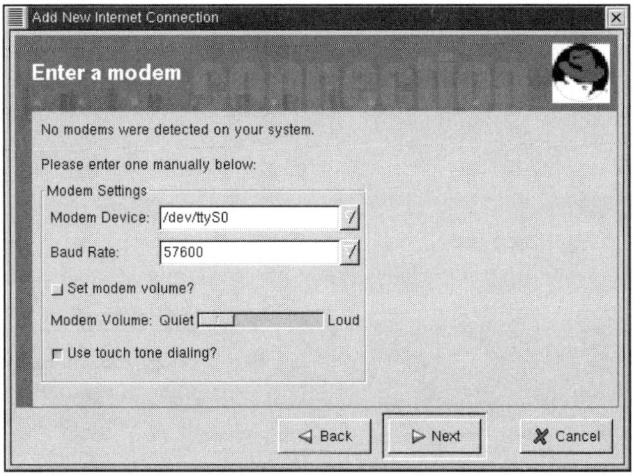

**FIGURE 16.12**

*Entering the manual settings for your modem.*

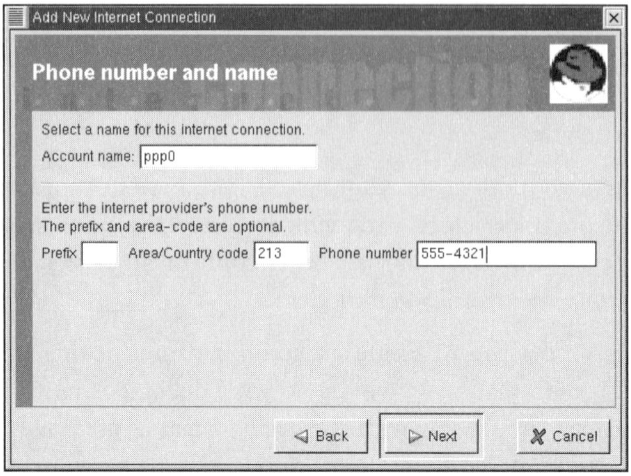

**FIGURE 16.13**

*Enter an account name for this particular dial-up account and the phone number of the ISP.*

Now enter the username and password for the account using the modem. These should be the username and password you defined for yourself under the PAP Connection Settings or they can also be the username and password you would normally use to Telnet or ssh into your Linux machine. If you normally use an alias for your e-mail, determine your unique username on the Linux system and enter that instead. For example, I would kjcox as my username rather than kerry.cox, which would be the prefix to my e-mail address and is simply an alias for kjcox.

**FIGURE 16.14**

*Insert your username and password to your Linux machine in the required fields.*

The rp3-config program next prompts you to choose an ISP (see Figure 16.15). Currently you can choose between a Normal ISP connection or AT&T Global Network Services. For now, you should choose the Normal ISP option.

The program prompts you to confirm your choices (see Figure 16.16). If the settings displayed match those that you have deemed correct, you may confirm your options and create the account by clicking Finish. You still have the option to return to earlier settings and modify your selections or to choose Cancel if you do not want to create the account now.

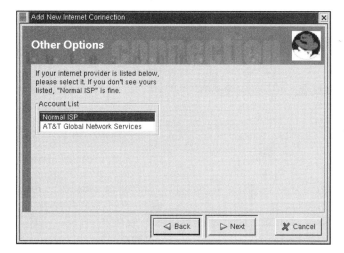

**FIGURE 16.15**

*Select the ISP of your choice. This option is still awaiting more choices and will be expanded to include other Internet Service Providers as they become available.*

**FIGURE 16.16**

*Confirm your options and create the unique dial-up account.*

The program now presents a window that shows your system's available modem connection (see Figure 16.17). The window shows not only your account name and the phone number of the ISP, but also the connection's current status. You may use this window to display your online status. Here, too, you may add, edit, delete, copy, or dial into any of the accounts that you created.

If you decide to change any of the accounts, highlight the particular account and click Edit. The Edit Internet Connection dialog box appears (see Figure 16.18). Here you can change the account name to something more descriptive or change the default username and password. If your ISP changes its default phone number, you may also edit that field.

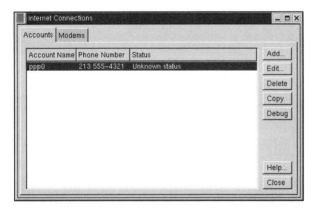

**FIGURE 16.17**

*The available Internet connections on your Linux machine. In this window, you can modify each account.*

**FIGURE 16.18**

*Edit each account's default information.*

If your modem requires additional information or if you wish to help automate the PPP daemon, the Advanced tab allows you to change supplementary options (see Figure 16.19). You can also enter DNS server information in the fields provided.

For more information on the modems detected or manually set up on your system, click the Modems tab of the Internet Connections dialog box (see Figure 16.20). You may add, edit, or delete the modems listed in this tab. If you have more than one modem attached to your system, you can select one to be the default modem that you normally use to dial out.

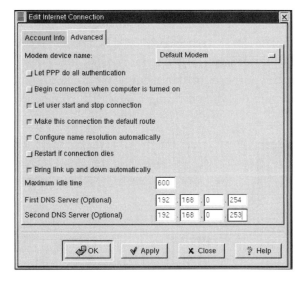

**FIGURE 16.19**

*Configure DNS settings and dial-up properties under the Advanced tab of the Edit Internet Connection dialog box.*

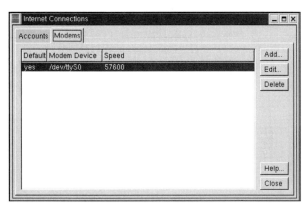

**FIGURE 16. 20**

*Edit the modem choices attached to your system.*

You can also edit any modems that you may have into which other users can dial. For example, if you have multiple phone lines, you can configure each modem attached to your system in the Modems tab

To change any setting on your modem, click the Edit button. The Edit Modem Properties dialog box appears (see Figure 16.21). In this dialog box, you make any alterations needed. If you do not already have a volume control on your modem, this dialog box enables you to raise or lower the settings. You can also disable touch-tone dialing, which is the *de facto* standard for most phone lines.

Once you have customized your modem, you can start your dial-up connection. The command to execute the dial-up connection is rp3. Any user can execute the PPP daemon and create a dial-up connection. From the command line or from the RH PPP Dialer icon located under the Programs, Internet you can execute the rp3 program. It will present you with a Choose dialog box enables you to select which interface to make active (see Figure 16.22). Select your account name, which in this case would be ppp0. Again, you can call the account name whatever you wish, but for the purposes of this example we are keeping it ppp0, much as the system itself would do when creating a new PPP connection.

**FIGURE 16.21**

*In the Edit Modem Properties dialog box, you can edit selected modem options, such as the volume, the unique device name, and the baud rate.*

**FIGURE 16.22**

*Choose your dial-up account name and start the PPP daemon.*

After your modem has dialed and successfully established a connection, a window appears that displays a small graph of bandwidth usage. By right-clicking the graph you can also disconnect or reconnect to your host provider. You can also configure the account and modem properties from under the same window. The rp3 program provides Linux users the same conveniences associated with the Windows operating system. Gnome continues to assist new users in converting to Linux and to make Linux into a user-friendly platform.

### Running kppp under KDE

With earlier releases tof KDE running under Red Hat, you are first prompted to enter the root password in a dialog box when starting the kppp program as a normal user. This corrects the security hole under previous releases that required you to use the chmod command and change the permissions on /usr/bin/kppp to 4711 so that regular users could also use kppp. Also, previously there was a security issue with the /etc/ppp/options file, which contained the word lock. The kppp program wanted to control this file itself and place the word lock in the file when initiated. This problem has since been resolved, and kppp runs as root instead.

To use kppp, follow these steps:

1. When first started, the program prompts you with the main kppp dialog box. Click the Setup button and begin entering the information regarding your ISP, as shown in Figure 16.23.

**FIGURE 16.23**

*Setting up kppp in the kppp Configuration dialog box.*

Figure 16.23 shows an entry created for a connection called My ISP. The name depends entirely upon your own hosting service, but it should be something easily identifiable if you have multiple connections to different ISPs.

2. You will want to edit this dial-up configuration and enter the appropriate DNS settings, phone numbers, passwords etc. Click on the Edit... button. This should bring up a Edit Account My ISP dialog box. Your own dialog box will be given the name you determined for your new account. Select the Dial tab under the Edit Account window. Then enter a phone number or the main access number of the ISP, as shown in Figure 16.24.

If you plan to configure the connection script yourself, be sure to choose the setting Script-based in the Authentication field of the Dial tab. You can also choose a Terminal-based setting, which allows you to type your username and password while connecting to the Internet Service Provider. Other alternatives include PAP- and CHAP-based authentication. These two alternatives query the contents of your pap-secrets and chap-secrets files located in the /etc/ppp directory. You can have kppp store your password so you do not have to input it each time that you wish to connect. However, this alternative poses a security risk if you do not want others using your connection for their own purposes. Within

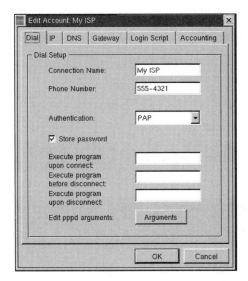

**FIGURE 16.24**

*Entering the unique phone number under the Dial tab in the kppp Configuration dialog box.*

the Dial tab, you can also give the pppd daemon other arguments and execute additional programs upon connect or disconnect.

3. Click the IP tab to display the screen shown in Figure 16.25. In the IP tab, you can configure your IP address to be either dynamically assigned or static. Most ISPs assign their user's dynamic addresses. If you have allocated a specific address from a range for your own use, click the Static IP Address option and enter the necessary information.

   Some users prefer having a static IP address when connected rather than a dynamic address. Although the latter type of address changes each time that you log in, a static IP address remains the same. A static address is useful for establishing a connection between home and business. If your ISP allows it, you can connect in the morning and still use telnet to access your machine at home, provided your machine is a Linux box. I often do this to transfer files between the two machines. The kppp program will also auto configure your machine's hostname based on the static IP address that you provide it. For most users, the dynamic IP address is the standard choice with nearly all ISP connections.

4. Click the DNS tab to display the screen shown in Figure 16.26. You must enter the domain name of your ISP and the DNS or name server information. Once you enter the first DNS IP address in the second field, you can add it to the DNS Address List.

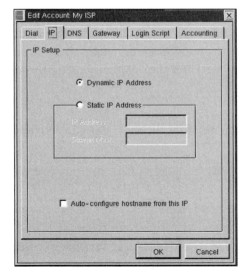

**FIGURE 16.25**

*Determine whether you will be using a dynamic or static IP address.*

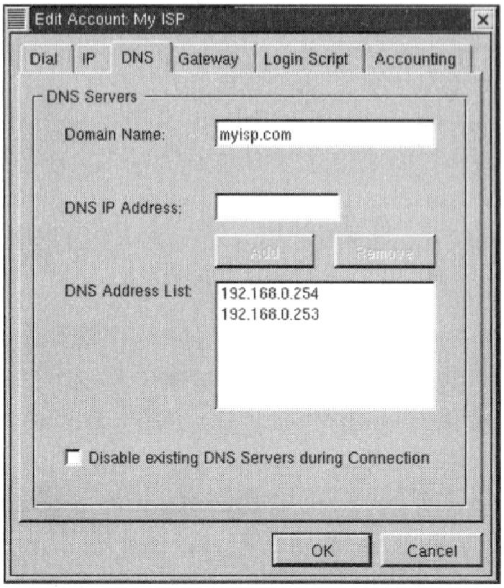

**FIGURE 16.26**

*Configuring your DNS servers for name server lookups.*

As with the /etc/resolv.conf file, the DNS tab requires the proper DNS domain or ISP domain and name server IP addresses. It also enables the user to disable any existing DNS servers, whether local or otherwise, defined under the text file. Then, when the user is connected to the ISP, only that user's DNS server is used.

5. Click the Gateway tab to display the screen shown in Figure 16.27. You can edit the settings in this tab to define which gateway your machine will use for routing purposes to other networks.

   Rather than attempting to define the gateway by hand or configure additional default gateways using a tool such as netcfg, you can provide kppp with either a default gateway or a static gateway going through another host.

6. Click the Login Script tab to display the screen shown in Figure 16.28. This tab includes settings that are often the most difficult to configure properly.

   If you chose to use the script-based method of connecting, you will need to properly insert the value requested by the ISP's server. These steps involve a series of Expect and Send requests. Usually an ogin: and an ord: value suffice for connecting. The former stands for *login*, and the latter for *password*. It is also wise to add a Timeout variable in case your script does not work or the ISP does not recognize your input.

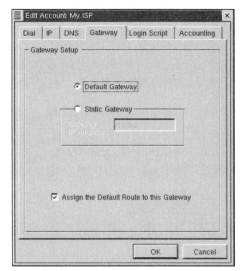

**FIGURE 16.27**

*Routing your packets through the ISP's default gateway.*

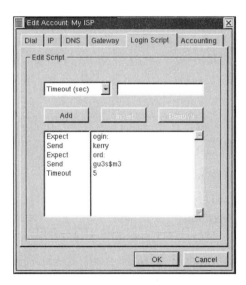

**FIGURE 16.28**

*Sending the remote modem the login variables.*

**7.** Click the Accounting tab to display the screen shown in Figure 16.29. This tab is designed for international users or those outside the United States where phone calls to an ISP are billed for the time of connection or where users are charged by the byte or kilobyte transferred. In the United States, customers are usually charged a flat rate for unlimited access, but customers in many countries overseas are billed a higher rate. Browsing the Internet can become more costly for these users.

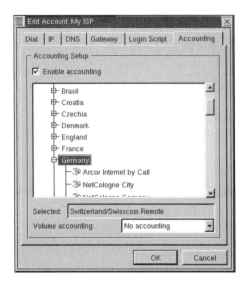

**FIGURE 16.29**

*Logging the connection time for billing purposes.*

Under kppp, international users can determine their typical cost per connection time and balance their Internet use accordingly. This feature is especially appealing to users who live in countries where the government regulates the phone rate and can charge more than a private company. Speaking from my own experiences in Germany, connecting the government-regulated phone system can be quite costly. Also in this tab, the Volume accounting field enables you to measure billing based on the amount of data flowing in or out or both in and out.

### Finishing the kppp Connection

Returning to the main kppp Configuration dialog box and clicking the Device tab (see Figure 16.30), you finish editing the setting for the modem itself and not just for the individual connection.

In the Device tab, you set the modem configuration to point to either your /dev/modem or to the real device name. For most users, the default choice will suffice. You also set flow control and line termination in the second and third fields. For most users, the defaults will also work fine. If you are using a generic modem, you should go with the settings that kppp provides. If you wish to edit these variables, check the settings in the modem's handbook or consult the manufacturer's page on the Internet.

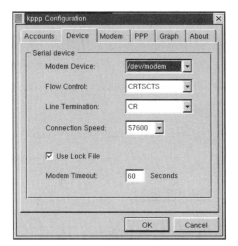

**FIGURE 16.30**

*Configuring the Device tab of the main kppp Configuration dialog box.*

## CAUTION

You should probably set the connection speeds only somewhat higher than your modem's defined speed. I have experienced problems with earlier versions and have been unable to successfully login after setting the speed higher than that of my own modem. As my local modem attempted to negotiate with the remote modem, it could not send the data stream correctly. If you find you are experiencing problems connecting, or are not connecting at all, try setting the speed to a lower rate.

The Modem tab provides additional settings for configuring the hardware (see Figure 16.31).

You can set the modem to wait a certain period of time before attempting to redial after receiving a busy signal. You can also decrease or increase the modem's volume so that you can either turn down the connection sounds or hear the handshaking more clearly. The kppp program allows you to send additional commands to the modem as it connects as well as query the modem and test its performance.

Figure 16.32 shows the PPP tab as it is used for editing the behavior of kppp under the KDE environment.

This tab features many useful options, such as keeping a docked version of kppp on the KDE toolbar or minimizing the dialog box upon connection. You can also configure kppp so that it either quits upon disconnect or redials. Also important

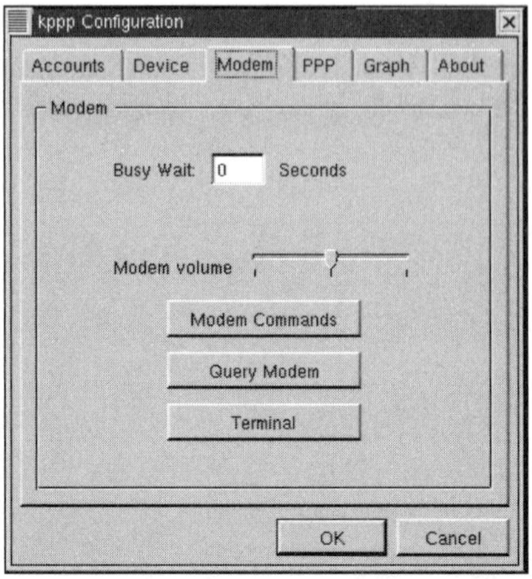

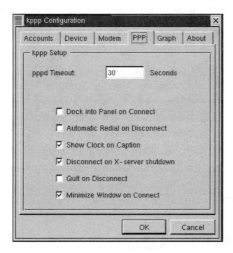

**FIGURE 16.31**

*Editing the modem variables under kppp.*

**FIGURE 16.32**

*Setting specific settings for kppp to operate under the KDE desktop environment.*

is kppp's ability to time out the ppp daemon so that it does not hang if the connection fails. Usually, the ppp daemon writes to a lock file so that another instance of itself will not start up while either connected or while attempting to connect. The timeout feature causes pppd to release the lock so that another instance can be started.

The Graph and About tabs provide further information. The former creates a graphical representation of the amount of data transferred between your local machine and the remote host. The latter tab explains more about the kppp program, including the names and e-mail addresses of the developers. If you have any comments or suggestions, or would simply like to locate the e-mail addresses of the KDE developers for their work and diligence in creating such a functional program, you can locate KDE's e-mail address here.

After properly entering and authorizing all the settings, you can begin trying out your connection. The default kppp window prompts you to enter your username and password (see Figure 16.33). Be sure to click the Setup button and then the Save Password button if you want to have kppp automatically connect you in the future so that you don't have to enter your password or configure the script each time.

If you have an external modem, make sure that it is turned on at this point, then click the Connect button. If you have set the volume under the settings at either medium or high range, you should be able to hear the modem as it dials, performs the handshaking, and then starts the ppp daemon. The kppp program will congratulate you with a small "connected" icon or minimize to the KDE toolbar, depending upon how you configured the options.

The kppp program is currently one of the most widely used dial-up connection programs. Much of the program's popularity is due to the fact that it comes installed with KDE, which is increasingly being used as the default window environment program under other Linux distributions. However, rp3 is also gaining in acceptance and notoriety due the advances being made in the Gnome desktop.

Similar tools are also available to use. XISP accomplishes much the same tasks as kppp and rp3. Several other tools are available on the Internet for free download. Any one of the many sites that host information about Linux programs could quickly point you to the latest download location or mirror.

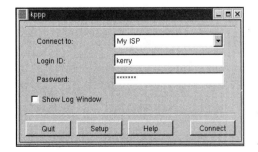

**FIGURE 16.33**

*Once all the settings have been entered, you will be given a main login window for connecting to your host provider.*

## Using the Dial Daemon

Another useful utility that you can use with rp3 and kppp is diald, or the Dial Daemon program. When you place a request for a Web page, service, or server connection outside your normal intranet, and if your modem is turned on, diald will automatically dial your default ISP's number or the number of the provider specified in any of your dial-up programs. It will also set up a PPP session between the two computers. The diald program can make it appear that you have a connection to the Internet over a SLIP or PPP link 24 hours a day, seven days a week. You can configure the program to keep your link up 24 hours a day in the face of problems with your phone lines, cause your modem to dial out whenever a connection is needed, or hang up the line again when it is no longer necessary.

Some ISPs frown upon redialing programs or the abuse of the phone privileges, so contact your ISP before instituting any such protocol.

As diald demonstrates once again, for any program that exists under Windows or any other system, an equivalent or superior counterpart is available for Linux.

### NOTE

For more information about diald, and to download this program, go to its Web site at http://diald.unix.ch/ or do a quick search on the Internet.

## Configuring Your Machine to Be a Stand-Alone PPP Server

Besides setting your Linux machine to talk PPP with an ISP's modem, you configure your own machine to talk PPP with another Linux box, thus providing connectivity to another machine and network and its bandwidth access. While some ISPs provide a vast array of equipment to connect to the Internet, including routers, switches, leased lines, and various other machinations to ensure the quickest connection to its customers, you can provide the same to yourself.

If you have a dedicated connection to the Internet and have an available analog line, you can set up a modem on any Red Hat Linux machine and have it answer any valid phone calls from either your home computer or from any other computer with a modem, thus establishing a valid dial-up connection and access to the Internet. Because so many of the tools available on Linux allow it to function as a server, you can also configure Linux to grant PPP access to individual dial-ups and give those machines the same access that Linux has. Linux can be a PPP server for any machine that knows how to speak PPP and TCP/IP.

For example, at my office I have a dedicated OC3 line to the Internet from which my Linux box can tap for bandwidth. At home I have a simple 33.6 modem connection—a slow but extremely reliable connection. Bypassing my ISP and dialing straight into the Linux box at work grants me a dedicated line to the Internet and prevents any busy signals I might encounter via the ISP. However, before you try to set up anything like this, first make sure that your line can be used successfully for this purpose.

To create a stand-alone PPP server, follow these steps:

1. Gather the necessary hardware, such as the modem, serial cable, analog phone line, and so on.

2. Properly configure your modem to answer incoming calls. Make certain it is not competing with another device such as a fax machine.

3. Verify that your system includes some sort of line monitoring device such as getty or mgetty.

4. Configure Linux to start the pppd daemon after a call is placed to the machine.

5. Properly configure your /etc/inittab file to watch for incoming calls.

Each step of these requirements is described in greater detail next.

This process involves two machines: the server and the client. You will be looking at the server in the greatest detail. This is the Linux machine that is connected to the Internet either via a LAN or high-speed connection. The client can be your Linux or Windows machine at home to which you wish to grant Internet connectivity.

On the server machine or the Linux box that will function as the stand-alone PPP server, make certain that you complete the following steps:

1. Verify that you have the PPP daemon installed. A simple rpm query will confirm this: **rpm -q ppp**.

2. Check to make sure you have PPP support compiled into your kernel. If you are using a default kernel that came with your Red Hat installation, you should already have modular PPP support enabled.

3. If you are using a custom kernel, turn PPP support on. You may also enable SLIP support if that is your preferred method of connection.

4. Make sure that all users can use pppd. Issue the following command: **chmod u+s /usr/sbin/pppd**.

5. Add this line to the /etc/bashrc file: **alias ppp="exec /usr/sbin/pppd - detach"**. With this option enabled, the PPP dameon can fork and run as a background process separate from the terminal that initiated it.

6. Make sure you have mgetty installed. Check in the /etc directory to see that you have an mgetty+sendfax/ directory. This directory contains several configuration files that you may need to change.

## Setting Up the Dial-Up Server

Now you can begin making the physical connection on your server. Either plug your modem into an available internal slot or attach your external modem to the appropriate COM port. My external modem is connected to COM1. Using the modemtool command resident in the Red Hat control panel, select the COM port that your modem will be using. This selection creates a symbolic link between the device name and the modem. You can accomplish this just as well by entering the following on the command line: **ln -s /dev/ttyS0 /dev/modem**.

Next, proceed to the /etc/ppp directory and examine its contents. There should be a file called options. You should copy this file to something more configurable and identifiable such as options.ttyS0. You can begin editing this new file.

On my own /etc/ppp/options.ttyS0 file, These must be viable IP addresses if you wish to have true Internet access.

You will want to place in the first field the IP address of the Linux server and then after the colon place the IP address you will be assigning to the dial-up client machine:

```
205.82.148.21:205.82.148.20
```

Next, check your /etc/mgetty+sendfax/login.config file. Make sure the following line is entered and customized to your specific filenames:

```
/AutoPPP/  -      ppp     /usr/sbin/pppd file /etc/ppp/options.srv
```

Now, check the contents of your /etc/ppp/options.srv file. Listing 16.1 shows an example of what you enter. Change the values to reflect your own system.

**Listing 16.1  A Sample options.srv File
Specifying Modem Requirements**

```
auth
-chap
+pap
login
asyncmap 0
:205.82.148.20
debug
modem
crtscts
ms-dns 205.82.148.253
ms-dns 205.82.148.254
proxyarp
```

Finally, check your /etc/inittab file and make sure to enter the last line shown in Listing 16.2.

**Listing 16.2  The /etc/inittab File with an Entry
to Spawn a Modem Connection**

```
# Run gettys in standard runlevels
1:2345:respawn:/sbin/mingetty tty1
2:2345:respawn:/sbin/mingetty tty2
3:2345:respawn:/sbin/mingetty tty3
4:2345:respawn:/sbin/mingetty tty4
5:2345:respawn:/sbin/mingetty tty5
6:2345:respawn:/sbin/mingetty tty6
# S0:2345:respawn:/sbin/mgetty ttyS0 -D /dev/ttyS0
# S0:2345:respawn:/sbin/uugetty -d /etc/default/uugetty.ttyS0 ttyS0
F115200 vt100
d1:345:respawn:/sbin/mgetty -n 1 ttyS0
```

The second- and third-to-last lines are commented out, but they too can accomplish the necessary connectivity. The last line is probably your best choice, as I had more success with it than with the other two. Web pages describing this same method cite the two commented lines for their example entries.

Next, create a user named dialup or remote or something that will identify that new user. Create this user using the /usr/sbin/adduser command and then assign that new user a unique password using the passwd command. Use a name that is not easily recognized.

The /etc/ppp/options.srv file includes a +pap entry, so you must add a line for that user in the /etc/ppp/pap-secrets file. Here is what a sample entry might look like:

```
# Secrets for authentication using PAP
# client         server   secret                 IP addresses
dialup    *      password   *
```

If you wish to give any other dial-up users access to your machine using a modem connection, enter their username and password in here as well. Replace the words dialup and password with the appropriate username and password of the client.

## Enabling IP Forwarding

Last item of business is to be sure to switch on IP forwarding. This option should be in your kernel, but you may have to start the module manually if you did not define it during your kernel recompilation. The file you want to edit is located at /etc/sysconfig/network under Red Hat. Here is what your configuration may look like:

```
NETWORKING=yes
FORWARD_IPV4=yes
HOSTNAME=quasi.astronomy.org
GATEWAY=205.82.148.1
GATEWAYDEV=
```

It is the second line that should be set to *yes*. Again, the IP address for the gateway has been changed for security purposes, although a simple nslookup on the name should show the entire address.

You also may need to switch on the proxy_arp setting:

```
echo 1 >/proc/sys/net/ipv4/conf/default/proxy_arp
```

In the latest Red Hat release, the variable FORWARD_IPV4 has been moved to the /etc/sysctl.conf file. Here several modular options are defined that affect networking. You can still leave the variable defined in /etc/sysconfig/network, but the system will automatically add the variable to the /etc.sysctl.conf file as well.

Here is what a sample entry looks like. Notice that the forward variable is defined although commented out. It is enabled only on the last line.

```
# Disables packet forwarding
# net.ipv4.ip_forward = 0
# Enables packet forwarding
# net.ipv4.ip_forward = 1
# Enables source route verification
net.ipv4.conf.all.rp_filter = 1
# Disables automatic defragmentation (needed for masquerading, LVS)
net.ipv4.ip_always_defrag = 0
# Disables the magic-sysrq key
kernel.sysrq = 0
# added by initscripts install on Thu Oct  19 13:46:24 MDT 2000
net.ipv4.ip_forward = 1
```

Once you have confirmed that the server is set up correctly, you can start configuring your client box at home or elsewhere. If you are using a Linux box, consult the previous "Setting Up the Dial-Up Server" section. If another machine on your network is using Microsoft Windows, use the provided Dial-Up Networking Tool. Enter in the numbers for the phone number into which your Linux modem is connected. If you are using a valid IP address for your system, be sure to provide the IP addresses of the DNS servers hosting your IP address.

---

**NOTE**

If you experience any problems, check the following files. Look at /var/log/mgetty. log.ttyS0 to see what kind of errors are being generated. If that file doesn't provide enough information, consult the messages in /var/log/messages. Otherwise look through all the files in /var/log.

Turn on the Debug option under the Linux dial-up connection and watch how your modem connects to the other remote modem. I noticed my own machine not sending the correct password for the user I was connecting as and was able to rectify the situation quickly.

# Sharing Modems with Multiple Users

One of the more dynamic features of Linux is *IP masquerading*—the ability to share one modem or Internet connection among users on a LAN network. IP masquerading works by assigning a range of nonviable IP addresses to some users or computers within an intranet. However, a Linux box translates these addresses into a viable address, thus allowing all within the intranet to share a common connection. The only limitation to these users' Internet connection is the amount of bandwidth through which the Linux box can transmit data.

Because IP masquerading is not only useful for sharing one modem and routing packets through a single connection, it is also practical for firewalling purposes. The Linux box that changes the internal addresses can also examine both incoming and outgoing packets and test all for compliance with a set of firewall rules or chains. For more information on configuring basic firewalls under Linux, see Chapter 19.

## Establishing Gateways and Clients for IP Masquerading

You must first determine which machine will function as the router or gateway to the outside world, and which machine will be the client or the internal machine. In this instance, Linux will be the gateway. Any other Linux box can be the client as well. In my own situation at work and at home, for example, other users might want to use Windows as their operating system. Configuring these machines is as simple as configuring Linux.

Let's first look at how you need to configure the clients. Because the instructions for setting up the gateway masquerading box are easily transferable to a Linux client as well, let's use a Windows box as a client and set up Linux as the gateway hosting the connection, whether it is a modem or a high-speed connection.

## Setting Up the Client

When configuring IP addresses for any machines that are located behind a firewall within an internet LAN and that are doing IP masquerading, they usually require a unique set of IP addresses. I normally choose the 192.168.xx.xx variety. In this manner, I can easily add additional subnets or other IP addresses later. I also do not work sequentially but increment the numbers on each machine by a series of 10, just in case I need to add additional machines later. It also helps when grouping the types of machines behind the masquerading Linux box. I place servers in the lower range, workstations in the mid- to upper range, and printers the upper region. IP address ranges can be arranged however you choose.

This example will use one Linux box named alpha and three Windows machines, called beta, gamma, and delta respectively, to sit behind the connection. Each of these machines requires an IP address within the 192.168 class B network. Assign the address 192.168.0.10 to alpha. Much like the alpha male of a pack of sled dogs, all the others follow behind. The beta, gamma, and delta machine are assigned 192.168.0.20, .30, and .40, respectively.

Next you must add these numbers to the Windows machines' network setup to make sure the machines know what number they are. These steps are only for the Windows machines, beta, gamma, and delta:

1. Turn off your computer, then insert the correct NIC card into an available slot. This card enables your Windows machine to communicate with the others via an Ethernet connection.

2. Turn the computer back on. When it is done loading, configure the new NIC by choosing Control Panel, Add New Hardware, if the machine did not already detect the card.

3. In the Control Panel, Network box under Configuration, add TCP/IP Protocol if it is not already there. Most Windows machines install this protocol by default now.

4. Select the TCP/IP Protocol and then click Properties.

5. Select the IP Address tab and type in the IP address that you chose for this machine. I placed 192.168.0.20 in the box labeled beta.

6. In the Netmask field, type **255.255.255.0**.

7. In the Gateway tab, type in the IP address that you assigned to the Linux router or gateway, which in this case is alpha. Here you would type **192.168.0.10**.

8. Click the DNS Configuration tab. Be sure to enable DNS, and in the hostname field type the name that you gave to this particular box. Feel free to follow any theme that you started with your own machines. To maintain continuity with my naming scheme, I will continue using Latin alphabetic names. Here I would type **beta**.

9. Place either an imaginary domain name in the domain field or use that of your ISP. Either name will suffice.

10. Enter the DNS server names of your ISP in their proper search order. You can also find these same values under /etc/resolv.conf on your Linux machine.

11. Connect each machine to the other physically be either running a null-modem cable from each Ethernet card to the other or by connecting them all into a simple network hub. The latter method is by far the best. Use a simple straight-through connection with RJ-45 connectors either made yourself or purchased at most any computer store. These type of cables do not require any sort of cross-over wiring. Pairing the same color-coding configuration on both ends is usually sufficient.

    You do not need to click the other dialog boxes or alter their fields.

12. Click OK on all dialog boxes to confirm your changes.

13. The program prompts you to restart your system. Rebooting is not necessary when you are changing network variables under Linux.

Complete this procedure on all the Windows machines, giving each a unique IP address. To enable each machine to see each other quicker, you can enter each machine's hostname and IP address in their respective hosts file in C:\Windows\ directory. For Windows NT, the same file is winnt\system32\drivers\etc\hosts. Verify that your Linux box also has the correct addresses and names in its configuration. Now make sure that each machine can see the others. If you have any questions on configuring the networking portion of your Linux box, refer to Chapter 15.

To test the connectivity of the Windows machines, under a console or xterm window on the Linux box, enter the following:

```
ping 192.168.0.20
```

You should see some response from the other machines. Do the same under the Windows machines. Choose Start, Run, then enter the same command, only specifying a different machine. Linux and Windows machines can ping themselves successfully, so be sure that you enter another IP address in the ping command aside from the machine's localhost IP address or the IP address assigned to that particular machine.

# Explaining the Syntax of ipchains

Once you have made certain that the computers are seeing each other, you need to make certain that your Linux box can connect to the Internet. See the section "Manually Configuring a Modem under Linux" if you have any questions about this.

After connecting to the Internet on your Linux box, you use a program called ipchains to allow the computers to talk through Linux. Verify that you have ipchains installed. Again, enter the **rpm -q ipchains** command to check for the most recent version of ipchains installed on your machine. If the program is not installed, either install the program from your distribution CD or download it from one of the many RPM distribution sites. The Red Hat distributors have many mirrored sites hosting all available and updated RPMs. The ipchains program allows your Linux machine to act as a gateway and router onto the Internet. It replaces ipfwadm, an older IP firewall administrative tool for doing IP masquerading.

The syntax associated with ipchains can be tricky at first. Table 16.1 lists the system targets associated with ipchains.

**Table 16.1  Available Targets Under ipchains**

| Arguments | Definition |
| --- | --- |
| ACCEPT | Allows a packet to come through |
| DENY | Drops the packet silently |
| REJECT | Notifies the sender that packet is dropped |
| MASQ | Masquerades the packet |
| REDIRECT | Sends the packet to a port on the firewall or the routing Linux machine. Mayalso receive a later command to send it to another port |
| RETURN | Transfer the packet to the end of the current chain and may be handled according to the chain's default target |

These are some of the main targets specified under ipchains. There are also a host of commands that you can use with the targets. Table 16.2 explains each.

**Table 16.2 Commands Used Under the ipchains Arguments**

| Commands | Definition |
| --- | --- |
| •A *chain* | Adds a rule to the chain |
| •D *chain rule_number* | Deletes a rule number from the chain |
| •I *chain rule_number* | Inserts a rule into the chain before the designated number |
| •R *chain rule_number* | Replaces the rule number in the chain |
| •F *chain* | Flushes the chain. Using this command is the same as sending a -D command to each chain one by one |
| •L *chain* | Lists the rules in the chain |
| •N *chain* | Creates a new user-defined chain |
| •X *chain* | Deletes a chain |
| •P *chain target* | Sets the default target |

Additional options are available for customizing ipchains even further. But for the purposes of this example, these tables cover the majority of the options.

## Setting Up the Host or Gateway

If you are to provide IP masquerading, support for the feature must be compiled into the kernel. Most Red Hat releases already provide IP masquerading. However, you may need to enable some customized options. If you need assistance to compiling a kernel, refer to Chapter 14.

For your convenience, Listing 16.3 shows the major steps needed to compile a kernel with IP masquerading enabled. You will need to provide the IP masquerading options in the kernel yourself.

**Listing 16.3 The Basic Steps Needed to Compile
a Kernel with IP Masquerading Enabled**

```
cd /usr/src/linux
make config        # or chose one of the two below
    make menuconfig
    make xconfig
make dep
make bzImage
    # edit your /etc/lilo.conf file now.
make modules
```

```
make modules_install
make install
/sbin/lilo
/sbin/shutdown now -r
```

You must compile in several options when setting up IP masquerading under the kernel. Due to the dynamic nature of kernel development, the options may have changed in the most up-to-date kernel from what is listed in the following. You should select all the IP masquerading options when prompted during the configuration routine.

The following set of options shown in Listing 16.4 is a sample of what you may see when you enter the make config command. When doing a normal compilation under the /usr/src/linux directory, you should enter Y (for *yes*) for each of the following options. As the kernel continues to mature and become less experimental, the options you in this listing may become more stable. You should also enable Ethernet support under the Networking portion of the kernel configuration that is not shown below. Again, be sure you know the make of your network interface card.

### Listing 16.4  What You May See When Entering the makecongif Command

```
CONFIG_EXPERIMENTAL
• this will allow you to select experimental ip_masq code compiled into
the kernel
• Enable loadable module support
CONFIG_MODULES
• This allows you to load modules
• Networking support
CONFIG_NET
• Network firewalls
CONFIG_FIREWALL
• TCP/IP networking
CONFIG_INET
• IP: forwarding/gatewaying
CONFIG_IP_FORWARD
• IP: firewalling
CONFIG_IP_FIREWALL
• IP: masquerading (EXPERIMENTAL?)
```

CONFIG_IP_MASQUERADE

• IP: always defragment

CONFIG_IP_ALWAYS_DEFRAG

• highly recommended

• Dummy net driver support

CONFIG_DUMMY

• recommended

After successfully compiling your kernel, copying it to the correct location and completing the other tasks associated with making a new kernel or modifying an existing one, you can begin configuring the network settings:

1. Create a loopback device and verify that network support is working correctly:

   ```
   # /sbin/ifconfig lo 127.0.0.1
   # /sbin/route add -host 127.0.0.1 lo
   ```

2. Now test your own network interface to make sure you can ping yourself:

   ```
   # ping 127.0.0.1
   ```

   Most systems will already have a loopback configuration set up, but check and/or add if necessary. If you receive a reply, your internal network is operational.

3. Now begin adding the hosts on your system to your own Linux settings:

   ```
   # /etc/hosts
   192.168.0.20    beta.astronomy.org    beta
   192.168.0.30    gamma.astronomy.org   gamma
   192.168.0.40    delta.astronomy.org   delta
   ```

4. Create a route for your client machines. After this command, you can simply add more clients as needed without ever needing to change (unless you have more than 255 clients in your small LAN, which may be unlikely).

   ```
   # /sbin/ifconfig eth0 192.168.0.20 netmask 255.255.255.0 up
      # /sbin/route add -net 192.168.0.0 eth0
   ```

5. Configure your Linux machine so that the client machines will "hide" their identity within the Linux machine. All packets will be routed through your Linux box and then go to your ISP and then to the Internet.

# Installing the Chains

I accomplished this by placing the correct sequence of ipchains at the end of my /etc/rc.d/init.d/network file. It is possible to run the script separately, but I wanted the feature available every time that I booted up or restarted the network configuration.

You can just as easily add a rc.masquerade script to the /etc/rc.d directory and then have the rc.local file call the script upon bootup. Copy all the lines needed for the masquerading to a file called /etc/rc.d/rc.masquerade.local.

Make the file executable by using the chmod command as follows:

```
chmod 700 /etc/rc.d/rc.masquerade.local
```

Place the file on a line toward the top of your /etc/rc.d/rc.local file. When the rc.local file starts, it will also parse through the script and start the masquerading process.

If you choose to run the masquerade script in your /etc/rc.d/init.d/network file, the lines shown in Listing 16.5 should appear just before the end of the file, immediately preceding the exit 0 line. This script makes starting and stopping the network connection very easy. This sample text also starts ipchains automatically. The lines preceded by a hash or pound sign (#) are comments and explain what each section accomplishes.

### Listing 16.5  A Sample Script Placed in the /etc/rc.d/init.d/network File that Enables IP Masquerading

```
echo "1" > /proc/sys/net/ipv4/ip_forward
echo "1" > /proc/sys/net/ipv4/ip_dynaddr


# MASQ timeouts
# 2 hrs timeout for TCP session timeouts
# 10 sec timeout for traffic after the TCP/IP "FIN""
# packet is received
# 60 sec timeout for UDP traffic (MASQ'ed ICQ users
```

```
# must enable a 30sec firewall timeout in ICQ itself)
#
ipchains -M -S 7200 10 60
# Enable simple IP forwarding and Masquerading
# NOTE: The following is an example for an internal
# LAN address in the 192.168.0.x
# network with a 255.255.255.0 or a "24" bit subnet mask.
#
# Please change this network number and subnet mask
# to match your internal LAN setup
#
ipchains -P forward DENY
ipchains -A forward -s 192.168.0.20/24 -j MASQ
# and
ipchains -A forward -i ppp0 -j MASQ
```

The first two lines enable the ip_forwarding and dynamic addressing modules. These modules are necessary for passing on information to the router and through to the network.

The next uncommented lines determine the timeout sequence when no traffic is being passed. Then the default policy is set up to deny all packets from being forwarded. The next rule then allows only packets from the internal LAN to forward masqueraded packets through the gateway as determined by their source IP address. The last rule specifies the device through which all packets are forwarded.

All you need do now is restart /etc/rc.d/init.d/network:

```
# /etc/rc.d/init.d/network restart
```

Now start an Internet browser on any of the Windows machines and make certain you can get onto the Internet. The telnet utility should also work.

However, IP masquerading does pose some problems to ICQ and FTP use. Using additional modules that come with the default installation of Red Hat Linux, you can modify this process to also include FTP and ICQ packet transfers. Choose these modules during the recompilation process if they are not available. To make FTP function through the masquerade, run the commands shown in Listing 16.6. These modules will remain active until you either reboot the machine or remove it using the rmmod command and the module name.

## Listing 16.6  Enabling Modules that Allow the Transfer of FTP and Other Packets through the Masquerade

```
/sbin/depmod -a
/sbin/modprobe /lib/modules/2.2.16/ipv4/ip_masq_ftp
/sbin/modprobe /lib/modules/2.2.16/ipv4/ip_masq_raudio
/sbin/modprobe /lib/modules/2.2.16/ipv4/ip_masq_irc
```

You can add these same lines to the /etc/rc.d/init.d/network script right below the entry in Listing 16.6. You can also place these commands in the /etc/rc.d/rc.local file as well so that every time Linux is rebooted these commands come up as well. For help with ICQ, Real Audio, and other processes that require a specific port, look for corresponding modules in the directory listed in Listing 16.6.

For a more detailed overview of IP masquerading, Listing 16.7 shows another standard script that accomplishes much the same thing as Listing 16.6. It, too, is designed to allow certain packets to masquerade using 192.168.0.10 as the gateway.

## Listing 16.7  A More Detailed ipchains Script that Accomplishes the Same Masquerading Process

```
# Flush
/sbin/ipchains -F input
/sbin/ipchains -F output
/sbin/ipchains -F forward
# Internal:
/sbin/ipchains -A input -s 192.168.0.10/24 -d 192.168.0.10/24 -j ACCEPT
/sbin/ipchains -A output -s 192.168.0.10/24 -d 192.168.0.10/24 -j ACCEPT
# Loopback:
/sbin/ipchains -A input -i lo -s 0/0 -d 0/0 -j ACCEPT
/sbin/ipchains -A output -i lo -s 0/0 -d 0/0 -j ACCEPT
# Masquerading:
/sbin/ipchains -A forward -s 192.168.0.10/24 -d 192.168.0.10/24 -j ACCEPT
/sbin/ipchains -A forward -s 192.168.0.10/24 -d 0/0 -j MASQ
/sbin/ipchains -P forward DENY
/sbin/ipchains -A input -s 192.168.0.10/24 -d 0/0 -j ACCEPT
/sbin/ipchains -A output -s 192.168.0.10/24 -d 0/0 -j ACCEPT
# TOS flags:
/sbin/ipchains -A output -p tcp -d 0/0 www -t 0x01 0x10
```

```
/sbin/ipchains -A output -p tcp -d 0/0 telnet -t 0x01 0x10
/sbin/ipchains -A output -p tcp -d 0/0 ftp -t 0x01 0x10
/sbin/ipchains -A output -p tcp -d 0/0 ftp-data -t 0x01 0x08
```

The last few lines accomplish much the same as that of the modules by allowing ftp data to be transmitted in and out of the system. This script is simply more verbose and allows data to be directed both in and out of the gateway machine.

> **NOTE**
>
> Some have raised the question about the ethics of using only one computer connection or just one viable IP address for more than one machine. If you are concerned about this, contact your ISP and ask what its acceptable use policies are. In any case, sharing an IP address with IP masquerading is a good thing, since it makes a limited number of IP addresses go a lot further. It is this same idea that drove the IETF to dump the class-based IP allotment scheme and come up with CIDR.

## Troubleshooting Your Masqueraded Connection

If you are still having problems and cannot get IP masquerading to work, here are a few suggestions that might help. They may not guarantee that you accomplish all that you want, but they might get you pointed in the right direction. If all else fails, read additional documentation provided on many sites, contact the newsgroups, and experiment with the other scripts provided in this book. The accompanying CD also provides several masquerading and firewalling scripts that you may use to your advantage.

◆ First check the physical connection between the computers. Make certain that the RJ-45 ends are plugged in correctly to both the machines and the hub.

◆ Try to ping your machines. Within a Linux xterm window, enter **ping 192.168.0.20**. You should receive echo replies from the Windows clients. You can stop this operation by pressing Ctrl-C. You can also try names such as ping beta or ping beta.astronomy.edu. If you do not receive any echo replies, double-check your network settings on both the Linux and Windows machines. Use /sbin/ifconfig on the Linux box along with /sbin/route -n to display the network card's settings and the current route. Make sure that there is a default gateway.

◆ Try to use Telnet to reach the Linux machine from the Windows machine. Click the Start button in the lower-left corner, select Run, then enter **telnet 192.168.0.10** in the box. An MS-DOS window should appear displaying the login prompt. If the message "Network unreachable" or a similar message appears, then you have not configured your network settings properly. If you get a prompt soon, there's surely some kind of traffic between your machines. Double-check that there are no extra settings in the /etc/hosts.allow and /etc/hosts.deny files that prevent other machines from using Linux services.

◆ Download a program called IPTraffic. You can find most Linux programs at the site http://freshmeat.net/. Freshmeat keeps an up-to-date log of all newly updated and current Linux programs. IPTraffic is a menu-based program that you can use to monitor Ethernet traffic. It can also check on the ppp0 device for PPP connections.

# Establishing Connectivity between Home and the Internet

Once you have established a connection between your home or work and either an ISP or your own system with access to the World Wide Web, you can start pulling down content from other servers and sites. Browsers and FTP sites provide quick access to Web content and programs. This chapter briefly deals with setting up and configuring a few simple browsers and then exploring command-line FTP requests.

## Text-Based Browsers

Long before Netscape or other browsers came on the scene, Linux was providing command-line interfaces to the Internet. Because Linux was originally developed as a console-based system with nearly all commands originating at the basic shell prompt, it was only natural that a text-based browser was to become the preferred method of browsing HTML pages and viewing text content on the Web. It was only with the further development of the X Window environment and similar movements in providing more graphically oriented sites that other browsers such as Netscape began to enjoy popularity as well. Still many people consider text-based browsers to be the more dynamic of the two types of browsers.

In addition to these simple command-line browsers, there were other pre-WWW interfaces that generated viewable text from information downloaded off the Web. These were tools such as archie, gopher, and veronica. Again, these browsers were not as dynamic as today's browsers, but for their time and for the machines on which they ran, these utilities were a vibrant method of exchanging simple text messages, downloading programs, etc.

Currently, the most popular text browser supported under Linux is lynx. It is operable under any console or xterm window. Most distributions provide it as a default option under installation. It generally installs via RPM, but can just as easily be installed via source code. The lynx browser runs under nearly any version of UNIX. Some of the latest releases also provide a color-coding scheme so that links are highlighted from within the text. Also, they differentiate between visited and unvisited links. You can use lynx to open HTML pages on the Web, but you can also use lynx to view local Web pages located on the hard drive.

Starting lynx is simple. Simply type in the name of the program and the page you would like to visit:

```
# lynx http://slashdot.org/
```

Most Linux-friendly pages are customized for both text-based browsers such as lynx as well as for graphically driven browsers. Once you have the page open, perusing its contents is simply a matter of pressing the arrow keys. Using the Tab key usually moves the cursor between the different links.

Some may feel that lynx has an ugly interface, but it is useful for testing ports and Web content from outside your own network. For example, friends throughout the country have provide accounts on Linux machines so that I can test my own firewall and routing from outside my network. To verify that an internal Web site is visible to the world, I like to fire up lynx and type in the URL.

◆ ◆ ◆

If you are unsure as to which page you should open or simply want to browse random sites, open lynx and then press G. The lynx program prompts you to specify which URL you would like to open. Now enter the name of any common search engine. The lynx program supports fields and forms, so inputting data should not be a problem. However, lynx does not handle frames well, so when presented with a choice between a framed and nonframed page, always choose the nonframed page. Many Linux users prefer Lynx for its speed and versatility as well as multiplatform capability. Not only can lynx be run on nearly any machine, but because it does not have to render any sort of graphic it quickly loads even the most stubborn of pages.

The lynx program, however, does not open secure sites or sites that have an https:// prefix. For pages such as these, you might want to try Netscape. With the recent release of the RSA encryption, you can expect to soon see more secure versions of lynx become available.

# Using Graphical Browsers

Some Linux users resisted Netscape's foray into the Linux world, as many of these users had already opted for other browsers such as lynx. However, once Netscape publicized plans to open its source code to all users, sentiment quickly changed. Now Netscape and its Communicator package have become one of the staples of the Linux installation. In fact, Netscape has become the model for most open-sourcing ventures. Many look to its success among Linux users and the quick development of new features as one of the greatest success stories of the open-source movement.

That is not to say, however, that Netscape has not experienced some difficult trials. Netscape still experiences memory leaks, though they are not as severe as those in the past. Also, the Linux community has not viewed Netscape's financial dealings with other Internet-related partners favorably. Still, Netscape has undeniably helped Linux substantially in influencing additional businesses and companies into considering open-sourcing their software.

The Netscape package for Linux has all the features found in its releases for Windows and Macintosh. Most users download the Communicator package, which is essentially three programs in one, or four if you count the address book utility. The standard programs that come with Communicator are the Netscape Browser, the Messenger (which provides e-mail and threaded news capability), and an HTML editor called the Composer.

For my own use around the office and at home, I use two of these tools almost every day. The quality provided by Netscape allows me to view nearly 100 percent of the pages I visit. The e-mail client allows me to check my e-mail, view attached documents, and save files to the hard drive. This client, which supports both POP3 and IMAP mail servers, is one of the simplest and best e-mail clients currently available for Linux. The news reader, which is now part of the e-mail client, is also quite useful and allows for a variety of news servers to be used for reading messages posted to newsgroups. The HTML editor is WYSIWYG (what you see is what you get), but can also be configured to view the content in text format. Some consider this editor to be the weakest link in the Communicator suite, yet it is extremely functional and can quickly generate HTML-coded text.

A typical download of the entire Communicator suite is around 15 megabytes, but for the functionality it provides, it is well worth it. The typical download for Linux does not include the source code but the binaries only. The latest developmental release of the Netscape browser is known as Mozilla. It is the precursor to the latest Netscape 6 release and is also the platform on which most new features for Netscape are added to the Communicator package. They run well, but Netscape has decided that for regular users to install the program quickly, sending just the binaries or compiled source with the executables is more efficient.

Installing Communicator is also simple. Once you have downloaded the entire code, unpack it in the /opt directory. This is where many of the latest programs have begun placing their default installation directories. First unzip the file, then untar it. This should create a Communicator directory within the opt/ directory. Be sure to read the readme file provided and make the necessary changes to the path and the /etc/profile after the program is fully installed so that you can execute Netscape from the command line.

Change to this new directory and run the file ./ns-install. You should do so as root so that Netscape can create the required directory for you. Normal installations will place everything into /opt/netscape. You can choose another directory, but as is the case with many Linux programs, it is sometime best to go with their default values. This directory is where the developers have tested the program under similar conditions and have certified that the program does indeed work.

You can either add /opt/netscape to your path or start the Netscape executable by typing in the absolute path. Netscape then makes a hidden directory called .netscape/ in your home directory. This directory stores the customized settings, including your bookmarks, cookies, and address books. Netscape also creates a mail directory called nsmail/ in your home directory. You can create individual mail folders for organizing incoming e-mail. Any of the many users on the same machine can use Netscape and personalize it to their tastes. Updating to newer releases involves simply deleting the /opt/netscape directory and then reinstalling the executable. Neither mail nor the individual settings are lost during upgrades.

One other complaint again Netscape on Linux has also been recently addressed. Because the Web has become so media-oriented, many of the standard plug-ins, such as Macromedia's Flash and audio plugins, are geared more toward the Windows user. However, now plug-ins are available that play most any audio or media file under Netscape on the Linux platform as well as generate most of the dynamic graphic renderings used on Web pages today. To download the latest plug-ins for Linux, go to the Netscape home page and review the available plug-ins. The two most common now used are the plugger and flash plug-ins. Both are quickly downloaded and extractable. Simply copying them over to the /opt/netscape/plugins directory and then restarting Netscape will usually enable them.

You can find further details regarding the customization of Netscape under Netscape's own home page. If you have any past experience using Netscape under other platforms, you will find that the Linux version does not differ much. Because Netscape uses the Motif libraries, the general look and feel might be a bit different. The upcoming version of Netscape will borrow the GTK libraries, thus helping to standardize the look of Netscape. Netscape was also ported to the QT libraries upon its initial source code release and has lately been revitalized by other KDE and QT enthusiasts. Thus efforts are already under way to improve Netscape's overall functionality and improve performance for all Linux users.

# Using Other Graphical Programs for Browsing

Other Web browsers besides Netscape are available for general download. One of the lesser known is Arena, which provides basic Web viewing using the HTML 1.0 general code. It does not provide as much versatility as Netscape offers, but it is small and efficient. The same is true of Amaya, which is one of the earliest Web browsers for Linux and came preinstalled on some of the older Red Hat releases.

Another favorite among Windows users is Opera, which is also extremely fast and versatile though it is stripped down in its graphic rendering ability. Opera is currently available for Linux and for a variety of other platforms. Opera is free for a limited time and is classified as shareware, meaning that after a certain period you are expected to pay for additional use.

It is encouraging to see that the general field of Internet browsing, once dominated by only one form of operating system, is now attracting other contenders. All told, more than 20 text- and graphic-based browsers are available for the Linux platform.

## Exchanging Data via FTP

Another method of transmitting information over the Internet is through the use of FTP (File Transfer Protocol). Whereas browsers are designed to send dynamic text and images through port 80, FTP is designed to transmit larger units of data through port 21. Through FTP you can download larger files more quickly and efficiently than you can by using a browser. Although Netscape offers a simplified version of an FTP client within its browser, it also allows for various other programs to plug into its program. When a certain feature is required, such as Telnet or FTP, you can launch an xterm window from within the Netscape program and then perform the necessary functions. Still, knowledge of FTP terminal commands is essential when you begin using Linux. If you opt not to install Netscape or some other browser during the initial install, knowing how to use FTP and download additional window managers, kernels, or browsers is necessary.

FTP is installed by default. The commands are part of the protocol that the various FTP clients implement. Packages such as ncftp significantly enhance the basic FTP client with scroll back, file viewing, command history, and other features. The commands associated with any FTP version are similar to normal Linux commands for moving through directories. The cd and ls commands also work under the FTP interface just like they do under the shell. Once you have successfully connected to the Internet or to the outside network, starting up FTP can be as simple as typing the following if you want to use FTP to access Netscape's home ftp directory:

```
# ftp ftp.netscape.com
```

After the machine resolves the name of this domain, the program prompts you to enter your username, which on most public FTP sites is "anonymous." Your password is generally your e-mail address. For security reasons, many people, rather than giving out their real e-mail address, opt for guest@anonymous.com.

After successfully logging in, you will usually be presented with a variety of directories. The standard directory where most files or programs are kept is pub/. If you wish to upload a file to the site, you may choose also to use the cd command to change into the incoming/ directory if there is one. However, the most common practice is to find the specific files from a certain ftp site under the pub/ directory. The directory often includes a message file that contains instructions and links for where to locate a particular file.

After locating the file in question, downloading involves a series of specific commands. The get and put commands are the simplest to use with FTP. If you wish to download a particular file, enter **get <filename>**. If you have access to that directory and wish to upload a file from your own machine, enter **put <filename>**. Make sure that the file you are uploading is located in the same directory that you were in when you connected to the FTP server.

If you need to change your local directories, simply enter **lcd /home/<username>** or **lcd <directory/name/>**. Changing directories on the remote FTP server is the same as under regular directories. A simple cd command followed by the directory name will work from that server also. The ls command is also useful to view the contents of the remote directory.

When you are downloading or uploading files, do not forget the bin and ascii commands if transferring data between UNIX and non-UNIX machines. The bin command stands for *binary* whereas the ascii command stands for simple ASCII text files. Depending on the type of file you are sending, convert the method of transport to the file type. If moving data between two Linux boxes you never need worry about setting the bin or ascii commands.

Some additional examples that help in downloading and uploading files are the following commands. To view the progress your download is making rather than waiting for the transfer to complete, use the hash or tick commands. Much like the hash option when using the rpm command, the hash command shows a steady stream of hash marks across your screen representing bytes of data received. The tick command uses a numeric format to show how many bytes of data have been downloaded. In this manner, the command's output presents a better representation of how far along your download is and how much is left.

When downloading multiple files from of a location instead of just one, you should use the mget or mput command. Here you can use wildcard options such as the following:

```
mget linux-2.2.*
```

If you are attempting to download all copies of the stable Linux kernel from the FTP site, the program will ask, after each download is complete, whether you want to download the next file. Depending on your answer, the program will either download the files successively or skip to the next file.

If you do not want the program to prompt you every time, you can use the prompt command to turn this feature off. Then the program will download all the files in rapid succession. To turn any of these features back off, simply retype the command. FTP will inform you that that particular feature has been turned off.

## Using GUI FTP Clients

For many converts to Linux, command-line programs are not enough, even though they may be more flexible to use. These new users require simplified GUIs. For this purpose, many FTP clients now run under the X Window interface. One of the better clients is IglooFTP. This client provides all the features of the command-line interface and yet is simple enough that anyone can use it. It is actually better than related counterparts that run under Windows. Because it is designed for Linux, it is more stable and robust than WS_FTP, one of the most popular Windows FTP clients. If you use FTP often and are frequently in the X Window environment, you may want to try either this FTP client or one of the many others.

The types of programs available for Linux users to access other servers or to gain access to Internet sites are manifold. It requires but a little research and testing to discover quickly how broad the field is for Internet use under Linux. Because Linux was designed for use as a server, you can provide the same services to others as are available for your own use.

# Conclusion

This chapter focused on creating dial-up networks and granting additional connectivity between the home, office, and Internet. As your skills in accessing the Internet from a Linux-based machine, you will also want to reciprocate in the information that you download. The next chapter focuses on one of the main bonding elements of the Internet community, e-mail. In particular, the chapter examines the sendmail program, a mainstay in electronic mail transfer agents (MTAs). Chapter 17 looks at how sendmail is installed by Red Hat, how to customize it to suit, how to free it up for your own use, and how to lock it down for added security.

# Chapter 17

## E-mail

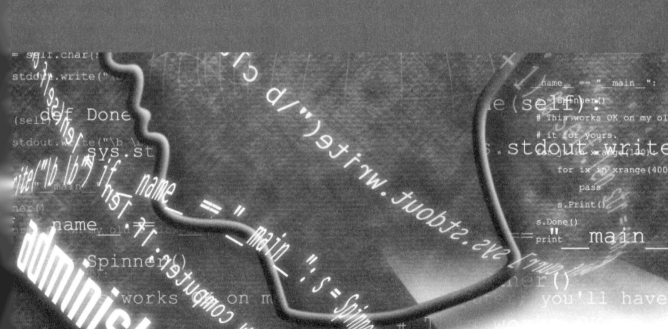

**E**lectronic mail has become an integral part of most people's lives. It links people from all over the globe, assists in gathering information we need, and provides a new means of communication that makes anonymous the sender from the sendee. It is known for both good and bad. From out of this free exchange of transmissions there has also arisen a barrage of junk and unsolicited electronic messages. Understanding how sendmail, the *de facto* mail utility for Linux, functions and how you as an administrator can tailor it to your needs is a crucial part of this chapter.

This chapter will examine the following areas:

◆ Obtaining the sendmail program and installing it via source or RPM

◆ Configuring the various enabling options for your domain

◆ Running sendmail from the command line or as a daemon

◆ Eliminating spam or unsolicited e-mail from your system

◆ Testing new configurations in your sendmail setup

◆ Sending mail from virtual domains within your system

◆ Checking and forwarding e-mail from your machine and others

# Understanding Mail Transfer Agents

As one of the oldest and most tried and proven mail transfer agents currently available, sendmail has an option for nearly every situation. Due to its age and the many incarnations it has undergone, it not only has become a standard bearer for e-mail delivery, but has so many features and variables that it requires a full chapter to cover the greater part of the many features it offers.

It is argued that sendmail is too convoluted for the present-day Internet. Many would prefer substituting a simpler program to handle the flood of e-mail currently awash through the networks. But with the many varying servers and e-mail clients delivering mail throughout the world, none can match sendmail in its robustness and stability.

One of the most popular uses of Linux is that of a mail server. Because of its dependability under high stress and load conditions and due to its low cost, it is customarily chosen to run the mail server of a company or organization. The preferred *Mail Transfer Agent* (*MTA*) that is responsible for handling incoming mail and properly sending it back out again is sendmail. Think of a mail server as one small post office where letters come in from all over the world. The sendmail program tackles all the traffic and properly sorts the messages either to drop them off within a local post office box or to ship them out again to a client that has relocated to another server. Such is the task and capacity of sendmail.

# Exploring the sendmail Program

The sendmail program is free for all to use. Though it has branched off subsidiary versions for commercial use and development, the main source code is still available to the public for download. Since it is licensed in its open-source incarnation, it too requires that any changes or improvements made to it must be released back to the community for its acceptance and/or disapproval. The developers, though, have final say in how sendmail will function and can revoke any change if they feel it compromises the security of the program. These checks and balances help to make sendmail not only more dependable but more efficient.

It is beyond the scope of this chapter to take an in-depth look at how each individual section of sendmail functions. Rather than look at the nuances of the program, this chapter instead examines some of the methods used to create a functioning version of sendmail, customizing its features under Linux while examining other mail programs. The chapter also looks at security issues posed by mail programs and at the way that mailing lists operate. Also, the chapter examines some of the methods employed both to view and handle mail on the server and client side. These methods include the use of POP3 and IMAP programs that manipulate incoming mail, along with the use of the pine program, which allows users to read and answer mail directly on the server.

## Installing sendmail

The sendmail program is a rather complicated mailing utility, but it is by far the most versatile and robust program available. What follows in this section are instructions for setting up sendmail on a standard Red Hat Linux machine. With most every distribution of Red Hat, sendmail comes preinstalled. The binary is already compiled either in RPM format or as a separate stand-alone binary, and the available options, such as the configuration file and other accessories, are already established. The instructions provided in this chapter will more closely examine the steps for compiling and running sendmail from source. For a truly manageable configuration of sendmail with all the settings determined by the user, compiling from source is the best option.

You first want to obtain the latest copy of sendmail from the main sendmail site:

```
http://www.sendmail.org/
```

You can also use ftp to receive the source code from the same domain:

```
ftp ftp.sendmail.org
```

Due to the active development of the sendmail source code, you cannot determine which release or version is the most stable. Unlike some of the other developmental software available for Linux, sendmail's developmental releases are quite reliable. You can download the most recent sendmail release and install it on your machine without any qualms. Usually the RPM version available from off the installation CD will accomplish all that is needed by most networks or systems for e-mail delivery. Otherwise, for those more adventurous souls are those administrators who tailoring the program exactly to the system's needs, it is recommended that they obtain the source code and install from scratch.

Unzip and untar the file anywhere on your server. I prefer keeping all source files in one location in case the program requires recompiling. Over time, a binary file can become corrupted, in which case the easiest way to fix the file is to create a new binary or copy the previous binary that you created over the corrupted file. I normally create a /usr/local/gnu directory on my Linux servers. Here I have all the source files for the latest developmental versions.

After unpacking the source code, change directories to the location of the new sendmail directory, ~/sendmail-8.11.0/src/. It is important that you first go to the src/ directory and customize the settings associated with the configuration and performance of sendmail. For complete instructions, read the install or readme file, but for a simplified version you can simply enter ./**Build** or **sh Build** to run the install. Make certain that your $PATH is correct so that the make command runs without a hitch. With the Red Hat Linux distributions, running the make command should be no problem.

# Building a Configuration File

Now edit the *.mc file in the ~/sendmail-8.11.0/cf/cf/ directory. The filename stands for the *m4 macro* file. This file determines your sendmail configuration and the variables that sendmail will require for operating your system. The sendmail program provides several different example .mc files that you may use for creating your own configuration. Most are configured for alternative UNIX platforms as well as for specific Linux needs, so look for the one that closely matches your own system.

The generic-linux.mc file will work for most Linux distributions and will generate a sendmail.cf file, or *configuration file*, from which the sendmail binary will look for instructions on how to handle specific requests. Otherwise, you can use the provided redhat.mc file for generating a customized sendmail.cf file specific to the Red Hat distribution. To create a viable sendmail.cf file, you must first edit the generic.mc file that comes with the source or edit the *.mc file that comes with the Red Hat distribution, if you installed all the sendmail packages. Then you must run the generic.mc file through a preprocessor, which, in turn, creates a generic sendmail.cf file.

Locate the sendmail.mc file in sendmail-8.11.0/cf/cf/generic-linux.mc. For the purposes of convenience, I copied the generic-linux.mc file to kerry-linux.mc so that I could edit it more easily. This way, if I made an error that I could not fix, I could always grab the pristine copy for further editing. In either case, it's a good idea to copy the distribution file to another filename so that you can edit it to suit your needs.

The generic sendmail.mc file is usually very limited. Here is the sum total of its contents:

```
divert(0)dnl
VERSIONID(`$Id: generic-linux.mc,v 8.1 1999/09/24 22:48:05
gshapiro Exp $')
OSTYPE(linux)dnl
DOMAIN(generic)dnl
MAILER(local)dnl
MAILER(smtp)dnl
```

You should either familiarize yourself with the options or look at one of the sample *.mc files provided. For a better understanding of what options can be compiled into the sendmail configuration, let's first look at the sendmail.mc file that comes with Red Hat and which already has several options provided (see Listing 17.1).

**Listing 17.1  A Generic sendmail.mc File with Several Options Provided for Generating a Secure sendmail.cf File**

```
divert(-1)
include('/usr/lib/sendmail-cf/m4/cf.m4')
define('confDEF_USER_ID', "8:12")
OSTYPE('linux')
undefine('UUCP_RELAY')
undefine('BITNET_RELAY')
define('confAUTO_REBUILD')
define('confTO_CONNECT', '1m')
define('confTRY_NULL_MX_LIST',true)
define('confDONT_PROBE_INTERFACES',true)
define('PROCMAIL_MAILER_PATH','/usr/bin/procmail')
FEATURE('smrsh','/usr/sbin/smrsh')
FEATURE(mailertable)
FEATURE('virtusertable','hash -o /etc/mail/virtusertable')
FEATURE(redirect)
FEATURE(always_add_domain)
FEATURE(use_cw_file)
FEATURE(local_procmail)
MAILER(procmail)
MAILER(smtp)
FEATURE('access_db')
FEATURE('blacklist_recipients')
FEATURE('accept_unresolvable_domains')
dnl FEATURE('relay_based_on_MX')
```

You can use the configuration in Listing 17.1 to define a custom *.mc file that you can name whatever you want. Though the options defined in this listing might appear rather confusing, it is easier to edit the generic *.mc file than to change the options in the generated sendmail.cf file. Many of these features are buried deep within the sendmail configuration file.

# Deciphering the sendmail Codex

To give you a better understanding of what each line accomplishes, this section looks at each line in the *.mc file in turn and explains how they operate under sendmail. You can find more specific uses can be found in the sendmail documentation.

```
divert(-1)
include('/usr/lib/sendmail-cf/m4/cf.m4')
```

The first line tells the m4 preprocessor where the actual configuration file begins. The second line includes the file, which defines the macro that you will need in order to parse the generic-linux.mc file into a human-readable format or into a standard sendmail.cf file.

```
define('confDEF_USER_ID',"8:12")
```

This line sets the default user and group ID for sendmail. The number 8 is the UID and the number 12 the GID of the user who will run the sendmail daemon. Check for your /etc/passwd for making detailed changes to this user configuration. For security reasons, it's a good idea to create a user and group just for the sendmail daemon, even though it normally runs as root. If you concerned about running sendmail as root, create a `sendmail` or `postmaster` user who controls the use of the daemon.

```
OSTYPE('linux')
```

This option tells the m4 prepocessor to include some standard settings for Linux.

```
undefine('UUCP_RELAY')
```

This line defines that sendmail will not accept or relay any UUCP-addressed e-mail. This is just the first of many relaying issues that come up with sendmail. In the past, many people abused the privileges associated with e-mail servers. Now developers are locking down all servers so that they do not allow relaying. If you do wish to allow a server to relay to any other host, you will have to define this yourself.

```
undefine('BITNET_RELAY')
```

**NOTE**

To relay e-mail is to allow a client from outside your domain or subnet class to use your mail server to send an e-mail or a block of e-mails to another server also outside your domain. Your mail server becomes the relay point. Administrators strongly frowned upon relaying e-mail because of abuses by unsolicited bulk e-mail distributors. The sendmail program disables relaying by default.

Likewise, this line specifies that sendmail does not accept any mail from .BITNET pseudodomains, or domains not supported by regular DNS entries.

```
define('confAUTO_REBUILD')
```

This line informs the sendmail program to rebuild the /etc/alias file automatically, if needed, after any setting is changed within that particular file. The alias file contains information about local e-mail aliases.

```
define('confTO_CONNECT', '1m')
```

This option sets the timeout for the initial connect() to 1 minute. This option can only shorten the connect timeout of the kernel. It should be safe to use this value.

```
define('confTRY_NULL_MX_LIST',true)
```

In case your mail server is the best MX or mail record for a host and the option is set to true, it will try to connect to the host directly. Hosts can have several mail servers in their MX records as defined under the name server entries. If the primary mail server is down, sendmail then transmits the mail to the next mail server in line defined in the DNS records for that system. For further clarification regarding name servers and MX records, consult Chapter 15.

```
define('confDONT_PROBE_INTERFACES',true)
```

If you set this option to true, sendmail will not add any local interfaces to the list of known equivalent addresses. It should be safe to leave this option at its default setting.

```
FEATURE('smrsh','/usr/sbin/smrsh')
```

This feature allows the use of a restricted shell to run local mailers (such as procmail). This option makes sendmail more secure because the local mailer will have only restricted access to other programs.

```
FEATURE('virtusertable','hash -o /etc/mail/virtusertable')
```

This feature allows the server to host virtual domains. The second part of the expression states the database format and the path to the file containing the virtual domains.

Virtual domains are domains not associated with the name of your server but which are hosted on your machine. With this setting, you can also set up mail aliases and allow e-mail to those virtual domains to be routed to viable e-mail addresses.

```
FEATURE(redirect)
```

This command rejects any mail that asks to be redirected. Use this option unless you want to support unsolicited e-mail—spam—and those who abuse unsuspecting mail servers. You should keep this option in place.

```
FEATURE(always_add_domain)
```

Always add your domain to unqualified addresses. You need to set this option if you want to masquerade your FROM addresses as they are sent out. This masquerade option is not like the ipchains masquerade option; instead it changes the outgoing e-mails to reflect your system's domain name.

```
FEATURE(use_cw_file)
```

This line tells sendmail to read the sendmail.cw file to get alternate names for the host. This file contains the names of other virtual domains that might be hosted on your system.

```
define('PROCMAIL_MAILER_PATH','/usr/bin/procmail')
```

If you wish to use procmail to sort, filter, and deliver your local mail, set its path here. The procmail program is a useful utility for routing e-mail to separate accounts and users.

```
FEATURE(local_procmail)
```

This feature allows procmail to deliver your local mail. Rather than letting your default mail program handle the incoming e-mail, you can define procmail as the default mail handler. Procmail has several advantages over the regular mail agent that comes installed on most Linux systems in that it is easier to define rules to route certain e-mails to different users and dispose of unwanted e-mail as well.

```
MAILER(procmail)
```

Use the interface to procmail.

```
MAILER(smtp)
```

Use the standard SMTP mailer (sendmail) for outgoing mail. This resides on port 25 and is defined in the /etc/services file.

```
FEATURE('access_db')
```

Use the access database, located at /etc/mail/access, to allow or refuse mail from certain domains. This database is also known as the spam-stomping utility in that you can drop e-mail from certain hosts or allow others to relay through your server. You must *rehash* or rebuild the database every time you edit the access file. To do so, enter the command **makemap -r hash access.db < access**. Under Red Hat Linux, this rehash option is already enabled for the sendmail RPM package with a default makefile. To rehash the default access file, simply enter **make** in the /etc/mail directory.

```
FEATURE('blacklist_recipients')
```

This command turns on the ability to block certain user/hostnames with access.db.

```
DOMAIN('generic')
```

In case you want to use the sendmail.cw file, keep this line in the *.mc file.

```
FEATURE(masquerade_envelope)
```

Masquerade the header and the envelope of your mail. The envelope contains the e-mail address to which external mail delivery subsystems will deliver error reports and warnings.

```
FEATURE(genericstable,'hash -o /etc/mail/genericstable')
```

This line specifies that sendmail use a hashed table with masquerading information. The unhashed file looks like this:

```
me       kerry@myisp.net
root     kerry@myisp.net
nobody   kerry@myisp.net
```

This file tells sendmail to rewrite the FROM addresses of your mail, so you will be able to relay all your mail over your ISP's mail server. The first column contains the local address, and the second one the address that sendmail should use instead. For sendmail to read this file, you have to hash it with this command: **makemap -r hash genericstable.db < genericstable**. Again, if this file is defined in your default RPM sendmail install, you can rehash the file using the make command located in /etc/mail.

```
GENERICS_DOMAIN_FILE('/etc/mail/genericsdomain')
```

You need to add your local domain name to this file so that sendmail knows what mail is local and what has to be masqueraded. To get your local domain, use the command hostname. Place this name within the /etc/mail/genericsdomain file.

```
define('SMART_HOST','mail.myisp.net')
```

The sendmail program uses this "smart" host to relay all your outgoing mail. Insert the mail server name of your ISP here if your box uses an external mail server.

```
FEATURE('accept_unresolvable_domains')
```

This line tells sendmail to accept all domains defined by the mail header, even if they can't be resolved either because your server is not online or connected to the Internet or because the name server does not respond. Do not use this line if your computer operates 24 hours a day, seven days a week. Allowing any form of e-mail without a viable domain is an invitation to host relaying for spammers.

```
FEATURE(`relay_based_on_MX')
```

This command tells sendmail to relay only from computers in your MX or mail domain. If you don't understand what this line means, don't use it.

```
define('confDIAL_DELAY','50s')
```

The sendmail program will delay the delivery of outgoing mail for a certain time. Use this line if you have a dial-up connection and want sendmail to connect to the Internet every time there is outgoing mail. (You will also have to install diald to automatically dial up your ISP periodically.)

If you want to send your outgoing mail every time you go online instead, use these lines instead of the dial delay:

```
define('confCON_EXPENSIVE','True')
define('SMTP_MAILER_FLAGS','e')
FEATURE('nocanonify')
```

The first line and second lines tell sendmail to put mail for an "expensive" mailer in the queue instead of sending it immediately and then mark the mailer for outgoing mail as "expensive." The last line tells sendmail not to convert or canonify mail addresses into a FQDN (Fully Qualified Domain Name), because this would include a DNS lookup, which can only be done online.

If you want to send mail only when you go online, you will also have to tell sendmail not to work through the queue after the specified number of minutes. You may have to start sendmail with the command **sendmail -bd** instead of **sendmail -bd -q30m** every time you start or restart it.

Because sendmail is started by init during startup, you will also have to change the /etc/sysconfig/sendmail file or redefine the /etc/rc.d/init.d/sendmail file under Red Hat to avoid having the queue checked every few minutes. Change the former file to the following:

```
DAEMON=yes
QUEUE=
```

Finally, add the command **/usr/sbin/sendmail -q** to /etc/ppp/ip-up.local, which may also be /etc/ppp/ip-up under non-Red Hat machines, in order to send all mail when you go online.

## Copying Over the New Configuration File

The details for the generic *.mc file as shown in the preceding section can be applied to the source code or customized to suit your particular server. Once you have added the necessary lines to your generic-linux.mc or the new file you created based on the existing generic-linux.mc file, you can run the m4 preprocessor program to parse through your macro and create a compiled sendmail.cf file.

If you are using a default *.mc file that came with your Red Hat distribution and if this is the file that you just edited, use the following command:

```
m4 /etc/sendmail.mc > /etc/sendmail.cf
```

If, however, you wish to use the source code as recommended, then use the following command. First make sure you are in the proper directory. The following example calls the *.mc file from its current location and then parses it to the same directory from which you issued the command:

```
m4 /usr/local/gnu/sendmail-8.11.0/cf/cf/kerry-linux.mc > kerry.cf
```

This gives me my own kerry.cf file, which will be renamed to sendmail.cf. Be sure and back up the distribution version of /etc/sendmail.cf by giving it a .dist extension or appending whatever you wish to the file. By naming your sendmail.cf something else first, you can edit the configuration file however you see fit without compromising the new file.

Back up your current /etc/sendmail.cf file before performing the next step:

```
cp /usr/local/gnu/sendmail-8.11.0/cf/cf/kerry.cf /etc/sendmail.cf
```

Once this new file has overwritten the old sendmail.cf file, you can now edit it by hand. The only sections of the sendmail.cf file that you should tackle for local customization are those that are listed before the Rewriting Rules. The first section of the file allows you to change the maximum e-mail size and similar variables. The Rewriting Rules, however, require a more detailed knowledge of the sendmail syntax than this chapter will supply.

## Installing the Binary

Now that the new sendmail.cf file is in place, you can copy over the sendmail binary that you created when you ran the ./Build sequence. Locate the binary file in the directory /usr/local/gnu/sendmail-8.11.0/obj.Linux.2.2.16.i586/sendmail/sendmail. It should be in the object directory created by sendmail and identified by the Linux title, the kernel number, and the processor type.

First, back up the distribution sendmail binary in case the newer one does not work. Backing up files is always an important precaution to take in case things do not work.

Copy the sendmail binary to the /usr/lib directory. Often the file /usr/lib/sendmail is a symbolic link to /usr/sbin/sendmail. Be aware of this while copying over the file. You may want to place the file in /usr/sbin instead thus preserve the symbolic links.

The sendmail binary is set with a sticky bit. An `ls -la` command shows it to have the following permissions:

```
# ls -la /usr/sbin/sendmail
   rwsr-sr-x  1 root    root    319908 Sep  1 07:40    /usr/sbin/sendmail
```

This output indicates that any child processes initiated by the file's owner (root) have the same permissions as the owner. Seasoned Linux veterans, who may recommend creating a new user rather than root run sendmail , discourage the use of a sticky bit.

To give the same sticky bit to the sendmail binary in /usr/lib or /usr/sbin, depending upon where you install it, you must issue the following command after copying the newer binary to its default location:

```
chmod 6755 /usr/sbin/sendmail
```

After checking the permissions, you should be ready to test your install.

## Testing the Installation

To verify that the new sendmail binary is now running on your system, first make sure that sendmail is even running on your server. You can test this by using the ps command. Enter the following command:

```
ps auxww | grep sendmail
```

You should see that the sendmail daemon is running. The reply might be something like the following:

```
sendmail: accepting connections on port 25.
```

The ww is also appended to the aux option in order to wrap the printout.

If sendmail is not running, you will either want to start it up by using the default startup method as defined by the distribution:

```
/etc/rc.d/init.d/sendmail start
```

Or, if you wish to start sendmail by hand, use the following command:

```
/usr/lib/sendmail -bd -q1h
```

The -bd option starts up sendmail as a daemon, which then runs in the background. The daemon awaits connections to port 25, at which time it will request information about the e-mail message itself and then either pass it along or drop it. You can use other options when starting up sendmail. Rather than running sendmail as a background daemon, you can use the commands describes in Table 17.1.

**Table 17.1  Options That You May Use to Define How sendmail Will Run**

| Mode | Alias | Description |
| --- | --- | --- |
| ba | | Use ARPAnet protocols |
| bD | | Run as a daemon, but do not fork |
| bd | smtpd | Run as a daemon |
| bH | purgestat | Purge persistent host status |
| bh | hoststat | Print persistent host status |
| bi | newaliases | Rebuild alias database |
| bm | | Be a mail sender |
| bp | mailq | Print contents of the mail queue |
| bs | | Run SMTP on standard input |
| bt | | Enter test mode and resolve addresses |
| bv | | Verify, but don't collect or deliver |

Many of these options are used to check the status of the running sendmail process or for debugging purposes. Also, instead of executing the absolute path to sendmail along with the options, you can simply use the alias name for the same command. The most popular of these is mailq, which prints the contents of the e-mail queued up and waiting to be delivered.

To test the running version of sendmail, use telnet to access port 25 on the localhost machine. This command verifies that the version is correct. In a terminal window of same machine on which you installed sendmail, enter the following:

```
telnet localhost 25
```

If the sendmail daemon is running, a message similar to the following will be printed to your display. Verify that the version number that you just installed is the same as that which is printed to your screen on the last line:

```
$ telnet localhost 25
Trying 127.0.0.1...
Connected to localhost.localdomain.
Escape character is '^]'.
220 antares.astronomy.org ESMTP Sendmail 8.11.0/8.11.0; Mon, 15 Aug
2000 10:30:00 -0700
```

You are now ready to try out your connection. Once you have a sendmail connection, enter the following:

```
helo antares.astronomy.org
```

Alternatively, enter the name of the server on which sendmail is running. The command should return the following message:

```
pleased to meet you.
```

Congratulations, you now have sendmail up and running. Try sending a message. If you have a viable Internet connection and your domain hostname is fully qualified, mail will proceed directly to its destination. Most sendmail commands or options use all uppercase letters. Here is an example e-mail from myself to another fictional user whose domain does actually exist:

```
MAIL FROM: kerry@antares.astronomy.org
250 kerry@antares.astronomy.org... Sender ok
RCPT TO: calvin@vega.nasa.gov
250 calvin@vega.nasa.gov... Recipient ok
DATA
    354 Enter mail, end with "." on a line by itself
This is just a test.
.

    250 MAA19900 Message accepted for delivery
quit
221 antares.astronomy.org closing connection
Connection closed by foreign host.
```

The sendmail program responds with the indented lines after receiving input. If you try to send e-mail to an unknown domain, sendmail complains because it also does name server lookups and attempts to resolve the domains, in most cases, before sending the e-mail. If sendmail cannot resolve a domain, it will either complain or place the mail in the queue for a later lookup.

If the mail went through just fine, then sendmail is operational on your system. You can now begin doing some tweaking to optimize its performance.

# Customizing the sendmail.cf File

You can tweak quite a few variables in the sendmail.cf file. Most are preceded by comments that explain the variables. Listing 17.2 shows just a few of the options that I find myself needing to adjust depending on the function of the Linux machine. You may customize these options to suit your own machine.

**Listing 17.2  Options within the sendmail.cf File That You Can Configure to Optimize the sendmail Program to Your Own Needs**

```
# maximum message size
O MaxMessageSize=2500000
# This sets the maximum size at 2.5 megabytes.  The default is set
at one megabyte.
# No email over 2.5 megabytes in size    will be allowed to pass.
# privacy flags
O PrivacyOptions=goaway
# This adjusts the types of connections users from outside might run
into.
# default UID (can be username or userid:groupid)
O DefaultUser=1:1
# If you want to run sendmail as root, the above settings will work.
# Remember that UID and GID 1 are both reserved for root.
# Here you can place an alternate user to run sendmail.
# maximum number of recipients per SMTP envelope
O MaxRecipientsPerMessage=100
# This option prevents a user from sending out emails to more than
100 people using the single email they wrote.
# This prevents those sending out spam and junk emails.
```

Once you have made any changes to the sendmail.cf file, your sendmail daemon must reread the configuration. To ensure that this occurs, you can either send the daemon the -HUP or kill -1 signal or else restart the daemon in the rc.d files. To use the former technique, first determine the PID of the sendmail process:

```
# ps aux | grep sendail | grep root
```

The added grep root command isolates the initial sendmail process and keeps it separate from any forked child processes. Once you have the PID, enter the following command:

```
# kill -HUP <PID>
```

Or, if you are using the sendmail RPM, simply restart the process:

```
# /etc/rc.d/init.d/sendmail restart
```

Make sure to verify that sendmail is still operational by using Telnet to access port 25 or by checking the status of the sendmail daemon:

```
# /etc/rc.d/init.d/sendmail status
```

These are but a few of the available options under the sendmail.cf file. Test out the variables yourself and locate those that work best for you.

# Securing a Mail Server

Two of the quickest methods for compromising a Linux server are to run an exploit against an older sendmail program or to exploit an older BIND program on a Linux box. The sendmail program has had a history of exploitable security concerns; however, if you remain current with the latest sendmail release, you can avoid many of the standard problems or security concerns. If you are not using your Linux box as a mail server, be certain to shut down the SMTP processes altogether. Leaving any sort of processes or ports open is another invitation to an attempt to compromise your machine.

This section looks at some of the other methods for securing the mail server processes if you will be running sendmail on your server.

## Preventing Relaying through Your Mail Server

One of the biggest obstacles to setting up a secure mail server is relaying through your system. Relaying is when someone either from within or without your system uses your mail system to pass on his or her e-mail to another external host. Your box acts as a relay between the two points. Linux machines that are open to relaying are subject to abuse by unscrupulous *spammers*. *Spam* is unsolicited junk e-mail that is distributed by negligent or naïve system administrators. Spammers seek out machines with older sendmail distributions with known problems or security holes. Before you might even realize that your box has been used for spamming purposes, tens of thousands of e-mails may already have passed through. You are then left with the mess of responding to the complaints from the many people who received the e-mail.

Fortunately, the latest version of sendmail denies relaying by default. This stops up a major security hole in some of the older versions. Unless you want others to relay through your mail server, which is highly inadvisable, sendmail will normally configure it so that you must open up specific domains or IP addresses to relaying.

## Improving upon the Access File

A marked improvement over previous releases of sendmail is the incorporation of the access file, normally located in the /etc/mail directory. Here you can place those domains or IP addresses of the machines you wish to allow to relay through you. You can also place in this file the known domains of notorious spammers and deny them access to your box as well. The access database frees a mail administrator to allow access to the mail server by individual domains.

As detailed on the main www.sendmail.org page, each database entry consists of a domain name or IP address as the *key* and an action as the *value*. Keys can be a fully or partly qualified host or domain names such as host.subdomain. domain.com, subdomain.domain.com, or domain.com. The last two forms match any host or subdomain under the specified domain. If the value FEA-TURE(relay_hosts_only) is set in your generic.mc file, only the first form works.

Keys can also be a network address or subnetwork, such as 205.199.2.250, 205.199.2, or 205.199. The latter two forms match any host in the indicated subnetwork. Notice that with IP addresses that are specific to a range rather than to just one IP address, you must add a period to the end of the domain range. This blocks or grants access to all users who have an address within that entire class.

Lastly, keys can also be user@host.domain to reject mail from a specific user. The last item is particularly crucial if you are attempting to block a specific user from distributing unwanted material.

Values can be any of the following:

◆ REJECT, refuses send requests from this host

◆ DISCARD, to accept the message but silently discard it (the sender will think it has been accepted)

◆ OK, to allow access and override other built-in checks

◆ RELAY, to allow access, including allowing SMTP to relay through your machine

◆ An arbitrary message such as "Spammers go away" to reject the mail specifically and send a quick message to the guilty party

Those attempting to connect using any domain that falls in this last category will see the message and should get the hint.

Table 17.2 lists keys and values that a good access file might contain.

**Table 17.2  A Sample List of Domains and IP Addresses of Those Users You Wish Either to Allow Access or Deny Service to Your Mail Server**

| Keys | Values |
| --- | --- |
| cyberpromo.com | REJECT |
| badpornsite.com | REJECT |
| friend@noname.org | DISCARD |
| nobody@mydomain.com | DISCARD |
| astronomy.org | RELAY |
| 206.71.77. | RELAY |
| spam@buyme.com | 550 Spammers go away! |
| adsgalore.com | Spamming not tolerated here |

The first two entries reject all mail from any host in the cyberpromo.com and badpornsite.com domain. Lists of known spamming domains are available on the Internet for download and incorporation into the access file. It is wise to take a look and make sure that you enter the more abusive ones into your access file. The third and fourth lines appear to the sender to have been received, but in actuality their e-mails were silently dropped. There is not much reason to use the DISCARD setting unless you wish to track down any offending parties. The fifth and sixth lines allow relaying to or from any host in the astronomy.org domain and from any IPs located in 206.71.77. The last two lines send a personalized message to any party attempting either to relay through the mail server or trying to send mail to a particular local user.

# Running the makemap Command

After customizing the access file to your specifications, you need to remake or rehash the database by using the hash command. If your access database is in /etc/mail, as is the standard in most Red Hat installs, you should run the following command:

```
# makemap -r hash /etc/mail/access.db < /etc/mail/access
```

This command automatically redoes the database with the new entries and allows sendmail to adjust to the changes. Be sure also to give the sendmail process the hangup or -HUP signal so that the program will reread any changed configuration files. If after changing the access file you find that you are still getting e-mail from a rejected domain, verify that you have redone your access file by using makemap.

# Verifying Your Configuration

To see whether your relay is open, try these simple tests. One thing to remember about sendmail is that it looks at the IP address of the host from which you are logging in. If you are going to test your system, try it from a domain or IP address entirely outside your system.

To check whether mail relay is open on the example domain, astronomy.org, try the following from a system outside the astronomy.org or respective domain address:

```
telnet astronomy.org 25
helo astronomy.org
MAIL FROM: kerry@astronomy.org
RCPT TO: spam@aol.com
quit
```

Your system should pass this test. This example assumes that the domain you are logging in from is the one that you are testing and that the system has a kerry username. The spam@aol.com is just a made-up e-mail, though the domain exists.

Now try relaying through your host from another system:

```
telnet astronomy.org 25
helo astronomy.org
MAIL FROM: joe@aol.com
RCPT TO: fredjwickerbill@yahoo.com
quit
```

If your host allows the recipient, fredjwickerbill@yahoo.com, to receive your test e-mail, then your relay is open.

> **NOTE**
>
> For more information on customizing the antirelaying features found in the latest sendmail version, you might want to consult Claus Aßmann's page at `http://www.sendmail.org/~ca/`. He has improved and documented many of the most complex sendmail features.

## Configuring the virtusertable File

To enable mail for *virtual domains,* or domains that do not actually exist except in name only, you will need to edit the virtusertable file located in the /etc/mail directory. For example, there might not be a machine that actually has the name astronomy.org but it can still be a registered domain, and name servers can still point to a valid IP address. By using any respectable Web server such as Apache, you can host a multitude of virtual domains on your Linux box. The sendmail program will also handle all incoming traffic for that virtual domain. For this purpose, you use the /etc/mail/virtusertable file. Make sure that you enabled this feature while creating your generic-linux.mc file or whatever file you used to create your default sendmail.cf file.

The syntax for this file is uncomplicated. For all usernames that are virtual, you must make a corresponding real account username on the mail server. For example, suppose that the mail server name is mail.mydomain.com and that it is hosting also the astronomy.org domain. If Joe Smith wants to have an e-mail address of joe@astronomy.org, this would be entered into the /etc/mail/virtusertable file along with Joe's real account name, which is jsmith@mydomain.com. Here is how the file would look:

```
joe@astronomy.org        jsmith@mydomain.com
```

The e-mail address on the left is the virtual address, and the one on the right is the real address on the host mail server. To access an incoming or outgoing mail message to or from the virtual domain, Joe must check the account jsmith@mydomain.com.

The user joe can also configure his e-mail client, whether it runs directly on Linux or on another operating system, so that any replies appear as if they were coming from the domain astronomy.org. If he did not do that, recipients might be confused as to why e-mails from joe were originating from the mydomain.com domain. If more than one e-mail address is associated with this domain, i.e.astronomy.org, you can set these up in the virtusertable file as well. For example, e-mails addressed to joe can also be addressed to joe.smith@ astonomy.org or skywatcher@astronomy.org. Either way, the user joe would receive those e-mails as defined in the virtusertable and directed to him.

In addition to the virtual accounts that go to real accounts, you should also create a *catch-all* address for any nonspecific e-mails coming into the virtual domain. Any indiscriminate e-mails directed to an unavailable user sent on the real server will be sent to the root or postmaster user. The same utility should also be available for virtual domains.

For example, any sort of e-mail such as abuse, info, questions or webmaster @astronomy.org should be received by a legitimate user, though the account itself is not defined. Listing 17.3 shows the same file with additional users.

### Listing 17.3  An Example virtusertable File with the Real Users and a Catch-All User

```
@astronomy.org        pdavis@mydomain.com
joe@astronomy.org     jsmith@mydomain.com
fred@astronomy.org    fjones@mydomain.com
pete@astronomy.org    pdavis@mydomain.com
mary@astronomy.org    mhurst@mydomain.com
```

Notice how the valid account pdavis@mydomain.com receives any e-mail not specifically addressed to a certain user.

Updating the virtusertable is much the same as updating the access file. As indicated in the definitions for the generic-linux.mc file, you build the virtual user table by entering the following command:

```
# makemap -o hash /etc/mail/virtusertable < /etc/mail/virtusertable.db
```

This command actually creates one or more nontext files. Typically it creates a /etc/mail/virtusertable.dir file and a /etc/mail/virtusertable.pag or /etc/virtusertable.db file, but does not actually change /etc/mail/virtusertable file itself.

If you would like to reverse-map local users for outbound mail—for example, to make it easier for them to send mail using their virtual domain—then you will need to add support for the genericstable to your *.mc file. According to the FAQ located on the main sendmail page, you should do the following:

```
FEATURE('genericstable', 'hash /etc/genericstable')dnl
GENERICS_DOMAIN_FILE('/etc/sendmail.cG')dnl
```

You will also need to create /etc/mail/genericstable, which is like /etc/mail/virtusertable except that the columns are reversed:

```
jsmith@mydomain.com          joe@astronomy.org
```

## Debugging the Files

When testing out the latest configuration, use the following command to verify the running version of sendmail:

```
/usr/lib/sendmail -d0.1 -bt < /dev/null
```

If the command hangs, use a Ctrl+C to return to the shell prompt.

In addition, it is also useful to use the diff utility to compare the sendmail.cf file to other sendmail.cf files that you might be making. For example, suppose that you want to make a new *.cf file based upon a different configuration of my *.mc file. You would first back up your /etc/sendmail.cf file to something new such as /etc/sendmail.cf.golden. You could then make the changes to your *.mc file, run m4, and generate another *.cf file. You would copy this new file to /etc as sendmail.cf, overwriting the original.

After creating a new sendmail.cf file, you can use diff to see what differences there are between the two files, sendmail.cf and sendmail.cf.golden.

Here's an example of two almost identical files.

```
# diff sendmail.cf sendmail.cf.golden
18c18
< ##### built by root@astronomy.org on Wed Jan 20 09:36:26
MST 2000
--
> ##### built by root@astronomy.org on Tue Jan 12 16:36:21
MST 2000
```

As you can see, the only difference between the two files is that they were built on different days. This utility is also useful for comparing the virtusertable and similar files located on other machines.

If you are using POP3 with sendmail, be sure to include your own computer's name in the /etc/sendmail.cw file. This will prevent any "we don't relay" messages.

To see what domains you are relaying, enter the following line at a shell prompt:

```
# echo '$=w' | /usr/lib/sendmail -bt -d0.4
```

You can also do use the | more option to scroll through the list.

## Forwarding E-mail

If a user is no longer on the mail server, yet still receives e-mail at his or her former address, you will want to implement a .forward file in that account. In this manner, that user can still receive e-mail sent to his or her former address at the new location. Although you could place an entry into the /etc/aliases file redirecting the mail to the new address, that file entry could quickly be overlooked. Instead, insert a .forward file in that user's home directory as soon as his or her account is deleted, leaving the home directory intact.

Be aware that the permissions on a .forward file should only be writable by that user and by no one else. It is simple enough for an attacker to send that user a file and then to become that user. Privileged users such as bin and root should never have a .forward file but should use an entry in the /etc/aliases file.

The regular syntax for a .forward file is to place the new e-mail address on the first line. If you want that user to retain e-mail delivered to the older address as well, simply enter a slash ( \ ) followed by the older account name.

For example, to have mail sent from jsmith's account on mydomain.com over to Joe's new e-mail address at joes@newdomain.com yet also retain the e-mail he received at mydomain.com for caching purposes, you need only place the following entries into his .forward file to make sure that the file is writable only by Joe:

```
# Joe's new email address
joes@newdomain.com
\jsmith
```

Now Joe will receive e-mail at his new address, but can also check for any cached messages that are stored as well at his old address.

## Adding Extra Security to Your Program

Under the FAQs on the main sendmail page, there is a very detailed explanation of some additional security issues associated with the sendmail program. This section is an excerpt taken from their page and edited slightly for clarity.

The sendmail program often gets blamed for many problems that are actually the result of other problems, such as overly permissive modes on directories. For this reason, sendmail checks the modes on system directories and files to determine whether they can be trusted. For sendmail to run without complaining, you *must* execute the following commands:

```
# chmod go-w / /etc /etc/mail /usr /var /var/spool /var/spool/mqueue
# chown root / /etc /etc/mail /usr /var /var/spool /var/spool/mqueue
```

You will probably have to tweak these commands for your environment. For example, some systems put the spool directory into /usr/spool instead of /var/spool and use /etc/mail directory for the aliases file instead of /etc. Under Red Hat Linux, the /var/spool directory is the location of mqueue/. If you set the RunAsUser option in your sendmail.cf, the RunAsUser will have to own the /var/spool/mqueue directory. As a general rule, after you have compiled sendmail, run the following command to initialize the alias database:

```
/usr/lib/sendmail -v -bi
```

This command might generate messages such as the following:

```
WARNING: writable directory /etc
WARNING: writable directory /usr/spool/mqueue
```

If so, the directories listed have inappropriate write permissions and you should secure them to avoid various possible security attacks.

Beginning with sendmail 8.9.x, these checks have become more strict to prevent users from being able to access files that they would normally not be able to read. In particular, .forward and :include: files, or files that redirect incoming e-mails to an executable file, in unsafe directory paths—directory paths to which groups or the world have write permission—will no longer be allowed. Therefore, if the user joe has a home directory that is writable by the group staff, sendmail will not use Joe's .forward file. You can alter this behavior, at the expense of system security, by setting the DontBlameSendmail option.

For example, to allow .forward files in group writable directories, enter the following line of code in the /etc/sendmail.cf file. Usually you need only uncomment the beginning of the line and add the extra variable:

```
O DontBlameSendmail=forwardfileingroupwritabledirpath
```

Or, to allow these files in both group and world writable directories, enter the following:

```
O DontBlameSendmail=forwardfileinunsafedirpath
```

Items from these unsafe .forward and :include: files are marked as unsafe addresses—the items cannot make deliveries to files or programs. You can alter this behavior also via the DontBlameSendmail option:

```
O DontBlameSendmail=forwardfileinunsafedirpath, forward-
fileinunsafedirpathsafe
```

The first flag allows the .forward file to be read, and the second allows the items in the file to be marked as safe for file and program delivery.

Other files affected by this strengthened security include class files, such as Fw, /etc/sendmail.cw, persistent host status files, and the files specified by the Error-Header and HelpFile options. Similar DontBlameSendmail flags are available for the class, ErrorHeader, and HelpFile files.

If you have an unsafe configuration of .forward and :include: files, you can make it safe by finding all such files and entering the command a **chmod go-w $FILE** for each. Also, enter the command **chmod go-w $DIR** for each directory in the file's path.

## Setting Up Mailing Lists

Several mailing list programs are available for use with large lists of members, but probably the most efficient is majordomo. The majordomo program handles mailing lists and requires that those who subscribe to the list authenticate their identity with a return e-mail. This is a marked improvement over other e-mail mailing list managers that do not require any sort of validation and as such allow anyone to subscribe using whatever e-mail address they wish. These older or less dynamic mailing lists other than majordomo can be particularly troublesome for system administrators who have users subscribe with a false or bogus e-mail address. Whenever a mailing is sent, all users who have signed up using root@localhost as their valid e-mail cause multiple bounces to the list. Major-domo bypasses this problem by forcing new subscribers to provide a valid e-mail and reply to a querying e-mail proving their identity. This way someone else can-not subscribe you to an unwanted mailing list.

The first step is to download the latest version of majordomo from the Internet. Here's the main URL for the official majordomo site:

```
http://www.greatcircle.com/majordomo/
```

About halfway down the page you will see where to download the source code. The latest version of majordomo also includes RPMs that you can download and use to facilitate the install process. In other situations, you can download the source code and compile it yourself.

Once you have the code, you will want to create the binary in one directory, then install it in another. I untar and unzip the source code in my home directory, /home/kerry, then determine my install directory to be /usr/local/etc/major-domo-1.95.5.

I could have chosen to name this latter directory majordomo/ instead of the full version name, but I wanted to know what the latest version was and when I should upgrade. If you wish instead to have a simple majordomo/ directory, create a symbolic link from the real directory to a directory without the version number. Use something similar to the following command:

```
# ln -s majordomo majordomo-1.94.5
```

Once I had the source code in hand, I needed to pick a user and group ID for majordomo to run under. I chose `majordom` and `daemon`. Then I edited the makefile so it would know where to look for my Perl libraries. I chose the following two variables for my Perl and compiler:

```
PERL = /usr/bin/perl
CC = gcc
```

Listing 17.4 shows a sample printout from the Makefile, including the prompts that majordomo offers.

### Listing 17.4  A Sample Printout from the majordomo Configuration File

```
W_HOME = /usr/local/etc/majordomo†$(VERSION)
# Where do you want man pages to be installed?
MAN = $(W_HOME)/man
# You need to have or create a user and group which majordomo will
run as.
# Enter the numeric UID and GID (not their names!) here:
W_USER = 104
W_GROUP = 12
# These set the permissions for all installed files and executables
(except
# the wrapper), respectively.  Some sites may wish to make these
more
# lenient, or more restrictive.
FILE_MODE = 644
EXEC_MODE = 755
```

It is a good idea to read through the install files and man pages to make sure the options you choose in the Makefile are really what you want. Next, edit the majordomo.cf file. As you might notice, this file is similar to the sendmail.cf file. The configuration routine is self-explanatory. As it proceeds through the various steps, the install routine asks various basic questions and essentially sets up the program for you.

The majordomo program is one of the most dynamic mailing list managers currently available. It runs many of the major developmental lists for emerging and stable Linux programs.

## Running Various E-mail Clients

The pine program is perhaps one of the most popular console-based e-mail clients. With it anyone can log in to the main mail server and check his or her mail on the fly. Rather than attempting to use a POP3 or IMAP client to download the user's mail onto his or her own system, the user can initiate a simple telnet or ssh session on the main computer to bring up a pine session. During this session, the user can read, delete, forward, or save mail in a customized mail folder.

Installing pine is as simple as using the RPM or downloading the pine source code from the main site at the University of Washington. The main home page for pine is at the following URL:

```
http://www.washington.edu/pine/
```

The pine source code no longer falls under the open-source category, yet developmental work continues forward. The code is free for all to use, but some of the code remains hidden from the public.

Both the RPM and source provide simple interfaces for setting up pine and getting it running in no time. Make sure that your sendmail connection is valid and that you can transmit and receive e-mail.

Figure 17.1 shows pine's main interface.

If you want to keep your mail on the main server rather than downloading it to your own machine, pine provides all the functionality to accomplish this. The pine program also provides a clickable mouse interface as well as support for both HTML documents and threaded news messages.

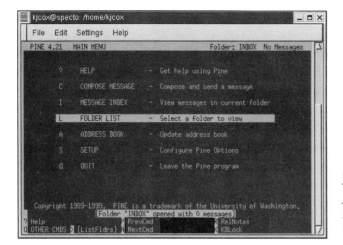

**FIGURE 17.1**

*An xterm window
showing the pine
interface.*

With the source code comes the latest POP3 and IMAP daemons. If you wish to create a POP3 or IMAP server on your Linux machine, pine provides the binaries to do so. After compiling the source to your specifications with working code, locate the imapd/ directory within the pine tree structure (no pun intended) and copy the ipop2d, ipop3d, and imapd binaries to a directory within your path. Make sure that your /etc/services file includes them and then add them to your /etc/inetd.conf file. Once you have used HUP to hang up your inetd daemon, you can test to make sure that these daemons are also running by logging in to their respective ports. The POP3 daemon runs under port 110, whereas imapd runs under port 143. Test these ports much as you would sendmail.

```
telnet localhost 110
```

or

```
telnet localhost 143
```

You should also verify that these ports are visible from the outside world by testing them from a separate server.

Once you have made certain that pine is configured correctly, you can set up individual mail accounts that users can log in to from their home machines and download their mail onto their home machines.

# Conclusion

Now that you can set up and receive e-mail on your machine, you should be feeling rather comfortable with your system. If you use Linux not only as a server for handling multitasking jobs, but also as a desktop operating system on which you perform many of your day-to-day operations, you will want to make it more personable and user-friendly. One method of accomplishing this is to configure your machine to play sound files and run audio clips and CDs through your sound card. Red Hat will recognize most any sound card and has made great progress in serving high-quality sound.

The next chapter will deal with the various methods of configuring sound under Red Hat, the types of tools available to listen to and modify audio files. The chapter also explains how to set up streaming media files. If you have a fast Internet connection and bandwidth to spare, any Red Hat machine can become its own webcasting server and function as a radio station.

# Chapter 18

**Sounding Off
on Linux**

Configuring sound under Linux used to be tiresome and unrewarding task. Before Red Hat developed many of the latest utilities and incorporated other programs developed by various users into its basic configuration, only a handful of sound cards ran successfully under Linux. Red Hat Linux now supports a wide variety of sound cards and can detect nearly any card using the kudzu utility after the initial install and can then configure them for sound by using the sndconfig program. As Red Hat continues to progress and more sound card manufacturers make their drivers available, cards will continue to become better supported and detected under Linux. Besides that, the Linux kernel continues to make more resources available for sound development.

This chapter will look at the following issues for configuring sound and setting up audio utilities under Linux:

◆ Checking your system for sound compatibility
◆ Configuring sound automatically using Red Hat utilities
◆ Testing sound files by piping directly to devices
◆ Setting up sound files to play under the various window managers
◆ Encoding audio files for transmission over the Internet
◆ Running various audio tools, such as CD, MP3, and .wav files, under Linux

# Wiring Linux for Sound

Setting up sound under Linux for your own enjoyment has become remarkably simple. Not so long ago, I remember spending hours trying out different drivers and options under the Linux kernel, reconfiguring settings in various files, and downloading program after program in the feeble attempt to get my plug and play sound card to work under an older Red Hat release. I finally did get it to function, but it is amazing how simple it has become to set up sound and play with audio files and streams under Linux.

Installing the sound card into the machine has now become the more difficult aspect of configuring sound. In many respects, it is now easier to set up sound under Linux than it is to configure a sound card properly under the latest Windows release. I now spend more time setting up an new sound card on my five-year-old's Windows machine than I do when installing a brand new sound card in my own Linux box. As you read through this chapter, I hope you will also see the beauty in the simplicity that has emerged from the Linux community in sound development.

## Checking for Compatibility

Before purchasing or installing any sort of sound card inside your Linux machine, verify that Linux supports that brand of sound card. Seldom, if ever, do I run across a card that Linux does not support to some degree. At the very least, I can get the card to emit some sort of garbled sound. However, nearly all my experiences in the past few years with both old and new sound cards have been highly favorable.

Consult the Red Hat hardware compatibility site (http://www.redhat.com/support/hardware/) and verify that it lists the sound card you wish for either installation or purchase. If this site does not list the sound card, then Red Hat does not support it. If you are unsure whether your card is supported or not, check with the newsgroups and ask others whether they have had any success with the sound card that you have chosen. I have found sound to be a highly active topic for many beginning users. Many Linux users are willing to share their time and effort to assist others to get sound working.

In addition to a card's own name, check for the proper chipset of the sound card. Many generic sound cards are available on the market are not listed on the hardware compatibility site, but which classify themselves as "Sound Blaster compatible" or similar to other major sound card brands. These can be made to work, but as with most any piece of computer hardware, purchasing name brands helps ensure that the device will function with the correct drivers. If one of these generic brands also includes a recognized chipset for its card, you will probably succeed.

Check the home page for the sound card in question and verify that its manufacturer provides support or drivers for the Linux platform. The technical support teams on many such sites are willing to assist in any problems that you might have. Check the FAQ page and read the documentation carefully and make certain that it doesn't cover your problem before sending any emails to the technical support team. If you require assistance from the technical support team, response times are usually good.

## Installing the Card

With some of the newer motherboards on the market, the sound card is already installed or it comes with the motherboard. This is nice in that you do not lose a PCI or ISA slot to an extra card. Instead, sound hardware is already placed on the motherboard. You simply need to plug in the speakers to the proper ports. These types of cards work well with Linux and should not pose a problem.

Otherwise, if your sound card is an ISA- or PCI-based card, install them as you would any other type of card. Making sure your machine is first powered down and that there is no chance any power might still connected to the machine, open your computer case and place the sound card in an available slot. If you also have a CD-ROM in your machine and would like to play CD audio files through the card, make sure that you have the correct CD audio cable type connected to the proper openings in both devices. With older cards, you may sometimes need to reverse the cable connection on the card. To do so, remove the white box into which the CD audio cable fits. If you cannot get sound to work properly using an older 16-bit Sound Blaster card, you may find it useful to try alternative fittings to your connector cable.

## Testing the Sound

After properly installing the card according to the manual specifications, power up your Linux machine. If you have chosen kudzu to run during the bootup phase, it will detect your new hardware device and configure it automatically for you. If you have not chosen to power up kudzu during the bootup, you can either choose it to start the next time you start up your machine by selecting it from the /usr/sbin/ntsysv program or by running it manually and having it detect the card itself. Superuser can start kudzu at any command line by entering **/usr/sbin/kudzu.**

Once kudzu determines that a new device is installed, it launches the /usr/sbin/sndconfig program. This utility, first introduced with the Red Hat 5.x releases, provides for dynamic configuration of sound cards. Incorporated into the program is the isapnptools program, which assists in setting up the proper settings for Plug and Play cards. Most any Plug and Play sound card is now fully configurable under Linux, whereas just a few years ago Linux was unable to run any sort of PnP card.

Once sndconfig has determined the sound card type, the program prompts you to confirm Red Hat's decision and then test for sound. Make sure that your speakers are plugged into the correct port and that they are powered. The sound card configuration routine plays a sample sound to verify that you can hear audio files. Red Hat plays a sound byte of Linus Thorvalds introducing himself and pronouncing the word *Linux*. If you wish to play this sound clip later or use it for your own purposes, you can find it in the directory /usr/share/sndconfig/ sample.au.

After confirming you hear the sound clip, the sound setup also plays a MIDI sound sequence, if your sound card supports MIDI. If you do not hear any sound. Linux prompts you to set the I/O Port, IRQ, DMA1, DMA2, and MPU I/O card settings manually. Chances are good that Linux will successfully play the sound file, but if you want a more flexible setup, you can configure the settings manually. After successfully configuring the card and confirming that you can hear both sound clips, the setup sequence exits.

### NOTE

There is still some dispute over the correct pronunciation of the operating system. Some favor pronouncing Linux as "line-ix," using the long *i* sound. This is a reflection of Linus Thovalds' own name, making the two names sound similar as they are pronounced in English. Others prefer making the short *i* sound, or "lin-ix." This pronunciation is similar to that of the word *minix* on which Thorvalds based his initial configuration for Linux. Or you may pronounce Linux as Thorvalds does, which sounds more like "lee-noox." Any of these pronunciations is acceptable.

Even the most recent sound cards are discovered by the latest Red Hat release. For example, under Red Hat 6.1, my Sound Blaster 512PCI card, newly released by Creative Labs, was not supported, nor could Red Hat configure any drivers for it. After installing Red Hat 6.2, the configuration setup detected this same card and installed the proper drivers. Testing it for sound, I found that it produced a rather garbled audio feed. The configuration was not fully optimized, but you can expect even the most recent card releases to be completely functional with the next Red Hat release, provided development continues its course.

There are two different methods for checking and validating your sound card's settings. The first involves checking a dynamic file and making sure that your system sees and correctly identifies the card. The second option involves sending a sound file directly to the audio port. Because all hardware is viewed as a device under Linux in the /dev directory, it is a simple task to send a file to a certain port in order to test whether or not that device is functional. Much like you test a printer by sending a file to the print device and ensuring that it prints, you test sound card settings by sending the sound file to a sound device to see whether it emits sound. To review the steps in configuring a printer under Linux, see Chapter 13.

The first method involves checking a dynamic file under the /dev directory. Use the following command to view the state of the sound card as Linux sees it:

```
# cat /dev/sndstat
```

If properly configured, you should see the output shown in Listing 18.1.

### Listing 18.1 Sample Output of the /dev/sndstat File on a Typical Linux Box with a Configured Sound Card

```
# cat /dev/sndstat
OSS/Free:3.8s2++-971130
Load type: Driver loaded as a module
Kernel: Linux quasi.astronomy.org 2.2.16 #1 Tue Mar 7 21:07:39 EST
2000 i686
Config options: 0

Installed drivers:

Card config:

Audio devices:
0: Sound Blaster 16 (4.16) (DUPLEX)

Synth devices:
0: AWE32-0.4.3 (RAM512k)

Midi devices:
0: Sound Blaster 16
1: AWE Midi Emu
```

```
Timers:
0: System clock


Mixers:
0: Sound Blaster
```

The sound card's configuration does not cover a few items in Listing 18.1, but these are normally enabled when the card is set up not to run as a sound module. Printing out the /dev/sndstat file is also a good method for debugging your sound card if your sound system is not working adequately.

The second method involves sending a sound file to the /dev/audio port. Red Hat Linux provides several tools for playing nearly every type of audio file available. One of the easiest sound files to play on the Linux operating system was designed originally for the Sun operating system. The .au file is simple to record and then play back. The sound byte featuring Linus Thorvalds' voice, discussed earlier, is saved in the .au format.

Locate any sort of audio file on the system by executing a locate or find command:

```
# locate *.au
# find / -name *.au -print
```

To test your sound capability, concatenate this same audio file to the audio device by using the cat command:

```
# cat /usr/share/sndconfig/sample.au > /dev/audio
```

You should hear the sample sound from your speakers. If you do not, try using another .au sound file and verify that the /dev/audio file does in fact exist. Make certain that no other audio programs are currently active on your system, as they will prevent the sample sound from being played.

You can also test other sound by executing the /usr/bin/play command. This is simpler to use than the cat command, and can also be run by any user. You can also use the play command with any sound file on your system under your window manager of choice. This is useful when you want to associate a certain sound file with a specific action, such as minimizing a window or when exiting the window manager. Most window managers have configuration options that allow you to combine the sound with the action or specify a certain command, such as play, with the sound file:

```
# play /usr/share/sndconfig/sample.au
```

**NOTE**

With the latest version of the Enlightenment window manager, the latest sound package will play multiple audio streams that can be mixed, matched, and played in overlapping fashion.

## Adding OSS Sound Modules

As you can see in the /dev/sndstat output shown in Listing 18.1, Red Hat runs most sound cards initially by configuring them as a sound module. The OSS Sound Module is a program developed by 4Front Technologies. OSS (Open Sound System) provides free sound card drivers for most popular sound cards under all flavors of Linux and FreeBSD. These drivers support the digital audio, MIDI, synthesizers, and mixers found on sound cards and comply with the Open Sound System API specification. It supports over 200 brand name sound cards, and provides automatic sound card detection, Plug-n-Play support, support for PCI audio sound cards, and support for full duplex audio. In all, it is a very dynamic program. If you experience any problems with Red Hat detecting your own card, the OSS drivers will assist in getting your card operating. If the free version provided in the Linux kernel does not accomplish the task of correctly configuring the sound, 4Front also has a commercial release, which supports nearly every card on the market. These drivers are available for around $30 and are well worth the cost if sound is an important issue on your Linux machine. When the Red Hat release I last installed did not support my sound card, I purchased and installed the latest drivers for the Sound Blaster 512PCI card and was able to get it to work with no problems whatsoever.

Red Hat uses an older version of OSS to recognize most sound cards as modules. The version it uses is called OSS/Free. This version does not offer technical support, nor can it recognize all the cards, including the latest PnP cards. If you desperately need to get the latest sound card working on your system and consider $20 U.S. worth the hassle of attempting to configure a sound card by hand, then try out the OSS drivers.

The OSS sound drivers are available at the 4Front Technologies site, http://www.opensound.com/.

# Adding Tools for Audible Entertainment

Now that you have a functioning sound card and can pipe sound files from your hard drive to speakers or audio devices, you can begin thinking about playing other forms of sound files on your own system. This section covers the installation and configuration of other useful tools that will allow you to play audio files for your own entertainment.

Linux provides a host of configurable CD or sound players that either come pre-installed with the distribution CD or are available for download. Many are designed specifically for use with a particular window manager but can be played on any interface of your choice. They may have options particular to that specific window manager. You can easily ignore, shut off, or optimize these sound players for the window manager depending upon how closely the sound programs are interrelated.

## Choosing CD Players

Some of the most basic CD players come with the basic Red Hat distribution. The XPlaycd program is a standard component on most all Red Hat releases. It plays regular audio CDs on all ATAPI CD-ROMs without any need to mount the media or reconfigure the device. With older Red Hat releases, you may have to allow yourself access to the device. Under older Red Hat releases you may have to grant yourself access to the CD-ROM by typing the following command as root. Otherwise, the CD-ROM should be accessible to any user:

```
# chmod 666 /dev/cdrom
```

This command enables you and all other users to read files from the CD-ROM.

Both Gnome and KDE offer their own CD players as well. You can call up Gnome by executing **gtcd** at the command line. Or, if you are within the Gnome desktop, you can select the CD player from under the Multimedia tab. Likewise, you can execute KDE's CD player, kscd, from within any window manager. Both have *CDDB support* — that is, if the host machine has Internet access, they can query any of the many CDDB (CD DataBase) servers and download additional information about the artist, CD title, and titles of the songs on the CD. You can either store these facts locally for later use or download them the next time the CD is installed.

You can also configure both CD players to dock to the either the Gnome or KDE panel. Both window managers also offer small docklets or applets that feature condensed CD players that can be called up from the respective window manager panel. These docklets make it easy to access and play selections from a CD.

Other window mangers such as Window Maker include additional docklets that feature smaller, stripped-down CD players where all the controls fit into a 64 × 64 pixel box or tile. You can dock these tiles under Window Maker and control the CD player via the tiled control panel.

Linux offers a plethora of simple CD players, each having its own strengths and weaknesses. If you are unhappy with the generic CD player that comes with Red Hat, you should have no trouble finding another one that will better suit your tastes.

## Choosing MP3 Players

One of the more popular recording formats to appear on the Internet audio scene is the mpeg1 layer 3 or MP3 format. This type of audio compression greatly reduces the amount of space required to play a single song. Under the older format used by regular audio CDs, a single song could require anywhere from 50 to 100 megabytes. Now, depending upon the level of compression and the bitrate used to encode the recording, a single song can require as little as 2 to 4 megabytes. This facilitates rapid and easy exchange of audio files throughout the Internet. Though the legality of copyrighted songs and their distribution via tools such as Napster and Gnutella remains in question, you can still record your own songs for local use. Many people prefer *ripping,* or encoding the regular CDs from purchased labels into MP3 format and then playing them from a hard drive or CD, then burning the songs onto a CD as data files. This allows my wife to listen to her music CDs at home while I can listen to the same songs on my work machine.

Currently, ATAPI CD-ROMs do not play CDs with MP3-formatted audio files. You must place the files on a hard drive or burn them onto a blank CD, mount the media on your Linux machine, and then use some other form of audio player to listen to the music. When these MP3 files are recorded at the standard 128 kilobytes per second, a regular user can fit nearly 150 songs onto a blank 650 megabyte CD. That is an improvement over regular audio CDs that save their audio files in .wav format. Wav audio compression allows between 10-12 songs to be placed on a regular CD.

One such popular MP3 player is xmms. Available for free download from http://www.xmms.org/, the xmms program provides support for mounted MP3 files on a CD or MP3s located on your hard drive. Either way, the quality is very good, and depending upon the quality of your encoding and sound card, nearly indistinguishable from a regular audio CD file.

The xmms program provides not only excellent to listen to, but is visually appealing. You can choose from and customize a variety of *skins* or graphical interfaces that are layered over the main program. Currently, hundreds of skins are available from which to choose, making your MP3 player more of a reflection of your tastes.

Initially fashioned after Winamp, the Windows MP3 player, xmms provides several other features aside from skins and audio quality. There are all sorts of visualization plug-ins that can generate a unique window display, showing cascading waterfalls that reflect the sound of the music in its patterns, to a blur scope, to a simple spectrum analyzer. Known as *eye-candy* to some pundits, these plug-ins really do nothing to improve the audio quality, but they do make your Linux desktop more aesthetically appealing.

Additional plug-ins are available, however, that will assist in making your xmms player into a more versatile program, allowing for sound recording, ripping of .wav files into MP3 format, and various other formatting utilities. Indeed, xmms is replete with a host of utilities and plug-ins that allow it to become your focal point for anything audio under Linux.

Another excellent MP3 deserving of mention is GQmpeg. This program offers much the same sort of utilities as xmms, but also enables you to save your favorite MP3 tunes to a play list that you can then access and sort according to your preferences. This program is available at `http://www.netpedia.net/hosting/gqview/mpeg-index.html`.

## Ripping Files to MP3 Format

As mentioned in the previous section, a Linux user can rip or convert audio files from a regular audio CD into MP3 format. These files can then be played on the user's local drive or saved onto a blank CD, if the user has a CD burner or some other form of large media backup. For detailed instructions on burning images or files onto a blank CD, refer to Chapter 9.

Linux offers several different types of audio rippers or programs for converting audio files. They range from simple Perl scripts to fully configurable GUI programs that run under your favorite window manager. The ripit program is used to create MP3 audio files from an audio CD. It is simply a front-end, written in Perl, for three excellent programs: cdparanoia, for ripping the audio CD tracks; bladeenc or lame, for encoding the MP3 files; and xmcd, for CDDB lookup. None of these files require any sort of GUI. The ripit program runs in text mode and does everything required to produce a set of MP3 files without any user intervention.

If you prefer a point-and-click interface, then use either grip or ripperX. Like ripit, these both require additional supporting programs to encode and rip the basic files. The two required programs are cdparanoia and bladeenc. You can install these programs either via the RPM release, usually provided with the Red Hat distribution, or by downloading the source code and compiling it yourself. Both grip and ripperX can be run as background processes, encoding your CD while you accomplish other tasks. The load that they place on the system is minimal and you may also determine the encoding level of choice. You should try these and other audio rippers and establish which method of encoding works best for you.

---

**NOTE**

As a matter of clarification, neither the author nor the publisher of this book condone in any way, shape, or form the encoding of MP3 files for distribution throughout the Internet. The author also does not support or advise the reader to engage in circulation of any audio MP3s made from copyrighted material. MP3s are allowable only for backup purposes or for private use under the condition that the original material was purchased by or is currently owned by the user.

---

# Streaming Audio

One of the latest innovations for use on Linux and the Internet is streaming audio. Though streams such as Real Audio and Streamworks have been available for years, it is only recently that Linux users whose machines had sufficient bandwidth have been able to configure their own nonproprietary audio streams. Such Linux users do not have to pay a licensing fee or purchase a proprietary streaming server to send out their audio sound or voice audio feeds to the Internet. Now virtually anyone can become his or her own radio station given a Linux box, a microphone or CD-Player, a sound card, and the proper software. The most popular version of audio streams available are those that encode the raw audio feed into MP3 format.

## Setting Up an Icecast Server

The two most popular streaming audio servers available for Linux are icecast and shoutcast. Because shoutcast is proprietary and requires the purchase of a license, many opt to use icecast. To set up this program, you should follow these steps:

1. Grab the latest tarred and zipped file from the main Icecast site at http://www.icecast.org/, and unpack it in a temporary directory. I prefer using /usr/local/gnu as my temporary directory for all source files.

   ```
   # cd /usr/local/gnu/
   # gunzip -c icecast-1.30.tar.gz | tar xvf -
   ```

2. After unpacking the file, you can start compiling the source. This is the order that I used after changing directories:

   ```
   # ./configure --with-crypt --with-libwrap
   # make
   # make install
   ```

This installs all necessary icecast files into the /usr/local/icecast/ directory.

Now edit the /usr/local/icecast/etc/icecast.conf file and then fire up the binary by issuing the following command in a virtual window:

```
# /usr/local/icecast/bin/icecast
```

This console or xterm window should then remain open if you wish to monitor the progress of the server and if you set up the configuration file to print the output to the console window.

The streaming server, liveice, must be built separately from the icecast server. The liveice server connects to the icecast server and then streams out the raw data. You may also use the shout program that is available from the icecast site, but which streams out the data in a similar format.

```
# cd /usr/local/gnu/icecast-1.30/liveice/
# ./configure
# make
```

You should now have a liveice binary in the same location as that of the source code, or /usr/local/gnu/icecast-1.30/liveice. Copy the liveice binary to /usr/local/icecast/bin/ and execute it from there. There should also be a file called liveice-configure.tk, which brings up a GUI. This utility is used to create a liveice.cfg file, which you can also edit manually. There is normally a liveice.cfg file elsewhere that has comments and explanations about each item, but the GUI tool will strip this file down to the basics.

## Configuring Sample Files for Streaming

Listing 18.2 shows a sample liveice.cfg file that works for the KSL's streaming audio server. This file is designed specifically to handle raw audio input and then translate it to MP3 format. A feed comes directly into the input jack on the back of the sound card. This raw audio is then encoded to MP3 format using the Fraunhofer codec. This proprietary codec is well worth its price of $200 because of the quality that it produces.

Other codecs are available, such as lame, which can also be configured to encode raw audio into MP3. Lame just recently released a stable version and it appears to produce high quality sound. The Fraunhofer codec also works well, though you will need to purchase the commercial version for extended broadcast periods. This particular MP3 streaming audio server was up and producing data for over 130 days without a restart or reboot of the system. The load was always under 0.5 and was handling over 150 clients connected simultaneously.

### Listing 18.2  An Example liveice.cfg File

```
# liveice configuration file
# Automatically generated
SERVER 206.81.144.133
# SERVER localhost
PORT 8000
NAME KSL_Radio
```

```
GENRE Live
URL http://icecast.ksl.com/
PUBLIC 1
X_AUDIOCAST_LOGIN
#ICY_LOGIN
PASSWORD my_secret_password
SAMPLE_RATE 24000
MONO
# uncomment this line if you want to listen to a playlist
## NO_SOUNDCARD
# uncomment this line if you want to listen to streams
SOUNDCARD
HALF_DUPLEX
# USE_LAME3 lame
USE_MP3ENC /usr/local/gnu/mp3enc31/mp3enc31
SOUND_DEVICE /dev/dsp
MOUNTPOINT live
BITRATE 24000
VBR_QUALITY 1
# uncomment this line if you want to listen to a playlist
## MIXER
# uncomment this line if you want to listen to streams
NO_MIXER
#PLAYLIST playlist
DECODER_COMMAND mpg123
# MIX_CONTROL_MANUAL
# CONTROL_FILE mix_command
# TRACK_LOGFILE track.log
# VERBOSE 10
```

Several items in this listing have been commented out either because their features have not yet been implemented or because they are not required on this particular server.

To create a playlist so that you can operate your system as a jukebox and send streaming MP3 static files located on your hard drive over the Internet, you will want to reverse the SOUNDCARD and MIXER features, which currently have double comments in front of them. To operate as a jukebox, remove the pound signs from in front of the MIXER and NO_SOUNDCARD features.

Listing 18.3 is the sample icecast.conf file that I have found works well for my purposes. I have removed most of the superfluous comments and have left only the pertinent entries. This file is located in the /usr/local/icecast/etc/ directory.

### Listing 18.3  A Sample icecast.conf File

```
############## Server Location and Responsible Person #############
location KSL Server Room
rp_email kerry.cox@ksl.com
server_url http://icecast.ksl.com/


######################### Server Limits #########################
max_clients 150
max_clients_per_source 150
max_sources 10
max_admins 5
throttle 10.0


###################### Stream Meta Data #######################
# use_meta_data 0
# streamurllock 0
# streamtitletemplate %s
# streamurl http://yp.icecast.org
# nametemplate %s
# desctemplate %s


##################### Server passwords #######################
client_password not_used
encoder_password uwMf7a2m3dmEo
admin_password uwMf7a2m3dmEo
oper_password uwMf7a2m3dmEo


#################### Directory servers ######################
#icydir yp.shoutcast.com
#icydir yp.breakfree.com
#icydir yp.musicseek.net
#icydir yp.van-pelt.com
```

```
#icydir yp.radiostation.de
#directory yp.icecast.org
touch_freq 5


########## Server IP/port configuration (IMPORTANT) ##############
#hostname 192.168.1.1
port 8000
server_name icecast.ksl.com


##################### Main Server Logfile ########################
logfile icecast.log
accessfile access.log
usagefile usage.log
logfiledebuglevel 0
consoledebuglevel 0


####################### Reverse Lookups #########################
# Set this to 1 if you want ip:s to be looked up (using reverse
lookup)
# or 0 if you just want the ip:s (which is slightly faster)
reverse_lookups 0


######################### Console mode ##########################
# Use 0 if you want stdin to become a local admin console with log
tailing
# Use 1 if you want stdin to become a local admin console
# Use 2 if you just want the console to become a log window
# Use 3 if you want the icecast server to be launched in the back-
ground (not available for Win32)
console_mode 0


####################### Client Timeout ##########################
# (How to deal with clients when no encoder is connected)
# A negative value means keep them forever
# 0 (zero) means kick them out instantly
# X > 0 means keep them X seconds
client_timeout 30
```

```
###################### Kicking clients ##########################
# If set to 1, then clients whose source has disconnected will
# be kicked. If set to 0, they will simply be moved to another
# stream. This has an effect only if client_timeout is <= 0.
kick_clients 0


################### Static file directory #######################
# This enables the http-server file streaming support in icecast.
# If you don't want to go through the trouble of setting up apache
# or roxen or whatever, then you can just specify a directory here,
# and then http://your_server:port/file/file.mp3 will be equivalent
# to /static_dir/file.mp3
# The http server support is of course very limited, don't try to
# do anything fancy. Also, only .mp3 files will be displayed.
#static_dir c:\windows\desktop
static_dir /tmp



########################### Statistics ##########################
# The icecast server dumps statistics to a file on a regular basis.
# You can specify how often (stats_time), and to what file
(stats_log)
# StatsTime (how often to dump stats, in seconds)
# 0 (zero) means to not dump stats
# X > 0 means dump stats every X seconds to the file specified by
stats_log
stats_log stats.log
statshtml_log stats.html
stats_time 60


########## Aliases (including virtual host support) #############
#alias radiofri http://195.7.65.207:6903


######################### Kick Relays ###########################
# How long to keep aliased sources when no clients are left
listening to it.
```

```
    kick_relays 10


    ######################### Transparent proxy #####################
    transparent_proxy 0


    #################### Access Control Lists #####################
    # You can specify acl rules either here in icecast.conf, or using
the
    # admin console. The syntax in icecast.conf is:
    # allow <all|client|source|admin> <hostmask>
    # deny <all|client|source|admin> <hostmask>
    # So, using the same rule as above (allowing only clients from
*.se)
    # deny <client> *
    # allow <client> *.se
    # When using the internal acl rules, you need to specify a policy.
    # This rule kicks in when no allow or deny rule affects a
connection.
    # If you set acl_policy to 0, then connections who are not allowed
by any
    # allow rule will be denied, and the other way around if you set it
to 1.
    acl_policy 1
    #deny all *
    #allow all *.ryd.student.liu.se


# EOF
```

While trying to get the encoder and the passwords to work, I discovered that you must to use the password encoding program that comes with icecast and encode the password in the liveice.conf file. In other words, decide what password you will use, place it unencoded in the liveice.cfg file, encrypt the password, then place the encrypted text within the body of this icecast.conf file. This is required if you use the --with-crypt option when compiling icecast initially from source.

# Conclusion

With the recent incursions and compromises of servers worldwide resulting in Denial of Service or DoS attacks against web sites and companies, it becomes all the more important to secure your Linux machine against any and all malicious hacking attempts. The next chapter will examine some of the standard procedures for configuring added security into your Red Hat release as well as taking proactive measures against crackers hoping to compromise your box. The chapter will also look at simple firewalling techniques and tools that will track any unauthorized use of system resources or breaches in Linux security.

# Chapter 19

## Linux Security

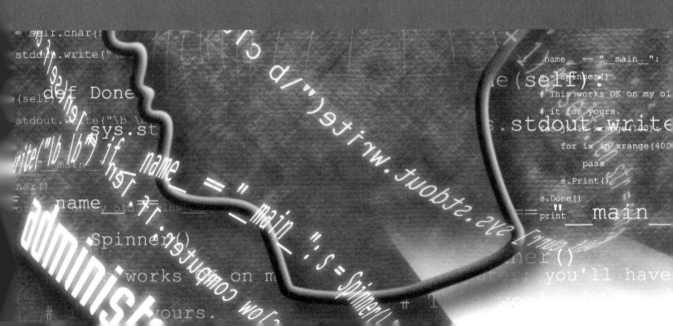

**P**robably the most pressing and troublesome issue to face any Linux administrator is that of security. The fear that someone can break into the system and abuse, destroy, or corrupt the data stored there can quickly become a nightmare for anyone. It is difficult enough protecting your own system from outside attempts at cracking your machine as well as protecting yourself from any foolish mistakes, but then to manage a system where others log in and also have access to data files can quickly make system administration more complicated. As an administrator, you need to be aware of not only how you are managing files kept on your system but how your users are also treating the system files. Keeping up-to-date on all current security issues and patching your files against any attacks both from within and without can be a time-consuming chore.

This chapter will cover the following topics:

◆ Understanding basic security under Red Hat Linux

◆ Managing users and keeping accounts secure

◆ Using packets sniffers and tracking users' history files

◆ Securing remote connections with ssh

◆ Logging unique events

◆ Creating simple firewalls for keeping out intruders

# Administering Passwords

Properly managing remote users and user accounts on all your Linux machines is one of the more difficult tasks for system administrators. Not only must you continually keep an eye outside your system checking for external attacks, you must also watch for internal abuses of system files by local users. This can be frustrating in that any users on your system should be considered at least semi-trustworthy. Unfortunately, you cannot always trust your system's users. Granting too much freedom to users who share your system with you can also be an invitation to abuse. You must walk a fine line between maintaining control over your system and allowing your system's users the freedom to accomplish their tasks.

# Examining Basic Security

It may seem strange to some administrators to be not only wary of external attacks but also to keep a close eye on users within the system. Attacks from your system's own users are perhaps the most insidious. You might think that users who already have access to a system would be content to leave their own system alone. But the siren call of root can be a powerful lure. Many users, called "script-kiddies" or crackers, desire only to compromise or trash the system for the pure joy of vandalism, or to use it to crack other systems. These are the users of whom you need to be aware.

Depending on your server's purpose and the types of users who share the system with you, your own security policy must be tuned to these groups of individuals. If your machine functions in a business setting and the users are few, you need not be as wary as in a commercial or ISP setting, where any user, with the right amount of money, can obtain an account legitimately.

As the Internet grows ever more pervasive and as servers increase in number, it becomes ever more simple to find a vulnerable server. The growth of the Internet has multiplied potential targets exponentially. Combine the explosion of software that scans entire blocks of IP addresses, and the huge (and growing) number of rank beginners with DSL and cable connections that are on constantly with little or no firewalling, and finding a vulnerable system becomes an effortless task. Many crackers now use drift-net methods for locating, identifying, and ensnaring vulnerable machines. The process is entirely automated and no system is immune. My own log files show hundreds of crack attempts daily against my system. Understanding some basic security measures is essential to reduce your own system's risk.

You must take several precautions to secure your Linux system. First, recognize and become familiar with the weaknesses of your particular system or Linux distribution. Stay current on any published security issues or concerns. Subscribe to *BugTraq* or any of the other vulnerability mailing lists.

Next, understand how these issues may affect your own system. What can someone possibly do to exploit your Linux box? What sorts of weaknesses does your release have over other later releases, and do those weaknesses justify an upgrade? Have you installed the latest security patches available from the Red Hat site?

Third, learn how to implement safety measures and take a proactive approach. Be aware also that you may need to be reactive in your handling of the system.

Know how to fix the system and clean up after a suspected break-in; be willing to reformat from scratch and restore all files if the crack is confirmed and is serious enough to warrant a total rewrite. Once your system's security has been breached and unless you clean up properly and ensure there are no other backdoors and that the exploits are no longer available to others, you are liable to suffer similar attacks and system failures if you don't install measures to verify your system's integrity and security.

And last, be able to prevent any future security breaches. It is all very fine to clean up a mess after someone gets in, but if you don't take the necessary steps to ensure that the same thing does not happen again, all your effort will have been in vain. Understand what the perpetrator accomplished and fix your system so that not only he or she cannot get back in but that no one else can profit from that cracker's efforts and from your negligence.

Knowing these few things will help make you a better administrator and keep your defenses well tuned. Though your users may not thank you, the best reward is never to have to explain to them why their data were lost or destroyed. This chapter will look at some of the easier examples and lessons to be learned in keeping your system secure. Though I cannot guarantee 100 percent security, but no one really can. There is no such thing as a 100 percent secure system.

## Knowing Your Linux Release

Before attempting to take on the external threats, you need to know and take care of the internal issues. As they are installed by default, many of the Linux distributions are wide open to security breaches. Red Hat often leaves certain programs running that should not enabled by default. Knowing the chinks and weak spots in your system's armors is the best way to start protecting yourself. Most Linux distributions keep an updated security page where they post information about the latest problems with their release. Red Hat is no different. Subscribing to Red Hat's newsletter and frequenting its page for news releases are the best methods of staying up to date on exploits. Red Hat also provides patches or upgrades to fix known issues. These fixes can come in the form of a simple command or can be a script run at the command line. More often, it is an RPM upgrade that directly updates the file or directory in question. Whenever a known bug or exploit comes to light that affects Red Hat, you should procure the latest update and fix the problem immediately.

One good site that keeps readers abreast of the latest Linux security issues and news stories is the *Linux Weekly News* page (http://lwn.net/). Every Thursday the site examines the latest public problems and shows what each Linux release or the community in general is doing to fix them. This site is also good for becoming familiar with basic Linux jargon, procedures, and tools. Any administrator worth his or her salt should spend at least some time becoming acquainted with his or her specific Linux distribution.

Another excellent source of security-related issues is the page formerly known as BugTraq that has in the past year or so transmogrified to SecurityFocus (http://www.securityfocus.com). This site not only provides users with the latest news and articles regarding UNIX and Linux security issues, but anything relating to security on most all platforms and on the Internet in general. It also provides links to many free tools allowing system administrators to check their own security protocols. Most importantly, this site provides a list of known vulnerabilities of most operating systems. Not only can you see what might be wrong or might have failed on other platforms, but you can see exactly how culprits can exploit weaknesses on your own system. The search engine provided on this site looks through all the entries provided by Bugtraq to give you the very latest exploits and examples on fixing your problem. It also provides a mailing-list subscription for daily email updates and contributions.

The CERT mailing list and security site (http://www.cert.org/) is another good example of developers dedicated to exposing weaknesses for the purpose of strengthening systems. The old adage of "security through obscurity" does not hold true in the day of open-source software. Point is, open source software now provides a viable alternative to diagnosing and repairing ills to the system without fear of exploitation. Without proper exposure and examination, security problems can quickly fester and become a cancerous body throughout the Internet. Only by diagnosing the illness can the tumor or security hole be diagnosed and removed.

## Keeping Users in Check

There are many aspects to implementing passwords under Linux. Creating and then making the users keep their passwords up-to-date is one of the more challenging facets to maintaining a secure system.

The best way to force users to update their passwords is to institute aging measures so that after a certain time users need to issue the system a new password.

With a certain amount of time left on their account (usually a week), they will be notified that they must change their password. After that time period, they can log in to the server manually and make the change. Some administrators do not allow Telnet access to their systems, in which case the administrator or someone else with direct access to the system must perform the updates. How these updates are implemented is usually left up to the administrator.

At one company that I worked at, I was very concerned by the weak passwords chosen by the users. They were able to pick their own passwords, which were then entered in the system by the tech support people, much to the dismay of the administrator. I took it upon myself to run the program crack, which attempts to decrypt the /etc/passwd and/or the /etc/shadow file and reveals each user's password. It generates a list of cracked passwords and their user. Based on this list, I sent an e-mail to all these users with compromised passwords and notified them to change their password quickly. A few weeks later nearly all the accounts had been updated.

For a review of basic rules involved in setting secure passwords, see Chapter 5.

If you insist on storing passwords, do so prudently. Do not write them down. One possible method of putting them in safekeeping is to store the files on your machine in some sort of encrypted program. Under Linux, a popular password program is gpasman. Here you can enter in the name of the host server, the username, the password, and a comment explaining the purpose or function of the password. Rather than having to memorize several different passwords for a range of machines, you must remember only one main password that then allows you to open the main encrypted file. Normally the passwords are hidden and only by clicking on the drop-down menu can you display all the passwords. This is in case anyone might be peering over your shoulder while you bring up the program. The gpasman program is just one of many password programs that encrypt text files. A simple search through a site such as http://freshmeat.net or any of the other sites that provide links to Linux programs will show the wide range of programs available.

It is never safe to write root passwords down, even when you are storing them in a safe place. You should simply memorize these passwords. Some workplaces insist on documenting passwords and then storing them in a safe. This creates an additional problem of memorizing the safe's combination. When the safe is opened and the passwords are consulted, you should change them immediately afterward, note the updates, then store the documented passwords again. If your company insists on documenting passwords, take whatever steps are necessary to keep them away from all prying eyes. It is easier to recover a well-protected password that is simply forgotten than to exercise damage control on your system if you lose a password to someone else.

# Managing Connections

Most all Linux servers carry certain security risks that you must take into account whenever outside users share system files. Whenever you share a server with other users, you must accept the liability that comes with multiuser systems. Users may attempt to access files that you would prefer to remain untouched, or run programs best installed and managed on a separate server or not at all. Keeping tabs on your users and monitoring the programs they use will help ensure that your own system remains untouched and semi-impervious from internal and external harm.

## Sniffing Packets

A normal terminal connection to any machine, including Linux machines, is extremely unsecure. Whenever a user logs in to a Linux machine, a Telnet client is transmitting unencrypted text across the LAN or Internet. The *packets*, or bits of data carrying the plain text, can be intercepted anywhere along the way and their contents examined. This is one way that passwords or sensitive data are exposed to malicious use. One means by which packets can be intercepted is a *packet sniffer*—a program that captures and views the packets as they are transmitted on your own machine Sniffers usually require root access because they need to enable promiscuous or eavesdropping mode on the NIC. Though any user can access the kernel's IP code, having a user place a sniffer on your network is akin to covertly gathering data and abusing the privacy of others. Though a packet sniffer can be a useful tool for debugging problem network machines, its power can still be abused in the wrong hands. Be wary of any user that installs or runs a sniffer on your network.

Though a normal connection does not print to the display or console the keys pressed when you enter a password, a *keyboard logger*—or program that track the keys pressed during your period of connectivity can also be a potential threat. Keep this in mind when using such commands as xhost + when sharing programs among machines. This means that passwords can be transmitted unsecurely to the system and can be viewed when in transit as well. These are usually limited to local machines and can be better controlled than network risks posed by packet sniffers.

Anyone with a packet sniffer on your line or network can determine your username and password. Some sniffers are limited to 256 characters, but others can continue monitoring additional keystrokes. This is a particularly acute security breach if you log in as yourself and then immediately become root. The best recommendation for discouraging eavesdroppers is to eliminate Telnet altogether due to its unprotected nature. Implement something analogous to ssh or openssh exclusively for viewing data on different machines in an unsecure environment.

To prevent this type of activity, make sure that you know what is running on your machine. Running the ps command periodically can identify both the process and the user. If someone is running an unattended process that appears unfamiliar or that you have not given prior approval, chances are that the user is doing something untoward. If that user is still actively connected to the system, attempt to determine the location from which the user connected. If the location is within the same domain as your system, then you can easily track that user down. For more information on using the ps command, refer to Chapter 7.

If you are connecting from outside your system, determine the user's connection by executing either a w or who command. If you wish to see exactly what process that user is running, perform the following command, substituting <username> with the user's real username:

```
# ps auxww | grep <username>
```

This command will also display the PID of the process and enable you both to kill the process by sending it a kill -9 signal and to remove the user from the system if the user appears to be abusing his or her privileges.

> **CAUTION**
>
> Be aware, though, that connections are easily spoofed, or falsified, to appear otherwise and that the IP address of the incoming connection can feign another IP address in the absence of other security measures. If your system is already cracked, this becomes a very simple matter. This means that anyone can pretend to be coming in from any other possible site. Details for spoofing addresses and feigning identities as well as steps to discourage such practices from occurring on your network are covered in greater detail at the SecurityFocus site, http://www.securityfocus.com/.
>
> Also, if someone has compromised your box, your display may not show a true representation of what processes are running on your machine or who is really logged in. The w and who commands use the /var/log/wtmp file, which is easy to forge or hack. Check for hidden dot files or ... directories that may be concealing secret directories and other binaries. Compare the binaries on your own system against those of a pristine install on another box and check for inconsistencies and size and location of standard files. Check security sites for exploits and look for dumped core files. All of these provide clues for seeking out solutions in the case of a hacked or suspected compromised system.

Packet sniffers can do untold damage, since you are never quite certain exactly what the program may or may not have been able to trace. If you can determine that a user has had a packet sniffer running on your system or has been monitoring your connections, change all passwords immediately. Also, inform other users to change their passwords as well. If you can pin down the times that the sniffer was running or when it was installed, you may need only to inform people who had logged in during those times. Run the last command to see who had logged in during that period and then contact those users.

> **CAUTION**
>
> Like the wtmp file, /var/log/lastlog is also easy to hack or replace with a forgery.

Dealing with a user who sniffs packets or monitors system use is left up to you as the administrator, but canceling that person's account and making sure that he or she stays away may not be too harsh a step to take. If that person is an employee or customer, you may want to contact his or her superiors and inform them.

I cannot condone an administrator using packet sniffing to test the activities of his or her clients, customers, or users. A good administrator needs to exercise some restraint, yet at the same time be aware of what users are doing. If users feel they cannot trust their administrator because everything they do might be watched, they may take their business elsewhere. However, if they feel totally unwatched, they might interpret this as *carte blanche* to do whatever they please. Any sort of monitoring needs to be done in measure and with a healthy dose of good judgment. Either way, too much or too little control can have adverse results.

## Securing Shells with ssh

One way to help anyone and everyone from finding out too much about your system is to use a secure shell. This is basically an encrypted connection from one machine to another. While a Telnet session transmits unencrypted data via the two machines, a secure connection prevents a mediocre cracker from gaining too much information from the connection. One of the most effective utilities currently available is *ssh*, short for *secure shell*.

The ssh utility is a secure login system and replaces such unsecure programs as telnet, rlogin, rsh, rcp, and rdist. The utility supports most encryption algorithms such as BlowFish, Triple DES, IDEA, and RSA and is easy to install. You can retrieve ssh from its parent site in Finland at the following address: http://www.ssh.fi/. You can either download the source code or the RPM version. I recommend compiling and installing ssh from source due to the varying configuration options. Additional support can be incorporated into the program and tuned to your own network.

The ssh utility runs as a background daemon and should be started upon bootup. Installing via the RPM automatically configures this secure utility for you. If you decide to compile ssh yourself, read the associated documentation carefully. This will usually provide you with sufficient instructions to get ssh installed and running. If you wish to have ssh start upon bootup, you will have to add it to your startup scripts in your /etc/rc.d files. Because ssh changes, you should read the documentation carefully to determine the file in which you want to place the startup script.

**NOTE**

Currently two versions of ssh are in active use: the *1.2.x* and *2.2.x* releases. Though many prefer the earlier (or lower-numbered) releases due to familiarity, you might be better off using the later (or higher-numbered) releases. The higher the version number goes, the more restrictive the license becomes. At the *2.2* level, there are significant legal implications if the user fails to read and heed the license. The 1.2 versions are user-friendlier. Alternatively, OpenSSH has no license restrictions and should be considered as a possible tool. It employs many of the same features as ssh and is considered open source, hence the name.

To configure and install the program, download the tarred and zipped file and place it in a secure directory. Unzip and untar in the location of your choice. Execute the following commands to create and install the binary:

```
# gunzip -c ssh-2.2.0.tar.gz | tar xvf -
# cd ssh-2.2.0/
# ./configure <options>
# make
# make install
```

This places a series of executable files in your /usr/local/bin directory or in the directory of your choice as determined by your initial configuration. These are the files that you use to connect to another ssh box. The files are considered part of the client package. Any user can implement ssh from your machine to another.

The daemon files that are initiated on bootup and are part of the ssh server process are located in /usr/local/sbin. One method of starting the ssh daemon on bootup is to add the following script to the top of the /etc/rc.d/rc.local file:

```
# Start SSH Daemon
#
if [ -f /usr/local/sbin/sshd ]; then
/usr/local/sbin/sshd;
echo "Starting SSH2"
fi
```

This allows other machines running with the ssh client to connect to your machine and establish a secure ssh link. To make your system doubly secure, disable Telnet or connections to port 23 by commenting out the appropriate line in the /etc/inetd.conf file. The only type of connections will then be through port 22, the port associated with ssh.

---

### NOTE

Be sure to send HUP or the `kill -1` signal to the inetd process after making changes to the /etc/inetd.conf file in order to effect the changes made.

---

## Editing the ssh Configuration Files

Two types of configuration files are available for modifying and improving the methods of connecting to your server and others. One is primed for the client and the other for server connections. Both are located in the /etc/ssh2/ directory, where both keys and config files are stored.

The first file, ssh2_config sets up the parameters used for connection to other servers or the client-side configuration. Listing 19.1 shows a sample file and the default parameters.

### Listing 19.1  A Sample ssh2_config File Display Options for Editing

```
# ssh2_config
# SSH 2.0 Client Configuration File

*:

        Port                    22
        Ciphers                 AnyStdCipher
        IdentityFile            identification
        Authorization           Fileauthorization
        RandomSeedFile          random_seed
        VerboseMode             no
        #PasswordPrompt         "%U@%H's password: "
        PasswordPrompt          "%U's password: "
        #LocalForward           "110:pop3.ssh.fi:110"
        #RemoteForward          "3000:foobar:22"
```

```
        Ssh1AgentCompatibility         none
        #Ssh1AgentCompatibility        traditional
        #Ssh1AgentCompatibility        ssh2
        #SshSignerPath                 ssh-signer2
        NoDelay                        no
        KeepAlive                      yes
        StrictHostKeyChecking          ask
#alpha*:
#       Host                           alpha.oof.fi
#       User                           user
#       PasswordPrompt                 "%U:s password at %H: "
#       Ciphers                        idea
#
#foobar:
#       Host                           foo.bar
#       User                           foo_user
```

Some of the more important variables that the administrator can configure are the port number, which should not be altered, the identity and authorization files, the password prompt, and compatibility with ssh1.

The second configuration file is longer and more detailed. It determines the variables for the ssh daemon and how others connect to your system. Listing 19.2 shows a sample configuration file that is available for editing purposes.

**Listing 19.2  A Sample sshd2_config File That Sets Up Incoming ssh Connections to Your System**

```
# sshd2_config
# SSH 2.0 Server Configuration File

*:

        Port                       22
        ListenAddress              0.0.0.0
        Ciphers                    AnyStd
#       Ciphers                    AnyCipher
#       Ciphers                    AnyStdCipher
#       Ciphers                    3des
        IdentityFileidentification
```

```
              AuthorizationFile          authorization
              HostKeyFile                hostkey
              PublicHostKeyFile          hostkey.pub
              RandomSeedFile             random_seed
              ForwardAgent                                          yes
              ForwardX11                                            yes
#   DEPRECATED                           PasswordAuthentication     yes
              PasswordGuesses            3
#             MaxConnections             50
#   0 == number of connections not limited
#             MaxConnections             0
#             PermitRootLogin            nopwd
              PermitRootLogin                                       yes
#   DEPRECATED                           PubkeyAuthentication       yes
#             AllowedAuthentications     publickey,password,hostbased
              AllowedAuthentications     publickey,password
#             RequiredAuthentications    publickey,password
              ForcePTTYAllocation                                   no
              VerboseMode                                           no
              PrintMotd                                             yes
              CheckMail                                             yes
              UserConfigDirectory        "%D/.ssh2"
#             UserConfigDirectory        "/etc/ssh2/auth/%U"
              SyslogFacility             AUTH
#             SyslogFacility             LOCAL7
              Ssh1Compatibility                                     yes
#             Sshd1Path                  <set by    configure>
#             AllowHosts                 localhost, foobar.com, friendly.org
#             DenyHosts                  evil.org, aol.com
#             AllowSHosts                trusted.host.org
#             DenySHosts                 not.quite.trusted.org
#             IgnoreRhosts                                          no
#             IgnoreRootRHosts                                      no
#   (the above, if not set, is defaulted to the value of IgnoreRHosts)
#             NoDelay                                               yes
#             KeepAlive                                             yes
              RequireReverseMapping                                 no
```

```
        UserKnownHosts                              yes
        MaxBroadcastsPerSecond      1
#       MaxBroadcastsPerSecond      0   # Default value
#       ChRootUsers                 ftp,guest
#       ChRootGroups                guest


# subsystem definitions
subsystem-sftp                      sftp-server
```

Listing 19.2 shows the different keys and files that ssh uses when authenticating incoming connections. Depending on your username when logging in to a machine running ssh, your hostkeys will be stored in that user's home directory in a .ssh2/ directory. This is a hidden directory that contains the public keys the server grants you for login purposes. The ssh program uses RSA to establish the shared secret keys, then a bulk data cipher such as IDEA/DES/Blowfish for the data. The keys are public/private key pairs. Similar to the SSL handshake, the client connects, the server sends back a public key which the client then compares to that one its record, i.e. in the ~/.ssh directory to guard against someone spoofing the server. The client then sends a message back to the server confirming to the server that a match is made. Once the connection is established, then additional data can be transmitted between the client and server in encrypted text mode.

## Logging in to Other Systems Using ssh

Using ssh to log in to another system is a simple matter. You must install and configure ssh to run on the client and sshd or the ssh daemon to run on the server. The *server* is normally the machine containing the data that you wish to access and which others will also log in to. The *client* machine is your own workstation and does not necessarily have to be a Linux box.

To log in to the server machine, which is running ssh as a daemon process, execute the command **ssh** from any terminal window, using the -l login option to specify your unique username and then state the name of the server. If, for example, I wanted to log in to the antares.astronomy.org server under the username of kerry, I would enter the following at a prompt:

```
$ ssh -l kerry antares.astronomy.org
```

This command would then generate a secure connection and prompt me for a password. After you have logged in, you have the same freedom as you would under a Telnet session. I can just as easily log in to the same box as another user, such as root, though on my client box I am still logged in as the user kerry:

```
$ ssh -l root antares.astronomy.org
```

The program would then prompt me for the root password on the box named antares.If you are connecting from the client box to the server, certain command-line options are available for optimizing the connection. Table 19.1 describes some of the flags associated with the command ssh.

### NOTE

When you first connect via ssh to another ssh-enabled box, you will notice the following message.

```
$ ssh antares.astronomy.org
Host key not found from database.
Key fingerprint:
xuvav-zetip-nahok-tytah-tupyk-sosuh-narim-munep-hebuz-bibeg-cexox
You can get a public key's fingerprint by running
% ssh-keygen -F publickey.pub
on the keyfile.
Are you sure you want to continue connecting (yes/no)?
```

This is a normal process and you should answer yes if you are connecting to the correct machine. Whenever you subsequently connect to this host, the program will not prompt you before establishing a connection. You can add additional machines to your known hosts configuration file beforehand and not receive this message from other machines.

## Securely Copying Files across Machines

As mentioned earlier, ssh is a replacement for other less secure methods of transmitting data across server connections. If you wish to grab data from another machine on your local network or from another subnet that also has ssh installed, you can use the scp command to copy over the data files remotely. The scp program is part of the ssh package.

**Table 19.1 The ssh Utility's Command Line Options**

| Option | Description |
|---|---|
| -a | Specifies that ssh will *not* use agent authentication forwarding |
| -c *cipher* | Specifies the method of encryption or the cipher preferred for the current session |
| -e *character* | Enables you to choose an alternate escape character |
| -f | Forks ssh into the background after you establish a connection and authenticate your session |
| -i *file* | Uses an alternate identity file |
| -l *user* | Specifies which user you wish to log in as |
| -n | Redirects input from /dev/null |
| -p *port* | Uses an alternate port for connecting (the default is 22) |
| -P | Requires ssh to connect on a nonprivileged port |
| -q | Sets ssh in quiet mode so that it does not print any warning messages to the console |
| -t | Instructs ssh to open a tty even if you are sending a single command |
| -v | Provides for verbose debugging to the console |
| -x | Disables X11 forwarding |

If you wish to copy a file from the box named web.astronomy.org and place it on quasi.astronomy.org, execute the following command. Use the scp command with the user and domain name of the target machines followed by the filename you wish to download. Follow this statement with the name of the local user and local machine's name as well as the selected file to be transferred.

```
    $ scp kerry@web.astronomy.org:apache_1.3.12.tar.gz joe@quasi.
astronomy.org:apache_1.3.12.tar.gz
    kerry@web.astronomy.org's password:
    joe@quasi.astronomy.org's password:
    apache_1.3.12.tar.gz                    | 1.6MB | 208.7 kB/s | TOC:
00:00:08 | 100%
```

After the system prompts you for the proper passwords, you will see a status bar appear that shows in percentages the amount of data successfully transferred. You may rename the file to be something else on your local system. The status bar will still show the original target name of the file, though the file will be saved as something else.

# Firewalling Your Machine

Linux provides several firewalling utilities on the kernel level in addition to the many programs that assist in creating generic scripts that also provide firewalling capabilities. In fact, considering its cost in comparison to other commercial systems and proprietary programs, Linux is a far more economical choice for establishing firewall protocols than any other system. Linux does not provide by default many of the standard tools that come with Checkpoint's Firewall-1 or PIX firewalls. However, some of the best-known firewalling utilities, including those that set up static *Name Address Translation* (*NAT*), are available as patches that you can apply to the kernel. With NAT you can provide non-routable IPs such as 192.168 addresses to machines within your internal and have those then route out through your gateway/firewall. Yet for all appearance to people outside your network these machines have routable addresses. This allows you to provide a nearly limitless number of unique addresses for internal boxes without purchasing expensive unique routable IP addresses. The patches for Linux that then provide NAT offer the same capabilities as their commercial equivalents. This section examines some of the basic principles involved in setting up a Linux firewall.

## Filtering Packets on the Server Level

The default method of creating a Linux firewall is with ipchains. The ipchains program is the successor to the earlier firewall program, ipfwadm. Development is also under way to implement a program named netfilter, which will accomplish both packet filtering and static NATing on the server level. The netfilter program is currently available in the latest 2.4 test kernels and should be included in its stable release. This program performs the same functions as ipchains, but is easier to use. Many of the commands associated with ipchains and firewalling are covered in Chapter 16.

Although ipchains is very useful for IP masquerading, it is more commonly implemented for closing ports and allowing traffic through from specified hosts. Because each user employs different methods of setting up a Linux firewall and has varying ideas of what should and should not be allowed to pass through, there is no single "right" way of creating an ipchains script. As long as you use the correct syntax and the system is operable, firewalls can attain varying levels of security.

Listing 19.3 is a sample ipchains script that configures a generic firewall under Linux. Because static NAT addresses, or retaining unique IPs both within and without the internal network, are still not available under the generic ipchains program, this script simply provides IP Masquerading and thus the address external hosts see coming from your network is simply the address assigned to your gateway or firewall machine.

Included with the script are several comments that should help in customizing it to suit. Several options have been commented out but you can readily add back in if your system requires them. The script includes a brief description of what each section does, but read carefully through the entire file, try some of the various options, and attempt to run it yourself.

### Listing 19.3 A Generic ipchains Script That Configures Linux as a Firewall

```
#!/bin/sh
# ---------Configuration--------
# Local Interface
# This is the interface that is the link to the world
LOCALIF="eth0"
# Internal Interface
# This is the interface for the local network
# NOTE: INTERNALNET is a *network* address. All host bits should
be 0
INTERNALNET="192.168.0.0/16"
# The location of ipchains.
IPCHAINS="/sbin/ipchains"
#--------End Configuration--------
```

```
      LOCALIP='ifconfig $LOCALIF | grep inet | cut -d : -f 2 | cut -d
\     -f 1'
      LOCALMASK='ifconfig $LOCALIF | grep Mask | cut -d : -f 4'
      LOCALNET="$LOCALIP/$LOCALMASK"
      echo "Internal: $INTERNALNET"
      echo "External: $LOCALNET"
      REMOTENET="0/0"
      # Flush everything, start from scratch -
      echo -n "Flushing rulesets.."
      # Incoming packets from the outside network
      $IPCHAINS -F input
      echo -n "."
      # Outgoing packets from the internal network
      $IPCHAINS -F output
      echo -n "."

      # Forwarding/masquerading
      $IPCHAINS -F forward
      echo -n "."

      echo "Done!"
      # Allow all connections within the network -
      echo -n "Internal.."
      $IPCHAINS -A input -s $INTERNALNET -d $INTERNALNET -j ACCEPT
      $IPCHAINS -A output -s $INTERNALNET -d $INTERNALNET -j ACCEPT
      echo -n ".."
      echo "Done!"
      # Allow loopback interface -
      echo -n "Loopback.."
      $IPCHAINS -A input -i lo -s 0/0 -d 0/0 -j ACCEPT
      $IPCHAINS -A output -i lo -s 0/0 -d 0/0 -j ACCEPT
      echo -n ".."
      echo "Done!"

      # Masquerading -
      echo -n "Masquerading.."
```

```
# don't masquerade internal-internal traffic
$IPCHAINS -A forward -s $INTERNALNET -d $INTERNALNET -j ACCEPT
echo -n "."
# don't Masquerade external interface direct
$IPCHAINS -A forward -s $LOCALNET -d $REMOTENET -j ACCEPT
echo -n "."

# masquerade all internal IPs going outside
$IPCHAINS -A forward -s $INTERNALNET -d $REMOTENET -j MASQ
echo -n "."
# set Default rule on MASQ chain to Deny
$IPCHAINS -P forward DENY
echo -n "."

# Allow all connections from the network to the outside -
$IPCHAINS -A input -s $INTERNALNET -d $REMOTENET -j ACCEPT
$IPCHAINS -A output -s $INTERNALNET -d $REMOTENET -j ACCEPT
echo -n ".."
echo "Done!"
# ----------Set telnet, www and FTP for minimum delay -
# This section manipulates the Type Of Service (TOS) bits of the
# packet. For this to work, you must have
# CONFIG_IP_ROUTE_TOS enabled in your kernel
echo -n "TOS flags.."
$IPCHAINS -A output -p tcp -d 0/0 www -t 0x01 0x10
$IPCHAINS -A output -p tcp -d 0/0 telnet -t 0x01 0x10
$IPCHAINS -A output -p tcp -d 0/0 ftp -t 0x01 0x10
echo -n "..."

# Set ftp-data for maximum throughput
$IPCHAINS -A output -p tcp -d 0/0 ftp-data -t 0x01 0x08
echo -n "."
echo "Done!"
# Trusted Networks -
# Add in any rules that specifically allow connections from
# hosts/nets that would otherwise be blocked.
# echo -n "Trusted Networks.."
```

```
# $IPCHAINS -A input -s [trusted host/net] -d $LOCALNET <ports>
# -j ACCEPT
# echo -n "."
# echo "Done!"

# Banned Networks -
# Add in any rules that specifically block connections
# from hosts/nets that have been known to cause you problems.
# These packets are logged.
# echo -n "Banned Networks.."

# This one is generic
# $IPCHAINS -A input -l -s [banned host/net] -d $LOCALNET
# <ports> -j DENY
# echo -n "."
# This one blocks ICMP attacks
# $IPCHAINS -A input -l -b -i $LOCALIF -p icmp -s [host/net]
# -d $LOCALNET -j DENY
# echo -n "."
# echo "Done!"

# Specific port blocks on the external interface -
# This section blocks off ports/services to the outside that have
# vulnerabilities. This will not affect the ability
# to use these services within your network.
echo -n "Port Blocks.."
# NetBEUI/Samba
$IPCHAINS -A input -p tcp -s $REMOTENET -d $LOCALNET 139 -j DENY
$IPCHAINS -A input -p udp -s $REMOTENET -d $LOCALNET 139 -j DENY
echo -n "."
# Microsoft SQL
$IPCHAINS -A input -p tcp -s $REMOTENET -d $LOCALNET 1433 -j DENY
$IPCHAINS -A input -p udp -s $REMOTENET -d $LOCALNET 1433 -j DENY
echo -n "."
# Postgres SQL
$IPCHAINS -A input -p tcp -s $REMOTENET -d $LOCALNET 5432 -j DENY
$IPCHAINS -A input -p udp -s $REMOTENET -d $LOCALNET 5432 -j DENY
```

```
    echo -n "."
    # Network File System
    $IPCHAINS -A input -p tcp -s $REMOTENET -d $LOCALNET 2049 -j DENY
    $IPCHAINS -A input -p udp -s $REMOTENET -d $LOCALNET 2049 -j DENY
    echo -n "."
    # X Displays :0-:2-
    $IPCHAINS -A input -p tcp -s $REMOTENET -d $LOCALNET 5999:6003 -j
DENY
    $IPCHAINS -A input -p udp -s $REMOTENET -d $LOCALNET 5999:6003 -j
DENY
    echo -n "."
    # X Font Server :0-:2-
    $IPCHAINS -A input -p tcp -s $REMOTENET -d $LOCALNET 7100 -j DENY
    $IPCHAINS -A input -p udp -s $REMOTENET -d $LOCALNET 7100 -j DENY
    echo -n "."
    # Back Orifice (logged)
    $IPCHAINS -A input -l -p tcp -s $REMOTENET -d $LOCALNET 31337 -j
DENY
    $IPCHAINS -A input -l -p udp -s $REMOTENET -d $LOCALNET 31337 -j
DENY
    echo -n "."
    # NetBus (logged)
    $IPCHAINS -A input -l -p tcp -s $REMOTENET -d $LOCALNET 12345:12346
-j DENY
    $IPCHAINS -A input -l -p udp -s $REMOTENET -d $LOCALNET 12345:12346
-j DENY
    echo -n "."
    echo "Done!"
    # High Unprivileged ports -
    # These are opened up to allow sockets created
    # by connections allowed by ipchains
    echo -n "High Ports.."
    $IPCHAINS -A input -p tcp -s $REMOTENET -d $LOCALNET 1023:65535 -j
ACCEPT
    $IPCHAINS -A input -p udp -s $REMOTENET -d $LOCALNET 1023:65535 -j
ACCEPT
    echo -n "."
```

```
echo "Done!"

# ------------------------------------------------------------- Basic
Services - echo -n "Services.."
    #ftp-data (20) and ftp (21)
    $IPCHAINS -A input -p tcp -s $REMOTENET -d $LOCALNET 20 -j ACCEPT
    $IPCHAINS -A input -p tcp -s $REMOTENET -d $LOCALNET 21 -j ACCEPT
    echo -n ".."
    #ssh (22)
    $IPCHAINS -A input -p tcp -s $REMOTENET -d $LOCALNET 22 -j ACCEPT
     echo -n "."
    #telnet (23)
    $IPCHAINS -A input -p tcp -s $REMOTENET -d $LOCALNET 23 -j ACCEPT
    echo -n "."
    #smtp (25)
    $IPCHAINS -A input -p tcp -s $REMOTENET -d $LOCALNET 25 -j ACCEPT
    echo -n "."
    # DNS (53)
    $IPCHAINS -A input -p tcp -s $REMOTENET -d $LOCALNET 53 -j ACCEPT
    $IPCHAINS -A input -p udp -s $REMOTENET -d $LOCALNET 53 -j ACCEPT
    echo -n ".."
    # DHCP on LAN side (67/68)
    # $IPCHAINS -A input -i $INTERNALIF -p udp -s $REMOTENET
-d 255.255.255.255/24 67 -j ACCEPT
    # $IPCHAINS -A output -i $INTERNALIF -p udp -s $REMOTENET
-d 255.255.255.255/24 68 -j ACCEPT
    # echo -n ".."
    #http (80)
    $IPCHAINS -A input -p tcp -s $REMOTENET -d $LOCALNET 80 -j ACCEPT
    echo -n "."
    #POP-3 (110)
    $IPCHAINS -A input -p tcp -s $REMOTENET -d $LOCALNET 110 -j ACCEPT
    echo -n "."
    #identd (113)
    $IPCHAINS -A input -p tcp -s $REMOTENET -d $LOCALNET 113 -j ACCEPT
    echo -n "."
    # nntp (119)
    # $IPCHAINS -A input -p tcp -s $REMOTENET -d $LOCALNET 119
```

```
# -j ACCEPT
# echo -n "."
# https (443)
# $IPCHAINS -A input -p tcp -s $REMOTENET -d $LOCALNET 443
# -j ACCEPT
# echo -n "."
# ICQ Services (it's a server service) (4000)
# $IPCHAINS -A input -p tcp -s $REMOTENET -d $LOCALNET 4000 -j
ACCEPT
# echo -n "."
echo "Done!"


# ------------------------- ICMP -
echo -n "ICMP Rules.."
# Use this to deny ICMP attacks from specific addresses
# $IPCHAINS -A input -b -i $EXTERNALIF -p icmp -s <address>
# -d 0/0 -j DENY
# echo -n "."
# Allow incoming ICMP
$IPCHAINS -A input -p icmp -s $REMOTENET -d $LOCALNET -j ACCEPT
$IPCHAINS -A input -p icmp -s $REMOTENET -d $LOCALNET -j ACCEPT
echo -n ".."
# Allow outgoing ICMP
$IPCHAINS -A output -p icmp -s $LOCALNET -d $REMOTENET -j ACCEPT
$IPCHAINS -A output -p icmp -s $LOCALNET -d $REMOTENET -j ACCEPT
$IPCHAINS -A output -p icmp -s $INTERNALNET -d $REMOTENET -j ACCEPT
$IPCHAINS -A output -p icmp -s $INTERNALNET -d $REMOTENET -j ACCEPT
echo -n "...."
echo "Done!"


# -- set default policy --
$IPCHAINS -A input -j DENY
$IPCHAINS -A output -j ACCEPT


echo ""
echo "Finished Establishing Firewall."
# End of file
```

# Explaining the Firewall Script

The first and second sections in Listing 19.3 define how the server connects to the outside world, its external interface, its network, its IP address, and the internal subnet mask. They also specify the location of the ipchains program and sets the previous addresses as environmental variables.

The next paragraph *flushes* or removes all previous chains or rules, allowing the system to begin anew. It then defines the incoming and outgoing packet rules.

The next three sections start the masquerading rules. Unlike the examples in Chapter 18, these rules do not comprise the whole of the script, but define only how the program will handle internal IP addresses. Here all internal nonvalid IPs are not masqueraded but allowed to retain the unique address when communicating with other internal hosts.

Next, the default rule on the masquerading chains is set to *deny*. This prevents internal nonvalid IPs from leaving the network.

Now, all connections from the inside to the outside are set to accept.

The following two sections allow for Web, Telnet, and FTP traffic to be set for minimum delay and maximum output of FTP data. This facilitates packets to route out of your system quickly without encapsulating additional headers to the packets. To have these sections apply to your system, you must set the specified variable in your kernel configuration.

The next three portions of the script are commented out. You must provide a list of networks that are either trusted or banned. The last portion also is a generic blocking chain that denies connectivity on all ports from a banned network or IP address.

Next, all ICMP attacks are denied. This precludes any sort of ability to ping the internal hosts. The standard practice with DoS (Denial of Service) attacks is to flood a host with so many ping queries that the host cannot respond to regular connection attempts, as it is spending all its resources on responding to pings. This rule partially prevents this sort of attack. It is currently commented out since it requires a specific host from which they should ignore all ICMP requests.

The following larger section defines port blocking against various services to the outside that have known vulnerabilities or for which there are published exploits. For the most part, there is no need to connect to the specified ports of the server. If the server is to function as a firewall, it should have fewer services running on it to minimize the risk of anyone compromising its purpose and breaking into the internal network.

The section following these denials allows other services to connect to higher unprivileged ports. This will be necessary for sending FTP packets back across the network, which create dynamic sockets for transmitting data.

The Basic Services section allows standard connections on needed ports within and outside the internal network. This facilitates regular communication between computers within the firewall-protected network to those hosts outside.

Again, the firewall chains are specific about ICMP attacks and define what ping requests are allowable on the network.

The next-to-last section defines the default policy for the chains or rules. All outgoing packets are accepted for transmission and routing, whereas all incoming packets are denied by default. This means that any packets seeking entry into your network must be defined as allowable. They must meet specific criteria as defined in the preceding chains.

The last section prints to the console the message that the basic firewall has been successfully configured. This lets the administrator know that the chains have been parsed through the available rules and have set each line as defined. To verify what rules are now operational, type the following at the command line:

```
# /sbin/ipchains -L
```

This command lists all valid chains. You may use the command to verify that a certain line or rule was correctly processed.

Most of the sections are relatively self-explanatory. The ipchains program identifies the various port numbers and the syntax that then allows or restricts the passage of packets through that port. More ports are listed here than you will probably need. You can leave the various sections commented or uncomment those that you wish to add. Either way, this script is flexible enough to start a working firewall and then configure it to your specific host system.

## Enabling the Script on Bootup

If you wish to execute this script upon system bootup, make it executable or type the command **chmod 700 <filename>**. Now place it someplace that it will not be easily overlooked. Then, in the /etc/rc.d/rc.local file, place a line that starts up the script. I placed my own rc.firewall.local script in the same directory as that of rc.local and called it in the following manner:

```
/etc/rc.d/rc.firewall.local
```

# Gaining Added Security

Aside from those already mentioned in this book, several other programs are available on the Internet and designed for Linux that will assist in keeping your system secure and in checking for intruders. Not all are free, either for you to use at your discretion or to distribute among others on the Internet, but the vast majority encourages users to proliferate their scripts throughout the Linux community and to make improvements or adjustments.

## Setting Off Tripwires

One commonly used program for checking the current files on your Linux system is Tripwire. This program generates a database of the existing directories and files on a newly installed system and then periodically checks for changes to the files. If any user changes a system file containing important or sensitive data, Tripwire will send you an email to notify you about the modification.

Tripwire is free for noncommercial use and is covered under the LGPL license. I have found Tripwire capable of keeping me informed of any system changes. Even those files that I modify myself or that are updated nightly are tracked and logged. For tracking individual files that are crucial to system integrity, this program and others like it are invaluable.

According to the Tripwire Web site, http://www.tripwiresecurity.com/, this program is a *system integrity checker*—a utility that compares properties of designated files and directories against information stored in a previously generated database. You should install this program immediately after installing Linux on any machine. It is not much use to install a system integrity checker if the system's integrity is already compromised; you would only be validating existing corrupted files. Any changes to pristine files that are logged in the generated database are flagged and logged, including those added or deleted. If Tripwire reports no changes, system administrators can conclude with a high degree of certainty that a given set of files remains free of unauthorized modifications.

To install Tripwire, go to the main site, fill out the agreement form, and then download the software. You must comply with the terms of the agreement and not distribute or resell the code. Tripwire does offer an older version of its same product with less restrictive issues. You can download this version from the same web page.

Installing Tripwire is a relatively simple process. Create a temporary directory in which to place the code. Root's home directory will do. Move the tarred and zipped code to this new location. Once the code is safely stored in a temporary directory, uncompress the file's contents.

```
# mkdir /root/tw/
# mv Tripwire_221_for_Linux_x86.tar.gz /root/tw/
# cd /root/tw/
# gunzip -c Tripwire_221_for_Linux_x86.tar.gz | tar xvf -
```

This will then unpack the contents into the current directory, where you can begin installing the program. Be sure to look through the readme file and verify that you can run this release on your machine.

You can install this program by executing the install.sh script. If the system does not detect your particular distribution, the program warns you but allow you to continue. The program then prompts you to read through the License.txt file and agree to its conditions. Next, the install program checks for files necessary to continue its operations, such as sendmail and vi, and then installs all program files in the /usr/TSS directory.

When the install is complete, you must enter a *passphrase*, or a password-type string, for both the site keyfile and local keyfile. These keys are needed for maintenance issues and to ensure that your database remains secure. Be sure to choose something secure with upper- and lowercase characters, digits, and punctuation marks.

Before starting the program, refer to the Tripwire configuration file, twcfg.txt, located in the /usr/TSS/bin/ directory. In this file, you can reconfigure how Tripwire operates.

To initiate the configuration to run the program and generate a database in the same directory, issue the following commands. The twadmin program initializes the files for first-time use.

```
# ./twadmin --create-cfgfile --site-keyfile ../key/site.key
twcfg.txt
    Please enter your site passphrase:
    Wrote configuration file: /usr/TSS/bin/tw.cfg
    # ./twadmin --create-polfile ../policy/twpol.txt
    Please enter your site passphrase:
    Wrote policy file: /usr/TSS/policy/tw.pol
```

Now, after creating your configuration files and your policy files, you can start Tripwire for the first time and generate your Tripwire database:

```
# ./tripwire --init
    Please enter your local passphrase:
    Parsing policy file: /usr/TSS/policy/tw.pol
    Generating the database...
    *** Processing Unix File System ***
    ......................
    Wrote database file: /usr/TSS/db/specto.ksl.com.twd
    The database was successfully generated.
```

You might see several error messages, depending on your configuration and what binaries are already installed on your machine. Note these and fix them by changing the rules in your policy file. You should fix them sooner rather than later because every time Tripwire runs it will generate the same messages. Otherwise, Tripwire will successfully generate a database for your use. To verify the integrity of your files use the following command from the newly installed directory:

```
# /usr/TSS/bin/tripwire --check
```

After a length of time, depending on your system speed and the amount of files hosted on your server, Tripwire will generate a report and place it in the ../report directory. Use the twprint command to view the report generated.

You should automate this process and have Tripwire to run nightly or periodically and send you the reports via email. The sample entry in root's crontab file will accomplish the task:

```
0 0 * * * /usr/TSS/bin/tripwire --check
```

Tripwire examines file permissions, the unique size of each file, its hash and other properties that a malicious user could alter. You should install Tripwire or a similar system integrity checker on every new system that you set up.

## Cracking Bad Passwords

In addition to Tripwire, which takes a proactive stance against changes made by users, several programs are available that take a reactive approach to changes already made on the system. For instance, you can use the program crack to test the passwords of your users and see whether any of them "crack" when run against dictionary lists and when tested with a decryption algorithm. Many such programs are available that can use against your password files to check for weak or easily decipherable passwords.

You can get more information about the crack program from the developer's site at http://www.users.dircon.co.uk/~crypto/index.html. The site provides links to FTP sites that provide the source code. I grabbed my copy from the site ftp://ftp.cerias.purdue.edu/pub/tools/unix/pwdutils/crack/.

Install the program as you would any other. Place it in a secure location, such as root's home directory, and then uncompress the file and its contents by using the standard command:

```
# gunzip -c crack5.0.tar.gz | tar xvf -
```

This will create a c50a/ directory. Change to this directory and read the manual.txt file for any specific notes. To generate the binary file, run the following command:

```
# ./Crack -makeonly
```

This command may seem a bit backwards in that it appears you are building a pre-compiled binary and the executable is already present. However, the Crack command will simply create a new binary.

> **NOTE**
>
> Under Red Hat distributions, you will have to uncomment the `-lcrypt` option in the Crack file before running the make command. Only then will the binary successfully compile.

When that command is complete, you need to create the dictionary files by entering the following command:

```
# ./Crack -makedict
```

Grab the password file from your machine and then run Crack against it:

```
# cp /etc/passwd passwd.txt
# ./Crack passwd.txt
```

You can check the status of the file and run a report to see whose files cracked by using the Reporter command. The output shows the results of your crack attempt. If you are using shadowed passwords, check the manual.txt file for converting the files into readable format.

## Securing Your Linux Box

Because some consider the Red Hat distribution to be rather unsecure straight out of the box, Jay Beale and the Bastille Project Developers developed a set of Perl scripts that shore up many of the most blatant security flaws or discretions. Bastille Linux aims to be the most comprehensive, flexible, and educational security hardening program for Red Hat Linux versions 6.1 and down. Virtually every task that it performs is optional, providing immense flexibility. Bastille Linux educates the administrator performing the install regarding the topic at hand before asking any questions. Its interactive nature allows the program to be more thorough when performing security tasks, whereas the educational component should produce an administrator who is less likely to compromise the increased security. For beginning system administrators, Bastille Linux offers you a method of fine-tuning your machine while increasing your knowledge.

You can download the Bastille scripts and files from the main site, http://bastille-linux.sourceforge.net/. After downloading the program, place it in a secure location, uncompress the files, and begin the installation. You can perform this operation only as root due to the nature of the files Bastille that modifies.

You have your choice between two different methods: You can choose the InteractiveBastille.pl text user interface (TUI) and then run the BackEnd.pl script, or choose the AutomatedBastille.pl script, which skips the BackEnd.pl script. To configure as many items by hand as possible, choose the first method.

As you read through each option, note the description and the instructions on how to implement each module of the script. The entire process is pretty much automated, and you need only approve or disapprove each step as you are prompted.

## Testing Your Own Machine

After installing a firewall or instituting additional security measures, you can best assess your own machine's vulnerability by attempting to crack your own box. A good way to measure your own machine's vulnerability is to install the Nmap program. Nmap is a *network scanner* in that it scans for available ports on your machine and reports back any security holes.

You can download the latest version of Nmap from http://www.insecure. org/nmap/. Though Nmap does not provide you with any exploits against your own system, it will show you any vulnerable ports and rate the degree of difficulty in accessing your system.

After downloading the file and storing it in a safe place, such as /root or /usr/local/gnu, you can begin uncompressing and installing by executing the following commands:

```
# gunzip -c nmap-2.54BETA2.tgz | tar xvf -
# ./configure ; make ; make install
```

These commands install the necessary libraries and place the executables in the /usr/local/bin/ directory. You can start Nmap at the command line and input the variables that you need. If you have any questions about the format you choose or options associated with the binary, enter **nmap --help**.

An easier interface with which to access the Nmap program is xnmap or NmapFE (Nmap Front End) (see Figure 19.1). You can click and choose the interfaces that you wish the port scanner to use, and the GUI displays the unique command-line settings as well.

**FIGURE 19.1**

*NmapFE, the GUI front-end program to the console-based Nmap program.*

You can select a single machine or a range of IP addresses to scan. Any option that you choose on the GUI will also appear directly above the lower window of the dialog box as a command-line option.

# Cleaning Up Compromised Boxes

No matter what measures you have taken and no matter how hard you tried to keep your system secure, you might still discover or be informed that a user is abusing your system and has gained control. This is not the end of the world nor does it immediately merit reformatting the system. It does require that you take some cautious steps in determining the damage. This section explains some the steps you should take to fix a compromised Linux machine.

## Assessing the Damage

If the worse-case scenario does occur and you discover that your machine has been cracked—that is, that someone has compromised the integrity of your system or was able to gain access to sensitive files—there are a few simple steps that you must take. First of all, disconnect your machine immediately from the network. If you can possibly afford to remove it from external sources, do so now. Even if you cannot afford to disconnect it from the network and deny others connectivity, you should consider the alternatives. If one person has gained access, it is uncertain how many others may have done the same. Do not restore any sort of network connectivity until you are *certain* that your security holes are plugged and that all compromised files are removed or restored to their previous state.

Next, take extreme care when becoming root. Do not immediately become superuser. If you do need to gain root access, always use absolute paths when executing any sort of application or command. Use commands such as the following, for example:

```
# /bin/ls -la
# /usr/bin/su
```

These commands will prevent any executables that the cracker may have modified or altered from further damaging your system or granting the cracker more power or knowledge of your system.

To prevent crackers from placing a fake or bogus su program in your $PATH, check your path and make sure that it is still the same as before. Make sure that you have the fewest files in your path.

```
# /usr/bin/echo $PATH        # should be only /usr/sbin:/usr/bin
```

After verifying that your path is still intact, you can become root and then go to that user's home directory, if that user has a directory. If not, then verify that the user has not changed the /etc/passwd file so that he or she has a UID of 0. If the program or file that the user was executing is not there, then locate the file by name by using either the find or locate command, again using the absolute pathname. The locate command may not be as effective since it is mainly used for files previously accessed or stored in a generated database. If the user is running a malicious program from an absolute path, it will be easier to track down.

If your box has been *rooted*—that is, if the root account has been compromised—you may have no other alternative than to reformat your machine. If you have been making regular backups, you should be in good shape. If not, hope for the best.

If you can see the cracker, than he or she can probably also see you, so if you want to sneak up on the cracker you will have to be quick. Once you have determined what program the cracker is running on your system or what files he or she has modified, you will want to check that program and see what it may do. You can be reasonably sure that he or she will be trying to execute it from out of his or her home directory or from the /tmp or /dev directory. Check these locations initially. Sometime the device files are substituted for directories. For example, a malicious program may be hidden in a directory named to hide among all the /dev/pty files. The file /dev/ptyva might be deleted and replaced with a directory whose contents are programs that systematically replace or destroy your own files.

Do not become that user in order to move to the cracker's home directory. If you do so, you will change that user's history file. If you do go to their home directory, do so as yourself or as superuser. Be careful when doing so. Often crackers like to append to the su program a few additional commands that will record your next few keystrokes and then mail them to that same user. In this manner, every time you become superuser using the su command, the cracker will see the new password. It is recommended that you use full paths if you feel the box not fully compromised and if you know you can trust the program. If you cannot trust any of the basic UNIX commands, use a tool such as Tripwire and check for modifications of files.

If you verify that the user has compromised root, then attempt to disconnect that user from off your system. Make sure that you know the cracker's point of origin, i.e. his IP address or domain from which he or she is gaining access to your box. Though these may be easily spoofed, you can at least frustrate his or her future attempts to log in. Then after kicking the cracker off the system, place an entry in your hosts.deny file, denying the user access from the last location. This is only a temporary solution, since chances are the cracker has already compromised other locations and can come at you from different domains, IP addresses, and usernames. Better yet, shut down all access from outside your network. If that user is from within your own network, remove that user immediately from your box and delete any entry or record of that user from your machine. If you have physical access to the box, make sure that that also has not been compromised.

Next, you must decide whether you should reformat your machine and restore needed files from a pristine backup, or make the best of what you have and attempt to clean up the system. The former choice is always the best, though in some instances you must make the best of a bad situation.

# Tracking Down the Culprit

If you decide to work with the existing system and fix any issues and if the damage does not appear to be too extensive, you will want to locate the method by which that user was able to gain access to your system. This method is usually something that the user placed on your system, and not something already there. If you have kept current on patches and updates, the program used to infiltrate your system's integrity will be from outside the operating system.

After locating the responsible program, check to see what it does. Use any text editor to view the contents. If it is a binary, then you can be 99 percent certain that it should not have been there to begin with. If the file is a shell script, then look through the file's text to determine exactly what it did. Use the strings program as well against the binary file and check to see if there are any questionable strings within the program, such as an e-mail address to forward snooped data on to another user outside your system. The strings command is useful for inspecting compiled data not normally accessible from a text editor. Make certain that the user is off the system and take the necessary steps to ensure he or she remains off.

If a customer or regular user proves to be the guilty party, you will probably want to get in contact with that person. If the cracker is a minor or juvenile, informing his or her parents may be enough to have the account canceled. You might even want to charge them for any cleanup effort. Most of the time, crackers are simply script-kiddies who grab a script from the Internet and then try to crack a box. Most compromises do not come from local or regular users; look for external breaches in your system's security.

If the culprit is a regular user who has a valid account on your system, then confront that person with proof or what he or she did. Often this is enough either to have the user barred from the system or to levy some sort of punishment if the crime is serious enough. Such punishment can either be dismissal from the workplace if the system is located in a business environment or possibly even criminal punishment.

If that person was not only doing damage to your system, but was utilizing company resources to advance his or her aims elsewhere, you should contact criminal authorities to pursue the matter more fully.

## Ransacking the Logs

Now check to see when the cracker last logged in or from where he or she may have logged in before either you kicked the user off your system or the user left the system after being discovered. Of course, do not consider these logs untouched as they may have been doctored or altered by the intruder. If the username of the cracker is joe, use the following command to see from whence joe last logged in:

```
# last joe | more
```

Now use the strings command to check out the /var/log/wtmp file. Because this file is a bit more difficult to parse, the strings command will extract all instances of this user and any additional data.

```
# strings /var/log/wtmp | grep joe > cracked.txt
```

If the cracker is not a regular user or does not have a valid account, you may have to do additional sleuthing outside these files to determine their last known login time and location.

Some crackers use a dial-up connection to achieve their aims. Contacting the cracker's ISP should also be enough to persuade the cracker to stay away. Good ISPs have a very low tolerance for people abusing their system or using their equipment to abuse others. They will usually provide you with enough information to track down the culprit and bill the user for the time that you spent cleaning up the system.

Now refer to the transfer or ftp log file, /var/log/xferlog. If not hacked or modified, this file should inform you of the sorts of things that the user has uploaded or downloaded from your system.  If your /etc/passwd or /etc/shadow file is among the files downloaded, you can basically say goodbye to your entire system. All passwords are now suspect. The best advice is to reinstall and give all users new passwords.

Check to see who recently has become superuser and look through any other files where the culprit could have left his or her mark. This may require some investigation on your part, but the challenge can be rewarding.

```
# cd /var/log/
```

```
# grep joe /var/log/secure* | more
# grep joe /var/log/messages* | more
```

Look in the /tmp directory to make sure that no one has been running an executable from that location. This directory is a common resource for users to start their own programs. It is the one place that users can initiate executables outside their home directory.

Make sure that no unattended processes are running on the system. Even though you may have killed off the process, it may have respawned or forked itself off. Certain IRC bots such as eggdrop are notorious for doing this. Check for any programs currently running on the system that are owned by the same intruder identity. Use the ps command in conjunction with grep to isolate any rogue processes.

```
# ps aux | grep joe
```

If you are unable either to kill off the process or stop it, do not reboot the system until you are certain that all the files are clean. This may take some time, but it will be well worth it if a critical file has been changed.

Look for known root kits. You can become acquainted with a list of the various programs available for compromising your system by consulting the Web page http://www.securityfocus.com/ and searching the Vulnerabilities section.

If, at the very worse, the suspect has gained root access and has already changed or destroyed files, then you can only hope for a recent backup. If you have been *root-kit'ed*—that is, if a cracker has placed a root kit program on your system from which the cracker has gained superuser access—then you can either try to clean up or simply wipe the files and start over. If the best you can do is replace all the directories affected before a time at which you can prove that the system was compromised, you will be glad you partitioned user directories in a separate locations. Usually you can simply wipe the /usr, /var, and / and start over recovering some of the configuration settings from backups. The best option, once again, is to reformat the entire machine completely and start over. Although this is a sad option, to say the least, starting from scratch may be the best solution in the case of a compromised Linux machine.

# Conclusion

Once you have shored up any security holes within your system, you can begin to breathe a bit easier. Though you may never have your Red Hat Linux machine impervious to outside hacking attempts, you will have defeated the majority of script-kiddies wanting to compromise your system's security. Continue to research and test new strategies. The next chapter covers exactly these items and provides pointers to other locations and Web sites that will help fill in any gaps that his book leaves behind.

# Chapter 20

**Updating Policies and Information**

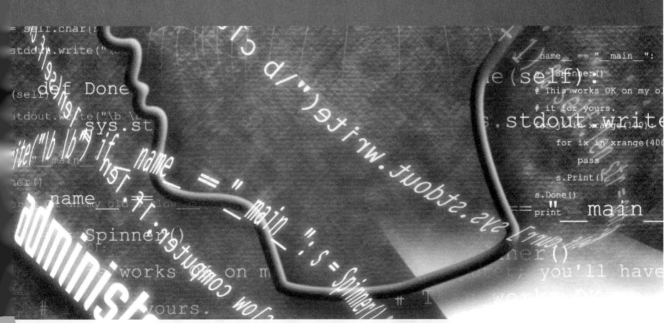

If you have been methodically working through this book from the first page onward, about now you should be finding yourself in the midst of Linux administration. It is at this point that many burgeoning administrators either throw up their hands in despair or have embraced Linux as their long-lost child. Hopefully, it is the latter instance you now find yourself.

This chapter will assist you in setting policies for beginning users and help you in maintaining the system. Some administrators may wish to have the system configured first and then allow users to share the resources. This chapter provides a brief overview of what administrators can do to manage their clientele as well as where to look for additional support.

This chapter will cover the following topics.

- ◆ Creating an acceptable use policy
- ◆ Making sure users are not abusing the system
- ◆ Setting quotas on user space
- ◆ Monitoring multiple servers and their reliability
- ◆ Tracking bandwidth use
- ◆ Providing helpful links to other Linux sites

# Providing File Access

Depending on your company's policies and the standards enforced by management, you may not have much say in how you govern your Linux machine. It is important to realize that just because users now can use Linux for file sharing, e-mail, or accessing the Internet, this does not give them *carte blanche* to do anything they want on the system that you administer. It remains your responsibility as a Linux system administrator to ensure that relevant files are accessible, but not to the point of being abused. It is important that you speak with your company's management and explain the freedoms that Linux offers and also the inherent risks involved.

If you have not already done so, now is the time to put in writing your company's acceptable use policy. This should cover the types of files you will allow to reside on your machine as well as the sorts of programs that can be run on your Linux box. Users should be aware of what constitutes acceptable use under the company's policy as defined by you and approved by management. The following section lays out stricter guidelines.

# Setting Standards

Now that you have successfully configured and are now maintaining an operational Linux system, you should consider instituting or enforcing policies and procedures. If your customers and users are well aware of what the system restrictions are up front and what they can do and should not do, your life will be much easier. Create a simple and well-defined acceptable-use policy. You should give this policy to each new user either as they sign up for service or when they are granted an account on the system. You should post these policies in a frequently visited area, such as the break room or another communal gathering place. This posting should be a friendly reminder about what is not tolerated and what is acceptable on your company or organization's work time.

Because working on the computer is clearly viewed as a common use of work time and because it is becoming increasingly more difficult to monitor each individual user, businesses and practices are becoming ever more stringent on the employee's use of productive computer time. Often the appearance of work is nothing more than frivolous game playing and Internet surfing. The World Wide Web has become increasingly more of a distraction to employees, and Linux systems are providing much of that traffic. It therefore becomes prudent for you as an administrator to monitor system usage and encourage more productive uses of the system. Internet access often is necessary for doing research or downloading material, including e-mail. However, you can simplify your monitoring of users by enabling keystroke logging, using proxy severs such as Squid that limit access to certain sites, and disabling Usenet or newsgroup access. First determine where your system's bandwdth is primarily squandered and then begin making the necessary restrictions.

This chapter outlines a few clear policies and offers some solutions to dealing with system abuse. Though it is nearly impossible to manage every workstation logged in to your system and to play Big Brother to all users, you can start by laying out what will and will not be allowed on your own system. What employees or users do on their own machines may be beyond your control, but you can at least check to make sure that they are not abusing your system.

## Defining Acceptable Use

Be specific as to what users may and may not use your system for. Pornographic material, bootlegged music copies (MP3 audio), video files, excessive e-mail use, and questionable software can all be verified on a Linux system. I often run find commands and check for miscellaneous *.gif, *.jpg, or *.mp3 files on my own system. A periodic test often turns up surprising results. You can run this test as a weekly night job with the output sent to a file, which is then stored in a secure directory. I frequently run this test on the weekend when users are not logged in, assuming that no regular user is monitoring the system.

You should consider running scans against user files only as a last resort, when less invasive measures and user education fail to accomplish the task. Also, consider that many users may treat your box as a storage facility and that not all MP3 audio files are pirated copies. I keep MP3 copies of CDs that I purchased myself on my system. Others may do the same.

A simple command such as the following is often enough to indicate who might be abusing the system by storing questionable graphic images:

```
# find / -name *.gif > /home/kerry/badpics.txt
```

Of course, you may customize this command to taste and to the specification of your box. But because the primary function of this particular Linux is to host text files and company documents, whenever I locate an image it immediately falls under suspicion. Much of the text generated is innocent enough, but sometimes I stumble across fairly explicit material. When this happens, it is best to bring it to the management's attention and perhaps inform the user, depending upon company policies. Some might tolerate a first offense, but others might show no leniency. How abuses are handled is up to your employers, or the matter may fall in your hands. However, I suspect that management can always trump the administrator's judgment.

The same is true of music files. MP3s are not only unethical to distribute if they are being sold or distributed illegally. Copies of personal files are tolerated by the music industry, but when your system begins providing them to others via FTP sites or by e-mail, then you may incur the wrath of lawyers. I have received cease and desist orders from lawyers representing the music industry in regard to a user who had set up an anonymous MP3 site. A simple e-mail message is usually enough to force their closure.

Excessive unsolicited e-mail, termed *spam* by disgruntled recipients, and the proliferation of humorous anecdotes or overzealous e-mail writers not only slows down your own mail server but also decreases that user's productivity. Keep tabs on the mail queue and the size and frequency of each user's outgoing e-mails. You may also want to institute an e-mail file size limit for both incoming and outgoing e-mails. While sendmail will e-mail the administrator of any bounced e-mails, you may not always see the size and frequency of the e-mails passing through your system. You can check on the system periodically by using the mailq command and viewing what is currently in the spool, looking at the /var/log/maillog file, and then using the grep command to single out frequent users. You can also institute a monitoring system. In your sendmail.cf file, locate the MaxMessageSize and MaxRecipientsPerMessage options and place a limit on their size. These two variables alone will reduce much of the e-mail traffic routed through your system, the former limiting the files of each e-mail allowed through and the latter reducing the number of messages that a user can carbon copy (cc) to other users. For more information on configuring the mail server variables as mentioned above, consult Chapter 17.

If you are also running a Web server and users have their own HTML directories, make certain that they understand the limits of free speech and what can and cannot prove libelous not only to themselves but also to your company or organization. Before becoming embroiled in freedom of speech issues, make certain that users understand that you reserve the right to remove any objectionable material from their site. Again, find or locate commands are useful for locating offensive content.

You may also want to install some sort of log analyzing program that tracks your Web server's use. Many commercial releases are available. For a high cost, they display exactly the number of "hits" a certain site is receiving on a daily, weekly, or monthly basis. There are also free open-source programs that accomplish much the same purpose.

My personal recommendation is to use webalizer, a free implementation of WebTrends. The webalizer program records and displays exactly what pages are receiving the most traffic and logs their hit count. You can download the latest copy from the webalizer home page at http://www.mrunix.net/webalizer/. Red

Hat ships webalizer with its Professional release and recommends it as well for logging HTML pages.

Another popular logging program is analog. Considered by some to be the most generic and commonly used Web page analysis tool, analog does not provide snazzy graphics, but can parse gigabytes worth of data in a matter of moments and generate a dynamic Web page displaying that information. You can download analog from http://www.statslab.cam.ac.uk/~sret1/analog/.

Empty threats are ineffective against users on your system. Rules should be enforceable and within reason. Keep these items in mind when instituting any sort of policy on your system. Some users may use your system because they have no choice, but often you may be catering to customers who have the choice and ability to go elsewhere to have their needs met.

> **NOTE**
>
> Depending on the type of company you work for and what is listed in your job description, you may be allowed to implement only the rules and policies that others create.

## Limiting Access through Quotas

Another area that you should be aware of is the amount of freedom that you give users on your system. Offering user or telnet access from any place or with any type of connection is always risky. Not only do you allow users to exploit certain processes that may not be as secure as you think, but you also grant them access to the resources of your system. Deciding upon the function of the Linux box—whether as a mail server, a file server, or Web server or all these purposes—depends upon you. If you decide to offer your Linux system for a particular purpose, understand what types of demands the users will make.

For example, if you use your Red Hat Linux box as a mail server, will you offer POP3 or IMAP services, or neither? Do you want to enable your system's users to download their e-mail from the box, or do you want to allow telnet access to the system as well? If so, will you make console e-mail programs available to your customers or users?

Providing this capability should be balanced against your own need for maintaining system security. If you do provide telnet access, how will you limit others from logging in? Will the hosts.allow and hosts.deny files be sufficient or do you want to enable ssh or some other form of secure login? The latter method is much more preferable. No server should allow telnet access from any place. Any ssh connections should be restricted to trusted users. Determine what your needs are and design the system accordingly.

If you allow users accounts on your file server, how will you allow them access their files? Will they be stored in a centralized location or will each user have his or her own directory? These are pertinent questions that will reflect upon your chore of maintaining system integrity.

The same applies to using your box as a Web server. How will you allow users to log in and upload or update their files? What sorts of services will you provide? If this Linux box is to be a virtual server, what sort of services will you offer users? Providing them access to a common cgi-bin is perhaps too much, but giving them their own cgi-bin might also compromise security. Above all, do not promise the user more than you are willing or able to deliver. You should allow most users only FTP access. You should not allow NFS connections, as NFS is still too insecure and can compromise system security.

# Monitoring Your Servers

Though setting up and configuring a Red Hat Linux machine can be a difficult task at first, if you do it well it is all the easier to maintain the server and keep all the services functioning. If you are like most administrators, you probably tend to the needs of more than just one machine. Many administrators need to monitor and maintain several Linux boxes. Keeping tabs on several Linux servers is sometimes a very thankless, but necessary, chore.

## Using Big Brother

One of the many monitoring programs that I have found works well for myself and others is Big Brother, a unique program that runs off a main Linux server and checks connectivity on any of a host of machines ranging from all UNIX varieties to Windows NT. Many find it preferable to run Big Brother under Linux and use the program to check on the other systems. You can read more about the Big Brother program and download the latest release at http://bb4.com/.

The Big Brother daemon gathers data about the most frequently used services, determining server status with ping, FTP, SMTP, HTTP, POP3, and so on. You can use Big Brother to monitor anything listed under /etc/services.

If a service or even a server goes down or if one of your servers seems to have an intermittent problem, Big Brother can both e-mail and page you. You can set up a series of rules as to what server certain people should be accountable for and when each should be notified. If specific servers are up at only certain times, such as dial-ups, you can customize Big Brother to test only at certain hours or simply to display the servers' connectivity status.

You can gather additional information from client machines by placing a running copy of Big Brother on them as well. The client box then transmits the information to the main Big Brother server. These statistics include CPU use, disk space, processes, and bad messages generated under /var/log/messages. One helpful feature of Big Brother is that it is fully customizable and can be tuned to nearly any server. The development team for this program also offers technical support and provides documentation for configuring the process. The team typifies the general attitude among open-source developers, seeking to offer a useful and productive product while gathering input from users for additional development. Big Brother's developers restrict redistribution of the code if it is done for commercial gain but allow most users to run the program for free. (However, they will gladly accept donations.)

From the main Big Brother page (see Figure 20.1), you can view a demonstration of what Big Brother can do.

Big Brother connects to the different ports and verifies that the services bound to each are running. You can manually set the run times to complete testing each client. If you need to monitor a host of sites and stay informed as to the problems of each or what might be down, Big Brother is just one of many Linux-based programs that can assist.

When you place information about your network on a Web page and make it accessible either to Internet or intranet users, it is prudent to password-protect

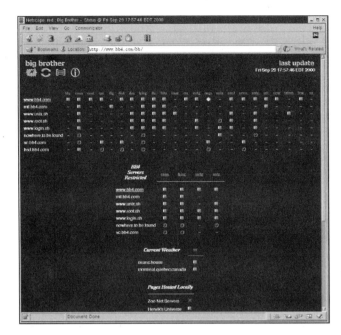

**FIGURE 20.1**

*A sample Big Brother Web page displaying the available servers and their current status.*

that page. This discourages others outside your system from gleaning information about your system. The standard Apache version that comes with the Red Hat Linux distribution offers password-protection capability. Using the htpasswd executable, you can create a flat text file that holds usernames and the encrypted passwords. In the page you wish to password-protect, simply place a .htaccess executable with the correct syntax.

The following is an example from my own Big Brother page. You should customize it to fit your own setup.

```
AuthName "Big Brother"
AuthType Basic
AuthUserFile /usr/local/apache/htdocs/password/bb
AuthGroupFile /dev/null
require valid-user
```

You will also want to make sure the htpasswd executable is in your PATH. The .htaccess file ensures that unauthorized users do not gather more information than necessary from your Web page.

> **NOTE**
>
> The Apache home page (http://www.apache.org/) provides additional information about configuring a .htaccess file.

The importance of gathering information from your system and network cannot be overstressed. It is important that you understand what is happening with your machines and that if something fails, that you are the first to know. Had it not been for the monitoring protocols that I implemented, things could have gone awry very quickly. Be sure always to know the status of your systems. Several other programs offer viable solutions with much the same functionality. A quick perusal of some of the sites in this section and a few queries will soon help you install the program that best suits your needs.

## Testing Router Status with MRTG

When you are monitoring bandwidth on a network, mrtg provides the tools necessary to test your routers and determine the amount of traffic both entering and leaving your system (see Figure 20.2). Designed with Cisco routers in mind, this program also monitors other router makes as well. When testing your system via a cron-based job, you can output the data generated by your router to a Web page.

Because mrtg gathers information from the network routers, which may not be as familiar to you as Linux, a quick summary of how to install mrtg follows.

1. Download the latest mrtg release from the following URL: http://ee-staff.ethz.ch/~oetiker/webtools/mrtg/mrtg.html.

2. Untar and unzip the file in a secure location. I chose the directory /usr/local/gnu/.

3. When the file is done uncompressing, relocate into the new directory by entering **cd /usr/local/gnu/mrtg-2.9.0**.

4. Enter the following commands: **./configure ; make**.

5. You may need the gd libraries from Tom Boutrell. The gd libraries are used to create .PNG images and dynamic images for graphing network use. These libraries should come installed on the Linux machine if everything was installed. You can either install them with the RPM or download the source from the gd main page, http://www.boutell.com/gd/.

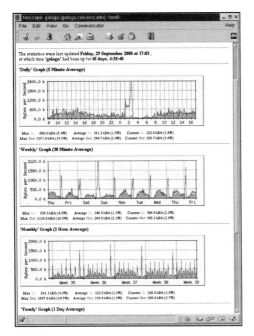

**FIGURE 20.2**

*A sample mrtg Web page displaying the amount of traffic being routed through your network.*

6. Define some parameters on your router. If you are using a Cisco router, the following rules will apply:

   a. The mrtg program uses snmp packets for monitoring traffic. You will need to enable this feature on your router. Log in to your router, type the **enable** password, then enter **conf t**. This command displays the current configuration.

   b. Now enter **snmp-server community public RO** or the variables of your choice. The community and public features are unsecure. Define something more unobvious.

   c. Save this information to your configuration by entering **exit** ; **write mem**.

7. Define on your Linux box a logs/ directory or make one in your mrtg directory. This is where you will be storing all data gathered from the router. Enter the following command: **cd /usr/local/gnu/mrtg/** ; **mkdir logs/**.

8. You can now create an mrtg.cfg or *configuration* file. Do this by changing directories to the mrtg run/ directory. Enter the command **cd /usr/local/ gnu/mrtg/run/.**

9. Check to verify that you can see snmp packets registering on your Linux system from the router. Use the snmpwalk command to test your router, 10.10.10.1, as follows: **snmpwalk -v1 10.10.10.1 public | more.**

10. Run the cfgmaker utility to create your own customized configuration file, by entering **/usr/local/gnu/mrtg/run/cfgmaker public@10.10.10.1 > mrtg.cfg.new.**

11. Be sure to edit this file after you create it. Specify a WorkDir on the second line from the top by entering the following:

    **WorkDir: /usr/local/gnu/mrtg/logs.**

12. You can now start running the indexmaker script, which will generate a graph displaying the router traffic. Use the following command to create the initial graph:

    **/indexmaker -t 'My Network' -r '.' -o /home/httpd/html/mrtg/index.html mrtg.cfg.new**

13. Place this script in a cron job and have it run every five minutes to create a continuous graph. This script calls the executable mrtg and then reads the configuration file that you created.

    ```
    # Run MRTG every five minutes.
    0,5,10,15,20,25,30,35,40,45,50,55 * * * *
    /usr/local/gnu/mrtg/run/mrtg  /usr/local/gnu/mrtg/run/mrtg.cfg.new
    ```

    You can customize the configuration file to your specifications. I have added the following two lines to my own configuration file to view additional information from the router:

    ```
    Options[10.10.10.1.1]: bits
    WithPeak[10.10.10.1.1]: wmy
    ```

14. If your router is located on the other side of a firewall from your Linux box, make sure that ports 161 and 162 are open and allow traffic to pass through from the router to your Linux box.

Here is a sample excerpt from my own mrtg.cfg.new file. You can change this to your own specifications.

```
# Add a WorkDir: /some/path line to this file


WorkDir: /usr/local/gnu/mrtg/logs



##############################################################
    # Description: Cisco Internetwork Operating System
Software IOS (tm) C5RSM Software (C5RSM-ISV-M), Version
12.0(3c)W5(8), RELEASE SOFTWARE Copyright (c) 1986-1999 by
cisco Systems, Inc. Compiled Mon 10-May-99 19:29 by integ
    #      Contact:
    # System Name: rsmb
    #      Location:


#...........................................................
......


    Target[10.10.10.1.1]: 1:public@10.10.10.1
    Options[10.10.10.1.1]: bits
    WithPeak[10.10.10.1.1]: wmy

    MaxBytes[10.10.10.1.1]: 12500000

    Title[10.10.10.1.1]: rsmb (No hostname defined for IP
address): Vlan0
    PageTop[10.10.10.1.1]: <H1>Traffic Analysis for Vlan0
    </H1>
    <TABLE>
      <TR><TD>System:</TD><TD>rsmb in </TD></TR>
      <TR><TD>Maintainer:</TD><TD></TD></TR>
      <TR><TD>Interface:</TD><TD>Vlan0 (1)</TD></TR>
      <TR><TD>IP:</TD><TD>No hostname defined for IP address
(127.0.0.4)</TD></TR>
```

```
<TR><TD>Max Speed:</TD>
    <TD>12.5 MBytes/s (ethernetCsmacd)</TD></TR>
</TABLE>
```

Again, be sure to password-protect all your pages.

# Conclusion

Now that we have covered nearly all the basics of Linux, including setting up, configuring, maintaining, and customizing, the appendix will mostly deal with terminology. It will also cover an assortment of topics that required too long a discussion to be incorporated in earlier chapters. For those terms unfamiliar to beginning Linux users, consult the appendix for a better understanding of the expressions used in Linux.

# PART V

## Appendixes

# Appendix A

### Linking to
### Informative Sites

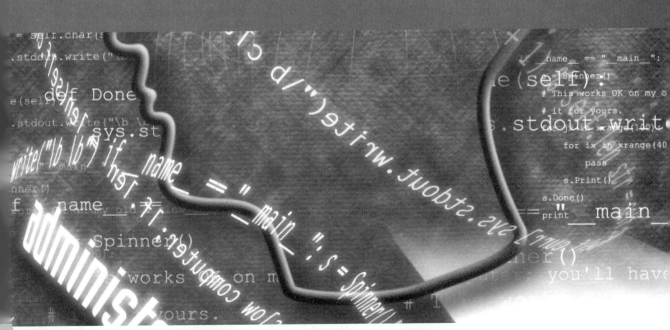

Gathering a comprehensive list of the many Linux sites throughout the Internet is by no means an easy task, nor does the list in this section represent a fraction of the information available. Every day new and innovative sites appear that provide additional information to users. This list reflects only a small percentage of those sites that many administrators have found useful for locating and gathering additional Linux code and updates. Many of these sites are cross-linked with a host of other URLs.

Linux is still in a state of flux and is continually evolving and developing, and the same can be said for the many Linux sites around the world. More sites are available than can ever be gathered in one source. I hope that the listed sites will assist you in learning more and gathering additional information. Many fellow Linux users are willing to help and provide the services that you need.

## Suggestions for News Sources

◆ Linux.com (http://www.linux.com/) is one of the many sites that offer both information and articles about Linux. It contains a plethora of links to other sites that offer additional news and information.

◆ Slashdot (http://slashdot.org/) promotes itself as "news for nerds, stuff that matters." It is also an excellent resource for gathering information about Linux.

◆ Linux Journal (http://www.linuxjournal.com/) is both an online and published magazine. You can get some of the latest articles via the Web site.

◆ Linux Gazette (http://metalab.unc.edu/mdw/LDP/LG/) is another Linux e-zine that provides insightful articles about various uses and implementations of Linux.

◆ LinuxNow (http://www.linuxnow.com/) is another informative site that provides news and tips.

◆ Linux Documentation Project (http://metalab.unc.edu/mdw/) is perhaps the most comprehensive site of them all. LDP hosts articles and links to nearly every Linux site available.

## Suggestions for Gathering News from Usenets

◆ Any of the newsgroups under the comp.os.linux.* category will provide you with ample opportunity both to post and reply to the myriad questions about Linux. Devoting some time to these groups and reading through the answers will help acclimate any beginner to the rigors of Linux administration.

◆ Doing a simple search for Linux under any news server will offer an array of Linux newsgroups in nearly all languages. Try out as many as you can.

## Suggestions for Kernel Resources

◆ Kernel.org (http://www.kernel.org/) tracks the very latest developments in the Linux kernel. This site offers cross-links to download sites and offers installation instructions.

◆ Kernelnotes (http://www.kernelnotes.org/) can keep you updated on what has changed since the previous release of the Linux kernel. This site provides additional information on utilizing the Linux kernel, including many "how to" pages on the subject.

## Suggestions for Program Archives

◆ Freshmeat (http://freshmeat.net/) offers a searchable database and links to sites.

◆ Linuxberg (http://www.linuxberg.com/) provides links and downloads of many Linux programs on the Internet.

◆ Tucows Linux (http://linux.tucows.com/) makes Linux programs accessible from the Internet.

◆ DaveCentral (http://linux.davecentral.com/) lists the many Linux programs available.

◆ Metalab (http://metalab.unc.edu/) is a clearinghouse of information and code for Linux systems and distribution. Currently, they are revamping their site and calling themselves ibiblio.org. (http://ibiblio.org/)

## Suggestions for Linux Sales

◆ Linuxmall (http://www.linuxmall.com/) is an excellent site for obtaining the latest Linux distribution for the least amount of money.

◆ CheapBytes (http://www.cheapbytes.com/) is also a quick and cheap way to obtain quality Linux products for a small price.

◆ GNUware (http://www.gnuware.com/) offers more than a thousand different Linux programs on one simple CD. This site is particularly useful for users with slow Internet connections.

# Appendix B

## Reviewing Linux Commands and Terminology

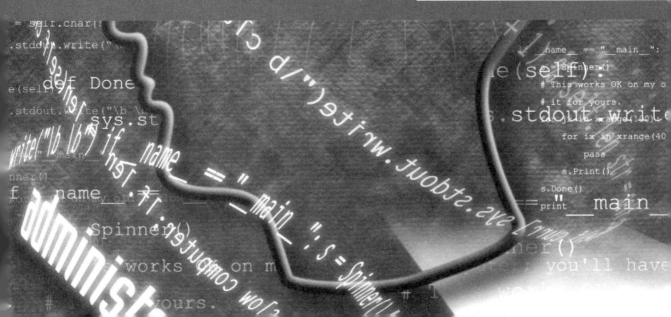

This appendix deals with the most basic Linux terminology and commands encountered when using a command-line interface. It defines the function of each command and term but does not explain any additional options or flags. Each command under Linux has a large assortment of possible choices as to how it can be executed. This chapter familiarizes you with only some of most commonly used expressions.

As mentioned in this appendix's introductory section, each command under Linux comes with a wide range of options and command-line flags that you can add to the command before you launch it. It is impossible to cover each flag of every command separately. For further information about what each program, command, or executable accomplishes, consult the manual pages for each. For example, to learn more about the ls command, enter **man ls**. This section provides examples as needed.

You can find the majority of these programs and commands in the /usr/bin directory. Those that require root in order to run can be found in /usr/sbin or /sbin.

**..**

Points to the parent directory of the directory that you currently are occupying. Using the cd command with this argument will take you one level higher.

**.**

This character represents the current directory or the one that you currently occupy. You use this character to run executables located in the same directory.

**&**

When executing any command, placing this character at the end of the command will place the program in the background. The shell prompt will then be free to execute other commands.

**>**

This character sends the standard output of any command that generates data to the screen to instead be saved in a file. Example: `find / -name *.bak > backup_files.txt`. Files that meet the criteria of the expression will be saved in a text file.

**<**

The input redirection operator is used to feed a program the contents of a file. This operator is useful with programs that require the input of several text files.

### >>

The output append operator appends data from one file to another. Rather than overwriting the file, it places the new data at the end of the file. You can also use this operator to append the output of a command to an existing file; if the file doesn't exist, it will be created.

### adduser

This command creates a new account on the system. When you are using the Red Hat Linux distribution, this command adds all the needed variable and files to a user's account. This command is run only by root with the new username following it.

### alias

This argument allows you to substitute another command in place of the typical Linux command. Entering **alias ls="ls -- color"** in the /etc/bashrc file defines a new ls command that will print out the different file types in varying colors.

### at

This command starts a certain process at a specified time. Rather than starting all processes manually, you can use this command to perform specific routines at certain periods or time increments. Unlike cron jobs, this command is designed for one-time commands only.

### atq

This command lists jobs waiting to be performed that have been scheduled with the at command.

### atrm

This command removes waiting at jobs from the queue.

### bash

The *Bourne Again SHell* shell is the shell most commonly used on Red Hat Linux terminal command lines.

### batch

Similar to the at command, this command runs jobs when a certain load average is reached as determined by the /proc/loadavg file. It will not run jobs if the load average exceeds a certain level.

### bg

This command forces a suspended process to the background. If the process was started without the & variable and you need the shell, you can issue a bg command to force it to the background or press Ctrl-Z if it is currently running in the foreground.

### bind

This command allows the user to change the behavior of certain key combinations. The command is often used to imitate other shell keystrokes. Bind is used under the bash and pdksh shells.

### cat

This command prints out the contents of a file to the screen. The output scrolls continuously unless parsed using the | more or | less options. You can also use this command with audio files and then output their contents to an audio device. Example: cat /usr/share/sndconfig/sample.au > /dev/audio.

### cd

Use this command to change directories under the Linux command line. When used with .., it ascends the directory structure. By itself, the cd command takes the user back to his or her home directory. With a dash (-) following the command, it returns to the previous directory location.

### chgrp

This command changes the group ownership for a particular file or directory. A single chgrp command can apply to a particular file or multiple files, or can apply recursively to a directory containing many files.

### chmod

This command changes the file permissions on a file or directory. A single chmod command can apply to a particular file or multiple files, or can apply recursively to a directory containing many files.

### chown

This command changes the ownership of a file or directory. A single chown command can apply to a particular file or multiple files, or can apply recursively to a directory containing many files.

### cp

Linux's copy command copies a file to another location as specified under the command line.

### cpio

This program is used to back up files and data from local or remote locations.

### cron

Cron, short for chronological, is a type of job or program that can be set up to run at predetermined times. The cron daemon checks a text file for entries, compares that against the current system time, and then executes the command when the two variables match.

### crontab

You can use this command to set up cron or automated jobs. It normally brings up a text editor and opens a temporary file in which commands can be placed along with the times at which they should be run.

### dd

Use the dd command to copy files or file systems to other devices. You can also use dd to convert file formats.

### deluser

This command deletes a user from the system. Normally, this command simply removes the specified username from of the /etc/passwd file and the /etc/group file. You may need to delete that user's home directory manually unless the proper flag is used.

### df

The df command lists the file systems on a given system along with the amount of space available, the space used, and the directory on which each file system.

### display

This command starts up the graphic editor ImageMagick. This program allows you to create, edit, and save images of most formats.

### dmesg

The dmesg command prints the most recent kernel messages, which might include the output of the Linux bootup. This command will show you the messages generated by the kernel as devices and processes are brought online.

### du

This command displays the amount of disk use on a given directory or for the entire hard drive. Followed by a directory, it will display how much space that folder occupies.

### dump

The dump command is a method of tape backup. It dumps the contents of a file system onto a backup media device.

### echo

This command prints strings to your display. It also is useful for printing out the environment variables. Example: echo $PATH.

### ed

This command invokes a very simple text editor.

### edquota

The edquota command allows root to change the amount of disk space available for use for each user.

### emacs

An extremely dynamic text editor, emacs is considered complicated to the uninitiated. You can use it either at the console or in an X Window environment. The emacs editor handles plug-ins allowing it to handle foreign languages or basic HTML. It also acts as a diary and calendar and supports programming, mail, and newsgroups.

### env

This command displays environment variables.

### fc

The fc command is used to edit the .history file. Depending upon the type of shell used, it can also execute any of the previously used commands.

### fdformat

You can use this command to perform a low-level format of a floppy disk. You must also place some form of file system on the floppy when the formatting is finished.

### fetchmail

This program retrieves mail from another mail server or from an ISP. You can program fetchmail to forward mail to appropriate users or to discard unwanted mail.

### fg

The reverse of bg, fg brings a process in the background to the foreground.

### file

When run against any type of file, this program informs you of the type of file that you are dealing with, whether it is simple text, zipped, or binary file.

### find

A useful tool for locating lost or misplaced file, find can be run locally within one directory or on the entire system.

### finger

Use this command to gather information about users on any system with finger enabled. It prints out each user's home directory, real name, and other information that the user has placed on the system.

### free

This command displays the amount of memory your system is using.

### ftp

The File Transfer Protocol allows you to move files quickly and efficiently from one server to another.

### grep

The grep (*global regular expression parse*) command allows you to search for a string of characters within files. The grep command works much like the find command, except it searches within files. You can also use grep with other commands to parse out the essential information. Example: `ps aux | grep sendmail`.

### groff

The groff program is the front end to a document-formatting program. By default, groff calls troff.

### groupadd

This command creates a new group definition to which users can then belong.

### gs

The *Ghostscript* interpreter can interpret and print PostScript documents for a variety of displays and non-PostScript printers.

### gunzip

This command uncompresses files that were zipped up using the gzip program.

### gv

A previewer for both PostScript and PDF files.

### gzip

This command by itself compresses files into smaller units, which can then be used for archival purposes or for saving transmission bandwidth.

### halt

The halt command shuts down the kernel preparatory to powering down the Linux machine. Only root can execute this command.

### head

The reverse of the tail command, the head command displays the first 10 lines of a text file by default.

### hostname

This command displays the current name of the host and domain of your Linux system.

### ical

The ical command invokes a calendaring program that is useful for marking events or tasks.

### ifconfig

This command is used to configure network interfaces. It displays the current network state.

## ispell

A simple spell checker used by programs such as emacs, ispell is also used by the crack program to test weak passwords.

## jed

This command invokes a simple text editor.

## joe

The joe command invokes another simple text editor reminiscent of WordStar.

## kill

This command sends certain signals to the processes on your system. The kill command is useful for slaying runaway processes or reinitializing others.

## less

Like the more option, less allows pagination through multiple screens. You use the less option when the output to the screen takes up more than one page.

## ln

This command either creates symbolic links (with its own inode) or hard links (sharing an inode). To determine whether a file is a symbolic link, run ls -l within the file's directory.

## locate

Like the find command, the locate command determines the location of specific files. It runs faster than the find command because it references the locatedb database in /var/lib.

## lpc

This command controls the order of files in the printer spooling queue. The lpc

command can also determine the status of the printers, spooling queues, and print daemons.

## lpd

This printer daemon normally starts with the system bootup. It uses the /etc/printcap file to find out more about the available printers.

## lpq

The lpq command lists the jobs currently awaiting processing in the printer spooling queue.

## lpr

The lpr command is the default command to send print jobs to the printer. If no specific printer is named, then the default printer is assumed.

## lprm

This command removes a specific print job from the printer spooling queue by identifying the print job ID number.

## ls

The ls command lists the files in the current directory. It can also list the contents of other directories by specifying their location.

## lsmod

This command displays the modules currently loaded in the running kernel.

## lynx

A text-based web browser, lynx is quicker and faster than Netscape when loading up pages since it ignores graphics. Specify a web address after the program name.

## mail

The most basic mail client available, mail is useful for sending simple messages to users on the system. For longer, more complex emails, use a mail client like pine.

## make

This program determines what parts of a program need to be recompiled and then uses the system compiler as defined by the user or Makefile to change the program from simple ASCII text to binary.

## man

The man command displays online manual pages. Invoking this command and the name of most any other program will bring up a helpful page that gives specific details about the specified program.

## mesg

This command controls the write access that others have to talk and write messages via the command line to other users on the system.

## mkdir

The mkdir command creates new directories where specified.

## mkfs

Use this command to create a Linux file system on devices such as floppy or hard disks. You must also specify the device name.

## modprobe

Use this command to load modules into the running kernel.

## more

The more command assists in paginating longer files within a single display window. You can scroll through succeeding lines by pressing the Enter key or scroll through the entire window by pressing the spacebar.

## mount

Executable only by root, the mount command enables you to place additional directories on your machine. Users can use this command to mount file systems that have the user option specified in /etc/fstab. Regular users can also use the bare mount command to get a listing of currently mounted file systems.

## mt

The mt (*magnetic tape*) command controls the magnetic tape drive. Depending on the available options that you specify, mt will erase, rewind, or retension the tape drive.

## mv

This command allows you to both move and/or rename files to different locations or names.

## netstat

The netstat command displays the status of the network connections. It is also used to display information about the routing table.

## newgrp

The newgrp command logs you in to a new group. This command allows you to become a member of a different group temporarily to access other files and file systems.

## nxterm

Similar to xterm, nxterm is a color-capable terminal emulator for the X Window environment. You can reconfigure nxterm's options through pop-up menus.

## passwd

Normal users use this command to change their own passwords. Root can use this command to change any user's password in the /etc/passwd file. The passwd file contains all the usernames and information about their home directory and real names.

## pico

The pico command invokes a simple, yet highly effective, text editor.

## pine

This command invokes a robust email client that supports a variety of options, including a newsreader and clickable links with emails to web pages.

## ping

The ping command offers a method of testing whether a site or IP address is alive. Sending out the ping command with an IP address or valid server name will identify whether the machine is operational. The ping command sends out small data packets and awaits their return. These packets are configurable by size and speed.

## procmail

The procmail utility processes incoming mail and allocates it to specific hosts or locations by searching through the mail messages for strings determined by the user. This utility can handle large amounts of incoming mail.

## ps

This command lists all the running processes on your system. It does not give a running display like the top command, but merely takes a snapshot of the system. You can use ps with other utilities to display specific sets of data. It will identify the PIDs for individual processes, which can then be sent as individual signals.

## pwd

This command displays the current working directory.

## quota

The quota command reports on the disk quota settings. This command notifies root how much space individual users are using on the system.

## quotacheck

The quotacheck command generates a report of disk usage. This command scans a specific directory structure and reports on the disk space being used. The quotacheck command works if the quota option is turned on.

## quotaoff

This command turns off disk quotas.

## quotaon

This command turns on disk quotas.

## repquota

The repquota command generates a specific report on the quota usage.

### restore

This command restores a dump backup. The restore command has an interactive option for determining which files should or should not be restored.

### rm

The rm command removes a file. With older Red Hat versions once you deleted a file there was little or no way to recover them With the latest release the rm command is aliased to "rm -i" and you will be prompted for confirmation as to whether or not you wish to delete a file.

### rmdir

This command removes an empty directory. If the directory still contains a file, rmdir will not complete its task successfully unless you include the -r option.

### route

The route command displays and configures the IP routing table. This command also allows you to communicate with the network interfaces on your system.

### rxvt

Another terminal emulator program, rxvt is similar to xterm.

### sed

The sed editor can change or manipulate streams or lines of text. You can use this editor to perform searches through text while dynamically changing or replacing specified variables.

### set

Use the set command to change an environment variable temporarily.

### shutdown

This command is used to shut down a Linux system or to issue a warm boot sequence.

### sort

The sort command generates an alphabetized list from a random text list. You can also use sort to create a sorted list in several different formats.

### stat

This command lists information about a given file. You can also use set to check the validity of symbolic links.

### strings

The strings command outputs all text strings within a binary file. This command is useful for gathering information about specific lines of text without running the binary program.

### su

This command enables a regular user to become superuser with all the privileges of root. Successful and failed attempts to become superuser are logged.

### swapoff

The swapoff command stops the swapping of data to a file or block device.

### swapon

This command turns on the swapping of data to a specific file or block device.

### tail

Like the head command, this command displays the last 10 lines of any text file by default.

### talk

The talk command allows any user to talk to another user. When two users make a connection on the same system, the terminal window is split and the users can chat synchronously. You can disable this feature in the /etc/inetd.conf file.

### tar

The tar (*tape archival*) program concatenates files and directories into one file.

### telnet

This protocol establishes a text-based connection to another system. You can also use telnet to connect to your own system. Then you can run programs and execute commands as if you were logged in via a local terminal.

### top

The top command runs a text display of the processes running along with the computer's uptime, memory use, and load on the system.

### touch

This command creates an empty file with a name specified by the user.

### tr

The tr command translates a set of characters specified by the user into another set of characters. Typical use might include changing the letters of a text file from all uppercase to all lowercase letters.

### tree

This command displays directory structures in a treelike form. The tree command is useful for seeing how your directories are arranged.

### ulimit

This command sets the resource limits on your system.

### umount

This command unmounts file partitions or media devices currently accessible on the system.

### uname

The uname command lists data about the running kernel, the date of the last compilation, and system information.

### unzip

This command lists, tests, and extracts information from a zipped archive.

### uptime

The uptime command lists the amount of time that the system has been up.

### vi

With most distributions, vi is the default text editor. The vi editor is highly versatile, but has a steep learning curve. With it you can edit text on most any UNIX-based server.

### vim

The vim editor is a souped-up version of **vi**. This editor is more responsive than vi in some respects.

### vmstat

This command prints out virtual memory statistics. It also displays the amount of disk space used by the system, usually by swap partition.

### w

The w command prints out a list of all the users currently logged in along with the same information displayed by the uptime command.

### wall

This command prints a message to the console connections of all users logged on to the system.

### wc

This program can count the amount of characters, words, or lines within your text file. It defaults to show all three variables, but you can use flags to specify which you want to display.

### who

This command shows who is logged on to the system and the system name from which those users are connecting.

### whoami

This whoami command displays your current user identity.

### xdm

The X11 Display Manager (xdm) configures the type of display shown when a user logs in to the graphical interface.

### xhost

This command grants clients access from a specific server.

### Xlock

The xlock program is both a screensaver and a terminal locking program requiring a password to open the display.

### xlsfonts

This command searches for and displays the fonts recognized by the X11 server.

### xmessage

This program displays short messages on your display window. You can use these messages much like post-it notes.

### xmodmap

This command modifies keyboards and mice to new configurations.

### xset

The xset command sets some of the options in an X Window session, including the background display image.

### xsetroot

This command changes the displayed image of your root window.

### zip

The zip utility is a utility that allows you to compress files similar to WinZip and PKZip.

# Appendix C

## A Sample Linux ipchains Firewall Configuration

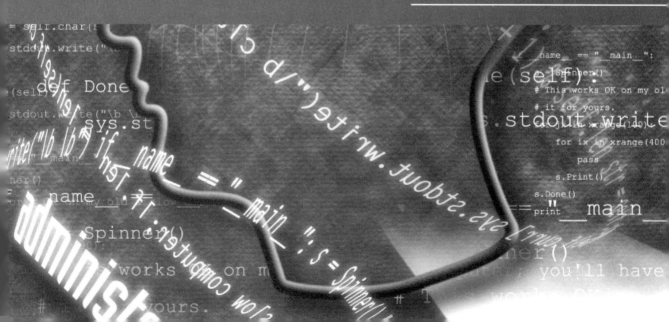

**A**s security becomes more of a concern for home users and as Internet connectivity is nearly constant, fortifying your Linux box against attacks is an absolute necessity. The following is a sample ipchains firewall configuration that can be used to lock down any Linux machine. It provides for IP Masquerading or sharing of a single connection and utilizing your Linux box as a gateway to the Internet.

## Listing C.1 The masq.sh Script for Configuring Dynamic Masquerading of Hosts and Ports

```
#!/bin/sh

# ---------Configuration--------
# Local Interface
# This is the interface that is the link to the world
LOCALIF="eth0"

# Internal Interface
# This is the interface for the local network
# NOTE: INTERNALNET is a *network* address. All host bits should be 0
INTERNALNET="172.16.0.0/16"

# The location of ipchains.
IPCHAINS="/sbin/ipchains"

#-------End Configuration--------

LOCALIP=`ifconfig $LOCALIF | grep inet | cut -d : -f 2 | cut -d \  -f 1`
LOCALMASK=`ifconfig $LOCALIF | grep Mask | cut -d : -f 4`
LOCALNET="$LOCALIP/$LOCALMASK"

echo "Internal: $INTERNALNET"
echo "External: $LOCALNET"


REMOTENET="0/0"

# Flush everything, start from scratch -
```

```
echo -n "Flushing rulesets.."

# Incoming packets from the outside network
$IPCHAINS -F input
echo -n "."

# Outgoing packets from the internal network
$IPCHAINS -F output
echo -n "."

# Forwarding/masquerading
$IPCHAINS -F forward
echo -n "."

echo "Done!"

# Allow all connections within the network -
echo -n "Internal.."
$IPCHAINS -A input -s $INTERNALNET -d $INTERNALNET -j ACCEPT
$IPCHAINS -A output -s $INTERNALNET -d $INTERNALNET -j ACCEPT
echo -n ".."
echo "Done!"

# Allow loopback interface -
echo -n "Loopback.."
$IPCHAINS -A input -i lo -s 0/0 -d 0/0 -j ACCEPT
$IPCHAINS -A output -i lo -s 0/0 -d 0/0 -j ACCEPT
echo -n ".."
echo "Done!"


# Masquerading -
echo -n "Masquerading.."

# don't masquerade internal-internal traffic
$IPCHAINS -A forward -s $INTERNALNET -d $INTERNALNET -j ACCEPT
echo -n "."

# don't Masquerade external interface direct
$IPCHAINS -A forward -s $LOCALNET -d $REMOTENET -j ACCEPT
echo -n "."
```

```
# masquerade all internal IP's going outside
$IPCHAINS -A forward -s $INTERNALNET -d $REMOTENET -j MASQ
echo -n "."

# set Default rule on MASQ chain to Deny
$IPCHAINS -P forward DENY
echo -n "."


# Allow all connections from the network to the outside -
$IPCHAINS -A input -s $INTERNALNET -d $REMOTENET -j ACCEPT
$IPCHAINS -A output -s $INTERNALNET -d $REMOTENET -j ACCEPT
echo -n ".."
echo "Done!"

# --------------------------------Set telnet, www and FTP for minimum delay -
# This section manipulates the Type Of Service (TOS) bits of the
# packet. For this to work, you must have CONFIG_IP_ROUTE_TOS enabled
# in your kernel

echo -n "TOS flags.."
$IPCHAINS -A output -p tcp -d 0/0 www -t 0x01 0x10
$IPCHAINS -A output -p tcp -d 0/0 telnet -t 0x01 0x10
$IPCHAINS -A output -p tcp -d 0/0 ftp -t 0x01 0x10
echo -n "..."

# Set ftp-data for maximum throughput
$IPCHAINS -A output -p tcp -d 0/0 ftp-data -t 0x01 0x08
echo -n "."

echo "Done!"

# Trusted Networks -
# Add in any rules to specifically allow connections from hosts/nets that
# would otherwise be blocked.
# echo -n "Trusted Networks.."
# $IPCHAINS -A input -s [trusted host/net] -d $LOCALNET <ports> -j ACCEPT
# echo -n "."
# echo "Done!"

# Banned Networks -
# Add in any rules to specifically block connections from hosts/nets that
```

```
# have been known to cause you problems. These packets are logged.
# echo -n "Banned Networks.."


# This one is generic

# $IPCHAINS -A input -l -s [banned host/net] -d $LOCALNET <ports> -j DENY
# echo -n "."


# This one blocks ICMP attacks
# $IPCHAINS -A input -l -b -i $LOCALIF -p icmp -s [host/net] -d $LOCALNET -j DENY
# echo -n "."
# echo "Done!"


# Specific port blocks on the external interface -
# This section blocks off ports/services to the outside that have
# vulnerabilities. This will not affect the ability to use these services
# within your network.

echo -n "Port Blocks.."

# NetBEUI/Samba
$IPCHAINS -A input -p tcp -s $REMOTENET -d $LOCALNET 139 -j DENY
$IPCHAINS -A input -p udp -s $REMOTENET -d $LOCALNET 139 -j DENY
echo -n "."

# Microsoft SQL
$IPCHAINS -A input -p tcp -s $REMOTENET -d $LOCALNET 1433 -j DENY
$IPCHAINS -A input -p udp -s $REMOTENET -d $LOCALNET 1433 -j DENY
echo -n "."

# Postgres SQL

$IPCHAINS -A input -p tcp -s $REMOTENET -d $LOCALNET 5432 -j DENY
$IPCHAINS -A input -p udp -s $REMOTENET -d $LOCALNET 5432 -j DENY
echo -n "."

# Network File System
$IPCHAINS -A input -p tcp -s $REMOTENET -d $LOCALNET 2049 -j DENY
$IPCHAINS -A input -p udp -s $REMOTENET -d $LOCALNET 2049 -j DENY
```

```
echo -n "."


# X Displays :0-:2-
$IPCHAINS -A input -p tcp -s $REMOTENET -d $LOCALNET 5999:6003 -j DENY
$IPCHAINS -A input -p udp -s $REMOTENET -d $LOCALNET 5999:6003 -j DENY
echo -n "."


# X Font Server :0-:2-
$IPCHAINS -A input -p tcp -s $REMOTENET -d $LOCALNET 7100 -j DENY
$IPCHAINS -A input -p udp -s $REMOTENET -d $LOCALNET 7100 -j DENY
echo -n "."


# Back Orifice (logged)
$IPCHAINS -A input -l -p tcp -s $REMOTENET -d $LOCALNET 31337 -j DENY
$IPCHAINS -A input -l -p udp -s $REMOTENET -d $LOCALNET 31337 -j DENY
echo -n "."


# NetBus (logged)
$IPCHAINS -A input -l -p tcp -s $REMOTENET -d $LOCALNET 12345:12346 -j DENY
$IPCHAINS -A input -l -p udp -s $REMOTENET -d $LOCALNET 12345:12346 -j DENY
echo -n "."


echo "Done!"


# High Unprivileged Ports -
# These are opened up to allow sockets created by connections allowed by
# ipchains

echo -n "High Ports.."
$IPCHAINS -A input -p tcp -s $REMOTENET -d $LOCALNET 1023:65535 -j ACCEPT
$IPCHAINS -A input -p udp -s $REMOTENET -d $LOCALNET 1023:65535 -j ACCEPT
echo -n "."


echo "Done!"


# ------------------------------------------------------------- Basic Services -

echo -n "Services.."


#ftp-data (20) and ftp (21)
$IPCHAINS -A input -p tcp -s $REMOTENET -d $LOCALNET 20 -j ACCEPT
$IPCHAINS -A input -p tcp -s $REMOTENET -d $LOCALNET 21 -j ACCEPT
```

```
echo -n ".."

#ssh (22)
$IPCHAINS -A input -p tcp -s $REMOTENET -d $LOCALNET 22 -j ACCEPT
echo -n "."

#telnet (23)
$IPCHAINS -A input -p tcp -s $REMOTENET -d $LOCALNET 23 -j ACCEPT
echo -n "."

#smtp (25)
$IPCHAINS -A input -p tcp -s $REMOTENET -d $LOCALNET 25 -j ACCEPT
echo -n "."

# DNS (53)
$IPCHAINS -A input -p tcp -s $REMOTENET -d $LOCALNET 53 -j ACCEPT
$IPCHAINS -A input -p udp -s $REMOTENET -d $LOCALNET 53 -j ACCEPT
echo -n ".."

   # DHCP on LAN side (67/68)
   # $IPCHAINS -A input -i $INTERNALIF -p udp -s $REMOTENET -d 255.255.255.255/24
67 -j ACCEPT
   # $IPCHAINS -A output -i $INTERNALIF -p udp -s $REMOTENET -d 255.255.255.255/24
68 -j ACCEPT
   # echo -n ".."

   #http (80)
   $IPCHAINS -A input -p tcp -s $REMOTENET -d $LOCALNET 80 -j ACCEPT
   echo -n "."

   #POP-3 (110)
   $IPCHAINS -A input -p tcp -s $REMOTENET -d $LOCALNET 110 -j ACCEPT
   echo -n "."

   #identd (113)
   $IPCHAINS -A input -p tcp -s $REMOTENET -d $LOCALNET 113 -j ACCEPT
   echo -n "."

   # nntp (119)
   # $IPCHAINS -A input -p tcp -s $REMOTENET -d $LOCALNET 119 -j ACCEPT
   # echo -n "."
```

```
# https (443)
# $IPCHAINS -A input -p tcp -s $REMOTENET -d $LOCALNET 443 -j ACCEPT
# echo -n "."

# ICQ Services (it's a server service) (4000)
# $IPCHAINS -A input -p tcp -s $REMOTENET -d $LOCALNET 4000 -j ACCEPT
# echo -n "."

echo "Done!"

# --------------------------------------------------------- ICMP -

echo -n "ICMP Rules.."

# Use this to deny ICMP attacks from specific addresses
# $IPCHAINS -A input -b -i $EXTERNALIF -p icmp -s <address> -d 0/0 -j DENY
# echo -n "."

# Allow incoming ICMP
$IPCHAINS -A input -p icmp -s $REMOTENET -d $LOCALNET -j ACCEPT
$IPCHAINS -A input -p icmp -s $REMOTENET -d $LOCALNET -j ACCEPT
echo -n ".."

# Allow outgoing ICMP
$IPCHAINS -A output -p icmp -s $LOCALNET -d $REMOTENET -j ACCEPT
$IPCHAINS -A output -p icmp -s $LOCALNET -d $REMOTENET -j ACCEPT
$IPCHAINS -A output -p icmp -s $INTERNALNET -d $REMOTENET -j ACCEPT
$IPCHAINS -A output -p icmp -s $INTERNALNET -d $REMOTENET -j ACCEPT
echo -n "...."

echo "Done!"

# --------------------------------------------------------- set default policy -

$IPCHAINS -A input -j DENY
$IPCHAINS -A output -j ACCEPT

echo ""
echo "Finished Establishing Firewall."
```

# Appendix D

**Using the
GNUware CD**

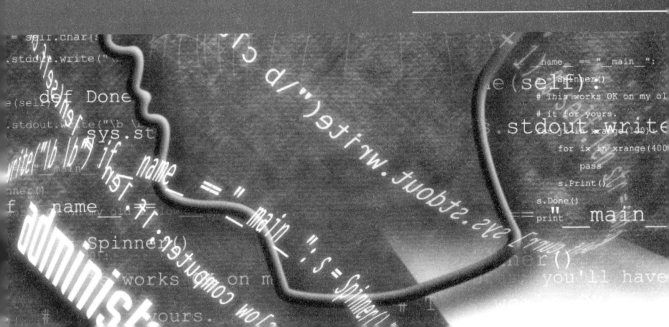

This section will explain how to access your GNUware CD. It is designed with the novice Linux user in mind. Accessing information from off a CD using Linux requires mounting the device. Because Linux treats different devices such as floppy drives and CD-ROMs as file systems, you need to mount the device itself into your partition table. Once you are through, be sure to unmount the device, otherwise you will encounter errors upon the next reboot.

The easiest way to mount a CD on your CD-ROM is to become root. After placing the CD in the drive, type the following:

```
mount -t iso9660 /dev/cdrom /mnt/cdrom
```

Change directories to the /mnt/cdrom directory. Using the ls command, you will be able to see the various directories containing the individual files. Copy the files from out of their respective directories to an install location. I recommend using your home directory, the /tmp directory, or a unique directory in /usr/local. Use the cp command as follows:

```
cp <filename> /usr/local/gnu/
```

When you are done copying the files down from off the CD, you will need to unmount the drive. First, make sure you are not accessing any files from within the /mnt/cdrom directory. Type the following:

```
umount /mnt/cdrom
```

Make sure you type it as "umount" and NOT "unmount". UNIX lost the "n" some time ago.

Another good way to peruse the contents of the CD is, after mounting the CD as per the instructions above, start up a Web browser. Netscape accomplishes this task quite well. Click on "File, Open Page..." and look for the file "/mnt/cdrom/index.html". This will allow you to look at the entire CD's contents using a javascript-enabled browser. It features a collapsible tree structure and further information on each program. You can then copy the file of choice after you have located it by holding down the Shift key and then clicking on the program with the left mouse button. Netscape will then prompt you for a default location to copy the file.

For instructions regarding uncompressing tarred and zipped programs, consult the sections "Comparing Archival Programs" and "Compression Utilities," in Chapter 9. For information about compiling programs from source code, review "Compiling Source," in Chapter 11.

Contents of the GNUware CD

The following is a breakdown of what's installed on the GNUware 1.8 CD included with this book. The four major sections, listed alphabetically, are Console, Kernel, Miscellaneous and X11.

- The Console section comprises those Linux programs that are designed for use as text-only or which can be run without the X Window Environment.
- The smaller section, labeled Kernel, contains only the stable and developmental Linux kernels along with a few kernel utilities.
- The Miscellaneous section contains a hodgepodge assortment of Linux programs that were either too new and could not be categorized or did not fall into the regular parameters.
- The last section, X11, contains programs designed specifically for use under the X Window Environment.

# Index